THE WORLD'S CLASSICS

FOUR RESTORATION
MARRIAGE PLAYS

BETWEEN 1660 and 1710 almost every major English comic dramatist wrote at least one comedy which centred on an anatomy of a marriage in crisis. This volume contains four of the finest and most original of these plays. They differ radically in the stories they tell, the settings they employ, the ways in which they represent matrimonial warfare, and the kinds of conclusions they bestow upon their discontented married couples. This collection illustrates the energetic diversity of English comedy in one of its greatest ages.

MICHAEL CORDNER is a Senior Lecturer in the Department of English and Related Literature at the University of York. He has edited editions of George Farquhar's *The Beaux' Stratagem*, the *Complete Plays* of Sir George Etherege, *Four Comedies* of Sir John Vanbrugh and, for the World's Classics series, *Four Restoration Marriage Comedies*. He has also co-edited *English Comedy* (Cambridge University Press, 1994) and is completing a book on *The Comedy of Marriage 1660–1737*.

RONALD CLAYTON lectures in History at the University of York.

PETER HOLLAND is Judith E. Wilson University Lecturer in Drama in the Faculty of English at the University of Cambridge.

MARTIN WIGGINS is a Fellow of the Shakespeare Institute and Lecturer in English at the University of Birmingham.

DRAMA IN WORLD'S CLASSICS

J. M. Barrie
Peter Pan and Other Plays

Ben Jonson
The Alchemist and Other Plays

Christopher Marlowe
Doctor Faustus and Other Plays

Arthur Wing Pinero
Trelawny of the 'Wells' and Other Plays

J. M. Synge
The Playboy of the Western World and Other Plays

Oscar Wilde
The Importance of Being Earnest and Other Plays

Chapman, Kyd, Middleton, Tourneur
Four Revenge Tragedies

Dryden, Lee, Otway, Southerne
Four Restoration Marriage Plays

THE WORLD'S CLASSICS

Four Restoration Marriage Plays

THOMAS OTWAY
The Soldiers' Fortune

NATHANIEL LEE
The Princess of Cleves

JOHN DRYDEN
Amphitryon; or The Two Sosias

THOMAS SOUTHERNE
The Wives' Excuse; or Cuckolds Make Themselves

Edited by
MICHAEL CORDNER
with
RONALD CLAYTON

General Editor
MICHAEL CORDNER
Associate General Editors
PETER HOLLAND   MARTIN WIGGINS

Oxford New York
OXFORD UNIVERSITY PRESS
1995

Oxford University Press, Walton Street, Oxford OX2 6DP

Oxford New York
Athens Auckland Bangkok Bombay
Calcutta Cape Town Dar es Salaam Delhi
Florence Hong Kong Istanbul Karachi
Kuala Lumpur Madras Madrid Melbourne
Mexico City Nairobi Paris Singapore
Taipei Tokyo Toronto
and associated companies in
Berlin Ibadan

Oxford is a trade mark of Oxford University Press

British Library Cataloguing in Publication Data
Data available

Library of Congress Cataloging in Publication Data
Data available
ISBN 0–19–282570–4

1 3 5 7 9 10 8 6 4 2

Typeset by Pure Tech Corporation, Pondicherry, India
Printed in Great Britain
by Biddles Ltd
Guildford and King's Lynn

CONTENTS

PREFATORY NOTE

The division of editorial responsibilities in this volume has been as follows. Michael Cordner edited and modernized the four play-texts and provided all the introductory materials. Michael Cordner and Ronald Clayton collaborated on the annotation and on checking the texts. Ronald Clayton compiled the glossary.

Michael Cordner
Ronald Clayton

ACKNOWLEDGEMENTS

We are deeply grateful for the help, encouragement, and expert information we have received from a wide range of colleagues and friends during the preparation of this edition. Our especial thanks to Richard and Marie Axton, Bernard Barr, John Bossy, Stuart Carroll, Niccy Cordner, Ruth Ellison, Nick Havely, Peter Holland, Dwyryd Jones, Jeremy Maule, Stephen Minta, J. S. F. Parker, John Roe, Richard Rowland, Peter Rycraft, J. A. Sharpe, Norman Stevenson, Lawrence Stone, Geoffrey Wall, and Nicole Ward Jouve. Anne Barton kindly read the introduction and suggested numerous improvements. The errors that remain are entirely our responsibility. Our greatest debt is to Jacques Berthoud for his constant enthusiasm and support.

Michael Cordner
Ronald Clayton

As the general editor of the series I would also wish to thank a number of people without whom the series would not have been brought to fruition. Kim Scott Walwyn at Oxford University Press courageously commissioned it and offered indispensable support in its early stages. Frances Whistler later took over its superintendence and was a tower of strength in offering encouragement, help, and sane advice to a general editor snowed under by a mountain of manuscripts. The final stages of the volumes' progress into print have been overseen with calm professionalism by Judith Luna and Susie Casement. At the early planning stages we benefited greatly from the counsel of Stanley Wells, and in the long journey to publication I have been deeply grateful for the industry and expertise of my associate general editors, Peter Holland and Martin Wiggins.

Michael Cordner

INTRODUCTION

IN each of the plays in this collection a married woman comes face to face with her would-be seducer. These roles were all originally played by a single pair of performers—the two greatest actors of the Restoration stage, Thomas Betterton and Elizabeth Barry. Although the earliest of the plays, Otway's *The Soldiers' Fortune*, was enormously popular, its successors are not simply recycling a proven formula. Instead, they so thoroughly reinvent that basic encounter between wife and gallant that each actor's mettle must have been formidably tested in meeting the new challenges the later scripts set them.

Betterton, for example, was required to switch from Otway's Beaugard, an angrily indigent English soldier, edgily proclaiming his alienation from his society, to impersonate in Dryden's *Amphitryon* the supreme ruler of the gods, Jupiter, suavely confident that whatever he desires in the universe is his for the taking. The rake roles provided for Betterton in Lee's *The Princess of Cleves* and Southerne's *The Wives' Excuse* are also radically distinct. Lee's Nemours is an extravagant zealot of the flesh, zestfully addicted to the extremes of sensual experience; while Southerne's Lovemore is a clinically exact manipulator, tirelessly calculating how to mould others to his own selfish ends. A yet more demanding task faced Elizabeth Barry. One can easily imagine a modern actress who could confidently undertake Dryden's Alcmena and Southerne's Mrs Friendall. But that an actress apt to those parts would also be happy to tackle the lead roles in the two other plays in this collection is much less likely. Few actresses of any period would be able to contemplate playing *both* Otway's Lady Dunce—quick-witted, streetwise, utterly exploitative of her husband, devoid of moral compunction—*and* Lee's Princess of Cleves—eloquently self-pitying, intricately guilt-ridden, haplessly incapable of concealing her true feelings from her husband for more than an instant. Reading these four great plays in a single volume should give the lie once and for all to the antique prejudice that 'In the matter of sexual relations Restoration comedy is entirely dominated by a narrow set of conventions'.[1]

[1] L. C. Knights, *Explorations: Essays in Criticism Mainly on the Literature of the Seventeenth Century* (Harmondsworth, 1964), 148.

No major period of our drama has been more repeatedly subjected to ill-founded generalization than the half-century between 1660 and 1710. Even enthusiasts for its achievements have often unwittingly collaborated in this by confining their attention to a narrow selection of material from the large body of surviving texts. A number of major book-length studies, for example, have been content to give detailed attention only to the plays of Etherege, Wycherley, and Congreve—three dramatists who between them wrote a mere eleven comedies. Hand in hand with this has gone a popular (and, too often, a scholarly) assumption that the essential dynamic of Restoration comedy is provided by the courtship manœuvres of one or more witty couples who may or may not eventually decide to risk embracing matrimony together. Many such plays do exist, and some of them are among the finest the period produced. But an analytical perspective focused so firmly on the courtship-game will have little of interest to say, for example, about a play as extraordinarily accomplished as Dryden's *Amphitryon*, which, to the detriment of its critical fortunes, neglects to include in its small cast of characters a pair of youthful lovers. As a result, a rich array of dramatic writing of the first rank has been shamefully neglected.[2]

Despite posterity's obsession with love-duel comedy, all the major, and most of the minor, dramatists writing between 1660 and 1710 produced at least one comedy which either centres on a marriage in crisis or balances a courtship action against a detailed anatomy of an irretrievably failed union. The sheer variety of the kinds of comedy thus generated is exhilarating. The settings can range from the most fashionable of courts, as in Dryden's *Marriage à la Mode*, to the traditional scenes of village comedy, as in Jevon's *The Devil of a Wife*. Adultery may be embraced with relative impunity, as in Ravenscroft's *The London Cuckolds* or Behn's *The Lucky Chance*, or be an action a wife may finally discover she lacks the courage and brazenness to commit, as in Vanbrugh's *The Provoked Wife*. Similarly, narratives can end in contrition for offences committed, reconciliation between previously quarrelsome partners, agreed or enforced separation, or a continuing state of war. The complex diversity of the ways in which marital crisis is represented and negotiated in these texts testifies to the brilliantly sustained energy and inventiveness with which marriage and its attendant woes were debated in the post-1660 playhouses.

[2] For a book which brilliantly redresses this neglect, see Robert D. Hume, *The Development of English Drama in the Late Seventeenth Century* (Oxford, 1976).

This collection offers the first modernized and comprehensively annotated editions of four of the most brilliant of these marriage plays. We have aimed to provide as stylistically and tonally various a selection as possible. Otway's and Lee's scripts are products of the early 1680s, while Dryden's and Southerne's belong to the early 1690s. Each bears the imprint of its immediate circumstances of origin. *The Soldiers' Fortune*, for example, engages intricately and wittily with the major crisis—the so-called Popish Plot and Exclusion Crisis—which was currently convulsing the political nation, while *The Princess of Cleves* is, in part, a response to the recent, premature death in 1680 of John Wilmot, Earl of Rochester, the masterly poet and notorious rake, who, for many contemporaries, epitomized Restoration licence, philosophical as well as sexual. *Amphitryon*, on the other hand, is a masterpiece provoked by the 1688 Revolution—an exhilarating meditation on the use and abuse of absolute power, interlaced with jokes about, and allusions to, William III's wresting of the throne from his father-in-law, the now exiled James II. *The Wives' Excuse*, too, derives its energy from the particular circumstances of the early 1690s, though in this case primarily theatrical ones. The mid- to late 1680s had produced a fairly small crop of interesting new comedies. The early 1690s were therefore a moment of stocktaking when dramatists pondered their Restoration inheritance and considered what new initiatives they might develop from it. Southerne's great play is part of that process. In it, he invents a new way of telling the story of an ill-matched wife which was in its turn to provide stimulus for other dramatists' inventiveness over the remainder of the decade.[3] The four plays in this volume, therefore, may indeed all focus on the possibility of a woman committing adultery; but the different dramatists bring to bear on that common situation a richly diverse array of preoccupations and stimuli.

Premièred in the spring of 1680, *The Soldiers' Fortune* 'took extraordinary well, and being perfectly *Acted*; got the Company great Reputation and Profit'.[4] The plot materials out of which Otway's triumph was built are scarcely novel. He combines an abrasive courtship-duel with a cuckolding plot involving a discontented wife, her elderly and loathed husband, and the man on whom her affections

[3] On this, see A. H. Scouten, 'Notes toward a History of Restoration Comedy', *Philological Quarterly*, 45 (1966), 62–70; Michael Cordner, 'Marriage Comedy after the 1688 Revolution: Southerne to Vanbrugh', *Modern Language Review*, 85 (1990), 273–89.

[4] John Downes, *Roscius Anglicanus* (London, 1708), 36.

were fixed before her parents compelled her to marry wealth. But his handling of these familiar elements is radically innovative. The two younger men are unemployed soldiers, desperately aware that penury threatens them. Robert D. Hume has observed that 'Poverty is . . . made *real*' in *The Soldiers' Fortune*; in place of the conventional 'airy younger son, scrambling to make his fortune', Otway's soldiers are grown men 'facing a bleak future in a desperately inhospitable world'.[5] The dramatist himself had obtained a military commission on 10 February 1678 in a regiment recruited for action in Flanders. It was, however, soon disbanded, and a disappointed Otway, like the soldiers in his comedy, found himself without employment and strapped for cash. In the epilogue to his *Caius Marius* (premièred in the autumn of 1679) he presented himself as one who '*t'other day . . . was a Captain*' but is now '*a poor Disbanded Souldier*' in search of anyone who will '*give him ready Money for's Debenture*'.[6]

More is involved here than simply a vigorous injection of autobiographical pain into a conventional story of preordained cuckolding. The disbanding of the army of 1678 was forced on an unwilling Charles II by a Parliament fearful that the expanded troops now potentially at the king's disposal provided a tool which could be used to consolidate royal power at Parliament's expense. The 'great Danger of *Arbitrary Power*'[7] is a constant leitmotiv in the political debates of the late 1670s and early 1680s. The propaganda of the Whig party, headed by the Earl of Shaftesbury, alleged a covert conspiracy to subvert the liberty and property of the subject. Fuelled by the revelations of Titus Oates, an elaborate and ingenious Popish Plot was detected, which included the assassination of Charles, his replacement by his Roman Catholic brother, James Duke of York (the future James II), the violent re-establishment of Catholicism as the state religion, and the extinction of all representative institutions.[8] A

---

[5] Robert D. Hume, *The Rakish Stage: Studies in English Drama, 1660–1800* (Carbondale and Edwardsville, Ill., 1983), 93–4.

[6] Thomas Otway, *Works*, ed. J. C. Ghosh (Oxford, 1932), i. 520.

[7] [John Nalson], *The Complaint of Liberty and Property Against Arbitrary Government* (London, 1681), 2.

[8] On the crisis, see David Ogg, *England in the Reign of Charles II* (Oxford, 1934); John Kenyon, *The Popish Plot* (London, 1972); Tim Harris, *Politics under the Later Stuarts: Party Conflict in a Divided Society 1660–1715* (London, 1993). The terms 'Whig' and 'Tory' were current from 1681 (see R. Willman, 'The Origins of "Whig" and "Tory" in English Political Language', *The Historical Journal*, 17 (1974), 247–64). The party formations they came to identify, however, were for Otway already securely in existence by 1680, and I have therefore freely used those two labels while discussing his play.

key agent in the plot's execution would have been the *'mercenary Army'* of 1678—'on foot, ready raised, and filled with Popish Officers, to have joyn'd that Party at an hours warning'.[9] A logical consequence of such views was the demonization of the majority of the soldiery. As Sir Thomas Meres asserted in the Commons in November 1678, 'What acting has here been to set up men to tear us in pieces and cut our throats'.[10] Whig pamphlets disseminated an image of the soldier as someone whose 'Interest makes him wish for a Standing Army, not considering any further than his own Pay and Plunder, and so helps to ruine you that way'.[11] Another partisan refined the point by claiming that the best 'Men of the Blade' for the plotters' ends were

Men of no Estates nor Principles; . . . For People are ever as valiant that have their Fortunes to raise, as those that have them to defend: nay, of the two they shall be more faithful to him [i.e. the Pope]; for they have no Property to be concern'd for, and will more zealously serve him, by reason their whole Interests and Estates lie in him.[12]

In 1681 the dramatist Thomas Durfey remarked that *'in this Age 'tis not a Poets Merit, but his Party that must do his business'*.[13] In *The Soldiers' Fortune* Otway reinvents the comedy of marriage for just such a politicized theatre-world. His soldiers are bruisingly explicit in their political partisanship. They trace their own lineage back to the 'old Cavaliers' whose civil war fidelity to the royalist cause brought them only the knowledge that 'loyalty and starving are all one' (1.1.14). They view with contempt the England of the 1680s, where honourable service such as theirs goes disregarded and where prosperity and advancement are monopolized by those whom they regard as the heirs of the men who brought Charles I 'to the block' in 1649 (2.1.346). Their set-piece diatribe against the insanity of their own times (2.1.314–79), treating it as a grotesque replaying of the mid-century crisis, echoes the characteristic Tory allegation that Whig tactics in the current struggle mimicked those used to

[9] [Henry Care], *The History of the Damnable Popish Plot* (London, 1680), 91.

[10] Anchitell Grey, *Debates of the House of Commons, From the Year 1667 to the Year 1684* (London, 1763), vi. 229.

[11] [Charles Blount], *An Appeal from the Country to the City; For the Preservation of His Majesties Person, Liberty, Property, and the Protestant Religion* (London, 1679), 2.

[12] [Elkanah Settle], *The Character of a Popish Successor* (London, 1681), 8–9.

[13] Thomas Durfey, *Sir Barnaby Whigg: Or, No Wit like a Womans* (London, 1681), sig. A3^r. A helpful analysis of the politics of the playhouse repertoire in these years can be found in Susan J. Owen, 'Interpreting the Politics of Restoration Drama', *The Seventeenth Century*, 8 (1993), 67–97.

destabilize English monarchy and society in the 1640s. Anti-Whig propaganda constantly warned that the nation risked condemning itself to reliving 'the whole course of the late War'.[14] Beaugard and Courtine go further. Their England is one in which the Whigs' ascendancy is so total that they have, in effect, already achieved victory without needing to resort again to arms. And in that England Beaugard and Courtine are irretrievably outsiders, raging helplessly at a world gone mad.

Their fury is aggravated by social disdain. Royalist mythology had always elaborated on the low origins of those who had allegedly masterminded and profited from the insurrection of the 1640s—men of 'obscure parentage, and education', which made 'them ignoble, and ignorant, to contempt'.[15] Otway's soldiers view the crisis of the 1680s through the same spectacles. Those whose current prosperity and political influence they lament are invariably, in their account, sprung from the humblest roots. One 'was my father's footman', another 'was born a vagabond, and no parish owned him' (2.1.325–6 and 340), and so on and on. As they see it, the social hierarchy has been turned upside down, and those of gentle birth, like Courtine and Beaugard—in Tory iconography, the country's natural rulers—are condemned to be the slaves of those born to be their servants. The disbanded soldiers live the bitter reality of this in scene after scene. They are subject to the disdain even of the 'parish bawd' (1.1.182) and, as vagrant men without employment, are spat at as a danger to the property of others. They may deride one of the new mighty as 'born a vagabond'; but they themselves are now vulnerable to similar abuse—as, for example, 'a poor, lousy, beggarly, disbanded devil', or (as Beaugard wryly translates) 'a vagabond' (i.e. a vagrant) who is likely to be 'hanged by next sessions' (2.1.100–6). These are men with a grudge to settle.

Otway casts the despised husband as his play's specimen Whig. As Lady Dunce explains, her spouse is 'one of those fools, forsooth, that are led by the nose by knaves to rail against the king and the government' (1.2.72–4). By one traditional comic logic, Sir Davy has already fully earned his cuckolding by using his wealth to entrap a woman who was already devoted to another man. But his Whig allegiances, in this Tory play, add an extra relish to his undoing. The

---

[14] [Sir Roger L'Estrange], *The Reformed Catholique: Or, The True Protestant* (2nd edn. London, 1679), 33.

[15] *A Letter From a Gentleman in Kent, Giving Satisfaction To a Friend in London, of the Beginning, Progresse, and End of the late great Action there* (London, 1648), 1.

ageing rich man stole Beaugard's future bride while the soldier was abroad fighting for his country. The story has been set up in a manner which ratifies Tory stigmatizing of the Whig as a kind of enemy within. Accordingly, a betrayal which is more than personal triggers a revenge which is both sexual and political.

Otway designed Sir Davy for a great comic actor, James Nokes, then at the height of his powers and, in Colley Cibber's account, a player of 'a quite different Genius from any I have ever read, heard of, or seen, since or before his Time'. Cibber describes how Nokes

scarce ever made his first Entrance in a Play, but he was received with an involuntary Applause, not of Hands only, for those may be, and have often been partially prostituted, and bespoken; but by a General laughter, which the very sight of him provok'd, and Nature cou'd not resist; yet the louder the Laugh, the graver was his Look upon it; and sure, the ridiculous Solemnity of his Features were enough to have set a whole Bench of Bishops into a Titter.

He also relates how, 'When he debated any matter by himself' onstage, 'he would shut up his Mouth with a dumb studious Powt, and roll his full Eye, into such a vacant Amazement, such a palpable Ignorance of what to think of it, that his silent Perplexity (which would sometimes hold him several Minutes) gave your Imagination as full Content, as the most absurd thing he could say upon it'. Cibber cites Sir Davy as a role Nokes 'particularly shone in',[16] and it is easy to see how brilliantly Otway has designed it to display to best advantage his distinctive repertoire of 'ridiculous Solemnity', 'vacant Amazement', 'palpable Ignorance', and 'silent Perplexity'. In the process, Otway harnesses Nokes's resplendent comic gifts to enact and confirm Tory derision for the alleged vacuity of the typical Whig camp-follower.

Sir Davy's docilely pliant mind makes him an ideal recipient of his party's anxiety-feeding propaganda. The play pillories his crass alacrity in swallowing and recycling a host of Whig-generated scare-stories. Implicit here is a rooted scepticism about the whole edifice of allegations and insinuations upon which the Popish Plot crisis had been erected. The play has a carefully calculated nemesis in store for Sir Davy's credulity. The fool manipulated by political knaves is also marked out to be the instrument, 'the property, the go-between' (1.2.127), of his wife's revenge on him through adultery.

[16] Colley Cibber, *An Apology for the Life of Colley Cibber*, ed. B. R. S. Fone (Ann Arbor, Mich., 1968), 82–4.

As the Whigs reduce him to a tool, so too the would-be adulterers deny him human status and render him merely 'instrumental' in their designs (1.2.117). His fate is treated as predestined, and, long before it is accomplished, he is announced as 'the monster that must be, the cuckold elect' (2.1.38). He is, in other words, not credited with possessing any resource which could defer his appointed destiny.

In the comedy's last two acts, this proposition is tested to extremes. Manipulated by Lady Dunce into agreeing to arrange Beaugard's murder, Sir Davy finds himself negotiating for this deed with fake assassins, who have, in fact, been schooled in their homicidal routine by his wife. Whig propaganda disseminated lurid tales of the host of mercenary swords in London that could be instantly mobilized to execute the dreaded Popish Plot. Otway, in comic retaliation, condemns his Whig buffoon to entering that imaginary underworld in order to hire a swordsman for his own nefarious purpose. It is a journey which scars him permanently. Encountering Bloody Bones's apparent lunacy and pain of conscience proves a contagious experience, and out of it is generated the insomniac Sir Davy of early Act 5, seeing visions and starting at the drop of a pin. An amazing new stage in the play's exploration of his mental pliability has been reached, which is then capped by Otway's extraordinary writing for Sir Davy when he finally knows that he is 'a cuckold, and that anybody may make bold with what belongs to me' (5.4.113–14). From one perspective, his giggling, nervously talkative compliance with his fate merely confirms the brutal prophecy that nature has marked him out to be an instrument of others' wills. But Otway elaborates so vividly on the symptoms of his disturbance, and allows him so much stage space in which to articulate them, that Sir Davy is apt to appear the key figure in the denouement, displacing Beaugard and Lady Dunce from centre-stage.

Reviewing a 1967 London revival, Tom Stoppard thought that the production went 'right against' the play's 'grain' in making the audience respond to Sir Davy at this point as something more than a comic butt, apt for all indignities.[17] Arthur Lowe, who played the part, did not understate the character's idiocy. To another reviewer, he appeared 'a joyfully bumbling dimhead, face like a crumbling dumpling and deep voice like an alarmed farmyard animal'.[18] Yet,

[17] Tom Stoppard, 'A Case of Vice Triumphant', *Plays and Players* (Mar. 1967), 17.
[18] Jeremy Kingston, review article, *Punch* (18 Jan. 1967), 99.

building on that base, Lowe's reading of the final scenes entered a new area of definition. In Hilary Spurling's words, he made 'Sir Davy's final writhing in betrayal and submission almost too hard to watch'.[19] Cibber's celebration of Nokes's skills contains a passage which is relevant here: 'In the ludicrous Distresses, which by the Laws of Comedy, Folly is often involv'd in, he sunk into such a mixture of piteous Pusillanimity, and a Consternation so rufully ridiculous and inconsolable, that when he had shook you, to a Fatigue of Laughter, it became a moot point, whether you ought not to have pity'd him'.[20] It is precisely this kind of ambiguous response which the text invites Nokes to explore. In the play's last speech, Sir Davy both celebrates with nervous laughter the 'very good jest' perpetrated on him and anticipates edgily Beaugard being 'cruel to him'. He then turns to the audience to beg ironically for fellow-feeling from at least 'one brother-cuckold' for his plight. This is uncomfortable writing. It does not seek a sudden switch of our sympathies in Sir Davy's favour; but the character is being registered in ways which make it impossible simply to pigeonhole him as the mere unthinking, unfeeling implement of another's plot.

Whig doctrine, in Tory eyes, converted the '*Liberty* and *Property* of the *Subject*' into 'The Peoples Queen; so Nice and Curious in her Dress, that Kings must approach her with more Softness and Distance, than they do their own Consorts'. The enemy of the subject's liberty and property, in Whig mythology, was '*Arbitrary Power*, *Mars* drawn in Horror', than which 'A Ruder Visage was never pencell'd'.[21] In the climax to Otway's play, '*Mars* drawn in horror', a soldier with his sword at the ready, invades Sir Davy's house, uses no 'Softness and Distance' in depriving him of his wife and converts him by threat of force into his obedient slave. To Sir Davy, no more comprehensive an invasion of his liberty and property could be devised. On one level, these events invite reading as a revengeful Tory fantasy, joyfully acting out on the comic stage a scenario pieced together from Whig nightmares. It is not only, however, the intricacy of Otway's handling of Sir Davy that suggests that the final effect is more multi-textured than that.

Basic to all the period's marriage plays is the knowledge that 'England in the early modern period was neither a separating nor a

[19] Hilary Spurling, 'What is this thing called froth?', *Spectator* (10 Jan. 1967), 72.
[20] Cibber, *Apology*, 84.
[21] *Truth and Honesty in Plain English* (London, 1679), 14 and 16.

divorcing society: death was virtually the sole agent for dissolving marriage'.[22] Beaugard, Sir Davy, and Lady Dunce are therefore fated to a perpetual *ménage à trois*. Sir Davy's legal title to her remains unbreakable, and the original wrong—the supplanting of the Tory soldier by the Whig interloper—can therefore never be rectified. In its place comes a permanent act of theft, upheld by the sword. Similarly, the play gives no hint that the manifold ills the soldiers so bitterly resent in contemporary England stand any chance of being remedied. Their political anger therefore remains unsolaced at the play's end. If within the Dunce household Sir Davy is now the victim of another's usurped authority, within the larger society Tory soldiers remain the victims of power-brokers whose right to control their destinies they do not acknowledge as justly founded.

Equally, if Sir Davy has been constantly manipulated by others' wills, Beaugard has scarcely been the author of his own fate. Throughout the play, whenever left to his own devices, he blunders; his successful moves are all scripted by someone else—either Lady Dunce or Sir Jolly Jumble. It is his willing indebtedness to the latter which signals most strongly the passivity of the role allotted to him by Otway. Essentially, apart from their phase of mutual mis-understanding in 2.1, Beaugard dances to the tune Sir Jolly sets. For example, the whores the pimp gathers up may revolt the passing bullies (1.1.289–302); but Beaugard, like Courtine, contentedly accepts them at the glamorous evaluation the knight puts on them. Comparing Beaugard with major rake-characters from the mid-1670s—Horner in Wycherley's *The Country Wife* (1675), for instance, Dorimant in Etherege's *The Man of Mode* (1676), or Don John in Shadwell's *The Libertine* (1676)—will swiftly indicate how lacking in initiative and ingenuity Otway has made him. The dramatic space he vacates is energetically colonized by Sir Jolly with a frenzied display of priapic anticipation. Here, in a weird reversal, the go-between comes to seem the prime mover; it can even paradoxically appear that his sexual desire and needs are more urgent than the soldiers'. Yet he is also finally a spent force, condemned by impotence to the imperfect delights of voyeurism. He truly lives only through imaginative participation in, and surreptitious witnessing of, the deeds the able-bodied young can commit. His ecstatic surveying of the soldiers' bodies loudly proclaims this. But it also indicates that Beaugard's prowess, as perhaps befits a son of Mars, is essentially physical. The

---

[22] Lawrence Stone, *Road to Divorce: England 1530–1987* (Oxford, 1990), 2.

qualities of 'a strong-built, well-made man' which gained him military employment also recommend him as 'a devilish fellow for a wench' (1.1.140–2). Of the capacity of his predecessor rakes to mould the world to their design through wit and invention he possesses no trace. Thus, Beaugard's history as adulterer echoes his experience as discarded soldier. In both, he is the plaything of forces over which he exerts no mastery.

Otway's deeply idiosyncratic conduct of the 'courtship' between Courtine and Sylvia explores similar territory. They are addicted to each other before the play begins, but each vainly strives not to give the other proof of this. Their encounters involve mutual insults, satiric annihilations of each other's conduct and person, and proclamations of their hatred of 'hideous marriage' (2.1.290). Raillery and stinging mockery were by 1680 customary parts of the way the stage presented the pre-marital wit-combats of the young. But no previous duet had been as savagely derisory in tone as this. The rich heiress struggles with her nausea at having fallen for 'a fellow with the mark of Cain upon him, which everybody knows him by, and is ready to throw stones at him for' (3.1.2–4). The penniless soldier deals with his own shaming subservience before her by sneering at her affectation, flightiness, and 'coxcomb-hunting' (3.1.21). Their mutual aggression is also a come-on. In this battle hostility and sexual excitement are closely yoked. But their encounters also map how totally each feels at risk of subjugation by the other. Nothing in the later action lays those fears to rest. Sylvia may announce that 'a true lover is to be found out like a true saint, by the trial of his patience' (4.2.3–4). But the humiliating trick she springs on a drunken Courtine in the same scene demonstrates nothing about him she does not already know. Instead, it acts out her own need to humble and embarrass, however briefly, the man to whom she will soon commit her fortune and herself. The tone of their eventual marriage-bargaining is similarly brutal. Her financial advantage over him is constantly harped on. He is about to become 'a poor jade' tied up in her stable; she might employ him as 'a husbandman' to 'cultivate' her 'farm'; he asks her for 'a bargain in a tenement of thine' (5.1.104–14). Throughout, it is clear to both that controlling and tethering him is a trick no legal contract can ensure. Sylvia embraces her fate with open eyes. In due course, Otway would write a sequel to *The Soldiers' Fortune*, *The Atheist* (1682), which explores the misery of the marriage they endure together. In courtship and adultery plots alike, *The Soldiers' Fortune* enmeshes its characters within entanglements of circumstance and passion to which its ending affords no lasting resolution.

Nathaniel Lee's *The Princess of Cleves* proved much less palatable to its original spectators than *The Soldiers' Fortune* had done. On its première in late 1681 or early 1682, it was '*well Acted, but succeeded not so well as*' earlier plays by Lee.[23] He later claimed that he had aimed to discomfort his audience. Expecting 'the most polished hero', it had been given instead 'a ruffian reeking from Whetstone's Park' (Dedication, l. 16). Those expectations had partly been shaped by the reputation of Lee's source—*La Princesse de Clèves*, the great novel of adulterous passion and self-deceit, published in Paris in 1678, and attributed by almost all authorities to Marie-Madeleine de Lafayette. At its centre is the tragic triangle linking the Princesse de Clèves, her husband, and the outstandingly gifted courtier, the Duc de Nemours. The book was an immediate success, and the centre of intense literary controversy. Battle was joined on many fronts, but especially focused on the difficulty of classification it posed. Should it be regarded as a novel, a history, a memoir, or a romance? Each of these labels seemed unsatisfactory. For instance, most of its major characters, including the Prince de Clèves, are derived from history, and Lafayette includes in her narrative many real events; but she also gives the Prince a fictitious wife and mother-in-law. The novel's sternest contemporary critics rebuked this interweaving of the verifiable and the fictional as deeply indecorous. Thus, Valincour, the first to publish a hostile critique, presumed 'that while authors have the right to embellish general historical events, they must never go against accepted accounts of those events'.[24]

An English translation was published as early as 1679,[25] and it was from this that Lee worked. He transforms his source ruthlessly. Anyone approaching the play in expectation of a faithful theatrical version of the original will be bitterly disappointed. A more sympathetic eye, however, will discern method and purpose in Lee's tactics. He radically promotes Nemours at the Princess's expense,

---

[23] Downes, *Roscius Anglicanus*, 38. For the dating of its first performance, see Hume, *Rakish Stage*, 113–18.

[24] William Ray, *Story and History: Narrative Authority and Social Identity in the Eighteenth-Century French and English Novel* (Oxford, 1990), 25.

[25] *The Princess of Cleve. The most famed Romance. Written in French by the greatest Wits of France. Rendred into English by a Person of Quality, at the Request of some Friends* (London, 1679). Subsequent quotations from the novel derive from this translation.

confining her to one of the play's two plots, while making him a dominant player in both. He also overlays Lafayette's original triangle with another consisting of the Princess, Nemours, and Marguerite, whom Nemours is engaged to marry. His dealings with Marguerite involve an extraordinary sequence of wit-combats, masked encounters, and stormy confrontations. In addition, the second of the play's plots—a wild cuckolding-action—is entirely Lee's invention, and conducted with a comic grotesquerie wholly antipathetic to the high-flown blank-verse world to which he restricts the Princess and her husband. Nemours moves between all these habitats with an improvisatory fluency which proclaims histrionic gifts of the highest order.

If Lafayette's novel controversially combined invention and history, Lee's play ambitiously complicates the mixture yet further by constantly invoking memories of the leading Court Wit, John Wilmot, Earl of Rochester, around whose flamboyant actions and free-thinking writing a potent rakish mythology had grown up during the preceding decade.[26] Rochester's recent, premature death, at the age of thirty-three, is recollected in the elegiac commemoration by Nemours and the Vidame of Count Rosidore, 'the life, the soul of pleasure'—a man who was 'the spirit of wit' and whose imaginative fluency was so great that he 'never spoke a witty thing twice' (1.2.92 and 104–6). In 1935, however, Montague Summers argued that Lee's portrait of Nemours is also modelled on Rochester, who is in this second representation 'seen steadily and as a whole', and therefore, in Summers's view, inevitably unflatteringly.[27] In the same interpretative tradition, Dustin Griffin has proposed that 'the witty and cynical Nemours is meant by Lee to embody the darker side of Rochester's character, as Rosidore embodies the brighter'.[28] Robert Hume goes further. For him, the mourning of Rosidore is indeed designed to bring Rochester to mind; but Lee's subsequent insinuation is that the real Rochester 'was a Nemours'—i.e. 'fatally attractive but vicious', and 'a scabrous swine'. Hume therefore reads the play as 'a savage attack on Rochester'.[29]

[26] For Rochester's biography, see Vivian de Sola Pinto, *Enthusiast in Wit: A Portrait of John Wilmot Earl of Rochester 1647–1680* (London, 1962); John Wilmot, Earl of Rochester, *Letters*, ed. Jeremy Treglown (Oxford, 1980), 1–37. On the Court Wit circle, see John Harold Wilson, *The Court Wits of the Restoration: An Introduction* (Princeton, NJ, 1948).

[27] Montague Summers, *The Playhouse of Pepys* (London, 1935), 301.

[28] Dustin H. Griffin, *Satires Against Man: The Poems of Rochester* (Berkeley, Calif., 1973), 287.

[29] Hume, *Rakish Stage*, 126, 131, and 127.

Lee had dedicated his first play, *Nero* (1674), to Rochester, hailing him as 'absolutely Lord of Wit', and informing him that his 'Writings are so exactly ingenious; Princes treasure them in their Memory, as things Divine'.[30] Whatever the immediate results of this bid for patronage, the longer-term dealings between Lee and Rochester were not to be as the former had desired. In his *Allusion to Horace* (1675–6) Rochester etched an annihilatingly disdainful judgement on the professional writer:

> When Lee makes temperate Scipio fret and rave,
> And Hannibal a whining amorous slave,
> I laugh, and wish the hot-brained fool
> In Busby's hands, to be well lashed at school.[31]

Such lofty dismissiveness may well have engendered in Lee an appetite for revenge which found an outlet after the victimizer's death. But we have no information about his attitude to Rochester in the early 1680s, beyond the play itself, to support such a hypothesis.

The libertine actions of Rochester's life were sufficiently notorious; but the manner of his dying converted the story into the stuff of legend. That a man who had lived so transgressively should on his deathbed embrace Christian piety and wish his writings burned was a boon to the sermonizers. Gilbert Burnet, the cleric who attended him in his last illness, and Robert Parsons, his mother's chaplain, soon committed to print the details of his sufferings, bodily and spiritual, and of his eventual recantation. They presented Rochester's volte-face as a just epitaph on the dangerous apostasy from faith and conventional morality of a highly visible, glamorously enticing group of young bloods—the so-called Court Wits—whose deeds epitomized for the likes of Burnet and Parsons everything in their society against which their Christian mission engaged them to war. Their theme was embellished by others. The Reverend Samuel Woodford, for example, offered a sickly image of 'Rochester in the LAMBS fresh blood new dy'd | All robed in white' as he 'sings Lauds to him whom he denyd'.[32] Other early memorialists saw things differently. Anne Wharton, for instance, could lament 'that lovely soul for ever fled' and Aphra Behn celebrate 'The Great, the God-like *Rochester*' without

---

[30] Nathaniel Lee, *Works*, ed. Thomas B. Stroup and Arthur L. Cooke (New Brunswick, NJ, 1954), i. 24.

[31] John Wilmot, Earl of Rochester, *Complete Poems*, ed. David M. Vieth (New Haven, Conn., and London, 1968), 122.

[32] David Farley-Hills (ed.), *Rochester: The Critical Heritage* (London, 1972), 127.

mentioning his sensational conversion.[33] For them, praising his genius did not entail collaborating in the dying man's wholesale denigration of the earlier achievements of his wit. In effect, they choose to erase his final days from the record.

When Lee wrote his play, therefore, a struggle for the possession of Rochester's memory was underway. *The Princess of Cleves* notoriously ends with a sneer at the untrustworthiness of deathbed repentances, clearly aimed at Burnet's triumphant image of the rake reclaimed for Christ as his life ebbs away. But this moment also calls in question the wisdom of assuming too simple an equivalence between Rochester and Nemours, since it is the latter who speaks the disdainful couplet:

> He well repents that will not sin, yet can;
> But death-bed sorrow rarely shows the man.
> (5.3.305–6)

If Nemours does in some way stand for Rochester, then it has to be a mythical Rochester who would scorn the eleventh-hour apostasy of the historical libertine. Similarly, Rosidore's death is one embraced without nerve-wracked contrition. Felled by 'his last debauch', he is now 'a nothing made | Huddled with worms, and swept to that cold den, | Where kings lie crumbled just like other men' (1.2.97–9). Whatever we make of that bleak vision, it is clearly not one which acknowledges the prospect of eternal judgement. Lee is building here on two of Rochester's most famous poems—'Upon Nothing' (with, for example, its unnerving description of 'turncoat Time' driving humankind back into the 'hungry womb' of 'primitive Nothing'), and his translation of the Act 2 Chorus from Seneca's *Troades* (especially lines 8–10): 'Dead, we become the lumber of the world, | And to that mass of matter shall be swept | Where things destroyed with things unborn are kept'. Also probably in Lee's mind is Rochester's 'Against Constancy', with its concluding boast that 'I'll change a mistress till I'm dead— | And fate change me to worms'.[34] Rosidore, as avatar of Rochester, has (unlike Rochester) died the death of a pagan agnostic, ecstatically embracing pleasure and the dissolution it brings with it. The tart irony is that it is Rosidore's death which is true to the principles Rochester himself enunciated at the height of his poetic powers. The allusive chain is further enriched by the fact that Lee, in the play he dedicated to Rochester, had himself translated the

---

[33] Ibid. 107 and 105.
[34] Rochester, *Complete Poems*, 118–20, 150–1, and 82.

Seneca chorus: 'Death's nothing; nothing after death will fall; | Time, and dark Chaos, will devour us all'.[35]

Death preoccupies Nemours, but he repeatedly declares his bravura defiance of its power to unnerve or subdue him. Thus, a rhapsodic assertion of his devotion to 'the generation of wit' and 'the extravagance of pleasure' is signed off by him with the following invocation: 'Let me dream of nothing but dimpled cheeks, and laughing lips, and flowing bowls. Venus be my star, and whoring my house, and, death, I defy thee. Thus sung Rosidore in the urn' (3.1.136–9). That final sentence abrasively rebuffs the Burnet mythology of deathbed contrition and, in effect, cultivates an image of Rochester resurrected, so that he can die again, this time true to his epicurean principles. David M. Vieth has seen in this passage a direct allusion to Rochester's 'Upon His Drinking a Bowl'.[36] The resemblances are not, in my view, compelling. I would surmise that Lee may instead have had in mind another poem which is now lost or a fragment of Rochester's own conversation or himself be inventing a statement Rochester might, or ought to have, made. In particular, missing from the Nemours speech is the characteristic Rochester note struck in the poem's final stanza:

> Cupid and Bacchus my saints are:
> May drink and love still reign.
> With wine I wash away my cares,
> And then to cunt again.[37]

Nemours' outburst contains no equivalent to Rochester's suggestion that drink is an anodyne for a pain which must be washed away before the erotic round can once again be resumed. In this sense, Lee's Nemours is a Rochester purged of many of the perturbations which haunt the latter's own verse and which, in some critical accounts, are taken to prefigure the need to seek a solace beyond the earthly which conquered him at the end. This effect is then disconcertingly compounded by having Nemours insouciantly and abruptly proclaim, in the play's last moments, his resolve to turn over a new leaf. The critical consensus has been wary about taking this at face value. But,

---

[35] Lee, *Works*, i. 56.

[36] David M. Vieth, *Attribution in Restoration Poetry: A Study of Rochester's 'Poems' of 1680* (New Haven, Conn., 1963), 405–6. The Lee passage is helpfully placed in a wider context by James Grantham Turner, 'The Libertine Sublime: Love and Death in Restoration England', *Studies in Eighteenth-Century Culture*, 19 (1989), 107.

[37] Rochester, *Complete Poems*, 107.

however we rate its authenticity or likely longevity, the key point surely is that, unlike Rochester's, Nemours' speech of recantation is made at the height of his bodily and mental powers, when his self-confidence is at its peak and his nerve uncracked by the imminence of an awful death. Nemours thus exits from the play swaggeringly insisting, as always, upon his right and ability to shape his future by the arbitrary exercise of his own will.

Those couplets from 'Upon His Drinking a Bowl' remind us of another difference between the poetry and the play. The verse circulating in manuscript under the names of rake poets in the period takes to itself a linguistic freedom never available to the dramatists of the time. The most famous four-letter words, for instance, could not be uttered on the stage, but are commonplaces in the poetry. The theatrical rake therefore is, in this and in other respects, a censored version of his historical equivalent. *The Princess of Cleves*, however, comes closer than any previous play to transcribing the full outrage of the rake's refusal to bow to conventional decorums. Lee's 1689 Dedication narrates how Nemours 'lays about him like the gladiator in the Park', i.e. a notorious statue of an amply naked gladiator. He adds mischievously that the spectators 'may walk by and take no notice' (ll. 20–1)—advice which may work for a statue, but not for a play. Offended playgoers may walk out of the theatre in protest, barrack the actors, call for the dramatist's head, or retreat into silent shock; but simply taking no notice is not an available option for them. Nemours cannot be allowed to mimic the gladiator in embracing literal nakedness—a step too far for even Lee to contemplate. But, in numerous other ways, he refuses to stoop to the limits of representation conventional in rake theatre of the 1670s. Nemours is, for instance, endowed with 'a polymorphous desire that attracts him promiscuously to *all* flesh',[38] so that even the fool Poltrot is subjected to caresses so intimate as to leave him wriggling to control an erection (1.2.167–8). Nemours is also flamboyantly unreticent in talking about his own sexuality, insisting that this is what divides a true gentleman from the common herd. Mankind is, for him, at one in its sexual drivenness; but, as he haughtily instructs the Vidame, almost all 'sneak with it under your cloaks like tailors and barbers', while 'I, as a gentleman should do, walk with it in my hand' (2.3.36–7). His mood influences even those rare scenes in which he does not appear.

---

[38] Harold Weber, *The Restoration Rake-Hero: Transformations in Sexual Understanding in Seventeenth-Century England* (Madison, Wis., 1986), 71.

Saint-André's erotic dream (4.2.68 ff.), for example, is graphic and explicit to an extent unparalleled in earlier writing for the Restoration public stage. At such moments, the gentlemanly rake's brazen self-exposure is fully matched by Lee's refusal to abide by the normal theatrical codes—his refusal, in other words, sneakingly to mask his characters' sexual needs and obsessions behind the cloak offered by conventional stage decorum. His play is the work of a dramatist heightenedly aware that he is repeatedly breaking rules and shattering conventions.

The abrasive frankness of his writing has prompted critics to label the play an angry exposé of all that Rochester had stood for. According to James Sutherland, for instance, 'Lee seems to be saying to his audience: "This is the sort of character you admire. Well, take a good look at him, and see what your precious Dorimants are really" '.[39] The problem is that a satirist seeking to indict Rochester was likely to discover that his choicest ammunition had already been used by the guilty man himself. Vieth has, for instance, observed that 'The Earl of Rochester's Conference with a Post Boy', a poem penned by Rochester himself, is a better satire on his conduct than his traducers proved able to write.[40] Anne Barton has mapped the paradoxical intricacy of its effects. She points out how its 'hyperbolic style . . . is persuasive and, at the same time, ironically conscious of its own exaggeration', managing 'simultaneously to magnify and deflate *both* its subject and the orthodox values by which that subject is being judged, to invite belief and to undercut it'. She also describes how bemused it leaves the reader as to how to take 'this mythologized Earl of Rochester', who brusquely claims as his own sins of which the poem's author was certainly guilty and others which are histrionically magnified and more apt to 'an allegorical figure of Lechery invented by some canting and overwrought divine':

He repels, but he also attracts. The poem is amusing; it is also horrifying. Even more perplexing: what is the point at which one should separate this dramatic character, the subject of the lampoon, from the witty poet of the same name who stage-managed the incident in the first place and who controls in so complex a fashion the tone and language of his self-presentation?[41]

---

[39] James Sutherland, *English Literature of the Late Seventeenth Century* (Oxford, 1969), 144.

[40] Vieth, *Attribution in Restoration Poetry*, 199.

[41] Anne Righter [Barton], 'John Wilmot Earl of Rochester', *Proceedings of the British Academy*, 53 (1967), 52–3.

Lee claimed to regard *The Princess of Cleves* as generically uncategorizable, calling it 'this farce, comedy, tragedy, or mere play' (Dedication, l. 14). Subsequent criticism has argued for the aptness of various other labels, including satire, tragicomedy, and black comedy; but the attempt seems foredoomed. In crucial ways, Lee's play poses its interpreters puzzles closely akin to those set by 'The Earl of Rochester's Conference with a Post Boy'. If the author of that poem had managed also to write an original stage play, it might very well have had something of the experimentally unruly, ethically provocative, Janus-faced nature of Lee's extraordinary improvisation.

One strain in modern commentary focuses on the damage Nemours does. In J. M. Armistead's words, he 'seriously disorders the lives of others'.[42] Such a view finds encouragement from Lee's 1689 Prologue with its myth of a decline from a golden age 'When truth and love with friendship did engage' (l. 2) to modern times when 'Men wait for men as dogs for foxes prey' (l. 9). Nemours' compunctionless exploitation of the Prince's friendship, as well as his numerous other smaller treacheries, eloquently exemplify such a fall from harmony and trust among men. But the rake hectoring the postboy also includes betrayal of a friend among his mistreadings (ll. 9–10)—an admission (or is it a boast?) which does not by itself prove sufficient to stabilize our judgement of him. In addition, the play's world seems in many ways constructed to confirm Nemours's confident self-evaluation. The forlorn inanity of Poltrot and Saint-André in affecting rakish attributes works, in a way familiar from 1670s comedy, to ratify their aristocratic model's assured possession of the powers they can only haplessly mimic. Similarly, Nemours proves irresistibly attractive to every woman in the play, including the Princess herself, while Lee includes no voice of real authority to rebuke him for his conduct or his philosophy. The Vidame comes nearest to this; but he is a covert libertine, seeking to hide his own erotic manœuvres from Nemours' gaze—potentially, therefore, himself a target for the latter's satire.

Lee's remodelling of the Lafayette novel is at its most radical in the final encounter between Nemours and the Princess. At first, it seems that she will sustain the poise and resolution to convince him, as in the novel, that 'his hopes were at end' (p. 257). Lee's writing here invites the full exercise of Elizabeth Barry's very considerable gifts. In Cibber's account, 'in Characters of Greatness' she 'had a presence

---

[42] J. M. Armistead, *Nathaniel Lee* (Boston, 1979), 148.

of elevated Dignity, her Mien and Motion superb, and gracefully majestick; her Voice full, clear, and strong, so that no Violence of Passion could be too much for her: And when Distress, or Tenderness possess'd her, she subsided into the most affecting Melody, and Softness'. In his judgement, 'In the art of exciting Pity, she had a Power beyond all the Actresses I have yet seen, or what your Imagination can conceive', and 'In Scenes of Anger, Defiance, or Resentment, while she was impetuous, and terrible, she pour'd out the Sentiment with an enchanting Harmony'.[43] Her guilt-stricken lament beside her husband's state and her first commanding responses to the 'cruel visit' of Nemours (5.3.68) seem designed to employ these resources at their fullest stretch and with great variety. But Lee then demands yet more from her. In effect, he asks her to destabilize the bravura effects she has just achieved—and, with it, the certainty with which Lafayette ends her narrative—by casting doubt on the sure-groundedness of all that she has just so eloquently expressed. She now admits that duty 'but subsists in thought' and wonders what 'time, with such a love as mine, | May work in' his 'behalf' (ll. 231–3). This startling undermining of her preceding conduct of the scene encourages and validates Nemours' brash and jeering confidence that she will now inevitably soon be his to command. From one perspective, Lee has annihilated the Princess's dignity and self-control and subjugated her to the whim of a libertine who is bound to pay her 'the cross returns of love' she has helplessly predicted (l. 188). From another, the rake's scorn for the hypocrisy with which lesser mortals seek to mask the true nature of their impulses behind a sneaking cloak has received another exemplification.

But there is also another dimension to the scene which must have registered with the original audience. Elizabeth Barry had been Rochester's mistress and borne him a child. Their relationship had been passionate, stormy, scarred by mutual suspicions of each other's infidelity, and, in the end, doomed. His surviving letters to her run the gamut from celebrating her as 'stark mad, and therefore the fitter for me to love' to asserting that 'I can see very woman in you, and from yourself am convinced I have never been in the wrong in my opinion of women'. One assures her that

Since nothing is so agreeable to my nature as seeking my own satisfaction, and since you are the best object of that I can find in the world, how can you

[43] Cibber, *Apology*, 92.

entertain a jealousy or fear? You have the strongest security our frail and daily changing frame can give, that I can live to no end so much as that of pleasing and serving you.[44]

Informing Nemours that he has 'a sense too nice for long enjoyment' (5.3.168) must have been weighted with personal implication for Barry. Indeed, the whole decision to cast her as the Princess adds another layer of complexity to the way in which Lee's script conjures Rochester's spirit to renewed life upon the stage. That effect was further complicated by the fact that Barry's lover appears also to have been her early patron. According to one tradition, he instructed her as an actress after her early stage appearances had been unsuccessful and in the process taught her that eloquent command of natural passion and pathos for which she was so noted and upon which Lee so palpably depends in his writing here.[45] That the Princess, in the face of Nemours' magnetism, should then deconstruct that 'presence of elevated Dignity' invites reading as yet another mark of the troubling potency of the dead man around whom this play's perplexed imagining revolves.

Amphitryon, Dryden's last and greatest comedy, was provoked by political disaster and financial exigency. In the 1680s Dryden had been a very public convert to Roman Catholicism and a key propagandist for the regime of James II. The Revolution of 1688, which displaced James in favour of his Protestant son-in-law and daughter, William and Mary, left Dryden out in the cold. Loyal to his new faith and deprived of his state offices of Poet Laureate and Historiographer Royal, he was now dependent once again on the printing press and the playhouse for his livelihood.[46] His masterly retelling of the cuckolding of Amphitryon by Jupiter, premièred in the autumn of 1690, was one of the first fruits of this unwelcome turn of fortune's wheel. It was an immediate triumph and remained a repertory piece throughout the eighteenth century.

In his dedication of the play to Leveson-Gower, Dryden pictures himself as politically marginalized, but with 'no disposition . . . to cry, while the mad world is daily supplying me with such occasions of

---

[44] Rochester, *Letters*, 98, 180, and 148.

[45] For a recent exploration of the theatrical implications of their relationship, see Elizabeth Howe, *The First English Actresses: Women and Drama 1660–1700* (Cambridge, 1992), 114 ff.

[46] For an authoritative account of Dryden during these years, see James Anderson Winn, *John Dryden and His World* (New Haven, Conn., 1987), 428–70.

laughter' (ll. 42–4). His plight echoes that of Otway's soldiers, his Tory predecessors of a decade earlier, who angrily mapped the lunacy of a world which spurned and impoverished them. But Dryden's response is totally distinct from theirs. He rejects the 'melancholic' philosopher in favour of the 'merry' one (ll. 41–2). His laughter at this 'mad world' will not be, like theirs, a covert expression of personal bile.

His insistence on this is partly politic in motivation. As his prologue makes clear, the post-revolutionary world was not one which encouraged a Jacobite satirist to indulge his 'rage' with 'noble vigour' or employ 'his sharp sting' freely (ll. 4 and 1). Those seeking to legitimate the Williamite regime had launched a massive propaganda offensive, the 'most sophisticated and extensive' effort of its kind 'thus far in the history of Western Europe'.[47] In the face of this, Dryden is learning to adjust to being permanently in opposition. He is also essaying the difficult art of assuring his new masters that they have nothing to fear from him. He remains faithful to his principles, but is also 'a patient sufferer, and no disturber of the government' (Dedication, ll. 33–4). This does not mean that his play is innocent of political implication. Its dialogue is peppered with allusions to the Revolution and the ideological ferment which accompanied it. The opening dialogue between Jupiter, Mercury, and Phoebus throws up aphorisms about the nature of royal prerogative (1.1.113–14) and that 'knock-down argument' of 'arbitrary power' (ll. 129–30), about 'grumbletonian morals' (l. 143), 'bumpkin patriots' (l. 138), and the rights subjects take to themselves to censure kings (l. 57). An ancient story is being made to yield contemporary meanings.

The tale of the desire of Jupiter, king of the gods, for Alcmena, the wife of the Theban general, Amphitryon, and Jupiter's enjoying her by assuming the bodily form of her husband is one of the most frequently dramatized of all classical myths.[48] Dryden explicitly cites two earlier versions—the *Amphitruo* of the Roman dramatist Plautus and a recent French masterpiece, the *Amphitryon* of Molière (1668). But the story was a familiar stage property long before Plautus, and

---

[47] Lois Schwoerer, 'The Glorious Revolution as Spectacle: A New Perspective', in Stephen B. Baxter (ed.), *England's Rise to Greatness* (Berkeley, Calif., 1983), 122.

[48] See L. R. Shero, 'Alcmena and Amphitryon in Ancient and Modern Drama', *Transactions of the American Philological Association*, 87 (1956), 192–238; Örjan Lindberger, *The Transformations of Amphitryon* (Stockholm, 1956); C. D. N. Costa, 'The Amphitryo Theme', in T. A. Dorey and Donald R. Dudley (eds.), *Roman Drama* (London, 1965), 87–122.

Molière's is only one of numerous seventeenth-century recyclings of it. Two other versions which Dryden perhaps knew are Thomas Heywood's *The Silver Age* (c.1611),[49] and Jean de Rotrou's *Les Sosies* (1638), which powerfully influenced Molière. Dryden's primary indebtedness, however, is to Plautus and Molière. Ned Bliss Allen calculated that 'only about two per cent of' his play 'contains material from Plautus, whereas nearly fifty per cent of it is from Molière'.[50] Such figures can be misleading, since Molière himself is building on Plautus. But they do roughly match Dryden's own statement that 'more than half of it is mine' (Dedication, ll. 64–5). Even where he is a direct inheritor from Plautus or Molière, however, Dryden is also a masterful transformer of the material he adopts. The result is 'one of the unrecognized masterpieces of English comedy'.[51] Two dimensions, in particular, of the story engaged Dryden's imagination. Central to the myth is the idea of a wife so contented in her marriage that the king of the gods can only enjoy her by impersonating her husband. Also implicit in it is the concept of an absolute power so devoted to its own purposes and desires that, to secure them, it will ruthlessly override all human rights and laws.

Dryden's Jupiter is supreme ruler of the universe, but he also bears many of the attributes of an earthly monarch. His own entry speech proposes the analogy between god and king (1.1.55–7), and the subsequent dialogue constantly plays on it. Dryden is cueing us to think in terms of contemporary parallels. At some points the key references seem to be retrospective. When Jupiter, for example, indulges the argument 'That when a monarch sins it should be secret, | To keep exterior show of sanctity, | Maintain respect, and cover bad example' (1.1.79–81), it seems apt to propose that the first spectators would naturally 'have thought of Jupiter as representing Charles II . . . , famous for the prodigality of his favours',[52] as also for the careless freedom with which he permitted his subjects to witness

---

[49] On the relationship between Heywood's play and Dryden's, see Margaret Kober Merzbach, 'The Third Source of Dryden's *Amphitryon*', *Anglia*, 73 (1955), 213–14.

[50] Ned Bliss Allen, *The Sources of Dryden's Comedies* (Ann Arbor, Mich., 1935), 226. Allen (pp. 273–81) provides a tabulated comparison of the three plays, as does John Dryden, *Works*, xv, ed. Earl Miner (Berkeley, Calif., 1976), 553–6.

[51] John Dryden, *Works*, xv. 472.

[52] John Loftis, 'Dryden's Comedies', in Earl Miner (ed.), *John Dryden* (London, 1972), 53.

[53] On this subject, see Paul Hammond, 'The King's Two Bodies: Representations of Charles II', in Jeremy Black and Jeremy Gregory (eds.), *Culture, Politics and Society in Britain, 1660–1800* (Manchester, 1991), 13–48.

his promiscuity.[53] The libertine heterosexual connoisseurship and athleticism with which Dryden endows Jupiter also point in the same direction. Contemporary satire characteristically painted William III as either impotent ('Not qualified for his wife, | Because of the cruel midwife's knife') or energetically addicted to young male flesh ('buggering of Benting doth please to the life').[54] Yet confining Jupiter to a parallel with Charles II would leave much of the play unexplained. Dryden's cleverness lies in the versatility with which he develops the role, invoking through it at different moments both Restoration monarchy and its Williamite supplanter. The original audience, however, can have had little doubt that his thoughts were primarily fixed on England post-1688.

Take, for example, the charged exchanges between Jupiter and his sons about the nature of fate. Jupiter justifies his adulterous love for Alcmena, 'because 'twas in the fates I should'—a manœuvre Phoebus mocks:

> Thus every wicked act in heaven or earth
> May make the same defence. But what is fate?
> Is it a blind contingence of events?
> Or sure necessity of causes linked
> That must produce effects? Or is't a power
> That orders all things by superior will,
> Foresees his work, and works in that foresight?

To which Jupiter brutally responds:

> Fate is, what I
> By virtue of omnipotence have made it;
> And power omnipotent can do no wrong—
> Not to myself, because I willed it so;
> Nor yet to men, for what they are is mine.

Which earns Mercury's ironic tribute: 'Here's omnipotence with a vengeance—to make a man a cuckold, and yet not to do him wrong' (1.1.92–111). In case the political applicability of this eludes the spectator, Phoebus points the moral: 'Since arbitrary power will hear no reason, 'tis wisdom to be silent' (ll. 127–8).

In Dryden's eyes, a recent 'wicked act' on the national stage had been validated by just such an appeal to 'power omnipotent'. A usurping monarch's seizure of the English throne had been justified

---

[54] William J. Cameron (ed.), *Poems on Affairs of State: Augustan Satirical Verse, 1660–1714, v. 1688–1697* (New Haven, Conn., 1971), 41–2.

by Anglican and Whig apologists via 'a theological interpretation of his undeniable success'—i.e. the prospering of his plan was read as demonstrating that it was 'the work of Providence'.[55] To Dryden, such arguments were mere impious rationalizations of theft; but, to those convinced of the necessity of William's actions but uncertain that rebellion could ever be deemed guiltless, such a providentialist stress on the nation's inherent passivity in the great events of 1688 was politically invaluable, since it 'allowed the mysteries of providence to wipe clear the crimes of rebellion and abjuration of oaths'.[56] It also helped reconcile the nation to the least palatable aspect of the Revolution—the fact that its trigger was a successful invasion by a foreign army. Williamite panegyric struggled to represent what could be considered a humiliating conquest as, instead, an event which guaranteed English liberties, as in Thomas Shadwell's 1689 celebration of the new king:

> H'*Invaded* us with *Force* to make us *free*,
> And in *anothers Realm* could *meet no Enemy*.[57]

Those effortful paradoxes reveal the (perhaps intractable) difficulty of the task Shadwell is attempting. In *Amphitryon* an external power, Jupiter, similarly invades '*another's Realm*', Amphitryon's home and marriage-bed; but, unlike Shadwell, Dryden feels no necessity to represent his actions as benign.

Dryden's elegant linking of the ancient story and contemporary politics does not depend upon rigorously consistent allegory. Any attempt to interpret Amphitryon as James II, for instance, will soon founder, although the plight of a husband and master finding his rights annexed by a rival who pretends a legitimate claim to them remains tantalizingly parallel to the fate which had overtaken Dryden's royal master. The inherited myth, however, ends with the restoration of Amphitryon's rights; so, even if Dryden had favoured an exact parallel earlier in his play, it would have broken down at that point. But such a simple matching of mythical and historical personages was never on Dryden's agenda. *Amphitryon* is, rather, fashioned as a teasingly suggestive meditation on the invasion of

[55] David Bywaters, *Dryden in Revolutionary England* (Berkeley, Calif., 1991), 61.

[56] Steven N. Zwicker, *Lines of Authority: Politics and English Literary Culture, 1649–1689* (Ithaca, NY, 1993), 177.

[57] Thomas Shadwell, 'A Congratulatory Poem On His Highness the Prince of Orange His Coming into England' (1689), *Works*, ed. Montague Summers (London, 1927), v. 340.

'*another's Realm*' by a force which cannot be withstood—constantly apposite, therefore, to the circumstances of post-1688 England, but scarcely ever commenting on them with naked directness. A dramatist who professes himself compelled by his society to write 'with one hand tied behind him' (Prologue, l. 11) is experimenting with that oblique, cryptic manner of invoking contemporary crises which modern scholarship has identified as typical of one mode of Jacobite writing in the 1690s.[58]

Happy to follow Plautus and Molière whenever it suits him, Dryden also energetically departs from their precedents in a number of decisive ways. One crucial example is his radical redesigning of Alcmena's role. In both Plautus and Molière we first meet Alcmena only as Jupiter leaves after their night together, whereas Dryden introduces us to her before she becomes the victim of Jupiter's deceit. Similarly, neither of the earlier dramatists includes her in their final scene. To them, the key focus for Jupiter's self-revelation and prophecy is the husband; the wife's feelings and reactions are disregarded. Dryden remedies this omission as well. Alcmena is onstage during his play's last pages, accorded an active role and also observed carefully by other characters. As a result, the journey his Alcmena goes on is a more ambitious and emotionally taxing one than had been assigned to her predecessors.

Her first words in the play are in soliloquy, a hymn of intensely devoted love to her husband, empathetically and anxiously imagining the dangers he confronts in war (1.2.1–11). Her subsequent welcome of the figure she takes to be Amphitryon adds to this a rich evocation of the tender, alert sexuality which bonds husband and wife, as in her rapt assertion that

> I am the fool of love, and find within me
> The fondness of a bride without the fear.
> My whole desires and wishes are in you.
> (1.2.114–16)

Such association of unalloyed contentment with 'the nuptial bed' (l. 121) is almost unique in post-1660 comedy. It is rendered darkly ironic here by being mistakenly addressed to the disguised predator god, Jupiter, who 'but laughs | At lovers' perjuries' (ll. 143–4). To

---

[58] See e.g. Howard Erskine-Hill, 'Literature and the Jacobite Cause: Was There a Rhetoric of Jacobitism?', in Eveline Cruickshanks (ed.), *Ideology and Conspiracy: Aspects of Jacobitism, 1689–1759* (Edinburgh, 1982), 49–53.

Jupiter his invasion of *'another's Realm'* is a form of heroic erotic comedy. His principal victims, however, experience it in another mode. Dryden so positions us that, through them, we gain an unnerving experience of 'a world in which the individual is open to forces more powerful than the self'.[59]

Dryden's Jupiter makes clear, as his predecessors do not, that it is indispensable to him that in their love-making Alcmena's sexual ardour should equal his own: she must 'meet my warmth' and 'give down' all 'her love' (1.1.193–4). In their night together the terms he sets are fully met, as is evident from her speeches and behaviour in 2.2—a scene in which Dryden takes many cues from Molière, but in which his Alcmena is far more sensually enraptured and erotically alive than reigning decorums allowed her French equivalent to be. What she at first experiences as a rapturous fulfilment of wedded love, however, is in fact her initiation into a far more dangerous knowledge. The divine revelation the libertine god vouchsafes her destabilizes her entire world. In 3.1, her husband returns, eager to embrace her 'as on our nuptial night' (l. 145); but now his courtship seems pallid to her, his kiss merely dutiful, beside the ecstatic delights in which the invading deity has instructed her. Without her volition or consent, her consciousness has been transformed by the whim of an 'arbitrary power' (1.1.129), and she is left to reckon the cost in the final words she speaks in the play:

> I know not what to hope, nor what to fear.
> A simple error is a real crime;
> And unconsenting innocence is lost.
>
> (5.1.383–5)

The Alcmenas of Plautus and Molière experience no such plangent desolation.

This is a pain Dryden's Jupiter was determined she should bear. In a scene greatly elaborated from Molière's version, he seeks the assurance that 'When you gave up yourself to love and me, | You thought not of a husband, but a lover' (2.1.356–7). Her newly instinctive dissatisfaction with Amphitryon's embraces is thus intrinsic to the god's game-plan. He is set not only on sexual consummation, but also on a form of spiritual colonization. As he expounds at his first parting from her,

---

[59] Greg Clingham, 'Another and the Same: Johnson's Dryden', in Earl Miner and Jennifer Brady (eds.), *Literary Transmission and Authority: Dryden and Other Writers* (Cambridge, 1993), 150.

> The being happy is not half the joy;
> The manner of the happiness is all!
> In me, my charming mistress, you behold
> A lover that disdains a lawful title,
> Such as of monarchs to successive thrones.
> The generous lover holds by force of arms
> And claims his crown by conquest.
>
> (ll. 372–7)

This speech, Dryden's invention, is characteristic of the deftness of his tactics throughout the play. On one level, Jupiter's elevating of a title gained 'by force of arms' over 'a lawful title' recalls the fierce contemporary debates over the nature of William's claim to the English throne. A right founded on conquest was not a favoured concept at the new Court, since it could only too easily be invoked to justify the title of any new conqueror who might in his turn overthrow William by force. But, to those of Dryden's convictions, conquest was precisely what had occurred in 1688. Indeed, imagery of rape is recurrent in Jacobite writing on the Revolution.[60] Jupiter's excited delight in achieving mastery by force, not mere legitimacy of title, would to Jacobite ears be an honest expression of the amoral principles upon which the new regime's power was based. To Dryden, Whig propaganda had impiously attempted to annex the authority of the Christian God to ratify the success of William's strategy, by pleading, in effect, that what thrived was providentially justified. *Amphitryon* teasingly derives from a familiar classical myth a theology to counterpoise this blasphemy, by staging the exploits of a pagan king of the gods who exults in the abrogation of others' rights and the invasion of others' property, proclaiming all the while the superiority of theft over mere legal possession. In the myth Jupiter's power is absolute; no human or divine force can gainsay it. Those who are its victims can no more elude their fates than those loyal to the pre-1688 regime could by sheer force of personal will decree the Revolution undone.

At the same time, however, Dryden also remains nimbly alert to all that makes the myth an incomplete parallel to England's contemporary fate. Alcmena, for instance, does, after all, experience in Jupiter's embraces an erotic joy far beyond anything Amphitryon can ever achieve with her. Attempting to deduce a political application from that would be labour ill-spent. Dryden's masterpiece

---

[60] Erskine-Hill, 'Literature and the Jacobite Cause', 49–50.

is a supremely ingenious balancing-act, in which he repeatedly but, as it were, discontinuously alludes to the Revolution and its aftermath, while also developing with fierce concision and brilliant invention the human drama which engulfs those on whom Jupiter's power operates. Again and again, he sharpens his characters' disturbance, renders their disarray more eloquent. When Amphitryon reels away from his first uncomprehending quarrel with his wife, Molière's Alcmène retains some of her aristocratic composure, though her disturbance is apparent: 'Je ne puis rien entendre: | Laisse-moi seule et ne suis point mes pas' ('I can listen to nothing; leave me alone and do not follow me'). Dryden substitutes at this point an intenser, more openly expressive response for his Alcmena:

> PHAEDRA Please you—that I—
> ALCMENA O, nothing now can please me.
> Darkness, and solitude, and sighs, and tears,
> And all the inseparable train of grief,
> Attend my steps forever.
>
> (3.1.325–9)

Similarly, in the final scene, Alcmena, confident that she can distinguish the true Amphitryon from the false, makes the correct choice, only to be brutally rebuffed by her husband with a cry of 'Away, adulteress!' (5.1.252). The disguised Jupiter exploits the situation with a guileful display of uxorious gentleness, which convinces Alcmena that she had been mistaken: 'The face might have deceived me in my choice; | Thy kindness is a guide that cannot err' (ll. 268–9). This provokes Amphitryon to another aggravated expression of fury and, therefore, to a further betrayal of that 'kindness' Alcmena associates with her husband. These emotional intricacies have no equivalent in Plautus and Molière. At moments like this we witness a great dramatist of emotional extremes confidently at work, suavely reshaping to his own imperatives a narrative already dramatized so often by others. Mistaken-identity plots often compel their principal characters 'to decide how they know who they are and how they can demonstrate their true identities to the world'.[61] Dryden insists on pressing his much further. Alcmena and Amphitryon have by the play's end lived through experiences which cannot be undone and which have not yet been absorbed. In its closing moments, as Mercury wryly observes, 'both stand mute, and know not how to take it' (5.1.402–3). It is integral to Dryden's

---

[61] Judith Sloman, *Dryden: The Poetics of Translation* (Toronto, 1985), 41.

mastery here that he refuses to conclude with easy gestures of reconciliation or peacemaking. A conventional closure of that kind would betray the distinction with which he has consistently evoked the world-transforming experience which has beset both husband and wife. The toughness of his vision makes of his play a masterpiece well worthy of a place on the world-stage beside the versions of Plautus and Molière.

Premièred late in 1691 or early in 1692, Thomas Southerne's *The Wives' Excuse* comprehensively disconcerted its original audience and consequently failed to secure a place in the repertory. Its virtues, however, found a potent advocate in Dryden, who wrote a judiciously complimentary verse epistle to accompany its publication in 1692. Another early tribute reported that 'good Judges commend the Purity of its Language'[62]—an emphasis which was to become recurrent in later accounts of Southerne's plays. According to a 1702 discussion of the post-1660 drama, for instance, 'there's a Spirit of Conversation in everything he writes'.[63] In recent commentary yet bolder claims have been made for *The Wives' Excuse*. It has been hailed as 'one of the five most considerable comedies written between 1660 and 1700', 'one of the toughest, most serious, and most original comedies of the seventeenth century', and 'one of the greatest, and most under-rated, Restoration comedies'.[64] To understand the justification for such heady praise, we must explore the circumstances of, and reason for, its original failure in the playhouse.

Its first cast was a brilliant one; it came adorned with specially composed, and dramatically apposite, music by Henry Purcell; it followed hard on the heels of Southerne's outstanding success of the preceding season, *Sir Anthony Love*; and those who read it ahead of the first performance 'thought well of it' (Dedication, l. 14). The omens must have seemed propitious indeed. Yet, with the benefit of hindsight, it is easy to see that Southerne was running great risks. Though his play everywhere invokes memories of earlier rake

---

[62] *The Gentleman's Journal Or The Monthly Miscellany . . . January 1691–2* (London, 1692), 52.

[63] *A Comparison Between the Two Stages* (London, 1702), 19.

[64] John Harrington Smith, *The Gay Couple in Restoration Comedy* (Cambridge, Mass., 1948), 144; Judith Milhous and Robert D. Hume, *Producible Interpretation: Eight English Plays 1675–1707* (Carbondale and Edwardsville, Ill., 1985), 256; Peter Holland, *The Ornament of Action: Text and Performance in Restoration Comedy* (Cambridge, 1979), 138.

comedy, it radically reinvents the way in which such stories might be dramatized. These transformations affect its every aspect, from how the narrative is concluded to the detailed, local control of dialogue rhythm and patterning. Yet, along the way, it often seems to encourage its audience to anticipate more conventional fare. Even its full title, *The Wives' Excuse; or, Cuckolds Make Themselves*, appears to promise that its action will include adultery, and that a husband's failings will provoke his wife, in despair and/or revenge, to cuckold him. It thus cues its audience to place the play in a clear line of descent from the numerous adultery comedies which had been popular in the late 1670s and early 1680s. But the distinction of Southerne's writing for Mrs Friendall is precisely that she cannot be subdued to such an easy formula. The proffered 'excuse' is one she principledly rejects as an insult to her capacity to make her own choices, to devise her own pattern for her life. His title records the proverbial lore of the society in which Mrs Friendall must perforce live; but its cynicism is invoked only to be rebuffed. The irony of the title can, however, only be comprehended retrospectively. In the meantime, an audience, anticipating one kind of play, found itself offered something so decisively different from its expectations and from dramatic precedent that it could not immediately make satisfactory sense of it. This is a comedy which 'challenges every one of the stock assumptions' usually made about the dramatic tradition to which it contributes.[65]

Restoration comedy contains many scenes of meetings for pleasure in public places—in St James's Park, in the Exchange, even the theatre itself. But no play before this chronicles such a wide and diverse range of such encounters in a single action. Some of these are familiar from earlier plays—the sauntering in the Mall in 3.2, for instance, or the masquerade in the last scene. Others reach the stage for the first time in this play, as, for instance, in the opening scenes at the music-meeting, itself a fairly recent innovation, or—another new fad—the private raffle Friendall arranges for the assembled company at the end of 4.1. Only a minority of the scenes concern intimate encounters in genuinely private places between two or three characters. The majority map the interaction of distinctly larger groups in places where the characters have gathered to relish the pleasures of society. The cumulative effect has been neatly described as 'Restoration Chekhov', in that the scenes 'are structured round very carefully notated social rituals rather than propelled by the demands of plot'.[66] Southerne's control of the plot is, in fact, immaculately precise; but he combines that mastery with a meticulous representation of the dynamics of the social gatherings which bring his principal characters into intimate contact.

The witty results of this include scenes like the encounter between Lovemore and Mrs Friendall in 4.1. No previous stage combat between an accomplished rake and discontented wife had been so precisely located domestically as this one. He comes upon her as she gives orders for the preparation of the boastfully expensive tea her husband desires to serve his friends. She can therefore mockingly greet him with 'Are you one of the gentlemen that love the tea with a hard name?' (ll. 76–7). Similarly, she eventually evades his intensest persuasions, as footmen enter *with a service of tea*, by announcing, 'My employment calls upon me. Are not you for tea?' (ll. 193–4). The wife's command of her household thus becomes an essential resource in checkmating the invading libertine, who insolently presumes that his old 'sly flattery' (l. 125) will once again be easily sufficient to ensure him victory. He has not yet understood how drastically the rules of the game have been rewritten.

Southerne's obsession with social rituals also yields more complicated effects. For example, the bravura intricacy of his marshalling of the interweavings and cross-movements of the eleven key figures at the music-meeting in 1.2 is without rival in seventeenth-century drama. Snatches of conversation from one group of characters intersect with longer exchanges between others, while, all the time, the groups repeatedly re-sort themselves into new configurations. Attempting this in a play's concluding scene, when all the characters are familiar to the audience, would be ambitious enough, and Southerne does, in fact, repeat the trick then; but in 1.2 we have not glimpsed any of these people before. Such tactics proclaim the work of a dramatist addicted to living dangerously.

In addition, Southerne arranges that a crucial encounter in this scene is unheard by us. Mrs Witwoud points out to us the extended, 'seriously engaged' conversation (l. 113) between Mrs Friendall and Lovemore. Like the other characters, we can see it in progress; but,

---

[66] Brean S. Hammond, reviewing the Jordan/Love edition of Southerne, *Review of English Studies*, NS 41 (1990), 250.

also like them, we never learn what they are saying. Few dramatists would risk being so reticent. Yet Southerne's positioning of us here is intrinsic to his conception of his play-world. That unheard duologue is effectively ventriloquized for us by several of the other characters. Springame, Mrs Friendall's brother, is uncensoriously confident that a seduction is underway, and that, although Lovemore may in the end not gain her 'consent to the business' (l. 55), sooner or later one of the gallants will. Witwoud makes the same assumption, though she is more confident of Lovemore's success (ll. 112–16). Their opinions echo the equally confident predictions of the footman in 1.1: 'Every man has hopes of a new-married woman. For she marries to like her man; and if upon trial she finds she can't like her husband, she'll find somebody else that she can like, in a very little time, . . . or change her men till she does' (ll. 75–9). The aphoristic form of the prophecy subdues the individuality of particular cases to a general law, which is presumed to be indisputable. To these observers, it would be unnecessary to hear the words of Lovemore and Mrs Friendall, since the roles of both are prescripted.

From one perspective, all this could be read as a parodic distillation of the blasé predictability of one kind of rake narrative—and, therefore, an early indication that Southerne is unlikely to follow that path himself, since identifying so clearly the predestined outcome would inevitably deprive the subsequent action of tension and conflict. Yet he is also making clear how widely diffused in the play-society these assumptions are—a point he reinforces later by having the pragmatic Mrs Teazall assure Mrs Friendall that husbands such as hers deserve cuckolding and that 'nobody will think you wrong him' (3.2.39). In a world where views like these command such broad assent, what reasons can a woman like Mrs Friendall find for refusing the licence so universally granted to her?

Throughout the play, Southerne's writing for Mrs Friendall is inventive and distinctive. At no point, for instance, does he make her employ Christian imperatives in her self-defence against Lovemore's worldly-wise sophistry, despite the fact that, in late seventeenth-century society, the most readily available arguments against marital infidelity were undoubtedly those religious ones which insisted on the divinely-decreed nature of the marriage oath. Southerne instead renders Mrs Friendall's consciousness immaculately secular. He also gives her formidable forensic gifts, as is shown by the efficiency with which she immobilizes Lovemore's 'sly flattery' and also manœuvres her husband to respond to Ruffle's insult as she desires (2.2.1–41). She is a strategist of suave social accomplishment.

She is also gifted by Southerne with the capacity to interrogate the institution of marriage itself with a scepticism far more incisive than any previous Restoration comedy wife had commanded. The most remarkable instance of this is the second of her brief soliloquies in 2.2:

How despicable a condition must that matrimony be, when the husband, whom we look upon as a sanctuary for a woman's honour, must be obliged to the discretion and management of a wife for the security of his own! . . . in a married state, as in the public, we tie ourselves up, indeed, but to be protected in our persons, fortunes and honours by those very laws that restrain us in other things; for few will obey, but for the benefit they receive from the government. (ll. 79–86)

Implicit here is a view of society as a contractual construct, in which the individual agrees to surrender hypothetical liberties and to endure some unwelcome restrictions in order to secure specific benefits, the possession of which the individual reckons will outweigh these losses. If, however, the terms of the original agreement are not fulfilled, the contract may be considered void. To many contemporaries, this would have seemed a dangerously unstable model on which to base the creation of a state; but calmly proceeding, by analogy between the 'public' and 'the married state', to apply the same thinking to the marriage bond would have been for them a yet more startling move. Mrs Friendall's was, after all, a society in which divorce, as we know it, was effectively unobtainable and in which marriage was therefore for life. Preachers were accordingly careful to insist that in marriage 'each side must look to what concerns themselves. Their Duties are Mutual, but not Conditional; so that we may not break with them, tho they break with us'.[67] Such doctrine is calmly disregarded by the thoroughgoing contractualism of Mrs Friendall's lucid speech.

That the 'condition' of her own marriage is as 'despicable' as she implies is clear from the preceding scenes. From her husband's 'government' she receives no 'benefit'. If her sane analysis could by itself produce the consequence she desires, her marriage would be instantly dissolved. Her society, however, does not order things so logically, and she must live with that fact. Consequently, even as she articulates her scepticism, she strives to censor her own mind—'Have a care of thinking that way' (l. 82), she instructs herself. Similarly, she seeks to prevent Friendall from publicly displaying the cowardice

[67] [John Kettlewell], *Of Christian Prudence, Or Religious Wisdom* (London, 1691), 161.

she suspects him of, so that she can tell herself that she does not '*know* that he is a coward' (2.2.44–5—my emphasis). Witwoud proclaims at one point that 'the understanding ought to be suited to the condition, to make anyone happy' and that her cousin Fanny 'has wit enough for a wife, and nothing else that I know of' (2.1.18–19). Mrs Friendall has too much wit to be Friendall's wife; and, in a failed attempt to make her 'condition' endurable, she strives to monitor, control, even cheat her own 'understanding'.

If her marriage is a prison, however, at no point does Southerne present the prospect of adultery with Lovemore as a compensating enfranchisement. The play's subtitle indeed declares the opposite. If '*Cuckolds Make Themselves*', then that reduces the wife to being merely a function of male behaviour. She becomes a kind of automaton propelled towards adultery by her husband's conduct. It is a thought repeatedly echoed by Lovemore, as, for example, in this brash advice to the audience:

> Thus, who a married woman's love would win
> Should with the husband's failings first begin:
> Make him but in the fault, and you shall find
> A good excuse will make most women kind.
>
> (1.3.68–71)

In this variation, the woman is twice puppet-mastered, since 'the husband's failings' which trigger her rebellion are themselves unmasked for her by the rake who wishes to bed her. It is a mythology which takes from her all self-control, all power over her own destiny. Southerne's exposure of its insolence towards women chimes with the parallel insistence of the pioneer feminist, Mary Astell, that 'nothing can justify the revenging the Injuries we receive from others, upon our selves' and that 'An ill Husband may deprive a Wife of the comfort and quiet of her Life; may give her occasion of exercising her Virtue, may try her Patience and Fortitude to the utmost, but that's all he can do: 'tis her self only can accomplish her Ruin'.[68] Southerne never deprives Mrs Friendall of the power, in this sense, to be the architect of her own destiny.

This takes him, however, into uncharted dramatic territory. Kenneth Muir has aptly praised him for the composure with which he evades precedent in the scene of Mrs Friendall's frank rejection of

[68] Bridget Hill (ed.), *The First English Feminist: 'Reflections Upon Marriage' and Other Writings by Mary Astell* (Aldershot, 1986), 91.

Lovemore's approaches: 'it is rare for a dramatist to deal with such a situation in such a cool and sensible way, without righteous indignation on the part of the woman and without the attempted use of force by the man'.[69] But that very avoidance of the conventional has made it difficult for critics to be confident about the cumulative dramatic effect of the final scenes.

That Southerne himself sensed danger here is suggested by his handling of Wellvile, who announces in 3.2 that he is himself writing a comedy called *The Wives' Excuse; or, Cuckolds Make Themselves* (l. 239). This admirable enterprise has been prompted by annoyance at the work of other playwrights:

I am scandalised extremely to see the women upon the stage make cuckolds at that insatiable rate they do in all our modern comedies, without any other reason from the poets, but because a man is married he must be a cuckold. Now, sir, I think the women are most unconscionably injured by this general scandal upon their sex. Therefore, to do 'em what service I can in their vindication, I design to write a play . . .

Yet he is unsure how to end it. Its story is, of course, that of Southerne's own play, and Friendall is self-damningly confident that it should climax with the unworthy husband's cuckolding, 'For such a character . . . will vindicate a wife in anything she can do to him'. Wellvile, referring both to Friendall's wife and the character in his play, claims to share this instinct: 'I am satisfied he ought to be a cuckold; and indeed, if the lady would take my advice, she should make him a cuckold'. So the 'vindication' Wellvile intends might simply enact the shabby moral in the play's subtitle. Yet, as he explains, other options remain open: 'I have not yet determined how to dispose of her. But, in regard to the ladies, I believe I shall make her honest at last' (ll. 230–59).

The two possible endings are nicely distinguished here. The cuckolding one reads as a natural nemesis for the husband's ineptitudes and worse. The 'honest' one is a species of compliment 'to the ladies'—projecting an image which is not necessarily probable, accurate, or exciting, but one which Wellvile still presumes to be culturally more acceptable to them. His instincts favour the first, his sense of decorum the second. Yet Friendall has predicted that the play's title, with its implication that adultery can be justified, is 'very

[69] Kenneth Muir, *The Comedy of Manners* (London, 1970), 91.

like to be popular among the women' (ll. 240–1), and Wellvile's own capacity to judge women has just been thrown into turmoil by Courtall's casual slandering of Mrs Sightly (ll. 158–78). As a playful and ironic self-portrait of the man who wrote the play in which he appears, Wellvile eloquently conveys the intricacy of Southerne's position, as a male writer seeking to create a representation of an unhappy wife which does not make her merely the plaything of male whims. Is he creating a comedy devoid of the sexual adrenalin and sense of rudimentary justice inflicted which are inherent to even the feeblest of cuckolding actions? Is he also in danger of fashioning an image of righteous female honesty which grows from a male sense of what is decorous, but which the women in the audience will find remote or unappealing? And is he creating a play which may be 'true among the men' (l. 242), i.e. satirically accurate about men's behaviour, but which will therefore be so directed towards a female constituency that it will have no pleasures to offer male spectators? Such witty self-scrutiny looks prophetic in the light of the comedy's failure in the contemporary playhouse. That he risked writing such a scene, however, may suggest that Southerne had thought long and hard about the difficulties and reckoned he had mastered them.

His treatment of Mrs Friendall in the final scene does not invite interpretation as simply 'a compliment to the ladies'. At two crucial moments in it the dramatic focus rests on her. The first involves her final plain speaking to Lovemore, in which she confesses her attraction to him, while making it clear he can expect nothing from her. In a key passage, she admits that 'Custom has fashioned' seduction 'into the way of living among the men', and that therefore his conduct 'may be i' th' right to all the town' (5.3.89–91). 'All the town' clearly does not mean only the men; custom has rendered unobjectionable, even acceptable, to fashionable women as well as men the freedoms the rakes take to themselves. She then pleads: 'let me be i' th' right too to my sex and to myself' (ll. 91–2). After the previous sentence, this one, with its echo-use of 'i' th' right', is in danger of sounding oddly abstract. Sustaining a self-defined integrity is one thing; but if her fellow women can tolerate the rakes' conduct, is it likely that they will also sincerely applaud hers? As a result, being 'i' th' right' seems most likely to mean something like 'true to an ideal of womanly integrity'. How the women in the play's society—and, also, in the audience—will respond to this exacting constancy is left unspecified and problematic.

In their 4.1 encounter Mrs Friendall had asked Lovemore:

> And would you have me lose that character,
> So 'worthy admiration', which even you,
> An enemy, must praise, when you would ruin?
> No, what I've done to raise this character
> May be an argument I will do more
> To heighten it, to the last act of life.
>
> (ll. 152–7)

In almost all the play's uses of it, 'character' means 'the image of one person in the eyes of one or more others', and hence, ultimately, 'the account of a person's nature and conduct current in their community'. In 4.1, the action they are discussing is not public knowledge; but Mrs Friendall speaks with a rapt and heightened rhetoric which suggests anticipation of future applause from some larger and sincerer audience than a single self-interested rake. The play's concluding moments bring Mrs Friendall face to face with that larger audience in the unhappiest of circumstances. Her entire strategy has been based on making what she can of a marriage which is a hollow charade, at whatever cost to her own understanding. This house of cards is brought tumbling down by the sheer inanity of Friendall's behaviour in the final scene; and her hesitant, troubled tone in her last major speech makes clear how unwelcome this denouement is to her (5.3.325–36). Their formal separation is swiftly agreed—an outcome another kind of Restoration comedy wife might greet delightedly for its promise of unrestricted liberty. To Mrs Friendall it represents bitter defeat. She has already rejected the adulterous option; but a woman, living apart from her husband, who does not seek sexual solace with another man, is a phenomenon her society finds it hard to credit and will not admire. Indeed, Mrs Friendall foresees the ultimate irony that 'if by separation we get free, | Then all our husband's faults are laid on us' (5.3.329–30). In claiming sympathetic attention for her plight, Mrs Friendall is thus forlornly requesting something her knowledge of her society suggests she is unlikely to receive.

Southerne's writing here does not seek to soften the blow. Hers may not be the speech of a woman confident of her society's understanding; but its every word makes clear that she still unavailingly desires to 'raise' her 'character' in its eyes. She insists on the suffering inherent in the 'hard condition of a woman's fate' (l. 331). But the only onstage response to that pained cry is a rake's mockery and her husband's crass celebration of his return to bachelor freedoms. This potent conflict of voices and perceptions is where the play leaves us. We are worlds away here from the simple either/or choices about endings debated by Friendall and Wellvile. Those would have been easily readable and, in their different ways, generically comfortable. Southerne's own ending eschews such easy options. With impeccable and unrelenting logic he has brought his action to this point. Now the spectators must make what they can of it. In *The Wives' Excuse*, as in the three other stunning plays in this volume, we encounter the work of a major dramatist who defies precedent in order to produce comic writing of the first rank.

Michael Cordner
York
1994

NOTE ON THE TEXTS

THE four plays in this volume were first published as follows: *The Soldiers' Fortune* in 1681, *The Princess of Cleves* in 1689, *Amphitryon* in 1690, and *The Wives' Excuse* in 1692. For each of them this first printed text offers the most authoritative basis for a modern edition, though subsequent quartos and/or collected editions often introduce apt corrections and emendations of the original quarto at particular points. Substantive departures from first quarto readings in the present edition, whether editorial or derived from subsequent seventeenth- or early eighteenth-century printings, are identified in the notes. The first quarto readings are identified in brackets (*1681* for *The Soldiers' Fortune*, and so on), and a similar style is employed to identify the later printing from which a reading has been admitted into the present texts.

The texts have been modernized in spelling and in punctuation. Standard forms have been adopted for characters' names both in entry/exit directions and in speech prefixes, and the necessary alterations to the quartos have been silently introduced. Similarly, apart from 'exit' and 'exeunt', Latin forms in stage directions and speech prefixes ('solus' and 'sola' for 'alone', 'manet' for 'remains', and 'omnes' for 'all') have been silently translated. In addition, at some points, the quartos have 'exit' for a multiple exit and 'exeunt' for a solitary one. Here too the necessary corrections have been silently made.

In all four plays the stage directions have been substantially amplified. It is fundamental to the principles of the series in which this edition appears that the reader should be offered all legitimate help possible to visualize the stage action the text demands. The first quartos are all relatively lightly equipped with stage directions, and on occasion those which are provided seem highly problematic. All editorial stage directions, as well as editorial alterations to first quarto stage directions, are signalled by being placed in square brackets. The stage directions have also been silently standardized to fit the series conventions. For instance, concluding directions to a scene take the form of a simple 'exit' or 'exeunt', regardless of whether the quarto did or did not specify the relevant characters' names.

A particularly taxing problem for the editor of the Lee and Southerne texts is the fluency with which in certain scenes they move

1

between verse and prose. The 1689 *Princess of Cleves* text lays some passages out as verse which seem scarcely to require this honour; whereas the 1692 *Wives' Excuse* text treats as prose passages which will strike most modern readers as verse. In the latter case, adjudicating exactly where the moves into verse and out again occur is a matter of especially delicate judgement. The versions printed here result from numerous experiments with other ways of dividing the relevant speeches and differ from the handling of the same problem in the Jordan and Love 1988 edition of the play. The nature of the problem means that absolute certainty is unobtainable. Here, in particular, readers and potential actors and directors need to listen carefully and be aware that alternative layouts are indeed possible.

In Lee's play a particular difficulty concerns how to handle French names in a modernized edition. Lee's title-page, for instance, announces it as 'The Princess of Cleve'. He derives this spelling from the 1679 translation of the novel, which uses 'Cleves' on its own title-page, but thereafter favours 'Cleve'. After much debate, we settled on 'Cleves', rather than 'Clèves' or 'Cleve', as a semi-Anglicized form (often, for instance, used in English historical accounts of Henry VIII's queen, Anne of Cleves), and therefore apt to the way Lee presumably intended it to be pronounced, but still staying loyal to the spelling of the French place-name. In contrast, in the case of the first quarto's 'St. André', we have used the proper French form, 'Saint-André', since here there is no pronunciation difference separating the two forms.

Of the plays in this volume only one—*The Soldiers' Fortune*—has been previously available in a modernized edition, and that was at the turn of the century, in a selection of Otway's works edited by Roden Noel for the Mermaid series in 1903. All four writers, however, have been awarded substantial old-spelling editions in the present century. Thus, in the 1930s J. C. Ghosh published a two-volume edition of Otway's *Works* (Oxford, 1932), which effectively displaced Montague Summers' three-volume edition of the previous decade (London, 1926); and, in the 1950s, Thomas B. Stroup and Arthur L. Cooke produced a two-volume edition of Lee's *Works* (New Brunswick, NJ, 1954). In the 1970s, volume xv, edited by Earl Miner, of the California edition of Dryden's *Works* (Berkeley, Calif., 1976) offered an authoritative edition of *Amphitryon*, and Ralph R. Thornton published a single-play edition of *The Wives' Excuse* (Wynnewood, Pa., 1973). This was followed fifteen years later by the two-volume edition of Southerne's *Works*, edited by Robert Jordan and Harold

Love (Oxford, 1988). We are inevitably deeply indebted to the impressive scholarship and industry of our predecessors; and, though we have departed from their precedents at numerous points in our handling of both texts and annotation, we have done this with a due sense of our own temerity.

THE RESTORATION STAGE

The playhouses for which these plays were written combined a scenic stage designed to display perspective scenery with a forestage projecting beyond the proscenium opening into the pit. This forestage area was substantial—in the 1674 Theatre Royal, Drury Lane, for example, it reached about twenty feet into the pit—and in comedy the majority of the acting took place on it. From the forestage the player was in intimate and easy contact with the audience. The smallest of gestures would register, and projection of the voice for an experienced performer was effortless. Some scholars see in this exploitation by players and playwrights of the advantages of physical proximity larger implications for the post-1660 comedy. Peter Holland, for instance, has argued that

Restoration comedy emphasised its close connections with its audience—and hence its claim, through its *vraisemblance* in acting and locale, to comment on its audience's morals—by placing the action principally on the forestage. Realistic as many of the sets must have been, especially for London locations like the New Exchange, Hyde Park or Covent Garden, the actors aligned themselves with the audience, especially through the use of the aside, so that the audience perceived the realism of the set as mediated through the action of the hybrid being, the actor-character. The audience saw the action as in a situation potentially analogous to their own, rather than in a totally fictive world. (*The Ornament of Action: Text and Performance in Restoration Comedy* (Cambridge, 1979), p. 29)

The scenic stage itself was unveiled after the speaking of the prologue by the drawing of the curtain, which then usually remained open until the performance's end. All changes of the scenes during the action took place, therefore, in full view of the audience. A particular setting (a private house, say, or St James's Park) was produced by manœuvring a pair of matching shutters (with the appropriate location painted on them) towards each other from either wing on grooves set in the stage-floor. Framed by side scenes ('wings'), these then provided a flat pictorial background to the action. The playhouses' stages were equipped with two shutter positions, at each of which three different sets of shutters could be sequentially displayed; so providing a variety of settings during a single performance was easily practicable. Thus, the direction 'the scene opens' means that one set of shutters opens to reveal another in place behind them, and so on. Sufficient space was available between the grooves to allow 'discovery scenes', i.e. the positioning of properties and/or players behind the previous shutters, to be revealed when the previous scene ends (as at the beginning of 2.1 of *The Wives' Excuse*) or during the course of a scene (as at 4.1.182–7 of *The Soldiers' Fortune*). These arrangements permitted a fluent transition from scene to scene within an act, and the stage would ordinarily only be bare of actors at the ends of acts, when the so-called 'act tunes'—i.e. instrumental pieces used to mark the act-interval—would be performed by the theatre-musicians. (The performance would also have been preceded by 'the first and second music'—i.e. a substantial overture. Curtis A. Price has provided an invaluable guide to the subject in his *Music in the Restoration Theatre* (Ann Arbor, Mich., 1979).)

The texts in this collection also include scenes where at least some, and perhaps all, of a scene seems designed to take place within the scenic stage. An example would be the opening of 5.3 of *The Princess of Cleves*, with the Princess and Irene framed beside the 'state'. How much of the following encounter between the Princess and Nemours was designed to be enacted within the scenic stage it is impossible now to determine.

The proscenium walls which flanked the scenic stage contained doors at stage level, and these were surmounted by balconies. The doors provided the easiest means of access to the forestage and were the most frequently used entry-points in comedy. The balconies too were mobilized whenever the script demanded some raised vantage-point for one or more of the characters. In addition, the proscenium walls could themselves enjoy a scenic function. Building on the effect of the image represented on the current pair of shutters, they could, for instance, represent the exterior of a house or houses or the interior of a house.

This was an intensely versatile playing-space which the four dramatists represented in this volume knew intimately and were able to exploit to full advantage. Further information on its lay-out and the uses to which it could be put can be found in the Introduction to Emmett L. Avery and Arthur H. Scouten, *The London Stage, 1660–1700* (Carbondale, Ill., 1968); Lee J. Martin, 'From Forestage to Proscenium: A Study of Restoration Staging Techniques', *Theatre Survey*, 4 (1963), 3–28; Peter Holland, *The Ornament of Action*, 19–54; Colin Visser, 'Scenery and Technical Design', in Robert D. Hume (ed.), *The London Theatre World, 1660–1800* (Carbondale and Edwardsville, Ill., 1980), 66–118; and Judith Milhous and Robert D. Hume, *Producible Interpretation: Eight English Plays 1675–1707* (Carbondale and Edwardsville, Ill., 1985).

THE CRITICAL INHERITANCE

The most comprehensive introduction to this period's drama is provided by Robert D. Hume, *The Development of English Drama in the Late Seventeenth Century* (Oxford, 1976). Hume has also written an important article investigating dramatic trends across the years during which the plays in this volume were produced, ' "The Change in Comedy": Cynical Versus Exemplary Comedy on the London Stage, 1678–1693', *Essays in Theatre*, 1 (1983), 101–18.

The treatment of marital crisis in comedies written for the post-1660 stage has been explored in a number of studies. These include Gellert Spencer Alleman, *Matrimonial Law and the Materials of Restoration Comedy* (Wallingford, 1942); A. H. Scouten, 'Notes towards a History of Restoration Comedy', *Philological Quarterly*, 45 (1966), 62–70; Maximillian E. Novak, 'Margery Pinchwife's "London Disease": Restoration Comedy and the Libertine Offensive of the 1670's', *Studies in the Literary Imagination*, 10 (1977), 1–23; Robert D. Hume, 'Marital Discord in English Comedy from Dryden to Fielding', *Modern Philology*, 74 (1976–7), 248–72; and Michael Cordner, 'Marriage Comedy after the 1688 Revolution: Southerne to Vanbrugh', *Modern Language Review*, 85 (1990), 273–89.

Otway and Lee were linked in a biographical study by Roswell Gray Ham, *Otway and Lee: Biography from a Baroque Age* (New Haven, Conn., 1931), which is critically dated, but still informative biographically. Up-to-date biographical surveys of both Otway and Lee are provided in J. Douglas Canfield, 'Thomas Otway', and Richard E. Brown, 'Nathaniel Lee', in Paula Backscheider (ed.), *Dictionary of Literary Biography, lxxx, Restoration and Eighteenth-Century Dramatists: First Series* (Detroit, 1989). Dryden has recently been the subject of a princely biography by James Anderson Winn, *John Dryden and his World* (New Haven, Conn., 1987). The best account of Southerne's life is provided as a preface to the first volume of the definitive edition of his *Works*, ed. Robert Jordan and Harold Love (Oxford, 1988).

Critical interest in Otway has tended to focus on his tragedies, but Robert D. Hume has written a striking essay on his comedies, 'Otway and the Comic Muse', *Studies in Philology*, 73 (1976), 87–116. Thomas B. Stroup had earlier published a survey of Otway's dramatic output which includes the comedies, 'Otway's Bitter Pessimism', in Daniel W. Patterson and Albrecht B. Strauss (eds.), *Essays in English Literature of the Classical Period Presented to Dougald MacMillan* (Chapel Hill, NC, 1967), 54–75. There is also a book-length study of his career by Kerstin P. Warner, *Thomas Otway* (Boston, Mass., 1982).

Scholarship on Lee has been similarly preoccupied with the non-comic work, but, once again, Robert D. Hume has stepped into the breach with an invaluable article on *The Princess of Cleves*, 'The Satiric Design of Nat. Lee's *The Princess of Cleve*', *Journal of English and Germanic Philology*, 75 (1976), 117–38.[1] In this case also, Thomas B. Stroup had earlier written on the topic, but this time less convincingly, in '*The Princess of Cleve* and Sentimental Comedy', *Review of English Studies*, 11 (1935), 200–3. J. M. Armistead has written a thoughtful book-length account of Lee, *Nathaniel Lee* (Boston, Mass., 1979), and two recent articles contain interesting material on the play: Richard E. Brown, 'Heroics Satirized by "Mad Nat. Lee" ', *Papers on Language and Literature*, 19 (1983), 385–401, and J. Douglas Canfield, 'Poetical Injustice in Some Neglected Masterpieces of Restoration Drama', in Canfield and J. Paul Hunter (eds.), *Rhetorics of Order/Ordering Rhetorics in English Neoclassical Literature* (Newark, NJ, 1989), 23–45. The latter also includes a section on *Amphitryon*.

James D. Garrison devotes a whole article to Dryden's play in 'Dryden and the Birth of Hercules', *Studies in Philology*, 77 (1980), 180–201, and Judith Milhous and Robert D. Hume, *Producible Interpretation: Eight English Plays 1675–1707* (Carbondale and Edwardsville, Ill., 1985) awards it a chapter. Other books which contain stimulating material on it include Irvin Ehrenpreis, *Acts of Implication: Suggestion and Covert Meaning in the Works of Dryden, Swift, Pope and Austen* (Berkeley, Calif., 1980); Judith Sloman, *Dryden: The Poetics of Translation* (Toronto, 1985); Bruce R. Smith, *Ancient Scripts & Modern Experience on the English Stage 1500–1700* (Princeton, NJ, 1988); and David Bywaters, *Dryden in Revolutionary England* (Berkeley, Calif., 1991). Anthony Kaufman writes on its epilogue, as also on the epilogue to *The Wives' Excuse*, in 'The Smiler with the Knife: Covert Aggression in Some Restoration Epilogues', *Studies in the Literary Imagination*, 17 (1984), 63–74.

[1] Hume's essays on marriage comedy, Otway's comedies and *The Princess of Cleves* have been helpfully reprinted in his *The Rakish Stage: Studies in English Drama, 1660–1800* (Carbondale and Edwardsville, Ill., 1983).

Articles with material of interest on *The Wives' Excuse* include Harold Love, '*The Wives' Excuse* and Restoration Comedy', *Komos*, 2 (1969–70), 148–56; Anthony Kaufman, ' "This Hard Condition of a Woman's Fate": Southerne's *The Wives' Excuse*', *Modern Language Quarterly*, 34 (1973), 36–47; Eugene M. Waith, 'Admiration in the Comedies of Thomas Southerne', in René Wellek and Alvaro Ribeiro (eds.), *Evidence in Literary Scholarship* (Oxford, 1979), 89–103; and Helga Drougge, ' "We'll learn that of the men": Female Sexuality in Southerne's Comedies', *Studies in English Literature*, 33 (1993), 545–63. Milhous and Hume, *Producible Interpretation*, provide an important chapter on it, and two books with significant sections devoted to it are Peter Holland, *The Ornament of Action: Text and Performance in Restoration Comedy* (Cambridge, 1979) and David Roberts, *The Ladies: Female Patronage of Restoration Drama 1660–1700* (Oxford, 1989). Holland particularly highlights the importance to the play's design of its original casting. (We now have at our disposal an invaluable array of information about Restoration performers in Philip H. Highfill, Jr., Kalman A. Burnim, and Edward A. Langhans (eds.), *A Biographical Dictionary of Actors, Actresses, Musicians, Dancers, Managers and Other Stage Personnel in London, 1660–1800* (16 vols.; Carbondale and Edwardsville, Ill., 1973–93).) Robert D. Hume has also published an interesting meditation on the implications of the Jordan/Love edition, 'The Importance of Thomas Southerne', *Modern Philology*, 87 (1989–90), 275–90.

In addition, books which cast their net widely across the post-1660 drama often contain useful material on one or more of the plays in this volume. Edward Burns, *Restoration Comedy: Crises of Desire and Identity* (London, 1987), for instance, writes on all of them, and Harold Weber, *The Restoration Rake-Hero: Transformations in Sexual Understanding in Seventeenth-Century England* (Madison, Wis., 1986) contains sections on the Lee and Southerne plays.

A CHRONOLOGY OF MARRIAGE PLAYS

THE following is a highly selective listing of plays, written between 1660 and the very early eighteenth century, in which at least one major plot centres on a marriage in disarray. The accompanying dates are those of certain or likely first performance.

George Etherege, *She Would If She Could* (1668)
Thomas Betterton, *The Amorous Widow* (*c.*1670)
John Dryden, *Marriage à la Mode* (1672)
Thomas Shadwell, *Epsom Wells* (1672)
John Dover, *The Mall* (1674)
William Wycherley, *The Country Wife* (1675)
Thomas Shadwell, *The Virtuoso* (1676)
William Wycherley, *The Plain Dealer* (1676)
[Thomas Rawlins?], *Tom Essence* (1676)
Thomas Durfey, *A Fond Husband* (1677)
Thomas Porter, *The French Conjuror* (1677)
Aphra Behn, *Sir Patient Fancy* (1678)
John Dryden, *Mr Limberham* (1678)
John Leanard, *The Rambling Justice* (1678)
Thomas Otway, *Friendship in Fashion* (1678)
Thomas Durfey, *The Virtuous Wife* (1679)
Thomas Shadwell, *The Woman Captain* (1679)
Thomas Otway, *The Soldiers' Fortune* (1680)
Aphra Behn, *The Roundheads* (1681)
Thomas Durfey, *Sir Barnaby Whig* (1681)
Edward Ravenscroft, *The London Cuckolds* (1681)
Nathaniel Lee, *The Princess of Cleves* (1681–2)
Thomas Otway, *The Atheist* (1682)
John Crowne, *The City Politiques* (1683)
Thomas Southerne, *The Disappointment* (1684)
Thomas Jevon, *The Devil of a Wife* (1686)
Aphra Behn, *The Lucky Chance* (1687)
Thomas Durfey, *A Fool's Preferment* (1688)
John Dryden, *Amphitryon* (1690)
William Mountfort, *Greenwich Park* (1691)
Thomas Southerne, *The Wives' Excuse* (1691–2)

Thomas Shadwell, *The Volunteers* (1692)
William Congreve, *The Old Bachelor* (1693)
Thomas Southerne, *The Maid's Last Prayer* (1693)
William Congreve, *The Double Dealer* (1694)
John Crowne, *The Married Beau* (1694)
William Congreve, *Love for Love* (1695)
Colley Cibber, *Love's Last Shift* (1696)
Mary Pix, *The Spanish Wives* (1696)
John Vanbrugh, *The Relapse* (1696)
Mary Pix, *The Innocent Mistress* (1697)
John Vanbrugh, *The Provoked Wife* (1697)
John Corye, *A Cure for Jealousy* (1699–1700)
William Burnaby, *The Reformed Wife* (1700)
William Congreve, *The Way of the World* (1700)
William Burnaby, *The Ladies' Visiting-Day* (1701)
Thomas Durfey, *The Bath* (1701)
Richard Steele, *The Funeral* (1701)
William Burnaby, *The Modish Husband* (1702)
Susanna Centlivre, *The Beau's Duel* (1702)
Richard Wilkinson, *Vice Reclaimed* (1703)
Colley Cibber, *The Careless Husband* (1704)
Richard Steele, *The Tender Husband* (1705)
John Vanbrugh, *The Confederacy* (1705)
Colley Cibber, *The Lady's Last Stake* (1707)
George Farquhar, *The Beaux' Stratagem* (1707)

THE SOLDIERS' FORTUNE

BY

THOMAS OTWAY

Quem recitas meus est O fidentine libellus,
Sed male cum recitas incipit esse tuus.°

[Martial]

THE DEDICATION

Mr Bentley,°

I have often, during this play's being in the press, been importuned for a preface; which you, I suppose, would have speak something in vindication of the comedy. Now, to please you, Mr Bentley, I will as briefly as I can speak my mind upon that occasion, which you may be pleased to accept of, both as a dedication to yourself, and next as a preface to the book.

And I am not a little proud that it has happened into my thoughts to be the first who in these latter years has made an epistle dedicatory to his stationer. It is a compliment as reasonable as it is just. For, Mr Bentley, you pay honestly for the copy; and an epistle to you is a sort of an acquittance, and may be probably welcome, when, to a person of higher rank and order, it looks like an obligation for praises, which he knows he does not deserve, and therefore is very unwilling to part with ready money for.

As to the vindication of this comedy, between friends and acquaintance, I believe it is possible that as much may be said in its behalf as heretofore has been for a great many others. But, of all the apish qualities about me, I have not that of being fond of my own issue. Nay, I must confess myself a very unnatural parent, for when it is once brought into the world, e'en let the brat shift for itself, I say.

The objections made against the merit of this poor play, I must confess, are very grievous.

First, says a lady that shall be nameless, because the world may think civilly of her,° 'Faugh! O sherru! 'Tis so filthy, so bawdy, no modest woman ought to be seen at it.° Let me die, it has made me sick'—when the world lies, Mr Bentley, if that very lady has not easily digested a much ranker morsel in a little alehouse towards Paddington,° and never made a face at it. But your true jilt is a creature that can extract bawdy out of the chastest sense, as easily as a spider can poison out of a rose.° They know true bawdy, let it be never so much concealed, as perfectly as Falstaff did the true prince by instinct.° They will separate the true metal from the allay, let us temper it as well as we can. Some women are the touchstones of filthiness. Though I have heard a lady° (that has more modesty than any of those she-critics, and I am sure more wit) say, she wondered at the impudence of any of her sex that would pretend to understand the thing called bawdy. So, Mr Bentley, for aught I perceive, my play may be innocent yet, and the lady mistaken in pretending to the knowledge of a mystery above her; though, to speak honestly, she has had besides her wit a liberal education, and (if we may credit the world) has not buried her talent neither.°

This is, Mr Bentley, all I can say in behalf of my play; wherefore I throw it into your arms. Make the best of it you can; praise it to your customers; sell ten thousand of them if possible—and then you will complete the wishes of

> Your friend and servant,
> Thomas Otway

THE CHARACTERS OF THE PLAY

Captain Beaugard°	*Mr Betterton*
Courtine°	*Mr Smith*
Sir Davy Dunce	*Mr Nokes*
Sir Jolly Jumble°	*Mr Leigh*
Fourbin,° *a servant to Beaugard*	*Mr Jevon*
Bloody Bones°	*Mr Richards*
Vermin, *servant to Sir Davy*	
A boy	
A Constable and Watch[men]	
[Frisk]	
[Drawer]	
[Will]	
[Chairman]	
[Bullies]	
[Passers-by in 2.1]	

Lady Dunce	*Mrs Barry*
Sylvia	*Mrs Price*
Maid	

[Musicians]

5

10

15

SCENE: LONDON

Prologue°

by Lord Falkland°

Forsaken dames with less concern reflect
On their inconstant hero's cold neglect,°
Than we (provoked by this ungrateful age)
Bear the hard fate of our abandoned stage.°
With grief we see you ravished from our arms,   5
And curse the feeble virtue of our charms;
Curse your false hearts, for none so false as they,
And curse the eyes that stole those hearts away.
Remember, faithless friends, there was a time
(But O the sad remembrance of our prime!)   10
When to our arms with eager joys ye flew,
And we believed your treacherous hearts as true
As e'er was nymph of ours to one of you.°
But a more powerful saint enjoys ye now,°
Fraught with sweet sins and absolutions too.   15
To her are all your pious vows addressed.
She's both your love's, and your religion's test,
The fairest prelate of her time and best.
We own her more deserving far than we,
A just excuse for your inconstancy.   20
Yet 'twas unkindly done to leave us so:
First to betray with love, and then undo—
A horrid crime you're all addicted to.
Too soon, alas, your appetites are cloyed,
And Phillis rules no more, when once enjoyed.°   25
But all rash oaths of love and constancy
With the too short, forgotten pleasures die,
Whilst she, poor soul, robbed of her dearest ease,
Still drudges on, with vain desire to please,
And restless follows you from place to place,   30
For tributes due to her autumnal face.
Deserted thus by such ungrateful men,
How can we hope you'll e'er return again?
Here's no new charm to tempt ye as before;
Wit now's our only treasure left in store,   35

And that's a coin will pass with you no more.
You who such dreadful bullies would appear
(True bullies!—quiet when there's danger near)
Show your great souls in damning poets here.

1.1

[*The Mall*]°

Enter Beaugard, Courtine and Fourbin

BEAUGARD A pox o' fortune! Thou art always teasing me about
fortune. Thou risest in a morning with ill luck in thy mouth; nay,
never eatest a dinner, but thou sighest two hours after it, with
thinking where to get the next. Fortune be damned, since the
world's so wide.   5

COURTINE As wide as it is, 'tis so thronged and crammed
with knaves and fools, that an honest man° can hardly get a living
in it.

BEAUGARD Do, rail, Courtine, do; it may get thee employment.

COURTINE At you I ought to rail. 'Twas your fault we left our   10
employments abroad° to come home, and be loyal, and now we as
loyally starve for it.

BEAUGARD Did not thy ancestors do it before thee, man? I tell thee,
loyalty and starving are all one. The old Cavaliers got such a trick
of it in the king's exile, that their posterity could never thrive   15
since.°

COURTINE 'Tis a fine equipage I am like to be reduced to. I shall be
ere long as greasy as an Alsatia bully°—this flopping° hat, pinned
up on one side, with a sandy weather-beaten peruke, dirty linen,
and to complete the figure, a long, scandalous iron sword° jarring   20
at my heels, like a—

BEAUGARD Snarling, thou meanest, like its master.

COURTINE My companion's the worthy knight of the most noble
order of the post°—your peripatetic philosophers of the Temple
walks, rogues in rags, and yet not honest; villains that undervalue   25
damnation, will forswear themselves for a dinner, and hang their
fathers for half a crown.

BEAUGARD I am ashamed to hear a soldier talk of starving.

COURTINE Why, what shall I do? I can't steal!

BEAUGARD Though thou canst not steal, thou hast other vices   30
enough for any industrious young fellow to live comfortably upon.

COURTINE What, wouldst thou have me turn rascal, and run cheating up and down the town for a livelihood? I would no more keep
a blockhead company and endure his nauseous nonsense in hopes
to get him, than I would be a drudge° to an old woman with   35

rheumatic eyes, hollow teeth, and stinking breath, for a pension.
Of all rogues, I would not be a foolmonger.

BEAUGARD How well this niceness becomes thee! I'd fain see thee
e'en turn parson in a pet, o' purpose to rail at all those vices which
I know thou naturally art fond of. Why, surely an old lady's   40
pension need not be so despicable in the eyes of a disbanded
officer, as times go, friend.

COURTINE I am glad, Beaugard, you think so.

BEAUGARD Why, thou shalt think so too, man. Be ruled by me, and
I'll bring thee into good company—families,° Courtine, families,   45
and such families, where formality's a scandal and pleasure is the
business, where the women are all wanton, and the men all witty,
you rogue.

COURTINE What, some of your worship's Wapping° acquaintance
that you made last time you came over for recruits and spirited   50
away your landlady's daughter, a-volunteering with you into
France?

BEAUGARD I'll bring thee, Courtine, where cuckoldom's in credit,
and lewdness laudable, where thou shalt wallow in pleasures and
preferments, revel all day, and every night lie in the arms of   55
melting beauty, sweet as roses, and as springs refreshing.

COURTINE Prithee don't talk thus. I had rather thou wouldst tell me
where new levies are to be raised.° A pox of whores, when a man
has not money to make 'em comfortable.

BEAUGARD That shall shower upon us in abundance. And for   60
instance, know to thy everlasting amazement, all this dropped out
of the clouds today.

COURTINE Ha! Gold, by this light!

FOURBIN Out of the clouds!

BEAUGARD (to Fourbin) Ay, gold! Does it not smell of the sweet hand   65
that sent it? Smell, smell, you dog!

> *Fourbin smells to the handful of gold, and gathers up some*
> *pieces in his mouth*

FOURBIN Truly, sir, of heavenly sweetness; and very refreshing.

COURTINE Dear Beaugard, if thou hast any good nature in thee, if
thou wouldst not have me hang myself before my time, tell me
where the devil haunts that helped thee to this, that I may go make   70
a bargain with him presently.° Speak, speak, or I am a lost man.

BEAUGARD Why, thou must know, this devil, which I have given my
soul to already, and must, I suppose, have my body very speedily,
lives I know not where, and may for aught I know be a real devil.

But if it be, 'tis the best-natured devil under Beelzebub's domi-   75
nion. That I'll swear to.

COURTINE But how came the gold then?

BEAUGARD To deal freely with my friend, I am lately happened into
the acquaintance of a very reverend° pimp, as fine a discreet, sober,
grey-bearded old gentleman as one would wish; as good a natured,   80
public-spirited person as the nation holds; one that is never so
happy as when he is bringing good people together, and promoting
civil understanding betwixt the sexes. Nay, rather than want
employment, he will go from one end of the town to t'other to
procure my lord's little dog to be civil to my lady's little   85
languishing bitch.

COURTINE A very worthy member of the commonwealth!

BEAUGARD This noble person one day—but Fourbin can give you a
more particular account of the matter. [To Fourbin] Sweet sir, if
you please, tell us the story of the first encounter betwixt you and   90
Sir Jolly Jumble. [To Courtine] You must know that's his title.

FOURBIN Sir, it shall be done. Walking one day upon the Piazza°
about three of the clock i' th'afternoon, to get me a stomach to my
dinner, I chance to encounter a person of goodly presence and
worthy appearance, his beard and hair white, grave and comely,   95
his countenance ruddy, plump, smooth and cheerful; who, perceiv-
ing me also equipped as I am with a mien and air which might well
inform him I was a person of no inconsiderable quality,° came very
respectfully up to me, and, after the usual ceremonies between
persons of parts° and breeding had passed, very humbly inquired   100
of me, 'What is it o'clock?' I, presently understanding° by the
question that he was a man of parts and business, told him I did
presume it was at most but nicely turned of three.

BEAUGARD Very court-like, civil, quaint, and new, I think.

FOURBIN The freedom of commerce increasing,° after some little   105
inconsiderable questions *pour passer le temps*° and so,° he was
pleased to offer me the courtesy of a glass of wine. I told him I
very seldom drank, but if he so pleased, I would do myself the
honour to present him with a dish of meat at an eating-house hard
by, where I had an interest.°   110

COURTINE Very well! I think this squire° of thine, Beaugard, is as
accomplished a person as any of the employment I ever saw.

BEAUGARD Let the rogue go on.

COURTINE In short, we agreed and went together. As soon as we
entered the room, 'I am your most humble servant, sir', says he.   115

'I am the meanest of your vassals, sir', said I. 'I am very happy in lighting into the acquaintance of so worthy a gentleman as you appear to be, sir', said he again. 'Worthy Sir Jolly', then came I upon him again o' t'other side (for you must know by that time I had groped out his title), 'I kiss your hands from the bottom of my heart, which I shall be always ready to lay at your feet'.   120

COURTINE Well, Fourbin, and what replied the knight then?

FOURBIN Nothing; he had nothing to say. His sense was transported with admiration of my parts. So we sat down, and after some pause, he desired to know by what title he was to distinguish° the person that had so highly honoured him.   125

BEAUGARD That is as much as to say, sir, whose rascal° you were.

FOURBIN Sir, you may make as bold with your poor slave as you please.—I told him those that knew me well were pleased to call me the Chevalier Fourbin, that I was a cadet of the ancient family of the Fourbinois, and that I had had the honour of serving the great monarch of France in his wars in Flanders, where I contracted great familiarity and intimacy with a gallant officer of the English troops in that service, one Captain Beaugard.°   130

BEAUGARD O, sir, you did me too much honour.—What a true-bred rogue's this!   135

COURTINE Well, but the money, Fourbin, the money.

FOURBIN 'Beaugard, hum, Beaugard', says he. 'Ay, it must be so. A black man,° is he not?' 'Ay', says I, 'blackish'. 'A dark brown, full-faced?' 'Yes.' 'A sly, subtle, observing eye?' 'The same.' 'A strong-built, well-made man?' 'Right.' 'A devilish fellow for a wench, a devilish fellow for a wench, I warrant him! A thundering rogue upon occasion, Beaugard! A thundering fellow for a wench! I must be acquainted with him.'   140

COURTINE But to the money, the money, man. That's the thing I would be acquainted withal.   145

BEAUGARD This civil gentleman of the chevalier's acquaintance comes yesterday morning to my lodging, and seeing my picture in miniature upon the toilet,° told me with the greatest ecstasy in the world, that was the thing he came to me about. He told me there was a lady of his acquaintance had some favourable thoughts of me, and 'Egad', says he, 'she's a hummer, such a *bona roba*, ah-h-h!' So without more ado begs me to lend it him till dinner, for we concluded to eat together. So away he scuttled with as great joy as if he had found the philosopher's stone.°   150

                    155

COURTINE Very well.

BEAUGARD At Locket's° we met again; where after a thousand grimaces to show how much he was pleased, instead of my picture, presents me with the contents aforesaid, and told me the lady desired me to accept of 'em for the picture, which she was much 160 transported withal,° as well as with the original.

COURTINE Ha!

BEAUGARD Now, whereabouts this taking quality lies in me, the devil take me, Ned, if I know—but the fates, Ned, the fates!

COURTINE A curse on the fates! Of all strumpets fortune's the basest. 165 'Twas fortune made me a soldier, a rogue in red, the grievance of the nation. Fortune made the peace just when we were upon the brink of a war. Then fortune disbanded us and lost us two months' pay.° Fortune gave us debentures° instead of ready money, and by very good fortune I sold mine and lost heartily by it, in hopes the 170 grinding, ill-natured dog that bought it will never get a shilling for't.

BEAUGARD Leave off thy railing, for shame. It looks like a cur that barks for want of bones. Come, times may mend, and an honest soldier be in fashion again. 175

COURTINE These greasy, fat, unwieldy, wheezing° rogues that live at home and brood over their bags,° when a fit of fear's upon 'em, then if one of us pass but by, all the family is ready at the door to cry, 'Heavens bless you, sir! The laird° go along with you'.

BEAUGARD 'Ah, good men, what pity 'tis such proper° gentlemen 180 should ever be out of employment!'

COURTINE But when the business is over, then every parish bawd that goes but to a conventicle twice a week, and pays but scot and lot to the parish, shall roar out, 'Faugh, ye lousy redcoat° rakehells! Hout, ye caterpillars, ye locusts of the nation! You are the dogs 185 that would enslave us all, plunder our shops, and ravish our daughters, ye scoundrels'.

BEAUGARD I must confess ravishing ought to be regulated. It would destroy commerce, and many a good, sober matron about this town might lose the selling of her daughter's maidenhead, which were a 190 great grievance to the people, and a particular branch of property lost.°—Fourbin!

FOURBIN Your worship's pleasure?

BEAUGARD Run like a rogue as you are, and try to find Sir Jolly, and desire him to meet me at the Blue Posts° in the Haymarket about 195 twelve. We'll dine together. I must inquire farther into yesterday's adventure.

[*Exit Fourbin*]

In the meantime, Ned, here's half the prize to be doing withal.
Old friends must preserve correspondence.° We have shared good
fortune together, and bad shall never part us.   200

COURTINE Well, thou wilt certainly die in a ditch for this. Hast thou
no more grace than to be a true friend, nay, to part with thy money
to thy friend? I grant you, a gentleman may swear and lie for his
friend, pimp for his friend, hang for his friend, and so forth; but
to part with ready money is the devil.   205

BEAUGARD Stand aside. Either I am mistaken, or yonder's Sir
Jolly coming. Now, Courtine, will I show thee the flower of
knighthood.

      Enter Sir Jolly Jumble

Ah, Sir Jolly!

SIR JOLLY My hero! My darling! My Ganymede!° How dost thou?   210
Strong! Wanton! Lusty! Rampant!° Ha, ah, ah! She's thine, boy;
od,° she's thine. Plump, soft, smooth, wanton! Ha, ah, ah! Ah
rogue, ah rogue! Here's shoulders, here's shape! There's a foot and
leg! Here's a leg, here's a leg! Qua-a-a-a-a!

      [*Sir Jolly*] *squeaks like a cat, and tickles Beaugard's legs*

COURTINE What an old goat's this!   215

SIR JOLLY Child, child, child, who's that? A friend of thine! A friend
o' thine? A pretty fellow; od, a very pretty fellow, and a strong
dog, I'll warrant him. How dost do, dear heart? Prithee let me kiss
thee. I'll swear and vow I will kiss thee. Ha, ha, he, he, he, he! A
toad, a toad, ah toa-a-a-ad!   220

COURTINE Sir, I am your humble servant.

BEAUGARD But the lady, Sir Jolly, the lady? How does the lady?
What says the lady, Sir Jolly?

SIR JOLLY What says the lady! Why, she says—she says—od, she has
a delicate° lip, such a lip, so red, so hard, so plump, so blub. I   225
fancy I am eating cherries every time I think on't—and for her
neck and breasts and her—od's life! I'll say no more, not a word
more. But I know, I know—

BEAUGARD I am sorry for that with all my heart. Do you know, say
you, sir, and would you put off your mumbled orts, your offal,   230
upon me?

SIR JOLLY Hush, hush, hush! Have a care. As I live and breathe, not
I. Alack and well-a-day, I am a poor old fellow, decayed and done.
All's gone with me, gentlemen, but my good nature. Od, I love to
know how matters go, though—now and then to see a pretty   235

wench and a young fellow touse and rouse and frowze and mouse.
Od, I love a young fellow dearly, faith, dearly!

COURTINE This is the most extraordinary rogue I ever met withal.

BEAUGARD But, Sir Jolly, in the first place, you must know I have
sworn never to marry.   240

SIR JOLLY I would not have thee, man. I am a bachelor myself, and
been a whoremaster all my life. Besides, she's married already,
man. Her husband's an old, greasy, untoward, ill-natured,
slovenly, tobacco-taking cuckold—but plaguy jealous.

BEAUGARD Already a cuckold, Sir Jolly?   245

SIR JOLLY No; that shall be, my boy. Thou shalt make him one, and
I'll pimp for thee, dear heart. And shan't I hold the door? Shan't
I peep, ha? Shan't I, you devil? You little dog, shan't I?

BEAUGARD What is it I'd not grant to oblige my patron?

SIR JOLLY And then—dost hear?—I have a lodging for thee in my   250
own house. Dost hear, old soul? In my own house. She lives the
very next door, man. There's but a wall to part her chamber and
thine. And then for a peep-hole, od's fish,° I have a peep-hole for
thee. 'Sbud, I'll show thee, I'll show thee.

BEAUGARD But when, Sir Jolly? I am in haste, impatient.   255

SIR JOLLY Why, this very night, man. Poor rogue's in haste, poor
rogue. But hear you—

COURTINE The matter?

SIR JOLLY Shan't we dine together?

BEAUGARD With all my heart.   260

SIR JOLLY The Maw° begins to empty. Get you before and bespeak
dinner at the Blue Posts, while I stay behind and gather up a dish
of whores for a dessert.

COURTINE Be sure that they be lewd, drunken, stripping whores, Sir
Jolly, that won't be affectedly squeamish and troublesome.   265

SIR JOLLY I warrant you.

COURTINE I love a well-disciplined whore, that shows all the tricks
of her profession with a wink, like an old soldier that understands
all his exercise by beat of drum.

SIR JOLLY Ah thief, sayest thou so! I must be better acquainted with 270
that fellow. He has a notable nose. A hard, brawny carl, true and
trusty, and mettle, I'll warrant him.

BEAUGARD Well, Sir Jolly, you'll not fail us?

SIR JOLLY Fail ye! Am I a knight? Hark ye, boys, I'll muster this
evening such a regiment of rampant, roaring, roisterous whores,   275
that shall make more noise than if all the cats in the Haymarket

were in conjunction—whores, ye rogues, that shall swear with you, drink with you, talk bawdy with you, fight with you, scratch with you, lie with you, and go to the devil with you. Shan't we be very merry, ha?   280

COURTINE As merry as wine, women and wickedness can make us.

SIR JOLLY Od, that's well said again, very well said. 'As merry as wine, women and wickedness can make us'! I love a fellow that is very wicked, dearly. Methinks there's a spirit in him. There's a sort of a tantara-rara,° tantara-rara, ah, ah-h-h! Well, and won't ye, 285 when the women come, won't ye? And shall I not see a little sport amongst you? Well, get ye gone. Ah rogues, ah rogues! Da, da. I'll be with you. Da, da.

> *Exeunt Beaugard and Courtine. Enter several Whores and*
> *three Bullies [from different directions]*

FIRST BULLY In the name of Satan, what whores are these in their copper trim,° yonder?   290

FIRST WHORE Well, I'll swear, madam, 'tis the finest evening. I love the Mall mightily.

SECOND BULLY Let's huzza the bulkers.

SECOND WHORE Really, and so do I—because there's always good company, and one meets with such civilities from every- 295 body.

THIRD BULLY Damned whores! Hout, ye filthies!

THIRD WHORE Ay, and then I love extremely to show myself here, when I am very fine, to vex those poor devils that call themselves virtues and are very scandalous and crapish,° I'll swear. O crimine, 300 who's yonder! Sir Jolly Jumble, I vow.

FIRST BULLY Faugh! Let's leave the nasty sows to fools and diseases.

> *[Exeunt Bullies]*

FIRST WHORE O Papa, Papa! Where have you been these two days, Papa?

SECOND WHORE You are a precious father indeed, to take no more 305 care of your children. We might be dead for all you,° you naughty Daddy, you.

SIR JOLLY Dead, my poor fubs! Od, I had rather all the relations I have were dead; adad I had. Get you gone, you little devils. Bubbies! O law,° there's bubbies! Od, I'll bite 'em; od, I will.   310

FIRST WHORE Nay, fie, Papa! I swear you'll make me angry, except you carry us and treat us° tonight. You have promised me a treat this week. Won't you, Papa?

SECOND WHORE Ay, won't you, Dad?

SIR JOLLY Od's so, od's so, well remembered! Get you gone, don't   315
stay talking, get you gone. Yonder's a great lord, the Lord
Beaugard, and his cousin the baron, the count, the marquis, the lord
knows what, Monsieur Courtine, newly come to town, od's so.

THIRD WHORE O law, where, Daddy, where? O dear, a lord!

FIRST WHORE Well, you are the purest° Papa. But when be dey   320
mun, Papa?°

SIR JOLLY I won't tell you, you gypsies, so I won't—except you
tickle me. 'Sbud, they are brave° fellows all, tall, and not a bit
small. Od, one of 'em has a devilish deal of money.

FIRST WHORE O dear, but which is he, Papa?   325

SECOND WHORE Shan't I be in love with him, Daddy?

SIR JOLLY What, nobody tickle me! Nobody tickle me? Not yet?
Tickle me a little, Mally.° Tickle me a little, Jenny. Do!
    They tickle him
He, he, he, he, he, he! No more! O dear, O dear! Poor rogues! So,
so, no more! Nay, if you do, if you do, od, I'll, I'll, I'll—   330

THIRD WHORE What, what will you do, trow?

SIR JOLLY Come along with me, come along with me. Sneak after
me at a distance, that nobody take notice. Swingeing fellows,
Mally—swingeing fellows, Jenny! A devilish deal of money! Get
you afore me then, you little didappers, ye wasps, ye wagtails! Get   335
you gone, I say! Swingeing fellows!
    Exeunt

[1.2]

[A room in Sir Davy Dunce's house]
Enter Lady Dunce and Sylvia

LADY DUNCE Die a maid, Sylvia! Fie for shame! What a scandalous
resolution's that! Five thousand pounds to your portion, and leave
it all to hospitals, for the innocent recreation hereafter of leading
apes in hell?° Fie for shame!

SYLVIA Indeed, such another charming animal as your consort, Sir   5
David, might do much with me. 'Tis an unspeakable blessing to
lie all night by a horse-load of diseases—a beastly, unsavoury, old,
groaning, grunting, wheezing wretch, that smells of the grave he's
going to already. From such a curse and hair-cloth next my skin,
good heaven deliver me!   10

LADY DUNCE Thou mistakest the use of a husband, Sylvia. They are
not meant for bedfellows. Heretofore, indeed, 'twas a fulsome
fashion to lie o' nights with a husband; but the world's improved
and customs altered.

SYLVIA Pray instruct then what the use of a husband is.   15

LADY DUNCE Instead of a gentleman-usher, for ceremony's sake, to
be in waiting on set days° and particular occasions. But the friend,
cousin, is the jewel unvaluable.

SYLVIA But Sir David, madam, will be difficult to be so governed. I
am mistaken if his nature is not too jealous to be blinded.   20

LADY DUNCE So much the better. Of all, the jealous fool is easiest
to be deceived. For observe, where there's jealousy there's always
fondness;° which if a woman, as she ought to do, will make the
right use of, the husband's fears shall not so awake him on one side
as his dotage shall blind him on the other.   25

SYLVIA Is your piece of mortality such a doting doodle? Is he so very
fond of you?

LADY DUNCE No; but he has the vanity to think that I am very fond
of him. And if he be jealous, 'tis not so much for fear I do abuse,
as that in time I may, and therefore imposes this confinement on   30
me—though he has other divertisements that take him off from my
enjoyment,° which make him so loathsome no woman but must
hate him.

SYLVIA His private divertisements I am a stranger to.

LADY DUNCE Then, for his person, 'tis incomparably odious. He has   35
such a breath, one kiss of him were enough to cure the fits of the
mother.° 'Tis worse than asafoetida.

SYLVIA O hideous!

LADY DUNCE Everything that's nasty he affects.° Clean linen, he
says, is unwholesome, and to make him more charming, he's   40
continually eating of garlic and chewing tobacco.

SYLVIA Faugh! This is love! This is the blessing of matrimony!

LADY DUNCE Rail not so unreasonably against love, Sylvia. As I have
dealt freely and acknowledged to thee the passion I have for
Beaugard, so methinks Sylvia need not conceal her good thoughts   45
of her friend. Do not I know Courtine sticks in your stomach?°

SYLVIA If he does, I'll assure you he shall never get to my heart. But
can you have the conscience to love another man now you are
married? What do you think will become of you?

LADY DUNCE I tell thee, Sylvia, I never was married to that   50
engine° we have been talking of. My parents indeed made me say

something to him after a priest once, but my heart went not along with my tongue. I minded not what it was. For my thoughts, Sylvia, for these seven years have been much better employed. Beaugard! Ah, curse on the day that first sent him into France! 55

SYLVIA Why so, I beseech you?

LADY DUNCE Had he stayed here, I had not been sacrificed to the arms of this monument of man, for the bed of death could not be more cold than his has been. He would have delivered me from the monster, for even then I loved him and was apt to think my 60 kindness not neglected.

SYLVIA I find indeed your ladyship had good thoughts of him.

LADY DUNCE Surely 'tis impossible to think too well of him, for he has wit enough to call his good nature in question, and yet good nature enough to make his wit be suspected. 65

SYLVIA But how do you hope ever to get sight of him? Sir David's watchfulness is invincible. I dare swear he would smell out a rival, if he were in the house, only by natural instinct; as some that always sweat when a cat's in the room. Then again, Beaugard's a soldier, and that's a thing the old gentleman, you know, loves 70 dearly.

LADY DUNCE There lies the greatest comfort of my uneasy life. He is one of those fools, forsooth, that are led by the nose by knaves to rail against the king and the government, and is mightily fond of being thought of a party.° I have had hopes this twelvemonth 75 to have heard of his being in the Gate-House° for treason.

SYLVIA But I find only yourself the prisoner all this while.

LADY DUNCE At present indeed I am so. But fortune, I hope, will smile, wouldst thou but be my friend, Sylvia.

SYLVIA In any mischievous design, with all my heart. 80

LADY DUNCE The conclusion, madam, may turn to your satisfaction. But you have no thoughts of Courtine?

SYLVIA Not I, I'll assure you, cousin.

LADY DUNCE You don't think him well-shaped, straight, and pro-portionable? 85

SYLVIA Considering he eats but once a week, the man is well enough.

LADY DUNCE And then wears his clothes, you know, filthily, and like a horrid sloven.

SYLVIA Filthily enough of all conscience, with a threadbare red coat, which his tailor duns him for to this day, over which a great, 90 broad, greasy buff belt, enough to turn anyone's stomach but a disbanded officer; a peruke tied up in a knot to excuse its want of

combing;° and then, because he has been a man-at-arms,° he must
wear two tuffles of a beard forsooth, to lodge a dunghill of snuff
upon, to keep his nose in good humour.   95

LADY DUNCE Nay, now I am sure that thou lovest him.

SYLVIA So far from it, that I protest eternally against° the whole sex.

LADY DUNCE That time will best demonstrate. In the meanwhile, to
our business.

SYLVIA As how, madam?   100

LADY DUNCE Tonight must I see Beaugard. They are this minute at
dinner in the Haymarket. Now to make my evil genius that haunts
me everywhere, my thing called a husband, himself to assist his
poor wife at a dead lift,° I think would not be unpleasant.

SYLVIA But 'twill be impossible.   105

LADY DUNCE I am apt to be persuaded, rather, very easy. You know
our good and friendly neighbour, Sir Jolly.

SYLVIA Out on him, beast! He's always talking filthily to a body. If
he sits but at the table with one, he'll be making nasty figures in
the napkins.   110

LADY DUNCE He and my sweet yoke-fellow are the most intimate
friends in the world; so that, partly out of neighbourly kindness,
as well as the great delight he takes to be meddling in matters of
this nature, with a great deal of pains and industry he has
procured° me Beaugard's picture, and given him to understand   115
how well a friend of his in petticoats, called myself, wishes him.

SYLVIA But what's all this to the making the husband instrumental?
For I must confess, of all creatures a husband's the thing that's
odious to me.

LADY DUNCE That must be done this night. I'll instantly to my   120
chamber, take my bed in a pet, and send for Sir David.

SYLVIA But which way then must the lover come?

LADY DUNCE Nay, I'll betray Beaugard to him, show him the picture
he sent me, and beg of him, as he tenders his own honour and my
quiet, to take some course to secure me from the scandalous   125
solicitations of that innocent fellow.

SYLVIA And so make him the property, the go-between, to bring the
affair to an issue the more decently.

LADY DUNCE Right, Sylvia; 'tis the best office a husband can do a
wife—I mean an old husband. Bless us! To be yoked in wedlock   130
with a paralytic, coughing, decrepit dotterel! To be a dry nurse all
one's lifetime to an old child of sixty-five! To lie by the image of
death a whole night, a dull immovable that has no sense of life but

through its pains! The pigeon's as happy that's laid to a sick man's
feet,° when the world has given him over. For my part, this shall   135
henceforth be my prayer:

    Cursed be the memory, nay, double cursed,
    Of her that wedded age for interest first.°
    Though worn with years, with fruitless wishes full,
    'Tis all day troublesome, and all night dull.   140
    Who wed with fools indeed lead happy lives;
    Fools are the fittest, finest things for wives.
    Yet old men profit bring as fools bring ease,
    And both make youth and wit much better please.
    [*Exeunt*]

2.[1]

[The Mall]

Enter Sir Jolly Jumble, Beaugard, Courtine and Fourbin

COURTINE Sir Jolly is the glory of the age.

SIR JOLLY Nay, now, sir, you honour me too far.

BEAUGARD He's the delight of the young and wonder of the old.

SIR JOLLY I swear, gentlemen, you make me blush.

COURTINE He deserves a statue in gold at the charge of the kingdom. 5

SIR JOLLY Out upon't, fie for shame! I protest I'll leave your company if you talk so. But, faith, they were pure whores, daintily dutiful strumpets. Ha! Ud's-bud, they'd—have stripped for t'other bottle.

BEAUGARD Truly, Sir Jolly, you are a man of very extraordinary 10
discipline. I never saw whores under better command in my life.

SIR JOLLY Pish, that's nothing, man, nothing. I can send for forty better when I please—doxies that will skip, strip, leap, trip, and do anything in the world, anything, old soul.

COURTINE Dear, dear Sir Jolly, where and when? 15

SIR JOLLY Od, as simply as° I stand here, her father was a knight.

BEAUGARD Indeed, Sir Jolly, a knight, say you?

SIR JOLLY Ay, but a little decayed.° I'll assure you she's a very good gentlewoman born.

COURTINE Ay, and a very good gentlewoman bred too. 20

SIR JOLLY Ay, and so she is.

BEAUGARD But, Sir Jolly, how goes my business forward? When shall I have a view of the quarry I am to fly at?

SIR JOLLY Alas-a-day, not so hasty. Soft and fair, I beseech you. Ah, my little son of thunder, if thou hadst her in thy arms now 25
between a pair of sheets, and I under the bed to see fair play, boy, gemini, what would become of me? What would become of me? There would be doings! O lawd, I under the bed!

BEAUGARD Or behind the hangings, Sir Jolly—would not that do as well? 30

SIR JOLLY Ah no; under the bed, against the world.° And then it would be very dark, ha!

BEAUGARD Dark to choose.°

SIR JOLLY No, but a little light would do well, a small, glimmering lamp, just enough for me to steal a peep by. O lamentable! 35

O lamentable! I won't speak a word more. There would be a trick!
O rare, you friend, O rare! Od's so, not a word more, od's so!
Yonder comes the monster that must be, the cuckold elect.° Step,
step aside, and observe him. If I should be seen in your company,
'twould spoil all.   40

    [Exeunt Sir Jolly Jumble and Courtine]

BEAUGARD For my part, I'll stand the meeting of him. One way to
promote a good understanding with a wife is first to get acquainted
with her husband.

    Enter Sir Davy Dunce

SIR DAVY *[aside]* Well, of all blessings a discreet wife is the greatest
that can light upon a man of years. Had I been married to anything   45
but an angel now, what a beast had I been by this time! Well, I am
the happiest old fool! 'Tis an horrid age that we live in, so that an
honest man° can keep nothing to himself. If you have a good
estate, every covetous rogue is longing for't. Truly, I love a good
estate dearly myself. If you have a handsome wife, every smooth-   50
faced coxcomb will be combing and cocking° at her. Flesh-flies are
not so troublesome to the shambles as those sort of insects are to
the boxes in the playhouse.° But virtue is a great blessing, an
unvaluable treasure. To tell me herself that a villain had tempted
her, and give me the very picture, the enchantment that he sent to   55
bewitch her, it strikes me dumb with admiration. Here's the villain
in effigy. (*Pulls out the picture*) Od, a very handsome fellow, a
dangerous rogue, I'll warrant him. Such fellows as these now
should be fettered like unruly colts, that they might not leap into
other men's pastures. Here's a nose now, I could find in my heart   60
to cut it off. Damned dog, to dare to presume to make a cuckold
of a knight! Bless us, what will this world come to! Well, poor Sir
David, down, down, on thy knees [*kneels*], and thank thy stars for
this deliverance.

BEAUGARD 'Sdeath, what's that I see? Sure 'tis the very pic-   65
ture which I sent by Sir Jolly. If so, by this light, I am damnably
jilted.

SIR DAVY *[aside]* But now if—

BEAUGARD Surely he does not see us yet.

FOURBIN See you, sir! Why, he has but one eye, and we are on his   70
blind side. I'll dumbfound him.°

    [Fourbin] strikes Sir Davy on the shoulder

SIR DAVY *[getting to his feet]* Who the devil's this? Sir, sir, sir, who
are you, sir?

BEAUGARD [*looking at the miniature in Sir Davy's hand*] Ay, ay, 'tis
the same. Now a pox of all amorous adventures! 'Sdeath, I'll go   75
beat the impertinent pimp that drew me into this fooling.

SIR DAVY Sir, methinks you are very curious.

BEAUGARD Sir, perhaps I have an extraordinary reason to be so.

SIR DAVY And perhaps, sir, I care not for you, nor your reasons
neither.   80

BEAUGARD Sir, if you are at leisure, I would beg the honour to speak
with you.

SIR DAVY With me, sir? What's your business with me?

BEAUGARD I would not willingly be troublesome, though it may be
I am so at this time.   85

SIR DAVY It may be so too, sir.

BEAUGARD But to be known to so worthy a person as you are
would be so great an honour, so extraordinary a happiness, that I
could not avoid taking this opportunity of tendering you my
service.   90

SIR DAVY (*aside*) Smooth rogue! Who the devil is this fellow? [*To
Beaugard*] But, sir, you were pleased to nominate business, sir. I
desire with what speed you can to know your business, sir, that
I may go about my business.

BEAUGARD Sir, if I might with good manners, I should be glad to   95
inform myself whose picture that is which you have in your hand.
Methinks it is very fine painting.

SIR DAVY Picture, friend, picture! Sir, 'tis the resemblance of a very
impudent fellow. They call him Captain Beaugard, forsooth. But
he is in short a rakehell, a poor, lousy, beggarly, disbanded devil.   100
Do you know him, friend?

BEAUGARD I think I have heard of such a vagabond.° The truth on't
is, he is a very impudent fellow.

SIR DAVY Ay, a damned rogue.

BEAUGARD O, a notorious scoundrel!   105

SIR DAVY I expect to hear he's hanged by next sessions.°

BEAUGARD The truth on't is, he has deserved it long ago. But did
you ever see him, Sir David?

SIR DAVY (*aside*) Sir—does he know me?

BEAUGARD Because I fancy that miniature is very like him. Pray, sir,   110
whence had it you? ·

SIR DAVY Had it, friend? Had it! Whence had it I! (*Compares the
picture with Beaugard's face*) [*Aside*] Bless us! What have I done
now! This is the° very traitor himself. If he should be desperate

now and put his sword in my guts! Slitting my nose will be as bad   115
as that. I have but one eye left neither, and may be—O, but this
is the king's court.° Od, that's well remembered. He dares not but
be civil here. I'll try to outhuff him. (*To Beaugard*) 'Whence had
it you?'

BEAUGARD Ay, sir, whence had it you? That's English in my   120
country,° sir.

SIR DAVY Go, sir, you are a rascal.

BEAUGARD How!

SIR DAVY Sir, I say you are a rascal, a very impudent rascal. Nay,
I'll prove you to be a rascal, if you go to that.°   125

BEAUGARD Sir, I am a gentleman and a soldier.

SIR DAVY So much the worse. Soldiers have been cuckold-makers
from the beginning. Sir, I care not what you are. For aught I know,
you may be a—come, sir, did I never see you? Answer me to that.
Did I never see you? For aught I know, you may be a Jesuit. There   130
were more in the last army beside you.°

BEAUGARD Of your acquaintance, and be hanged!°

SIR DAVY Yes, to my knowledge, there were several at Hounslow
Heath,° disguised in dirty petticoats,° and cried brandy.° I knew a
sergeant of foot that was familiar with one of them all night in a   135
ditch, and fancied him a woman; but the devil is powerful.

BEAUGARD In short, you worthy villain of worship,° that picture is
mine, and I must have it; or I shall take an opportunity to kick
your worship most inhumanly.

SIR DAVY Kick, sir?

BEAUGARD Ay, sir, kick. 'Tis a recreation I can show you.   140

SIR DAVY Sir, I am a free-born subject of England, and there are
laws, look you, there are laws. So I say you are a rascal again,° and
now how will you help yourself? Poor fool!

BEAUGARD Hark you, friend, have not you a wife?   145

SIR DAVY I have a lady, sir. O, and she's mightily taken with this
picture of yours. She was so mightily proud of it, she could not
forbear showing it me, and telling too who 'twas sent it her.

BEAUGARD And has she been long a jilt? Has she practised the trade
for any time?   150

SIR DAVY Trade! Humph, what trade? What trade, friend?

BEAUGARD Why, the trade of whore and no whore—caterwauling in
jest, putting out Christian colours, when she's a Turk under deck.°
A curse upon all honest women in the flesh, that are whores in the
spirit.   155

SIR DAVY [*aside*] Poor devil! How he rails! Ha, ha, ha! [*To Beaugard*]
Look you, sweet soul, as I told you before, there are laws, there
are laws. But those are things not worthy your consideration.
Beauty's your business. But, dear vagabond, trouble thyself no
further about my spouse. Let my doxy rest in peace; she's meat   160
for thy master, old boy. I have my belly full of her every night.

BEAUGARD Sir, I wish all your noble family hanged, from the bottom
of my heart.

SIR DAVY Moreover, Captain Swash, I must tell you my wife is an
honest woman, of a virtuous disposition, one that I have loved   165
from her infancy, and she deserves it by her faithful dealing in this
affair; for that° she has discovered loyally to me the treacherous
designs laid against her chastity and my honour.

BEAUGARD By this light, the beast weeps.

SIR DAVY Truly, I cannot but weep for joy, to think how happy I   170
am in a sincere, faithful and loving yoke-fellow. She charged me
too to tell you into the bargain, that she is sufficiently satisfied
of° the most secret wishes of your heart.

BEAUGARD I am glad on't.

SIR DAVY And that 'tis her desire that you would trouble yourself no   175
more about the matter.

BEAUGARD With all my heart.

SIR DAVY But henceforward behave yourself with such discretion as
becomes a gentleman.

BEAUGARD O, to be sure, most exactly!   180

SIR DAVY And let her alone to° make the best use of those innocent
freedoms I allow her, without putting her reputation in hazard.

BEAUGARD As how, I beseech you?

SIR DAVY By your impertinent and unseasonable address.

BEAUGARD And this news you bring me by a particular commission   185
from your sweet lady?

SIR DAVY Yea, friend, I do, and she hopes you'll be sensible, dear
heart, of her good meaning by it. These were her very words. I
neither add nor diminish, for plain dealing is my mistress's friend.

BEAUGARD Then all the curses I shall think on this twelvemonth   190
light on her, and as many more on the next fool that gives credit
to the sex.°

SIR DAVY [*aside*] Well, certainly I am the happiest toad! How
melancholy the monkey stands now! Poor pug, hast thou lost her?

BEAUGARD [*aside*] To be so sordid a jilt, to betray me to such a   195
beast as that! Can she have any good thoughts of such a swine?

Damn her! Had she abused me handsomely,° it had never vexed me.

SIR DAVY Now, sir, with your permission I'll take my leave.

BEAUGARD Sir, if you were gone to the devil, I should think you very   200
well disposed of.

SIR DAVY If you have any letter or other commendation to the lady
that was so charmed with your resemblance there, it shall be very
faithfully conveyed by—

BEAUGARD Fool!   205

SIR DAVY Your humble servant, sir. I'm gone. I shall disturb you no
further. Your most humble servant, sir.

          Exit [Sir Davy Dunce]

BEAUGARD Now poverty, plague, pox and prison fall thick upon the
head of thee!—Fourbin!

FOURBIN Sir!   210

BEAUGARD Thou hast been an extraordinary rogue in thy time.

FOURBIN I hope I have lost nothing in your honour's service, sir.

BEAUGARD Find out some way to revenge me on this old rascal, and
if I do not make thee a gentleman—

FOURBIN That you have been pleased to do long ago, I thank you;   215
for I am sure you have not left me one shilling in my pocket these
two months.

BEAUGARD Here, here's for thee to revel withal.

          [Beaugard gives Fourbin money]

FOURBIN Will your honour please to have his throat cut?

BEAUGARD With all my heart.   220

FOURBIN Or would you have him decently hanged at his own door,
and then give out to the world he did it himself?°

BEAUGARD That would do very well.

FOURBIN Or I think—to proceed with more safety—a good stale
jakes° were a very pretty expedient.   225

BEAUGARD Excellent, excellent, Fourbin.

FOURBIN Leave matters to my discretion, and if I do not—

BEAUGARD I know thou wilt. Go, go about it, prosper and be
famous.

          Exit [Fourbin]

Now, ere I dare venture to meet Courtine again, will I go by   230
myself, rail for an hour or two, and then be good company.

          Exit [Beaugard.] Enter Courtine and Sylvia

SYLVIA Take my word, sir. You had better give this business over. I
tell you there's nothing in the world turns my stomach so much

25

as the man, that man that makes love to° me. I never saw one of
your sex in my life make love, but he looked so like an ass all the   235
while, that I blushed for him.

COURTINE I am afraid your ladyship then is one of those dangerous
creatures they call she-wits, who are always so mightily taken with
admiring themselves, that nothing else is worth their notice.

SYLVIA O, who can be so dull not to be ravished with that roisterous   240
mien of yours? That ruffling air in your gait, that seems to cry
where'er you go, 'Make room, here comes the captain'? That face
the which bids defiance to the weather? Bless us! If I were a poor
farmer's wife in the country now, and you wanted quarters,° how
would it fright me! But as I am young, not very ugly, and one you   245
never saw before, how lovingly it looks upon me.

COURTINE Who can forbear to sigh, look pale and languish, where
beauty and wit unite both their forces to enslave a heart so tractable
as mine is? First, for that modish swim of your body, the victorious
motion of your arms and head, the toss of your fan, the glancing of   250
the eyes, bless us! If I were a dainty, fine-dressed coxcomb with a
great estate and a little or no wit, vanity in abundance, and good for
nothing, how would they melt and soften me! But as I am a
scandalous honest rascal, not fool enough to be your sport, nor rich
enough to be your prey, how gloatingly they look upon me!   255

SYLVIA Alas, alas! What pity 'tis your honesty should ever do you
hurt, or your wit spoil your preferment.

COURTINE Just as much, fair lady, as that your beauty should make
you be envied at, or your virtue provoke scandal.

SYLVIA Well, the more I look, the more I'm in love with you.   260

COURTINE The more I look, the more I am out of love with you.

SYLVIA How my heart swells when I see you!

COURTINE How my stomach rises° when I'm near you!

SYLVIA Nay, then let's bargain.

COURTINE With all my heart. What?   265

SYLVIA Not to fall in love with each other, I assure you, Monsieur
Captain.

COURTINE But to hate one another constantly and cordially.

SYLVIA Always when you are drunk, I desire you to talk scandalously
of me.   270

COURTINE Ay, and when I am sober too. In return whereof,
whene'er you see a coquette of your acquaintance, and I chance to
be named, be sure you spit at the filthy remembrance, and rail at
me as if you loved me.

SYLVIA In the next place, whene'er we meet in the Mall, I desire you   275
    to humph, put out your tongue, make ugly mouths, laugh aloud,
    and look back at me.

COURTINE Which if I chance to do, be sure at next turning to pick
    up some tawdry fluttering fop or another.

SYLVIA That I made acquaintance withal at the music-meeting.°   280

COURTINE Right—just such another spark to saunter by your side
    with his hat under his arm.

SYLVIA Harkening to all the bitter things I can say to be revenged.

COURTINE Whilst the dull rogue dare not so much as grin to
    oblige you, for fear of being beaten for it, when he is out of his   285
    waiting.°

SYLVIA Counterfeit your letters from me.

COURTINE And you, to be even with me for the scandal, publish to
    all the world I offered to marry you.

SYLVIA O hideous marriage!   290

COURTINE Horrid, horrid marriage!

SYLVIA Name, name no more of it.

COURTINE At that sad word let's part.

SYLVIA Let's wish all men decrepit, dull and silly.°

COURTINE And every woman old and ugly.   295

SYLVIA Adieu!

COURTINE Farewell!

    Enter [Frisk,] a young fellow affectedly dressed, several others
    with him

SYLVIA Ah me, Mr. Frisk!

FRISK Mademoiselle Sylvia! Sincerely, as I hope to be saved, the
    devil take me, damn me, madam, who's that?   300

SYLVIA Ha, ha, ha, hea!

    Exit [Sylvia] with Frisk [and the other gallants]

COURTINE True to thy failings always, woman! How naturally is the
    sex fond of a rogue! What a monster was that for a woman to
    delight in! Now must I love her still, though I know I am a
    blockhead for't, and she'll use me like a blockhead too, if I don't   305
    prevent her. What's to be done? I'll have three whores a day, to
    keep love out of my head.

    Enter Beaugard

Beaugard, well met again! How go matters? Handsomely?

BEAUGARD O very handsomely! Had you but seen how handsomely
    I was used just now, you would swear so. I have heard thee rail in   310
    my time. Would thou wouldst exercise thy talent a little at present.

27

COURTINE At what?

BEAUGARD Why, canst thou ever want a subject! Rail at thyself, rail at me. I deserve to be railed at.

A clumsy° fellow marches over the stage dressed like an officer
See there! What thinkest thou of that engine, that moving lump of   315
filthiness, miscalled a man?

COURTINE Curse on him for a rogue! I know him.

BEAUGARD So.

COURTINE The rascal was a retailer of ale but yesterday, and now he is an officer and be hanged.° 'Tis a dainty° sight in a morning to   320
see him with his toes turned in, drawing his legs after him, at the head of a hundred lusty fellows. Some honest gentleman or other stays now, because that dog had money to bribe some corrupt colonel withal.°

Enter another, gravely dressed

BEAUGARD There, there's another of my acquaintance. He was my   325
father's footman not long since, and has pimped for me oftener than he prayed for himself. That good quality recommended him to a nobleman's service, which, together with flattering, fawning, lying, spying and informing, has raised him to an employment of trust and reputation, though the rogue can't write his name, nor   330
read his neck verse,° if he had occasion.

COURTINE 'Tis as unreasonable to expect a man of sense should be preferred,° as 'tis to think a hector can be stout, a priest religious, a fair woman chaste, or a pardoned rebel loyal.°

Enter two more, seeming earnestly in discourse

BEAUGARD That's seasonably thought on. Look there. Observe but   335
that fellow on the right hand, the rogue with the busiest° face of the two. I'll tell thee his history.

COURTINE I hope hanging will be the end of his history, so well I like him at the first sight.

BEAUGARD He was born a vagabond, and no parish owned him. His   340
father was as obscure as his mother public—everybody knew her, and nobody could guess at him.

COURTINE He comes of a very good family, heaven be praised.

BEAUGARD The first thing he chose to rise by was rebellion. So a rebel he grew, and flourished a rebel, fought against his king, and   345
helped to bring him to the block.°

COURTINE And was he not religious too?

BEAUGARD Most devoutly! He could pray till he cried, and preach till he foamed, which excellent talent made him popular,° and at

last preferred him to be a worthy member of that never-to-be-   350
forgotten Rump Parliament.°

COURTINE Pray, sir, be uncovered° at that, and remember it with
reverence.

BEAUGARD In short, he was committee-man, sequestrator- and
persecutor-general of a whole county, by which he got enough, at   355
the king's return to secure himself in the general pardon.°

COURTINE Nauseous vermin! That such a swine with the mark of
rebellion in his forehead should wallow in his luxury,° whilst
honest men° are forgotten!

BEAUGARD Thus forgiven, thus raised, and made thus happy, the   360
ungrateful slave disowns the hand that healed him, cherishes
factions to affront his master,° and once more would rebel against
the head which so lately saved his from a pole.

COURTINE What a dreadful beard and swinging° sword he wears!

BEAUGARD 'Tis to keep his cowardice in countenance.° The rascal   365
will endure kicking most temperately for all that. I know five or
six more of the same stamp, that never come abroad° without
terrible long spits by their sides, with which they will let you bore
their own noses if you please. But let the villain be forgotten.

COURTINE His co-rogue I have some knowledge of. He's a tattered,   370
worm-eaten case-putter. Some call him lawyer. One that takes it
very ill he is not made a judge.

BEAUGARD Yes, and is always repining that men of parts are not
regarded.

COURTINE He has been a great noise-maker in factious clubs these   375
seven years,° and now I suppose is courting that worshipful rascal
to make him recorder of some factious town.°

BEAUGARD To teach tallow-chandlers and cheesemongers how far
they may rebel against their king by virtue of Magna Charta.°

COURTINE But, friend Beaugard, methinks thou art very splenetic of   380
a sudden. How goes the affair of love forward? Prosperously, ha?

BEAUGARD O, I assure you, most triumphantly. Just now, you must
know, I am parted with the sweet, civil, enchanted lady's husband.

COURTINE Well, and what says the cuckold? Is he very kind and
good-natured, as cuckolds use to be?°   385

BEAUGARD Why, he says, Courtine, in short, that I am a very silly
fellow—and truly I am very apt to believe him—and that I have
been jilted in this affair most unconscionably. A plague on all
pimps, I say! A man's business never thrives so well as when he is
his own solicitor.   390

Enter Sir Jolly Jumble and Boy

SIR JOLLY [*to Beaugard*] Hist, hist, captain, captain, captain.—Boy!

BOY Sir.

SIR JOLLY Run and get two chairs° presently. Be sure you get two chairs, sirrah, do you hear?

[*Exit Boy*]

Here's luck, here's luck. Now or never, captain, never if not now, 395 captain! Here's luck.

BEAUGARD Sir Jolly, no more adventures, sweet Sir Jolly. I am like to have a very fine time on't, truly.

SIR JOLLY The best in the world, dear dog, the very best in the world. 'Sbud, she's here hard by, man, stays on purpose for thee, 400 finely disguised. The cuckold has lost her too; and nobody knows anything of the matter but I, nobody but I, and I, you must know, I am I, ha! And I, you little toad, ha—

BEAUGARD You are a very fine gentleman.

SIR JOLLY The best-natured fellow in the world, I believe, of my 405 years! Now does my heart so thump for fear this business should miscarry. Why, I'll warrant thee, the lady is here, man; she's all thy own. 'Tis thy own fault if thou art not *in terra incognita* within this half-hour. Come along, prithee come along. Fie for shame! What, make a lady lose her longing! Come along, I say, you—out upon't! 410

BEAUGARD Sir, your humble. I shan't, sir.

SIR JOLLY What? Not go!

BEAUGARD No, sir, no lady for me.

SIR JOLLY Not go! I should laugh at that, faith.

BEAUGARD No, I will assure you; not go, sir. 415

SIR JOLLY Away, you wag; you jest, you jest, you wag. 'Not go', quotha?

BEAUGARD No, sir, not go, I tell you. What the devil would you have more?

SIR JOLLY Nothing, nothing, sir, but I am a gentleman.° 420

BEAUGARD With all my heart.

SIR JOLLY And do you think then that I'll be used thus?

BEAUGARD Sir!

SIR JOLLY Take away my reputation and take away my life. I shall be disgraced forever. 425

BEAUGARD I have not wronged you, Sir Jolly.

SIR JOLLY Not wronged me! But you shall find you have wronged me, and wronged a sweet lady, and a fine lady. I shall never be trusted again, never have employment more! I shall die of the

spleen.° Prithee now be good-natured, prithee be persuaded. Od,   430
I'll give thee this ring; I'll give thee this watch—'tis gold. I'll give
thee anything in the world. Go!

BEAUGARD Not one foot, sir.

SIR JOLLY [*aside*] Now that I durst but murder him.—Well, shall I
fetch her to thee? What shall I do for thee?   435

     Enter Lady Dunce

Od's fish, here she comes herself. Now, you ill-natured churl, now,
you devil, look upon her, do but look upon her. What shall I say
to her?

BEAUGARD E'en what you please, Sir Jolly.

SIR JOLLY [*aside*] 'Tis a very strange monster, this. [*Goes to Lady*   440
Dunce] Madam, this is the gentleman; that's he. Though,° as one
may say, he's something bashful; but I'll tell him who you are.
(*Goes to Beaugard*) If thou art not more cruel than leopards, lions,
tigers, wolves, or Tartars, don't break my heart, don't kill me. This
unkindness of thine goes to the soul of me. (*Goes to Lady Dunce*)   445
Madam, he says he's so amazed at your triumphant beauty, that
he dares not approach the excellence that shines from you.

LADY DUNCE [*aside*] What can be the meaning of all this?

SIR JOLLY [*to Beaugard*] Art thou then resolved to be remorse-
less? Canst thou be insensible? Hast thou eyes? Hast thou a heart?   450
Hast thou anything thou shouldst have? Od, I'll tickle thee.
Get you to her, you fool, get you to her, to her, to her, to her. Ha,
ha, ha.

LADY DUNCE Have you forgot me, Beaugard?

SIR JOLLY [*to Beaugard*] So, now, to her, again I say, to her, to her,   455
and be hanged. Ah rogue, ah rogue! Now, now, have at her, now
have at her.

    [*Sir Jolly propels Beaugard towards Lady Dunce*]

There it goes, there it goes. Hey, boys!

LADY DUNCE Methinks this face should not so much be altered, as
to be nothing like what once I thought it—the object of your   460
pleasure and subject of your praises.

SIR JOLLY [*aside*] Cunning toad! Wheedling jade! You shall see now
how by degrees she'll draw him into the whirlpool of love. Now
he leers upon her, now he leers upon her. O law! There's eyes!
There's your eyes! I must pinch him by the calf of the leg.   465

BEAUGARD Madam, I must confess I do remember that I had once
acquaintance with a face, whose air and beauty much resembled
yours; and if I may trust my heart, you are called Clarinda.

LADY DUNCE Clarinda I was called till my ill fortune wedded me. Now you may have heard of me by another title; your friend there, 470 I suppose, has made nothing a secret to you.

BEAUGARD And are you then that kind, enchanted, fair one who was so passionately in love with my picture, that you could not forbear betraying me to the beast your husband, and wrong the passion of a gentleman that languished for you, only to make your monster 475 merry? Hark you, madam. Had your fool been worth it, I had beaten him, and have a month's mind to be exercising my parts that way upon your go-between, your male bawd there.

SIR JOLLY [aside] Ah lord, ah lord! All's spoiled again, all's ruined. I shall be undone forever. Why, what a devil is the matter now? 480 What have I done? What sins have I committed?

LADY DUNCE And are you that passionate adorer of our sex who cannot live a week in London without loving? Are you the spark that sends your picture up and down to longing ladies, longing for a pattern of your person? 485

BEAUGARD Yes, madam, when I receive so good hostages as these are (*shows the gold*), that it shall be well used. Could you find out nobody but me to play the fool withal?

SIR JOLLY [aside] Alack-a-day!

LADY DUNCE Could you pitch upon nobody but that wretched 490 woman that has loved you too well to abuse you thus?

SIR JOLLY [aside] That ever I was born!

BEAUGARD Here, here, madam, I'll return you your dirt. [*Attempts to return the money*] I scorn your wages, as I do your service.

LADY DUNCE Fie for shame! What, refund? That is not like a soldier 495 to refund. Keep, keep it to repay your seamstress° withal.

SIR JOLLY [aside] His seamstress! Who the devil is his seamstress? Od, what would I give to know that now?

LADY DUNCE There was a ring too, which I sent you this afternoon. If that fit not your finger, you may dispose of it some 500 other way, where it may give no occasion of scandal, and you'll do well.

BEAUGARD A ring, madam!

LADY DUNCE A small trifle. I suppose Sir David delivered it to you when he returned you your miniature. 505

BEAUGARD I beseech you, madam—

LADY DUNCE Farewell, you traitor.

BEAUGARD As I hope to be saved, and upon the word of a gentleman—

LADY DUNCE Go, you are a false, ungrateful brute, and trouble me 510
no more.
  Exit [Lady Dunce]
BEAUGARD Sir Jolly, Sir Jolly, Sir Jolly—
SIR JOLLY Ah, thou rebel!
BEAUGARD Some advice, some advice, dear friend, ere I'm
ruined. 515
SIR JOLLY Ev'n two pennyworth of hemp° for your honour's supper;
that's all the remedy that I know.
BEAUGARD But prithee hear a little reason.
SIR JOLLY No, sir, I ha' done; no more to be said. I ha' done. I am
ashamed of you. I'll have no more to say to you. I'll never see your 520
face again. Good-bye.
  Exit Sir Jolly Jumble
BEAUGARD Death and the devil, what have my stars been doing
today! A ring! Delivered by Sir David! What can that mean? Pox
on her for a jilt! She lies, and has a mind to amuse° and laugh at
me a day or two longer. Hist, here comes her beast once more. I'll 525
use him civilly, and try what discovery I can make.
  Enter Sir Davy Dunce
SIR DAVY [*aside*] Ha, ha, ha! Here's the captain's jewel. Very well.
In troth I had like to have forgotten it. Ha, ha, ha! How damn-
able mad he'll be now, when I shall deliver him his ring again.
Ha, ha! Poor dog, he'll hang himself at least. Ha, ha, ha! Faith, 'tis 530
a very pretty stone, and finely set. Humph, if I should keep it now!
I'll say I have lost it. No, I'll give it him again, o' purpose to vex
him. Ha, ha, ha!
BEAUGARD [*doffing his hat*] Sir David, I am heartily sorry.
SIR DAVY O sir, 'tis you I was seeking for. Ha, ha, ha! [*Aside*] What 535
shall I say to him now to terrify him?
BEAUGARD Me, sir?
SIR DAVY Ay, you, sir, if your name be Captain Beaugard. [*Aside*]
How like a fool he looks already!
BEAUGARD What you please, sir. 540
SIR DAVY Sir, I should speak° a word with you, if you think fit.
[*Aside*] What shall I do now to keep my countenance?°
BEAUGARD Can I be so happy, sir, as to be able to serve you in
anything?
SIR DAVY No, sir—ha, ha, ha!—I have commands of service to you, 545
sir. O lord! Ha, ha, ha!
BEAUGARD Me, sir?

SIR DAVY Ay, sir, you, sir. But put on your hat, friend, put on your hat; be covered.

BEAUGARD Sir, will you please to sit down on this bank?°   550

SIR DAVY No, no, there's no need, no need. For all I have a young wife, I can stand upon my legs, sweetheart.

BEAUGARD Sir, I beseech you.

SIR DAVY By no means. I think, friend, we had some hard words just now. 'Twas about a paltry baggage; but she's a pretty baggage, and   555 a witty baggage, and a baggage that—

BEAUGARD Sir, I am heartily ashamed of all misdemeanour on my side.

SIR DAVY You do well. Though are not you a damned whoremaster, a devilish, cuckold-making fellow? Here, here, do you see this?   560 Here's the ring you sent a-roguing. Sir, do you think my wife wants anything that you can help her to? Why, I'll warrant this ring cost fifty pound. What a prodigal fellow are you to throw away so much money? Or didst thou steal it, old boy? I believe thou may'st be poor; I'll lend thee money upon't, if thou think'st fit, at   565 thirty in the hundred,° because I love thee. Ha, ha, ha!

BEAUGARD Sir, your humble servant, I am sorry 'twas not worth your lady's acceptance. [Aside] Now what a dog am I!

SIR DAVY I should have given it thee before; but, faith, I forgot it—though it was not my wife's fault in the least, for she says, as   570 thou likest this usage she hopes to have thy custom again, child. Ha, ha, ha!

BEAUGARD Then, sir, I beseech you tell her that you have made a convert on me,° and that I am so sensible of my insolent behaviour towards her—   575

SIR DAVY Very well, I shall do it.

BEAUGARD That 'tis impossible I shall ever be at peace with myself till I find some way how I may make her reparation.

SIR DAVY Very good. Ha, ha, ha!

BEAUGARD And that if ever she find me guilty of the like offence   580 again—

SIR DAVY No, sir, you had not best; but proceed. Ha, ha, ha!

BEAUGARD Let her banish all good opinion of me forever.

SIR DAVY No more to be said. Your servant. Good-bye.

BEAUGARD One word more, I beseech you, Sir Davy.   585

SIR DAVY What's that?

BEAUGARD I beg you tell her that the generous reproof she has given me has so wrought upon me—

SIR DAVY Well, I will.

BEAUGARD That I esteem this jewel, not only as a wreck redeemed   590
from my folly, but that for her sake I will preserve it to the utmost
moment of my life.

SIR DAVY With all my heart, I vow and swear.

BEAUGARD And that I long to convince her I am not the brute she
might mistake me for.   595

SIR DAVY Right. (*Aside*) Well, this will make the purest sport.—Let
me see: first you acknowledge yourself to be a very impudent
fellow.

BEAUGARD I do so, sir.

SIR DAVY And that you shall never be at rest till you have satisfied   600
my lady.

BEAUGARD Right, sir!

SIR DAVY Satisfied her! Very good. Ha, ha, ha! And that you will
never play the fool any more. Be sure you keep your word, friend.

BEAUGARD Never, sir.   605

SIR DAVY And that you will keep that ring for her sake as long as
you live, ha!

BEAUGARD To the day of my death, I'll assure you.

SIR DAVY I protest that will be very kindly done. And that you long,
mightily long, to let her understand that you are anotherguess   610
fellow than she may take you for.

BEAUGARD Exactly, sir; that is the sum and end of my desires.

SIR DAVY Well, I'll take care of your business; I'll do your business,
I'll warrant you. (*Aside*) This will make the purest sport when I
come home—no? [*To Beaugard*] Well, your servant. Remember;   615
be sure you remember. Your servant.
    [*Exit Sir Davy Dunce*]

BEAUGARD So, now I find a husband is a delicate° instrument,
rightly made use of. To make her old, jealous coxcomb pimp for
me himself! I think 'tis as worthy an employment as such a noble
consort can be put to.   620
    Ah, were ye all such husbands and such wives,
    We younger brothers should lead better lives.
    [*Exit*]

3.[1]

Covent Garden°

Enter Sylvia and Courtine [from different directions]

SYLVIA *[aside]* To fall in love, and to fall in love with a soldier! Nay, a disbanded soldier too, a fellow with the mark of Cain upon him,° which everybody knows him by, and is ready to throw stones at him for.

COURTINE *[aside]* Damn her; I shall never enjoy her without ravishing. If she were but very rich and very ugly, I would marry her. *[Seeing Sylvia]* Ay, 'tis she. I know her mischievous look too well to be mistaken in it.—Madam!

SYLVIA Sir.

COURTINE 'Tis a very hard case, that you have resolved not to let me be quiet.

SYLVIA 'Tis very unreasonably done of you, sir, to haunt me up and down everywhere at this scandalous rate. The world will think we are acquainted shortly.

COURTINE But, madam, I shall fairly take more care of my reputation, and from this time forward shun and avoid you most watchfully.

SYLVIA Have you not haunted this place these two hours?

COURTINE 'Twas because I knew it to be your ladyship's home then, and therefore might reasonably be the place you least of all frequented. One would imagine you were gone a-coxcomb-hunting by this time to some place of public appearance or other. 'Tis pretty near the hour; 'twill be twilight presently, and then the owls° come all abroad.

SYLVIA What need I take the trouble to go so far a-fowling when there's game enough at our own doors?

COURTINE What, game for your net, fair lady?

SYLVIA Yes, or any woman's net else that will spread it.

COURTINE To show you how despicably I think of the business, I will here leave you presently, though I lose the pleasure of railing at you.

SYLVIA Do so, I would advise you. Your raillery betrays your wit, as bad as your clumsy civility does your breeding.

COURTINE Adieu!

SYLVIA Farewell!

COURTINE Why do not you go about your business?

SYLVIA Because I would be sure to be rid of you first, that you might not dog me.

COURTINE Were it but possible that you could answer me one question truly, and then I should be satisfied. 40

SYLVIA Anything for composition to be rid of you handsomely.

COURTINE Are you really honest? Look in my face and tell me that.

SYLVIA Look in your face and tell you! For what? To spoil my stomach to my supper?

COURTINE No, but to get thee a stomach to thy bed, sweetheart. I 45 would, if possible, be better acquainted with thee, because thou art very ill-natured.

SYLVIA Your only way to bring that business about effectually is to be more troublesome, and if you think it worth your while to be abused substantially, you may make your personal appearance this 50 night.

COURTINE How? Where? And when? And what hour, I beseech thee?

SYLVIA Under the window, between the hours of eleven and twelve exactly.

COURTINE Where shall these lovely eyes and ears 55
Hear my plaints and see my tears?

SYLVIA At that kind hour thy griefs shall end,
If thou canst know thy foe from thy friend.
        Exit Sylvia

COURTINE Here's another trick of the devil now! Under that window between the hours of eleven and twelve exactly! I am a damned 60 fool, and must go. Let me see: suppose I meet with a lusty beating! Pish, that's nothing for a man that's in love. Or suppose she contrive some way to make a public coxcomb of me and expose me to the scorn of the world, for an example to all amorous blockheads hereafter? Why, if she do, I'll swear I have lain with her, beat her 65 relations if they pretend to vindicate her,° and so there's one love intrigue pretty well over.
        Exit Courtine. Enter Sir Davy Dunce and Vermin

SIR DAVY Go, get you in to your lady now, and tell her I am coming.

VERMIN Her ladyship, right-worshipful,° is pleased not to be at home. 70

SIR DAVY How's that? My lady not at home! Run, run in and ask when she went forth, whither she is gone, and who is with her. Run and ask, Vermin.

VERMIN She went out in her chair presently after you this afternoon.

SIR DAVY Then I may be a cuckold still for aught I know. What will   75
become of me? I have surely lost and ne'er shall find her more. She
promised me strictly to stay at home till I came back again. For
aught I know, she may be up three pair of stairs in the Temple
now.°

VERMIN Is her ladyship in law then, sir?   80

SIR DAVY Or, it may be, taking the air as far as Knightsbridge with
some smoothfaced rogue or another. 'Tis a damned house, that
Swan; that Swan at Knightsbridge is a confounded house, Vermin.

VERMIN Do you think she is there then?

SIR DAVY No, I do not think she is there neither; but such a thing   85
may be, you know. Would that Barn Elms was under water too.
There's a thousand cuckolds a year made at Barn Elms, by
Rosamond's Ponds.° The devil! If she should be there this evening,
my heart's broke.

Enter Sir Jolly Jumble

SIR JOLLY [*aside*] That must be Sir Davy. Ay, that's he, that's he.   90
Ha, ha, ha! Was ever the like heard of? Was ever anything so
pleasant?

SIR DAVY I'll lock her up three days and three nights without meat,
drink or light; I'll humble her in the devil's name.

SIR JOLLY [*pretending to search for Sir Davy*] Well, could I but meet   95
my friend Sir Davy, it would be the joyfullest news for him.

SIR DAVY Who's there that has anything to say to me?

SIR JOLLY Ah my friend of friends, such news, such tidings.

SIR DAVY I have lost my wife, man.

SIR JOLLY Lost her! She's not dead, I hope.   100

SIR DAVY Yes, alas, she's dead, irrecoverably lost.

SIR JOLLY Why, I parted with her within this half-hour.

SIR DAVY Did you so? Are you sure it was she? Where was it? I'll
have my Lord Chief Justice's warrant and a constable presently.

SIR JOLLY And she made the purest° sport now with a young fellow,   105
man, that she met withal accidentally.

SIR DAVY O lord! That's worse and worse. A young fellow! My wife
making sport with a young fellow! O lord! Here are doings! Here
are vagaries! I'll run mad; I'll climb Bow steeple presently, bestride
the dragon,° and preach cuckoldom to the whole city.   110

SIR JOLLY The best of all was too, that it happened to be an idle°
coxcomb that pretended° to be in love with her, neighbour.

SIR DAVY Indeed! In love with her! Who was it? What's his name? I
warrant you won't tell a body. I'll indict him in the Crown Office.°

No, I'll issue warrants to apprehend him for treason upon the 115
statute of Edward 19th.° Won't you tell me what young fellow it
was? Was it a very handsome young fellow, ha?

SIR JOLLY Handsome? Yes, hang him; the fellow's handsome
enough. He is not very handsome neither; but he has a devilish
leering black eye. 120

SIR DAVY O lord!

SIR JOLLY His face too is a good riding face.° 'Tis no soft, effeminate
complexion indeed; but his countenance is ruddy, sanguine and
cheerful. A devilish fellow in a corner,° I'll warrant him.

SIR DAVY Bless us, what will become of me! Why the devil did I 125
marry a young wife? Is he very well-shaped too, tall, straight and
proportionable, ha?

SIR JOLLY Tall? No, he's not very tall neither. Yet he is tall enough
too. He's none of your overgrown, lubberly Flanders jades,° but
more of the true English breed—well-knit, able, and fit for service, 130
old boy. The fellow is well-shaped truly, very well-proportioned,
strong and active. I have seen the rogue leap like a buck.°

SIR DAVY Who can this be? Well, and what think you, friend? Has he
been there? Come, come, I'm sensible she's a young woman, and I
am an old fellow, troth a very old fellow. I signify little or nothing 135
now. But do you think he has prevailed? Am I cuckold, neighbour?

SIR JOLLY Cuckold? What! A cuckold in Covent Garden? No, I'll
assure you, I believe her to be the most virtuous woman in the
world. But if you had but seen!

SIR DAVY Ay, would I had! What was it? 140

SIR JOLLY How like a rogue she used him. First of all comes me up
the spark to her. 'Madam', says he, and then he bows down, thus.
'How now', says she, 'what would the impertinent fellow have?'

SIR DAVY Humph! Ha! Well, and what then?

SIR JOLLY 'Madam', says he again, bowing as he did before, 'my 145
heart is so entirely yours, that except you take pity of my
sufferings, I must here die at your feet'.

SIR DAVY So, and what said she again, neighbour? Ha!

SIR JOLLY 'Go, you are a fop.'°

SIR DAVY Ha, ha, ha! Did she indeed? Did she say so indeed? I am 150
glad on't, troth I am very glad on't. Well, and what next? And
how, and well, and what? Ha!

SIR JOLLY 'Madam', says he, 'this won't do. I am your humble
servant, for all this; you may pretend to be as ill-natured as you
please, but I shall make bold'. 155

SIR DAVY Was there ever such an impudent fellow?

SIR JOLLY With that, 'Sirrah',° says she, 'you are a saucy jackanapes, and I'll have you kicked'.

SIR DAVY Ha, ha, ha! Well, I would not be unmarried again to be an angel.   160

SIR JOLLY But the best jest of all was, who this should be at last.

SIR DAVY Ay, who indeed? I'll warrant you, some silly° fellow or other. Poor fool!

SIR JOLLY E'en a scandalous rakehell that lingers up and down the town by the name of Captain Beaugard; but he has been a bloody   165 cuckold-making scoundrel in his time.

SIR DAVY Hang him, sot; is it he? I don't value him thus, not a wet finger,° man. To my knowledge she hates him, she scorns him, neighbour; I know it, I am very well satisfied in the point. Besides, I have seen him since that, and outhectored him. I am to   170 tell her from his own mouth that he promises never to affront her more.

SIR JOLLY Indeed.°

SIR DAVY Ay, ay.

        Enter Lady Dunce, paying her Chairman

CHAIRMAN God bless you, madam; thank your honour.   175

        [*Exit Chairman*]

SIR JOLLY [*to Sir Davy*] Hush, hush, there's my lady. I'll be gone; I'll not be seen. Your humble servant. Good-bye.

SIR DAVY No, faith, Sir Jolly, e'en go into my house now, and stay supper with me. We han't supped together a great while.

SIR JOLLY Ha! Say you so? I don't care if I do; faith, with all my   180 heart. [*Aside*] This may give me an opportunity to set all things right again.

SIR DAVY My dear!

LADY DUNCE Sir!

SIR DAVY You have been abroad, my dear, I see.   185

LADY DUNCE Only for a little air. Truly, I was almost stifled within-doors. I hope you will not be angry, Sir David, will you?

SIR DAVY Angry, child! No, child, not I. What should I be angry for?

LADY DUNCE I wonder, Sir David, you will serve me at this rate. Did you not promise me to go in my behalf to Beaugard and   190 correct him according to my instructions for his insolence?

SIR DAVY So I did, child. I have been with him, sweetheart; I have told him all to a tittle. I gave him back again the picture too; but as the devil would have it, I forgot the ring, faith I did.

LADY DUNCE Did you purpose, Sir Sodom,° to render me ridiculous   195
  to the man I abominate? What scandalous interpretation, think
  you, must he make of my retaining any trifle of his sent me on so
  dishonourable terms?

SIR DAVY Really, my lamb, thou art in the right. Yet I went back
  afterwards, dear heart, and did the business to some purpose.   200

LADY DUNCE I am glad that you did, with all my heart.

SIR DAVY I gave him his lesson, I'll warrant him.

LADY DUNCE Lesson! What lesson had you to give him?

SIR DAVY Why, I told him, as he liked that usage he might come
  again. Ha, ha, ha!   205

LADY DUNCE Ay, and so let him.

SIR DAVY With all my heart; I'll give him free leave, or hang me.
  Though thou wouldst not imagine how the poor devil's altered. La
  you there now!° But, as certainly as I stand here, that man is
  troubled that° he swears he shall not rest day nor night till he has   210
  satisfied thee. Prithee be satisfied with him if 'tis possible, my dear;
  prithee do. I promised him before I left him to tell thee as much,
  for the poor wretch looks so simply.° I could not choose but pity
  him, I vow and swear. Ha, ha, ha!

SIR JOLLY [aside] Now, now, you little witch, now, you chits-   215
  face! Od, I could find in my heart to put my little finger in your
  bubbies.

LADY DUNCE Sir David, I must tell you that I cannot but resent
  your so soon reconcilement with a man that I hate worse than
  death, and that if you loved me with half that tenderness which   220
  you profess, you would not forget an affront so palpably and so
  basely offered me.

SIR DAVY Why, chicken, where's the remedy? What's to be done?
  How wouldst thou have me deal with him?

LADY DUNCE Cut his throat.   225

SIR DAVY Bless us forever! Cut his throat? What, do murder?

LADY DUNCE Murder?—yes, anything to such an incorrigible enemy
  of your honour, one that has resolved to persist in abusing of you.
  See here this letter. This I received since I last parted with you.
  Just now it was thrown into my chair by an impudent lackey of   230
  his, kept o' purpose for such employments.

SIR DAVY Let me see. A letter indeed! [Reads] 'For the Lady Dunce.'
  Damned rogue, treacherous dog! What can he say in the inside
  now? Here's a villain.
    [Sir Davy starts to open the letter]

41

LADY DUNCE Yes, you had best break it open, you had so; 'tis like   235
the rest of your discretion.

SIR DAVY Lady, if I have an enemy, it is best for me to know what
mischief he intends me. Therefore, with your leave, I will break it
open.

LADY DUNCE Do, do, to have him believe that I was pleased   240
enough with it to do it myself. If you have the spirit of a gentleman
in you, carry it back, and dash it as it is in the face of that
audacious fellow.

SIR JOLLY [aside] What can be the meaning of this now?

SIR DAVY A gentleman; yes, madam, I am a gentleman, and the   245
world shall find that I am a gentleman. [Aside] I have certainly the
best woman in the world.

LADY DUNCE What do you think must be the end of all this? I have
no refuge in the world but your kindness. Had I a jealous husband
now, how miserable must my life be!   250

SIR JOLLY [aside] Ah rogue's nose! Ah devil! Ah toad! Cunning thief,
wheedling slut! I'll bite her by and by.

SIR DAVY Poor fool! No, dear, I am not jealous, nor never will be
jealous of thee. Do what thou wilt, thou shalt not make me jealous.
I love thee too well to suspect thee.   255

LADY DUNCE Ah, but how long will you do so?

SIR DAVY How long! As long as I live, I warrant thee, I—don't talk
to a body so. I cannot hold out if thou dost; my eyes will run over.
Poor fool, poor bird's-nie! Poor lambkin!

LADY DUNCE But will you be so kind to me to answer my   260
desires?° Will you once more endeavour to make that traitor
sensible that I have too just an esteem of you, not to value his
addresses as they deserve?

SIR DAVY Ay, ay, I will.

LADY DUNCE But don't stay away too long, dear; make what haste   265
you can. I shall be in pain till I see you again.

SIR DAVY My dear, my love, my babby, I'll be with thee in a moment.
How happy am I above the rest of men!—Neighbour, dear neighbour, walk in with my wife, and keep her company till I return
again.—Child, don't be troubled; prithee don't be troubled. Was   270
there ever such a wife? Well, da, da, da. Don't be troubled, prithee,
don't be troubled, prithee don't be troubled. Da, da.

Exeunt [Sir Davy Dunce and Vermin]

LADY DUNCE Sir Jolly, Sir Jolly, Sir Jolly.

SIR JOLLY 'Don't be troubled, prithee don't be troubled. Da, da.'

LADY DUNCE But, Sir Jolly, can you guess whereabout my wander- 275
ing officer may be probably found now?

SIR JOLLY Found, lady? He is to be found, madam; he is to be at
my house presently. Lady, he's certainly one of the finest fellows
in the world.

LADY DUNCE You speak like a friend, Sir Jolly. 280

SIR JOLLY His friend, lady? No, madam, his foe, his utter enemy. I
shall be his ruin; I shall undo him.

LADY DUNCE You may, if you please, then come both and play at
cards this evening with me for an hour or two, for I have contrived
it so that Sir David is to be abroad at supper tonight; he cannot 285
possibly avoid it. I long to win some of the captain's money
strangely.°

SIR JOLLY Do you so, my gamester? Well, I'll be sure to bring him,
and for what he carries about him° I'll warrant you—od, he's a
pretty fellow, a very pretty fellow. He has only one fault. 290

LADY DUNCE And what is that, I beseech you, sir?

SIR JOLLY Only too loving, too good-natured; that's all. 'Tis certainly the best-natured fool breathing. That's all his fault.

LADY DUNCE Hist, hist, I think I see company coming. If you please,
Sir Jolly, we'll go in. 295

    Enter Beaugard, followed by Sir Davy Dunce [and] Vermin

SIR JOLLY Mum, mum, mum. 'Tis he himself, the very same. Od's
so, Sir Davy after him too. Hush, hush, hush. Let us be gone, let
us retire. Do but look upon him now; mind him a little. There's
a shape, there's an air, there's a motion! Ah rogue! Ah devil! Get
you in, get you in. I say there's a shape for you! 300

    Exeunt [Sir Jolly Jumble and Lady Dunce]

BEAUGARD [*aside*] What the devil shall I do to recover this day's loss
again? My honourable pimp too, my pander knight, has forsaken
me. Methinks I am quandaried like one going with a party to
discover the enemy's camp, but had lost his guide upon the
mountains. [*Seeing Sir Davy*] Curse on him; old Argus° is here 305
again. There can be no good fortune towards me when he's at my
heels.

SIR DAVY Sir, sir, sir, one word with you, sir! Captain, captain, noble
captain, one word, I beseech you.

BEAUGARD With me, friend? 310

SIR DAVY Yes, with you, my no friend.

BEAUGARD Sir David, my intimate, my bosom physician—

SIR DAVY [*aside*] Ah rogue! Damned rogue!

BEAUGARD My confessor, my dearest friend I ever had—

SIR DAVY [*aside*] Dainty wheedle! Here's a fellow for ye.   315

BEAUGARD One that has taught me to be in love with virtue and
shown me the ugly inside of my follies.

SIR DAVY Sir, your humble servant.

BEAUGARD Is that all? If you are as cold in your love as you are in
your friendship, Sir Davy, your lady has the worst time on't of   320
anyone in Christendom.

SIR DAVY So she has, sir, when she cannot be free from the insolent
solicitations of such fellows as you are, sir.

BEAUGARD As me, sir? Why, who am I, good Sir Domine Doddlepate?   325

SIR DAVY [*to Vermin*] So, take notice he threatens me. I'll have
him bound to the peace° instantly.—Will you never have
remorse of conscience, friend? Have you banished all shame from
your soul? Do you consider my name is Sir Davy Dunce? That I
have the most virtuous wife living? Do you consider that? [*Aside*] 330
Now, how like a rogue he looks again! What a hangdog° leer was
that!

BEAUGARD Your virtuous wife, sir? You are always harping upon
that string, Sir Davy.

SIR DAVY No, 'tis you would be harping upon that string, sir. See   335
you this? Cast your eyes upon this, this letter, sir. [*Sir Davy gives
Beaugard the letter*] Did not you promise this very day to abandon
all manner of proceedings of this nature tending to the dishonour
of me and my family?

BEAUGARD Letter, sir? [*Aside*] What the devil does he mean now?   340
Let me see. [*Reads*] 'For the Lady Dunce.' This is no scrawl of
mine, I'll be sworn. By Jove, her own hand!° What a dog was I!
Forty to one, but I had played the fool and spoiled all again. Was
there ever so charming a creature breathing! [*To Sir Davy*] Did
your lady deliver this to your hands, sir?   345

SIR DAVY Ev'n her own self in person, sir, and bade me tell you, sir,
that she has too just an esteem of me, sir, not to value such a fellow
as you are as you deserve.

BEAUGARD Very good. (*Reads the letter*) 'I doubt not but this letter
will surprise you'—[*aside*] in troth, and so it does extremely—'but 350
reflect upon the manner of conveying it to your hand as kindly as
you can'.

SIR DAVY Ay, a damned thief, to have it thrown into the chair by a
footman!

BEAUGARD (*reads*)° 'Would Sir Davy were but half so kind to you as   355
I am.'

SIR DAVY Say you so, you insinuating knave?

BEAUGARD (*reads*) 'But he, I am satisfied, is so severely jealous, that
except you contrive some way to let me see you this evening, I fear
all will be hopeless.'   360

SIR DAVY Impudent traitor! I might have been a monster° yet before
I had got my supper in my belly.

BEAUGARD (*reads*) 'In order to which either appear yourself, or
somebody for you, half an hour hence in the Piazza, where more
may be considered of. Adieu.'   365

SIR DAVY Thanks to you, noble sir, with all my heart. You are come,
I see, accordingly. But, as a friend, I am bound in conscience to
tell you the business won't do,° the trick won't pass, friend. You
may put up your pipes° and march off. [*Aside*] O lord! He lie with
my wife! Pugh-h-h! He make Sir Davy Dunce a cuckold! Poor   370
wretch! Ha, ha, ha!
      Enter Sir Jolly Jumble

SIR JOLLY [*aside, to Beaugard*] Hist, hist, hist.
      Enter Lady Dunce, and Fourbin (disguised)

LADY DUNCE (*to Fourbin*) That's he, there he is! Succeed and be
rewarded.

FOURBIN [*aside*] Other people may think what they please; but, in   375
my own opinion, I am a very pretty° fellow now. If my design but
succeed upon this old baboon, I'll be canonized. [*To Sir Davy*] Sir,
sir, sir.

SIR DAVY Friend! With me? Would you speak with me, friend?

FOURBIN Sir, my commands were to attend your worship.   380

SIR JOLLY [*aside, to Beaugard*] Beaugard, Beaugard! Hist, hist! Here,
here! Quickly! Hist!
      Exeunt Beaugard and Sir Jolly Jumble

SIR DAVY Where do you live, sweetheart, and who do you belong
to?

FOURBIN Sir, I am a small instrument of the city. I serve the Lord   385
Mayor in his office there.

SIR DAVY How! The Lord Mayor!

FOURBIN Yes, sir, who desires you by all means to do him the
honour of your company at supper this evening.

SIR DAVY It will be the greatest honour I ever received in my life.   390
What, my Lord Mayor invite me to supper? I am his lordship's
most humble servant.

FOURBIN Yes, sir, if your name be Sir Davy Dunce, as I have the
    honour to be informed it is. He desires you moreover to make what
    haste you can, for that he has some matters of importance to   395
    communicate° to your honour which may take up some time.

LADY DUNCE [aside] I hope it will succeed.

SIR DAVY Communicate with me! He does me too noble a favour.
    I'll fly upon the wings of ambition to lay myself at his footstool.
    [Aside] My Lord Mayor sends himself to invite me to supper—to   400
    confer with me too! I shall certainly be a great man.

FOURBIN What answer will your worship charge me back withal?

SIR DAVY Let his lordship know that I am amazed, and confounded,
    at his generosity, and that I am so transported with the honour he
    does me, that I will not fail to wait on him in the roasting of an   405
    egg.°

FOURBIN I am your worship's lowly slave.
       [Exit Fourbin]

SIR DAVY Vermin, go get the coach ready. Get me the gold medal
    too and chain which I took from the Roman Catholic officer for a
    popish relic.°   410
       [Exit Vermin]
    I'll be fine; I'll shine and drink wine that's divine. My Lord Mayor
    invite me to supper!

LADY DUNCE My dearest, I'm glad to see thee returned in safety,
    from the bottom of my heart. Hast thou seen the traitor?

SIR DAVY Seen him? Hang him; I have seen him. Pox on him! Seen   415
    him!

LADY DUNCE Well, and what is become of him? Where is he?

SIR DAVY Why dost thou ask me where he is? What a pox care I
    what becomes of him? Prithee don't trouble me with thy imper-
    tinence;° I am busy.   420

LADY DUNCE You are not angry, my dear, are you?

SIR DAVY No; but I am pleased, and that's all one—very much
    pleased, let me tell you. But that I am only to sup with my Lord
    Mayor; that's all—nothing else in the world. Only the business of
    the nation calls upon me; that's all. Therefore, once more I say,   425
    don't be troublesome, but stand off.

LADY DUNCE You always think my company troublesome; you
    never stay at home to comfort me. What think you I shall do
    alone by myself all this evening, moping in my chamber? Pray, my
    joy, stay with me for once. (Aside) I hope he won't take me at my   430
    word.

SIR DAVY I say again and again, tempter, stand off. I will not lose
my preferment for my pleasure. Honour is towards me, and flesh
and blood are my aversion.

LADY DUNCE But how long will you stay then?   435

SIR DAVY I don't know; maybe an hour, maybe all night—as his
lordship and I think fit. What's that to anybody?

LADY DUNCE You are very cruel to me.

SIR DAVY I can't help it. Go, get you in and pass away the time with
your neighbour. I'll be back again before I die. In the meantime   440
be humble and conformable. Go.

    [Enter Vermin]

Is the coach ready?

VERMIN Yes, sir.

SIR DAVY *[to Lady Dunce]* Well, your servant. What, nothing to my
Lady Mayoress! You have a great deal of breeding indeed, a great 445
deal. Nothing to my Lady Mayoress?

LADY DUNCE *[weeping]* My service to her, if you please.

SIR DAVY Well, da, da. The poor fool cries, o' my conscience! Adieu.
Do you hear? Farewell.

    Exeunt [Sir Davy and Vermin]

LADY DUNCE As well as what I love can make me.   450

    Enter Sir Jolly

SIR JOLLY Madam, is he gone?

LADY DUNCE In post-haste, I assure.

SIR JOLLY In troth, and joy go with him.

LADY DUNCE Do you then, Sir Jolly, conduct the captain hither,
whilst I go and dispose of the family,° that we may be private.   455

    Exeunt, [in different directions]

[3.2]

    [Sir Davy Dunce's house]

    Enter Sir Davy Dunce

SIR DAVY Troth, I had forgot my medal and chain, quite and clean
forgot my relic. I was forced to come up these backstairs, for fear
of meeting my wife again. It is the troublesom'st loving fool. I
must into my closet° and write a short letter too. 'Tis post-night;° I had
forgot that. Well, I would not have my wife catch me for a guinea.   5

    Exit [Sir Davy Dunce.] Enter Beaugard and Lady Dunce

BEAUGARD Are you very certain, madam, nobody is this way? I fancy,
as we entered, I saw the glimpse of something more than ordinary.

LADY DUNCE Is it your care of me, or your personal fears, that make
you so suspicious? Whereabouts was the apparition?

BEAUGARD There, there, just at the very door.   10

LADY DUNCE Fie for shame! That's Sir Davy's closet, and he, I am
satisfied, is far enough off by this time. I'm sure I heard the coach
drive him away. But, to convince you, you shall see now. (*Knocking
at the closet-door*) Sir Davy, Sir Davy, Sir Davy!—Look you there.
You a captain, and afraid of a shadow. Come, sir, shall we call for   15
the cards?

BEAUGARD And what shall we play for, pretty one?

LADY DUNCE E'en what you think best, sir.

BEAUGARD Silver kisses or golden joys? Come, let us make stakes a
little.°   20

> *Enter Sir Jolly Jumble, [unobserved by Beaugard and Lady
> Dunce]*

SIR JOLLY [*aside*] Ah rogue, ah rogue! Are you there? Have I caught
you in faith? Now, now, now!

LADY DUNCE And who shall keep them?°

BEAUGARD You, till Sir Davy returns from supper.

LADY DUNCE That may be long enough, for our engine, Fourbin,   25
has orders not to give him over° suddenly, I assure you.

BEAUGARD And is't to yourself then I'm obliged for this blessed
opportunity? Let us improve° it to love's best advantage.

SIR JOLLY [*aside*] Ah-h-h-h! Ah-h-h-h!

BEAUGARD Let's vow eternal, and raise our thoughts to expectation   30
of immortal pleasures. In one another's eyes let's read our joys till
we've no longer power o'er our desires, drunk with this dissolving—O!—

> *Enter Sir Davy Dunce from his closet*

LADY DUNCE (*squeaks*) Ah!

BEAUGARD By this light, the cuckold! Presto! Nay then, halloo!°   35

> [*Beaugard*] *gets up° and runs away*

SIR DAVY O lord, a man! A man in my wife's chamber! Murder,
murder! Thieves, thieves! Shut up my doors! Madam! Madam!
Madam!

SIR JOLLY [*coming forward*] Ay, ay, thieves, thieves! Murder, murder! Where, neighbour, where, where?   40

> *Lady Dunce catches up Beaugard's sword which he had left
> behind him in the hurry, and presents it to Sir Davy*

LADY DUNCE Pierce, pierce this wretched heart hard to the hilts. Dye this in deepest crimson of my blood. Spare not a miserable woman's life, whom heaven designed to be the unhappy object of the most horrid usage man e'er acted.

SIR DAVY What in the name of Satan does she mean now?   45

LADY DUNCE Curse on my fatal beauty! Blasted ever be these two baneful eyes, that could inspire a barbarous villain to attempt such crimes as all my blood's too little to atone for! Nay, you shall hear me.

SIR DAVY Hear you, madam? No, I have seen too much, I thank you   50
heartily. Hear you, quotha!

LADY DUNCE Yes, and before I die too, I'll be justified.°

SIR DAVY Justified! O lord, justified!

LADY DUNCE Notice being given me of your return, I came with speed to this unhappy place, where I have oft been blessed with   55
your embraces, when from behind the arras out starts Beaugard. How he came there, heaven knows.

SIR DAVY I'll have him hanged for burglary. He has broken my house, and broke the peace upon my wife. Very good!

LADY DUNCE Straight in his arms he grasped me fast. With much   60
ado I plunged and got my freedom, ran to your closet-door, knocked and implored your aid, called on your name, but all in vain.

SIR DAVY Ha!

LADY DUNCE Soon again he seized me, stopped my mouth, and with   65
a conqueror's fury—

SIR DAVY O lord! O lord! No more, no more, I beseech thee. I shall grow mad, I will grow mad, and very mad. I'll plough up rocks and adamantine iron bars. I'll crack the frame of nature, sally out like Tamburlaine upon the Trojan Horse, and drive the pygmies   70
all like geese before me.° O lord, stop her mouth! Well! And how? And what then? Stopped thy mouth! Well! Ha!

LADY DUNCE No, though unfortunate, I still am innocent. His cursed purpose could not be accomplished. But who will live so injured? No, I'll die, to be revenged on myself. I ne'er can hope   75
that I may see his streaming gore; and thus I let out my own.

[Lady Dunce] offers to run upon the sword

SIR DAVY [*preventing her*] Ha! What wouldst thou do, my love? Prithee don't break my heart. If thou wilt kill, kill me. I know thou art innocent; I see thou art. Though I had rather be a cuckold a thousand times than lose thee, poor love, poor dearee, poor baby.   80

SIR JOLLY (*weeps*) Alack-a-day!

LADY DUNCE [*sinking to her knees*] Ah me!

SIR DAVY Ah, prithee be comforted now; prithee do. Why, I'll love
thee the better for this, for all this, mun. Why shouldst be troubled
for another's ill doings? I know it was no fault of thine.   85

SIR JOLLY No, no more it was not, I dare swear.

SIR DAVY See, see, my neighbour weeps too; he's troubled to see
thee thus.

LADY DUNCE O, but revenge!

SIR DAVY Why, thou shalt have revenge. I'll have him murdered. I'll   90
have his throat cut before tomorrow morning, child. Rise now;
prithee rise.

SIR JOLLY Ay, do, madam, and smile upon Sir Davy.

LADY DUNCE But will you love me then as well as e'er you did?

SIR DAVY Ay, and the longest day I live too.   95

LADY DUNCE And shall I have justice done me on that prodigious
monster?

SIR DAVY Why, he shall be crows' meat by tomorrow night; I tell
thee he shall be crows' meat by midnight, chicken.

LADY DUNCE [*rising*] Then I will live, since so 'tis something   100
pleasant,
      When I in peace may lead a happy life
      With such a husband—

SIR DAVY   I with such a wife.

      [*Exeunt*]

4.[1]

The tavern

Enter Beaugard, Courtine and Drawer

DRAWER Welcome, gentlemen, very welcome, sir. Will you please to walk up one pair of stairs?

BEAUGARD Get the great room ready presently. Carry up too a good stock of bottles beforehand, with ice to cool our wine and water to refresh our glasses.

DRAWER It shall be done, sir. [*Customers call offstage*] Coming, coming there, coming. [*To Servants offstage*] Speak up in the Dolphin,° somebody!

[*Exit Drawer*]

BEAUGARD Ah, Courtine, must we be always idle? Must we never see our glorious days again? When shall we be rolling in the lands of milk and honey,° encamped in large, luxuriant vineyards, where the loaded vines cluster about our tents; drink the rich juice, just pressed from the plump grape, feeding on all the fragrant golden fruit that grow in fertile climes, and ripened by the earliest vigour of the sun?°

COURTINE Ah, Beaugard, those days have been. But now we must resolve to content ourselves at an humble rate. Methinks it is not unpleasant to consider how I have seen thee in a large pavilion, drowning the heat of the day in Champagne° wines, sparkling sweet as those charming beauties whose dear remembrance every glass recorded, with half a dozen honest fellows more. Friends, Beaugard, faithful, hearty friends—things as hard to meet with as preferment here. Fellows that would speak truth boldly, and were proud on't, that scorned flattery, loved honesty, for 'twas their portion,° and never yet learned the trade of ease and lying. But now—

BEAUGARD Ay, now we are at home in our natural hives and sleep like drones. But there's a gentleman on the other side the water that may make work for us all one day.°

COURTINE But in the meanwhile—

BEAUGARD In the meanwhile, patience, Courtine; that is the Englishman's virtue. Go to the man that owes you money, and tell him you are necessitated; his answer shall be, 'A little patience, I beseech you, sir'. Ask a cowardly rascal satisfaction° for a sordid

injury done you; he shall cry, 'Alas-a-day, sir, you are the strangest   35
man living; you won't have patience to hear one speak'. Complain
to a great man that you want° preferment, that you have forsaken
considerable advantages abroad in obedience to public edicts;° all
you shall get of him is this, 'You must have patience, sir'.

COURTINE But will patience feed me, or clothe me, or keep me   40
clean?

BEAUGARD Prithee no more hints of poverty. 'Tis scandalous.
'Sdeath, I would as soon choose to hear a soldier brag as complain.
Dost thou want any money?

COURTINE True, indeed I want no necessaries to keep me alive; but   45
I do not enjoy myself with that freedom I would do. There is no
more pleasure in living at stint° than there is in living alone. I
would have it in my power, when he needed me, to serve and assist
my friend. I would to my ability deal handsomely too by the
woman that pleased me.   50

BEAUGARD O, fie for shame! You would be a whoremaster. Friend,
go, go; I'll have no more to do with you.

COURTINE I would not be forced neither at any time to avoid a
gentleman that had obliged me, for want of money to pay him a
debt contracted in our old acquaintance. It turns my stomach to   55
wheedle with the rogue I scorn when he uses me scurvily, because
he has my name in his shop-book.°

BEAUGARD As, for example, to endure the familiarities of a rogue
that shall cock his greasy hat° in my face, when he duns me, and
at the same time vail it to an overgrown deputy of the ward,°   60
though a frowzy fellmonger.

COURTINE To be forced to concur with his nonsense too, and laugh
at his parish jests.°

BEAUGARD To use respects and ceremonies to the milch-cow his
wife, and praise her pretty children, though they stink of their   65
mother, and are uglier than the issue of a baboon. Yet all this must
be endured.

COURTINE Must it, Beaugard?

BEAUGARD And since 'tis so, let's think of a bottle.

COURTINE With all my heart, for railing and drinking do much   70
better together than by themselves. A private room, a trusty friend
or two, good wine and bold truths, are my happiness. But where's
our dear friend and intimate, Sir Jolly, this evening?

BEAUGARD To deal like a friend, Courtine, I parted with him but
just now. He's gone to contrive me a meeting, if possible this   75

night, with the woman my soul is most fond of. I was this evening just entering upon the palace of all joy, when I met with so damnable° a disappointment. In short, that plague to all well-meaning women, the husband, came unseasonably and forced a poor lover to his heels, that was fairly making his progress another way, Courtine. The story thou shalt hear more at large hereafter.

COURTINE A plague on him! Why didst thou not murder the presumptuous cuckold? Saucy, intruding clown! To dare to disturb a gentleman's privacies! I would have beaten him into sense of his transgression, enjoyed his wife before his face, and a° taught the dog his duty.

BEAUGARD Look you, Courtine, you think you are dealing with the landlord of your winter quarters in Alsatia° now? Friend, friend, there is a difference between a freeborn English cuckold, and a sneaking wittol of a conquered province.

COURTINE O, by all means! There ought to be a difference observed between your arbitrary whoring and your limited fornication.°

BEAUGARD And but reason; for, though we may make bold with another man's wife in a friendly way, yet nothing upon compulsion, dear heart.

COURTINE And now Sir Jolly, I hope, is to be the instrument of some immortal plot, some contrivance for the good of thy body and the old fellow's soul, Beaugard; for all cuckolds go to heaven—that's most certain.

BEAUGARD Sir Jolly! Why, on my conscience, he thinks it as much his undoubted right to be pimpmaster-general to London and Middlesex, as the estate he possesses is. By my consent, his worship should e'en have a patent° for it.

COURTINE He is certainly the fittest for the employment in Christendom. He knows more families by their names and titles than all the bellmen within and without the walls.

BEAUGARD Nay, he keeps a catalogue of the choicest beauties about town, illustrated with a particular account of their age, shape, proportion, colour of hair and eyes, degrees of complexion, gunpowder-spots and moles.

COURTINE I wish the old pander were bound to satisfy my experience° what marks of good nature my Sylvia has about her.

[*Enter Sir Jolly Jumble*]

SIR JOLLY My captains! My sons of Mars, and imps of Venus!° Well encountered! What, shall we have a sparkling bottle or two, and

use fortune like a jade? Beaugard, you are a rogue, you are a dog.
I hate you; get you gone, go.

BEAUGARD But, Sir Jolly, what news from paradise, Sir Jolly? Is
there any hopes I shall come there tonight?

SIR JOLLY Maybe there is, maybe there is not. I say, let us have a   120
bottle, and I will say nothing else without a bottle. After a glass or
two my heart may open.

COURTINE Why then, we will have a bottle, Sir Jolly.

SIR JOLLY Will? We'll have dozens and drink till we're wise and
speak well of nobody, till we are lewder than midnight-whores and   125
outrail disbanded officers.

BEAUGARD Only one thing more, my noble knight, and then we are
entirely at thy disposal.

SIR JOLLY Well, and what's that? What's the business?

BEAUGARD This friend of mine here stands in need of thy assistance.   130
He's damnably in love, Sir Jolly.

SIR JOLLY In love! Is he so? In love! Od's my life! Is he!° What's
her name? Where does she live? I warrant you I know her; she's
in my table-book, I'll warrant you. (*Pulls out a table-book*) Virgin,
wife, or widow?   135

COURTINE In troth, Sir Jolly, that's something a difficult question;
but as virgins go now, she may pass for one of them.

SIR JOLLY Virgin—very good. Let me see. Virgin, virgin, virgin—O
here are the virgins. Truly, I meet with the fewest of this sort of any.
Well, and the first letter of her name now! For a wager, I guess her.   140

COURTINE Then you must know, Sir Jolly, that I love my love with
an S.

SIR JOLLY S. S. S. O here are the Esses. Let me consider now.
Sappho?

COURTINE No, sir.   145

SIR JOLLY Selinda?

COURTINE Neither.

SIR JOLLY Sophronia?

COURTINE You must guess again, I assure you.

SIR JOLLY Sylvia?   150

COURTINE Ay, ay, Sir Jolly, that's the fatal name—Sylvia, the fair,
the witty, the ill-natured. Do you know her, my friend?

SIR JOLLY Know her? Why, she is my daughter, and I have adopted
her these seven years. Sylvia—let me look. [*Reads*] 'Light brown
hair, her face oval and Roman, quick sparkling eyes, plump,   155
pregnant, ruby lips, with a mole on her breast, and the perfect

likeness of a heart-cherry on her left knee.' Ah villain! Ah sly-cap! Have I caught you? Are you there, i'faith? Well, and what says she? Is she coming? Do her eyes betray her? Does her heart beat, and her bubbies rise, when you talk to her, ha? 160

BEAUGARD Look you, Sir Jolly, all things considered, it may make a shift to come to a marriage in time.

SIR JOLLY I'll have nothing to do in it; I won't be seen in the business of matrimony. Make me a matchmaker, a filthy marriage-broker? Sir, I scorn; I know better things. Look you, friend, to 165 carry her a letter from you or so, upon good terms, though it be in a church I'll deliver it; or when the business is come to an issue, if I may bring you handsomely together, and so forth, I'll serve thee with all my soul, and thank thee into the bargain—thank thee heartily, dear rogue. I will, you little cocksparrow;° faith and troth, 170 I will. But no matrimony, friend; I'll have nothing to do with matrimony. 'Tis a damned invention, worse than a monopoly,° and a destroyer of civil correspondence.°

Enter Drawer

DRAWER Gentlemen, your room is ready, your wine and ice upon the table. Will your honours please to walk in? 175

SIR JOLLY Ay, wine, wine, give us wine. A pox on matrimony! Matrimony, in the devil's name!

COURTINE [*to Drawer*] But if an honest harlot or two chance to inquire for us, friend—

SIR JOLLY Right, sirrah, if whores come never so many, give 'em 180 reverence and reception. But nothing else; let nothing but whores and bottles come near us, as you tender your ears.

They go within the scene, where is discovered table and bottles°

BEAUGARD Why, there's, there's the land of Canaan° now in little. Hark you, drawer, dog, shut, shut the door, sirrah—do you hear?—shut it so close, that neither cares nor necessities may peep 185 in upon us.

[*The scene closes upon Beaugard and Courtine.*] *Enter Sir Davy Dunce, Fourbin and Bloody Bones*

FOURBIN [*aside, to Bloody Bones*] Bloody Bones, be you sure to behave yourself handsomely and like your profession. Show yourself a cut-throat of parts, and we'll fleece him.

BLOODY BONES My lady says we must be expeditious. Sir Jolly has 190 given notice to the captain by this time, so that nothing is wanting but the management of this overgrown gull to make us hectors-at-large and keep the whore Fortune under.

DRAWER Welcome, gentlemen, very welcome, sir. Will't please you
to walk into a room? Or shall I wait upon your honours' pleasure   195
here?

SIR DAVY Sweetheart, let us be private, and bring us wine hither.
   [*Exit Drawer, who returns with wine and glasses and then
   exits again*]
So. (*Sits down*) From this moment, war, war, and mortal dudgeon
against that enemy of my honour and thief of my good name called
Beaugard. [*To Fourbin*] You can cut a throat upon occasion, you   200
say, friend?

FOURBIN Sir, cutting of throats is my hereditary vocation. My father
was hanged for cutting of throats before me, and my mother for
cutting of purses.°

SIR DAVY No more to be said. My courage is mounted like a little   205
Frenchman upon a great horse; and I'll have him murdered.

FOURBIN Sir, 'murdered' you say, sir?

SIR DAVY Ay, 'murdered' I say, sir—his face flayed off and nailed to
a post in my great hall in the country, amongst all the other
trophies of wild beasts slain by our family since the Conquest.°   210
There's never a whoremaster's head there yet.

FOURBIN Sir, for that let me recommend this worthy friend of mine
to your service. He's an industrious gentleman and one that will
deserve your favour.

SIR DAVY He looks but something ruggedly though, methinks.   215

FOURBIN But, sir, his parts will atone for his person. Forms and
fashions are the least of his study. He affects a sort of philosophical
negligence indeed; but, sir, make trial of him, and you'll find him
a person fit for the work of this world.

SIR DAVY What trade are you, friend?   220

BLOODY BONES No trade at all, friend; I profess murder.° Rascally
butchers make a trade on't; 'tis a gentleman's divertisement.

SIR DAVY Do you profess murder?

BLOODY BONES Yes, sir, 'tis my livelihood. I keep a wife and six
children by it.   225

SIR DAVY [*drinks to him*] Then, sir, here's to you with all my heart.
[*Aside*] Would I had done with these fellows.

FOURBIN Well, sir, if you have any service for us, I desire we may
receive your gold and your instructions so soon as is possible.

SIR DAVY Soft and fair,° sweetheart, I love to see a little how I lay   230
out my money. Have you very good trading nowadays in your way,
friend?

BLOODY BONES In peaceable times a man may eat and drink comfortably upon't; a private murder done handsomely is worth money. But now that the nation's unsettled, there are so many 235 general undertakers, that 'tis grown almost a monopoly.° You may have a man murdered almost for little or nothing, and nobody e'er know who did it neither.

SIR DAVY Pray what countryman are you? Where were you born, most noble sir? 240

BLOODY BONES Indeed my country is foreign. I was born in Algier;° my mother was an apostate Greek, my father a renegado English-man,° who by oppressing of Christian slaves grew rich; for which when he lay sick, I murdered him one day in his bed, made my escape to Malta, where, embracing the faith,° I had the honour 245 given me to command a thousand horse aboard the galleys of that state.

SIR DAVY O lord, sir! My humble service to you again.

FOURBIN He tells you, sir, but the naked truth.

SIR DAVY I doubt it not in the least, most worthy sir. (*Aside*) These 250 are devilish fellows, I'll warrant 'em.

FOURBIN War, friend, and shining honour has been our province, till rusty peace reduced us to this base obscurity. Ah, Bloody Bones! Ah, when thou and I commanded that party at the siege of Philippsburgh,° where in the face of the army we took the 255 impenetrable half-moon!

BLOODY BONES Half-moon, sir! By your favour, 'twas a whole moon.

FOURBIN Brother, thou art in the right. 'Twas a full moon—and such a moon, sir! 260

SIR DAVY I doubt it not in the least, gentlemen; but in the meanwhile to our business.

FOURBIN With all my heart, so soon as you please.

SIR DAVY Do you know this Beaugard? He's a devilish fellow, I can tell you but that. He's a captain. 265

FOURBIN Has he a heart, think you, sir?

SIR DAVY O, like a lion! He fears neither God, man, nor devil.

BLOODY BONES I'll bring it you for your breakfast tomorrow. Did you never eat a man's heart, sir?

SIR DAVY Eat a man's heart, friend! 270

FOURBIN Ay, ay, a man's heart, sir. It makes absolutely the best ragout in the world. I have eaten forty of 'em in my time without bread.

SIR DAVY O lord! A man's heart! My humble service to you both,
gentlemen.   275

BLOODY BONES Why, your Algerine pirates eat nothing else at
sea; they have them always potted up like venison. Your well-
grown Dutchman's heart makes an excellent dish with oil and
pepper.

SIR DAVY O lord! O lord! [*To Fourbin*] Friend, friend, a word with   280
you. How much must you and your companion have to do this
business?

FOURBIN What, and bring you the heart home to your house?

SIR DAVY No, no, keeping the heart for your own eating. [*Aside*] I'll
be rid of 'em as soon as possible I can.   285

FOURBIN You say, sir, he's a gentleman?

SIR DAVY Ay, such a sort of gentleman as are about this town. The
fellow has a pretty handsome outside, but, I believe, little or no
money in his pockets.

FOURBIN Therefore we are like to have the honour to receive the   290
more from your worship's bounty.

BLOODY BONES For my part I care for no man's bounty. I expect to have my bargain performed, and I'll make as good a one as
I can.

SIR DAVY Look you, friend, don't you be angry, friend, don't be   295
angry, friend, before you have occasion. You say you'll have—let's
see how much will you have now? [*Aside*] I warrant the devil and
all by your good will.

FOURBIN Truly, Sir David, if, as you say, the man must be well
murdered without any remorse or mercy, betwixt Turk and Jew it   300
is honestly worth two hundred pounds.

SIR DAVY Two hundred pounds! Why, I'll have a physician shall kill
a whole family for half the money.

BLOODY BONES Damme, sir, how do ye mean?

SIR DAVY Damme, sir, how do I mean? Damme, sir, not to part with   305
my money.

BLOODY BONES Not part, brother!

FOURBIN Brother, the wight is improvable, and this must not be
borne withal.

BLOODY BONES Have I for this dissolved Circean charms,°   310
Broke iron durance, whilst from these firm legs
The well-filed, useless fetters dropped away
And left me master of my native freedom?

SIR DAVY What, what does he mean now?

FOURBIN Truly, sir, I am sorry to see it with all my heart. 'Tis a   315
distraction that frequently seizes him, though I am sorry it should
happen so unluckily at this time.

SIR DAVY Distracted, say you! Is he so apt to be distracted?

FOURBIN O, sir, raging mad. We that live by murder are all so. Guilt
will never let us sleep. I beseech you, sir, stand clear of him; he's   320
apt to be very mischievous at these unfortunate hours.

BLOODY BONES Have I been drunk with tender infants' blood
And ripped up teeming wombs? Have these bold hands
Ransacked the temples of the gods and stabbed
The priests before their altars? Have I done this?   325
Ha!

SIR DAVY No, sir, not that I know, sir. I would not say any such
thing for all the world, sir. [To Fourbin] Worthy gentleman, I
beseech you, sir—you seem to be a civil person—I beseech you,
sir, to mitigate his passion. I'll do anything in the world; you shall   330
command my whole estate.

FOURBIN Nay, after all, sir, if you have not a mind to have him quite
murdered, if a swingeing drubbing to bed-rid him, or so, will serve
your turn, you may have it at a cheaper rate a great deal.

SIR DAVY Truly, sir, with all my heart, for methinks now I consider   335
matters better, I would not by any means be guilty of another
man's blood.

FOURBIN Why then, let me consider. To have him beaten substantially, a beating that will stick by him, will cost you—half the
money.   340

SIR DAVY What, one hundred pounds! Sure the devil's in you, or
you would not be so unconscionable.

BLOODY BONES The devil! Where? Where is the devil? Show me.
I'll tell thee, Beelzebub, thou hast broke thy covenant.
Didst thou not promise me eternal plenty,   345
When I resigned my soul to thy allurements?

SIR DAVY Ah, lord!

BLOODY BONES Touch me not yet. I've yet ten thousand murders
To act before I'm thine. With all those sins
I'll come with full damnation to thy caverns   350
Of endless pain and howl with thee forever.

SIR DAVY Bless us! What will become of this mortal body of mine?
Where am I? Is this a house? Do I live? Am I flesh and blood?

BLOODY BONES There, there's the fiend again! Don't chatter so,
And grin at me. If thou must needs have prey,   355

Take here, take him, this tempter that would bribe me
With shining gold
To stain my hands with new iniquity.

SIR DAVY Stand off, I charge thee, Satan, whereso'er thou art. Thou
hast no right nor claim to me. I'll have thee bound in necromantic   360
charms. [*To Fourbin*] Hark you, friend, has the gentleman given
his soul to the devil?

FOURBIN Only pawned it a little; that's all.

SIR DAVY Let me beseech you, sir, to dispatch, and get rid of him
as soon as you can. I would gladly drink a bottle with you, sir; but   365
I hate the devil's company mortally. As for the hundred pound,
here, here it is ready. [*Gives Fourbin the money*] No more words.
I'll submit to your good nature and discretion.

FOURBIN [*to Bloody Bones*] Then, wretch, take this [*giving him
money*], and make thy peace with the infernal king; he loves riches.   370
Sacrifice and be at rest.

BLOODY BONES 'Tis done. I'll follow thee; lead on. Nay, if thou
smile, I more defy thee. Fee, fa, fum.°

     Exit [*Bloody Bones*]

FOURBIN 'Tis very odd, this.

SIR DAVY Very odd indeed. I'm glad he's gone though.   375

FOURBIN Now, sir, if you please, we'll refresh ourselves with a
cheerful glass, and so *chaqu'un chez lui*. [*Aside*] I would fain make
the gull drunk a little to put a little mettle into him.

SIR DAVY With all my heart, sir; but no more words of the devil, if
you love me.   380

FOURBIN The devil's an ass,° sir, and here's a health [*drinks*] to all
those that defy the devil.°

SIR DAVY With all my heart, and all his works too.

FOURBIN [*pouring Sir Davy a drink*] Nay, sir, you must do me right,°
I assure you.   385

SIR DAVY Not so full, not so full; that's too much, of all conscience.°
In troth, friend, these are sad times, very sad times. But here's to
you.

    [*Sir Davy drinks*]

FOURBIN Pox o' the times. The times are well enough so long as a
man has money in his pocket.   390

SIR DAVY 'Tis true. Here I have been bargaining with you about a
murder, but never consider that idolatry is coming in full speed
upon the nation.° Pray what religion are you of, friend?

FOURBIN What religion am I of, sir? Sir, your humble servant.°

[*Fourbin toasts Sir Davy*]

SIR DAVY Truly, a good conscience° is a great happiness. And so I'll   395
pledge you. [*Drinks and chokes*] Hemph, hemph! But shan't the dog
be murdered this night?

FOURBIN My brother rogue is gone by this time to set him,° and the
business shall be done effectually, I'll warrant you. [*Drinks*] Here's
rest his soul.   400

SIR DAVY With all my heart. [*Drinks*] Faith, I hate to be unchrarit-
able.

    Enter Courtine and Drawer

COURTINE Look you, 'tis a very impudent thing not to be drunk
by this time. Shall rogues stay in taverns to sip pints, and be
sober, when honest gentlemen are drunk by gallons? I'll have   405
none on't.

SIR DAVY (*sits up in his chair*) O lord, who's there?

DRAWER [*to Courtine*] I beseech your honour; our house will be
utterly ruined by this means.

COURTINE Damn your house, your wife and children, and all your   410
family, you dog! (*To Sir Davy*) Sir, who are you?

SIR DAVY Who am I, sir? What's that to you, sir? Will you tickle my
foot,° you rogue?

COURTINE I'll tickle your guts,° you poltroon, presently.

SIR DAVY Tickle my guts, you madcap? I'll tickle your toby° if you   415
do.

COURTINE What, with that circumcised band? That grave hypocritical beard of the Reformation cut?° Old fellow, I believe you're
a rogue.

SIR DAVY Sirrah, you are a whore, an errant bitch-whore. I'll use you   420
like a whore. I'll kiss you, you jade; I'll ravish you, you buttock.°
I am a Justice of the Peace, sirrah, and that's worse.

COURTINE Damn you, sir, I care not if you were a constable and all
his watch. What, such a rogue as you send honest fellows to prison
and countenance whores in your jurisdiction for bribery,° you   425
mongrel! I'll beat you, sirrah. I'll brain you; I'll murder you, you
mooncalf.

    [*Courtine*] *throws the chairs after* [*Sir Davy Dunce*]

SIR DAVY Sir, sir, sir! Constable! Watch! Stokes,° Stokes, Stokes!
Murder!

    Exit [*Sir Davy Dunce*]

COURTINE Huzza, Beaugard!   430

    [*Exit Courtine.*] *Enter Beaugard, Sir Jolly Jumble*

FOURBIN Well, sir, the business is done. We have bargained to murder you.

BEAUGARD Murdered! Who's to be murdered? Ha, Fourbin!

SIR JOLLY You are to be murdered, friend; you shall be murdered, friend.   435

BEAUGARD But how am I to be murdered? Who's to murder me, I beseech you?

FOURBIN Your humble servant, Fourbin. I am the man, with your worship's leave. Sir David has given me this gold to do it handsomely.   440

BEAUGARD Sir David! Uncharitable cur! What, murder an honest fellow for being civil to his family? What can this mean, gentlemen?

SIR JOLLY No, 'tis for not being civil to his family—that it means, gentleman. Therefore are you to be murdered tonight, and buried abed with my lady, you Jack Straw, you.   445

BEAUGARD I understand you, friends. The old gentleman has designed to have me butchered, and you have kindly contrived to turn it to my advantage in the affair of love. I am to be murdered but as it were, gentlemen, ha!

FOURBIN Your honour has a piercing judgment. Sir, Captain Court-   450
ine's gone.

BEAUGARD No matter; let him go. He has a design to put in practice this night too, and would perhaps but spoil ours. But when, Sir Jolly, is this business to be brought about?

SIR JOLLY Presently; 'tis more than time 'twere done already. Go,   455
get you gone, I say. Hold, hold, let's see your left ear° first. Hum. Ha! You are a rogue, you're a rogue. Get you gone, get you gone, go.

  Exeunt

[4.2]

Covent Garden Piazza [outside Sir Davy Dunce's house]
Enter Sylvia and Maid in the balcony°

MAID But why, madam, will you use him so inhumanly? I'm confident he loves you.

SYLVIA O, a true lover is to be found out like a true saint, by the trial of his patience. Have you the cords ready?

MAID Here they are, madam.   5

SYLVIA Let 'em down, and be sure, when it comes to trial, to pull
     lustily.
          [*The Maid lets the cords down from the balcony*]
     Is Will the footman ready?
WILL [*offstage*] At your ladyship's command, madam.
SYLVIA I wonder he should stay so long; the clock has struck twelve.   10
          Enter Courtine [*below*]
COURTINE (*sings*) *And was she not frank and free,*
                    And was she not kind to me,
                    To lock up her cat in her cupboard,
                    And give her key to me, to me;
                    To lock up her cat in her cupboard,   15
                    And give her key to me?
SYLVIA This must be he. Ay, 'tis he, and, as I am a virgin, roaring
     drunk. But if I find not a way to make him sober—
COURTINE Here, here's the window. Ay, that's hell-door, and my
     damnation's in the inside. [*Calls*] Sylvia, Sylvia, Sylvia! Dear imp   20
     of Satan, appear to thy servant.
SYLVIA Who calls on Sylvia in this dead of night,
     When rest is wanting to her longing eyes?
COURTINE 'Tis a poor wretch can hardly stand upright,
     Drunk with thy love, and if he falls he lies.   25
SYLVIA Courtine, is't you?
COURTINE Yes, sweetheart, 'tis I. Art thou ready for me?
SYLVIA Fasten yourself to that cord there. There, there it is.
COURTINE Cord! Where? O, O, here, here. [*Fastens himself*] So, now
     to heaven in a string.   30
SYLVIA Have you done?
COURTINE Yes, I have done, child, and would fain be doing° too,
     hussy.
SYLVIA [*to the servants*] Then pull away. Hoa up, hoa up, hoa up.
          [*Courtine is pulled halfway up to the balcony*]
     So, avast there.° [*To Courtine*] Sir.   35
COURTINE Madam?
SYLVIA Are you very much in love, sir?
COURTINE O, damnably, child, damnably.
SYLVIA I'm sorry for't with all my heart. Good night, captain.
          [*Exeunt Sylvia and Maid*]
COURTINE Ha, gone! What, left in Erasmus' paradise° between   40
     heaven and hell? If the constable should take me now for a
     straggling monkey hung by the loins, and hunt me with his cry of

watchmen!° Ah woman, woman, woman! Well, a merry life, and a short; that's all. (*Sings*)

> God prosper long our noble king,   45
> Our lives and safeties all.°

I am mighty loyal tonight.

Enter Fourbin and Bloody Bones, as from Sir Davy Dunce's house

FOURBIN Murder, murder, murder! Help, help, murder!

COURTINE Nay, if there be murder stirring, 'tis high time to shift for myself.   50

[Courtine] climbs up to the balcony [and exits]

SYLVIA [*offstage*] (*squeaking*) Ah-h-h-h!

BLOODY BONES Yonder, yonder he comes. Murder, murder, murder!

Exeunt Bloody Bones and Fourbin. Enter Sir Davy Dunce

SIR DAVY 'Tis very late; but murder is a melancholy business, and night is fit for't. I'll go home.

[Sir Davy Dunce] knocks [at his house-door]

VERMIN (*inside*) Who's there?   55

SIR DAVY 'Who's there?' Open the door, you whelp of Babylon.°

VERMIN [*opening the door*] O sir, you're welcome home; but here is the saddest news! Here has been murder committed, sir.

SIR DAVY Hold your tongue, you fool, and go to sleep. Get you in, do you hear? You talk of murder, you rogue? You meddle with   60
state-affairs?° Get you in.

[Exeunt]

[4.3]

[Sir Davy's house]

The scene opens [to show] the middle of the house and discovers Sir Jolly Jumble and Lady Dunce putting Beaugard in order as if he were dead°

SIR JOLLY Lie still, lie still, you knave. Close, close,° when I bid you. You had best quest and spoil the sport, you had!

BEAUGARD But pray how long must I lie thus?

LADY DUNCE I'll warrant you, you'll think the time mighty tedious.   5

BEAUGARD Sweet creature, who can counterfeit death when you are near him?

SIR JOLLY You shall, sirrah, if a body desires you a little,° so you
shall; we shall spoil all else. All will be spoiled else, man, if you do
not. Stretch out longer, longer yet, as long as ever you can. So, so.   10
Hold your breath, hold your breath. Very well.
  Enter Maid
MAID Madam, here comes Sir David.
  [*Exit Maid*]
SIR JOLLY Od's so, now close again as I told you. Close, you
devil! Now stir if you dare. Stir but any part about you if you
dare now. Od, I hit you such a rap if you do. Lie still, lie   15
you still.
  Enter Sir Davy Dunce
SIR DAVY My dear, how dost thou do, my dear? I am come.
LADY DUNCE Ah sir! What is't you've done? You've ruined me, your
family, your fortune; all is ruined. Where shall we go, or whither
shall we fly?   20
SIR DAVY 'Where shall we go?' Why, we'll go to bed, you little
jackadandy. Why, you are not a wench, you rogue; you are a boy,
a very boy, and I love you the better for't, sirrah, hey!
LADY DUNCE Ah sir, see there.
SIR DAVY Bless us, a man! And bloody! What, upon my hall-   25
table!°
LADY DUNCE Two ruffians brought him in just now, pronouncing
the inhuman deed was done by your command. Sir Jolly came in
the distracting° minute, or sure I had died with my distracting
fears. How could you think on a revenge so horrid?   30
SIR DAVY As I hope to be saved, neighbour, I only bargained with
'em to bastinado him in a way, or so, as one friend might do
another. But do you say that he is dead?
SIR JOLLY Dead, dead as clay; stark stiff and useless all. Nothing
about him stirring, but all's cold and still. I knew him a lusty fellow   35
once, a very mettled fellow. 'Tis a thousand pities.
SIR DAVY What shall I do? I'll throw myself upon him, kiss his wide
wounds and weep till blind as buzzard.°
LADY DUNCE O come not near him. There's such horrid antipathy
follows all murders, his wounds would stream afresh should you   40
but touch him.°
SIR DAVY Dear neighbour, dearest neighbour, friend, Sir Jolly, as
you love charity, pity my wretched case, and give me counsel. I'll
give my wife and all my estate to have him live again. Or shall I
bury him in the arbour at the upper end of the garden?   45

SIR JOLLY Alas-a-day, neighbour, never think on't, never think on't. The dogs will find him there, as they scrape holes to bury bones in. There is but one way that I know of.

SIR DAVY [*kneeling*] What is it, dear neighbour? What is it? You see I am upon my knees to you. Take all I have and ease me of my   50
fears.

SIR JOLLY Truly, the best thing that I can think of is putting of him to bed, putting him into a warm bed, and try to fetch him to life again. A warm bed is the best thing in the world. My lady may do much too. She's a good woman and, as I've been told, understands   55
a green wound° well.

SIR DAVY My dear, my dear, my dear!

LADY DUNCE Bear me away, O send me hence far off, where my unhappy name may be a stranger, and this sad accident no more remembered to my dishonour.   60

SIR DAVY Ah, but, my love, my joy, are there no bowels° in thee?

LADY DUNCE What would you have me do?

SIR DAVY Prithee do so much as try thy skill. There may be one dram of life left in him yet. Take him up to thy chamber, put him into thy own bed, and try what thou canst do with him.   65
Prithee do. If thou canst but find motion in him, all may be well yet. I'll go up to my closet in the garret and say my prayers in the meanwhile.

LADY DUNCE Will ye then leave this ruin on my hands?

SIR DAVY Pray, pray, my dear. [*To Sir Jolly*] I beseech you,   70
neighbour, help to persuade her if it be possible.

SIR JOLLY Faith, madam, do; try what you can do. I have a great fancy you may do him good. Who can tell but you may have the gift of stroking?° Pray, madam, be persuaded.

LADY DUNCE I'll do whate'er's your pleasure.   75

SIR DAVY That's my best dear. I'll go to my closet and pray for thee heartily. Alas, alas, that ever this should happen!

    Exit [*Sir Davy Dunce*]

BEAUGARD So, is he gone, madam, my angel?

SIR JOLLY What, no thanks, no reward for old Jolly now? Come hither, hussy, you little canary-bird,° you little hop-o'-my-thumb,   80
come hither. Make me a curtsy, and give me a kiss now. Ha! Give me a kiss, I say. Od, I will have a kiss, so I will; I will have a kiss if I set on't.° [*They kiss*] Shoo, shoo, shoo! Get you into a corner when I bid you. Shoo, shoo, shoo!

    Lady Dunce goes to Beaugard

What, there already? Well, I ha' done, I ha' done. This 'tis to be   85
an old fellow now.

BEAUGARD And will you save the life of him you've wounded?

LADY DUNCE Dare you trust yourself to my skill for a cure?

Sir Davy Dunce appears at a window above

SIR JOLLY Hist, hist! Close, close, I say again! Yonder's Sir Davy.
Od's so!   90

SIR DAVY My dear, my dear! My dear!

LADY DUNCE Who's that calls? My love, is't you?

SIR DAVY Ah, some comfort, or my heart's broke. Is there any hopes
yet? I've tried to say my prayers and cannot. If he be quite dead,
I shall never pray again. Neighbour, no hopes?   95

SIR JOLLY Truly little or none. Some small pulse I think there is
left, very little. There's nothing to be done if you don't pray. Get
you to prayers, whatever you do. Get you gone. Nay, don't stay
now. Shut the window, I tell you.

SIR DAVY Well, this is a great trouble to me; but good-night.   100

SIR JOLLY Good-night to you, dear neighbour.

[*Exit Sir Davy Dunce*]

(*To Beaugard and Lady Dunce*) Get ye up, get ye up, and be gone
into the next room. Presently; make haste. But don't steal away till
I come to you. Be sure ye remember; don't ye stir till I come. Pish,
none of this bowing and fooling; it but loses time. I'll only bolt the   105
door that belongs to Sir Davy's lodgings, that he may be safe, and
be with you in a twinkle. Ah-h-h-h!

[*Exeunt Beaugard and Lady Dunce*]

So, now for the door. [*Bolts the door*] Very well, friend, you are
fast. (*Sings*)

      Bonny lass, gin° thou wert mine,
      And twenty thoosand poonds aboot thee, &c.°   110

    [*Exit*]

5.[1]

Sylvia's chamber

Courtine bound on a couch

COURTINE [*waking up*] Hey ho! Hey ho! Ha! Where am I? Was I drunk or no last night? Something leaning that way. But where the devil am I? Sincerely, in a bawdy house. Faugh! What a smell of sin is here! Let me look about. If there be ever a Geneva Bible or a *Practice of Piety*° in the room, I am sure I have guessed right. 5 What's the matter now? Tied fast! Bound too! What tricks have I played to come into this condition! I have lighted into the territories of some merrily-disposed chambermaid or other, and she in a witty fit forsooth hath trussed me up thus. Has she pinned no rags to my tail, or chalked me upon the back, trow? Would I 10 had her mistress here at a venture.

[*Enter Sylvia and Maid*]

SYLVIA What would you do with her, my enchanted knight, if you had her? You are too sober for her by this time. Next time you get drunk, you may perhaps venture to scale her balcony, like a valiant captain as you are. 15

COURTINE Hast thou done this, my dear destruction? And am I in thy limbo?° I must confess, when I am in my beer, my courage° does run away with me now and then. But let me loose and thou shalt see what a gentle, humble animal thou hast made me. Fie upon't! What, tie me up like an ungovernable cur to the frame of 20 a table. Let, let thy poor dog loose, that he may fawn and make much of thee a little.

SYLVIA What, with those paws which you have been ferreting Moorfields withal,° and are very dirty still? After you have been daggling yourself abroad for prey and can meet with none, you 25 come sneaking hither for a crust, do you?

MAID Shall I fetch the whip and the bell,° madam, and slash him for his roguery soundly?

COURTINE Indeed, indeed! Do you long to be firking of man's flesh, Madam Flea-trap? Does the chaplain° of the family use you to the 30 exercise, that you are so ready for it?

SYLVIA If you should be let loose and taken into favour now, you would be for rambling° again so soon as you had got your liberty?

68

COURTINE Do but try me, and if ever I prove recreant more, let me   35
be beaten and used like a dog in good earnest.

SYLVIA Promise to grant me but one request, and it shall be done.

COURTINE Hear me but swear.

SYLVIA That anybody may do ten thousand times a day.

COURTINE Upon the word of a gentleman. Nay, as I hope to get   40
money in my pocket.

SYLVIA There I believe him leally. You'll keep your word, you
say?

COURTINE If I don't, hang me up in that wench's old garters.

SYLVIA [untying him] See, sir, you have your freedom.   45

COURTINE Well, now name the price. What must I pay for't?

SYLVIA You know, sir, considering our small acquaintance, you have
been pleased to talk to me very freely of love matters.

COURTINE I must confess I have been something to blame that way;
but if ever thou hearest more of it from my mouth after this night's   50
adventure, would I were well out of the house!

SYLVIA Have a care of swearing, I beseech you; for you must
understand that, spite of my teeth,° I am at last fallen in love most
unmercifully.

COURTINE And dost thou imagine I am so hard-hearted a villain as   55
to have no compassion of thee?

SYLVIA No, for I hope he's a man you can have no exceptions
against.

COURTINE Yes, yes, the man is a man, I'll assure you; that's one
comfort.   60

SYLVIA Who do you think it may be now? Try if you can guess him.

COURTINE Whoever he is, he's an honest fellow, I'll warrant him,
and I believe will not think himself very unhappy neither.

SYLVIA If a fortune of five thousand pounds, pleasant nights, and
quiet days can make him happy, I assure you he may be so. But   65
try once to guess at him.

COURTINE But if I should be mistaken?

SYLVIA Why, who is it you would wish me to?

COURTINE You have five thousand pound, you say?

SYLVIA Yes.   70

COURTINE Faith, child, to deal honestly, I know well enough who
'tis I wish for. But, sweetheart, before I tell you my inclinations,
it were but reasonable that I knew yours.

SYLVIA Well, sir, because I am confident you will stand my friend in
the business, I'll make a discovery. And, to hold you in suspense   75

no longer, you must know I have a month's mind to an armful of
your dearly beloved friend and brother captain. What say you to't?

COURTINE Madam, your humble servant, good-bye; that's all.

SYLVIA What, thus cruelly leave a lady that so kindly took you in in
your last night's pickle into her lodging? Whither would you rove   80
now, my wanderer?

COURTINE Faith, madam, you have dealt so gallantly in trusting me
with your passion, that I cannot stay here without telling you that
I am three times as much in love with an acquaintance of yours as
you can be with any friend of mine.   85

SYLVIA Not with my waiting-woman, I hope, sir.

COURTINE No, but it is with a certain kinswoman of thine, child.
They call her my Lady Dunce, and I think this is her house too.
They say she will be civil° upon a good occasion. Therefore prithee
be charitable, and show me the way to her chamber a little.   90

SYLVIA What, commit adultery, captain? Fie upon't! What, hazard
your soul?

COURTINE No, no, only venture my body a little; that's all. Look
you, you know the secret, and may imagine my desires. Therefore,
as you would have me assist your inclinations, pray be civil and   95
help me to mine. Look you, no demurring upon the matter, no
qualms; but show me the way. [*To Maid*] Or you, hussy, you shall
do't. Any bawd will serve at present, for I will go.
        [*Exit Maid*]

SYLVIA But you shan't go, sir.

COURTINE 'Shan't go', lady?   100

SYLVIA No, shan't go, sir. Did I not tell you, when once you had got
your liberty, that you would be rambling again?

COURTINE Why, child, wouldst thou be so uncharitable to tie up a
poor jade to an empty rack in thy stable, when he knows where to
go elsewhere and get provender enough?   105

SYLVIA Any musty provender, I find, will serve your turn, so you
have it but cheap, or at another man's charges.

COURTINE No, child, I had rather my ox should graze in a field of
my own than live hidebound upon the common, or run the hazard
of being pounded every day for trespasses.   110

SYLVIA Truly, all things considered, 'tis great pity so good a
husbandman as you should want a farm to cultivate.

COURTINE Wouldst thou be but kind and let me have a bargain in a
tenement° of thine, to try how it would agree with me.

SYLVIA And would you be contented to take a lease for your life?   115

COURTINE So pretty a lady of the manor and a moderate rent.

SYLVIA Which you'll be sure to pay very punctually.

COURTINE If thou doubtest my honesty, faith e'en take a little earnest beforehand.

       [Courtine offers to kiss her]

SYLVIA Not so hasty neither, good tenant. Imprimis: you shall oblige   120
yourself to a constant residence, and not, by leaving the house uninhabited, let it run to repairs.

COURTINE Agreed.

SYLVIA Item: for your own sake you shall promise to keep the estate well-fenced and enclosed, lest sometime or other your neighbour's   125
cattle break in and spoil the crop on the ground, friend.

COURTINE Very just and reasonable, provided I don't find it lie too much to common° already.

SYLVIA Item: you shall enter into strict covenant not to take any other farm upon your hands without my consent and approbation;   130
or if you do, that then it shall be lawful for me to get me another tenant, how and where I think fit.

COURTINE Faith, that's something hard though, let me tell you but that, landlady.

SYLVIA Upon these terms we'll draw articles.°   135

COURTINE And when shall we sign 'em?

SYLVIA Why, this morning, as soon as the ten o' clock office in Covent Garden° is open.

COURTINE A bargain. But how will you answer your entertainment of a drunken redcoat in your lodgings at these unseasonable hours?   140

SYLVIA That's a secret you will be hereafter obliged to keep for your own sake; and, for the family, your friend Beaugard shall answer for us there.

COURTINE Indeed I fancied the rogue had mischief in his head, he behaved himself so soberly last night. Has he taken a farm lately   145
too?

SYLVIA A trespasser, I believe, if the truth were known, upon the provender you would fain have been biting at just now.

       Enter Maid

MAID Madam, madam, have a care of yourself. I see lights in the great hall, whatever is the matter.° Sir Davy and all the family are   150
up.

       [Exit Maid]

COURTINE I hope they'll come and catch me here. Well, now you have brought me into this condition, what will you do with me, ha?

SYLVIA You won't be contented for a while to be tied up like a jade
to an empty rack without hay, will you?   155

COURTINE Faith, e'en take me and put thy mark upon me quickly,
that if I light into strange hands they may know me for a sheep of
thine.

SYLVIA What, by your wanting a fleece,° do you mean? If it must be
so, come, follow your shepherdess. Ba-a-a.   160
   Exeunt

[5.2]

[Another room in Sir Davy Dunce's house]
Enter Sir Davy Dunce and Vermin

SIR DAVY I cannot sleep, I shall never sleep again. I have prayed too
so long, that were I to be hanged presently, I have never a prayer
left to help myself.° I was no sooner lain down upon the bed just
now, and fallen into a slumber, but methought the devil was
carrying me down Ludgate Hill a-gallop, six puny fiends with   5
flaming fire-forks running before him like linkboys, to throw me
headlong into Fleet-ditch,° which seemed to be turned into a lake
of fire and brimstone. Would it were morning!

VERMIN Truly, sir, it has been a very dismal night.°

SIR DAVY But didst thou meet never a white thing upon the stairs?   10

VERMIN No, sir, not I; but methoughts I saw our great dog Towser,
with his brass collar on, stand at the cellar-door as I came along
the old entry.

SIR DAVY It could never be. Towser has a chain; had this thing a
chain on?   15

VERMIN No, sir, no chain; but it had Towser's eyes for all the world.

SIR DAVY What, ugly, great, frightful eyes?

VERMIN Ay, ay, huge saucer eyes, but mightily like Towser's.°

SIR DAVY O lord! O lord! Hark! Hark!

VERMIN What? What, I beseech you, sir!   20

SIR DAVY What's that upon the stairs? Didst thou hear nothing?
Hist, hark! Pat, pat, pat. Hark, hey!

VERMIN Hear nothing? Where, sir?

SIR DAVY Look! Look! What's that! What's that! In the corner there?

VERMIN Where?   25

SIR DAVY There.

VERMIN What, upon the iron chest?

SIR DAVY No, the long black thing up by the old clock-case. See! See! Now it stirs, and is coming this way.

VERMIN Alas, sir, speak to it—you are a Justice o' Peace—I beseech 30 you. I dare not stay in the house. I'll call the watch and tell 'em Hell's broke loose. What shall I do? O!

>   *Exit [Vermin]*

SIR DAVY O Vermin, if thou art a true servant, have pity on thy master, and do not forsake me in this distressed condition. Satan, be gone; I defy thee. I'll repent and be saved. I'll say my prayers; 35 I'll go to church. Help! Help! Help! Was there anything, or no? In what hole shall I hide myself?

>   *Exit [Sir Davy Dunce.] Enter Sir Jolly Jumble, Fourbin and Bloody Bones*

SIR JOLLY That should be Sir Davy's voice. The waiting-woman indeed told me he was afraid and could not sleep. Pretty fellows, pretty fellows both, you've done your business handsomely. What, 40 I'll warrant you have been a-whoring together now, ha! You do well, you do well; I like you the better for't. What's o'clock?

FOURBIN Near four, sir; 'twill not be day yet these two hours.

SIR JOLLY Very well. But how got ye into the house?

FOURBIN A ragged retainer of the family—Vermin I think they call 45 him—let us in as physicians sent for by your order.

SIR JOLLY Excellent rogues! And then I hope all things are ready as I gave directions?

FOURBIN To a tittle, sir. There shall not be a more critical° observer of your worship's pleasure than your humble servant, the Cheva- 50 lier Fourbin.

SIR JOLLY Get you gone, you rogue. You have a sharp nose and are a nimble fellow. I have no more to say to you. Stand aside, and be ready when I call. Here he comes. Hist! Hem, hem, hem.

>   *[Exeunt Bloody Bones and Fourbin.] Enter Sir Davy Dunce*

SIR DAVY Ha! What art thou? 55
>   Approach thou like the rugged Bankside bear,
>   The Eastcheap bull, or monster shown in fair;
>   Take any shape but that, and I'll confront thee.°

SIR JOLLY Alas, unhappy man! I am thy friend.

SIR DAVY Thou canst not be my friend, for I defy thee. Sir Jolly! 60 Neighbour! Ha! Is it you? Are you sure it is you? Are you? Yourself? If you be, give me your hand. Alas-a-day, I ha' seen the devil.

SIR JOLLY The devil, neighbour!

SIR DAVY Ay, ay, there's no help for't. At first I fancied it was a young
white bear's cub dancing in the shadow of my candle. Then it was   65
turned to a pair of blue breeches with wooden legs on, stamped about
the room as if all the cripples in town had kept their rendezvous there,
when all of a sudden it appeared like a leathern serpent,° and with a
dreadful clap of thunder flew out of the window.

SIR JOLLY Thunder! Why, I heard no thunder.   70

SIR DAVY That may be too. What, were you asleep?

SIR JOLLY 'Asleep', quotha! No, no, no sleeping this night for me,
I assure you.

SIR DAVY Well, what's the best news then? How does the man?

SIR JOLLY E'en as he did before he was born—nothing at all. He's   75
dead.

SIR DAVY Dead! What, quite dead?

SIR JOLLY As good as dead, if not quite dead. 'Twas a horrid°
murder—and then the terror of conscience, neighbour.

SIR DAVY And, truly, I have a very terrified one, friend, though I   80
never found I had any conscience at all till now. Pray whereabout
was his death's wound?

SIR JOLLY Just here, just under his left pap; a dreadful gash.

SIR DAVY So very wide?

SIR JOLLY O, as wide as my hat. You might have seen his lungs,   85
liver and heart, as perfectly as if you had been in his belly.

SIR DAVY Is there no way to have him privately buried and conceal
this murder? Must I needs be hanged by the neck like a dog,°
neighbour? Do I look as if I would be hanged?

SIR JOLLY Truly, Sir Davy, I must deal faithfully with you; you do   90
look a little suspiciously at present. But have you seen the devil,
say you?

SIR DAVY Ay, surely, it was the devil; nothing else could have
frighted me so.

SIR JOLLY Bless us and guard us all the angels! What's that?   95
      [*Sir Davy Dunce*] *kneels, holding up his hands and muttering*
      as if he prayed

SIR DAVY *Potestati sempiternae cuius benevolentia servantur gentes, et*
cuius misericordia.°

SIR JOLLY Neighbour, where are you, friend, Sir Davy?

SIR DAVY Ah, whatever you do, be sure to stand close to me. Where,
where is it?   100

SIR JOLLY Just, just there, in the shape of a coach and six horses
against the wall.

SIR DAVY Deliver us all. He won't carry me away in that coach and six, will he?

SIR JOLLY Do you see it?

[Exit Sir Jolly Jumble]

SIR DAVY See it! Plain, plain. Dear friend, advise me what I shall do? Sir Jolly, Sir Jolly, do you hear nothing? Sir Jolly! Ha! Has he left me alone? Vermin!

[Enter Vermin]

VERMIN Sir.

SIR DAVY Am I alive? Dost thou know me again? Am I thy quondam master, Sir Davy Dunce?

VERMIN I hope I shall never forget you, sir.

SIR DAVY Didst thou see nothing?

VERMIN Yes, sir, methought the house was all o' fire, as it were.

SIR DAVY Didst thou not see how the devils grinned and gnashed their teeth at me, Vermin?

VERMIN Alas, sir, I was afraid one of 'em would have bit off my nose, as he vanished out of the door.

SIR DAVY Lead me away. I'll go to my wife; I'll die by my own dear wife. Run away to the Temple and call Counsellor, my lawyer. I'll make over my estate presently—I shan't live till noon—I'll give all I have to my wife, ha, Vermin!

VERMIN Truly, sir, she's a very good lady.

SIR DAVY Ah much, much too good for me, Vermin. Thou canst not imagine what she has done for me, man. She would break her heart if I should give anything away from her; she loves me so dearly. Yet if I do die, thou shalt have all my old shoes.°

VERMIN I hope to see you live many a fair day yet though.

SIR DAVY Ah my wife, my poor wife! Lead me to my poor wife.

Exeunt

[5.3]

[Lady Dunce's bedchamber]

Scene draws and discovers Beaugard and Lady Dunce in her chamber, Sir Jolly [watching]°

LADY DUNCE What think you now of a cold, wet march over the mountains, your men tired, your baggage not come up, but at night a dirty, watery plain to encamp upon, and nothing to shelter you but an old leaguer cloak, as tattered as your colours?° Is not this much better now than lying wet and getting the sciatica? 5

BEAUGARD The hopes of this made all fatigue easy to me. The thoughts of Clarinda have a thousand times refreshed me in my solitude. Whene'er I marched, I fancied still it was to my Clarinda! When I fought, I imagined it was for my Clarinda! But when I came home, and found Clarinda lost! How could you think of 10 wasting but a night in the rank, surfeiting arms of this foul-feeding monster, this rotten trunk of a man, that lays claim to you?

LADY DUNCE The persuasion of friends and the authority of parents!

BEAUGARD And had you no more grace than to be ruled by a father and mother? 15

LADY DUNCE When you were gone, that should have given me better counsel, how could I help myself?

BEAUGARD Methinks then you might have found out some cleanlier shift° to have thrown away yourself upon, than nauseous old age and unwholesome deformity. 20

LADY DUNCE What, upon some overgrown, full-fed country fool, with a horse face, a great ugly head, and a great fine estate? One that should° have been drained and squeezed, and jolted up and down the town in hackneys with cheats and hectors, and so sent home at three o' clock every morning like a lolling booby, 25 stinking, with a belly full of stummed wine, and nothing in's pockets?

BEAUGARD You might have made a tractable beast of such a one; he would have been young enough for training.

LADY DUNCE Is youth then so gentle if age be stubborn? Young 30 men, like springs wrought by a subtle workman, easily ply to what their wishes press 'em; but, the desire once gone that kept 'em down, they soon start straight again, and no sign's left which way they bent before.

SIR JOLLY (*at the door, peeping*) So, so. Who says I see anything now? 35 I see nothing, not I. I don't see, I don't see; I don't look, not so much as look, not I.

Enter Sir Davy Dunce. [*Sir Jolly Jumble comes forward*]°

SIR DAVY I will have my wife. Carry me to my wife; let me go to my wife. I'll live and die with my wife, let the devil do his worst. Ah, my wife, my wife, my wife! 40

LADY DUNCE [*aside, to Beaugard*] Alas, alas, we are ruined. Shift for yourself. Counterfeit the dead corpse once more, or anything.

[*Beaugard feigns dead*]

SIR DAVY Ha! Whatsoe'er thou art, thou canst not eat me! Speak to
me. Who has done this? Thou canst not say I did it.°

SIR JOLLY 'Did it'? Did what? Here's nobody says you did anything   45
that I know, neighbour. What's the matter with you? What ails
you? Whither do you go? Whither do you run? I tell you here's
nobody says a word to you.

SIR DAVY Did you not see the ghost just now?°

SIR JOLLY Ghost! Prithee now, here's no ghost. Whither would   50
you go? I tell you, you shall not stir one foot farther, man; the
devil take me if you do. Ghost! Prithee, here's no ghost at all. A
little flesh and blood indeed there is—some old, some young,
some alive, some dead, and so forth. But ghost! Pish, here's no
ghost.   55

SIR DAVY But, sir, if I say I did see a ghost, I did see a ghost. An
you go to that,° why, sure, I know a ghost when I see one. [*To
Lady Dunce*] Ah my dear, if thou hadst but seen the devil half so
often as I have seen him.

LADY DUNCE Alas, Sir Davy, if you ever loved me, come not, O   60
come not near me. I have resolved to waste the short remainder of
my life in penitence, and taste of joys no more.

SIR DAVY Alas, my poor child! [*To Sir Jolly*] But do you think then
there was no ghost indeed?

SIR JOLLY Ghost! Alas-a-day, what should a ghost do here?   65

SIR DAVY And is the man dead?

SIR JOLLY Dead? Ay, ay, stark dead. He's stiff by this time.

LADY DUNCE Here you may see the horrid, ghastly spectacle—the
sad effects of my too rigid virtue and your too fierce resentment.

SIR JOLLY Do you see there?   70

SIR DAVY Ay, ay, I do see. Would I had never seen him. Would he
had lain with my wife in every house between Charing Cross and
Aldgate,° so this had never happened.

SIR JOLLY In troth, and would he had. But we are all mortal,
neighbour, all mortal. Today we are here, tomorrow gone, like the   75
shadow that vanisheth, like the grass that withereth, or like the
flower that fadeth,° or indeed like anything, or rather like nothing.
But we are all mortal.

SIR DAVY Heigh!

LADY DUNCE [*aside to Beaugard*] Down, down that trap-door. It   80
goes into a bathing-room. For the rest, leave it to my conduct.
     [*Beaugard descends through the trap-door,° unseen by Sir
     Davy Dunce*]

SIR JOLLY 'Tis very unfortunate that you should run yourself into this praemunire, Sir David.

SIR DAVY Indeed, and so it is.

SIR JOLLY For a gentleman, a man in authority, a person in years, 85
one that used to go to church with his neighbours.

SIR DAVY Every Sunday, truly, Sir Jolly.

SIR JOLLY Pay scot and lot to the parish.

SIR DAVY Six pounds a year to the very poor without abatement or
deduction. 'Tis very hard, if so good a commonwealth's man° 90
should be brought to ride in a cart° at last and be hanged in a
sunshiny morning, to make butchers and suburb apprentices a
holiday. I'll e'en run away.

SIR JOLLY Run away! Why, then your estate will be forfeited; you'll
lose your estate, man. 95

SIR DAVY Truly, you say right, friend, and a man had better be half
hanged than lose his estate, you know.

SIR JOLLY Hanged! No, no, I think there's no great fear of hanging
neither. What, the fellow was but a sort of an unaccountable fellow
as I heard you say. 100

SIR DAVY Ay, ay, a pox on him. He was a soldierly sort of a
vagabond. He had little or nothing but his sins to live upon. If I
could have had but patience, he would have been hanged within
these two months, and all this mischief saved.

> *Beaugard rises up like a ghost at a trap-door, just before Sir
> Davy Dunce*

SIR DAVY Ah lord! The devil, the devil, the devil! 105

> [*Sir Davy Dunce*] *falls upon his face.* [*Beaugard goes down
> the trap-door*]

SIR JOLLY Why, Sir Davy, Sir Davy, what ails you? What's the
matter with you?

SIR DAVY Let me alone, let me lie still. I will not look up, to see an
angel. Oh-h-h!

LADY DUNCE My dear, why do you do these cruel things to affright 110
me? Pray rise and speak to me.

SIR DAVY I dare not stir. I saw the ghost again just now.

LADY DUNCE 'Ghost again'! What ghost? Where?

SIR DAVY Why, there, there.

SIR JOLLY Here has been no ghost. 115

SIR DAVY Why, did you see nothing then?

LADY DUNCE See nothing! No, nothing but one another.°

SIR DAVY Then I am enchanted, or my end near at hand, neighbour.
For heaven's sake, neighbour, advise me what I shall do to be at
rest.   120

SIR JOLLY Do! Why, what think you if the body were removed?

SIR DAVY Removed! I'd give a hundred pound the body were out of
my house. Maybe then the devil would not be so impudent.

SIR JOLLY I have discovered a door-place in the wall betwixt my
lady's chamber and one that belongs to me. If you think fit, we'll   125
beat it down and remove this troublesome lump of earth to my
house.

SIR DAVY But will ye be so kind?

SIR JOLLY If you think it may by any means be serviceable to you.

SIR DAVY Truly, if the body were removed and disposed of privately   130
that no more might be heard of the matter. [*Aside*] I hope he'll be
as good as his word.

SIR JOLLY Fear nothing; I'll warrant you. But, in troth, I had utterly
forgot one thing, utterly forgot it.

SIR DAVY What's that?   135

SIR JOLLY Why, it will be absolutely necessary that my lady stayed
with me at my house for one day till things were better settled.

SIR DAVY Ah Sir Jolly! Whatever you think fit—anything of mine
that you have a mind to. Pray take her, pray take her; you shall be
very welcome.—Hear you, my dearest. There is but one way for   140
us to get rid of this untoward business, and Sir Jolly has found it
out. Therefore, by all means go along with him, and be ruled by
him, and whatever Sir Jolly would have thee do, e'en do it, so
heaven prosper ye. Good-bye, good-bye till I see you again.

        Exit [Sir Davy Dunce]

SIR JOLLY This is certainly the civillest° cuckold in city, town or   145
country.

        [Beaugard] steps out [of the trap-door]

BEAUGARD Is he gone?

LADY DUNCE Yes, and has left poor me here.

BEAUGARD In troth, madam, 'tis barbarously done of him, to commit
a horrid murder on the body of an innocent poor fellow, and then   150
leave you to stem the danger of it.

SIR JOLLY Od, an I were as thee, sweetheart, I'd be revenged on him
for it, so I would. Go, get ye together. Steal out of the house as
softly as you can. I'll meet ye in the Piazza presently. Go. Be sure
ye steal out of the house, and don't let Sir Davy see you.   155

The scene shuts [upon Lady Dunce and Beaugard,] and Sir
Jolly Jumble comes forwards
Bloody Bones!
        Enter Bloody Bones
BLOODY BONES I am here, sir.
SIR JOLLY Go you and Fourbin to my house presently. Bid Mon-
    sieur Fourbin remember that all things be ordered according to my
    directions. Tell my maids too I am coming home in a trice. Bid   160
    'em get the great chamber, and the banquet I spoke for, ready
    presently, and—d'ye hear?—carry the minstrels° with ye too, for
    I'm resolved to rejoice this morning.
        Exit Bloody Bones
    Let me see—
        Enter Sir Davy Dunce
    Sir Davy?   165
SIR DAVY Ay, neighbour, 'tis I. Is the business done? I cannot be
    satisfied till I am sure. Have you removed the body? Is it gone?
SIR JOLLY Yes, yes, my servants conveyed it out of the house just
    now. Well, Sir Davy, a good morning to you. I wish you your
    health with all my heart, Sir Davy. The first thing you do, though,   170
    I'd have you say your prayers by all means if you can.
SIR DAVY If I can possibly, I will.
SIR JOLLY Well, God-b'-w'-y'.
SIR DAVY God-b'-w'-y' heartily, good neighbour.
        Exit Sir Jolly
    Vermin, Vermin!   175
        Enter Vermin
VERMIN Did your honour call?
SIR DAVY Go, run, run presently over the square, and call the
    constable presently. Tell him here's murder committed, and that
    I must speak with him instantly.
        [*Exit Vermin*]
    I'll e'en carry him to my neighbour's, that he may find the dead   180
    body there, and so let my neighbour be very fairly hanged in my
    stead. Ha! A very good jest, as I hope to live. Ha, ha, ha! Hey,
    what's that?
WATCHMEN (*at the door*) Almost four o'clock, and a dark, cloudy
    morning. Good-morrow, my masters all, good-morrow.   185
        Enter Constable and Watchmen
CONSTABLE How's this! A door open! Come in, gentlemen.—Ah, Sir
    Davy! Your honour's humble servant! I and my watch, going my

morning rounds, and finding your door open, made bold to enter
to see there were no danger. Your worship will excuse our care. A
good morning to you, sir.   190

SIR DAVY O Mr Constable, I'm glad you're here. I sent my man just
now to call you. I have sad news to tell you, Mr Constable.

CONSTABLE I am sorry for that, sir. Sad news?

SIR DAVY O ay, sad news, very sad news truly. Here has been
murder committed.   195

CONSTABLE Murder! If that's all, we are your humble servants, sir;
we'll bid you good-morrow. Murder's nothing at this time o' night
in Covent Garden.

SIR DAVY O, but this is a horrid, bloody murder, done under my
nose; I cannot but take notice of it—though I am sorry to tell you   200
the authors of it, very sorry truly.

CONSTABLE Was it committed here near hand?

SIR DAVY O, at the very next door. A sad murder indeed. After they had
done, they carried the body privately into my neighbour Jolly's house
here. I am sorry to tell it you, Mr Constable, for I am afraid it will look   205
but scurvily on his side—though I am a Justice o' Peace, gentlemen, and
am bound by my oath to take notice of it; I can't help it.

FIRST WATCHMAN I never liked that Sir Jolly.

CONSTABLE He threatened me t'other day, for carrying a little, dirty,
draggle-tailed whore to Bridewell,° and said she was his cousin.   210
Sir, if your worship thinks fit, we'll go search his house.

SIR DAVY O by all means, gentlemen, it must be so. Justice must
have its course; the king's liege-subjects must not be destroyed.—
Vermin, carry Mr Constable and his dragons into the cellar and
make 'em drink. I'll but step into my study, put on my face of   215
authority, and call upon ye instantly.

ALL WATCHMEN We thank your honour.

    [*Exeunt*]

[5.4]

[Sir Jolly Jumble's house]

*A banquet. Enter Sir Jolly Jumble, Beaugard and Lady
Dunce [and Musicians]*

SIR JOLLY So, are ye come? I am glad on't. Od, you're welcome,
very welcome; od, ye are. Here's a small banquet, but I hope 'twill

please you. Sit ye down, sit ye down, both together—nay, both
together. A pox o' him that parts ye, I say.

BEAUGARD Sir Jolly, this might be an entertainment for Antony and   5
Cleopatra,° were they living.

SIR JOLLY Pish! A pox of Antony and Cleopatra! They are dead and
rotten long ago. Come, come, time's but short, time's but short,
and must be made the best use of; for [*sings*]

> Youth's a flower that soon does fade,   10
> And life is but a span;
> Man was for the woman made,
> And woman made for man.

Why, now we can be bold, and make merry, and frisk, and be brisk,
rejoice and make a noise, and—od, I am pleased, mightily pleased;   15
od, I am.

LADY DUNCE Really, Sir Jolly, you are more a philosopher than I
thought you were.

SIR JOLLY Philosopher, madam! Yes, madam, I have read books
in my times. Od, Aristotle,° in some things, had very pretty   20
notions; he was an understanding fellow. Why don't ye eat? Od,
an ye don't eat! Here, child, here's some ringoes. Help, help your
neighbour a little. Od, they are very good, very comfortable, very
cordial.

BEAUGARD Sir Jolly, your health.   25

SIR JOLLY With all my heart, old boy.

LADY DUNCE Dear Sir Jolly, what are these? I never tasted of these
before.

SIR JOLLY That! Eat it, eat it—eat it when I bid you. Od, 'tis the
root satyrion, a very precious plant. I gather 'em every May   30
myself. Od, they'll make an old fellow of sixty-five cut a caper°
like a dancing-master. Give me some wine.° Madam, here's a
health, here's a health, madam; here's a health to honest Sir Davy,
faith and troth. Ha, ha, ha!

> *Dance.*° [*Then*] *enter Bloody Bones,* [*as the Musicians exit*]

BLOODY BONES Sir, sir, sir! What will you do? Yonder's the   35
constable and all his watch at the door, and threatens demolish-
ment, if not admitted presently.

SIR JOLLY Od's so! Od's so! The constable and his watch! What's to
be done now? Get ye both into the alcove there.° Get ye gone
quickly, quickly. No noise, no noise—d'ye hear? The constable and   40
his watch! A pox on the constable and his watch! What the devil
have the constable and his watch to do here?

Enter Constable, Watchmen and Sir Davy Dunce. Scene shuts [upon Lady Dunce and Beaugard.] Sir Jolly Jumble comes forward

CONSTABLE This way, this way, gentlemen. Stay one of ye at the door, and let nobody pass, do you hear?—Sir Jolly, your servant. 45

SIR JOLLY What! This outrage, this disturbance committed upon my house and family! Sir, sir, sir! What do you mean by these doings, sweet sir? Ho!

CONSTABLE Sir, having received information that the body of a murdered man is concealed in your house, I am come, according 50 to my duty, to make search and discover the truth. [*To the Watchmen*] Stand to my assistance, gentlemen.

SIR JOLLY A murdered man, sir!

SIR DAVY Yes, a murdered man, sir. Sir Jolly, Sir Jolly, I am sorry to see a person of your character and figure in the parish concerned 55 in murder, I say.

SIR JOLLY Here's a dog! Here's a rogue for you! Here's a villain! Here's a cuckoldly son of his mother! I never knew a cuckold in my life, that was not a false rogue in his heart. There are no honest fellows living but whoremasters. Hark you, sir, what a pox do you 60 mean? You had best play the fool and spoil all, you had. What's all this for?

SIR DAVY When your worship's come to be hanged, you'll find the meaning on't, sir. I say once more, search the house.

CONSTABLE It shall be done, sir. Come along, friends. 65
Exeunt Constable and Watchmen, [with Sir Davy]

SIR JOLLY Search my house! O lord, search my house! What will become of me? I shall lose my reputation with man and woman, and nobody will ever trust me again. O lord, search my house! All will be discovered, do what I can. I'll sing a song like a dying swan, and try to give 'em warning. [*Sings*] 70

> *Go from the window, my love, my love, my love,*°
> *Go from the window, my dear.*
> *The wind and the rain*
> *Has brought 'em back again,*
> *And thou canst have no lodging here.*

75

O lord, search my house!

SIR DAVY [*offstage*] Break down that door. I'll have that door broke open. Break down that door, I say.
Knocking within

SIR JOLLY Very well done! Break down my doors! Break down my
walls, gentlemen! Plunder my house! Ravish my maids! Ah, cursed   80
be cuckolds, cuckolds, constables and cuckolds!
> *Scene draws and discovers Beaugard and Lady Dunce.*
> [*Enter Sir Davy, Constable and Watchmen*]

BEAUGARD [*drawing his sword*] Stand off! By heaven, the first that
comes here comes upon his death.

SIR DAVY Sir, your humble servant. I am glad to see you are alive
again with all my heart. [*To the Constable and Watchmen*]   85
Gentlemen, here's no harm done, gentlemen; here's nobody murdered, gentlemen. The man's alive again, gentlemen. But here's my
wife, gentlemen, and a fine gentleman with her, gentlemen and Mr
Constable. I hope you'll bear me witness, Mr Constable.

SIR JOLLY (*aside*) That he's a cuckold, Mr Constable.   90

BEAUGARD Hark ye, ye curs. Keep off from snapping at my heels, or
I shall so feague ye.

SIR JOLLY Get ye gone, ye dogs, ye rogues, ye night-toads of the
parish dungeon. Disturb my house at these unseasonable hours!
Get ye out of my doors; get ye gone, or I'll brain ye. Dogs, rogues,   95
villains!
> *Exeunt Constable and Watchmen*

BEAUGARD And next, for you, Sir Coxcomb. You see I am not
murdered, though you paid well for the performance. What think
you of bribing my own man to butcher me?
> *Enter Fourbin and Bloody Bones*

Look ye, sir, he can cut a throat upon occasion; and here's another   100
dresses a man's heart with oil and pepper, better than any cook in
Christendom.

FOURBIN Will your worship please to have one for your breakfast
this morning?

SIR DAVY With all my heart, sweetheart. Anything in the world, faith   105
and troth. [*Aside*] Ha, ha, ha! This is the purest sport. Ha, ha, ha!
> *Enter Vermin*

VERMIN O, sir, the most unhappy and most unfortunate news! There
has been a gentleman in Madam Sylvia's chamber all this night,
who, just as you went out of doors, carried her away; and whither
they are gone, nobody knows.   110

SIR DAVY With all my heart, I am glad on't, child. I would not care
if he had carried away my house and all, man. [*Aside*] 'Unhappy
news', quotha! Poor fool, he does not know I am a cuckold, and
that anybody may make bold with what belongs to me. Ha, ha, ha!

I am so pleased. Ha, ha, ha! I think I was never so pleased in all 115
my life before. Ha, ha, ha!

BEAUGARD Nay, sir, I have a hank upon you. There are laws for
cut-throats, sir; and as you tender your future credit, take this
wronged lady home, and use her handsomely—use her like my
mistress, sir, do you mark me?—that when we think fit to meet 120
again, I hear no complaint of you. This must be done, friend.

SIR JOLLY In troth, and it is but reasonable, very reasonable in troth.

LADY DUNCE Can you, my dear, forgive me one misfortune?

SIR DAVY Madam, in one word, I am thy ladyship's most humble
servant and cuckold, Sir Davy Dunce, knight, living in Covent 125
Garden. [*Aside*] Ha, ha, ha! Well, this is mighty pretty. Ha, ha, ha!

Enter Sylvia, followed by Courtine

SYLVIA Sir Jolly, ah Sir Jolly, protect me, or I'm ruined.

SIR JOLLY My little minikin, is it thy squeak?

BEAUGARD My dear Courtine, welcome.

SIR JOLLY Well, child, and what would that wicked fellow do to 130
thee, child? Ha, child, child, what would he do to thee?

SYLVIA O, sir, he has most inhumanly seduced me out of my uncle's
house, and threatens to marry me.

COURTINE Nay, sir, and she, having no more grace before her
eyes° neither, has e'en taken me at my word. 135

SIR JOLLY In troth, and that's very uncivilly done. I don't like these
marriages; I'll have no marriages in my house, and there's an end
on't.

SIR DAVY And do you intend to marry my niece, friend?

COURTINE Yes, sir, and never ask your consent neither. 140

SIR DAVY In troth, and that's very well said. I am glad on't with all
my heart, man, because she has five thousand pound to her
portion, and my estate's bound to pay it. Well, this is the happiest
day. Ha, ha, ha!
Here, take thy bride; like man and wife agree; 145
And may she prove as true—as mine to me.
Ha, ha, ha!

BEAUGARD Courtine, I wish thee joy. Thou art come opportunely to
be a witness of a perfect reconcilement between me and that
worthy knight, Sir Davy Dunce; which to preserve inviolate [*to Sir* 150
Davy], you must, sir, before we part, enter into such covenants for
performance as I shall think fit.

SIR DAVY No more to be said; it shall be done, sweetheart. But don't
be too hard upon me. Use me gently,° as thou didst my wife.

Gently! Ha, ha, ha! A very good jest, i'faith! Ha, ha, ha! Or if he   155
should be cruel to me, gentlemen [*addressing the men in the
audience*], and take this advantage over a poor cornuto to lay me in
a prison or throw me in a dungeon, at least
   I hope amongst all you, sirs, I shan't fail
   To find one brother-cuckold out for bail.   160

Epilogue

With the discharge of passions much oppressed,
Disturbed in brain, and pensive in his breast,
Full of those thoughts which make th'unhappy sad,
And by imagination half grown mad,
The poet led abroad his mourning muse   5
And let her range, to see what sport she'd choose.
Straight—like a bird got loose and on the wing,
Pleased with her freedom—she began to sing;
Each note was echoed all the vale along,
And this was what she uttered in her song.   10
'Wretch, write no more for an uncertain fame,
Nor call thy muse, when thou art dull, to blame.
Consider with thyself how th'art unfit
To make that monster of mankind, a wit.
A wit's a toad, who, swelled with silly pride,   15
Full of himself, scorns all the world beside;
Civil would seem, though he good manners lacks,
Smiles on all faces, rails behind all backs.
If e'er good-natured, nought to ridicule,
Good nature melts a wit into a fool;   20
Placed high, like some Jack Pudding in a hall
At Christmas revels, he makes sport for all.
So much in little praises he delights,
But when he's angry draws his pen and writes.
A wit to no man will his dues allow: 25
Wits will not part with a good word that's due.
So whoe'er ventures on the ragged coast°
Of starving poets certainly is lost:
They rail like porters at the penny-post.°
At a new author's play see one but sit   30
Making his snarling froward face of wit;
The merit he allows, and praise he grants,
Comes like a tax from a poor wretch that wants.
O poets, have a care of one another;
There's hardly one amongst ye true to t'other.   35
Like Trincalos and Stephanos, ye play°
The lewdest tricks each other to betray—

Like foes detract, yet, flattering, friendlike smile,
And all is one another to beguile
Of praise, the monster of your barren isle.   40
Enjoy the prostitute ye so admire,
Enjoy her to the full of your desire,
Whilst this poor scribbler wishes to retire,
Where he may ne'er repeat his follies more,
But curse the fate that wrecked° him on your shore'.   45
    Now you, who this day as his judges sit,
After you've heard what he has said of wit,
Ought for your own sakes not to be severe,
But show so much to think he meant none here.

THE PRINCESS OF CLEVES

BY

NATHANIEL LEE

tuque dum procedis, 'io Triumphe'!,
non semel diemus, 'io Triumphe!',
civitas omnis, dabimusque divis
tura benignis.°

(Horace)

To the Right Honourable Charles, Earl of Dorset and Middlesex,°
Lord Chamberlain of His Majesty's Household, and one of His
Majesty's most honourable Privy Council, &c.

May it please your lordship,

This play, when it was acted, in the character of the Princess of
Jainville had a resemblance of Marguerite in *The Massacre of Paris*,
sister to Charles IX, and wife to Henry IV, King of Navarre—that
fatal marriage which cost the blood of so many thousand men and the   5
lives of the best commanders. What was borrowed in the action is left
out in the print and quite obliterated in the minds of men. But *The
Duke of Guise*, who was notorious for a bolder fault, has wrested two
whole scenes from the original, which after the vacation he will be
forced to pay.° I was, I confess, through indignation forced to limb   10
my own child, which time, the true cure for all maladies and injustice,
has set together again. The play cost me much pains, the story is true,
and I hope the object will display treachery in its own colours. But
this farce, comedy, tragedy, or mere play, was a revenge for the
refusal of the other; for when they expected the most polished hero   15
in Nemours,° I gave 'em a ruffian reeking from Whetstone's Park.°
The fourth and fifth acts of *The Chances*, where Don John is pulling
down; *Marriage à la Mode*, where they are bare to the waist; *The
Libertine*, and *Epsom Wells*, are but copies of his villainy.° He lays
about him like the gladiator in the park;° they may walk by and take   20
no notice. I beg your lordship to excuse this account, for indeed, 'tis
all to introduce *The Massacre of Paris* to your favour, and approve it
to be played in its first figure.

      Your lordship's humble and obedient servant,
      Nat. Lee   25

THE CHARACTERS OF THE PLAY

Prince of Cleves	*Mr Williams*	
Duke Nemours	*Mr Betterton*	
Bellamore°		
Jacques		
Saint-André°	*Mr Leigh*	5
Vidame of Chartres°	*Mr Gillow*	
Poltrot°	*Mr Nokes*	
[Pedro]		
[Boy]		
[Thomas]		10
[Servants]		
Princess of Cleves	*Mrs Barry*	
Tournon°	*Mrs Leigh*	
Marguerite, [Princess of Jainville]°	*Lady Slingsby*	
Elianor	*Mrs Betterton*	15
Celia		
Irene		
La March°		

[Maskers, Musicians]

SCENE: PARIS

Prologue°

[by John Dryden]

Ladies, I hope there's none behind to hear.
I long to whisper something in your ear,
A secret which does much my mind perplex:
There's treason in the play against our sex.
A man that's false to love, that vows and cheats,   5
And kisses every living thing he meets!
A rogue in mode—I dare not speak too broad—°
One that does something to the very bawd.°
Out on him, traitor, for a filthy beast.
Nay, and he's like the pack of all the rest—   10
None of 'em stick at mark; they all deceive.°
Some Jew has changed the text, I half believe;°
Their Adam cozened our poor grandam, Eve.
To hide their faults, they rap out oaths and tear;
Now, though we lie, we're too well-bred to swear.   15
So we compound for half the sin we owe;
But men are dipped for soul and body too,°
And (when found out) excuse themselves, pox cant 'em,°
With Latin stuff, *perjuria ridet amantum*.°
I'm not book-learned to know that word in vogue,   20
But I suspect 'tis Latin for a rogue.
I'm sure I never heard that screech-owl hollowed
In my poor ears, but separation followed.
How can such perjured villains e'er be saved?
Achitophel's not half so false to David.°   25
With vows and soft expressions to allure,
They stand like foremen of a shop, demure;
No sooner out of sight, but they are gadding
And for the next new face ride out a-padding.°
Yet, by their favour, when they have been kissing,   30
We can perceive the ready money missing.°
Well, we may rail, but 'tis as good e'en wink;°
Something we find, and something they will sink.°
But since they're at renouncing, 'tis our parts
To trump their diamonds, as they trump our hearts.°   35

Prologue

Trust was the glory of the foremost age,°
When truth and love with friendship did engage;
When man to man could walk with arms entwined
And vent their griefs in spaces of the wind,
Express their minds, and speak their thoughts as clear   5
As Eastern mornings opening to the year.
But since that law and treachery came in,
And open honesty was made a sin,
Men wait for men as dogs for foxes prey,
And women wait the closing of the day.   10
There's scarce a man that ventures to be good,
For truth by knaves was never understood;
For there's the curse, when vice o'er virtue rules,
That all the world are knaves or downright fools.
So they may make advantage of th'allay,°   15
They'll take the dross and throw the gold away.
Women turn usurers with their own affright,
And want's the hag that rides 'em all the night.°
The little mob, the city waistcoateer,°
Will pinch the back to make the buttock bare,   20
And drain the last poor guinea from her dear.°
Thus times are turned upon a private end;
There's scarce a man that's generous to his friend.°
But there's a monarch on a throne sublime,
That makes truth law, and gives the poets rhyme.°   25
Be his the business of our little fates,
Our mean contentions, and their high debates.
By sea and land our most imperial lord,
With all the praises blessed that hearts afford,
With laurels crowned, unconquered by the sword: 30
William, the sovereign of our whole affairs,
Our guide in peace, and counsel in the wars.

1.1

[*The palace of Nemours*]

[*Enter*] *Nemours and Bellamore. Fiddles playing*°

NEMOURS [*to the Musicians*] Hold there you, Monsieur Devol.
Prithee leave off playing fine in consort, and stick to time and
tune.° So, now the song. Call in the eunuch.°

[*Enter Singer*]

Come, my pretty stallion, hem and begin.

SONG

> *All other blessings are but toys*°   5
> *To his that in his sleep enjoys,*°
> *Who in his fancy can possess*°
> *The object of his happiness.*
> *The pleasure's purer, for he spares*
> *The pains, expenses, and the cares.*   10
>
> *Thus when Adonis got the stone,*°
> *To love the boy still made his moan.*
> *Venus, the queen of fancy, came,*°
> *And as he slept she cooled his flame.*
> *The fancy charmed him as he lay,*
> *And fancy brought the stone away.*   15

[*Exeunt Singer and Musicians*]

NEMOURS [*to Bellamore*] Sirrah, stick to clean pleasures, deep sleep,
moderate wine, sincere whores, and thou art happy. Now by this
damask cheek I love thee. Keep but this gracious form of thine in
health, and I'll put thee in the way of living like a man. What I   20
have trusted thee with—my love to the Princess of Cleves—treasure it as thy life. Nor let the Vidame of Chartres know it. For,
however I seem to cherish him because he has the knack of telling
a story maliciously and is a great pretender to nature,° I cast him
off here. 'Tis too much for him. Besides, he is her uncle and has   25
a sort of affected honour that would make him grin° to see me leap
her.—Hey, Jacques!

[*Enter Jacques*]

When Madam Tournon comes, bring her in. And, hark you, sir,
whoever comes to speak with me, while she is with me—

JACQUES What if the dauphin° comes?   30

NEMOURS What if his father comes! Dog, slave, fool! What if Paris
were afire, the President and Council of Sixteen° at the door! I'm
sick, I'm not within, I'm a hundred mile off.
    [*Exit Jacques*]
    [*To Bellamore*] My bosom dear—so young, and yet I trust thee too.
But away, to the Princess of Cleves. Thou art acquainted with her   35
women. Watch her motions, my sweet-faced pimp, and bring me
word of her rising.

BELLAMORE She is a prize, my lord; and, O, what a night of pleasure
has Cleves had with her—the first too!

NEMOURS Anything but what makes such a pleasure, would I give   40
for such another. But be gone, and no more of this provoking
discourse, lest ravishing should follow thee at the heels and spoil
my sober design.°
    *Exeunt [Nemours and Bellamore] severally. Enter Tournon
    [and] La March [with Jacques]*

JACQUES Madam, my lord was just now asking for you.

TOURNON Go tell him I'm coming. Is he dressed?   45

JACQUES Yes; but your ladyship knows that's all one to him.

TOURNON Honest Jacques, 'tis pity such honesty should not be
encouraged.
    [*Tournon gives Jacques money*]

JACQUES [*aside*] This comes of pimping, which she calls honesty.
    Exit Jacques

TOURNON Thus thou may'st see the method of the queen.° We are   50
the lucky sieves where fond° men trust their hearts, and so she sifts
'em through us.

LA MARCH What of Nemours, whom you thus early visit?

TOURNON The queen designs to rob him of a mistress, Marguerite
the Princess of Jainville, whom he keeps from the knowledge of   55
the court, and (if the queen be a judge) is contracted to her.°
The dauphin loves her too, whereon the queen,
Who works the court quite round by womankind
And thinks this way to mould his supple soul,
Resolves, if possible, to gain her for him.   60

LA MARCH But how is't possible to work the princess from the Duke
Nemours, who loves him as the queen affects ambition?°

TOURNON Why thus. She knows Nemours his soul° is bent upon
variety. Therefore, to gain her ends, she has made me sacrifice my
honour. Nay, I'm become his bawd, and ply him every day with   65

95

some new face to wean his heart from Marguerite's form. Nor must you longer be without your part.°

LA MARCH Employ me, for you know the queen commands me.

TOURNON There was a letter dropped in the tennis-court out of Nemours his pocket, as I'm told, and read last night in the presence.° 'Tis your task slyly to insinuate with Marguerite. This note which came from some abandoned mistress is certainly the duke's.

LA MARCH Then jealousy's the ground on which you build.

TOURNON Right; we must make 'em jealous of each other. Jealousy breeds disdain in haughty minds, and so from the extremes of violent love proceeds to fiercest hate.

    Enter Saint-André [and Boy]

But see the gay, the brisk, the topping gallant, Saint-André, here—cousin to Poltrot, who arrived from England with a pretty wife last week and lodges in the palace of this his related fool. Saint-André has a wife too of my acquaintance. Both for the duke, my dear.

    [Enter Jacques]

But haste, I'm called.

    Exit La March

JACQUES Madam—

TOURNON I go.

    Exit Tournon

SAINT-ANDRÉ Monsieur Jacques, your most obliged, faithful, humble servant. What, his grace continues the old trade, I see, by the flux° of bawds and whores that choke up his avenues. And I must confess, excepting myself, there's no man so built for whoring as his grace—black, sanguine, brawny; a Roman nose; long foot; and a stiff—calf of a leg.

JACQUES Your lordship has all these in perfection.

SAINT-ANDRÉ Sir, your most faithful, obliged, humble servant.— Boy!

BOY My lord.

SAINT-ANDRÉ How many bottles last night?

BOY Five, my lord.

SAINT-ANDRÉ Boy!

BOY My lord.

SAINT-ANDRÉ How many whores?

BOY Six, my lord.

SAINT-ANDRÉ Boy!

BOY My lord.

SAINT-ANDRÉ What quarrels? How many did I kill?

BOY Not one, my lord. But the night before you hamstrung a beadle,   105
and run a link-man in the back.

SAINT-ANDRÉ What, and no blood nor blows last night?

BOY O yes, my lord, now I remember me. You drew upon a
gentleman that knocked you down with a bottle.

SAINT-ANDRÉ [to the Boy, aside] Not so loud, you urchin, lest I twist   110
your neck round.—Monsieur Jacques, is his grace stirring?

JACQUES My lord, he's at Council.°

SAINT-ANDRÉ Od, I beg his pardon. Pray give my duty to him, and
tell him, if he pleased to hear a languishing air or two, I am at the
Princess of Cleves' with a serenade.° [To the Boy] Go, rascal, go   115
to Monsieur Poltrot. Tell him he'll be too late.

[Exit Boy]

Black, airy shape—but then Madame Cleves is virtuous, chaste,
cold. Gad, I'll write to her, and then she's mine directly, for 'tis
but reason of course, that he that has been yoked to so many
duchesses should at last back a princess. [To Jacques] Sir, your   120
most obliged, faithful and very humble servant, sir.

Exeunt, [in different directions]

1.2

[The palace of Nemours]°

[Enter] Nemours [and] Tournon

TOURNON Undone, undone! Will your sinful grace never give over?
Will you never leave ruining of bodies and damning of souls?
Could you imagine that I came for this? What have you done?

NEMOURS No harm, pretty rogue, no harm. Nay, prithee leave
blubbering.   5

TOURNON 'Tis blubbering now, plain blubbering; but before you
had your will 'twas another tone. 'Why, madam, do you waste
those precious tears? Each falling drop shines like an orient pearl
and sets a gaiety on a face of sorrow.'

NEMOURS Thou art certainly the pleasantest° of womankind, and I   10
the happiest of men. Dear, delightful rogue, let's have another
main. Like a winning gamester, I long to make it t'other hundred
pound.

TOURNON Inconsiderate, horrid° peer, will you damn your soul
deeper and deeper? Can you be thus insensible of your crime?   15

NEMOURS Why, there's it.° I was as a man may be, very dry, and
thou, kind soul, gav'st me a good draught of drink. Now 'tis
strange to me, if a man must be damned for quenching his thirst.

TOURNON Ha, ha! Well, I'll swear you are such another man.° Who
would have thought you could delude a woman thus, and a woman   20
of honour too, that resolved so much against it? Ah my lord! Your
grace has a cunning tongue.

NEMOURS No cunning, Tournon. My way is downright, leaving
body, state and spirit, all for a pretty woman; and when grey hairs,
gout and impotence come, no more but this—drink away pain, and   25
be gathered to my fathers.

TOURNON O thou dissembler, give me your hand, this soft, this
faithless, violating hand. Heaven knows what this hand has to
answer for.

NEMOURS [*taking her hand*] And for this hand, with these long,   30
white, round, pretty bobbins, 't'has the kindest grip, and I so love
it, now Gad's blessing on't—that's all I say. But come tell me:
what, no new game? For thou knowest I die directly without
variety.

TOURNON Certainly never woman loved like me, who am not   35
satisfied with sacrificing my own honour, unless I rob my delights
by undoing others'.

NEMOURS Come, come, out with it. I see thou art big° with some
new intrigue, and it labours for a vent.

TOURNON What think you of Saint-André's lady?   40

NEMOURS That I'm in bed with her, because thou dar'st befriend
me.

TOURNON Nay, there's more. Monsieur Poltrot lodges in his house
with a young English wife of the true breed,° and the prettier of
the two.   45

NEMOURS Excellent creature! But command me something extravagant,° as thy kindness, state, life and honour.°

TOURNON Yet all this will be lost when you are married to
Marguerite.

NEMOURS Never! By heaven I'm thine, with all the heat and vigorous   50
inspiration of an unfleshed lover—and so will be while young limbs
and lechery hold together; and that's a bond methinks should last
till doomsday.

TOURNON But do you believe if Marguerite should know—

NEMOURS The question's too grave. When and where shall I see the   55
  gems thou hast in store?

TOURNON By noon or thereabouts. Take a turn in Luxembourg
  Garden,° and one, if not both, shall meet you.

NEMOURS And thou'lt appear in person?

TOURNON With colours flying,° a handkerchief held out—and yet   60
  methinks it goes against my conscience.

NEMOURS Away! That serious look has made thee old.
  Conscience and consideration—in a young woman too?°
  It makes a bawd of thee before thy time.
  Nay, now thou put'st me in poetic rapture,   65
  And I must quote Ronsard to punish thee.°
  Call all your wives to council, and prepare
  To tempt, dissemble, flatter, lie and swear.
  To make her mine, use all your utmost skill.
  Virtue, an ill-bred crossness in the will;   70
  Honour a notion, piety a cheat!
  Prove but successful bawds and you are great.°
  Come, thou wilt meet me.

TOURNON 'Tis resolved I will. Till which time, thou dear man—

NEMOURS Thou pretty woman—   75

TOURNON Thou very dear man—

NEMOURS Thou very pretty woman, one kiss.
    [*They kiss*]

TOURNON Hey ho.

NEMOURS Now all the gods go with thee.

TOURNON A word, my lord. You are acquainted with these fops. Set   80
  'em in the modish way of abusing their wives. They are turning
  already,° and that will certainly bring 'em about.

NEMOURS Bellamore shall do't with less suspicion. Farewell.
    Exit Tournon
  Hey, Jacques!
    Enter Jacques with the Vidame. [*Exit Jacques*]
  Ha, my grave Lord of Chartres! Welcome as health, as wine, and   85
  taking whores! And tell me now the business of the court.

VIDAME Hold it, Nemours, for ever at defiance.
  Fogs of ill humour, damps of melancholy,
  Old maids of fifty choked with eternal vapours,
  Stuff it with fulsome honour. Dozing virtue   90
  And everlasting dullness husk it round,
  Since he that was the life, the soul of pleasure,

Count Rosidore, is dead.°
NEMOURS   Then we may say
Wit was and satire is a carcase now.
I thought his last debauch would be his death.   95
But is it certain?
VIDAME   Yes, I saw him dust.
I saw the mighty thing a nothing made,
Huddled with worms, and swept to that cold den,
Where kings lie crumbled just like other men.°
NEMOURS Nay then, let's rave and elegize together,   100
Where Rosidore is now but common clay,
Whom every wiser emmet bears away,
And lays him up against a winter's day.
He was the spirit of wit, and had such an art in gilding his failures,   105
that it was hard not to love his faults. He never spoke a witty thing
twice, though to different persons. His imperfections were catch-
ing, and his genius was so luxuriant, that he was forced to tame it
with a hesitation in his speech° to keep it in view. But O how
awkward, how insipid, how poor and wretchedly dull is the
imitation of those that have all the affectation° of his verse and   110
none of his wit.
        Enter Jacques
JACQUES My lord, Monsieur Poltrot desires to kiss your grace's
hand.
NEMOURS Let's have him, to drive away our melancholy.
        [*Exit Jacques*]
VIDAME I wonder what pleasure you can take in such dull dogs,   115
asses, fools.
NEMOURS But this is a particular fool, man, fate's own fool, and
perhaps it will never hit the like again. He's ever the same thing,
yet always pleasing. In short, he's a finished fool, and has a fine
wife. Add to this his late leaving the court of France, and going to   120
England to learn breeding.°
        Enter Poltrot [and Jacques]
POLTROT My lord duke, your grace's most obedient, humble
servant. My Lord of Chartres, and Monsieur Jacques, yours,
monsieur. Saint-André desires your grace's presence at a serenade
of mine and his together. And I must tell your grace by the way,   125
he is a great master, and the fondest thing of my labours.
NEMOURS And the greatest oaf in the world.
POLTROT How, my lord!

VIDAME The whole court wonders you will keep him company.

NEMOURS Such a passive rascal. He had his shins broke last night in   130
the presence; and, were it not feared you would second him,° he
would be kicked out of all society.

POLTROT I second him, my lord! I'll see him damned ere I'll be
second to any fool in Christendom. For, to tell your grace the
truth, I keep him company and lie at his house, because I intend   135
to lie with his wife—a trick I learnt since I went into England,
where, o' my conscience, cuckoldom is the destiny of above half
the nation.

NEMOURS Indeed!

POLTROT O, there's not such another drinking, scowering, roaring,   140
whoring nation in the world. And for little London, to my
knowledge, if a bill were taken of the weekly cuckolds,° it would
amount to more than the number of christenings and burials put
together.

VIDAME What, and were you acquainted with the wits?   145

POLTROT O lord, sir, I lived in the city a whole year together. My
Lord Mayor and I, and the Common Council, were sworn
brothers.° I could sing you twenty catches and drolls that I made
for their feast-days; but at present I'll only hint you one or two.

NEMOURS Pray do us the favour, sir.   150

POLTROT Why, look you, sir, this is one of my chief ones, and I'll
assure your grace, 'twas much sung at court too. [Sings] 'O to bed
to me, to bed to me, &c.'°

NEMOURS Excellent, incomparable.

POLTROT Why, is it not, my lord? This is no kickshaw; there's   155
substance in the air and weight in the words. Nay, I'll give your
grace a taste of another. The tune is, let me see—ay, ay—[sings]
'Give me the lass that is true country-bred'.° But I'll present your
grace with some words of my own, that I made on my wife before
I married her, as she sat singing one day in a low parlour and   160
playing on the virginals.

NEMOURS [caressing and tickling Poltrot] For heaven's sake oblige us,
dear, pleasant creature.

POLTROT I'll swear I'm so ticklish you'll put me out, my lord, for I
am as wanton as any little Bartholomew boar-pig.°   165

VIDAME [following suit] Dear, soft, delicate rogue, sing.

POLTROT Nay, I protest, my lord, I vow and swear, but you'll make
me run to a whore. Lord, sir, what do you mean?

NEMOURS Come then, begin.

POLTROT (*sings*)
>   *Phillis is soft, Phillis is plump,*   170
>   *And beauty made up this delicate lump.*
>   *Like a rose-bud she looks, like a lily she smells,*
>   *And her voice is a note above sweet Philomel's.*°

Now a little smutty, my lord, is the fashion. [*Sings*]
>   *Her breasts are two hillocks, where hearts lie and pant,*   175
>   *In the herbage so soft, for a thing that they want.*
>   *But mum, sir, for that, though a notable jest,*
>   *For if I should name it you'd call me a beast.*

>   *Enter Saint-André without his hat and wig*°

SAINT-ANDRÉ My lord, the serenade is just begun; and if you
don't come just in the nick—I beg your grace's pardon for   180
interrupting you. But if you have a mind to hear the sweetest airs
in the world—

NEMOURS With all my heart, sir.

POLTROT Nay, since your grace has put my hand in,° I'll sing you,
my lord, before you go, the softest thing—composed in the nonage   185
of my muse, yet such a one as our best authors borrow from. Nay,
I'll be judged by your grace, if they do not steal their dying from
my killing.°

SAINT-ANDRÉ Nay, prithee, Poltrot, thou art so impertinent.

POLTROT No more impertinent° than yourself, sir. Nor do I doubt,   190
sir, but my character shall be drawn by the poets for a man of wit
and sense,° sir, as well as yourself, sir.

VIDAME Ay, I'll be sworn, shall it.

POLTROT For I know how to repartee with the best, to rally my wife,
to kick her too if I please, sir, to make similes as fast as hops, sir,   195
though I lay a-dying—slap-dash, sir, quickly off and quickly on,
sir, and as round as a hoop,° sir.

SAINT-ANDRÉ I grant you, dear bully, all this. But let's have your
song another time, because mine are begun.

POLTROT Nay, look you, dear rogue, mine is but a prologue to your   200
play; and by your leave his grace has a mind to hear it, and he shall
hear it, sir.

NEMOURS Ay, and will hear it, sir, though the great Turk were at
St Denis's Gate.° Come along, my Orpheus;° and then, sir, we'll
follow you to the Prince of Cleves'.   205

[POLTROT] [*sings*] '*When Phoebus had fetched, &c.*'°
>   *Exeunt, singing*

1.3

The Prince of Cleves' palace
Music

SONG°

> *In a room for delight, the landscape of love,*
> > *Like a shady old lawn,*
> > *With the curtains half drawn,*
> *My love and I lay, in the cool of the day,*
> > *Till our joys did remove.°*   5

> *So fierce was our fight, and so smart every stroke,*
> > *That love, the little scout,°*
> > *Was put to the rout.*
> *His bow was unbent, every arrow was spent,*
> > *And his quiver all broke.*   10

Enter the Vidame [and] Nemours

NEMOURS I have lost my letter, and by your description it must be
that which the queen read at court. But are you sure the Princess
of Cleves has seen it?

VIDAME Why are you so concerned? Does your wild love turn that
way too? She is too grave.   15

NEMOURS Too grave? As if I could not laugh with this, and cry° with
that, and veer with every gust of passion. But has she seen it?

VIDAME She has the letter; the queen dauphin° sent it her.

NEMOURS Then you must own it on occasion,° and whatever else I
shall put upon your person.°   20

VIDAME Why?

NEMOURS Lest it should reach the ears of Marguerite. For, O my
Vidame, 'tis such a ranting devil. If she believes this letter mine,
when next we meet, beware my locks and eyes. No more but this:
remember that you own it.°   25

Exit [Nemours.] Enter Saint-André and Poltrot

SAINT-ANDRÉ and POLTROT (*singing*) '*His bow was unbent, &c.*'

SAINT-ANDRÉ [*to Poltrot*] Come, my lord, we'll have all over again.

Enter the Prince of Cleves

VIDAME See, we have raised the Prince of Cleves.—My lord, good-
morrow.

PRINCE [*greeting the Vidame*] Good-morrow, my good lord.°   30

103

POLTROT Give you joy, my lord. What, a little blue under the eyes.
Ha, ha!

SAINT-ANDRÉ Give you joy, my lord. (*Holds up three fingers*)° Ha,
my lord, ha!

POLTROT (*holding up five fingers*) Ha, my lord, ha!   35

PRINCE You are merry, gentlemen. I am not in the vein; therefore,
dear Chartres, take these fingers hence.

SAINT-ANDRÉ My lord, you look a little heavy. Shall we dance, sing,
fence, take the air, ride?

VIDAME Come away, sir; the prince is indisposed.   40

SAINT-ANDRÉ Gad, I remember, now I talk of riding. At the
tournament° of Metz, as I was riding the great horse°—

VIDAME Leave off your lying, and come along.

SAINT-ANDRÉ With three pushes of pike and six hits of sword, I
wounded the Duke of Ferrara, Duke of Milan, Duke of Parma,   45
Prince of Cleves—

PRINCE My lord, I was not there.

SAINT-ANDRÉ My lord—I beg your lordship's pardon. I meant the
Vidame of Chartres.

VIDAME You lie; I was then at Rome.   50

SAINT-ANDRÉ My lord—

POLTROT Ha, ha! Lord, lord, how this world is given to lying! Ha!
Come, come; you're damnably out.° Come away.

SAINT-ANDRÉ My lord, I beg your pardon; I see you are indisposed.
Besides, the queen obliged me this morning to let 'em choose   55
colours° for my complexion.

VIDAME Hark you. Will you go, or (*pulling him off by the nose*) shall
I—

SAINT-ANDRÉ My friend, my lord, you see, is a little familiar. But I
am ever your highness's most humble, faithful, obedient servant.   60
> *Exeunt* [*the Vidame, Saint-André and Poltrot.*] *The Prince of*
> *Cleves remains*

PRINCE Full of himself, the happy man is gone.
Why was not I too cast in such a mould?
To think like him, or not to think at all.
> *Enter the Princess of Cleves*, [*unobserved by the Prince*]

Had he a bride like me, earth would not bear him;
But, O, I wish that it might cover me,   65
Since Chartres cannot love me. O, I found it!°
Last night I found it in her cold embraces,
Her lips, too, cold—cold as the dew of death;

And still whene'er I pressed her in my arms,
I found my bosom all afloat with tears. 70
PRINCESS [aside] He weeps, O heaven!—My lord, the Prince of
Cleves.
PRINCE My life, my dearest part!
PRINCESS   Why sighs my lord?
What have I done, sir, thus to discompose you?
PRINCE Nothing.
PRINCESS   Ah, sir, there is a grief within,
And you would hide it from me.
PRINCE Nothing, my Chartres, nothing here but love. 75
PRINCESS Alas, my lord, you hide that secret from me
Which I must know or think you never loved me.
PRINCE Ah princess! That you loved but half so well!
PRINCESS I have it then. You think me criminal 80
And tax my honour.
PRINCE   O, forbid it, heaven.
But since you press me, madam, let me ask you
Why, when the princess led you to the altar,°
Why caked the tears upon your bloodless face?
Why sighed you when your hand was clasped with mine? 85
As if your heart, your heart refused to join.
PRINCESS Ah, sir!
PRINCE   Behold, you're dashed with the remembrance.
Why, when my hopes were fierce and joys grew strong,
Why were you carried like a corpse along?
When like a victim by my side you lay, 90
Why did you gasp, why did you swoon away?
O, speak!
You have a soul so open and so clear,°
That if there be a fault it must appear.
PRINCESS Alas, you are not skilled in beauty's cares, 95
For, O, when once the god his wrath declares,°
And stygian oaths have winged the bloody dart°
To make its passage through the virgin's heart,
She hides her wound; and, hasting to the grove,
Scarce whispering to the winds her conscious love,° 100
The touch of him she loves she'll not endure,
But weeps and bleeds, and strives against the cure.
So judge of me when any grief appears;
Believe my sighs are kind, and trust my tears.

PRINCE Vanish my doubts, and jealousies be gone.   105
On thy loved bosom let me break my joy.
> [*He embraces her*]
O only sweets that fill, but never cloy!
And was it, was it only virgin's fear?
But speak for ever and I'll ever hear.
Repeat, and let the echoes deal it round,   110
While listening angels bend to catch the sound.
Nay, sigh and weep, drain all thy precious store;
Be kind, as now, and I'll complain no more.
> *Exit* [*the Prince of Cleves*]

PRINCESS Was ever man so worthy to be loved,
So good, so gentle, soft a disposition,   115
As if no gall had mixed with his creation;°
So tender and so fearful to displease,
No barbarous heart but thine would stop his entrance.
But thou, inhuman, banished him from his own;
And while the lordly master lies without,   120
> *Enter Irene* [*with a letter*]
Thou, traitress, riot'st with a thief within.°

IRENE Ah, madam, what new grief?

PRINCESS   Alas, Irene,
Thou treasurer of my thoughts,
What shall I do? How shall I chase Nemours,
That robber, ravisher of my repose?   125

IRENE For the great care you wish, may I inquire°
Whether you think the duke insensible,°
Indifferent to the rest of womankind?

PRINCESS I must confess I did not think him so,
Though now I do—but would give half my blood   130
To think him otherwise.

IRENE   Without the expense,
There take your wish—
> [*Gives the Princess the letter*]
                    a letter which he dropped
In the tennis-court, given the queen dauphin
By her page, and sent to you to read
For your diversion.

PRINCESS   Alas, Irene,   135
Why trembles thus my hand? Why beats my heart?

But let us read. (*Reads*) 'Your affection has been divided betwixt
me and another. You are false, a traitor to the truest love. Never
see me more.' Ah, 'tis too plain. I thought as much before; but, O,
we are too apt to excuse the faults of those we love, and fond of   140
our own undoing.
　　Support me, O, to bear this dreadful pang,
　　This stab to all my gathered resolution.
IRENE Read it again, and call revenge to aid you.
PRINCESS Perhaps he makes his boast too of the conquest,   145
　　For, O, my heart he knows too well, my passion—
　　But as thou hast inspired me, I'll revenge
　　Th'affront, and cast him from my poisoned breast,
　　To make him room that merits all my thoughts.
　　　　Enter the Prince of Cleves with Nemours
PRINCE Madam, there is a letter fallen by accident into your hands.   150
　　My friend comes in behalf of the Vidame of Chartres to retrieve
　　it. [*To Nemours*] When I am dismissed from the king, my lord, I'll
　　wait you here again.°
NEMOURS [*offering to accompany him*] My lord—
PRINCE Not a step further.   155
　　　　Exit the Prince of Cleves
NEMOURS Madam, I come most humbly to inquire whether the
　　dauphin queen sent you a letter which the Vidame lost.
PRINCESS Sir, you had better
　　Find the queen dauphin out, tell her the truth,
　　For she's informed the letter is your own.   160
NEMOURS Ah, madam, I have nothing to confess
　　In this affair—or, if I had, believe me,
　　Believe these sighs that will not be kept in,
　　I should not tell it to the dauphin queen.
　　But to the purpose. Know my Lord of Chartres   165
　　Received the note you saw from Madame Tournon,
　　A former mistress. But the secret's this:
　　The sister of our Henry long has loved him.
PRINCESS I thought the king intended her for Savoy.°
NEMOURS True, madam, but the Vidame is beloved.   170
　　In short, he dropped the letter, and desired,
　　For fear of her he loves, that I would own it.
　　I promised too to trace the business for him,
　　And, if 'twere possible, regain the letter.

PRINCESS The Vidame then has shown but small discretion,   175
    Being engaged so high.°
    Why did he not burn the letter?
NEMOURS But, madam, shall I dare presume to say,
    'Tis hard to be in love and to be wise?
    O, did you know like him—like him? like me—   180
    What 'tis to languish in those restless fires.
PRINCESS Irene, Irene, restore the duke his letter.
       [*The Princess gives the letter to Irene, who hands it to*
       Nemours]°
NEMOURS Madam, you've bound me ever to your service.
    But I'll retire and study to repay,
    If aught but death can quit the obligation.   185
       Exit [*Nemours*]
PRINCESS O, 'tis too much; I'm lost, I'm lost again.
    The duke has cleared himself, to the confusion
    Of all my settled rage and vowed revenge;
    And now he shows more lovely than before.
    He comes again to wake my sleeping passion,   190
    To rouse me into torture. O the racks
    Of hopeless love! It shoots, it glows, it burns,
    And thou, alas, shalt shortly close my eyes.
IRENE Alas, you're pale already.
PRINCESS   O Irene,
    Methinks I see fate set two bowls before me—   195
    Poison and health, a husband and Nemours.
    But see with what a whirl my passions move.
    I loathe the cordial of my husband's love;
    But when Nemours my fancy does recall,
    The bane's so sweet that I could drink it all.   200
       [*Exeunt*]

2.1

[*The Court*]°

[*Enter*] *Tournon* [*and*] *La March*

TOURNON It works, my dear; it works beyond belief.
The letter which he lost has sprung a mine
That shatters all the court. Each jealous duchess
Concludes her man concerned, and straight employs
A confidant to find the mystery out.
But that which takes the queen, and makes me die° 5
With pleasure, is, that Marguerite thinks,
Spite of the imprecations of Nemours,
The letter sent to him.

LA MARCH I see 'em move this way. 10

TOURNON Haste to Saint-André's palace. Watch their wives till I appear. I have promised Nemours an afternoon assignation with 'em in Luxembourg Garden; but I will antedate the business as he is waiting, and set Marguerite upon him just as he meets 'em, which will heighten the design.° Be gone, while I attend the 15 business here.

Exeunt La March [*and Tournon in different directions.*]
Enter Marguerite, Nemours [*followed by the Vidame*]

MARGUERITE Away! You have combined to ruin me.
You have conspired the death of her you hate.
But tell me—O, confess, and I'll forgive thee;
Say it was thine. Nay, look not on the Vidame.
There is discourse in eyes—consent, denial, 20
All understood by looks. Say it was thine;
Confess, and lay this tempest with a word.
Not yet? Why then, I'll have it in despite
Of thee and him. I'll sell my soul to hell—
If woman can be worth the devil's purchase, 25
After she has been blown upon by man—
That I may tell thee, as I sink for ever,
'Thou hast been false'.

NEMOURS   You have heard me more than once
Affirm. The Vidame, if you'll give him leave,
Will own it to your face. 30

MARGUERITE   Hear, hear him, heaven.

By all extremes, thou art false. Therefore be gone,°
For if I look upon thee in this rage,
I shall do mischief. Speak not, but away.

Nemours beckons the Vidame. They steal off. Enter Tournon°

TOURNON Madam, the duke has taken you at your word, and is gone   35
with the Vidame. I made bold to overhear part of your discourse,
because I have more of his infidelity to tell you. Betwixt one and
two in Luxembourg Garden he has appointed some ladies.°

MARGUERITE Furies and hell!

TOURNON Have patience for an hour. I'll bring you to the place,   40
where, if you please, you may flesh your fingers in the blood of
those young women whom he meets to enjoy.

MARGUERITE No, no, I have a better cast, if I can conquer this rising
spleen.° How long will it be ere you call me?

TOURNON An hour or thereabouts.   45

MARGUERITE And by that time I'll put on a disguise. Fail not.

TOURNON But what do you intend?

MARGUERITE I know not yet myself. Revenge.

TOURNON You had a lover° once, Francis the dauphin.

MARGUERITE Be that then the last card. I know not what.   50
The dauphin shall—I'll do't, and openly affront him,
And as the little worshippers adore me,
Spy the duke out, and (leaning on the prince)°
Inquire, 'Who's that?' It shall be so; I will.
Revenge, revenge, and show thyself true woman.   55
Down then, proud heart; down, woman, down. I'll try;
I'll do't. I've sworn to curb my will or die.°

Exeunt

2.2

[*Saint-André's palace*]

[*Enter*] *Saint-André, Poltrot* [*and*] *Bellamore*

BELLAMORE Well, gentlemen, good-morrow, and remember my
counsel.

POLTROT What, to bear ourselves like men of wit and sense, snub
our wives, rally 'em, and be as witty as the devil?

SAINT-ANDRÉ With all my heart. 'Tis not my time of assignation yet   5
with my duchesses, and this is very fashionable.

BELLAMORE I've put you in the way. And so good-morrow.
    Exit [Bellamore]
POLTROT They come, they come.
    Enter Elianor and Celia
    Walk by 'em. Take no notice, and repeat verses.°
    'Phillis did in so strange a posture lie,   10
    Panting and breathless, languishing her eye;
    She seemed to live, and yet she seemed to die.'
SAINT-ANDRÉ I grow sick of the wife. Prithee, Poltrot, let's go.
POLTROT Whither thou wilt, so we get rid of 'em. 'Slife, I am as
weary of mine as a modish lady of her old clothes.   15
CELIA What, does the maggot bite? You must be jogging from this
place of little ease?° Yet I am resolved to know some reason why
a wife may not be as good company as a wench.
POLTROT Prithee, spouse, do not provoke me, for I'm in the witty
vein and shall repartee thee to the devil.   20
ELIANOR Pray, Saint-André, leave tricing your curls,° your affected
nods, grimaces, taking of snuff, and answer me. Why are we not
as pleasing as formerly?
SAINT-ANDRÉ Why, Nell—Gad, 'tis special, this amarum° is very
pungent—why, Nell, I can give no more reason for my change of   25
humour than for the turning of a weather-cock. Only this: I love
whoring, because I love whoring.
POLTROT Nay, since you provoke us, know I can give a reason. We
run after whores, because you bar us from 'em—as some take
pleasure to go a-deer-stealing that have fine parks of their own.—   30
Gad, and there I was with her.°—This itch of the blood, spouse,
is nothing but a spice of the first great jilt, your grandmother Eve.
We long for the fruit, because it is forbidden.
SAINT-ANDRÉ Nay, that's not all, for misses° are really more pleasant
than a wife can be. *Probatum est.* A wife dares not assume the   35
liberty of pleasing like a miss, for fear of being thought one. A wife
may pretend to dutiful affection and bustle below,° but must be
still at night. 'Tis miss alone may be allowed flame and rapture,
and all that.
CELIA Yet how do you know but a wife may have flame and rapture,   40
and all that?
POLTROT 'Tis impossible. 'Tis the nature of a wife to be as cold as
a stone. There's slap-dash for you.
CELIA Yet out of a stone a man of sense would strike fire.—There's
slap-dash for you.   45

ELIANOR Will you be constant to us, if we make it appear by your own confession that we can please as well as the subtlest she that ever charmed you?

SAINT-ANDRÉ Till which miracle come to pass, since 'twas your own proposition, I Saint-André and thou Elianor come not between a pair of sheets.   50

ELIANOR How should they know then?

POLTROT Nor I Anthony with thee Celia.

ELIANOR But we hope you are not in earnest. You cannot be so inhuman.   55

CELIA 'Tis a curse beyond all curses, to have a man that can and will not. 'Tis worse than teaching a fool, or leading the blind.

ELIANOR To marry and live thus is to be like fish in frosty weather—have water, but pine for want of air.

CELIA Yet who knows but heaven may send some kind, good man   60
that in mere pity may break the ice and give us a breathing?°

ELIANOR Can you be so hard-hearted?

POLTROT Come, bully, let's away, for fear we should melt. Look ye, spouses of ours: if our wenches prove ill-humoured, we'll come back to you.   65

SAINT-ANDRÉ Agreed. Rather than grow rusty, let our wives file us. But I thank heaven 'tis not come to that yet. There's no such want. I'll have you to know, Nell, there's no woman can resist me if she would. No duchess 'scapes me, if I make it my business to compass° her.   70

POLTROT Any man of wit and sense like us charms all women, as one key unlocks all doors at court.° Nay, I'll say a bold word for myself. Turn me to the sharpest shrew that ever bit or scratched. If I do not make her feed out of my hand like a tame pigeon, may I be condemned to lie with my wife.   75

ELIANOR Flesh and blood can endure no longer. You are the vainest lying fellows that ever lived. You compass a duchess! There's not a footman but would shame you.

SAINT-ANDRÉ 'Sdeath and fury, if they should try!

CELIA You pitiful, sneaking, rascally cuckolds,° countenanced°   80
scoundrels, that dare bespatter ladies of honour thus! For heaven sake, what are you? How do you live, and where do you spend your time? In tennis-courts, taverns, eating-houses, bawdy-houses, where you quarrel in drink for your trulls, who, while you manfully fight their cause, they run away with your hats   85
and belts.

ELIANOR Then you come home and swear you'll be revenged on this
  lord, or that duke, that assaulted you single with all his footmen.

CELIA And, says my gentleman, 'If I had not been the most skilful
  person alive, my body had been by this time like an old-fashioned   90
  suit, pinked all over and full of eyelet-holes'.

ELIANOR But did he not disarm my lord at last?

CELIA By all means, and made him beg his life.

ELIANOR When indeed he compounded with the constable for his
  own liberty.   95

CELIA You, persons of quality! What person of honour would keep
  company with such debauchees?° 'Slife, madam, an orange-wench
  is above their ambition.

ELIANOR An orange-wench!° If they can but run in her debt, and the
  poor creature come dunning 'em to their lodgings, they'll swear   100
  they lay with her, when they dare not be known that they are
  within.

CELIA Sometimes lie lolling upon a long scarf in the playhouse,
  talking loud and affectedly, and swear at night they had the
  prettiest thing just come out of the country.   105

ELIANOR And wish themselves damned if she did not smell of the
  grass.

CELIA When in truth 'twas some disguised bawd that met 'em there
  according to assignation.

POLTROT Hark you, Potiphar's wife of mine.° By Pharaoh's lean   110
  kine,° thou shalt starve for this.

SAINT-ANDRÉ And for thee, Nell, mark me. Thou shalt dream and
  be tormented with imagination, like one that, having drunk hard,
  is thirsty in the night, dreams of vessels brim-full, and drinks and
  drinks, yet never is satisfied.   115

POLTROT For my part, I'll serve my damned wife as Tantalus° was
  punished. The fruit shall bob at her lips, which she shall never
  enjoy.

        Exeunt Saint-André [and] Poltrot

ELIANOR Very well. The world's come to a fine pass. If this be
  marrying, would I were a maid again. Men take wives now as they   120
  snatch up a gazette—look it over and then fling it by.

CELIA They forget us in a day or two; or if they read us over again,
  'tis only to rub up remembrance, and commonly they fall asleep so.

ELIANOR What's to be done, child? For rather than live thus—

CELIA Rather than live thus, let's do anything.   125

ELIANOR Anything, rogue? Why, cuckolds are things.

CELIA Perhaps they think we have no such thing as flesh and blood
about us; but we'll make 'em know, a young woman in the flower
of her age is not like painted fruit in a glass, only to be looked on.
Perhaps you are a more contemplative person, and will go farther   130
about.°

ELIANOR What, dear rogue, dost think I will leave thee? By this kiss,
not I.

CELIA Thus then. We'll slip on long scarves and black gowns, put on
masks, and ramble about.°   135

ELIANOR Rare rogue, let me kiss thee again. Certainly, intriguing° is
the pleasantest part of life. To meet a gallant abroad in a summer's
evening and laugh away an hour or two in a garden bower, where
nobody sees nor nobody knows—methinks 'tis so pretty and
harmless. Lord, how it works in my fancy.   140

CELIA We must tell Madame Tournon by all means.

ELIANOR I believe her secret° and know her very good-natured. But,
for all that, methinks she has the cant of a refined Florence bawd.°
     Enter Tournon

CELIA The better for our purpose. She comes as wished.

TOURNON Dear precious rosebuds, your servant. Now for all the   145
world you look as you were new-blown. And how do ye, my pretty
primroses? 'Tis a whole day since I saw ye.

CELIA O, madam, we have a suit to your ladyship.

TOURNON I grant it, whate'er it be. Speak, my hyacinth.

ELIANOR Our husbands are worse than ever.   150

CELIA They use us as if we had neither beauty nor portion.

TOURNON What's this I hear? O ingrate and ignoble! Revenge
yourselves, sweetings. 'Tis time to pule and put finger in eye when
you are past propagation; but, my ladybirds, you are in your prime.
Let me touch your delicate hands. Well, and do not these humid   155
palms claim a man? Nay, and your breasts! Lord, lord, how
swollen and hard they are! How they heave and pant now, by
Cynthia,° as if they were ready to burst! Look to't; have a care of
a cancer. Draw 'em down, draw 'em down; for let me tell you,
jewels, it may be dangerous for you to go thus long without   160
cultivation.

ELIANOR What would you have us do, madam?

TOURNON Do, violet? Why, do as all the world does beside. Lose no
time, catch him by the forelock°—get a man to your mind. I'll
acquaint you with one that's as true as the day, that will fight like   165
a lion, and love like a sparrow.° He has eyes as black as sloes—you

can hardly look on 'em—and a skin so white, and soft as satin with
the grain. And for thee, tulip—

CELIA For me, madam!

TOURNON For thee, honeysuckle, such a man. Well, I shall never   170
forget him. Such a straight bole of a body, such a trunk, such a
shape, such a quick strength. He will over anything he can lay his
hand on, and vaults° to admiration.

ELIANOR But, madam, will you provide us lodgings on occasion?

TOURNON The richest in the town—the costliest hangings, great   175
glasses,° china-dishes,° silver tables, silver stands, and silver
urinals. And then these gallants are the closest° lovers, so good at
keeping a secret. Well, give me your man that says nothing, but
minds the business in hand; for a secret lover's like a gun charged
with white powder°—does execution but makes no noise.   180

CELIA Well, and let me tell you that's the point, madam.

TOURNON Ay, and 'tis a precious point, a feeling point, and a
pleasing point. You shall know him. You must know him. I shall
die if you don't know him. He has the fling of a gentleman.

ELIANOR Pray, madam, how's that?   185

TOURNON Why thus, apricot. Into your arms, then stops your mouth
with a double-tongued English kiss,° that you can't be angry with
him for your blood.

CELIA I know 'tis my filthy country way; but I'll assure you, if he
should serve me so, my blood would rise at him.   190

TOURNON But then you'd repent and fall before him, for he has the
most particular, obliging way, and she whom he particularly loves
is so obliged with his particular—well, for my part, my twins of
beauty, I set an infinite value on their caresses, distresses° and
addresses. Nay, I could refuse a quilt imperial° to be obliged by   195
them, though on the bare boards or the cold stones.

ELIANOR But, madam, are they in being?

TOURNON They are, my blossoms. Then they kiss beyond imagination, just for all the world as when you cut a pure, juicy China
orange the goodness runs over. Lord, now it comes in my   200
cogitation! I'm just now going to take a view of 'em in Luxembourg Garden, where, if you please to walk, they shall sun
themselves in your smiles. Come, my carnations.

  [*Celia and Elianor wait for Tournon to take precedence*]
Nay, I protest I will not go before ye.

CELIA But, madam, we're at home.   205

TOURNON O lord, beauties, I know not the way.

ELIANOR Indeed, madam, you must—or we shall use violence.

TOURNON Well, ladies, since 'tis your command, I dare not but obey.

> *Exeunt, [Tournon taking the lead]*

2.3

[The Prince of Cleves' palace]

[Enter] Nemours [and] Bellamore

NEMOURS *[embracing Bellamore]* Thou dear soft rogue, my spouse, my Hephaestion, my Ganymede!° Nay, if I die tonight, my dukedom's thine. But art thou sure the Princess of Cleves withdraws here after dinner?

BELLAMORE One of her women whom I have debauched tells me 'tis   5
her custom. You may slip into the closet and overhear all. And yet methinks 'tis hard, because the Prince of Cleves loves you as his life.

NEMOURS I saved his life, sweetheart, when he was assaulted by a mistake in the dark. And shall he grudge me a little fooling with his wife for so serious an obligation?   10

> *Enter the Vidame*

A pox upon him! Here comes the Vidame with his sour morals.

VIDAME *[to himself]* 'Tis certain I like her. She's very pretty, and Tournon shall help me to her.

NEMOURS In love, by my lechery! Ay, and she shall help thee to her. But who, but who is't, my man of principles?   15

VIDAME To tell your grace, I am sure, were to be a man of none for myself—you that are the whores' engrosser. Let me see. There's Tournon your ubiquitary whore, your bawd, your bawd-barber or bawd-surgeon,° for you're ever under her hands, and she plasters you every day with new wenches. Then there's your domestic   20
termagants,° Elianor and Celia, with something new in chase. Why, you outdo Caesar himself in your way and dictate to more whores at once than he did to knaves. Believe me, sir, in a little time you'll be nicked the town-bull.

NEMOURS Why, there's the difference betwixt my sense and yours.   25
Would I were, and your darkling mistress the first should come in my way. Jove and Europa,° I'd leap her in thy face. Why, how now, Vidame, what devil has turned thee grave—the devil of love, or the devil of envy?

VIDAME Friendship, mere friendship and care of your soul. I thought   30
it but just to tell you the whole town takes notice of your way.

NEMOURS Why, then the whole town does me wrong, because I take
no notice of theirs. Thus t'other night I was in company with two
or three well-bred fops that found fault with my obscenity and
protested, ' 'Twas such a way'. Why, 'tis the way of ye all. Only   35
you sneak with it under your cloaks like tailors and barbers; and I,
as a gentleman should do, walk with it in my hand. For prithee
observe, does not your priest the same thing? Did not I see Father
Patrick,° declaiming against flesh in Lent, strip up to the elbow
and, telling the congregation he had ate nothing but fish these   40
twenty years, yet protest to the ladies, that fat arm of his, which
was a chopping one, was the least member about him?

VIDAME Faith, and it may be so too.

NEMOURS Does not your politician, your little great man of business,
that sets the world together by the ears, after all his plotting,   45
drudging and sweating at lying, retire to some little punk and
untap at night?

VIDAME I submit to the weight of your reasons, and confess the
whole world does you injustice; wherefore I judge it fit that they
bring your grace their wives and daughters to make you amends.   50

NEMOURS Why, now thou talk'st like an honest fellow, for never let
business flatter thee, Frank, into nonsense. Women are the sole
pleasure of the world. Nay, I had rather part with my whole estate,
health and sense, than lose an inch of my love. I was t'other day
at a pretty entertainment,° where two or three grave, politic rogues   55
were wondering why women should be brought into plays. I as
gravely replied, 'The world was not made without 'em'. He full
pop° upon me, 'But, sir, it had been better if it had'.

VIDAME And then no doubt a gloomy smile arose.

NEMOURS These are your rogues, Frank, that would be thought   60
critics, that are never pleased but with something new (as they call
it), just, proper, and never as men speak—your out-of-the-way
men that hate us rogues with a way.

VIDAME But after all this they'll run you down and say your grace is
no scholar.   65

NEMOURS Why, faith, nor would be, if learning must wrench a man's
head quite round. I understand my mother-tongue well enough,
and some others, just as I do women—not to be married to 'em,
but to serve my turn. What's good in 'em never 'scapes me; but as
for points and tags,° for which those solemn fops are to be valued,   70

I slight 'em, nor would remember 'em if I could; for he that once
listens to jingling, ten to one if ever he gets it out of his head while
he lives. But prithee be gone, and leave me to my musing. Find
Tournon out, my Vidame, and bid her remember the handkerchief. Away! Thou art concerned in the business; therefore, away!   75

    Exeunt the Vidame [and] Bellamore. Enter the Princess of
    Cleves [and] Irene

[*Aside*] She comes, ye gods, with what a pompous state;°
The stars and all heaven's glories on her wait.
That's out-of-the-way too—but now for my closet.

    Exit [Nemours]

PRINCESS No, no, I charge thee pity me no longer,
But on the earth let us consult our woes;   80
For earth I shall be shortly. Sit and hear me,
    [*They sit together on the ground*]
While on thy faithful bosom thus I lean
My aching head, and breathe my cruel sorrows.

IRENE Speak, madam, speak. They'll strangle if contained.

PRINCESS As late I lay upon a flowery bank,   85
My head a little heaved beyond the verge
To look my troubles in the rockless stream,°
I slept and dreamt I saw
The bosom of the flood unfold.
I saw the naked nymphs ten fathom down,   90
With all the crystal thrones in their green courts below,
Where in their busy arms Nemours appeared,
His head reclined, and swollen as he were drowned,°
While each kind goddess dewed his senseless face
With nectar's drops to bring back life in vain;   95
When on a sudden the whole synod rose
And laid him to my lips. O my Irene!
Forgive me, honour, duty—love, forgive me!
I found a pleasure I ne'er felt before,
Dissolving pains, and swimming, shuddering joys,   100
To which my bridal night with Cleves was dull.°
    Enter the Prince of Cleves

IRENE [*rising*] Behold him, madam.

PRINCE   Ha, my Chartres, how!
Why on the earth?

PRINCESS   Because, my lord, it suits
The humble posture of my sad condition.

PRINCE These starts again. But why thy sad condition?   105
  O rise and tell me why this melancholy?
  Why fall those tears? Why heaves this bosom thus?
  Nay, I must then constrain thee with my arms.
     [The Prince helps the Princess to rise and embraces her]°
  Is't possible? Does then thy load of grief
  Oppress thee so, thou canst not speak for sighing?   110
  Ah, Chartres, Chartres! Then thou didst but soothe me.
  There is some cause, too frightful to be told,
  And thou hast learnt the art too to dissemble.
PRINCESS O heavens, dissemble—when I strip my soul,
  Show it all bare and trembling to your view!   115
  Can you suspect me, sir, for a dissembler?
PRINCE By all my hopes, doubts, jealousies and fears,
  I know not what to think. I think thou show'st
  Thy inmost thought, and now I think thou dost not.
  I think there is a bosom secret still   120
  And have a dawn of it through all thy folds
  That hide it from my view. O, trust me, Cleves!
  Trust me, whate'er it be. I love thee more
  Than thou lov'st help for that which thus enthrals thee.
  Trust thy dear husband. O, let loose the pain   125
  That makes thee droop, though it should be my death!
  By thy dear self I'll welcome it to ease thee.
PRINCESS Thou best of all thy kind, why should you rack me,
  Who dare not, cannot speak? No more but this:
  Take me from Paris, from the court.
PRINCE   Ha, Chartres, how!   130
  What, from the court of Paris? Why?
PRINCESS   Because—
  My mother's death-bed counsel so advised me,°
  Because the court has charms, because I love
  A grotto best, because 'tis best for you
  And me and all the world.
PRINCE   Because, O heaven,   135
  Because there is some cursèd charm at court,
  Which you love better than me and all the world.
  The reason's plain, for which you would remove—
  To lose the memory of some lawless love.
PRINCESS Why then am I detained, if that's your fear?   140
PRINCE It is, it ought, and shall, and, O, you must

Confess this horrid falsehood to my face.

PRINCESS Never, my lord, never confess a lie.
By heavens, I love your life above my own.

PRINCE Not that, not that. Speak home and fly not wide.°   145
Swear by thyself, thou dearly purchased pleasure,
Swear by those chaster sweets thy mother left thee,
Swear that thy soul, which cannot hide a treason,
Prefers me even to all the world. Hold, precious.
Swear that thou lov'st him more—and only lov'st him,   150
And in such sense as not to love another.

PRINCESS [kneeling] Ah, sir, why will you sink me to your feet,
Where I must lie and groan my life away?

PRINCE Speak, Chartres, speak. Nor let the name of husband
Sound terror to thy soul; for by my hopes   155
Of paradise, howe'er thou usest me,
I am thy creature, still to make and mould me,°
Thy cringing, crawling slave, and will adore°
The hand that kills me.

PRINCESS   O you are too good!
And I must never hope for pardon. Yet   160
I could excuse it; but, my lord, I will not.
Know then—I cannot speak.

PRINCE   Nor I, by heaven.

PRINCESS I love—

PRINCE   Go on.

PRINCESS   I love you as my soul.

PRINCE Ha—but the rest?

PRINCESS   Alas, alas, I dare not.

PRINCE Why then, farewell for ever.

PRINCESS   Stay and take it—   165
Take the extremest pang of tortured virtue;
Take all. I love, I love thee, Cleves, as life;
But, O, I love, I love another more.

PRINCE O, Chartres, O.

PRINCESS   Why did you rack me then?
You were resolved, and now you have it all.   170

PRINCE All, Chartres! All! Why, can there then be more?
But rise, and know I by this kiss forgive thee.
      [He compels her to rise and embraces her]
Thou hast made me wretched by the clearest proof
Of perfect honour that e'er flowed from woman.

But crown the misery which you have begun,   175
And let me know who 'tis you would avoid,
Who is the happy man that had the power
To burn that heart which I could never warm.
PRINCESS Forgive me, sir; in this prudence commands
    Eternal silence.
PRINCE   Ha! If silent now,   180
Why didst thou speak at all? If here thou stop'st,
I shall conclude that which I thought thy virtue
A start of passion which thou couldst not hide,
And now vexation gnaws thy guilty soul
With a too-late repentance for confessing.   185
His name?°
PRINCESS   You shall not know it. Yes, my lord,
Now a too-late repentance tears my soul
And tells me I have done amiss to trust you.
Yet, by my hopes of ease at last by death,
I swear my love has never yet appeared   190
To any man but you.
PRINCE Weep not, my Chartres, for howe'er my tongue
Upbraid thy fame, my heart still worships thee;
And by the blood that chills me round, I swear,
From this sad moment I'll ne'er urge thee more.   195
All that I beg of thee is not to hate me.
PRINCESS The study of my life shall be to love you.
PRINCE Never, O never! I were mad to hope it.
Yet thou shalt give me leave to fold thy hand,
To press it with my lips, to sigh upon it,   200
And wash it with my tears.
PRINCESS I cannot bear this kindness without dying.
PRINCE Nay, we will walk and talk sometimes together.
Like age, we'll call to mind the pleasures past—
Pleasures, like theirs, which never shall return.   205
For, O, my Chartres, since thy heart's estranged,
The pleasure of thy beauty is no more.
Yet I each night will see thee softly laid,
Kneel by thy side, and when thy vows are paid,
Take one last kiss, ere I to death retire,   210
Wish that the heavens had given us equal fire,
Then sigh, 'It cannot be', and so expire.
        Exeunt [the Prince and Princess of Cleves.] Enter Nemours

NEMOURS She loves, she loves, and I'm the happy man.
    She has avowed it, past all precedent,
    Before her husband's face.   215
    Ha! But from love like hers, such daring virtue,
    That, like a bleeding quarry lately chased,°
    Plunges among the waves, or turns at bay,
    What is there to expect? But let it come,
    The worst can happen; yet 'tis glorious still°   220
    To bring to such extremes so chaste a mind,
    And charm to love the wisest of her kind.
        Enter the Vidame
    Ah, Vidame! I could tell thee such a story of such a friend of mine,
    the oddest, prettiest, out-of-the-way business.° But thou art so
    flippant there's no trusting thee.   225
VIDAME Tournon says the flag's held out.°
NEMOURS Tournon be damned! Know then, but be secret, there is
    a friend of mine beloved, but by a soul so virtuous—
VIDAME That was too much.
NEMOURS That, quite from the method of all womankind, she told   230
    it to her husband.
VIDAME That's strange indeed. And how did her husband like it?
NEMOURS Why, after a tedious, passionate discourse, approved her
    carriage,° and swore he loved her more than ever. So they cried
    and kissed, and went away most lovingly together.   235
VIDAME Why, then she cuckolds him to rights, nor can he take the
    law of her; and I'll be judge by any bawd in Christendom.° And
    so, my lord, farewell. I have business of my own, and Tournon
    waits you.
NEMOURS But hark you, Frank. I have occasion for you and must   240
    press thee, I hope, to no unwelcome office—only a second.
VIDAME With all my heart, my lord. The time and place?
NEMOURS Just now in Luxembourg Garden, betwixt one and two—a
    challenge from a couple, the smartest, briskest, prettiest tilting ladies.
VIDAME Your servant, sir.° And as you thrive, let me hear from your 245
    grace, and so fate speed your plough.
        Exit [Vidame.] Enter Tournon with Marguerite, [masked]
NEMOURS [*aside*] And so fate speed your plough, an you go to
    that.° And I shall tell you, sir, 'twas not handsomely done, to leave
    me thus to the mercy of two unreasonable women at once.
TOURNON [*aside, to Marguerite*] You have him now in view, and so 250
    I leave you.

Exit Tournon

MARGUERITE Stand, sir.

NEMOURS To a lady, while I have breath.

MARGUERITE Would you not fall to a lady too, if she should ask the
favour?   255

NEMOURS Ay, Gad, any pretty woman may bring me upon my knees
at her pleasure.°

MARGUERITE [*aside*] O devil.

NEMOURS Prithee, my dear, soft, warm rogue, let thee and I be
kind—   260

MARGUERITE And kiss, you were going to say.

NEMOURS [*aside*] 'Slife, how pat she hits me.°—[*To her*] Why, thou
and I were made for one another. Let's try how our lips fit.
       [*They kiss*]

MARGUERITE Is that your fitting?

NEMOURS [*aside*] 'Fore heaven, she's wondrous quick.—[*To her*]   265
Nay, my dear, an you go to that,° I can fit you every way.

MARGUERITE You are a notorious talker.

NEMOURS And a better doer. Prithee try.

MARGUERITE As if that were to do now.

NEMOURS Nay, then I'm sure of thee;° for never was a woman mine   270
once, but was mine always.

MARGUERITE Know then you are a heavy, sluggish fellow. But I see
there is no more faith in man than woman, cork and feathers.°

NEMOURS Make a shuttlecock—that's woman. Let me, if you please,
be battledore, and, by Gad, for a day and a night I'll keep up with 275
any fellow in Christendom.°

MARGUERITE Come away then, and I'll keep count, I warrant you.
[*Aside*] Monster! Villain!

NEMOURS [*aside*] Now is the devil and I as great as ever. [*To her*] I
come, my dear. [*Aside*] But what then becomes of my other dears, 280
for whom I was primed and charged?

MARGUERITE Why don't you come, my dear?

NEMOURS [*aside*] There with that sweet word she cocked me.

MARGUERITE Lord, how you tremble!

NEMOURS [*aside*] There the pan flashed.   285

MARGUERITE I'll set my teeth in you.

NEMOURS [*aside*] Now I go off.° O man! O woman! O flesh! O devil!
       [*Exeunt*]

3.1

[Luxembourg Garden]

[Enter] the Vidame [and] Tournon

TOURNON A woman in love with another, and confess it to her husband! What would I give to know her! Without all question Nemours is the person beloved.

VIDAME That's plain by his eagerness in the discovery. He forced me to hear him, whether I would or no. Yet what I so admire in his temper° is, that, for all the former heat, I no sooner mentioned you, but he flew from it and run upon another scent, as if the first had never been.

TOURNON Where did you find him?

VIDAME At the Princess of Cleves'; and my heart tells me that's the lady that acquainted her husband how she was determined to make him a cuckold—if he pleased to give his consent.

TOURNON My judgement, which is most sagacious in these matters, is most positive in your opinion, for by his whitely cast the Prince of Cleves must be the man forked in the book of fate.°

VIDAME And yet 'tis odd that Nemours, of all men, should have such luck at this lottery.

TOURNON O, to choose,° my lord! Because she's nice and precise.° Your demure ladies that are so squab in company are devils in a corner. They are a sort of melancholy birds that ne'er peep abroad by day, but they tu-whit, tu-woo it at night. Nay, to my particular knowledge, all grave women love wild men. And if they can but appear civil at first, they certainly snap 'em. For mark their language: 'The man is a handsome man, if he had but grace', 'The man has wit, parts and excellent gifts, if he would but make a right use of 'em'. Why, all these ifs are but civil pimps to a most bawdy conclusion. But see, I descry him with a mask yonder.

VIDAME You'll remember Saint-André's lady for this discovery.

TOURNON If she be not yours tonight, never acquaint me with a mystery again.

VIDAME Not a word to the duke. My gravity gets me a hank over him. Therefore, if you tell him of any love matters of mine, you must never hope for more secrets.

TOURNON Trouble not your head, but away.

Exit the Vidame

So. This gets me a diamond from the queen, an ambassador's   35
merit° at least. Confess to her husband! Alas, poor princess. See,
they come. But that which startles me is how a woman of
Marguerite's sex° can contain° all this while as she seems to do.
But perhaps she designs to pump him—or has some further end,
which I must learn.   40

    [Exit Tournon.] Enter Nemours and Marguerite, [masked]

MARGUERITE But did you never promise thus before?

NEMOURS Never. But why these doubts? Thou hast all the wit in the
    world. Thou know'st I love thee without protestations. Why then
    this delay?

MARGUERITE I have not conversed with you an hour, and you are   45
    for running over me.° No, sir; but if you can have patience till the
    ball—[*aside*] O, I shall burst.

NEMOURS Patience? I must. But if it were not for the clog of thy
    modesty, we might have been in the third heaven by this, and have
    danced at the ball beside. Ha, you faint. Take off your mask.   50

MARGUERITE Unhand me, or—But pray, ere we part, let me ask you
    a serious question. What if you should have picked up a devil
    incarnate?°

NEMOURS Why, by your loving to go in the dark thus, you make me°
    begin to suspect you. But be a devil, an thou wilt. If we must be   55
    damned together, who can help it?

MARGUERITE [*aside*] I shall not hold.°

NEMOURS Yet, now I think on't, thou canst be no devil; thou art so
    'fraid of a sinner. For you refused me just now, when I proffered
    to sell myself and seal the bargain with the best of my blood.°   60

MARGUERITE But if I should permit you, could you find in your
    heart to engender with a damned spirit?

NEMOURS Yes, marry, could I, for all you ask the question so
    seriously. For know, thou bewitching creature, I have longed any
    time this seven years to be the father of a succubus.   65

MARGUERITE [*aside*] Fiend, and no man!

NEMOURS Besides, madam, don't you think a feat devil of yours and
    my begetting would be a prettier sight in a house than a monkey
    or a squirrel? Gad, I'd hang bells about his neck and make my valet
    spruce up his brush-tail every morning as duly as he combed my   70
    head.°

MARGUERITE But is it possible—for I know you have a mistress, a
    convenience as you call her—that you could leave her for me, who
    may be ugly, diseased, or a devil indeed, for aught you know?

NEMOURS Why, since you tax me with truth, I must answer like a   75
man of honour. I could leave her for thee or any else of your tribe,
so they were all like you.

MARGUERITE But in the name of reason, what is there in us
runners-at-all,° that a wife, or a mistress of that nature, may not
possess with more advantage?   80

NEMOURS Why, the freedom, wit and roguery, and all sort of
acting,° as well as conversation.° In a domestic she, there's no
gaiety, no chat, no discourse, but of the cares of this world and its
inconveniencies. What we do we do, but so dully. By Gad, my
thing asked me once, when my breeches were down, what the stuff   85
cost a yard.

  [Exit Marguerite]

Ha, what now, upon the gog again? Nay, then have with you at all
adventures°—at least to put you in mind of the ball.

  Exit [Nemours.] Enter Tournon

TOURNON [*watching offstage*] Ha, yonder she lost him. See. What can
she intend by keeping herself so close?° But see, La March has   90
seized her, and now the mystery will open of itself.

  Enter Marguerite with La March

LA MARCH But have you found him false?

MARGUERITE°   Curses, damnation,
The racks of woman's wits, when her soul°
Is balked of vengeance, wait on his desires.

LA MARCH Why did you leave him so upon the sudden?   95

MARGUERITE Because I found my passion move too strongly.
My foolish heart would not obey my will.
I found my eyes grow full, my sighs had choked me,
And I was dying in his arms.

LA MARCH   But now
You have got breath, what is your purpose, madam?   100

MARGUERITE To meet him as I promised, to enjoy him
With the last pang of a revengeful pleasure;
And let him know—°
Then make him damn himself with thousand oaths
That he'll ne'er see forsaken Marguerite more,   105
The cursed, fond, foolish, doting Marguerite.
For thus with an extorted gallantry°
I'll force him to revile me to my face,
Then throw the mask away, and vent my rage,
Tell him he is a fiend, devil, devil, devil,   110

Or what is worse, a man—
And leave him to the horror of his soul.
    Exit [Marguerite]

TOURNON I've heard her rave and must applaud thy conduct.
To the next task then. When she has satisfied°
This odd figary of revenge and pleasure,   115
Take her in the height of her disdain
And ply her with the dauphin. Then tell Nemours
Of her resolve to cast him further off.
Millions to one we carry the design.
But haste and scout, while I attend the duke,   120
That harps upon the loss of his new mistress.
    [Exit La March.] Enter Nemours

NEMOURS Death and the devil! We went talking along so pleasantly,
when of a sudden, whispering she would not fail me at the ball,
she sprung from me at yon dark corner and vanished. Well, if she
be a devil, hell by her should be a merry place; or perhaps she has   125
not been there yet, but fell this morning and took earth in her way.
My comfort is, I shall make a new discovery if she keeps her word;
and she has too much wit to break it before she tries me.

TOURNON And where are you to make this new discovery?

NEMOURS At the ball in masquerade.° Thus would I have time roll   130
still all in these lovely extremes, the corruption of reason being the
generation of wit, and the spirit of wit lying in the extravagance of
pleasure. Nay, the two nearest ways to enter the closet of the gods,
and lie even with the fates themselves, are fury° and sleep.
Therefore, the fury of wine and fury of women possess me waking   135
and sleeping. Let me dream of nothing but dimpled cheeks, and
laughing lips, and flowing bowls. Venus be my star, and whoring
my house,° and, death, I defy thee. Thus sung Rosidore in the
urn.° But where, and when, with my fops' wives? Be quick. Thou
know'st my appointment with this unknown, and the minute's   140
precious.

TOURNON Why, I have contrived you the sweetest wight in the
world, if you dare.

NEMOURS Dare, and in a woman's cause! Why, I have no drop of
blood° about me, but must out in their service, and what matter   145
is't which way?

TOURNON Know, Poltrot's lady has informed me how Saint-André
walks in his sleep, and that her husband last night attempted to
cuckold him, that she watched and overheard the whole matter,

but Poltrot could not find the door before Saint-André returned. 150
She doubts not but he will try again tonight. Now, if you can nick
the time when Poltrot rises, and steal to her, ten to one but she'll
be glad to be revenged.

NEMOURS Or she would not have told thee the business. There
wants but speaking with her, taking her by the hand, and 'tis a 155
bargain.

    Enter Celia [and] Elianor, masked; Poltrot [and]
    Saint-André following

TOURNON Step, step aside. They are upon the hunt for you, and
their husbands have 'em in the wind.° Stand by a while to observe,
and I'll turn you loose upon 'em.

    [*Exeunt Tournon and Nemours*]

SAINT-ANDRÉ Ha, Tournon! By my honour, a prize. Let's board 160
'em.

POLTROT Be not too desperate, my little frigate, for I am that I am,°
a furious man of honour.

CELIA Now heaven defend us. What, will you give us a broadside?

ELIANOR Lord, how I dread the guns of the lower tier! 165

SAINT-ANDRÉ Such notable marksmen too—we never miss hitting
between wind and water.

CELIA I'll warrant they carry chain-shot. Pray heaven they do not
split us, sister.°

POLTROT Yield then, yield quickly, or no mercy. We have been so 170
shattered today already by two she-pirates, that we are grown
desperate.

ELIANOR But what alas have we done, that you should turn your
revenge upon us poor harmless innocents, that never wronged you,
never saw you before? 175

CELIA If you should deal unkindly with us, 'twould break our hearts,
for we are the gentlest things.

SAINT-ANDRÉ And we will use you so gently, so kindly, like little
birds. You shall never repent the loss of your liberty.

ELIANOR I'll warrant, sister, they'll put us in a cage, or tie us by the 180
legs.

POLTROT No, upon the word of a man of honour, your legs shall be
at liberty.

CELIA What, will you pinion our wings then, and let us hop up and
down the house? 185

SAINT-ANDRÉ Not in the house where we live, pretty soul, for
there's two ravenous sow-cats will eat you.

ELIANOR Your wives, you mean.

POLTROT Something like—two melancholy things that sit purring in
the chimney-corner and, to exercise their spite, kill crickets.   190

CELIA O, for God-sake keep us from your wives.

SAINT-ANDRÉ I'll warrant thee, little Rosamond,° safe from my
jealous Elianor.

POLTROT And if any wife in Europe dares but touch a hair of thee,
I say not much, but that wife were better be a widow.   195

ELIANOR But are your wives handsome and well-qualitied? For,
whatever you say to us, when you have had your will you'll home
at night, and for my part I cry, 'All or none'.

POLTROT And all thou shalt have, dear rogue. Never fear my wife's
beauty or good nature. They are things to her like saints and   200
angels, which she believes never were nor never will be. She's a
basin of water against lechery, and looks so sharp whenever I see
her, like vinegar she makes me sweat.

SAINT-ANDRÉ And mine's so fulsome, that a goat with the help of
cantharides would not touch her.   205

CELIA But then for their qualities—

SAINT-ANDRÉ Such scolds, like thunder they turn° all the drink in
the cellar.

POLTROT Such niggards, they eat kitchen-stuff and candles' ends.
Once indeed, raving mad, my wife seemed prodigal, for, a rat   210
having ate his way through an old cheese, she baited a trap for him
with a piece of paring. But, having caught him, by the lord she ate
him up without mercy, tail and all.

ELIANOR [aside, to Celia] Are they not even with us, sister?°

SAINT-ANDRÉ 'Tis hoped, though, the hangman will take 'em off of   215
our hands, for they are shrewdly suspected for witches. Mine
'noints herself every night, sets a broomstaff in the chimney, and
opens the window. For what purpose but to fly?

POLTROT Gad, and my wife has teats in the wrong place.° She's
warted all over like a pumpled orange.   220

CELIA Yet sure, gentlemen, you told these hags another story once,
and made as deep protestations to them as you do to us?

SAINT-ANDRÉ Never, by this hand. The salt souls fell in lust with us
and hauled us to matrimony like bears to the stake.

POLTROT Where they set a long black thing° upon us that cried,   225
'Have and hold'.

ELIANOR Put the question° they had been handsome, brought you
great portions, were pleasant and airy and willing to humour you—

Enter Nemours with the Vidame

NEMOURS Nay, then I can hold no longer. 'Sdeath, there's it, madam!
Willing! That willingness spoils all, my dear, my honey, my jewel.   230
It palls the appetite like sack at meals. Give me the smart, disdainful
she that, like brisk Champagne or sprightly Burgundy, makes me
smack my lips after she's down and long for t'other glass.

SAINT-ANDRÉ Nay, if your grace come in, there's no dallying.
[*Taking hold of Elianor*] I'll make sure of one.   235

POLTROT Nay, and for my part I am resolved to secure another.
[*Taking hold of Celia*] Come, madam, no striving, for I am like a
lion. When I lay hold, if the body come not willingly, I pull a
whole limb away.

NEMOURS Yes, madam, he speaks truth. Take it on my word who   240
am a rational creature: he is a great, furious, wild beast.

CELIA Pray heaven he be not a horned beast.° Is the monster
married?

VIDAME Yes, ladies, they are both married.

ELIANOR Married! For heaven sake, gentlemen, save us from the   245
cattle.

POLTROT Why, what, is the breeze° in your tails? 'Sdeath, ladies,
we'll not eat you.

CELIA Say you so? But we'll not trust you. I am sure you both look
hungrily.   250

VIDAME It may be their wives use 'em unkindly.

ELIANOR And the poor good-natured things take it to heart.

CELIA I swear 'tis pity. They have both promising looks.

NEMOURS Proceed, sweet souls; we'll defend you to death. Spare 'em
not.   255

ELIANOR Or it may be we mistake all this while, and their pitiful
looks are caused by loving too much.

VIDAME Right, madam; a little too uxorious. Ha, ha!

SAINT-ANDRÉ [*aside, to Poltrot*] Now have not I one word to say, but
stand to endure all jerks like a schoolboy with my shirt up.°   260

POLTROT I'll have one fling at 'em, though I die for't. [*To Elianor
and Celia*] Why, ladies, you'll overshoot yourselves at this rate.
Must we only be the butts to bear all your raillery? Methinks you
might spend one arrow at random and take off that daw that
chatters so near you.—Gad, and I think I paid 'em there.   265

CELIA Butts and daw! Let me never laugh again, if they be not witty
too. Why, you pleasant rogues! 'Slife, I could kiss 'em if they did
not stink of matrimony.

SAINT-ANDRÉ [*aside to Poltrot*] Mum, mum, mum. Did not I tell you
'twas a madness to speak to 'em? 270

ELIANOR They envy my friend too here, this pleasant companion.

CELIA This dear, agreeable person.

NEMOURS Ay, damme, madam, the rogues envy us.

ELIANOR What a gentle aspect!

CELIA How proper and airy!° 275

ELIANOR See, here's blood in this face.

VIDAME Pure blood, madam, at your service.

CELIA [*to Nemours*] Will you walk, dear sir? Give me your hand.

ELIANOR [*to the Vidame*] And me yours.

NEMOURS Come, you dear ravishing rogues.—Your servant, Mr 280
Butts.

VIDAME Gentle Mr Butts.

ELIANOR Adieu, sweet Mr Butts.

CELIA Witty Mr Butts. Ha, ha, ha!
Exeunt Nemours, the Vidame, Celia [and] Elianor

SAINT-ANDRÉ Well, I'll to a duchess. 285

POLTROT Lord, thou art always so high-flown. Hast thou never a
cast° countess for me?

SAINT-ANDRÉ Come along to the ball and thou shalt see. The Duke
of Nemours is the gallant tonight and treats at his palace, because
'tis the king's birthday. Let me see. What new fancy° for the 290
masquerade? O, I have it. Because the town is much taken with
fortune-telling, I'll act the dumb man, the highlander° that made
such a noise, and thou shalt be my interpreter. Come along, and
as we go I'll instruct thee in the signs.

POLTROT Dear rogue, let's practise a little before we stir—as, what 295
sign for lechery, because we may nick our wives?

SAINT-ANDRÉ Why thus. [*Demonstrating*] That's a glancing,°
squeezed eye. Or thus, for a moist hand. Or thus, for a whore in
a corner. Or thus, for downright cuckolding.

POLTROT Well, I swear this will be rare sport. And so, my damned 300
spouse, I am resolved to tickle her with a squeezed eye and a moist
hand—and a whore in a corner°—till she confess herself guilty of
downright cuckoldom; then, in revenge for her last impudence, sue
for a divorce,°

 And, holding to her face the flying label,° 305
 Call her in open court the Whore of Babel.°
Exeunt

3.2

[*The Prince of Cleves' palace*]

[*Enter*] *the Prince and Princess of Cleves*

PRINCE Madam, the king commands me to attend
His daughter into Spain, and further adds,
Because no princess rivals you in fame,
You will oblige the court in going with me.

PRINCESS My lord, I am prepared, and leave the court   5
With such a joy as would admit no bounds.

PRINCE As would admit no bounds! And why? Because
It takes you from the charms which you would shun.
This is a virtue of such height indeed,
As none but you can boast nor I deplore.   10
But, madam, rumour says the king intends
To join another with me.

PRINCESS   Who, my lord?

PRINCE 'Twas thought at first the Chevalier de Guise.°

PRINCESS He is your friend, nor could the king choose better.

PRINCE I say at first 'twas thought the Duke of Guise.   15
But I was since instructed by the queen,
That honour's fixed upon the Duke Nemours.

PRINCESS Nemours, my lord?

PRINCE   Most certain.

PRINCESS   For what reason?

PRINCE Because I moved the dauphin queen to gain him.

PRINCESS 'Twas rashly done, against your interest moved.   20

PRINCE Perhaps 'tis not too late yet to supplant him.

PRINCESS Do't then; be quick. Nemours will share your honours,
Eclipse your glory.

PRINCE   Ha! I must confess
The soldiers love him, and he bears the palm
Already from the marshals of the field.°   25

PRINCESS And in the court he's called the rising star.
You see each night at every entertainment
Where he moves, what troops of beauties follow,
How the queens praise him, and all eyes admire him.

PRINCE Ha, Chartres!

PRINCESS   Ah, my lord, what have I done?   30

PRINCE Nothing, my Chartres, but admire Nemours!

O heaven and earth! And if I had but patience
To hear you out, how had you lost yourself
On that eternal object of your love?
No, madam, no, 'tis false; 'tis not Nemours.°   35
'Twas my invention to find out the truth.
Your trouble has convinced me 'tis Nemours,
Which cursed discovery in another woman
I should have made by her too eager joy.
Why speak you not? You're shocked with your own virtue.   40
The resolution of your justice awes you,
Which cannot, dares not give itself the lie.

PRINCESS My lord, my love, my life. Alas, my Cleves!
     [Kneels]
O pity me! I know not what to answer.
I'm mortally ashamed. I'm on the rack.   45
But spare this humble passion. Take me with you,
Where I may never see a man again.

PRINCE O rise, my Chartres! Rise, if possible.
I'll force thee to be mine in spite of fate.
     [Raises her]
My constant martyrdom and deathless kindness,   50
My more than mortal patience in these sufferings,
Shall poise his noblest qualities. O heaven!°
No fear, my Chartres, though these sorrows fall,
That I suspect thy glory. Thou hast strength
To curb this passion in, that else may end us.   55
All that I ask thee is to bend thy heart.

PRINCESS I'll break it.

PRINCE   Turn it from Nemours, Nemours—
But, O, that name presents thy danger greater.
Look to thy honour then, and look to mine.
I ask it as thy lover and thy husband.
I beg it as a man whose life depends   60
Upon thy breath, that offers thee a heart
All bleeding with the wounds of mortal love,°
All hacked and gashed, and stabbed and mangled o'er—
And yet a heart so true, in spite of pain,
As ne'er yet loved, nor ever shall again.   65
    Exit the Prince of Cleves. Enter Irene

IRENE Ha, madam, speak. How is it with your heart?

PRINCESS As with a timorous slave, condemned to torments,

That still cries out, he cannot, will not bear it,
And yet bears on.
IRENE   Ah, madam, I would speak,   70
  If you could bear the dreadful news I bring.
PRINCESS Alas, thou canst not add to grief like mine.
IRENE May I demand then if you have not told
  The secret to your husband?
PRINCESS   Ha, Irene—
  Why dost thou ask?   75
IRENE Because but now—Tournon, a lady of the queen's,
  Told me 'tis blazed at court—Nemours confessed
  He is beloved by one of such nice virtue,°
  That, fearing lest the passion might betray her,
  She owned, confessed, and told it to her husband.   80
PRINCESS Death and despair! But does Nemours avow it?
IRENE He owned it to the Vidame, who again
  Told it to Madame Tournon, she to others.
  'Tis true, Nemours told not the lady's name,
  Nor would confess himself to be the party;   85
  But yet the court in general does believe it.
PRINCESS I am undone. My fame is lost for ever,°
  And death, Irene, must be my remedy.
  'Tis true indeed, I laid my bosom open.
  I showed my heart to that ungrateful Cleves,   90
  Who since, in dangerous search of him I love,
  To the eternal ruin of my honour,
  Has trusted a third person. But away.
  I hear his tread, and am resolved to tax him.
    [*Exit Irene.*] *Enter the Prince of Cleves*°
  Ah, sir, what have you done? If you must kill me,   95
  Are there not daggers, poison? But the jealous
  Are cruel still, and thoughtful in revenge;°
  And single death's too little. Must your will
  Of knowing names my duty durst not tell you
  Oblige you to betray me to another,   100
  So to divulge the secret of my soul,
  That the whole court must know it?
PRINCE   Ha! Know what?
  Know my dishonour? Have you told it then?
PRINCESS No, 'tis yourself; 'tis you revealed it, sir,
  To gain a confidant for more discovery.   105

A lady of the queen's just now declared it.
To your eternal shame you have divulged it.
She had it from the Vidame, sir, of Chartres,
And he from the Duke Nemours.

PRINCE   Nemours!
How, madam, said you? What, Nemours! Nemours!   110
Does Nemours know you love him? Hell and furies!
And that I know it too, and not revenge it!

PRINCESS That's yet to seek. He will not own himself°
To be concerned; he offers not at names.°
But yet 'tis found, 'tis known, believed by all.   115
He cannot hold it; 'twill be shortly posted°
That, Cleves, your wife's that cursed, dishonoured she
You told him of.

PRINCE   Is't possible I told him?
Peace, peace; and if it lies in human power
To reason calmly, tell me, murderess, tell me—   120
Compose that face of flushed hypocrisy,
And answer to a truth. Was it my interest
To speak of this? Was I not rather tied
To wish it buried in the grave in hell,
Whence it might never rise to blot my honour?   125
But you have seen him. By my hopes of heaven,
You have met and interchanged your secret souls;
On that complotted, since I bore so tamely
Your first confession, I should bear the latter.

PRINCESS Believe it if you please.   130

PRINCE   I must believe it.
This last proceeding has unmasked your soul.
He sees you every hour and knows you love him.
Nay, for your greater freedom, you have joined
To make this loathed, detested Cleves your stale.
Ha! I believed you might o'ercome this passion,   135
So well you knew to charm me with the show°
Of seeming virtue, till I lost my reason.

PRINCESS 'Tis likely, sir, it was but seeming virtue,
And you did ill to judge so kindly of me.
I was mistaken too in that confession,   140
Because I thought that you would do me justice.

PRINCE You were mistaken when you thought I would.
Sure you forgot that I was desperate,

Sentenced and doomed by fate, or rather damned
To love you to my grave—and could I bear   145
A rival? What, and when I was your husband,
And when you owned your passion to my face,
Confessed you loved me much, but loved him more?
Ha! Is not this enough to make me mad?

PRINCESS   You have the power to set all right again.   150
Why do you not end me?

PRINCE   No, I'll end myself.
My thoughts are grown too violent for my reason.
By this last usage, O, thou hast undone me.
I know not what—this ought not to be thine—°
I have offended and would sue for pardon.   155
But yet I blush; the treason is too gross.
After that most unnatural confession,
I wonder now that I have lived so long.
Confess and then divulge! Make me your bawd!
It scents too far; the god of love flies wide,°   160
He gets the wind, and stops the nose at this.
No more; farewell. False Chartres, false Nemours,
False world, false all, since Chartres is not true!
But you your wish with loved Nemours shall have,
And shortly see your husband in the grave.   165

          Exit [the Prince of Cleves]

PRINCESS (*alone*) False world, false Cleves, false Chartres, false
Nemours,
Farewell to all, a long and last farewell.
From all converse, to deserts let me fly,
And in some gloomy cave forgotten lie.
My bower at noon the shade of some old trees   170
With whistling winds to indulge my pomp of ease,°
And lulling murmurs rolled from neighbouring seas,
Where I may sometimes hasten to the shore
And to the rocks and waves my loss deplore,
Where when I feel my hour of fate draws on,   175
Lest the false world should claim a parting groan,
My mother's ghost may rise to fix my mind
And leave no thought of tenderness behind.

          [*Exit*]

4.1

[*The palace of Nemours*]

Music, songs, maskers, &c.° [*Enter*] *Nemours with music,*°
Celia

NEMOURS He has confessed to me he intends to cuckold Saint-André
when he walks in his sleep. Therefore, if love should inspire me
to nick the opportunity, I hope you will not bar the door which
your husband opens.

CELIA Ingrateful monster!   5

NEMOURS Ingrateful, that's certain, and it lies in your power to make
him a monster.°

CELIA I dare not—

NEMOURS What?

CELIA Trust you.   10

NEMOURS Nay, then I am sure thou wilt. Let me but in to show the
power you have over me.

CELIA As how, my lord?

NEMOURS Why, when I have thee in my arms, by heaven I'll quit
my joys at thy desire.   15

CELIA That will indeed be a perfect trial of your love. Come then
through the garden backstairs, and when you see the candle put
out, thrust open the door.

NEMOURS By heaven, I'll eat thy hand. Thou dear, sweet seducer,
how it fires my fancy to steal into a garden, to rustle through the   20
trees, to stumble up a narrow pair of backstairs, to whisper through
the hole of the door, to kiss it open, and fall into thy arms with a
flood of joy.

CELIA Farewell; the company comes. I must leave you a while, to
engage with my husband. You'll fall asleep before the hour.   25

NEMOURS If I do, the very transport of imagination shall carry me
in my sleep to thy bed, and I'll wake in the act.

 Exit Celia

So, there's one in the fernbrake; and if she stir till morning, I have
lost my aim.°

 Enter Tournon in the habit of a Huguenot,° [*Marguerite,*
 masked, and others]

But now—why, what have we here? A Huguenot whore, by this   30
light! Have I the forward° brisk she that promised me the ball

assignation, that said there was nothing like slipping out of the crowd into a corner, breathing short an ejaculation,° and returning as if we came from church. Let me see. I'll put on my mask, fling my cloak over my shoulder, and view 'em as they pass.—Not thou nor thou—   35

TOURNON Ah, thou unclean person, have I hunted thee there like a hart from the mountains to the valleys, and thou wouldst not be found?° Verily, thou hast been amongst the daughters of the Philistines.° Nay, if you are innocent, stand before me, and reply   40
to the words of my mouth.

NEMOURS I shall, truly.

TOURNON Say then: hast thou not defiled thyself with any Delilah,° since last you felt upon my neck and loved much?

NEMOURS Nay, verily.   45

TOURNON Have you not overheated your body with adulterate wines? Have you not been at a play, nor touched fruit after the lewd orange-women?°

NEMOURS I am unpolluted.

TOURNON And yet methinks there is not the same colour in your   50
cheeks, nor does the spirit dance in your eye as formerly. Why do you not approach me? (*Unmasking*)

NEMOURS Tournon turned heretic! Why, thou dear rascal, this is such a new frolic, that, though I am engaged as deep as damnation to another, thou shalt not 'scape me.   55

          Marguerite claps him on the shoulder

MARGUERITE I love a man that keeps the commandment of his word.

NEMOURS And I a woman that breaks hers with her husband, yet loves her neighbour as herself.° I would fain be in private with you.

          [*Exit Tournon*]

MARGUERITE° And I with you, because I am resolved never to see   60
you more.

NEMOURS Never to see me more? The reason?

MARGUERITE Because I hate you.

NEMOURS And yet I believe you love me too, because you are precise to the minute.   65

MARGUERITE True; yet I hate you justly, heartily, and maliciously.

NEMOURS By Gad, and I'll love thee as heartily, justly, and maliciously as thou canst love me for thy blood. Come away, riddle, and I'll unfold thee.

Exeunt [Marguerite and Nemours. Enter Poltrot [and]
Saint-André disguised, with Elianor [and] Celia coming up to
'em

ELIANOR But is it true indeed that your friend can tell all the   70
actions of our life past, present, and to come, yet cannot speak one
word?

POLTROT O he's infallible! Why, what, did you never hear of your
second-sight° men, your dumb highlanders that tell fortunes? Why,
you would think the devil in hell were in him, he speaks so exactly.°   75

ELIANOR I thought you had said he was dumb?

POLTROT Right; but I am his interpreter, and when the fit comes on
him, he blows through me like a trunk,° and straight I become his
speaking trumpet.

CELIA Pray, sir, may not I have my fortune told me too?   80

POLTROT Ay, an there were a thousand of you, he will run you 'em
over like the criss-cross-row° and never miss a tittle. He shall tell
ye his name that cried, 'God bless you', when you sneezed last, tell
you when you winked last, when and where you scratched last, and
where you sat o' Saturday.   85

ELIANOR Pray let him tell us then—for we are sisters—our tempers
and conditions, whether married or unmarried, with all the
impertinences thereunto belonging.°

POLTROT I'll speak to him.—Son of the sun, and emperor of the
stars!   90

SAINT-ANDRÉ Ha, ha!

POLTROT Look ye, look ye; he's pleased to tell you. But you must
go near him, for he must look in your hand, touch your face,
breasts, and wherever else he pleases.

Saint-André makes horns with both his hands, puts his finger
in his mouth and laughs

In nomine domini bomine,° I protest I am confounded. Well, ladies,   95
I could not have thought it had been in you. But 'tis certainly true,
and I must out with it. First he says, you are both married, you
are both libidinous beyond example, and your husbands are the
greatest cornutoes° in Christendom.

ELIANOR and CELIA Indeed.   100

POLTROT Ay, indeed, indeed and indeed. He says you are a couple
of Messalinas,° and the stews cannot satisfy you. He says your
thoughts are swelled with a carnosity. Nay, you have the green
sickness of the soul, which runs upon nothing but neighing°
stallions, churning boars, and bellowing bulls.   105

CELIA O, I confess, I confess. But for heaven sake, dear sir, let it not take air,° for then we are both undone.

ELIANOR O, undone, undone, sir, if our husbands should know it, for they are a couple of the jealousest, troublesome, impertinent cuckolds alive.   110

POLTROT [*aside*] Alack, alack! O Jezebel!° But I will have my eunuchs fling her from the window, and the dogs shall eat her.

CELIA But pray, sir, ask him how many times—

POLTROT What, how many times you have cuckolded 'em?

ELIANOR Spare our modesty. You make the blood so flush in our   115
faces.

POLTROT [*aside*] But by Jove I'll let it out. I'll hold her by the muzzle and stick her like a pig.

CELIA Will you speak to him, sir?

POLTROT See; he understands you without it. He says your iniqui-   120
ties are innumerable, your fornications like the hairs of your head, and your adulteries like the sands on the sea-shore; that you are all fish downward;° that Lot's wife° is fresh to you; and that when you were little girls of seven, you were so wanton, your mothers tied your hands behind you.   125

ELIANOR All this we confess to be true. But we confess too, if fate had found out any sort of tools but those leaden rogues, our husbands—

CELIA Whose wits are as dull as their appetites—

ELIANOR Mine such a utensil as is not fit to wedge a block—   130

CELIA Nor mine the beetle to drive him.°

SAINT-ANDRÉ [*removing his disguise*] Nay, then 'tis time to uncase and be revenged.

POLTROT [*following suit*] Hark you, strumpet—

ELIANOR Ha, ha, ha! Are you not fitted finely?°   135

CELIA You must turn fortune-tellers, must you?

ELIANOR And think we could not know you?

CELIA Well, gentlemen, shall homely Beck go down with you at last?

POLTROT But didst thou know me then indeed?

CELIA As if that sweet voice of yours could be disguised in any shape.   140

POLTROT Nay, I confess I have a whirl in my voice, a warble that is particular.

ELIANOR And what say you, sir? Shall musty wife come into grace again?

SAINT-ANDRÉ She shall, and here's my hand on't. All friends, Nell.   145
And when I leave thee again, may I be cuckold in earnest.

POLTROT [*aside*] Certain as I live, all this proceeded from his lady; my dreaming cuckold wife could never think on't. Well, I am resolved this very night, when he rambles in his sleep, to watch him, slip to his wife and say nothing. [*To the others*] Hey! Come, come; where are these dancers? A little diversion, and then for bed.   150

[*Dancers and Musicians perform a*] *Dance*. [*Enter Tournon*]

TOURNON [*aside*] (*to Elianor*) I have locked the Vidame in your closet, who will be sure to watch your husband's rising. Therefore, be not surprised.

Exit Tournon

SAINT-ANDRÉ Come, well, let's away to bed.   155

ELIANOR And what then?

SAINT-ANDRÉ Nay, Gad, that I can't tell, for, what with dancing, singing, fencing, and my last duchess, I am very drowsy.

POLTROT And so am I. Perhaps our wives have given us opium, lest we should disturb 'em in the night.   160

ELIANOR [*aside, to Celia*] Don't these men deserve to be fitted?°

CELIA They do, and fortune grant they may. Hear us, O hear us, good heaven, for we pray heartily.

Exeunt [*Poltrot, Saint-André, Celia and Elianor*], *as
Nemours and Marguerite enter*

NEMOURS Was ever man so blessed with such possession,
Thou ebbing, flowing, ravishing, racking joy!   165
A skin so white and soft, the yielding mould
Lets not the fingers stay upon the dint,
But from the beauteous dimples slips 'em down
To pleasures that must be without a name.
Yet hands, and arms, and breasts we may remember,   170
And that which I so love, no smelling art,°
But sweet by nature, as just peeping violets
Or opening buds.

MARGUERITE   Then you do love me?

NEMOURS O, I could die methinks this very hour,
But for the luscious hopes of thousand more,   175
And all like these. Yet when I must go out,
Let it be thus, with beauty laughing by me,
Songs, lutes, and canopies, while I sacrifice°
To thee the last, dear, ebbing drop of love.
But show me now that face.   180

MARGUERITE No; you dissemble. You say the same thing to everyone you meet. I thought once indeed to have fixed my heart

upon you; but I'm off again, and am resolved you shall never see
me.

NEMOURS You dally. Come, by all the kindness past.   185

MARGUERITE Swear then.

NEMOURS What?

MARGUERITE Never to touch your dear domestic she,
That lives in shades to all the world but me.
Do you guess I know you now?   190

NEMOURS I do, and swear. But are these equal terms: that you shall
never touch a man but me?

MARGUERITE I will. But how can you convince me? Oaths with you
libertines of honour are to little purpose.

NEMOURS But this must satisfy thee. There is more pleasure in thee   195
after enjoyment than in her and all womankind before it. Thou
hast inspiration, ecstasy, and transport, all these bewitching joys
that make men mad.

MARGUERITE (*unmasking*) And thou villainy, treachery, perjury, all
those monstrous, diabolical arts that seduce young virgins from   200
their innocent homes, to set 'em on the highway to hell and
damnation.

NEMOURS Ha, ha! My Marguerite! Is't possible?

MARGUERITE Call me not yours, nor think of me again.
I am convinced you're traitors all alike,   205
And from this hour renounce you—
Not but I'll be revenged.°
Yes, I will try the joys of life like you,
But not with men of quality, you devils of honour.
No, I will satisfy   210
My pride, disdain, rage and revenge more safely;
By all the powers of heaven and earth, I will.
I'll change my loving, lying, tinsel lord
For an obedient, wholesome, drudging fool.°

NEMOURS Why, this will make the matter easy to both.   215
Take you your ramble, madam, and I'll take mine.°
But is't possible for one of your nice taste
To bed a fool?

MARGUERITE   To choose, to choose, my lord.
A fool! Now, by my will and pride of heart,
There's freedom, fancy and creation in't—°   220
He truckles to the frown and cries, 'Forgive me'—
Besides the moulding of him without blushing.

And what would woman more? Now view the other,
Your man of sense that vaunts despotic power,
That reels precisely home at break of day,   225
Thunders the house, brains half the family,
Cries, 'Where's my whore? What, will she stew till doomsday?';
When she appears and kindly goes to help him,
Roars out, 'A shop, a walking-shop of scents,
Flavours of physic and the clammy bath,   230
The stench of orange-flowers, the devil pulvillio!
These, these', he cries, 'are the blessed husband's joys!'

NEMOURS I swear, most natural and unaffected. Ha, ha!

MARGUERITE But if he chance to use her civilly,
Take heed. There's covert malice in his smiles.   235
Millions to one, the villain has been whoring,
And comes to try experiments on her,
Besides a thousand under-plots and crosses.°
Prescribing silence still where'er he comes,
'No chat', he cries, 'of colours, points or fashions'.   240

NEMOURS Preach on, divine. Ha, ha!

MARGUERITE 'Let me not hear you ask my sickly lady
Whether she found obstructions at the waters.'°

NEMOURS Fie, that's obscene.

MARGUERITE Thus damns the affectation of our prattle,   245
And swears he'll gag the clack, or—what is worse—

NEMOURS Nay, hold!

MARGUERITE   Send for the new-found lock.°

NEMOURS   What, mad?

MARGUERITE Do, villain, traitor—
Contrive this mischief, if thou canst, for me.
Send thou the padlock; but I'll find the key.   250
        Exit [Marguerite]

NEMOURS Where goes the partridge on the purring wing?
Yet when I see my time I must recall her. For she has many
admirable things in her, such as, if I gain not the Princess of
Cleves, may fix me to her,° without nauseating the vice of
constancy.   255
        Enter Bellamore
Ha, Bellamore! What news, my dear? Ha, hast thou found her?
Speak.

BELLAMORE I have.

NEMOURS   Where, how, when and by what means?

BELLAMORE After I had inquired after the prince's health,
　　I asked a woman of his lady, who told me   260
　　She was retired into the great bower in the garden.
NEMOURS The very place where first I saw and loved her,
　　When, after I had saved the prince's life,
　　He brought me late one evening to the view.
　　There love and friendship first began.   265
　　My love remains—and friendship, as
　　Much as man can have for his cuckold.
　　Nay, I know not that man upon earth I love so well, or could take
　　so much from, as this hopeful Prince of Cleves. Didst thou see her
　　in the garden?   270
BELLAMORE My lord, I did, where she appeared like her that gave
　　Actaeon horns,° with all her nymphs about her, busy in tying knots
　　which she took from baskets of ribbons that they brought her; and
　　methought she tied and untied 'em so prettily, as if she had been
　　at cross-questions, or knew not what she did. Her face, her neck   275
　　and arms quite bare—
NEMOURS No more. If I live I'll see her tonight, for the heroic vein
　　comes upon me. Death and the devil, what shall become of the
　　backstair lady then? Hark thee, Bellamore. Take this key. Dost
　　thou hear, rogue? Go to Saint-André's house, through the garden   280
　　up the backstairs, push open the door and be blessed. Hell! Can't
　　I be in two places at once? Hark thee. Give her this [*embracing and
　　kissing Bellamore*], and this, and this; and when thou bitest her with
　　a parting blow,° sigh out, 'Nemours'.
BELLAMORE I'll do't.   285
　　　　　Enter the Prince of Cleves
NEMOURS Go to Tournon for the rest. She'll instruct thee in the
　　management. Away!
　　　　　Exit Bellamore
　　Ha! He comes up but slowly; yet he sees me.
　　Perhaps he's jealous. Why, then I'm jealous too.
　　Hypocrisy and softness, with all the arts of woman,   290
　　Tip my tongue.
PRINCE I come, my lord, to ask you if you love me.
NEMOURS Love thee, my Cleves! By heaven, ere yet I saw thee,
　　Thus were my prayers still offered to the fates:
　　'If I must choose a friend, grant me, ye powers,   295
　　The man I love may seize my heart at once.
　　Guide him the perfect temper of yourselves,°

With every manly grace and shining virtue.
Add yet the bloom of beauty to his youth,
That I may make a mistress of him too—'   300
PRINCE O heaven!
NEMOURS   'That at first view our souls may kindle
And, like two tapers, kindly mix their beams.'°
I knelt and prayed and wept for such a blessing,
And they returned me more than I could ask,
All that was good or great or just in thee.   305
PRINCE You say you love me. I must make the proof,
For you have brought it to a doubt.
NEMOURS   In what?
PRINCE In this: you have not given me all your heart.
You muse of late. Even on my bridal-day
I saw you sit with a too-thoughtful brow.   310
You sighed and hung your head upon your hand.
Nay, in the midst of laughter,
You started, blushed and cried 'twas wondrous well,
And yet you knew not what. Speak like a friend.
What is the cause, my lord?   315
NEMOURS Shall I deal plainly with you? I'm not well.
PRINCE I do believe it. How happened the distemper?
NEMOURS It is too deep to search, nor can I tell you.
PRINCE Then you're no friend.
Should Cleves thus answer to Nemours, 'I cannot'?   320
Say rather that you will not trust a man
You do not love.
NEMOURS   By heaven I do.
PRINCE By heaven you do? Yet 'tis too deep to search
For such a shallow friend.
NEMOURS   Of all mankind
You ought not—
PRINCE   Nay, the rest.
NEMOURS   It is not fit.   325
Be satisfied. I'll bear it to my grave
Whate'er it be.
PRINCE   You are in love, my lord.
And if you do not swear—but where's the need?
You start, you change, you are another man.
You blush, you're all constraint, you turn away.   330
NEMOURS Why, take it then. 'Tis true, I am in love,

In torture, racks, in all the hells of love,
Of hopeless, restless and eternal love.

PRINCE Her name, my lord?

NEMOURS   Her name, my lord, to you?

PRINCE To me? Confusion, plagues and death upon me!   335
Why not to me? And wherefore did you say,
Of all mankind I ought not? There you stopped,
But would have said, 'To pry into this business'.
Yet speak to ease the troubles of my soul.
By all our friendship, by the life thou gav'st me,   340
I do conjure thee: thunder in my ears°
'Tis Chartres that thou lov'st, Chartres my wife.

NEMOURS Your wife, my lord?

PRINCE My wife, my lord, and I must have you own it.

NEMOURS I will not tell you, sir, who 'tis I love.   345
Yet think me not so base, were it your wife,
That all the subtlest wit of earth or hell
Should make me vent a secret of that nature
To any man on earth, much less to you.

PRINCE Yet you could basely tell it to the Vidame,   350
And he to all the court. But I waste time.
By all the boiling venom of my passion,
I'll make you own it ere we part. Dispatch!
Say thou hast whored my wife. Damnation on me!
Pronounce me cuckold.   355

NEMOURS   But then I give myself the lie,
Who told you just before I would not speak,
Though I had done it—which I swear I have not.
Beside, I fear you are going mad.

PRINCE [drawing his sword] Draw then and make it up,   360
For if thou dost not own what I demand,
What you both know and have complotted on me,
Though neither will confess, I swear again
That one of us must fall.

NEMOURS   Then take my life.

PRINCE I will, by heaven, if thou refuse me justice.   365
Draw then, for if thou dost not I will kill thee,
And tell my wife thou basely didst confess
Thy guilt at last, in hopes to save thy life.

NEMOURS That is a blast indeed that honour shrinks at.
        [Nemours draws his sword]

Therefore I draw, but—O, be witness, heaven— 370
With such a trembling hand and bleeding heart,
As if I were to fight against my father.
Therefore I beg thee by the name of friend—
Which once with half this suit would have dissolved thee—°
I beg thee, gentle Cleves, to hold thy hand. 375

PRINCE I'm deaf as death that calls for one or both.
    [They fight.] The Prince of Cleves is disarmed. Nemours gives
    him his sword again

NEMOURS Then give it me. I arm thy hand again
Against my heart, against this heart that loves thee.
Thrust then, for, by the blood that bears my life,
Thou shalt not know the name of her I love— 380
Not but I swear upon the point of death,°
Your wife's as clear from me as heaven first made her.°

PRINCE No more, my lord. You've given me twice my life.

NEMOURS Are you not hurt?

PRINCE   Alas, 'tis not so well.
I have no wound but that which honour makes. 385
And yet there's something cold upon my heart.
I hope 'tis death, and I shall shortly pay you
With Chartres' love, for you deserve her better.

NEMOURS No, sir, you shall not. You shall live, my lord,
And long enjoy your beauteous, virtuous bride. 390
You shall, dear prince. Why are you then so cold?

PRINCE I cannot speak—
But thus, and thus, there's something rises here.°

NEMOURS I'll wait you home. Nay, shake these drops away,°
And hang upon my arm.

PRINCE   I will do anything, 395
So you will promise never to upbraid me.

NEMOURS I swear I will not.

PRINCE   But will you love me too
As formerly?

NEMOURS   I swear, far more than ever.

PRINCE Thou know'st my nature soft. Yet, O, such love,
Such love as mine, and injured as I thought,
Would spleen the gall-less turtle, would it not?° 400

NEMOURS It would, by heaven. (*Weeping*) You make a woman of me.

PRINCE Why, anything thou say'st to humour me,
  Yet it is kind, and I must love these tears.

I hope my heart will break, and then we're even.   405
Yet if this cruel love thy Cleves should kill,
Remember after death thou lov'st me still.
    Exeunt

4.2

[The palace of Saint-André]
Enter Tournon with the Vidame

TOURNON So. Let that corner be your post, and as soon as ever you
see Saint-André come stalking in his dream, slip to his lady; and
when you have agreed upon the writings,° I'll be ready to bring
you off with a witness.°

VIDAME Thou dear, obliging—   5

TOURNON No more o' that. Away!
    [The Vidame goes to his waiting-post]
Mark but how easily those that are gifted with discretion bring
things about. In the name of goodness let men and women have
their risks, but still be careful of the main.° Here's a hot-headed
lord goes mad for a prating girl, treats her, presents her,° flames   10
for her, dies for her, till the fool complies for pure love and, when
the business fails, is forced to live at last by the love of his
footmen.° But she that makes a firm bargain is commonly thought
a great soul, for my lord, having consider'd on't, thinks her a
person of depth and so resolves to have it out of her.° But why do   15
I talk so myself, when there's something to do? Certainly I
should have made a rare speaker° in a parliament of women, or a
notable head to a female jury, when his lordship gravely puts the
question, whether it be *satis* or *non satis* or *nunquam satis*, and we
bring it in *ignoramus*.° Ha, but who comes here? I must attend for   20
Bellamore.
    [Exit Tournon.] Enter Poltrot, [followed by] Celia overhearing

POLTROT My wife and I went to bed together, and I'll warrant
full she was of expectation, so white and clean, and much inclined
to laugh, and lay at her full length, as who would say, 'Come eat
me'.   25

CELIA *[aside]* Said she so, sweet sir?

POLTROT Not a bit, by the lord! Not I, not I!

CELIA *[aside]* Alas! Nice gentleman!

POLTROT A farmer would say this was barbarously done, because he
loves beef; but I have plover in reserve.° Ha, Saint-André! Hark,   30
I hear him bustle. O lord, how my heart goes pit-a-pat! Nay, I
dreamt last night I was gelt.

    Enter Saint-André in his sleep

'Tis he, 'tis he. By the twilight I see him.

    The Vidame goes in

Ay, now the politic head goes. It shall be branched° by and by.
What was that stop for? There's neither gate nor stile in your way.   35
Now, by that sudden stretch, he seems as if he would take a jump
or practise on the high rope.° O, your humble servant, sir. I'll but
do a little business for you and be with you again. Nay, look you,
sir, I have as many bobs as Democritus when he cried, 'Poor jack!'°
There's more pride in a Puritan's band, short hair, and cap   40
pinched, than under a king's crown. 'Poor jack!' Citizens, citizens,
look to your wives—the courtiers come. Look to 'em; they'll do
'em.° Look to 'em; they'll do 'em. 'Poor jack!'

    Exit Poltrot

SAINT-ANDRÉ [*in his sleep*] Ha, ha! You'll tickle me to death. Nay,
prithee, Pen, your mistress will hear us. Thou art the wantonest   45
rogue.

    Enter Tournon with Bellamore

TOURNON Madam.

CELIA Here's.°

TOURNON Here's a thief I took in your chamber.

BELLAMORE Ah, madam, retire for a moment, and I'll make you the   50
whole confession.

CELIA Confess, and you know what follows.° However, I am resolved
to hear what you can say for yourself.

    [*Exeunt Bellamore and Celia in one direction, and Tournon
    in another*]

SAINT-ANDRÉ [*in his sleep*] 'Nay, pish, nay, fie, sweet-heart.'
But I'll kiss you if I can.   55
'I did not take you for to be
Such a kind of a man.'

    Enter Poltrot

'But I'll go call my mother as loud as I can cry.
Why, mother, mother, mother! Out upon you! Fie!'

POLTROT O lord! O lord! I had like to have trod upon a serpent that   60
would have bit me to death. I went to take up the clothes as gently
as I could for my life, when a great, huge, hoarse voice flew in my

face with 'Damme, you son of a whore, I'll cut your throat'. You
may guess I withdrew, for, o' my conscience, the fright had almost
made me unclean. But I'll to my own spouse; and if the lord be   65
pleased to bring me off safe this bout, I'll never, never go
a–cuckold–making again while my eyes are open.

    Exit [*Poltrot*]

SAINT-ANDRÉ [*in his sleep*] Hark, my wife's coming upstairs. Help up
with my breeches. So, so smoothe the bed. What damned luck's
this! So, fall a-rubbing the room again.—Hark you, wife. Celia has   70
been upon the hunt for you all this day. She's below in the garden.
Go, go! We'll kiss when you come back.—Now, sirrah, now, you
rogue, she's gone. Come, come, lose not your opportunity. I'll keep
on my breeches for fear. Ay? No, no, not upon the bed. Pish!
Against the back of this chair. Won't it? How can you tell? Try.   75
I'll buy thee a new gown, and a fan, and a laced petticoat, and pay
thee double wages. O, thou dear, pretty, soft, sweet, wriggling
rogue! What, wouldst thou dodge me? Gad, but I'll have thee.
Gad, but I'll catch thee. Ay, and have at thee again and again.

    Exit [*Saint-André.*] *Enter Poltrot*

POLTROT Was ever man of honour thus unfortunately met with? I   80
went into my chamber and trod as softly as a half-starved mouse,
for fear of waking my cat, when, coming close to my bedside,
methought it rocked to and fro like a great cradle, and the clothes
heaved as if some beast lay blowing there. But the beast was by the
bedside, it seems. Yes, I am—and who can help it?—as very a   85
cornuto as e'er was grafted. I heard my beloved wife too—the
plagues of Egypt° on her!—speak so lovingly and angrily together.
'Nay, prithee, my dear. Nay, now you are tiresome.° I shall be
ashamed to look you in the face again!' Why, how will she look
upon me then? O lord, O lord, what shall I do? Shall I stand thus   90
like a cuckoldly son of a whore, with my horns in my pocket, and
not be revenged?

    Enter Saint-André

But here comes as very a cuckold as myself. I am resolved to wake
him, and we'll fall upon 'em together.—'Alloo,° Saint-André,
Saint-André!   95

SAINT-ANDRÉ [*in his sleep*] 'Ti-'ti-'tis im-im-im-possible I-I-I should
be the man, fo-fo-for I cannot speak a plain word.

POLTROT You're a cuckold, a cuckold, a cuckold.

SAINT-ANDRÉ [*in his sleep*] Why, lo-lo-look you, I said it co-co-could
not be me, for, sir, I, all the world knows, I am no cu-cu-cu-ckold. 100

POLTROT Wake, wake, I say, or I'll shake the bones out of your
body. Your horns are a-growing, your bed is a-going, your heifer's
a-ploughing.°

SAINT-ANDRÉ [*in his sleep*] Why, let her plo-plo-plough on. If the
se-se-seed be well sown, we shall have a good cro-crop.   105

POLTROT Worse and worse. Why, then I will roar out directly and
raise the neighbours.—Help! Ho, help! Murder, murder! Fire, fire,
fire! Cuckoldom, cuckoldom! Thieves! Murder! Rapes! Cuckoldom!
> *Enter the Vidame and Bellamore. The Vidame comes up to*
> *Poltrot, shoots off a pistol. Saint-André and Poltrot fall down*
> *together. Tournon enters with Elianor and Celia.° Tournon*
> *leads off the Vidame and Bellamore*

CELIA Thieves, thieves! Ho! Jacques! Pedro! Thomas!
> [*Enter Servants*]

ELIANOR Thieves, thieves! Wake, wake, my lord!   110

SAINT-ANDRÉ (*waking*) Why, what a devil's the matter? Where
am I?

ELIANOR O, you'll never leave this ill habit of walking in your sleep.
'Tis a mercy we had not all been murdered. You went down in
your shirt, sir, opened the door, and let in rogues that had like to   115
have cut all our throats. But, for the future, I am resolved to tie
you to me with the bed-cord rather than endure this.

SAINT-ANDRÉ Where's Poltrot?

CELIA Murdered, sir! Here, here, here! One of the villains discharged
a pistol just in his belly.   120

SAINT-ANDRÉ Shot in the guts! Lord bless us!—Here, Thomas, a
light! Light, light!—Shot in the guts, say you?

POLTROT O, O! Lower, lower, lower! Feel, feel, search me, lower,
lower!

SAINT-ANDRÉ Cold hereabouts! Let's bear him to his bed, and send   125
for a surgeon.
> [*Saint-André and the Servants lift Poltrot*]

POLTROT Softly, softly, softly! [*To Celia*] Come not near me,
crocodile.° O, O!

SAINT-ANDRÉ Unhappy chance! Nowhere but just in the guts?

POLTROT Yes, yes, yes. In the head too. In the head, man, in the   130
head. Nay, and let me tell you, you had best search your own. But
bear me off or I shall swoon. I feel something trickle, trickle in my
breeches. O, O, O!
> *Exeunt*

4.3

[*The Prince of Cleves' palace*]
Enter Nemours; Pedro listening

NEMOURS Alas, poor prince! I protest the violence of his passion has
cast him in a fever. He dies of it. And how then? Shall I marry the
Princess of Cleves, or stick to Marguerite as we are? For 'tis most
certain she has rare things in her, which I found by my last
experiment; and I love her more than ever, almost to jealousy.   5
Besides, Tournon tells me the dauphin begins to buzz about her
again; and who knows but in this heat of hers, as she says, she will
hang herself out to sale? But he may nick the time and buy her. I
like not that. No, I'll throw boldly, clear the table if I can.° If not,
'tis but at last forswearing play, shake off my new acquaintance,   10
and be easy with my reserve.
      [*Music from offstage*]
Hark, I am just upon the bower. Music!

PEDRO [*aside*] I have hitherto obeyed my master's order, but I'm
resolved to dog him till he's lodged.

NEMOURS Now do I know the precise° will call me damned rogue   15
for wronging my friend, especially such a soft, sweet-natured friend
as this gentle prince. Verily, I say they lie in their throats. Were the
gravest of 'em in my condition, and thought it should never be
known, they would rouse up the spirit, cast the dapper cloak,° leave
off their humming and haing, and fall to like a man of honour.   20
      Exit [*Nemours*]

PEDRO I'll face him° till he enters the bower, and then call my lord.
      Exit

4.4

The bower. Lights
[*Enter*] *the Princess of Cleves* [*and*] *Irene*

SONG

> *Lovely Selina, innocent and free°*
> *From all the dangerous arts of love,*
> *Thus in a melancholy grove*

Enjoyed the sweetness of her privacy,
Till th'envious gods, designing to undo her,° 5
Dispatched the swain, not unlike them, to woo her.
It was not long ere the design did take.
A gentle youth, born to persuade,
Deceived the too, too easy maid.
Her scrip and garlands soon she did forsake 10
And rashly told the secrets of her heart,
Which the fond man would ever more impart.
'False Florimel, joy of my heart', said she
' 'Tis hard to love and love in vain,
To love and not be loved again.° 15
And why should love and prudence disagree?
Pity, ye powers that sit at ease above,
If e'er you knew what 'tis to be in love'.

PRINCESS Alas, Irene, I do believe Nemours
  The man thou represents him. Yet, O heaven, 20
  And O my heart, in spite of my resolves,
  Spite of those matchless virtues of my husband,
  I love the man my reason bids me hate.
  Yet grant me some few hours, ye saints, to live,
  That I may try what innocence so armed 25
  As mine with vows can do in such a cause!
  The war's begun, the war of love and virtue,
  And I am fixed to conquer or to die.
IRENE Your fate is hard, and since you honoured me
  With the important secret of your life, 30
  I've laboured for the remedy of love.°
PRINCESS I must to death own thee my better angel.
  Thou know'st the strugglings of my wounded soul,
  Hast seen me strive against this lawless passion,
  Till I have lain like slaves upon the rack, 35
  My veins half burst, my weary eyeballs fixed,
  My brows all covered with big drops of sweat,
  Which strangling grief wrung from my tortured brain.
IRENE Alas, I weep to see you thus again.
PRINCESS Thou hast heard me curse the hour, when first I saw 40
  The fatal, charming face of loved Nemours,
  Hast heard the death-bed counsel of my mother.
  Yet what can this avail, spite of my soul,

The nightly warnings from her dreadful shroud?°
I love Nemours. I languish for Nemours.   45
And when I think to banish him my breast,
My heart rebels, I feel a gorging pain
That chokes me up, tremblings from head to foot—
A shog of blood and spirits, madmen's fears,
Convulsions, gnawing griefs and angry tears.   50
     Enter Nemours
Ha, but behold! My lord!
NEMOURS   O, pardon me.
Spare me a minute's space and I am gone.
PRINCESS Is this a time, sir?
NEMOURS   O, I must speak or die.
PRINCESS Die then, ere thus presume to violate
The honour of your friend, your own and mine.   55
NEMOURS Yet hear me, and I swear by all things sacred
Never to see you more.
PRINCESS   Speak then—and keep your word.
     [*Enter the Prince of Cleves above*]°
PRINCE [*aside*] Horror and death!
NEMOURS Did you but know what 'tis to love like me,   60
Without a dawn of bliss to dream all day,
To pass the night in broken sleeps away,
Tossed in the restless tides of hopes and fears,
With eyes for ever running o'er with tears;
To leave my couch and fly to beds of flowers,   65
T'invoke the stars, to curse the dragging hours,
To talk like madmen to the groves and bowers.
Could you know this, yet blame my tortured love,
If thus it throws my body at your feet?
     [*Kneels before her*]°
O, fly not hence.   70
Vouchsafe but just to view me in despair.
I ask not love, but pity from the fair.
     [*Exit the Prince of Cleves*]
PRINCESS O heavens, inspire my heart.
NEMOURS   The heavenly powers
Accept the poorest sacrifice we bring.
A slave to them's as welcome as a king.   75
Behold a slave that glories in your chains.
Ah, with some show of mercy view my pains.

Your piercing eyes have made their splendid way,
Where lightning could not pass.
Even through my soul their pointed lustre goes   80
And sacred smart upon my spirit throws.
Yet I your wounds with as much zeal desire,
As sinners that would pass to bliss through fire.
Yes, madam, I must love you to my death;
I'll sigh your name with my last gasp of breath.   85

PRINCESS No more. I have heard you, sir, as you desired.
    Enter the Prince of Cleves [and Pedro below, unobserved by
    the Princess of Cleves and Nemours]
Reply not, but withdraw, if possible.
Fix to your word, and let us trust our fates.
Be gone, I charge you. Speak not, but retire.
    Exit Nemours

PRINCE Excellent woman, and, O, matchless friend!   90
Love, friendship, honour, poison, daggers, death—
    [The Prince] falls

PRINCESS O heaven! Irene, help! Help the prince my lord.—
My dearest Cleves, wake from this dream of death,
And hear me speak.

PRINCE   Curse on my disposition
That thus permits me bear the wounds of honour!   95
And, O, thou foolish, gentle, love-sick heart,
Why didst thou let thy hand from stabbing both?°

PRINCESS Behold. 'Tis yet, my lord, within your power
To give me death.

PRINCE   I do entreat thee leave me.
I'm bound for death myself, and I would make   100
My passage easy, if you would permit me.
All that I ask thee for the heart I gave thee,
And for the life I love in thy behalf,
Is, that thou'dst leave me to myself a while,
And this poor, honest friend.

PRINCESS   I would obey you,   105
But cannot stir. I know, I know, my lord,
You think that I designed to meet Nemours
This night, but by the powers above I swear—

PRINCE O, do not swear, for, Chartres, credit me,
There is a power that can and will revenge.   110
Therefore, dear soul, for I must love thee still,

155

If thou wilt speak, confess, repent thy fault,
And thou, perhaps, may'st find a door of mercy.
For me, by all my hopes of heaven, I swear
I freely now forgive thee. O, my heart!   115
Pedro, thy arm.
      [Pedro assists the Prince to rise]
          Let me to bed—
PRINCESS And do you then refuse my help?
PRINCE In honour, Chartres, after such a fall,
  I ought not to permit that thou shouldst touch me.
PRINCESS But, sir, I will. Your arm? I'll hold you all   120
      [Embracing him]
  Thus in the closest, strictest, dearest clasps.
  Nor shall you die believing my dishonour.
  I swear I knew not of Nemours his coming;
  Nor had I spoke those words, which yet were guiltless,
  Had he not vowed never to see me more.   125
  By our first meeting, by our nuptial joys,
  By my dead mother's ghost, by your own spirit
  (Which, O, I fear, is taking leave for ever),
  I swear that this is true.
PRINCE   I do believe thee.
  Thou hast such power, such charms in those dear lips,   130
  As might persuade me that I am not dying.
  Off, Pedro.
      [Pedro stands aside]
          By my most untimely fate
  I swear, I'm reconciled. And hark thee, Cleves,
  If thou dost marry—ha, I cannot speak.
  Away to bed. Yet love my memory.   135
PRINCESS To bed! And must we part then?
PRINCE   O, we must.
  Were I to live, I should not see thee more;
  But since I am dying, by this kiss I beg thee—
  Nay, I command thee—part. Be gone and leave me.
PRINCESS I go, and leave this farewell prayer behind me.   140
  For me, if all I've said be not most true,
  True as thou think'st me false, all curses on me—
  The whips of conscience, and the stings of pleasure,
  Sores and distempers, disappointments plague me!
  May all my life be one continued torment,   145

And that more racking than a woman's labour.
In meeting death may my least trouble be
As great as now my parting is with thee.
　　　　Exeunt severally

5.1

[The palace of Saint-André]

[Enter] Poltrot [and] Bellamore

BELLAMORE Come, come; take her into grace again. 'Twas but a slip.

POLTROT Take her into grace again? Why, sure you would have her bring me to that pass she did in England, when my Lord Harebrain° used to keep me in awe, stand biting my lips, twisting my hat, playing with my thumbs, while they were at it, and I durst not look behind me.   5

BELLAMORE Mere jealousy! You say yourself you saw nothing.

POLTROT No, sir, I thank you; I had more care of my throat. Neither is this the first fault. For once upon a time, a little while after we were married, at London—a pox o' that cuckolding Trojan race°—   10 she was talking to me one day out of her window more pleasantly than ordinary, and acted with her head and body wondrous prettily, butting at me like a little goat, while I butted at her again. I, being glad to find her in so good humour, what did I, sir, but stole away and came softly up the backstairs, thinking to cry 'Boo!'.   15 But, O lord, how was I thunder-struck, to find my Lord Harebrain there all in a sweat, kissing and smacking, puffing and blowing so hard, you would have sworn they had been at hot-cockles.°

BELLAMORE A little familiar perhaps. Things of custom!°

POLTROT Ay, sir, kiss my wife and welcome; but for that zeal in her   20 shogging and butting, '*Noli me tangere*',° I cry. I am sure it ran so in my imagination, I have been horn-mad ever since. Therefore spare your pains, for I am resolute.

Enter Celia

BELLAMORE See where she comes, my lord. But you are resolved, you say. However, let me advise you: have a care of making her   25 desperate.

Exit [Bellamore]

POLTROT Desperate! Damn her, polluter of my sheets, damn her.

CELIA Seek not to shun me, for, where'er you fly,°
I'll follow, hang upon thy knees and die.
[She kneels]
Poltrot, behold. Ah, canst thou see me kneel,   30
And yet no bowels of compassion feel?
Why dost thou bluster by me like a storm

And ruffle into frowns that godlike form?
Why dost thou turn away those eyes of thine,
In which love's glory and his conquests shine?   35
POLTROT What is this thing called woman? She is worse
Than all ingredients rammed into a curse.
Were she a witch, a bawd, a noseless whore,°
I could forgive her, so she were no more.°
But she's far worse and will in time forestall   40
The devil, and be the damning of us all.
CELIA Yet honour bids you sink with her you call
So foul, whose frailties you too sharply named.
Like Adam, you should choose with her to fall
And in mere generosity be damned.°   45
POLTROT No; by thyself, and all alone, be cursed,
And by the winds thy venom dust be hurled.
For thou'rt a serpent equal to the first
And hast the will to damn another world.
CELIA But am I not thy wife? Let that atone.   50
POLTROT My dear, damned wife, I do confess thou art
Flesh of my flesh, and bone too of my bone.°
Would mine had all been broke when first thou wert.
CELIA [rising] Why, then I'll cringe no longer. Hark you, sir. Leave
off your swelling and frowning and awkward ambling, and tell me   55
in fine whether you'll be reconciled or no, for I am resolved to
stoop no longer to an ungrateful person.
POLTROT To your husband, to your head, to your lord and master, you
will not, Goody° Bathsheba.° But you could stoop your swine's flesh,
last night you could, to your rank bravado, that would have struck his   60
tusks in my guts. He had you with a beck, a snort. Nay, o' my
conscience, thou wouldst not give him time to speak, but hunched
him on the side like a full-acorned boar, cried 'O!' and mounted.°
CELIA Are you resolved then, never to take me into grace again for
one slip?   65
POLTROT No, I'm the son of a carted bawd° if I do. A slip, do you
call it? What, when I heard the bed crack with the violence of my
cuckoldom! No, I will ascend the judge of my own cause, proceed
to condemnation, and banish thee for ever the confines of our
benevolence.°   70
CELIA What, here, before the Vidame here?°
POLTROT Yes, impudence; before the Vidame and the Duke
Nemours. Nay, to thy eternal confusion, I will post thee° in the

market-place. But, first, I'll find out Saint-André and tell him the
whole matter, that he may know too what a ram his blessed ewe   75
has made him. And then—

CELIA And then I'll have your throat cut.

POLTROT Ha! Tigress! Cut my throat! Why, thou she-bear! Thou
dam of lion's whelps, thou cormorant of cormorants!° Why, what,
wilt thou devour me horns and all?   80

CELIA He that missed your guts in the dark shall take better aim at
your gullet by day-light. Nay, to thy terror of heart be it known,
thou monster of ill nature, if I would have consented last night to
have run his fortune,° which is no small one, he would have
murdered thee in thy bed. For I heard him speak these very words,   85
'Let him lie *in mortuis et in limbo patrum*',° where I must have
prayed for that unthankful soul, or thou wouldst have been
damned to all eternity, dying suddenly and without repentance.

POLTROT O lord, O lord! '*In mortuis et in limbo patrum*'. What, to be
tossed on burning pitchforks for my sins? Why, what a bloody-   90
minded son of Belial° is this?

CELIA In fine, since you will have the truth, he has long had a design
upon both our bodies—to ravish mine, and rip open yours.

POLTROT Why, then he's a cannibal! Lord, lord, lord, lord! Why,
what pleasure can it be to any man to rip me open? To ravish thee   95
indeed, there's some sense in that. But there's none in ripping me
open. Why, this is such a brutish cruelty—

CELIA Rogue, and so I told him. Therefore, when he found that
nothing could make me consent to your murder, he swore, and
caught me by the hair, if I stirred or made the least noise, he would   100
murder us all, set the house o' fire, and so leave us to ourselves.

POLTROT And so thou wert forced to consent! Why then, by this kiss,
I swear from my soul, which might have been damned (as thou
say'st) but for thee, I forgive thee. And what was he that cuckolded
Saint-André? Such another Mephistopheles° as this too?   105

CELIA O, my dear, there are not such a pair of fiends upon earth
again. Why, they look upon't as a favour to our sex if they ravish
a woman, for you must know they were formerly heads of the
banditti.

POLTROT Well, and I must praise thy discretion in sacrificing thy   110
body. For, o' my conscience, if they had seen this smock-face of
mine, I had gone to pot too° before my execution.

CELIA They sent their pages this morning to know whether it was
our pleasure to have your throats cut. But we answered 'em, all

was well, and desired 'em, as ever they hoped to see us again, to   115
stir no further in the matter.

POLTROT Mum, mum. Dear, sweet soul, secure my life and thou
shalt command me for the future with as full a swinge as thou
canst desire. Only, like those that use that exercise,° let it be to
and fro, sometimes at home and sometimes abroad, and we'll be as   120
merry as the day is long.

CELIA Be thou but true to me, and, like the Indian wives, I'll not
outlive thee.°

POLTROT And I'll swear now, that was kindly said, as I hope for
mercy. But it makes me weep. What, burn for me! And shall I not   125
return? I will, I will, I will return when thou dost burn.

    Enter Saint-André [and] Elianor
Nay, when thy body in the fire appears,
My ghost shall rise and quench it with his tears.

SAINT-ANDRÉ All flesh is grass;° that's certain. We're all mortal. The
court's in mourning for the Prince of Cleves. The Vidame of   130
Chartres is extremely grieved.—Hark you, Poltrot. Sure as I am
alive, he died of jealousy.—Well, Nell, for this last care of thine, I
swear to be constant to thy sheets; and, as thou say'st, I think it
will not be amiss to tie me to thee now and then for fear of the
worst.—Ha, Poltrot!   135

POLTROT Ha! Bully, I heard your kind expressions to your Nell, and
I'll swear I'll vie with thee who shall love most, for I'll swear these
daily examples make my hair stand on end. Cut my throat and rip
me open! He shall cuckold me all over first, like the man in the
almanac.° Nay, he shall ravish her while I hold the door° to my   140
own deflowering.

    [Exeunt]

5.2

    [The palace of Nemours]
    [Enter] Tournon [and] Nemours

NEMOURS Resolved never to see me more, and give up her honour
to the dauphin, that puling, snivelling prince, that looks as if he
sucked still, or were always in a milk diet for the sins of his
Florentine mother!°

TOURNON Bless me! You are jealous.   5

NEMOURS I confess it. The last time I had her in disguise, she made
such discoveries as I shall never forget. Lose her I must not. No,
I'll lose a limb first. Therefore go tell her—tell her the Prince of
Cleves' death has wrought my conversion, I grow weary of my wild
courses, repent of my sins, am resolved to leave off whoring and   10
marry his wife.

TOURNON So the town talks indeed.

NEMOURS The town is as it always was and will be—a talk, a
hum, a buzz, and a great lie. Do as I bid thee, and tell her, just as
you left me, I was going to make my court to the princess   15
upon her husband's tomb, which is true too—I mean, a visit by
the way of consolation.° Not but I knew it the only opportunity
to catch a woman in the undress of her soul. Nay, I would
choose such a time for my life, and 'tis like the rest of those starts
and one of the secrets of their nature. Why, they melt. Nay, in   20
plagues, fire, famine, war, or any great calamity—mark it—let a
man stand but right before 'em, and like hunted hares they run
into his lap.

TOURNON But who's the instrument to bring you to her?

NEMOURS Her uncle, the Vidame. She lies at his house, immured in   25
a dark room, with her husband's image in her view, and so
resolves, he says, for death. However, I'll sound her in the ebb of
her soul. If my boat run aground, 'tis but calling for Marguerite,
and she'll weep a tide that shall set me afloat again. As thus: I'll
lay the dauphin in her dish,° nose her in the tiptoe of her pride,° 30
railing, lying, laming, hanging, drowning, dying, and she comes
about again.

    Exit [*Nemours*]

TOURNON Go thy ways, Petronius.° Nay, if he were dying too, with
his veins cut, he would call for wine, fiddles and whores, and laugh
himself into the other world.   35

    Enter La March

Where's Marguerite?

LA MARCH She follows like a wind, with swollen cheeks, ruffled hair
and glaring eyes. The Princess of Cleves has found her fury,° nor
will she yet believe it.

    [*Exeunt*]

5.3

[*The Vidame's house*]

[*Enter*] *the Princess of Cleve* [*and*] *Irene in mourning.* [*A*]
song [*is performed*] *as the Princess kneels at the state*°

SONG

Weep, all ye nymphs, your floods unbind,°
  For Strephon's now no more.°
Your tresses spread before the wind,
  And leave the hated shore.
See, see, upon the craggy rocks   5
  Each goddess stripped appears.
They beat their breasts, and rend their locks,
  And swell the sea with tears.

The god of love that fatal hour,
  When this poor youth was born,   10
Had sworn by Styx to show his power:°
  He'd kill a man ere morn.
For Strephon's breast he armed his dart
  And watched him as he came.
He cried, and shot him through the heart,   15
  'Thy blood shall quench my flame'.

On Stella's lap he laid his head;
  And, looking in her eyes,
He cried, 'Remember, when I'm dead,
  That I deserve the prize'.   20
Then down his tears like rivers ran.
  He sighed, 'You love, 'tis true.
You love perhaps a better man;
  But, ah, he loves not you'.

CHORUS

Why should all things bow to love,   25
Men below, and gods above?
Why should all things bow to love?
Death and fate more awful move,
Death below, and fate above,

> _Death below, and fate above._ 30
> _Mortals, mortals, try your skill,_
> _Seeking good or shunning ill._
> _Fate will be the burden still,°_
> _Will be the burden still._
> _Fate will be the burden still._ 35
> _Fate will be the burden still._

PRINCESS Dead, thou dear lord—yet from thy throne of bliss,
    If anything on earth be worth thy view,
    Look down and hear me, hear my sighs and vows,
    Till death has made me cold and wax like thee. 40
    Water shall be my drink and herbs my food,
    The marble of my chapel be my bed,
    The altar's steps my pillows, while all night,
    Stretched out, I groaning lie upon the floor,
    Beat my swollen breasts and thy dear loss deplore. 45
IRENE Ah, madam, what a life have you proposed!
PRINCESS Too little all for an offence like mine.
    Yet death will shortly purge my dross away,
    For, O, Irene, where's the joy? I find it here.°
    Yes, I shall die without those violent means 50
    That might have hazarded my soul. O heaven,°
    O thou that seest my heart and know'st my terrors,
    Wilt thou forgive those crimes I could not help
    And would not hide?
IRENE   Doubt not but your account
    Shall stand as fair in His eternal book 55
    As any saint's above.
PRINCESS   Take, take me then
    From this bad world. Quench these rebellious thoughts.
    For, O, I have a pang, a longing wish
    To see the luckless face of loved Nemours,°
    To gaze a while and take one last farewell, 60
    Like one that is to lose a limb. 'Tis gone.
    It was corrupt, a gangrene to my honour.
    Yet I methinks would view the bleeding part,
    Shudder a little, weep, and grudge at parting.
    But by the soul of my triumphant saint 65
    I swear this longing is without a guilt,
    Nor shall it ever be by my appointment.

Enter Nemours, [unseen by the Princess and Irene]

IRENE But if he should attempt this cruel visit,
  How would your heart receive him?

PRINCESS   With such temper,°
  So clear and calm in height of my misfortune,   70
  As thou thyself perhaps wouldst wonder at.

IRENE Ha, but he's here!

PRINCESS   Is't possible, my lord?
  Has then my uncle thus betrayed my honour?

NEMOURS Start not, nor wonder, madam, but forgive
  The Vidame who has thus entrapped your virtue,   75
  To end a lingering wretch that dies for love.

PRINCESS For love, my lord? Is this a time for love,
  In tears and blacks, the livery of death?
  But what's your hope, if I should stay to hear you?
  Ah, what can you expect from rigorous virtue,   80
  From chastity as cold as Cleves himself?
  You that are made, my lord, for other pleasures.

NEMOURS Is this then the reward of all my passion?
  As if there could be any happiness
  For this disconsolate, despairing wretch,   85
  But in your love alone?

PRINCESS   You're pleased, my lord,
  That I should entertain you, and I will,°
  Before this dear remembrancer of Cleves.
  We'll talk of murdered love, and you shall hear,
  From this abandoned part of him that was,   90
  How much you have been loved.

NEMOURS   Ha, madam!

PRINCESS   Yes,
  Sighing I speak it, sir. You have inspired me
  With something which I never felt before,
  That pleased and pained, the quickenings of first love;°
  Nor feared him then, when with his infant beams°   95
  He dawned upon my chill and senseless blood.
  But, O, when he had reached his fierce meridian,
  How different was his form! That angel face,
  With his short rays, shot to a glaring god.
  I grew inflamed, burnt inward, and the breath   100
  Of the grown tyrant parched my heart to ashes.
  Nor need I blush to make you this confession,

Because, my lord, 'tis done without a crime.
NEMOURS [*kneeling*] Because for this most blessed discovery°
    I am resolved to kneel an age before you.   105
PRINCESS Rise, I conjure you, rise. I've told you nothing
    But what you knew, my lord, too well before;
    Not but I always vowed to keep those rules°
    My duty should prescribe.
NEMOURS   Strike me not dead
    With duty's name. By heaven, I swear you're free   110
    As air, as waters, winds or open wilds.
    There is no form of obligation now.
    Nay, let me say, for duty—O, forgive me—
    'Tis utmost duty now to keep that love
    You have confessed for me.
PRINCESS   'Tis duty's charge,   115
    The voice of honour and the cry of love,
    That I should fly from Paris as a pest,°
    That I should wear these rags of life away
    In sunless caves, in dungeons of despair,
    Where I should never think of man again—   120
    But more particularly that of you,°
    For reasons yet unknown.
NEMOURS   Unknown they are,
    And would to heaven they might be ever so,
    Since 'tis impossible they should be just.
    Nay, madam, let me say, the ghost of Cleves—   125
PRINCESS Ah, sir, how dare you mention that dear name
    That drains my eyes and cries to heaven for blood?
    Name it no more without the consequence.°
    For 'tis but too, too true, you were the cause
    Of Cleves' untimely death, I swear I think   130
    No less than if you had stabbed him through the heart.
NEMOURS O cruel princess! But why should I answer,
    When thus you raise the shadow of a reason
    To ruin me for ever? Is it a fault
    To love? Then blame not me—no, madam, no—   135
    But blame yourself, who told it to your husband.
    But, O, you would not argue thus against me
    If ever you had loved.
    You have deceived yourself and flattered me.
    Why am I thrown else from the glorious height,   140

Snatched in a moment from my blissful state
And hurled like lightning by the hand of fate?
PRINCESS Be satisfied, my lord. You are not flattered.
   I have such love for you, that duty's bar
   Would prove too weak to hinder our engagement.°   145
   But there is more.
NEMOURS   More fancy, more chimera!°
   But let it come. I'll stand the stalking nothing;
   And when the bladdered air would turn the balance,
   I'll cast in love substantial, ponderous love,
   Eternal love, and hurl him to the beam.°   150
   But speak. And if a hell of separation
   Must part my soul and body, do not rack me;
   But let the poison steal into my veins,
   And damn me mildly, madam, as you can.
PRINCESS Hear then my bosom thought. 'Tis the last time   155
   I e'er shall see you, and 'tis a poor reward
   For such a love. Yet, sir, 'tis all I have,
   And you must ask no more.
NEMOURS   Be witness, heaven,
   Of my obedience. I will ask her nothing.
PRINCESS Know then, my lord, you're free, and I am so,   160
   Free from the eternal bond of marriage.°
   My heart too is inclined by love like yours,
   Nor can I fear the censuring world should blame us.°
   But now, my lord, what power on earth can give
   Security that bond shall prove eternal?   165
NEMOURS Ha! Madam—
PRINCESS   Silence, silence, I command you.
   No, no, Nemours; I know the world too well.
   You have a sense too nice for long enjoyment.°
   Cleves was the man that only could love long.°
   Nor can I think his passion would have lasted,   170
   But that he found I could have none for him.
   'Tis obstacle, ascent, and lets and bars,
   That whet the appetite of love and glory.
   These are the fuel for that fiery passion;
   But when the flashy stubble we remove,   175
   The god goes out and there's an end of love.
NEMOURS Ah, madam, I'm not able to contain,
   But must perforce break your commands to answer.

Once to be yours is to be for ever yours,
Yours only, without thought of other women.° 180
PRINCESS Why, this sounds well and natural, till you're cloyed.
But, O, when once satiety has palled you,°
You sicken at each view, and every glance
Betrays your guilty soul and says you loathe her.
I know it, sir. You have the well-bred cast 185
Of gallantry and parts to gain success;
And do but think, when various forms have charmed you,
How I should bear the cross returns of love?°
NEMOURS Ah, madam, now I find you're prejudiced°
To blast my hopes.
PRINCESS   'Tis reason, all calm reason. 190
Nature affirms no violent thing can last.
I know't, I see't; every new face that came
Would charm you from me. Ha, and could I live
To see that fatal day and see you scorn me,
To hear the ghost of Cleves each hour upbraid me? 195
No, 'tis impossible, with all my passion,
Not to submit to these almighty reasons.
For this I brave your noblest qualities.°
I'll keep your form at distance, curb my soul,
Despair of smiles and tears, and prayers and oaths, 200
And all the blandishments of perjured love.
I will, I must, I shall, nay, now I can
Defy to death the lovely traitor, man.
NEMOURS No, madam, think not you shall carry't thus.
'Tis not allowable; 'tis past example.° 205
'Tis most unnatural, unjust and monstrous.
And were the rest of women thus resolved,
You would destroy the purpose of creation.
What, when I have the happiness to please,
When heaven and earth combine to make us happy, 210
Will you defeat the aim of destiny
By most unparalleled extremes of virtue,
Which therefore take away its very being?°
PRINCESS Away! I must not answer, but conjure you
Never to seek occasion more to see me. 215
Farewell. 'Tis past.
NEMOURS   I cannot let you go.
I'll follow on my knees and hold your robe,

Till you have promised me that I shall see you,
To show you how each day by slow degrees
I die away. This you shall grant, by heaven,   220
Or you shall see my blood let out before you.

PRINCESS Alas, Nemours! O heaven, why must it be
  That I should charge you with the death of Cleves?
  Alas, why met we not ere I engaged
  To my dead lord? And why did fate divide us?   225

NEMOURS Fate does not. No;
  'Tis you that cross both fortune, heaven, and fate.
  'Tis you obstruct my bliss. 'Tis you impose
  Such laws as neither sense nor virtue warrant.

PRINCESS 'Tis true, my lord, I offer much to duty,   230
  Which but subsists in thought. Therefore have patience.
  Expect what time, with such a love as mine,°
  May work in your behalf. My husband's death
  So bleeding, fresh I see him in the pangs.
  Nay, look—methinks I see his image rise   235
  And point an everlasting separation.
  Yet, O, it shall not be without a tear.

NEMOURS O, stay!

PRINCESS   Let go. Believe, no other man
  Could thus have wrought me, but yourself, to love.

NEMOURS Stay then.

PRINCESS   I dare not. Think I love you still.   240

NEMOURS I do. But stay and speak it o'er again.

PRINCESS Believe that I shall love you to my death.

NEMOURS I will. But live and love me.

PRINCESS   Off, I charge you.
  Believe this parting wounds me like the fate
  Of Cleves or worse. Believe—but, O, farewell.   245

NEMOURS Believe—but what? That last thought I implore.

PRINCESS Believe that you shall never see me more.

          Exit [*the Princess of Cleves.*] *Enter the Vidame*

VIDAME Well, and how goes the game? What, on the knee,° a
  gathered brow, and a large dew upon it? Nay, then you are a
  loser.   250

NEMOURS [*rising*] Didst thou see her pass?

VIDAME I did. She wrung me by the hand and sighed,
  Then looked back twice,
  And tottered on the threshold at the door.

NEMOURS 'Believe that you shall never see me more.' She lies. I'll   255
  wager my state° I bed her eighteen months three weeks hence at
  half an hour past two in the morning.
VIDAME Why, faith, and that's as exact as e'er an astrologer of 'em
  all.
NEMOURS Give me thy hand, Vidame. I know the souls of women   260
  better than they know themselves. I know the ingredients just that
  make 'em up, all to loose grains,° the subtlest volatile atoms, with
  the whole mish-mash of their composition. Hark there without—
  the voice of Marguerite. Now thou shalt see a battle worth the
  gazing. Mark but how easily my reason flings her; and yet at last   265
  I'll swing into friendship because I love her.°
      Enter Bellamore
BELLAMORE The Princess! Shall I stop her?
NEMOURS   No, let her come,
  With flying colours and with beat of drum,
  Like the fanatic. I'll but rub me down,°
  And then have at her.—Vidame, stay you here.   270
  By heaven, I'm jealous of this changeable stuff.° Therefore the hits
  will be the livelier o' both sides. The dauphin—but no more: she
  comes, she comes.
      Enter Marguerite, pushing Bellamore
MARGUERITE Be gone, villain, devil, fury, monster of a man!
NEMOURS But hear me but six words in private.   275
      [*Nemours and Marguerite speak apart.*] *Enter Poltrot, Celia,*
      [*Saint-André and Elianor*]
POLTROT And I swear by this lascivious bit of beauty, I will cleave
  to my Celia for better for worse, in serge, grogram or crepe,
  though a queen should come in my way in beaten gold.
NEMOURS [*rejoining them*] What then, gentlemen, I perceive there
  have been wars at home?   280
POLTROT Not a battle, my lord. Only a charge, a charge sounded or
  so.
NEMOURS What, was it a trumpet, or through a horn, sir?
POLTROT A horn, sir, a horn, sir! No, sir, 'twas not a horn, sir. Only
  my Celia was a little disdainful. But we are friends again, sir. And   285
  what then, sir?
NEMOURS Come, come; all friends. Were Tournon here, I would
  forgive her. A little scorn in a pretty woman, so it be not too
  much affected, is a charm to new friendship. Therefore [*taking*

Marguerite's hand] let each man take his fair one by the hand, thus   290
lay it to his lips, and swear a whole life's constancy.

SAINT-ANDRÉ [*following suit*] As I will to my Nell, though I haul cats
at sea, or cry small-coal.° And for him that upbraids her, I'll have
more bobs than Democritus when he cried 'Poor jack!'. There's
more pride in Diogenes,° or under a Puritan's cap, than in a king's   295
crown.

NEMOURS For my part, the death of the Prince of Cleves, upon
second thoughts, has so truly wrought a change in me, as nothing
else but a miracle could. For, first, I see and loathe my debau-
cheries. Next, while I am in health, I am resolved to give   300
satisfaction to all I have wronged—and first to this lady, whom I
will make my wife before all this company ere we part. This, I
hope, whenever I die, will convince the world of the ingenuity° of
my repentance, because I had the power to go on.

 He well repents that will not sin, yet can;
 But death-bed sorrow rarely shows the man.°   305

Epilogue

[by John Dryden]

A qualm of conscience brings me back again
To make amends to you bespattered men!°
We women love like cats, that hide their joys
By growling, squalling, and a hideous noise.
I railed at wild young sparks; but, without lying,   5
Never was man worse thought-on for high-flying.°
The prodigal of love gives each her part
And, squandering, shows at least a noble heart.°
I've heard of men who in some lewd lampoon
Have hired a friend to make their valour known.   10
That accusation straight this question brings:
What is the man that does such naughty things?
The spaniel lover, like a sneaking fop,
Lies at our feet; he's scarce worth taking up.
'Tis true such heroes in a play go far;   15
But chamber-practice is not like the bar.°
When men such vile, such faint petitions make,
We fear to give, because they fear to take.
Since modesty's the virtue of our kind,
Pray let it be to our own sex confined.   20
When men usurp it from the female nation,
'Tis but a work of supererogation.
We showed a princess in the play, 'tis true,
Who gave her Caesar more than all his due,°
Told her own faults; but I should much abhor   25
To choose a husband for my confessor.°
You see what fate followed the saint-like fool
For telling tales from out the nuptial school.°
Our play a merry comedy had proved,
Had she confessed as much to him she loved.   30
True Presbyterian wives the means would try;°
But damned confessing is flat Popery.

Epilogue

What is this wit which Cowley could not name?°
The rare inducement to a perfect fame;°
The art of nature curious in a frame.°
Is it a Whig, a Trimmer, or a Tory,°
Or an old fop forgotten in the story?°   5
'Tis honour veiled in honesty's disguise,°
Or Caesar like a fencer in a prize.°
'Tis Pindar's ramble, nature in misrule,°
A politician acted by a fool.°
'Tis all variety that arts can give,   10
The Danaid's filling of a leaky sieve,°
The valley's sweets and the distilling spring,
The brimming Bacchus that the Muses bring
To drink the health of England's glorious king.
A statesman thoughtful for a clown reviled;°   15
A pestle and a mortar for a child.°
'Tis a true principle, but hardly shown,°
An artificial sigh, a virgin's groan,°
When the first night her lover lays her on.°
'Tis like a lass that gads to gather May.°
'Tis like the comedy you have today—   20
A bulling gallant in a wanton play.

AMPHITRYON;
OR
THE TWO SOSIAS

BY

JOHN DRYDEN

Egregiam vero laudem, et spolia ampla refertis;
Una dolo divum si femina victa duorum est.°
(Virgil)

To the Honourable
Sir William Leveson-Gower, Baronet°

There is one kind of virtue which is inborn in the nobility, and indeed in most of the ancient families of this nation: they are not apt to insult on the misfortunes of their countrymen. But you, sir, I may tell it you without flattery, have grafted on this natural commiseration and raised it to a nobler virtue. As you have been pleased to honour me, for a long time, with some part of your esteem and your good will, so in particular, since the late Revolution,° you have increased the proofs of your kindness to me, and not suffered the difference of opinions,° which produce such hatred and enmity in the brutal part of humankind, to remove you from the settled basis of your good nature and good sense. This nobleness of yours, had it been exercised on an enemy, had certainly been a point of honour, and as such I might have justly recommended it to the world. But that of constancy to your former choice, and the pursuance of your first favours, are virtues not overcommon amongst Englishmen. All things of honour have, at best, somewhat of ostentation in them, and self-love; there is a pride of doing more than is expected from us, and more than others would have done. But to proceed in the same tract of goodness, favour, and protection is to show that a man is acted by a thorough principle.° It carries somewhat of tenderness in it, which is humanity in a heroical degree; 'tis a kind of unmoveable good nature—a word° which is commonly despised, because it is so seldom practised. But after all, 'tis the most generous virtue, opposed to the most degenerate vice, which is that of ruggedness and harshness to our fellow creatures.

'Tis upon this knowledge of you, sir, that I have chosen you, with your permission, to be the patron of this poem. And, as, since this wonderful Revolution, I have begun with the best pattern of humanity, the Earl of Leicester,° I shall continue to follow the same method in all to whom I shall address, and endeavour to pitch on such only as have been pleased to own me in this ruin of my small fortune; who, though they are of a contrary opinion themselves, yet blame not me for adhering to a lost cause° and judging for myself what I cannot choose but judge, so long as I am a patient sufferer and no disturber of the government. Which, if it be a severe penance, as a great wit has told the world,° 'tis at least enjoined me by myself; and Sancho

Panza,° as much a fool as I, was observed to discipline his body no
farther than he found he could endure the smart.

You see, sir, I am not entertaining you, like Ovid, with a lamentable
epistle from Pontus.° I suffer no more than I can easily undergo; and,
so long as I enjoy my liberty, which is the birthright of an English-   40
man, the rest shall never go near my heart. The merry philosopher is
more to my humour than the melancholic;° and I find no disposition
in myself to cry, while the mad world is daily supplying me with such
occasions of laughter. The more reasonable sort of my countrymen
have shown so much favour to this piece that they give me no doubt   45
of their protection for the future.°

As you, sir, have been pleased to follow the example of their
goodness in favouring me, so give me leave to say that I follow yours
in this dedication to a person of a different persuasion. Though I must
confess withal that I have had a former encouragement from you for   50
this address; and the warm remembrance of your noble hospitality to
me at Trentham, when some years ago I visited my friends and
relations in your country,° has ever since given me a violent temptation to this boldness.

'Tis true, were this comedy wholly mine, I should call it a trifle,   55
and perhaps not think it worth your patronage; but when the names
of Plautus and Molière° are joined in it—that is, the two greatest
names of ancient and modern comedy—I must not presume so far on
their reputation to think their best and most unquestioned° produc-
tions can be termed little. I will not give you the trouble of   60
acquainting you what I have added or altered in either of them, so
much it may be for the worse; but only that the difference of our stage
from the Roman and the French did so require it. But I am afraid,
for my own interest, the world will too easily discover that more than
half of it is mine, and that the rest is rather a lame imitation of their   65
excellencies than a just translation. 'Tis enough, that the reader know
by you that I neither deserve nor desire any applause from it. If I have
performed anything, 'tis the genius of my authors that inspired me;
and if it has pleased in representation,° let the actors share the praise
amongst themselves. As for Plautus and Molière, they are dangerous   70
people; and I am too weak a gamester to put myself into their form
of play.° But what has been wanting on my part has been abundantly
supplied by the excellent composition of Mr Purcell,° in whose
person we have at length found an Englishman equal with the best
abroad. At least my opinion of him has been such, since his happy   75
and judicious performances in the late opera, and the experience I

have had of him in the setting my three songs for this *Amphitryon*; to
all which, and particularly the composition of the 'Pastoral Dialogue',
the numerous choir of fair ladies gave so just an applause on the
third day.° I am only sorry, for my own sake, that there was one star   80
wanting, as beautiful as any in our hemisphere—that young
Berenice,° who is misemploying all her charms on stupid country
souls that can never know the value of them, and losing the triumphs
which are ready prepared for her in the court and town. And yet I
know not whether I am so much a loser by her absence, for I have   85
reason to apprehend° the sharpness of her judgment, if it were not
allayed with the sweetness of her nature; and after all, I fear she may
come time enough to discover a thousand imperfections in my play,
which might have passed on vulgar understandings. Be pleased to use
the authority of a father over her, on my behalf; enjoin her to keep   90
her own thoughts of *Amphitryon* to herself, or at least not to compare
him too strictly with Molière's. 'Tis true, I have an interest in this
partiality of hers; but, withal, I plead some sort of merit for it in being
so particularly as I am,

   Sir,   95
   Your most obedient, humble servant,
   John Dryden.
          October 24, 1690

THE CHARACTERS OF THE PLAY

Jupiter°	*Mr Betterton*
Mercury°	*Mr Leigh*
Phoebus°	*Mr Boman*
Amphitryon°	*Mr Williams*
Sosia	*Mr Nokes*
Gripus	*Mr Sandford*
Polydas	*Mr Bright*
Tranio	*Mr Bowen*
Alcmena°	*Mrs Barry*
Phaedra	*Mrs Mountfort*
Bromia	*Mrs Corey*
Night	*Mrs Butler*

5

10

[Musicians and Dancers]

[SCENE: THEBES]°

Prologue

Spoken by Mrs Bracegirdle°

The labouring bee, when his sharp sting is gone,
Forgets his golden work, and turns a drone.
Such is a satyr, when you take away°
That rage in which his noble vigour lay.
What gain you by not suffering him to tease ye?°   5
He neither can offend you now, nor please ye.
The honey-bag and venom lay so near,
That both together you resolved to tear,
And lost your pleasure, to secure your fear.°
How can he show his manhood, if you bind him   10
To box, like boys, with one hand tied behind him?
This is plain levelling of wit, in which
The poor has all th'advantage, not the rich.°
The blockhead stands excused, for wanting sense;
And wits turn blockheads in their own defence.   15
Yet, though the stage's traffic is undone,
Still Julian's interloping trade goes on:°
Though satire on the theatre you smother,°
Yet in lampoons you libel one another.
The first produces still a second jig;   20
You whip 'em out, like schoolboys, till they gig—°
And with the same success, we readers guess,
For every one still dwindles to a less.
And much good malice is so meanly dressed,
That we would laugh, but cannot find the jest.   25
If no advice your rhyming rage can stay,
Let not the ladies suffer in the fray.
Their tender sex is privileged from war;
'Tis not like knights, to draw upon the fair.°
What fame expect you from so mean a prize?   30
We wear no murdering weapons, but our eyes.
Our sex, you know, was after yours designed,°
The last perfection of the Maker's mind:
Heaven drew out all the gold for us, and left your dross behind.
Beauty for valour's best reward He chose,   35

Peace after war, and after toil repose.
Hence, ye profane, excluded from our sights;
And charmed by day with honour's vain delights,
Go, make your best of solitary nights.
Recant betimes, 'tis prudence to submit;   40
Our sex is still your overmatch in wit.
We never fail, with new, successful arts,
To make fine fools of you and all your parts.

1.1

Thebes°

Mercury and Phoebus descend in several machines°

PHOEBUS Know you the reason of this present summons?
'Tis neither council-day, nor is this heaven.
What business has our Jupiter on earth?
Why more at Thebes than any other place?
And why we two of all the herd of gods   5
Are chosen out to meet him in consult?°
They call me god of wisdom;
But Mars and Vulcan, the two fools of heaven,°
Whose wit lies in their anvil and their sword,
Know full as much as I.   10

MERCURY And Venus may know more than both of us,°
For 'tis some petticoat affair, I guess.°
I have discharged my duty, which was to summon you, Phoebus.
We shall know more anon, when the Thunderer comes down. 'Tis
our part to obey our father; for, to confess the truth, we two are   15
little better than sons of harlots;° and if Jupiter had not been
pleased to take a little pains with our mothers, instead of being
gods, we might have been a couple of link-boys.

PHOEBUS But know you nothing farther, Hermes? What news in
court?   20

MERCURY There has been a devilish quarrel, I can tell you, betwixt
Jupiter and Juno.° She threatened to sue him in the spiritual court°
for some matrimonial omissions; and he stood upon his prerogative.° Then she hit him on the teeth of° all his bastards; and your
name and mine were used with less reverence than became our   25
godships. They were both in their cups;° and at the last the matter
grew so high, that they were ready to have thrown stars at one
another's heads.

PHOEBUS 'Twas happy for me that I was at my vocation, driving
daylight about the world; but I had rather stand my father's   30
thunderbolts than my stepmother's railing.

MERCURY When the tongue-battle was over, and the championess
had harnessed her peacocks to go for Samos° and hear the prayers
that were made to her—

PHOEBUS By the way, her worshippers had a bad time on't. She was   35
in a damnable humour for receiving petitions.°

MERCURY Jupiter immediately beckons me aside, and charges me,
that as soon as ever you had set up° your horses, you and I should
meet him here at Thebes. Now, putting the premises together, as
dark as it is, methinks I begin to see daylight.   40

PHOEBUS As plain as one of my own beams. She has made him
uneasy at home, and he is going to seek his diversion abroad. I see
heaven itself is no privileged place for happiness, if a man must
carry his wife along with him.

MERCURY 'Tis neither better nor worse, upon my conscience. He is   45
weary of hunting in the spacious forest of a wife, and is following
his game incognito in some little purlieu here at Thebes. That's
many an honest man's case on earth too, Jove help 'em—as indeed
he does, to make 'em cuckolds.

PHOEBUS But if so, Mercury, then I, who am a poet, must indite his   50
love-letter; and you, who are by trade a porter, must convey it.

MERCURY No more. He's coming down souse upon us, and hears as
far as he can see too. He's plaguy hot upon the business; I know
it by his hard driving.

    Jupiter descends

JUPITER What, you are descanting upon my actions?   55
Much good may do you with your politics.°
All subjects will be censuring their kings.
Well, I confess I am in love. What then?

PHOEBUS Some mortal, we presume, of Cadmus' blood,
Some Theban beauty, some new Semele,   60
Or some Europa.°

MERCURY I'll say that for my father—he's constant to an handsome
family. He knows when they have a good smack with 'em, and
snuffs up incense so savourly, when 'tis offered him by a fair hand.

JUPITER Well, my familiar sons, this saucy carriage°   65
I have deserved; for he who trusts a secret
Makes his own man his master.
I read your thoughts;
Therefore you may as safely speak as think.

MERCURY Mine was a very homely thought. I was considering into   70
what form your almightyship would be pleased to transform
yourself tonight. Whether you would fornicate in the shape of a
bull, or a ram, or an eagle, or a swan.° What bird or beast you
would please to honour, by transgressing your own laws in his

likeness. Or, in short, whether you would recreate° yourself in   75
feathers or in leather?

PHOEBUS Any disguise to hide the king of gods.

JUPITER I know your malice, Phoebus. You would say
That when a monarch sins it should be secret,
To keep exterior show of sanctity,   80
Maintain respect, and cover bad example;
For kings and priests are in a manner bound,
For reverence sake, to be close hypocrites.°

PHOEBUS But what necessitates you to this love,
Which you confess a crime, and yet commit?   85
For to be secret makes not sin the less.
'Tis only hidden from the vulgar view—°
Maintains, indeed, the reverence due to princes,
But not absolves the conscience from the crime.

JUPITER I love, because 'twas in the fates I should.   90

PHOEBUS With reverence be it spoke, a bad excuse.
Thus every wicked act in heaven or earth
May make the same defence. But what is fate?
Is it a blind contingence of events?
Or sure necessity of causes linked   95
That must produce effects? Or is't a power
That orders all things by superior will,
Foresees his work, and works in that foresight?°

JUPITER Fate is, what I
By virtue of omnipotence have made it;   100
And power omnipotent can do no wrong—
Not to myself, because I willed it so;
Nor yet to men, for what they are is mine.
This night I will enjoy Amphitryon's wife;
For, when I made her, I decreed her such   105
As I should please to love. I wrong not him
Whose wife she is; for I reserved my right
To have her while she pleased me. That once past,
She shall be his again.

MERCURY Here's omnipotence with a vengeance°—to make a man a   110
cuckold, and yet not to do him wrong. Then I find, father Jupiter,
that when you made fate, you had the wit to contrive a holiday for
yourself now and then. For you kings never enact a law, but you
have a kind of an eye to your own prerogative.°

PHOEBUS If there be no such thing as right and wrong,   115

Of an eternal being,° I have done;
But if there be—
JUPITER   Peace, thou disputing fool.
    Learn this. If thou couldst comprehend my ways,
    Then thou wert Jove, not I. Yet, thus far know,
    That, for the good of humankind, this night   120
    I shall beget a future Hercules,
    Who shall redress the wrongs of injured mortals,
    Shall conquer monsters, and reform the world.°
MERCURY Ay, brother Phoebus; and our father made all those
    monsters for Hercules to conquer, and contrived all those vices on   125
    purpose for him to reform too. There's the jest on't.
PHOEBUS Since arbitrary power will hear no reason, 'tis wisdom to
    be silent.
MERCURY Why, that's the point. This same arbitrary power is a
    knock-down argument. 'Tis but a word and a blow. Now methinks   130
    our father speaks out like an honest barefaced god, as he is. He lays
    the stress in the right place—upon absolute dominion. I confess, if
    he had been a man, he might have been a tyrant, if his subjects
    durst have called him to account. But you, brother Phoebus, are
    but a mere country gentleman that never comes to court, that   135
    are abroad all day on horseback, making visits about the world, are
    drinking all night and in your cups are still railing at the
    government.° O these patriots,° these bumpkin patriots, are a very
    silly sort of animal.
JUPITER My present purpose and design you heard—   140
    T'enjoy Amphitryon's wife, the fair Alcmena.
    You two must be subservient to my love.
MERCURY (to Phoebus) No more of your grumbletonian° morals,
    brother. There's preferment coming. Be advised and pimp duti-
    fully.   145
JUPITER Amphitryon, the brave Theban general,
    Has overcome his country's foes in fight,
    And in a single duel slain their king.
    His conquering troops are eager on their march,
    Returning home; while their young general,   150
    More eager to review his beauteous wife,°
    Posts on before, winged with impetuous love,
    And, by tomorrow's dawn, will reach this town.
MERCURY That's but short warning, father Jupiter. Having made no
    former advances of courtship to her, you have need of your   155

omnipotence, and all your godship, if you mean to be beforehand
with him.

PHOEBUS Then how are we to be employed this evening?
　　Time's precious, and these summer nights are short.
　　I must be early up to light the world.　　　　　　　　　　160

JUPITER You shall not rise; there shall be no tomorrow.

MERCURY Then the world's to be at an end, I find.

PHOEBUS Or else a gap in nature, of a day.

JUPITER A day will well be lost to busy man:
　　Night shall continue sleep, and care shall cease.　　　　165
　　So, many men shall live, and live in peace,
　　Whom sunshine had betrayed to envious sight,°
　　And sight to sudden rage, and rage to death.°
　　Now, I will have a night for love and me,
　　A long luxurious night, fit for a god　　　　　　　　　　170
　　To quench and empty his immortal heat.

MERCURY I'll lay on° the woman's side for all that, that she shall love
　　longest tonight, in spite of your omnipotence.

PHOEBUS I shall be cursed by all the labouring trades
　　That early rise; but you must be obeyed.　　　　　　　　175

JUPITER No matter for the cheating part of man;
　　They have a day's sin less to answer for.

PHOEBUS When would you have me wake?

JUPITER Why, when Jove goes to sleep. When I have finished,°
　　Your brother Mercury shall bring you word.　　　　　　　180
　　　　　Exit Phoebus on his chariot

JUPITER (*to Mercury*) Now, Hermes, I must take Amphitryon's form,
　　T'enjoy his wife.
　　Thou must be Sosia, this Amphitryon's slave,
　　Who, all this night, is travelling to Thebes
　　To tell Alcmena of her lord's approach　　　　　　　　185
　　And bring her joyful news of victory.

MERCURY But why must I be Sosia?

JUPITER Dull god of wit, thou statue of thyself!
　　Thou must be Sosia, to keep out Sosia,
　　Who, by his entrance, might discover Jove,°　　　　　　190
　　Disturb my pleasures, raise unruly noise,
　　And so distract Alcmena's tender soul,
　　She would not meet my warmth, when I dissolve
　　Into her lap, nor give down half her love.°

MERCURY Let me alone; I'll cudgel him away.°　　　　　　195

But I abhor so villainous a shape.°

JUPITER Take it; I charge thee on thy duty, take it.
Nor dare to lay it down, till I command.
I cannot bear a moment's loss of joy.

Night appears above in her chariot

Look up. The night is in her silent chariot,   200
And rolling just o'er Thebes. Bid her drive slowly,
Or make a double turn about the world,
While I drop Jove and take Amphitryon's dress,
To be the greater, while I seem the less.

Exit Jupiter

MERCURY (*to Night*) Madam Night, a good even to you. Fair and   205
softly, I beseech you, madam. I have a word or two to you, from
no less a god than Jupiter.

NIGHT O, my nimble-fingered god of theft, what make you here on
earth at this unseasonable hour? What banker's shop° is to be
broken open tonight? Or what clippers, and coiners,° and conspir-   210
ators have been invoking your deity for their assistance?

MERCURY Faith, none of those enormities; and yet I am still in my
vocation, for you know I am a kind of jack-of-all-trades. At a word,
Jupiter is indulging his genius tonight with a certain noble sort of
recreation called wenching. The truth on't is, adultery is its proper 215
name.

NIGHT Jupiter would do well to stick to his wife Juno.

MERCURY He has been married to her above these hundred
years; and that's long enough in conscience to stick to one
woman.   220

NIGHT She's his sister too, as well as his wife—that's a double tie of
affection to her.

MERCURY Nay, if he made bold with his own flesh and blood, 'tis
likely he will not spare his neighbours'.

NIGHT If I were his wife, I would raise a rebellion against him for   225
the violation of my bed.

MERCURY Thou art mistaken, old Night; his wife could raise no
faction. All the deities in heaven would take the part of the
cuckold-making god, for they are all given to the flesh most
damnably. Nay, the very goddesses would stickle in the cause of   230
love; 'tis the way to be popular—to whore and love. For what dost
thou think old Saturn was deposed,° but that he was cold and
impotent, and made no court to the fair ladies. Pallas° and Juno
themselves, as chaste as they are, cried shame on him. I say unto

thee, old Night, woe be to the monarch that has not the women   235
on his side.°

NIGHT   Then by your rule, Mercury, a king who would live happily
must debauch his whole nation of women.

MERCURY   As far as his ready money° will go, I mean; for Jupiter
himself can't please all of 'em. But this is beside my present   240
commission. He has sent me to will and require you to make a
swingeing long night for him, for he hates to be stinted in his
pleasures.

NIGHT   Tell him plainly, I'll rather lay down my commission. What,
would he make a bawd of me?   245

MERCURY   Poor ignorant! Why, he meant thee for a bawd when he
first made thee. What art thou good for, but to be a bawd? Is not
daylight better for mankind, I mean as to any other use, but only
for love and fornication? Thou hast been a bawd too, a reverend,
primitive, original bawd, from the first hour of thy creation!   250
And all the laudable actions of love have been committed under
thy mantle. Prithee for what dost thou think that thou art
worshipped?

NIGHT   Why, for my stars and moonshine.

MERCURY   That is, for holding a candle to° iniquity. But if they were   255
put out, thou wouldst be double worshipped by the willing,
bashful virgins.

NIGHT   Then for my quiet, and the sweetness of my sleep.

MERCURY   No, for thy sweet waking all the night, for sleep comes not
upon lovers till thou art vanished.   260

NIGHT   But it will be against nature, to make a long winter's night at
midsummer.

MERCURY   Trouble not yourself for that. Phoebus is ordered to make
a short summer's day tomorrow; so in four-and-twenty hours all
will be at rights again.   265

NIGHT   Well, I am edified° by your discourse; and my comfort is, that
whatever work is made, I see nothing.

MERCURY   About your business then. Put a spoke into your chariot-
wheels, and order the seven stars° a halt, while I put myself into
the habit of a servingman and dress up a false Sosia to wait upon   270
a false Amphitryon. Good-night, Night.

NIGHT   My service to Jupiter.° Farewell, Mercury.

Night goes backward.° Exit Mercury

1.2

Amphitryon's palace

Enter Alcmena alone

ALCMENA Why was I married to the man I love!
For, had he been indifferent to my choice,°
Or had been hated, absence had been pleasure.
But now I fear for my Amphitryon's life;
At home, in private, and secure from war,   5
I am amidst an host of armèd foes,
Sustaining all his cares, pierced with his wounds,°
And if he falls (which O ye gods avert)
Am in Amphitryon slain! Would I were there,
And he were here. So might we change our fates,   10
That he might grieve for me, and I might die for him!

Enter Phaedra, running

PHAEDRA Good news, good news, madam! O such admirable news,
that if I kept it in a moment, I should burst with it!

ALCMENA Is it from the army?

PHAEDRA No matter.   15

ALCMENA From Amphitryon?

PHAEDRA No matter, neither.

ALCMENA Answer me, I charge thee, if thy good news be anything
relating to my lord. If it be, assure thyself of a reward.

PHAEDRA Ay, madam, now you say something to the matter. You   20
know the business of a poor waiting-woman, here upon earth, is
to be scraping up something against a rainy day called the day of
marriage. Everyone in our own vocation.° But what matter is it to
me if my lord has routed the enemies, if I get nothing of their
spoils?   25

ALCMENA Say, is my lord victorious?

PHAEDRA Why, he is victorious. Indeed I prayed devoutly to Jupiter
for a victory, by the same token that° you should give me ten
pieces of gold, if I brought you news of it.

ALCMENA They are thine—supposing he be safe too.   30

PHAEDRA Nay, that's a new bargain; for I vowed to Jupiter, that then
you should give me ten pieces more. But I do undertake for my
lord's safety, if you will please to discharge his godship Jupiter of
the debt and take it upon you to pay.

ALCMENA When he returns in safety, Jupiter and I will pay your   35
vow.

PHAEDRA And I am sure I articled with Jupiter, that if I brought you
news that my lord was upon return, you should grant me one small
favour more that will cost you nothing.

ALCMENA Make haste, thou torturer. Is my Amphitryon upon   40
return?

PHAEDRA Promise me that I shall be your bedfellow tonight, as I
have been ever since my lord's absence—unless I shall be pleased
to release you of your word.

ALCMENA That's a small request. 'Tis granted.   45

PHAEDRA But swear by Jupiter.

ALCMENA But why by Jupiter?

PHAEDRA Because he's the greatest. I hate to deal with one of
your little baffling gods that can do nothing but by permission.
But Jupiter can swinge you off, if you swear by him and are   50
forsworn.

ALCMENA I swear by Jupiter.

PHAEDRA Then I believe he is victorious, and I know he is safe; for
I looked through the keyhole and saw him knocking at the gate,
and I had the conscience to let him cool his heels there.   55

ALCMENA And wouldst thou not open to him! O thou traitress!

PHAEDRA No, I was a little wiser. I left Sosia's wife to let him in, for
I was resolved to bring the news and make my pennyworths° out
of him—as time shall show.

> Enter Jupiter, in the shape of Amphitryon,° with Sosia's wife,
> Bromia. He kisses and embraces Alcmena

JUPITER O let me live for ever on those lips!—   60
The nectar of the gods to these is tasteless.°
I swear that, were I Jupiter, this night
I would renounce my heaven to be Amphitryon.

ALCMENA Then, not to swear beneath Amphitryon's oath
(Forgive me, Juno, if I am profane),   65
I swear I would be what I am this night,
And be Alcmena rather than be Juno.

BROMIA Good my lord, what's become of my poor bedfellow, your
man Sosia? You keep such a billing and colling here, to set one's
mouth a-watering. What, I say, though I am a poor woman, I have   70
a husband as well as my lady, and should be as glad as she of a
little honest recreation.

PHAEDRA And what have you done with your old friend and my old
sweetheart, Judge Gripus? Has he brought me home a crammed
purse that swells with bribes? If he be rich, I'll make him welcome, 75

like an honourable magistrate; but if he has not had the wit to sell
justice, he judges no causes in my court, I warrant him.

ALCMENA My lord, you tell me nothing of the battle?
Is Thebes victorious? Are our foes destroyed?
For now I find you safe, I should be glad   80
To hear you were in danger.

JUPITER (*aside*) A man had need be a god, to stand the fury of three
talking women! I think, in my conscience, I made their tongues of
thunder.

BROMIA (*pulling him on one side*) I asked the first question. Answer   85
me, my lord.

PHAEDRA (*pulling him on t'other side*) Peace. Mine's a lover, and yours
is but a husband; and my judge is 'my lord' too. The title shall
take place,° and I will be answered.

JUPITER Sosia is safe; Gripus is rich; both coming.   90
I rode before 'em with a lover's haste.
(*Aside*) Was e'er poor god so worried! But for my love,°
I wish I were in heaven again with Juno.

ALCMENA Then I, it seems, am last to be regarded?

JUPITER Not so, my love; but these obstreperous tongues   95
Have snatched their answers first. They will be heard;
And surely Jove would never answer prayer
That women made, but only to be freed
From their eternal noise. Make haste to bed.
There let me tell my story in thy arms.   100
There in the gentle pauses of our love,
Betwixt our dyings, ere we live again,°
Thou shalt be told the battle and success,°
Which I shall oft begin and then break off;
For love will often interrupt my tale   105
And make so sweet confusion in our talk,
That thou shalt ask, and I shall answer, things
That are not of a piece, but patched with kisses,
And sighs, and murmurs, and imperfect speech;
And nonsense shall be eloquent, in love.   110

BROMIA (*to Phaedra*) My lord is very hot upon't. This absence is
a great friend to us poor neglected wives. It makes us new
again.

ALCMENA I am the fool of love, and find within me
The fondness of a bride without the fear.°
My whole desires and wishes are in you.   115

PHAEDRA (*aside*) My lady's eyes are pinking to bedward too. Now is she to look very sleepy, counterfeiting yawning; but she shall ask me leave first.

ALCMENA Great Juno, thou whose holy care presides   120
Over the nuptial bed, pour all thy blessings
On this auspicious night.

JUPITER Juno may grudge, for she may fear a rival
In those bright eyes; but Jupiter will grant,
And doubly bless this night.   125

PHAEDRA (*aside*) But Jupiter should ask my leave first, were he here in person.

ALCMENA Bromia, prepare the bed.
The tedious journey has disposed my lord
To seek his needful rest.   130

   Exit Bromia

PHAEDRA 'Tis very true, madam. The poor gentleman must needs be weary; and, therefore, 'twas not ill contrived that he must lie alone tonight, to recruit himself with sleep and lay in enough for tomorrow night, when you may keep him waking.

ALCMENA (*to Jupiter*) I must confess I made a kind of promise.   135

PHAEDRA (*almost crying*) A kind of promise, do you call it? I see you would fain be coming off.° I am sure you swore to me, by Jupiter, that I should be your bedfellow, and I'll accuse you to him too, the first prayers I make. And I'll pray o' purpose° too, that I will, though I have not prayed to him this seven years.   140

JUPITER O, the malicious hilding!

ALCMENA I did swear indeed, my lord.

JUPITER Forswear thyself, for Jupiter but laughs
At lovers' perjuries.°

PHAEDRA The more shame for him if he does. There would be a fine 145
god indeed for us women to worship, if he laughs when our sweethearts cheat us of our maidenheads. No, no, Jupiter is an honester gentleman than you make of him.

JUPITER I'm all on fire, and would not lose this night
To be the master of the universe.   150

PHAEDRA Ay, my lord, I see you are on fire; but the devil a° bucket shall be brought to quench it without my leave. You *may* go to bed, madam; but you shall see how heaven will bless your night's work, if you forswear yourself. Some fool, some mere elder brother,° or some blockheadly hero, Jove, I beseech thee, send her. 155

JUPITER (*aside*) Now I could call my thunder to revenge me,

But that were to confess myself a god,
And then I lost my love!—Alcmena, come;
By heaven, I have a bridegroom's fervour for thee,
As I had ne'er enjoyed.°

ALCMENA (*sighing*)   She has my oath;   160
And sure she may release it if she please.

PHAEDRA Why, truly, madam, I am not cruel in my nature to poor
distressed lovers, for it may be my own case another day. And
therefore, if my lord pleases to consider me—

JUPITER Anything, anything; but name thy wish and have it.   165

PHAEDRA Ay, now you say 'Anything, anything'; but you would tell
me another story tomorrow morning. Look you, my lord, here's a
hand open to receive. You know the meaning of it. I am for
nothing but the ready.°

JUPITER Thou shalt have all the treasury of heaven.   170

PHAEDRA Yes, when you are Jupiter to dispose of it.

JUPITER (*aside*) I had forgot, and showed myself a god.
This love can make a fool of Jupiter.

PHAEDRA You have got some part of the enemy's spoil, I warrant
you. I see a little trifling diamond upon your finger, and I am   175
proud enough to think it would become mine too.

JUPITER (*taking a ring off his finger and giving it*)
Here, take it. This is a very woman.°
Her sex is avarice, and she, in one,
Is all her sex.

PHAEDRA Ay, ay, 'tis no matter what you say of us. What, would you   180
have your money out of the treasury without paying the officers
their fees?° Go, get you together, you naughty couple, till you are
both weary of worrying one another,° and then tomorrow morning
I shall have another fee for parting you.

          Phaedra goes out before Alcmena with a light

JUPITER (*alone*) Why, now I am, indeed, the lord of all;   185
For what's to be a god, but to enjoy?
Let humankind their sovereign's leisure wait;
Love is, this night, my great affair of state.
Let this one night of providence be void;°
All Jove, for once, is on himself employed.   190
Let unregarded altars smoke in vain,
And let my subjects praise me or complain.
Yet, if betwixt my intervals of bliss
Some amorous youth his orisons address,

His prayer is in an happy hour preferred;°   195
And when Jove loves, a lover shall be heard.
    Exit

2.1

Night-scene of [Amphitryon's] palace

[Enter] Sosia with a dark-lanthorn; [and, unseen by Sosia,] Mercury, in Sosia's shape, with a dark-lanthorn also [and a cudgel]

SOSIA Was not the devil in my master, to send me out in this dreadful dark night to bring the news of his victory to my lady? And was not I possessed with ten devils, for going on his errand without a convoy for the safeguard of my person? Lord, how am I melted into sweat with fear! I am diminished of my natural weight, above two stone. I shall not bring half my self home again to my poor wife and family. I have been in an ague-fit ever since shut of evening, what with the fright of trees by the highway, which looked maliciously like thieves by moonshine, and what with bulrushes by the riverside, that shaked like spears and lances at me. Well, the greatest plague of a servingman is to be hired to some great lord! They care not what drudgery they put upon us, while they lie lolling at their ease abed, and stretch their lazy limbs in expectation of the whore which we are fetching for them.

MERCURY (*aside*) He is but a poor mortal that suffers this! But I, who am a god, am degraded to a foot-pimp, a waiter° without-doors—a very civil° employment for a deity!

SOSIA The better sort of 'em will say 'Upon my honour' at every word. Yet ask 'em for our wages, and they plead the privilege of their honour and will not pay us, nor let us take our privilege of the law upon them. These are a very hopeful sort of patriots, to stand up as they do for liberty and property of the subject.° There's conscience for you!

MERCURY (*aside*) This fellow has something of the republican spirit° in him.

SOSIA (*looking about him*) Stay; this methinks should be our house, and I should thank the gods now for bringing me safe home. But I think I had as good let my devotions alone, till I have got the reward for my good news, and then thank 'em once for all; for if I praise 'em before I am safe within doors, some damned mastiff dog may come out and worry me, and then my thanks are thrown away upon 'em.

MERCURY (*aside*) Thou art a wicked rogue and wilt have thy bargain beforehand.° Therefore thou get'st not into the house this night; and thank me accordingly as I use thee.   35

SOSIA Now am I to give my lady an account of my lord's victory. 'Tis good to exercise my parts beforehand and file my tongue into eloquent expressions, to tickle her ladyship's imagination.

MERCURY (*aside*) Good! And here's the god of eloquence° to judge of thy oration.   40

SOSIA (*setting down his lanthorn*) This lanthorn, for once, shall be my lady—because she is the lamp of all beauty and perfection.

MERCURY (*aside*) No, rogue, 'tis thy lord is the lanthorn° by this time, or Jupiter is turned fumbler.°

SOSIA Then thus I make my addresses to her. (*Bows*) 'Madam, my   45
lord has chosen me out, as the most faithful, though the most unworthy of his followers, to bring your ladyship this following account of our glorious expedition.' Then she. (*In a shrill tone*) 'O my poor Sosia, how am I overjoyed to see thee!' She can say no less. 'Madam, you do me too much honour, and the world will   50
envy me this glory.' Well answered on my side. 'And how does my lord Amphitryon?' 'Madam, he always does like a man of courage, when he is called by honour.' There I think I nicked it. 'But when will he return?' 'As soon as possibly he can; but not so soon as his impatient heart could wish him with your ladyship.'   55

MERCURY (*aside*) When Thebes is an university, thou deservest to be their orator.°

SOSIA 'But what does he do, and what does he say? Prithee tell me something more of him.' 'He always says less than he does, madam, and his enemies have found it to their cost.' Where the   60
devil did I learn these elegancies and gallantries?

MERCURY [*aside*] So. He has all the natural endowments of a fop, and only wants the education!

SOSIA (*staring up to the sky*) What, is the devil in the night! She's as long as two nights. The seven stars are just where they were seven   65
hours ago! High day°—high night, I mean, by my favour. What, has Phoebus been playing the good-fellow° and overslept himself, that he forgets his duty to us mortals?

MERCURY [*aside*] How familiarly the rascal treats us gods! But I shall make him alter his tone immediately.   70

> *Mercury comes nearer and stands just before him*

SOSIA (*seeing him, and starting back: aside*) How now? What, do my eyes dazzle, or is my dark lanthorn false to me! Is not that a giant before our door? Or a ghost of somebody slain in the late battle? If he be, 'tis unconscionably done, to fright an honest man thus, who never drew weapon wrathfully in all my life! Whatever wight he be, I am devilishly afraid, that's certain. But 'tis discretion to keep my own counsel. I'll sing, that I may seem valiant. 75

Sosia sings and, as Mercury speaks, by little and little drops his voice

MERCURY What saucy companion is this, that deafens us with his hoarse voice? What midnight ballad-singer have we here? I shall teach the villain to leave off caterwauling. 80

SOSIA [*aside*] I would I had courage, for his sake; that I might teach him to call my singing caterwauling. An illiterate rogue. An enemy to the muses and to music.

MERCURY There is an ill savour that offends my nostrils, and it wafteth this way. 85

SOSIA [*aside*] He has smelt me out: my fear has betrayed me into this savour. I am a dead man; the bloody villain is at his 'fee, fa, fum'° already.

MERCURY Stand. Who goes there?

SOSIA A friend.

MERCURY What friend? 90

SOSIA Why, a friend to all the world that will give me leave to live peaceably.

MERCURY I defy peace and all its works.° My arms are out of exercise; they have mauled nobody these three days. I long for an honourable occasion to pound a man and lay him asleep at the first 95 buffet.

SOSIA (*aside*) That would almost do me a kindness, for I have been kept waking without tipping one wink of sleep these three nights.

MERCURY Of what quality are you, fellow? 100

SOSIA Why, I am a man, fellow. [*Aside*] Courage, Sosia.

MERCURY What kind of man?

SOSIA Why, a two-legged man.° What man should I be? (*Aside*) I must bear up to him; he may prove as errant a milksop as myself.

MERCURY Thou art a coward, I warrant thee. Do not I hear thy teeth 105 chatter in thy head?

SOSIA Ay, ay, that's only a sign they would be snapping at thy nose. (*Aside*) Bless me, what an arm and fist he has, with great thumbs too, and golls and knuckle-bones of a very butcher.

MERCURY Sirrah, from whence come you, and whither go you? 110 Answer me directly, upon pain of assassination.

SOSIA I am coming from whence I came, and am going whither I
go—that's directly home. Though this is somewhat an uncivil
manner of proceeding at the first sight of a man, let me tell you.

MERCURY Then, to begin our better acquaintance, let me first make   115
you a small present of this box o' the ear.

    [Mercury] strikes him

SOSIA If I were as choleric a fool as you now, here would be fine work
betwixt us two; but I am a little better-bred than to disturb the
sleeping neighbourhood, and so (*going [towards the palace]*) good-
night, friend.   120

MERCURY (*stopping him*) Hold, sir. You and I must not part so easily.
Once more: whither are you going?

SOSIA Why, I am going as fast as I can, to get out of the reach of
your clutches. Let me but only knock at that door there.

MERCURY What business have you at that door, sirrah?   125

SOSIA This is our house; and when I am got in, I'll tell you more.

MERCURY Whose house is this, sauciness, that you are so familiar
with to call it *ours*?

SOSIA 'Tis mine, in the first place; and next, my master's—for I lie
in the garret, and he lies under me.   130

MERCURY Have your master and you no names, sirrah?

SOSIA His name is Amphitryon. Hear that and tremble.

MERCURY What, my lord general?

SOSIA O, has his name mollified you? I have brought you down a peg
lower already, friend.°   135

MERCURY And your name is—

SOSIA Lord, friend, you are so very troublesome. What should my
name be but Sosia?

MERCURY How—Sosia, say you? How long have you taken up that
name, sirrah?   140

SOSIA Here's a fine question. Why, I never took it up, friend; it was
born with me.

MERCURY What, was your name born Sosia? Take this remem-
brance° for that lie.

    [Mercury] beats him

SOSIA Hold, friend. You are so very flippant° with your hands; you   145
won't hear reason. What offence has my name done you, that you
should beat me for it? S.O.S.I.A. They are as civil, honest,
harmless letters as any are in the whole alphabet.

MERCURY I have no quarrel to the name, but that 'tis e'en too good
for you, and 'tis none of yours.   150

SOSIA What, am not I Sosia, say you?

MERCURY No.

SOSIA I should think you are somewhat merrily disposed, if you had
not beaten me in such sober sadness.° You would persuade me out
of my heathen name,° would you?   155

MERCURY Say you are Sosia again at your peril, sirrah.

SOSIA I dare say nothing; but thought is free. But whatever I am
called, I am Amphitryon's man, and the first letter of my name is
S. too. You had best tell me that my master did not send me home
to my lady with news of his victory.   160

MERCURY I say he did not.

SOSIA Lord, lord, friend, one of us two is horribly given to lying—
but I do not say which of us, to avoid contention.

MERCURY I say my name is Sosia, and yours is not.

SOSIA I would you could make good your words, for then I should   165
not be beaten, and you should.

MERCURY I find you would be Sosia if you durst; but if I catch you
thinking so—

SOSIA I hope I may think I was Sosia; and I can find no difference
between my former self and my present self, but that I was plain   170
Sosia before, and now I am laced Sosia.°

MERCURY Take this, for being so impudent to think so.

    [*Mercury*] *beats him*

SOSIA (*kneeling*) Truce a little, I beseech thee! I would be a stock or
a stone now by my good will,° and would not think at all, for
self-preservation. But will you give me leave to argue the matter   175
fairly with you? And promise me to depose that cudgel, if I can
prove myself to be that man that I was before I was beaten?

MERCURY Well, proceed in safety. I promise you I will not beat
you.

SOSIA In the first place then, is not this town called Thebes?   180

MERCURY Undoubtedly.

SOSIA And is not this house Amphitryon's?

MERCURY Who denies it?

SOSIA I thought you would have denied that too, for all hangs upon
a string. Remember then that those two preliminary articles are   185
already granted. In the next place, did not the foresaid Amphitryon
beat the Teleboans, kill their King Pterelas,° and send a certain
servant, meaning somebody that for sake-sake shall be nameless, to
bring a present to his wife, with news of his victory and of his
resolution to return tomorrow?   190

MERCURY This is all true, to a very tittle.° But who is that certain
servant? There's all the question.

SOSIA Is it peace or war betwixt us?

MERCURY Peace.

SOSIA I dare not wholly trust that abominable cudgel. But 'tis a   195
certain friend of yours and mine, that had a certain name before
he was beaten out of it. But if you are a man that depends
not altogether upon force and brutality, but somewhat also
upon reason, now do you° bring better proofs that you are that
same certain man. And in order to it, answer me to certain   200
questions.

MERCURY I say I am Sosia, Amphitryon's man. What reason have
you to urge against it?

SOSIA What was your father's name?

MERCURY Davus, who was an honest husbandman, whose sister's   205
name was Harpage,° that was married and died in a foreign
country.

SOSIA So far you are right, I must confess. And your wife's name
is—

MERCURY Bromia, a devilish shrew of her tongue, and a vixen of her   210
hands, that leads me a miserable life, keeps me to hard duty abed,
and beats me every morning when I have risen from her side
without having first—

SOSIA I understand you, by many a sorrowful token. (*Aside*) This
must be I.   215

MERCURY I was once taken upon suspicion of burglary, and was
whipped through Thebes and branded for my pains.

SOSIA [*aside*] Right me again. [*To Mercury*] But if you are I, as I
begin to suspect, that whipping and branding might have been
passed over in silence for both our credits.° [*Aside*] And yet now I   220
think on't, if I am I (as I am I), he cannot be I. All these
circumstances he might have heard; but I will now interrogate him
upon some private passages.° [*To Mercury*] What was the present
that Amphitryon sent by you or me—no matter which of us—to
his wife Alcmena?   225

MERCURY A buckle of diamonds, consisting of five large stones.

SOSIA And where are they now?

MERCURY In a case, sealed with my master's coat of arms.

SOSIA This is prodigious, I confess. (*Aside*) But yet 'tis nothing, now
I think on't, for some false brother° may have revealed it to him.   230
[*To Mercury*] But I have another question to ask you, of somewhat

that passed only betwixt myself and me. If you are Sosia, what
were you doing in the heat of battle?

MERCURY What a wise man should, that has a respect for his
own person. I ran into our tent and hid myself amongst the   235
baggage.

SOSIA [aside] Such another cutting answer, and I must provide myself of another name. (To Mercury) And how did you pass your
time in that same tent? You need not answer to every circumstance
so exactly now. You must lie a little, that I may think you the   240
more me.

MERCURY That cunning shall not serve your turn, to circumvent me
out of my name. I am for plain naked truth. There stood a
hogshead of old wine, which my lord reserved for his own
drinking—   245

SOSIA (aside) O the devil! As sure as death, he must have hid himself
in that hogshead, or he could never have known that!

MERCURY And by that hogshead, upon the ground, there lay the
kind inviter and provoker of good drinking—

SOSIA Nay, now I have caught you. There was neither inviter nor   250
provoker, for I was all alone.

MERCURY A lusty gammon of—

SOSIA (sighing) Bacon. [Aside] That word has quite made an end of
me.° Let me see. This must be I, in spite of me. But let me view
him nearer.   255

    [Sosia] walks about Mercury with his dark lanthorn

MERCURY What are you walking about me for with your dark
lanthorn?

SOSIA No harm, friend. I am only surveying a parcel of earth here,
that I find we two are about to bargain for. [Aside] He's damnable
like me; that's certain. Imprimis: there's the patch upon my nose,° 260
with a pox to him. Item: a very foolish face with a long chin at end
on't. Item: one pair of shambling legs, with two splay feet
belonging to them. And summa totalis: from head to foot all my
bodily apparel.° (To Mercury) Well, you are Sosia; there's no
denying it. But what am I then? For my mind gives me° I am   265
somebody still, if I knew but who I were.

MERCURY When I have a mind to be Sosia no more, then thou
may'st be Sosia again.

SOSIA I have but one request more to thee, that, though not as Sosia,
yet as a stranger, I may go into that house and carry a civil message 270
to my lady.

MERCURY No, sirrah; not being Sosia, you have no message to deliver, nor no lady in this house.

SOSIA Thou canst not be so barbarous, to let me lie in the streets all night, after such a journey and such a beating—and therefore I am resolved to knock at the door in my own defence.   275

MERCURY If you come near the door, I recall my word and break off the truce; and then expect—

    [Mercury] holds up his cudgel

SOSIA No; the devil take me if I do expect.° I have felt too well what sour fruit that crab-tree bears.° I'll rather beat it back upon the hoof to my Lord Amphitryon, to see if he will acknowledge me for Sosia. If he does not, then I am no longer his slave. There's my freedom dearly purchased with a sore drubbing. If he does acknowledge me, then I am Sosia again. So far 'tis tolerably well. But then I shall have a second drubbing, for an unfortunate ambassador as I am; and that's intolerable.   280 285

    Exit Sosia

MERCURY (*alone*) I have fobbed off his excellency° pretty well. Now let him return, and make the best of his credentials.° I think too I have given Jupiter sufficient time for his consummation. O, he has taken his cue, and here he comes as leisurely and as lank° as if he had emptied himself of the best part of his Almightyship.°   290

    Enter Jupiter leading Alcmena, followed by Phaedra; Pages
    with torches before them

JUPITER (*to the Pages*) Those torches are offensive. Stand aloof.°
  (*To her*) For, though they bless me with thy heavenly sight,
They may disclose the secret I would hide.
The Thebans must not know I have been here.   295
Detracting crowds would blame me that I robbed°
These happy moments from my public charge,
To consecrate to thy desired embrace;
And I could wish no witness but thyself,
For thou thyself art all I wish to please.   300

ALCMENA So long an absence, and so short a stay!
What, but one night! One night of joy and love
Could only pay one night of cares and fears;
And all the rest are an uncancelled sum!
Curse on this honour and this public fame;   305
Would you had less of both, and more of love!

JUPITER Alcmena, I must go.

ALCMENA   Not yet, my lord.
JUPITER Indeed I must.
ALCMENA   Indeed you shall not go.
JUPITER Behold the ruddy streaks o'er yonder hill.
    Those are the blushes of the breaking morn   310
    That kindle daylight to this nether world.
ALCMENA No matter for the day. It was but made
    To number out the hours of busy men.
    Let 'em be busy still, and still be wretched,
    And take their fill of anxious, drudging day.   315
    But you and I will draw our curtains close,°
    Extinguish daylight, and put out the sun.
    Come back, my lord; in faith, you shall retire.
    You have not yet lay long enough in bed°
    To warm your widowed side.°   320
PHAEDRA (*aside*) I find my lord is an excellent schoolmaster; my lady
is so willing to repeat her lesson.
MERCURY (*aside*) That's a plaguy little devil. What a roguish eye she
has! I begin to like her strangely.° She's the perquisite of my place
too; for my lady's waiting-woman is the proper fees of my lord's   325
chief gentleman. I have the privilege of a god too: I can view her
naked through all her clothes. Let me see. Let me see. I have
discovered something that pleases me already.
JUPITER Let me not live but thou art all enjoyment!
    So charming and so sweet, that not a night,   330
    But whole eternity, were well employed,
    To love thy each perfection as it ought.
ALCMENA (*kissing him*) I'll bribe you with this kiss to stay a while.
JUPITER A bribe indeed that soon will bring me back.
    But, to be just, I must restore your bribe.   335
        (*Kissing her*)
    How I could dwell for ever on those lips!
    O, I could kiss 'em pale with eagerness!
    So soft, by heaven, and such a juicy sweet,
    That ripened peaches have not half the flavour.
ALCMENA Ye niggard gods, you make our lives too long.   340
    You fill 'em with diseases, wants and woes,
    And only dash 'em with a little love,
    Sprinkled by fits, and with a sparing hand.
    Count all our joys, from childhood even to age,

They would but make a day of every year.   345
Take back your seventy years (the stint of life),
Or else be kind, and cram the quintessence
Of seventy years into sweet seventy days;
For all the rest is flat, insipid being.

JUPITER But yet one scruple pains me at my parting.   350
I love so nicely, that I cannot bear°
To owe the sweets of love which I have tasted
To the submissive duty of a wife.
Tell me, and soothe my passion ere I go,
That in the kindest moments of the night,   355
When you gave up yourself to love and me,
You thought not of a husband, but a lover.

ALCMENA But tell me first why you would raise a blush
Upon my cheeks by asking such a question.

JUPITER I would owe nothing to a name so dull   360
As husband is, but to a lover all.

ALCMENA You should have asked me then, when love and night,
And privacy, had favoured your demand.

JUPITER I ask it now, because my tenderness
Surpasses that of husbands for their wives.   365
O, that you loved like me! Then you would find
A thousand, thousand niceties in love.°
The common love of sex to sex is brutal;
But love refined will fancy to itself
Millions of gentle cares and sweet disquiets.   370
The being happy is not half the joy;
The manner of the happiness is all!
In me, my charming mistress, you behold
A lover that disdains a lawful title,
Such as of monarchs to successive thrones.   375
The generous lover holds by force of arms
And claims his crown by conquest.°

ALCMENA Methinks you should be pleased, I give you all
A virtuous and a modest wife can give.

JUPITER No, no; that very name of wife and marriage   380
Is poison to the dearest sweets of love.
To please my niceness, you must separate
The lover from his mortal foe, the husband.
Give to the yawning husband your cold virtue,
But all your vigorous warmth, your melting sighs,   385

Your amorous murmurs, be your lover's part.
ALCMENA I comprehend not what you mean, my lord;
But only love me still, and love me thus,
And think me such as best may please your thought.
JUPITER There's mystery of love in all I say.   390
Farewell; and when you see your husband next
Think of your lover then.

    Exeunt Jupiter and Alcmena severally. Phaedra follows her

MERCURY (*alone*) Now I should follow him; but love has laid a
lime-twig for me, and made a lame god of me.° Yet why should I
love this Phaedra? She's interessed, and a jilt into the bargain.   395
Three thousand years hence, there will be a whole nation of such
women, in a certain country that will be called France; and there's
a neighbour island too, where the men of that country will be all
interest.° O, what a precious generation will that be, which the
men of the island shall propagate out of the women of the   400
continent!

    Phaedra re-enters

And so much for prophecy; for she's here again, and I must love
her in spite of me. And since I must, I have this comfort, that the
greatest wits are commonly the greatest cullies, because neither of
the sexes can be wiser than some certain parts about 'em will give   405
'em leave.
PHAEDRA Well, Sosia, and how go matters?
MERCURY Our army is victorious.
PHAEDRA And my servant, Judge Gripus?
MERCURY A voluptuous gourmand.   410
PHAEDRA But has he gotten wherewithal to be voluptuous? Is he
wealthy?
MERCURY He sells justice as he uses, fleeces the rich rebels, and
hangs up the poor.°
PHAEDRA Then, while he has money, he may make love to me. Has   415
he sent me no token?
MERCURY Yes, a kiss; and, by the same token, I am to give it you as
a remembrance from him.
PHAEDRA How now, impudence! A beggarly servingman presume to
kiss me?   420
MERCURY Suppose I were a god, and should make love to you?
PHAEDRA I would first be satisfied whether you were a poor god or
a rich god.
MERCURY Suppose I were Mercury, the god of merchandise?

PHAEDRA What, the god of small wares and fripperies, of pedlars and   425
pilferers?

MERCURY (*aside*) How the gypsy despises me!

PHAEDRA I had rather you were Plutus, the god of money, or Jupiter
in a golden shower.° There was a god for us women! He had the
art of making love. Dost thou think that kings, or gods either, get   430
mistresses by their good faces? No, 'tis the gold and the presents
they can make. There's the prerogative they have over their fair
subjects.

MERCURY All this notwithstanding, I must tell you, pretty Phaedra,
I am desperately in love with you.   435

PHAEDRA And I must tell thee, ugly Sosia, thou hast not wherewithal
to be in love.

MERCURY Yes; a poor man may be in love, I hope?

PHAEDRA I grant a poor rogue may be in love, but he can never make
love. Alas, Sosia, thou hast neither face to invite me, nor youth to   440
please me, nor gold to bribe me. And, besides all this, thou hast a
wife, poor miserable Sosia! [*Calling offstage*] What ho, Bromia!

MERCURY O thou merciless creature, why dost thou conjure up that
sprite° of a wife?

PHAEDRA To rid myself of that devil of a poor lover. Since you are   445
so lovingly disposed, I'll put you together, to exercise your fury
upon your own wedlock. [*Calling offstage*] What, Bromia, I say,
make haste. Here's a vessel of yours, full freighted, that's going off
without paying duties.

MERCURY Since thou wilt not let me steal custom,° she shall have all   450
the cargo I have gotten in the wars. But thou mightst have lent me
a little creek to smuggle in.

PHAEDRA Why, what have you gotten, good gentleman soldier,
besides a legion of—
    [*Phaedra*] *knaps her fingers*°

MERCURY When the enemy was routed, I had the plundering of a   455
tent.

PHAEDRA That's to say, a house of canvas, with moveables of straw.
[*Calling offstage*] Make haste, Bromia.

MERCURY But it was the general's own tent.

PHAEDRA You durst not fight, I'm certain, and therefore came last   460
in, when the rich plunder was gone beforehand. [*Calling offstage*]
Will you come, Bromia?

MERCURY Prithee do not call so loud. A great goblet that holds a
gallon.

PHAEDRA Of what was that goblet made? Answer quickly, for I am 465
just calling very loud. [*Calling offstage*] Bro—

MERCURY Of beaten gold. Now call aloud, if thou dost not like the
metal.

PHAEDRA (*very softly*) Bromia.

MERCURY That struts in this fashion, with his arms akimbo, like a 470
city magistrate, and a great bouncing belly, like an hostess with
child of a kilderkin of wine. Now what say you to that present,
Phaedra?

PHAEDRA Why, I am considering—

MERCURY What, I prithee? 475

PHAEDRA Why, how to divide the business equally°—to take the gift,
and refuse the giver. Thou art so damnably ugly and so old.

MERCURY (*aside*) Now the devil take Jupiter for confining me to this
ungodly shape today! (*To her*) But Gripus is as old and as ugly too.

PHAEDRA But Gripus is a person of quality and my lady's uncle, and 480
if he marries me I shall take place of° my lady. Hark! Your wife!
She has sent her tongue before her. I hear the thunderclap already;
there's a storm approaching.

MERCURY Yes, of thy brewing; I thank thee for it. O, how I should
hate thee now if I could leave loving thee! 485

PHAEDRA Not a word of the dear golden goblet, as you hope
for—you know what, Sosia.

MERCURY You give me hope then?

PHAEDRA Not absolutely hope neither; but gold is a great cordial in
love matters, and the more you apply of it, the better. (*Aside*) I am 490
honest;° that's certain. But when I weigh my honesty against the
goblet, I am not quite resolved on which side the scale will turn.
    Exit Phaedra

MERCURY [*calling after her*] Farewell, Phaedra. Remember me to my
wife, and tell her—
    Enter Bromia

BROMIA Tell her what, traitor! That you are going away without 495
seeing her?

MERCURY That I am doing my duty and following my master.

BROMIA Umph! So brisk too! Your master did his duty to my lady
before he parted. He could leave his army in the lurch and come
galloping home at midnight to have a lick at the honeypot, and 500
steal to bed as quietly as any mouse, I warrant you. My master
knew what belonged to a married life. But you, sirrah—you
trencher-carrying rascal, you worse than dunghill-cock,° that stood

clapping your wings and crowing without doors, when you should
have been at roost, you villain—   505

MERCURY Hold your peace, Dame Partlet, and leave your cackling.
My master charged me to stand sentry without-doors.

BROMIA My master! I dare swear thou beliest him. My master's
more a gentleman than to lay such an unreasonable command upon
a poor distressed married couple, and after such an absence too.   510
No, there's no comparison between my master and thee, thou
sneaksby.

MERCURY No more than there is betwixt my lady and you, Bromia.
You and I have had our time in a civil way,° spouse, and much
good love has been betwixt us. But we have been married fifteen   515
years, I take it; and that highty-toighty business ought, in
conscience, to be over.

BROMIA Marry come up,° my saucy companion! I am neither old nor
ugly enough to have that said to me.

MERCURY But will you hear reason, Bromia? My lord and my lady   520
are yet in a manner bride and bridegroom; they are in honeymoon
still. Do but think in decency what a jest it would be to the family,
to see two venerable old married people lying snug in a bed
together and sighing out fine tender things to one another!

BROMIA How now, traitor, dar'st thou maintain that I am past the   525
age of having fine things said to me?

MERCURY Not so, my dear; but certainly I am past the age of saying
'em.

BROMIA Thou deserv'st not to be yoked with a woman of honour, as
I am, thou perjured villain.   530

MERCURY Ay, you are too much a woman of honour, to my
sorrow. Many a poor husband would be glad to compound for less
honour in his wife, and more quiet. Prithee be but honest and
continent in thy tongue, and do thy worst with everything else
about thee.   535

BROMIA Thou wouldst have a woman of the town, wouldst thou!—to
be always speaking my husband fair, to make him digest his
cuckoldom more easily.° Wouldst thou be a wittol, with a vengeance to thee? I am resolved I'll scour thy hide for that word.

       [*Bromia*] *holds up her ladle at him*

MERCURY Thou wilt not strike thy lord and husband, wilt thou?   540

BROMIA Since thou wilt none of the meat, 'tis but justice to give thee
the bastings° of the ladle.

       She courses him about

MERCURY (*running about: aside*) Was ever poor deity so henpecked
as I am! Nay, then, 'tis time to charm her asleep with my
enchanted rod—before I am disgraced or ravished.   545
    [*Mercury*] *plucks out his caduceus° and strikes her upon the*
    shoulder with it

BROMIA What, art thou rebelling against thy anointed wife?° I'll
make thee—How now—What, has the rogue bewitched me! I grow
dull and stupid° on the sudden. I can neither stir hand nor foot. I
am just like him; I have lost the use of all my—members.
(*Yawning*) I can't so much as wag my tongue—neither, and that's   550
the last liv—ing part about a—woman.
    [*Bromia*] *falls down*

MERCURY (*alone°*) Lord, what have I suffered, for being but a
counterfeit married man one day! If ever I come to this house as
a husband again—then—and yet that *then* was a lie too, for while
I am in love with this young gypsy, Phaedra, I must return. But   555
lie thou there, thou type° of Juno—thou that want'st nothing of
her tongue, but the immortality. If Jupiter ever let thee set foot in
heaven, Juno will have a rattling second° of thee, and there will
never be a fair day in heaven or earth after it.

    For two such tongues will break the poles asunder,   560
    And, hourly scolding, make perpetual thunder.
    Exit

3.1

Before Amphitryon's palace

[Enter] Amphitryon and Sosia

AMPHITRYON Now, sirrah, follow me into the house; thou shalt be
convinced at thy own cost, villain! What horrible lies hast thou told
me! Such improbabilities, such stuff, such nonsense!—that the
monster with two long horns that frighted the great king, and the
devil at the stone-cutter's,° are truths to these! 5

SOSIA I am but a slave, and you are master; and a poor man is always
to lie, when a rich man is pleased to contradict him. But as sure
as this is our house—

AMPHITRYON So sure 'tis thy place of execution. Thou art not made
for lying neither. 10

SOSIA That's certain; for all my neighbours say I have an honest
face,° or else they would never call me cuckold, as they do.

AMPHITRYON I mean thou hast not wit enough to make a lie that
will hang together. Thou hast set up a trade that thou hast not
stock enough to manage. O, that I had but a crab-tree cudgel for 15
thy sake!

SOSIA How, a cudgel, said you! The devil take Jupiter for inventing
that hard-hearted, merciless, knobby wood.

AMPHITRYON The bitterness is yet to come; thou hast had but a half
dose of it. 20

SOSIA I was never good at swallowing physic, and my stomach
wambles at the very thought of it. But, if I must have a second
beating, in conscience let me strip first, that I may show you the
black and blue streaks upon my sides and shoulders. I am sure I
suffered them in your service. 25

AMPHITRYON To what purpose wouldst thou show them?

SOSIA Why, to the purpose that you may not strike me upon the sore
places, and that as he beat me last night cross-ways, so you would
please to beat me long-ways, to make clean work on't, that at least
my skin may look like chequer-work. 30

AMPHITRYON This request is too reasonable to be refused. But,
that all things may be done in order, tell me over again the same
story, with all the circumstances of thy commission, that a blow
may follow in due form for every lie. To repetition, rogue, to
repetition. 35

SOSIA No, it shall be all a lie if you please, and I'll eat my words to save my shoulders.

AMPHITRYON Ay, sirrah, now you find you are to be disproved; but 'tis too late. To repetition, rogue, to repetition.

SOSIA With all my heart, to any repetition but the cudgel. But would you be pleased to answer me one civil question? Am I to use complaisance to you,° as to a great person that will have all things said your own way? Or am I to tell you the naked truth alone, without the ceremony of a farther beating?

AMPHITRYON Nothing but the truth, and the whole truth, so help thee cudgel.°

SOSIA That's a damned conclusion of a sentence; but since it must be so—back and sides, at your own peril. I set out from the port in an unlucky hour, the dusky canopy of night enveloping the hemisphere.

Amphitryon strikes him

AMPHITRYON Imprimis: for fustian. Now proceed.

SOSIA I stand corrected. In plain prose then, I went darkling, and whistling to keep myself from being afraid, mumbling curses betwixt my teeth for being sent at such an unnatural time of night.

AMPHITRYON How, sirrah, cursing and swearing against your lord and master! (*Going to strike*) Take—

SOSIA Hold, sir! Pray consider if this be not unreasonable—to strike me for telling the whole truth, when you commanded me. I'll fall into my old dog-trot of lying again, if this must come of plain-dealing.

AMPHITRYON To avoid impertinences,° make an end of your journey, and come to the house. What found you there a' God's name?

SOSIA I came thither in no god's name at all; but in the devil's name I found before the door a swingeing fellow with all my shapes and features, and accoutred also in my habit.

AMPHITRYON Who was that fellow?

SOSIA Who should it be but another Sosia! A certain kind of other me, who knew all my unfortunate commission precisely to a word, as well as I Sosia, as being sent by yourself from the port upon the same errand to Alcmena.

AMPHITRYON What gross absurdities are these!

SOSIA O lord, O lord, what absurdities! As plain as any packstaff.° That other me had posted himself there before me me. You won't give a man leave to speak poetically now; or else I would say that I was arrived at the door before I came thither.

AMPHITRYON This must either be a dream, or drunkenness, or madness in thee. Leave your buffooning and lying; I am not in humour to bear it, sirrah.

SOSIA I would you should know I scorn a lie, and am a man of honour in everything, but just fighting. I tell you once again in 80 plain sincerity and simplicity of heart, that before last night I never took myself but for one single individual Sosia; but, coming to our door, I found myself, I know not how, divided, and (as it were) split into two Sosias.

AMPHITRYON Leave buffooning. I see you would make me laugh, 85 but you play the fool scurvily.

SOSIA That may be; but if I am a fool, I am not the only fool in this company.

AMPHITRYON How now, impudence! I shall—

SOSIA Be not in wrath, sir. I meant not you. I cannot possibly be the 90 only fool; for if I am one fool, I must certainly be two fools, because, as I told you, I am double.

AMPHITRYON That one should be two is very probable!

SOSIA Have not you seen a sixpence split into two halves by some ingenious schoolboy, which bore on either side the impression of 95 the monarch's face? Now, as those moieties were two threepences, and yet in effect but one sixpence—

AMPHITRYON No more of your villainous tropes and figures.

SOSIA Nay, if an orator must be disarmed of his similitudes—

AMPHITRYON A man had need of patience to endure this gibberish. 100 Be brief, and come to a conclusion.

SOSIA What would you have, sir? I came thither, but the t'other I was there before me; for that there was two I's is as certain as that I have two eyes in this head of mine. This I, that am here, was weary; the t'other I was fresh. This I was peaceable, and t'other I 105 was a hectoring bully I.

AMPHITRYON And thou expect'st I should believe thee?

SOSIA No, I am not so unreasonable; for I could never have believed it myself, if I had not been well beaten into it. But a cudgel, you know, is a convincing argument in a brawny fist. What shall I say, 110 but that I was compelled at last to acknowledge myself! I found that he was very I, without fraud, cozen, or deceit. Besides, I viewed myself, as in a mirror, from head to foot—he was handsome, of a noble presence, a charming air, loose and free° in all his motions—and saw he was so much I, that I should have 115 reason to be better satisfied with my own person, if his hands had not been a little of the heaviest.

AMPHITRYON Once again, to a conclusion. Say you passed by him and entered into the house.

SOSIA I am a friend to truth and say no such thing. He defended° 120
the door, and I could not enter.

AMPHITRYON How, not enter!

SOSIA Why, how should I enter, unless I were a sprite to glide by him and shoot myself through locks, and bolts, and two-inch boards?

AMPHITRYON O coward! Didst thou not attempt to pass? 125

SOSIA Yes, and was repulsed and beaten for my pains.

AMPHITRYON Who beat thee?

SOSIA I beat me.

AMPHITRYON Didst thou beat thyself?

SOSIA I don't mean I here; but the absent me beat me here present. 130

AMPHITRYON There's no end of this intricate piece of nonsense.

SOSIA 'Tis only nonsense because I speak it who am a poor fellow; but it would be sense, and substantial sense, if a great man said it, that was backed with a title and the eloquence of ten thousand 135
pounds a year.

AMPHITRYON No more; but let us enter. Hold. My Alcmena is coming out, and has prevented me! How strangely will she be surprised to see me here so unexpectedly!

Enter Alcmena and Phaedra

ALCMENA (*to Phaedra*) Make haste after me to the temple, that we 140
may thank the gods for this glorious success which Amphitryon has had against the rebels. (*Seeing him*) O heavens!

AMPHITRYON Those heavens, and all their blessed inhabitants,
(*Saluting her*)°
Grant, that the sweet rewarder of my pains
May still be kind, as on our nuptial night. 145

ALCMENA So soon returned!

AMPHITRYON 'So soon returned!' Is this my welcome home?
(*Stepping back*)
'So soon returned' says I am come unwished.
This is no language of desiring love.
Love reckons hours for months, and days for years, 150
And every little absence is an age.

ALCMENA What says my lord?

AMPHITRYON   No, my Alcmena, no.
True love by its impatience measures time,
And the dear object never comes too soon.

ALCMENA Nor ever came you so, nor ever shall. 155

But you yourself are changed from what you were,
Palled in desires, and surfeited of bliss.
Not so I met you at your last return,
When, yesternight, I flew into your arms
And melted in your warm embrace.

AMPHITRYON   How's this?   160

ALCMENA Did not my soul even sparkle at my eyes
And shoot itself into your much-loved bosom?
Did I not tremble with excess of joy?
Nay, agonize with pleasure at your sight,
With such inimitable proofs of passion   165
As no false love could feign!

AMPHITRYON   What's this you tell me?

ALCMENA Far short of truth, by heaven!
And you returned those proofs with usury,°
And left me, with a sigh, at break of day.
Have you forgot?

AMPHITRYON   Or have you dreamt, Alcmena?   170
Perhaps some kind, revealing deity
Has whispered in your sleep the pleasing news
Of my return, and you believed it real!
Perhaps too, in your dream, you used me kindly;
And my preventing image reaped the joys°   175
You meant awake to me.

ALCMENA Some melancholy vapour, sure, has seized
Your brain, Amphitryon, and disturbed your sense;
Or yesternight is not so long a time,
But you might yet remember, and not force   180
An honest blush into my glowing cheeks,
For that which lawful marriage makes no crime.

AMPHITRYON I thank you for my melancholy vapour.

ALCMENA 'Tis but a just requital for my dream.

PHAEDRA (*aside*) I find my master took too much of the creature° last   185
night, and now is angling for a quarrel, that no more may be
expected from him tonight, when he has no assets.

> *In the meantime Amphitryon and Alcmena walk by*
> *themselves and frown at each other as they meet*

AMPHITRYON You dare not justify it to my face.

ALCMENA Not what?

AMPHITRYON   That I returned before this hour.

ALCMENA You dare not, sure, deny you came last night,   190

And stayed till break of day.

AMPHITRYON   O impudence!—
Why, Sosia!

SOSIA Nay, I say nothing; for all things here may go by enchantment
(as they did with me), for aught I know.

ALCMENA Speak, Phaedra. Was he here?   195

PHAEDRA You know, madam, I am but a chambermaid; and by my
place, I am to forget all that was done overnight in love-
matters—unless my master please to rub up my memory with
another diamond.

AMPHITRYON Now in the name of all the gods, Alcmena,   200
A little recollect your scattered thoughts,°
And weigh what you have said.

ALCMENA I weighed it well, Amphitryon, ere I spoke;
And she, and Bromia, all the slaves and servants,
Can witness they beheld you when you came.   205
If other proof were wanting, tell me how
I came to know your fight, your victory,
The death of Pterelas in single combat?
And, farther, from whose hands I had a jewel,
The spoils of him you slew?

AMPHITRYON   This is amazing!   210
Have I already given you those diamonds,
The present I reserved?

ALCMENA   'Tis an odd question:
You see I wear 'em. Look.

AMPHITRYON   Now answer, Sosia.

SOSIA Yes, now I can answer with a safe conscience, as to that point.
All the rest may be art magic;° but, as for the diamonds, here they   215
are, under safe custody.

ALCMENA (to Sosia) Then what are these upon my arm?

SOSIA Flints, or pebbles, or some such trumpery of enchanted
stones.

PHAEDRA [aside] They say the proof of a true diamond is to glitter   220
in the dark. I think my master had best take my lady into some
by-corner, and try whose diamond will sparkle best.

SOSIA Yet now I think on't, madam, did not a certain friend of mine
present 'em to you?

ALCMENA What friend?   225

SOSIA Why, another Sosia—one that made himself Sosia in my
despite, and also unsociated° me.

AMPHITRYON Sirrah, leave your nauseous nonsense. Break open the
    seal, and take out the diamonds.

SOSIA More words than one to a bargain, sir;° I thank you. That's   230
    no part of prudence for me to commit burglary upon the seals. Do
    you look first upon the signet, and tell me in your conscience
    whether the seals be not as firm as when you clapped the wax upon
    them.

AMPHITRYON (*looking*) The signature is firm.   235

SOSIA (*giving him the casket*) Then take the signature into your own
    custody, and open it; for I will have nothing done at my proper
    peril.

AMPHITRYON (*breaking open the seal*) O heavens! Here's nothing but
    an empty space, the nest where they were laid.   240

SOSIA Then if the birds are flown, the fault's not mine. Here has
    been fine conjuring work; or else the jewel, knowing to whom it
    should be given, took occasion to steal out, by a natural instinct,
    and tied itself upon that pretty arm.

AMPHITRYON Can this be possible?   245

SOSIA Yes, very possible. You, my Lord Amphitryon, may have
    brought forth another you my Lord Amphitryon, as well as I Sosia
    have brought forth another me Sosia; and our diamonds may have
    procreated these diamonds—and so we are all three double.

PHAEDRA (*aside*) If this be true, I hope my goblet has gigged another   250
    golden goblet; and then they may carry double upon all four.°

ALCMENA My lord, I have stood silent, out of wonder
    What you could wonder at.

AMPHITRYON (*aside*) A chilling sweat, a damp of jealousy,
    Hangs on my brows and clams upon my limbs.   255
    I fear; and yet I must be satisfied—
    And, to be satisfied, I must dissemble.

ALCMENA Why muse you so, and murmur to yourself?
    If you repent your bounty, take it back.

AMPHITRYON Not so; but, if you please, relate what passed   260
    At our last interview.

ALCMENA That question would infer you were not here.

AMPHITRYON I say not so;
    I only would refresh my memory,
    And have my reasons to desire the story.   265

PHAEDRA [*aside*] So. This is as good sport for me as an examination
    of a great belly before a magistrate.°

ALCMENA The story is not long. You know I met you,

Kissed you, and pressed you close within my arms
With all the tenderness of wifely love.   270
AMPHITRYON (*aside*) I could have spared that kindness.
  (*To her*) And what did I?
ALCMENA You strained me with a masculine embrace,
  As you would squeeze my soul out.
AMPHITRYON   Did I so?
ALCMENA You did.   275
AMPHITRYON (*aside*) Confound those arms that were so kind.
  (*To her*) Proceed, proceed.
ALCMENA You would not stay to sup, but, much complaining of
  your drowsiness and want of natural rest—
AMPHITRYON Made haste to bed. Ha, was't not so? Go on—   280
  (*Aside*) And stab me with each syllable thou speak'st.
PHAEDRA [*aside*] So. Now 'tis coming, now 'tis coming.
ALCMENA I have no more to say.
AMPHITRYON   Why, went we not to bed?
ALCMENA Why not?
  Is it a crime for husband and for wife   285
  To go to bed, my lord?
AMPHITRYON   Perfidious woman!
ALCMENA Ungrateful man!
AMPHITRYON   She justifies it too!
ALCMENA I need not justify. Of what am I accused?
AMPHITRYON Of all that prodigality of kindness,
  Given to another, and usurped from me.   290
  So bless me heaven, if since my first departure
  I ever set my foot upon this threshold.
  So am I innocent of all those joys
  And dry of those embraces.
ALCMENA   Then I, it seems, am false?
AMPHITRYON As surely false as what thou say'st is true.   295
ALCMENA I have betrayed my honour, and my love?
  And am a foul adulteress?
AMPHITRYON   What thou art,
  Thou stand'st condemned to be by thy relation.
ALCMENA Go, thou unworthy man; for ever go.
  No more my husband, go, thou base impostor,
  Who tak'st a vile pretence to taint my fame,°   300
  And, not content to leave, wouldst ruin me.
  Enjoy thy wished divorce. I will not plead

My innocence of this pretended crime.
I need not. Spit thy venom. Do thy worst.   305
But know: the more thou wouldst expose my virtue,
Like purest linen laid in open air,
'Twill bleach the more and whiten to the view.
AMPHITRYON 'Tis well thou art prepared for thy divorce;
For know thou too, that after this affront,   310
This foul indignity, done to my honour,
Divorcement is but petty reparation.
But, since thou hast with impudence affirmed
My false return, and bribed my slaves to vouch it,
The truth shall, in the face of Thebes, be cleared.   315
Thy uncle, the companion of my voyage,
And all the crew of seamen, shall be brought,
Who were embarked and came with me to land,
Nor parted till I reached this cursèd door.
So shall this vision of my late return   320
Stand a detected lie; and woe to those
Who thus betrayed my honour.
SOSIA Sir, shall I wait on you?°
AMPHITRYON No, I will go alone. Expect me here.°
         Exit Amphitryon
PHAEDRA (*to Alcmena*) Please you—that I—   325
ALCMENA O, nothing now can please me.
Darkness, and solitude, and sighs, and tears,
And all the inseparable train of grief,
Attend my steps for ever.
         Exit Alcmena
SOSIA (*aside*) What if I should lie now, and say we have been here   330
before? I never saw any good that came of telling truth.
PHAEDRA (*aside*) He makes no more advances to me. I begin a little
to suspect that my gold goblet will prove but copper.
SOSIA (*aside*) Yes, 'tis resolved; I will lie abominably, against the light
of my own conscience. For suppose the t'other Sosia has been   335
here. Perhaps that strong dog has not only beaten me, but also has
been predominant° upon my wife, and most carnally misused her!
Now, by asking certain questions of her, with a side wind,° I may
come to understand how squares go,° and whether my nuptial bed
be violated.   340
PHAEDRA (*aside*) Most certainly he has learned impudence of his
master, and will deny his being here. But that shall not serve his

turn, to cheat me of my present! [*To him*] Why, Sosia! What, in a
brown study?°

SOSIA A little *cogitabund*, or so, concerning this dismal revolution in
our family!

45

PHAEDRA But that should not make you neglect your duty to me,
your mistress.

SOSIA Pretty soul, I would thou wert—upon condition that old
Bromia were six foot under ground.

50

PHAEDRA What! Is all your hot courtship to me dwindled into a poor
unprofitable wish? You may remember I did not bid you absolutely
despair.

SOSIA No; for all things yet may be accommodated,° in an amicable
manner, betwixt my master and my lady.

55

PHAEDRA I mean, to the business betwixt you and me—

SOSIA Why, I hope we two never quarrelled?

PHAEDRA Must I remember° you of a certain promise that you made
me at our last parting?

SOSIA O, when I went to the army: that I should still° be praising
thy beauty to Judge Gripus, and keep up his affections to thee.

60

PHAEDRA No; I mean the business betwixt you and me this morning—that you promised me.

SOSIA That I promised thee. (*Aside*) I find it now. That strong
dog, my brother Sosia, has been here before me, and made love
to her.

65

PHAEDRA You are considering whether or no you should keep your
promise.

SOSIA That I should keep my promise? (*Aside*) The truth on't is,
she's anotherguess morsel than old Bromia.

70

PHAEDRA And I had rather you should break it, in a manner, and as
it were, and in some sense—

SOSIA 'In a manner, and as it were, and in some sense', thou say'st?
(*Aside*) I find the strong dog has only tickled up her imagination,
and not enjoyed her; so that with my own limbs I may perform
the sweetness of his function with her. (*To her*) No, sweet creature,
the promise shall not be broken; but what I have undertaken, I will
perform like a man of honour.

75

PHAEDRA Then you remember the preliminaries of the present?

SOSIA Yes, yes, in gross I do remember, something; but this disturbance of the family has somewhat stupefied my memory. Some
pretty *quelque chose*, I warrant thee; some acceptable toy, of small
value.

80

PHAEDRA You may call a gold goblet a toy; but I put a greater value
upon your presents.   385

SOSIA A gold goblet, say'st thou! Yes, now I think on't, it was a kind
of a gold goblet—as a gratuity after consummation.

PHAEDRA No, no; I had rather make sure of one bribe beforehand
than be promised ten gratuities.

SOSIA Yes, now I remember. It was, in some sense, a gold goblet, by   390
way of earnest; and it contained—

PHAEDRA One large—

SOSIA How, one large—?

PHAEDRA Gallon.

SOSIA No; that was somewhat too large, in conscience. It was not a   395
whole gallon; but it may contain, reasonably speaking, one large—
thimbleful. But gallons and thimblefuls are so like, that, in
speaking, I might easily mistake them.

PHAEDRA Is it come to this? Out, traitor!

SOSIA I had been a traitor, indeed, to have betrayed thee to the   400
swallowing of a gallon. But a thimbleful of cordial-water is easily
sipped off; and then this same goblet is so very light too, that it
will be no burden to carry it about with thee in thy pocket.

PHAEDRA O apostate to thy love! O perjured villain!

Enter Bromia

What, are you here, Bromia! I was telling him his own.° I was   405
giving him a rattle for his treacheries to you, his love. You see I
can be a friend, upon occasion.

BROMIA Ay, chicken, I never doubted of thy kindness. But, for this
fugitive—this rebel—this miscreant—

SOSIA A kind welcome to an absent lover, as I have been.   410

BROMIA Ay; and a kind greeting you gave me at your return, when
you used me so barbarously this morning.

SOSIA (*aside*) The t'other Sosia has been with her too, and has used
her barbarously—barbarously, that is to say, uncivilly: and uncivilly—I am afraid that means, too civilly.°   415

PHAEDRA You had best deny you were here this morning! And by
the same token—

SOSIA Nay, no more tokens, for heaven's sake, dear Phaedra. (*Aside*)
Now must I ponder with myself a little, whether it be better for
me to have been here, or not to have been here, this morning.   420

Enter a Servant

SERVANT Phaedra, my lord's without, and will not enter till he has
first spoken with you.

Exit Servant

PHAEDRA O that I could stay to help worry thee for this abuse; but
the best on't is, I leave thee in good hands. (*To him in private*)
Farewell, thimble.—To him, Bromia.   425

Exit Phaedra

BROMIA No; you did not beat me, and put me into a swoon, and
deprive me of the natural use of my tongue for a long half-hour.
You did not beat me down with your little wand. But I shall teach
you to use your rod another time, I shall.

SOSIA (*aside*) Put her into a swoon with my little wand, and so forth?   430
That's more than ever I could do. These are terrible circumstan-
ces° that some Sosia or another has been here. Now, if he has
literally beaten her, gramercy, brother Sosia. He has but done what
I would have done, if I had durst. But I am afraid it was only a
damned love-figure,° and that the wand that laid her asleep might   435
signify the peace-maker.°

BROMIA Now you are snuffling upon a cold scent, for some pitiful
excuse. I know you: twenty to one, but you will plead a drunkenness. You are used to be pot-valiant.

SOSIA [*aside*] I was pumping; and I thank her—she has invented for   440
me. [*To her*] Yes, Bromia, I must confess I was exalted;° and,
possibly, I might scour upon thee, or perhaps be a little more
familiar with thy person, by the way of kindness, than if I had been
sober. But, prithee, inform me what I did, that I may consider
what satisfaction I am to make thee.   445

BROMIA Are you there, at your dog-tricks! You would be forgetting,
would you? Like a drunken bully that affronts over-night, and,
when he is called to account the next morning, remembers nothing
of the quarrel, and asks pardon, to avoid fighting.

SOSIA By Bacchus,° I was overtaken;° but I should be loth that I   450
committed any folly with thee.

BROMIA (*crying*) I am sure I kept myself awake all night, that I did,
in expectation of your coming.

SOSIA But what amends did I make thee, when I came?

BROMIA You know well enough, to my sorrow; but that you play the   455
hypocrite.

SOSIA I warrant I was monstrous kind to thee.

BROMIA Yes, monstrous kind indeed. You never said a truer word;
for, when I came to kiss you, you pulled away your mouth and
turned your cheek to me.   460

SOSIA Good.

BROMIA How, good! Here's fine impudence. He justifies!

SOSIA Yes, I do justify, that I turned my cheek, like a prudent person, that my breath might not offend thee; for, now I remember, I had eaten garlic.   465

BROMIA Ay, you remember, and forget, just as it makes for you, or against you.° But, to mend the matter,° you never spoke one civil word to me, but stood like a stock, without sense or motion.

SOSIA (*aside*) Yet better.

BROMIA After which I lovingly invited you to take your place in your   470
nuptial bed, as the laws of matrimony oblige you, and you inhumanly refused me.

SOSIA Ay, there's the main point of the business! Art thou morally certain that I refused thee? Look me now in the face, and say I did not commit matrimony with thee!   475

BROMIA I wonder how thou canst look me in the face after that refusal!

SOSIA Say it once again, that I did not feloniously come to bed to thee!

BROMIA No, thou cold traitor, thou know'st thou didst not.   480

SOSIA [*aside*] Best of all. [*To her*] 'Twas discreetly done of me to abstain.

BROMIA What, do you insult upon me too!

SOSIA No, I do not insult upon you; but—

BROMIA But what? How was it discreetly done then? Ha!   485

SOSIA Because it is the received opinion of physicians, that nothing but puling chits and booby-fools are procreated in drunkenness.

BROMIA A 'received opinion', snivel-guts! I'll be judged by all the married women of this town, if any one of 'em has received it. The devil take the physicians, for meddling in our matters. If a husband   490
will be ruled by them, there are five weeks of abstinence in dog-days too,° for fear a child that was got in August should be born just nine months after, and be blear-eyed, like a May kitten.°

SOSIA Let the physicians alone; they are honest men, whatever the   495
world says of 'em.° But, for a certain reason that I best know, I am glad that matter ended so fairly and peaceably betwixt us.

BROMIA Yes, 'twas very fair and peaceable—to strike a woman down, and beat her most outrageously.

SOSIA Is it possible that I drubbed thee!   500

BROMIA I find your drift. You would fain be provoking me to a new trial now; but, i'faith, you shall bring me to no more handy blows.

I shall make bold to trust to my tongue hereafter. You never durst have offered to hold up a finger against me, till you went a-trooping.°

SOSIA (*strutting*) Then I am a conqueror, and I laud my own courage. This renown I have achieved by soldiership and stratagem. Know your duty, spouse, henceforward, to your supreme commander.

Enter Jupiter and Phaedra, attended by Musicians and Dancers

PHAEDRA [*to Jupiter*] Indeed I wondered at your quick return.

JUPITER Even so almighty Love will have it, Phaedra,
And the stern goddess of sweet-bitter cares,°
Who bows our necks beneath her brazen yoke.
I would have manned my heart, and held it out;°
But, when I thought of what I had possessed—
Those joys that never end, but to begin—
O, I am all on fire to make my peace,
And die, Jove knows, as much as I can die,°
Till I am reconciled.

PHAEDRA I fear 'twill be in vain.

JUPITER   'Tis difficult;
But nothing is impossible to love,
To love like mine; for I have proved° his force,
And my Alcmena too has felt his dart.
If I submit, there's hope.

PHAEDRA 'Tis possible I may solicit° for you.

JUPITER But wilt thou promise me to do thy best?

PHAEDRA (*curtsying*) Nay, I promise nothing—unless you begin to promise first.

JUPITER I won't° be ungrateful.

PHAEDRA Well; I'll try to bring her to the window. You shall have a fair shoot at her. If you can bring her down, you are a good marksman.

JUPITER That's all I ask.
And I will so reward thee, gentle Phaedra—

PHAEDRA What, with cats' guts and rosin! This sol-la is but a lamentable, empty sound.°

JUPITER (*throwing her a purse*) Then there's a sound will please thee better.

PHAEDRA Ay, there's something of melody in this sound. I could dance all day to the music of chink, chink.

Exit Phaedra

JUPITER Go, Sosia, round our Thebes,

To Polydas, to Tranio, and to Gripus,
Companions of our war. Invite 'em all
To join their prayers to smoothe Alcmena's brow,
And, with a solemn feast, to crown the day.

SOSIA (*taking Jupiter about the knees*) Let me embrace you, sir.   545
          Jupiter pushes him away
Nay, you must give me leave to express my gratitude. I have not
eaten, to say eating, nor drunk, to say drinking, never since our
villainous encamping so near the enemy. 'Tis true I 'scaped the
bloody flux,° because I had so little in my bowels to come out; and
I durst let nothing go, in conscience, because I had nothing to   550
swallow in the room on't.°

JUPITER You, Bromia, see that all things be prepared
With that magnificence as if some god
Were guest or master here.

SOSIA Or rather, as much as if twenty gods were to be guests or   555
masters here.

BROMIA That you may eat for today and tomorrow.

SOSIA Or, rather again, for today and yesterday, and as many months
backwards as I am indebted to my own belly.

JUPITER Away, both of you.   560
          Exeunt Sosia and Bromia severally
Now I have packed him hence, thou, other Sosia—
Who, though thou art not present, hear'st my voice—
Be ready to attend me at my call
And to supply his place.
          *Enter Mercury to Jupiter. Alcmena and Phaedra appear
          above,° Jupiter seeing Alcmena*
                    See, she appears.   565
This is my bribe to Phaedra. When I made
This gold, I made a greater god than Jove,
And gave my own omnipotence away.
          Jupiter signs to the Musicians, [*who perform a*] *song*

SONG

> *Celia, that I once was blessed°*
> *Is now the torment of my breast,*   570
> *Since, to curse me, you bereave me*
> *Of the pleasures I possessed.*
> *Cruel creature, to deceive me!*
> *First to love, and then to leave me!*

Had you the bliss refused to grant,   575
Then I had never known the want;
But possessing once the blessing
Is the cause of my complaint.
Once possessing is but tasting;
'Tis no bliss that is not lasting.   580

Celia now is mine no more;
But I am hers, and must adore.
Nor to leave her will endeavour.
Charms, that captived me before,
No unkindness can dissever.   585
Love that's true, is love for ever.

[*The musicians accompany the dancers in a*] *dance, after
which Alcmena withdraws, frowning*

JUPITER O stay.

MERCURY   She's gone, and seemed to frown at parting.

JUPITER Follow, and thou shalt see her soon appeased;
For I, who made her, know her inward state.
No woman, once well-pleased, can throughly hate.   590
I gave 'em beauty to subdue the strong—
A mighty empire, but it lasts not long.
I gave 'em pride to make mankind their slave;
But, in exchange, to men I flattery gave.
The offending lover, when he lowest lies,   595
Submits, to conquer, and but kneels, to rise.

    [*Exeunt*]

4.1

[Before Amphitryon's palace]

Enter Jupiter, following Alcmena; Mercury and Phaedra

JUPITER O stay, my dear Alcmena; hear me speak.

ALCMENA No, I would fly thee, to the ridge of earth,
And leap the precipice to 'scape thy sight.°

JUPITER For pity—

ALCMENA   Leave me, thou ungrateful man.

JUPITER I cannot leave you; no, but, like a ghost   5
Whom your unkindness murdered, will I haunt you.

ALCMENA Once more, be gone. I'm odious to myself
For having loved thee once.

JUPITER Hate not the best and fairest of your kind.
Nor can you hate your lover, though you would.   10
Your tears, that fall so gently, are but grief.
There may be anger; but there must be love.
The dove, that murmurs at her mate's neglect,
But counterfeits a coyness, to be courted.

ALCMENA Courtship from thee, and after such affronts!   15

JUPITER Is this that everlasting love you vowed
Last night, when I was circled in your arms?
Remember what you swore.

ALCMENA Think what thou wert, and who could swear too much?
Think what thou art, and that unswears it all.   20

JUPITER Can you forsake me for so small a fault?
'Twas but a jest, perhaps too far pursued.
'Twas but at most a trial of your faith,
How you could bear unkindness.
'Twas but to get a reconciling kiss,   25
A wanton stratagem of love.

ALCMENA See how he doubles, like a hunted hare.
A jest, and then a trial, and a bait—
All stuff and daubing!

JUPITER   Think me jealous then.

ALCMENA O, that I could; for that's a noble crime,   30
And which a lover can, with ease, forgive.
'Tis the high pulse of passion, in a fever—
A sickly draught, but shows a burning thirst.

Thine was a surfeit, not a jealousy;
And, in that loathing of thy full-gorged love,   35
Thou saw'st the nauseous object with disdain.

JUPITER O think not that, for you are ever new.
Your fruits of love are like eternal spring
In happy climes, where some are in the bud,
Some green, and ripening some, while others fall.   40

ALCMENA Ay, now you tell me this,
When roused desires, and fresh recruits of force,°
Enable languished love to take the field.
But never hope to be received again.
You would again deny you were received,   45
And brand my spotless fame.

JUPITER I will not dare to justify my crime,
But only point you where to lay the blame:
Impute it to the husband, not the lover.

ALCMENA How vainly would the sophister divide,   50
And make the husband and the lover two!

JUPITER Yes, 'tis the husband is the guilty wretch:
His insolence forgot the sweets of love,
And, deeming them his due, despised the feast.
Not so the famished lover could forget: 55
He knew he had been there, and had been blessed
With all that hope can wish, or sense can bear.

ALCMENA Husband, and lover, both alike I hate.

JUPITER And I confess I have deserved that hate.
    (*Kneeling*)
Too charming fair, I kneel for your forgiveness.   60
I beg by those fair eyes,
Which gave me wounds that time can never cure—
Receive my sorrows, and restore my joys.

ALCMENA Unkind, and cruel! I can speak no more.

JUPITER O, give it vent, Alcmena, give it vent.   65
I merit your reproach; I would be cursed.
Let your tongue curse me, while your heart forgives.

ALCMENA Can I forget such usage?

JUPITER   Can you hate me?

ALCMENA I'll do my best; for sure I ought to hate you.

JUPITER That word was only hatched upon your tongue;°   70
It came not from your heart. But try again;
And if, once more, you can but say 'I hate you',

My sword shall do you justice.
ALCMENA   Then, I hate you.
JUPITER Then you pronounce the sentence of my death?
ALCMENA I hate you, much; but yet I love you more.   75
JUPITER To prove that love, then say that you forgive me;
   For there remains but this alternative—
   Resolve to pardon, or to punish me.
ALCMENA Alas, what I resolve appears too plain:
   In saying that I cannot hate, I pardon.   80
JUPITER But what's a pardon worth without a seal?
   Permit me, in this transport of my joy—
       [*Jupiter*] *kisses her hand*
ALCMENA (*putting him gently away with her hand*)
   Forbear. I am offended with myself,
   That I have shown this weakness. Let me go,
   Where I may blush alone.
       Going, and looking back on him
                           But come not you,   85
   Lest I should spoil you with excess of fondness,°
   And let you love again.
       Exit Alcmena
JUPITER (*aside*) Forbidding me to follow, she invites me.
   This is the mould of which I made the sex.°
   I gave 'em but one tongue, to say us nay,   90
   And two kind eyes, to grant. (*To Mercury*) Be sure that none
   Approach, to interrupt our privacy.
       Exit Jupiter after Alcmena. Mercury and Phaedra remain
MERCURY Your lady has made the challenge of reconciliation to my
   lord. Here's a fair example for us two, Phaedra.
PHAEDRA No example at all, Sosia; for my lady had the diamonds   95
   aforehand, and I have none of the gold goblet.
MERCURY The goblet shall be forthcoming, if thou wilt give me
   weight for weight.
PHAEDRA Yes, and measure for measure too, Sosia—that is, for a
   thimbleful of gold a thimbleful of love.   100
MERCURY What think you now, Phaedra? (*Pulling out the goblet in a
   case from under his cloak*) Here's a weighty argument of love for you.
PHAEDRA (*taking it in both hands*) Now Jupiter, of his mercy, let me
   kiss thee, O thou dear metal!
MERCURY And Venus, of her mercy, let me kiss thee, dear, dear   105
   Phaedra.

PHAEDRA Not so fast, Sosia! There's a damned proverb in your
way. 'Many things happen betwixt the cup and the lips',° you
know.

MERCURY Why, thou wilt not cheat me of my goblet?   110

PHAEDRA Yes; as sure as you would cheat me of my maidenhead. I
am yet but just even with you for the last trick you played me.
And, besides, this is but a bare retaining-fee. You must give me
another, before the cause is opened.°

MERCURY Shall I not come to your bedside tonight?   115

PHAEDRA No, nor tomorrow-night neither. But this shall be my
sweetheart in your place. 'Tis a better bedfellow, and will keep me
warmer in cold weather.

    Exit Phaedra

MERCURY (*alone*) Now, what's the god of wit in a woman's hand?
This very goblet I stole from Gripus; and he got it out of bribes   120
too. But this is the common fate of ill-gotten goods, that as they
came in by covetousness, they go out by whoring.

    Enter Amphitryon

O, here's Amphitryon again; but I'll manage him above in the
balcony.

    Exit Mercury

AMPHITRYON Not one of those I looked for, to be found!   125
As some enchantment hid 'em from my sight!°
Perhaps, as Sosia says, 'tis witchcraft all.
Seals may be opened, diamonds may be stolen;
But how I came, in person, yesterday
And gave that present to Alcmena's hands—   130
That which I never gave, nor ever came—
O, there's the rock on which my reason splits.
Would that were all! I fear my honour, too!
I'll try her once again. She may be mad—
A wretched remedy, but all I have   135
To keep me from despair.

    [*Enter Mercury above*]

MERCURY (*from the balcony, aside*) This is no very charitable action
of a god—to use him ill, who has never offended me. But my
planet disposes me to malice;° and when we great persons do but
a little mischief, the world has a good bargain of us.   140

AMPHITRYON How now! What means the locking-up of my doors at
this time of day?

    [*Amphitryon*] *knocks* [*at the door*]

MERCURY Softly, friend, softly. You knock as loud, and as saucily,
as a lord's footman, that was sent before him to warn the family
of his honour's visit. Sure you think the doors have no feeling!   145
What the devil are you, that rap with such authority?

AMPHITRYON Look out, and see. 'Tis I.

MERCURY You. What you?

AMPHITRYON No more, I say, but open.

MERCURY I'll know to whom first.   150

AMPHITRYON I am one that can command the doors open.

MERCURY Then you had best command 'em, and try whether they
will obey you.

AMPHITRYON Dost thou not know me!

MERCURY Prithee, how should I know thee? Dost thou take me for   155
a conjuror?

AMPHITRYON What's this? Midsummer moon?° Is all the world
gone a-madding?° Why, Sosia!

MERCURY That's my name indeed. Didst thou think I had forgot it!

AMPHITRYON Dost thou see me?   160

MERCURY Why, dost thou pretend to go invisible? If thou hast any
business here, dispatch it quickly. I have no leisure to throw away
upon such prattling companions.

AMPHITRYON Thy companion, slave? How dar'st thou use this
insolent language to thy master!   165

MERCURY How! Thou my master? By what title? I never had any
other master but Amphitryon.

AMPHITRYON Well. And for whom dost thou take me?

MERCURY For some rogue° or other; but what rogue I know not.

AMPHITRYON Dost thou not know me for Amphitryon, slave!   170

MERCURY How should I know thee, when I see thou dost not know
thyself! Thou Amphitryon? In what tavern hast thou been? And
how many bottles did thy business, to metamorphose thee into my
lord?

AMPHITRYON I will so drub thee for this insolence!   175

MERCURY How now, impudence! Are you threatening your betters!
I should bring you to condign punishment, but that I have a great
respect for the good wine, though I find it in a fool's noddle.°

AMPHITRYON What, none to let me in? Why, Phaedra! Bromia!

MERCURY Peace, fellow. If my wife hears thee, we are both undone.   180
At a word, Phaedra and Bromia are very busy—one in making a
caudle for my lady, and the other in heating napkins, to rub down
my lord, when he rises from bed.

AMPHITRYON Amazement seizes me.

MERCURY At what art thou amazed? My master and my lady had a   185
falling-out, and are retired, without seconds, to decide the quarrel.
If thou wert not a meddlesome fool, thou wouldst not be thrusting
thy nose into other people's matters. Get thee about thy business,
if thou hast any; for I'll hear no more of thee.

    Exit Mercury from above

AMPHITRYON Braved by my slave, dishonoured by my wife,   190
  To what a desperate plunge am I reduced,
  If this be true the villain says! But why
  That feeble *if*! It must be true. She owns it.
  Now, whether to conceal, or blaze th'affront?
  One way, I spread my infamy abroad;   195
  And, t'other, hide a burning coal within,
  That preys upon my vitals. I can fix
  On nothing but on vengeance.

    Enter to him Sosia, Polydas, Gripus, Tranio

GRIPUS Yonder he is, walking hastily to and fro before his door—like
a citizen° clapping his sides before his shop in a frosty morning.   200
'Tis to catch a stomach,° I believe.

SOSIA I begin to be afraid that he has more stomach to my sides and
shoulders than to his own victuals. How he shakes his head and
stamps! And what strides he fetches! He's in one of his damned
moods again. I don't like the looks of him.   205

AMPHITRYON [*seeing Sosia*] O, my mannerly, fair-spoken, obedient
slave, are you there! I can reach you now, without climbing. Now
we shall try who's drunk, and who's sober.

SOSIA Why, this is as it should be. I was somewhat suspicious that
you were in a pestilent humour. Yes, we will have a crash at the   210
bottle,° when your lordship pleases. I have summoned 'em, you
see; and they are notable topers, especially Judge Gripus.

GRIPUS Yes, 'faith; I never refuse my glass in a good quarrel.

AMPHITRYON (*to Sosia*) Why, thou insolent villain! I'll teach a slave
how to use his master thus.   215

SOSIA Here's a fine business towards.° I am sure I ran as fast as ever
my legs could carry me, to call 'em. Nay, you may trust my
diligence in all affairs belonging to the belly.

GRIPUS He has been very faithful to his commission, I'll bear him
witness.   220

AMPHITRYON How can you be witness, where you were not present?
  [*To Sosia*] The balcony! Sirrah, the balcony!

SOSIA Why, to my best remembrance, you never invited the balcony.

AMPHITRYON What nonsense dost thou plead for an excuse of thy
foul language and thy base replies!   225

SOSIA You fright a man out of his senses first, and blame him,
afterwards, for talking nonsense. But 'tis better for me to talk
nonsense than for some to do nonsense. I will say that, whate'er
comes on't. Pray, sir, let all things be done decently. What, I hope,
when a man is to be hanged, he is not trussed upon the gallows,   230
like a dumb dog,° without telling him wherefore.

AMPHITRYON [*preparing to beat Sosia*] By your pardon, gentlemen;
I have no longer patience to forbear him.

SOSIA Justice, justice, my Lord Gripus; as you are a true magistrate,
protect me. Here's a process° of beating going forward without   235
sentence given.

GRIPUS My Lord Amphitryon, this must not be. Let me first
understand the demerits of the criminal.

SOSIA Hold you to that point, I beseech your honour, as you
commiserate the case of a poor, innocent malefactor.   240

AMPHITRYON To shut the door against me in my very face; to deny
me entrance; to brave me from the balcony; to laugh at me; to
threaten me—what proofs of innocence call you these? But if I
punish not this insolence—

> [*Amphitryon*] *is going to beat him and is held by Polydas and*
> *Tranio*

I beg you let me go.   245

SOSIA I charge you in the king's name, hold him fast; for you see he's
bloodily disposed.

GRIPUS Now, what hast thou to say for thyself, Sosia?

SOSIA I say, in the first place, be sure you hold him, gentlemen; for
I shall never plead° worth one farthing, while I am bodily afraid.   250

POLYDAS Speak boldly; I warrant thee.°

SOSIA Then, if I may speak boldly, under my lord's favour,° I do not
say he lies neither—no, I am too well-bred for that—but his
lordship fibs most abominably.

AMPHITRYON Do you hear his impudence? Yet will you let me go?   255

SOSIA No impudence at all, my lord; for how could I, naturally
speaking, be in the balcony, and affronting you, when at the same
time I was in every street of Thebes, inviting these gentlemen to
dinner?

GRIPUS Hold a little. How long since was it that he spoke to you   260
from the said balcony?

AMPHITRYON Just now; not a minute before he brought you hither.

SOSIA Now speak, my witnesses.

GRIPUS I can answer for him for this last half-hour.

POLYDAS And I.

TRANIO And I.   265

SOSIA Now judge equitably, gentlemen, whether I was not a civil, well-bred person, to tell my lord he fibs only?

AMPHITRYON Who gave you that order to invite 'em?

SOSIA He that best might—yourself. By the same token, you bid old   270
Bromia provide an° 'twere for a god, and I put in for a brace or a lease. No, now I think on't, it was for ten couple of gods, to make sure of plenty.°

AMPHITRYON When did I give thee this pretended commission?

SOSIA Why, you gave me this pretended commission, when you were   275
just ready to give my lady the fiddles and a dance, in order, as I suppose, to your second bedding.

AMPHITRYON Where, in what place, did I give this order?

SOSIA Here, in this place, in the presence of this very door and of
that balcony; and if they could speak, they would both justify it.   280

AMPHITRYON O heaven, these accidents are so surprising, that the more I think of 'em, the more I am lost in my imagination.

GRIPUS Nay, he has told us some passages, as he came along, that seem to surpass the power of nature.

SOSIA What think you now, my lord, of a certain twin brother of   285
mine, called Sosia? 'Tis a sly youth. Pray heaven you have not just such another relation within-doors called Amphitryon. It may be it was he that put upon me in your likeness; and perhaps he may have put something upon your lordship too, that may weigh heavy upon the forehead.°   290

AMPHITRYON (to those that hold him) Let me go. Sosia may be innocent, and I will not hurt him.
      [They release him]
Open the door; I'll resolve my doubts immediately.

SOSIA The door is peremptory that it will not be opened without keys; and my brother on the inside is in possession and will not   295
part with 'em.

AMPHITRYON Then 'tis manifest that I am affronted. Break open the door there.

GRIPUS Stir not a man of you to his assistance.

AMPHITRYON Dost thou take part with my adulteress too, because   300
she is thy niece?

GRIPUS I take part with nothing but the law; and to break the doors
open is to break the law.

AMPHITRYON Do thou command 'em then.

GRIPUS I command nothing without my warrant; and my clerk is not   305
here to take his fees for drawing it.

AMPHITRYON (*aside*) The devil take all justice-brokers. I curse him
too when I have been hunting him all over the town to be my
witness! But I'll bring soldiers to force open the doors by my own
commission.   310
        Exit Amphitryon

SOSIA [*aside*] Pox o' these forms of law, to defeat a man of a dinner,
when he's sharp-set! 'Tis against the privilege of a free-born
stomach,° and is no less than subversion of fundamentals.°
        [*Enter*] *Jupiter above in the balcony*

JUPITER O, my friends, I am sorry I have made you wait so long.
You are welcome, and the door shall be opened to you immediately.   315
        Exit Jupiter

GRIPUS Was not that Amphitryon?

SOSIA Why, who should it be else?

GRIPUS In all appearance it was he; but how got he thither?

POLYDAS In such a trice too!

TRANIO And after he had just left us?   320

GRIPUS And so much altered for the better in his humour?

SOSIA Here's such a company of foolish questions, when a man's
a-hungry. You had best stay° dinner till he has proved himself to
be Amphitryon in form of law. But I'll make short work of that
business, for I'll take mine oath 'tis he.   325

GRIPUS I should be glad it were.

SOSIA How, 'glad it were'? With your damned interrogatories, when
you ought to be thankful that so it is!

GRIPUS (*aside*) That I may see my mistress Phaedra and present her
with my great gold goblet.   330

SOSIA If this be not the true Amphitryon, I wish I may be kept
without-doors, fasting, and biting my own fingers for want of
victuals; and that's a dreadful imprecation! I am for the inviting, and eating, and treating Amphitryon. I am sure 'tis he that
is my lawfully begotten lord. And if you had an ounce of true   335
justice in you, you ought to have laid hold on t'other Amphitryon, and committed him for a rogue, and an impostor, and a
vagabond.
        The door is opened

MERCURY (*from within*) Enter quickly, masters. The passage on the right hand leads to the gallery, where my lord expects you—for I am called another way.

Gripus, Tranio, and Polydas go into the house

SOSIA I should know that voice by a secret instinct. 'Tis a tongue of my family, and belongs to my brother Sosia. It must be so, for it carries a cudgelling kind of sound in it. But put the worst; let me weigh this matter wisely. Here's a beating, and a bellyful— against no beating, and no bellyful. The beating is bad; but the dinner is good. Now, not to be beaten is but negatively good; but not to fill my belly is positively bad. Upon the whole matter, my final resolution is to take the good and the bad as they come together.

[Sosia] is entering; Mercury meets him at the door

MERCURY Whither now, you kitchen-scum? From whence this impudence, to enter here without permission?

SOSIA Most illustrious sir, my ticket is my hunger. Show the full bowels of your compassion to the empty bowels of my famine.

MERCURY Were you not charged to return no more? I'll cut you into quarters and hang you upon the shambles.

SOSIA You'll get but little credit by me. Alas, sir, I am but mere carrion! Brave Sosia, compassionate° coward Sosia, and beat not thyself in beating me.

MERCURY Who gave you that privilege, sirrah, to assume my name? Have you not been sufficiently warned of it? And received part of punishment already?

SOSIA May it please you, sir, the name is big enough for both of us; and we may use it in common, like a strumpet. Witness heaven, that I would have obeyed you, and quitted my title to the name; but, wherever I come, the malicious world will call me Sosia in spite of me. I am sensible there are two Amphitryons; and why may not there be two Sosias? Let those two cut one another's throats at their own pleasure; but you and I will be wiser, by my consent, and hold good intelligence together.°

MERCURY No, no, two Sosias would but make two fools.

SOSIA Then let me be the fool, and be you the prudent person; and choose for yourself some wiser name. Or you shall be the elder brother, and I'll be content to be the younger, though I lose my inheritance.

MERCURY I tell thee I am the only son of our family.

SOSIA   Then let me be your bastard brother and the son of a whore.
  I hope that's but reasonable.

MERCURY   No, thou shalt not disgrace my father; for there are few   380
  bastards nowadays worth owning.°

SOSIA   Ah! Poor Sosia! What will become of thee?

MERCURY   Yet again profanely using my proper name?

SOSIA   I did not mean myself. I was thinking of another Sosia, a poor
  fellow, that was once of my acquaintance, unfortunately banished   385
  out of doors, when dinner was just coming upon the table.

  Enter Phaedra

PHAEDRA   Sosia, you and I must—Bless me! What have we here?
  A couple of you! Or do I see double?

SOSIA   I would fain bring it about, that I might make one of 'em.°
  But he's unreasonable and will needs incorporate me° and swallow   390
  me whole into himself. If he would be content to be but one and
  a half, 'twould never grieve me.

MERCURY   'Tis a perverse rascal. I kick him and cudgel him to no
  purpose; for still he's obstinate to stick to me,° and I can never
  beat him out of my resemblance.°   395

PHAEDRA   Which of you two is Sosia? For t'other must be the devil.

SOSIA   You had best ask him that has played the devil with my back
  and sides.

MERCURY   You had best ask him who gave you the gold goblet.

PHAEDRA   No, that's already given. But he shall be my Sosia, that   400
  will give me such another.

MERCURY   I find you have been interloping, sirrah.

SOSIA   No, indeed, sir. I only promised her a gold thimble, which was
  as much as comes to my proportion of being Sosia.

PHAEDRA   This is no Sosia for my money. Beat him away, t'other   405
  Sosia. He grows insufferable.

SOSIA   (*aside*) Would I were valiant, that I might beat him away, and
  succeed him at the dinner, for a pragmatical son of a whore as he
  is!

MERCURY   What's that you are muttering betwixt your teeth, of a   410
  'son of a whore', sirrah?

SOSIA   I am sure I meant you no offence; for, if I am not Sosia, I am
  the son of a whore, for aught I know. And, if you are Sosia, you
  may be the son of a whore, for aught you know.

MERCURY   Whatever I am, I will be Sosia as long as I please. And   415
  whenever you visit me, you shall be sure of the civility of the
  cudgel.

SOSIA If you will promise to beat me into the house, you may begin
when you please with me. But, to be beaten out of the house at
dinner-time, flesh and blood can never bear it.   420

> *Mercury beats him about, and Sosia is still making towards
> the door; but Mercury gets betwixt, and at length drives him
> off the stage*

PHAEDRA In the name of wonder, what are you, that are Sosia and
are not Sosia?

MERCURY If thou wouldst know more of me, my person is freely at
thy disposing.

PHAEDRA Then I dispose of it to you again; for 'tis so ugly, 'tis not   425
for my use.

MERCURY I can be ugly or handsome, as I please—go to bed old, and
rise young. I have so many suits of persons by me, that I can shift
'em° when I will.

PHAEDRA You are a fool then to put on your worst clothes, when   430
you come a-wooing.

MERCURY Go to. Ask no more questions. I am for thy turn;° for I
know thy heart, and see all thou hast about thee.

PHAEDRA Then you can see my back-side too; there's a bargain for
you.°   435

MERCURY In thy right pocket—let me see—three love letters from
Judge Gripus, written to the bottom on three sides, full of fustian
passion and hearty nonsense; as also, in the same pocket, a letter
of thine intended to him, consisting of nine lines and a half,
scrawled and false-spelled, to show thou art a woman, and full of   440
fraudulence, and equivocations, and shoeing-horns° of love to him,
to promise much and mean nothing—to show, over and above, that
thou art a mere° woman.

PHAEDRA Is the devil in you, to see all this? Now, for heaven's sake,
do not look into t'other pocket.   445

MERCURY Nay, there's nothing there but a little godly prayer-book,
and—a bawdy lampoon—and—

PHAEDRA (*giving a great frisk*) Look no farther, I beseech you.

MERCURY And a silver spoon—

PHAEDRA (*shrieking*) Ah!   450

MERCURY Which you purloined last night from Bromia.

PHAEDRA (*holding up her hands to him*) Keep my counsel, or I am
undone for ever.

MERCURY No; I'll mortify thee, now I have a handle to thy iniquity,°
if thou wilt not love me.   455

PHAEDRA Well, if you'll promise me to be secret, I will love you—because indeed I dare do no other.

MERCURY 'Tis a good girl. I will be secret; and, further, I will be assisting to thee in thy filching, for thou and I were born under the same planet.°   460

PHAEDRA And we shall come to the same end too, I'm afraid.

MERCURY No, no; since thou hast wit enough already to cozen a judge, thou needst never fear hanging.

PHAEDRA And will you make yourself a younger man, and be handsome too, and rich? For you that know hearts must needs   465
know that I shall never be constant to such an ugly old Sosia.

MERCURY Thou shalt know more of that another time. In the meanwhile, here's a cast of my office° for thee.

*He stamps upon the ground.° Some dancers come from
underground, and others from the sides of the stage.*

MERCURY'S SONG TO PHAEDRA°

*Fair Iris I love, and hourly I die,
But not for a lip, nor a languishing eye.*   470
*She's fickle and false, and there we agree;
For I am as false, and as fickle as she.
We neither believe what either can say;
And, neither believing, we neither betray.*

'Tis civil to swear, and say things of course;°   475
*We mean not the taking for better for worse.°
When present, we love; when absent, agree—
I think not of Iris, nor Iris of me.
The legend of love no couple can find°
So easy to part, or so equally joined.°*   480

After [the song] a fantastic dance.° [Then exeunt dancers]

PHAEDRA This power of yours makes me suspect you for little better than a god; but if you are one, for more certainty, tell me what I am just now thinking.

MERCURY Why, thou art thinking—let me see—for thou art a woman, and your minds are so variable that 'tis very hard even for   485
a god to know them. But, to satisfy thee, thou art wishing now for the same power I have exercised, that thou mightest stamp, like me, and have more singers come up for another song.

PHAEDRA Gad, I think the devil's in you. Then I do stamp in somebody's name, but I know not whose. (*Stamps*) Come up,   490
gentlefolks, from below, and sing me a pastoral dialogue, where the

woman may have the better of the man, as we always have in love-matters.

New singers come up and sing a song

A PASTORAL DIALOGUE BETWIXT THYRSIS AND IRIS°

THYRSIS *Fair Iris and her swain*
Were in a shady bower, 495
Where Thyrsis long in vain
Had sought the shepherd's hour.°
At length his hand advancing upon her snowy breast,
He said, 'O kiss me longer,
And longer yet, and longer, 500
If you will make me blessed.'

IRIS *'An easy yielding maid*
By trusting is undone;
Our sex is oft betrayed
By granting love too soon. 505
If you desire to gain me, your sufferings to redress,
Prepare to love me longer,
And longer yet, and longer,
Before you shall possess.'

THYRSIS *'The little care you show* 510
Of all my sorrows past
Makes death appear too slow,
And life too long to last.
Fair Iris, kiss me kindly, in pity of my fate,
And kindly still, and kindly, 515
Before it be too late.'

IRIS *'You fondly court your bliss,*
And no advances make.
'Tis not for maids to kiss,
But 'tis for men to take. 520
So you may kiss me kindly, and I will not rebel,
And kindly still, and kindly,
But kiss me not and tell.'

A RONDEAU

CHORUS *Thus at the height we love and live,°*
And fear not to be poor; 525

> *We give, and give, and give, and give,*
>   *Till we can give no more.*
> *But what today will take away,*
>   *Tomorrow will restore.*
> *Thus at the height we love and live,*   530
>   *And fear not to be poor.*

[*Exeunt singers*]

PHAEDRA Adieu. I leave you to pay the music.° Hope well, Mr
Planet; there's a better heaven in store for you.° I say no more, but
you can guess.

Exit [*Phaedra*]

MERCURY (*alone*) Such bargain-loves as I with Phaedra treat   535
Are all the leagues and friendships of the great:
All seek their ends, and each would other cheat.
They only seem to hate, and seem to love;
But interest° is the point on which they move.
Their friends are foes, and foes are friends again—   540
And, in their turns, are knaves and honest men.
Our iron age is grown an age of gold:
'Tis who bids most, for all men would be sold.°

Exit

5.1

[*A courtyard inside Amphitryon's palace*]

Enter Gripus, Phaedra. Gripus has the goblet in his hand

PHAEDRA You will not be so base to take it from me?

GRIPUS 'Tis my proper chattel;° and I'll seize my own, in whatever hands I find it.

PHAEDRA You know I only showed it you to provoke your generosity, that you might outbid your rival with a better present. 5

GRIPUS My rival is a thief; and I'll indict you for a receiver of stolen goods.

PHAEDRA Thou hidebound lover!

GRIPUS Thou very mercenary mistress!

PHAEDRA Thou most mercenary magistrate! 10

GRIPUS Thou seller of thyself!

PHAEDRA Thou seller of other people! Thou weather-cock of government, that when the wind blows for the subject point'st to privilege,° and when it changes for the sovereign, veers to prerogative!°

GRIPUS Will you compound, and take it as my present? 15

PHAEDRA No; but I'll send thy rival to force it from thee.

GRIPUS When a thief is rival to his judge, the hangman will soon decide the difference.

Exit Phaedra. Enter Mercury, with two swords

MERCURY (*bowing*) Save your good lordship.

GRIPUS From an impertinent coxcomb. I am out of humour and am 20
in haste. Leave me.

MERCURY 'Tis my duty to attend on your lordship, and to ease you of that undecent burden.

GRIPUS Gold was never any burden to one of my profession.

MERCURY By your lordship's permission, Phaedra has sent me to 25
take it from you.

GRIPUS What, by violence?

MERCURY (*still bowing*) No; but, by your honour's permission, I am to restore it to her, and persuade your lordship to renounce your pretensions to her. 30

GRIPUS Tell her flatly, I will neither do one, nor t'other.

MERCURY O my good lord, I dare pass my word° for your free consent to both. Will your honour be pleased to take your choice of one of these?

GRIPUS Why, these are swords. What have I to do with them?   35

MERCURY Only to take your choice of one of them—which° your
lordship pleases—and leave the other to your most obedient
servant.

GRIPUS What, one of these ungodly weapons? Take notice: I'll lay
you by the heels,° sirrah. This has the appearance of an unlawful,   40
bloody challenge.°

MERCURY You magistrates are pleased to call it so, my lord; but,
with us swordmen, 'tis an honourable invitation to the cutting of
one another's throats.

GRIPUS Be answered: I have no throat to cut. The law shall decide   45
our controversy.

MERCURY By your permission, my lord, it must be dispatched this way.

GRIPUS I'll see thee hanged before I give thee any such permission
to dispatch me into another world.

MERCURY At the least, my lord, you have no occasion to complain   50
of my want of respect to you. You will neither restore the goblet
nor renounce Phaedra. I offer you the combat; you refuse it. All
this is done in the forms of honour.° It follows that I am to affront,
cudgel you, or kick you, at my own arbitrement; and I suppose you
are too honourable not to approve of my proceeding.   55

GRIPUS Here's a new sort of process that was never heard of in any
of our courts.

MERCURY This, my good lord, is law in shorthand, without your
long preambles and tedious repetitions that signify nothing but to
squeeze the subject.° Therefore, with your lordship's favour, I   60
begin.

[Mercury] fillips him under the chin

GRIPUS What's this for?

MERCURY To give you an occasion of returning me a box o' th'ear,
that, so, all things may proceed methodically.°

GRIPUS I put in no answer, but suffer a non-suit.°   65

MERCURY No, my lord; for the costs and charges are to be paid. Will
you please to restore the cup?

GRIPUS I have told thee: no.

MERCURY Then from your chin I must ascend to your lordship's
ears.   70

GRIPUS [as Mercury pulls his ears] O, O. O, O. Wilt thou never leave
lugging me by the ears?

MERCURY (pulling again) Not till your lordship will be pleased to
hear reason.

GRIPUS Take the cup; and the devil give thee joy on't.   75

MERCURY (*still holding him*) And your lordship will farther be graciously pleased to release all claims, titles, and actions whatsoever to Phaedra. You must give me leave (*pulling him again*) to add one small memento for that too.

GRIPUS I renounce her; I release her.   80

> *Enter Phaedra*

MERCURY (*to her*) Phaedra, my lord has been pleased to be very gracious, without pushing matters to extremity.

PHAEDRA I overheard it all. But give me livery and seisin° of the goblet in the first place.

MERCURY There's an Act of Oblivion° should be passed too.   85

PHAEDRA Let him begin to remember quarrels, when he dares. Now I have him under my girdle,° I'll cap verses with him to the end of the chapter.°

> *Enter Amphitryon and Guards*

AMPHITRYON (*to Gripus*) At the last I have got possession without your lordship's warrant. Phaedra, tell Alcmena I am here.   90

PHAEDRA I'll carry no such lying message. You are not here, and you cannot be here; for, to my knowledge, you are above with my lady in the chamber!

AMPHITRYON All of a piece,° and all witchcraft! Answer me precisely: dost thou not know me for Amphitryon?   95

PHAEDRA Answer me first: did you give me a diamond and a purse of gold?

AMPHITRYON Thou know'st I did not.

PHAEDRA Then, by the same token, I know you are not the true Amphitryon. If you are he, I am sure I left you in bed with your   100
own wife. Now you had best stretch out a leg, and feel about for a fair lady.

AMPHITRYON I'll undo this enchantment with my sword, and kill the sorcerer. (*To the Guards*) Come up, gentlemen, and follow me.

PHAEDRA I'll save you the labour, and call him down to confront   105
you, if you dare attend him.

> *Exit Phaedra*

MERCURY (*aside*) Now the spell is ended, and Jupiter can enchant no more; or else Amphitryon had not entered so easily.

> *Gripus is stealing off*

Whither now, Gripus? I have business for you. If you offer to stir, you know what follows.   110

> *Enter Jupiter, followed by Tranio and Polydas*

JUPITER Who dares to play the master in my house?
    What noise is this, that calls me from above,
    Invades my soft recess and privacy,
    And, like a tide, breaks in upon my love?
AMPHITRYON O heavens, what's this I see?   115
TRANIO What prodigy!
POLYDAS   How, two Amphitryons!
GRIPUS I have beheld the appearance of two suns;
    But still the false was dimmer than the true.
    Here both shine out alike.
AMPHITRYON This is a sight that like the Gorgon's head°   120
    Runs through my limbs and stiffens me to stone.
    I need no more inquire into my fate;
    For what I see resolves my doubts too plain.
TRANIO Two drops of water cannot be more like.
POLYDAS They are two very sames.   125
MERCURY (aside) Our Jupiter is a great comedian;° he counterfeits
    most admirably. Sure his priests have copied their hypocrisy from
    their master.
AMPHITRYON Now I am gathered back into myself,
    My heart beats high, and pushes out the blood   130
    (Drawing his sword)
    To give me just revenge on this impostor.
    (To the Guards)
    If you are brave, assist me.—Not one stirs.
    What, are all bribed to take the enchanter's part?
    'Tis true, the work is mine; and thus—
        [Amphitryon is] going to rush upon Jupiter, and is held by
        Tranio and Polydas
POLYDAS It must not be.   135
JUPITER Give him his way. I dare the madman's worst.
    But still take notice, that it looks not like
    The true Amphitryon, to fly out at first
    To brutal force. It shows he doubts his cause,
    Who dares not trust his reason to defend it.   140
AMPHITRYON (struggling) Thou base usurper of my name and bed,
    No less than thy heart's blood can wash away
    The affronts I have sustained.
TRANIO   We must not suffer
    So strange a duel as Amphitryon
    To fight against himself.   145

POLYDAS Nor think we wrong you, when we hold your hands.
We know our duty to our general;
We know the ties of friendship to our friend.
But who that friend, or who that general is,
Without more certain proofs betwixt you two,   150
Is hard to be distinguished by our reason,
Impossible by sight.

AMPHITRYON I know it, and have satisfied myself.
I am the true Amphitryon.

JUPITER   See again.
He shuns the certain proofs, and dares not stand   155
Impartial judgment and award of right.
But since Alcmena's honour is concerned,
Whom more than heaven and all the world I love,
This I propose, as equal to us both.°
Tranio and Polydas, be you assistants.   160
The guards be ready to secure th'impostor,
When once so proved, for public punishment;
And, Gripus, be thou umpire of the cause.

AMPHITRYON I am content. Let him proceed to examination.

GRIPUS (aside to Mercury) On whose side would you please that I   165
should give the sentence?

MERCURY (aside to him) Follow thy conscience for once—but not to
make a custom of it neither, nor to leave an evil precedent of
uprightness to future judges. (Aside) 'Tis a good thing to have a
magistrate under correction.° Your old fornicating judge dare   170
never give sentence against him that knows his haunts.

GRIPUS Let the true Amphitryon answer first.

JUPITER and AMPHITRYON (together) My lord, I told him—

GRIPUS Peace, both of you.—'Tis a plain case: they are both true, for
they both speak together. But, for more certainty, let the false   175
Amphitryon speak first.

MERCURY Now they are both silent.

GRIPUS Then it's as plain on t'other side, that they are both false
Amphitryons.

MERCURY Which Amphitryon shall speak first?   180

GRIPUS Let the choleric Amphitryon speak, and let the peaceable
hold his peace.

AMPHITRYON (to Polydas) You may remember that I whispered you
not to part from the stern one single moment.

POLYDAS You did so.   185

GRIPUS No more words then; I proceed to sentence.

JUPITER 'Twas I that whispered him, and he may remember I gave him this reason for it: that if our men were beaten, I might secure my own retreat.

POLYDAS You did so.   190

GRIPUS Now again he's as true as t'other.

TRANIO You know I was paymaster. What directions did you give me the night before the battle?

GRIPUS To which of the you's art thou speaking?

MERCURY (aside) It should be a double U; but they have no such   195
letter in their tongue.°

AMPHITRYON I ordered you to take particular care of the great bag.

GRIPUS Why, this is demonstration.

JUPITER The bag that I recommended to you was of tiger's skin, and   200
marked *Beta*.

GRIPUS In sadness° I think they are both jugglers. Here's nothing, and here's nothing; and then *hiccius doccius*° and they are both here again.

TRANIO You peaceable Amphitryon, what money was there in that   205
bag?

JUPITER The sum in gross amounted just to fifty Attic talents.

TRANIO To a farthing!°

GRIPUS Paugh! Obvious, obvious.

AMPHITRYON Two thousand pieces of gold were tied up in a   210
handkerchief by themselves.

TRANIO I remember it.

GRIPUS Then 'tis dubious again.

JUPITER But the rest was not all silver; for there were just four thousand brass halfpence.   215

GRIPUS Being but brass, the proof is inconsiderable. If they had been silver, it had gone on your side.

AMPHITRYON (to Jupiter) Death and hell, you will not persuade me that I did not kill Pterelas?

JUPITER Nor you me, that I did not enjoy Alcmena?   220

AMPHITRYON (aside) That last was poison to me.
[To Jupiter] Yet there's one proof thou canst not counterfeit:
In killing Pterelas, I had a wound
Full in the brawny part of my right arm,
Where still the scar remains. Now blush, impostor;   225
For this thou canst not show.

[*Amphitryon*] *bares his arm and shows the scar, which they all look on*

ALL This is the true Amphitryon.

JUPITER May your lordship please—

GRIPUS No, sirrah, it does not please me. Hold your tongue, I charge you; for the case is manifest.

JUPITER By your favour then, this shall speak for me.   230

[*Jupiter*] *bares his arm and shows it*

TRANIO 'Tis just in the same muscle.

POLYDAS Of the same length and breadth, and the scar of the same blueish colour.

GRIPUS (*to Jupiter*) Did not I charge you not to speak? 'Twas plain   235
enough before; and now you have puzzled it again.

AMPHITRYON Good gods, how can this be!

GRIPUS For certain there was but one Pterelas; and he must have been in the plot against himself too, for he was killed first by one of them, and then rose° again out of respect to t'other Amphitryon,   240
to be killed twice over.

Enter Alcmena, Phaedra, and Bromia

ALCMENA (*turning to Phaedra and Bromia*) No more of this; it sounds impossible

That two should be so like, no difference found.

PHAEDRA You'll find it true.

ALCMENA Then where's Alcmena's honour and her fame?   245
Farewell, my needless fear. It cannot be.
This is a case too nice for vulgar sight.°
But let me come; my heart will guide my eyes
To point and tremble to its proper choice.°
(*Seeing Amphitryon, goes to him*)
There neither was, nor is, but one Amphitryon;   250
(*Goes to take him by the hand*)
And I am only his.

AMPHITRYON (*pushing her away from him*) Away, adulteress!

JUPITER My gentle love, my treasure and my joy,
Follow no more that false and foolish fire°
That would mislead thy fame to sure destruction!   255
Look on thy better husband, and thy friend,
Who will not leave thee liable to scorn,
But vindicate thy honour from that wretch
Who would by base aspersions blot thy virtue.

ALCMENA (*going to him, who embraces her*)

247

I was indeed mistaken; thou art he!   260
Thy words, thy thoughts, thy soul is all Amphitryon.
The impostor has thy features, not thy mind.
The face might have deceived me in my choice;
Thy kindness is a guide that cannot err.

AMPHITRYON What, in my presence to prefer the villain!   265
O execrable cheat! I break the truce,
And will no more attend your vain decisions.°
To this [*drawing his sword*], and to the gods I'll trust my cause.
    [*Amphitryon*] *is rushing upon Jupiter, and is held again*

JUPITER Poor man, how I contemn those idle threats!
Were I disposed, thou might'st as safely meet   270
The thunder launched from the red arm of Jove
(Nor Jove need blush to be Alcmena's champion).
But in the face of Thebes she shall be cleared;
And what I am, and what thou art, be known.
Attend, and I will bring convincing proof.   275

AMPHITRYON Thou wouldst elude my justice, and escape.
But I will follow thee through earth and seas,
Nor hell shall hide thee from my just revenge.

JUPITER I'll spare thy pains. It shall be quickly seen,
Betwixt us two, who seeks and who avoids.—   280
Come in, my friends—and thou who seem'st Amphitryon—
That all who are in doubt may know the true.
    Jupiter re-enters the house; with him Amphitryon, Alcmena,
    Polydas, Tranio, and Guards

MERCURY (*to Gripus and Bromia, who are following*)
Thou Gripus, and you Bromia, stay with Phaedra;
Let their affairs alone, and mind we ours.
Amphitryon's rival shall appear a god;   285
But know beforehand I am Mercury,
Who want not heaven, while Phaedra is on earth.

BROMIA But, an't please your lordship, is my fellow Phaedra to be
exalted into the heavens, and made a star?

PHAEDRA When that comes to pass, if you look up a-nights, I shall   290
remember old kindness and vouchsafe to twinkle on you.
    Enter Sosia, peeping about him, and, seeing Mercury, is
    starting back

SOSIA [*aside*] Here he is again; and there's no passing by him into the
house, unless I were a sprite, to glide in through the keyhole.
[*Beginning to leave*] I am to be a vagabond, I find.

MERCURY Sosia, come back. 295

SOSIA No, I thank you. You may whistle me long enough; a beaten dog has always the wit to avoid his master.

MERCURY I permit thee to be Sosia again.

SOSIA 'Tis an unfortunate name, and I abandon it. He that has an itch to be beaten, let him take it up for Sosia. What have I said 300 now! I mean for me; for I neither am nor will be Sosia.

MERCURY But thou may'st be so in safety; for I have acknowledged myself to be God Mercury.

SOSIA You may be a god, for aught I know; but the devil take me if ever I worship you, for an unmerciful deity as you are.° 305

MERCURY You ought to take it for an honour to be drubbed by the hand of a divinity.

SOSIA I am your most humble servant, good Mr God. But, by the faith of a mortal, I could well have spared the honour that you did me. But how shall I be sure that you will never assume my shape 310 again?

MERCURY Because I am weary of wearing so villainous an outside.

SOSIA Well, well; as villainous as it is, here's old Bromia will be contented with it.

BROMIA Yes, now I am sure that I may chastise you safely, and that 315 there's no god lurking under your appearance.

SOSIA Ay; but you had best take heed how you attempt it; for as Mercury has turned himself into me, so I may take the toy into my head to turn myself into Mercury, that I may swinge you off condignly. 320

MERCURY In the meantime, be all my witnesses that I take Phaedra for my wife of the left hand°—that is, in the nature of a lawful concubine.

PHAEDRA You shall pardon me for believing you, for all you are a god;° for you have a terrible ill name below, and I am afraid you'll 325 get a footman, instead of a priest, to marry us.

MERCURY But here's Gripus shall draw up articles betwixt us.

PHAEDRA But he's damnably used to false conveyancing. Well, be it so; for my counsel shall overlook 'em before I sign. Come on, Gripus, that I may have him under black and white.° 330

Here Gripus gets ready pen, ink, and paper

MERCURY With all my heart, that I may have thee under black and white hereafter.

PHAEDRA (*to Gripus*) Begin, begin. Heads of articles to be made, &c., betwixt Mercury, god of thieves——

MERCURY And Phaedra, queen of gypsies. Imprimis: I promise to   335
buy and settle upon her an estate containing nine thousand acres
of land, in any part of Boeotia, to her own liking.

PHAEDRA Provided always that no part of the said nine thousand
acres shall be upon or adjoining to Mount Parnassus;° for I will
not be fobbed off with a poetical estate.°   340

MERCURY Memorandum: that she be always constant to me and
admit no other lover.

PHAEDRA Memorandum: unless it be a lover that offers more; and
that the constancy shall not exceed the settlement.

MERCURY Item: that she shall keep no male servants in her house.   345
Item: no rival lap-dog for a bedfellow. Item: that she shall never
pray to any of the gods.

PHAEDRA What, would you have me an atheist?

MERCURY No devotion to any he-deity, good Phaedra.

BROMIA Here's no provision made for children yet.   350

PHAEDRA Well remembered, Bromia. I bargain that my eldest son
shall be a hero, and my eldest daughter a king's mistress.

MERCURY That is to say, a blockhead and a harlot, Phaedra.

PHAEDRA That's true; but who dares call 'em so? Then for the
younger children—But, now I think on't, we'll have no more but   355
Mas and Miss;° for the rest would be but chargeable, and a burden
to the nation.

MERCURY Yes, yes. The second shall be a false prophet: he shall have
wit enough to set up a new religion, and too much wit to die a
martyr for it.°   360

PHAEDRA O, what had I forgot? There's pin-money, and alimony,
and separate maintenance,° and a thousand things more to be
considered, that are all to be tacked to this Act of Settlement.°

SOSIA I am a fool, I must confess; but yet I can see as far into a
millstone as the best of you.° I have observed that you women-wits   365
are commonly so quick upon the scent, that you often over-run it.
Now I would ask of Madam Phaedra, that in case Mr Heaven there
should be pleased to break these articles, in what court of
judicature she intends to sue him?

PHAEDRA The fool has hit upon't. Gods, and great men, are never   370
to be sued, for they can always plead privilege of peerage.° And
therefore [to Sosia] for once, monsieur, I'll take your word, for as
long as you love me you'll be sure to keep it; and in the meantime
I shall be gaining experience how to manage some rich cully, for
no woman ever made her fortune by a wit.   375

It thunders; and the company within-doors—Amphitryon,
Alcmena, Polydas, and Tranio—all come running out and
join with the rest, who were on the theatre° before

AMPHITRYON Sure 'tis some god. He vanished from our sight,
And told us we should see him soon return.

ALCMENA I know not what to hope, nor what to fear.
A simple error is a real crime;
And unconsenting innocence is lost. 380

> *A second peal of thunder. After which Jupiter appears in a*
> *machine*

JUPITER Look up, Amphitryon, and behold above
Th'impostor god, the rival of thy love.
In thy own shape see Jupiter appear,
And let that sight secure thy jealous fear.°
Disgrace and infamy are turned to boast. 385
No fame in Jove's concurrence can be lost:°
What he enjoys he sanctifies from vice,
And, by partaking, stamps into a price.°
'Tis I who ought to murmur at my fate—
Forced by my love my godhead to translate,° 390
When on no other terms I could possess,
But by thy form, thy features, and thy dress.
To thee were given the blessings that I sought,
Which else not all the bribes of heaven had bought.
Then take into thy arms thy envied love,
And, in his own despite,° triumph o'er Jove. 395

MERCURY (*aside*) Amphitryon and Alcmena both stand mute, and
know not how to take it.

SOSIA (*aside*) Our sovereign lord Jupiter is a sly companion; he knows
how to gild a bitter pill. 400

JUPITER From this auspicious night shall rise an heir,
Great, like his sire, and like his mother, fair—
Wrongs to redress, and tyrants to disseize—
Born for a world that wants a Hercules.°
Monsters and monster-men he shall engage, 405
And toil and struggle through an impious age.
Peace to his labours shall at length succeed;
And murmuring men, unwilling to be freed,
Shall be compelled to happiness—by need.

> *Jupiter is carried back to heaven*

ALL We all congratulate Amphitryon. 410

MERCURY Keep your congratulations to yourselves, gentlemen. 'Tis a nice point, let me tell you that; and the less that is said of it, the better. Upon the whole matter, if Amphitryon takes the favour of Jupiter in patience, as from a god, he's a good heathen.

SOSIA I must take a little extraordinary pains tonight, that my spouse   415
may come even with her lady and produce a squire to attend on young Hercules, when he goes out to seek adventures; that when his master kills a man, he may stand ready to pick his pockets, and piously relieve his aged parents. Ah, Bromia, Bromia, if thou hadst been as handsome and as young as Phaedra—I say no more, but   420
somebody might have made his fortunes as well as his master, and never the worse man neither.

> For, let the wicked world say what they please,
> The fair wife makes her husband live at ease:
> The lover keeps him too, and but receives,   425
> Like Jove, the remnants that Amphitryon leaves.
> 'Tis true the lady has enough in store
> To satisfy those two, and eke, two more.
> In fine, the man who weighs the matter fully
> Would rather be the cuckold than the cully.   430

[*Exeunt*]

Epilogue

Spoken by Phaedra (Mrs Mountfort)

I'm thinking (and it almost makes me mad),
How sweet a time those heathen ladies had.
Idolatry was even their gods' own trade;
They worshipped the fine creatures they had made.
Cupid was chief of all the deities;   5
And love was all the fashion in the skies.
When the sweet nymph held up the lily hand,
Jove was her humble servant at command.
The treasury of heaven was ne'er so bare,
But still there was a pension for the fair.   10
In all his reign adultery was no sin,
For Jove the good example did begin.°
Mark too, when he usurped the husband's name,
How civilly he saved the lady's fame.
The secret joys of love he wisely hid;   15
But you, sirs, boast of more than e'er you did.
You tease your cuckolds, to their face torment 'em;
But Jove gave his, new honours to content 'em,
And, in the kind remembrance of the fair,
On each exalted son bestowed a star.°   20
For those good deeds, as by the date appears,
His godship flourished full two thousand years.
At last, when he and all his priests grew old,
The ladies grew in their devotion cold,
And that false worship would no longer hold.   25
    Severity of life did next begin
(And always does, when we no more can sin).
That doctrine, too, so hard in practice lies,
That the next age may see another rise.
Then pagan gods may, once again, succeed;   30
And Jove or Mars be ready, at our need,
To get young godlings, and so mend our breed.°

THE WIVES' EXCUSE;
OR
CUCKOLDS MAKE THEMSELVES

BY
THOMAS SOUTHERNE

Nihil est his, qui placere volunt,
tam adversarium, quam expectatio.°
(Cicero)

To the Right Honourable
Thomas Wharton, Esq.,°
Comptroller of His Majesty's Household

Sir,

Every man of fortune° has the power of doing a good turn; but there must be more in the man one would choose to be obliged to. I have a thousand obligations to you, and have confessed 'em upon every occasion, with as much satisfaction as I received 'em. I have enjoyed the benefit of your favours, and have the pride of 'em yet in my heart, that you have not thought so much good nature thrown away upon me. I would make you what amends I could, and a dedication is all that I have in my power to return. 'Tis a poetical payment indeed, which, while it discharges one debt, is running into another, begging your protection for a play which will almost need your interest° to defend. I won't contend a point, where most voices are to carry it;° but as I designed this play for you, when some people° thought well of it, I hope it does not lessen the present, that everybody does not. 'Tis only the capacity and commendation of the common mistresses to please everybody, to whom I will leave some of my critics, who were affronted at Mrs Friendall. For those sparks who were most offended with her virtue in public are the men that lose little by it in private; and if all the wives in town were of her mind, those mettled gentlemen would be found to have the least to do in making 'em otherwise. But if she was of evil example, Witwoud makes amends for her in the moral of her character, where the women are manifestly safer in the possession of a lover than in the trust and confidence of a friend.° But she was no more understood to the advantage of the men than the wife was received in favour of the women. As to the music-meeting,° I always thought it an entertainment reasonably grown up into the liking of the town. I introduced it as a fashionable scene of bringing good company together, without a design of abusing what everybody likes, being in my temper so far from disturbing a public pleasure, that I would establish twenty more of 'em, if I could. And for the billet-doux that was put into Mrs Sightly's hand upon leading her out,° I have heard of such a thing in a church before now, and never thought the worse of the place.

These, sir, are capital objections against me. But they hit very few 35
faults; nor have they mortified me into a despair of pleasing the more
reasonable part of mankind. If Mr Dryden's judgement goes for
anything, I have it on my side; for, speaking of this play, he has
publicly said, the town was kind to *Sir Anthony Love*,° I needed 'em
only to be just to this. And to prove there was more than friendship 40
in his opinion, upon the credit of this play with him, falling sick last
summer, he bequeathed to my care the writing of half the last act of
his tragedy of *Cleomenes*,° which, when it comes into the world, you
will find to be so considerable a trust, that all the town will pardon
me for defending this play that preferred me to it.° If modesty be 45
sometimes a weakness, what I say can hardly be a crime. In a fair
English trial both parties are allowed to be heard; and, without this
vanity of mentioning Mr Dryden, I had lost the best evidence of my
cause.° Sir, I have the privilege of a dedication to say some fine things
of my patron. But I will be as little impertinent as I can,° and only 50
beg leave to say some true ones, and no more than I have always
declared in the absence of Mr Wharton: that (without the advantage
of your family and fortune) you are the very man I would choose to
be, if I could. I would have the force of your understanding and
knowledge of mankind, to make a fortune out of the public business 55
of the world. Or if I were to mend my condition more to my own
humour, and a way I should like better than through the hurry of a
crowd,° your wit and conversation, your person and address, would
best recommend me to the women. I don't know, sir, how successful
you have been with that fair sex;° but I would not have it lie at any 60
fair lady's door (who has a mind to be justified in disposing of herself)
that she could not distinguish in your favour against all the pre-
tenders° of the town. If you have any enemies among the women, I
must think 'tis in a great measure because it was impossible to engage
'em all to be your friends. Sir, I am a well-wisher to all your interests; 65
and be pleased to accept of this dedication of my respects, as an
offering of my inclination,° as well as a duty from my gratitude.
    I am, sir, Your very much obliged humble servant,
    Thomas Southerne

To Mr Southerne; on his comedy, called
The Wives' Excuse

Sure there's a fate in plays; and 'tis in vain
To write, while these malignant planets reign.°
Some very foolish influence rules the pit,
Not always kind to sense, or just to wit.
And whilst it lasts, let buffoonery succeed,°   5
To make us laugh; for never was more need.
Farce, in itself, is of a nasty scent;
But the gain smells not of the excrement.
The Spanish nymph, a wit and beauty too,°
With all her charms bore but a single show.   10
But, let a monster Muscovite appear,°
He draws a crowded audience round the year.
Maybe thou hast not pleased the box and pit;
Yet those who blame thy tale commend thy wit.
So Terence plotted; but so Terence writ.°   15
Like his, thy thoughts are true, thy language clean;
Even lewdness is made moral in thy scene.°
The hearers may for want of Nokes repine;°
But rest secure, the readers will be thine.
Nor was thy laboured drama damned or hissed,°   20
But with a kind civility dismissed—
With such good manners as the wife did use,
Who, not accepting, did but just refuse.
There was a glance at parting, such a look
As bids thee not give o'er for one rebuke.°   25
But if thou wouldst be seen as well as read,
Copy one living author and one dead.
The standard of thy style let Etherege be;
For wit, th'immortal spring of Wycherley.°
Learn after both to draw some just design,   30
And the next age will learn to copy thine.

John Dryden

THE CHARACTERS OF THE PLAY

Lovemore°	Mr Betterton	
Wellvile°	Mr Kynaston	
Wilding	Mr Williams	
Courtall	Mr Boman	
Springame°	Mr Michael Leigh	5
Friendall	Mr Mountfort	
Ruffle°	Mr Bright	
Music-Master	Mr Harris	
Mrs Friendall	Mrs Barry	
Mrs Sightly°	Mrs Bracegirdle	10
Mrs Witwoud°	Mrs Mountfort	
Mrs Teazall°	Mrs Corey	
Fanny, her niece		
Betty, Witwoud's maid	Mrs Richardson	

Two Pages, [Seven] Footmen, [Musicians, Three Lords],   15
        and Linkboys

SCENE: LONDON

Prologue

Spoken by Mr Betterton

Gallants, you're welcome to our homely cheer.
If you have brought your English stomachs here,
We'll treat you, as the French say, *chere entière*.°
And what we want of humour or of wit,
Make up with your she-neighbours in the pit;°   5
For on the stage whate'er we do or say,
The vizard-masks can find you better play.
With all our pains we can but bring 'em in;
'Tis you must take the damsels out again.
And when we've brought you kindly thus together,   10
'Tis your fault if you're parted by foul weather.°
We hope these natural reasons may produce,
In every whoremaster, a kind excuse
For all our faults, the poet's and the players'.
(*To the Maskers*)°
You'll pardon us, if you can find out theirs.°   15
But to the gentler men, who love at sight
And never care to come to closer fight—
We have provided work for them tonight.
With safety they may draw their cannon down
And into a surrender bomb the town.   20
From both side-boxes play their batteries,
And not a bullet shot, but burning eyes;
Those they discharge with such successful arts,
They fire, three deep, into the ladies' hearts.°
Since each man here finds his diversion,   25
Let not the damning of our play be one.
But to the ladies, who must sit it out
To hear us prate and see the oglers shoot,
Begging their favour, we have this to say
In hopes of their protection for the play: 30
'Here is a music-meeting every day'.

1.1

The outward room to the music-meeting°

Several footmen at hazard,° some rising from play

WELLVILE'S FOOTMAN° A pox on these music-meetings! There's no
fifth act here, a free cost,° as we have at the playhouses, to make
gentlemen of us and keep us out of harm's way. Nothing but lice
and link-boys in this antechamber, or a merry main° to divert us;
and that merry main, as you call it, makes most of us sad all the   5
week after.

FRIENDALL'S FOOTMAN Why, what hast thou done, Gill?

WELLVILE'S FOOTMAN Undone myself, and a very good friend of
mine, my belly, for a week forward. I am hungry already in the
apprehension of wanting a supper;° for my board-wages° is gone   10
to the devil with his bones.°

WILDING'S FOOTMAN Six is the main, gentlemen.

COURTALL'S FOOTMAN (*rising from play*) That was my last tester.

LOVEMORE'S FOOTMAN (*rising from play*) I'll play no more.

WILDING'S FOOTMAN Set out my hand;° don't leave me so,   15
gentlemen.

FOOTMAN Come, sir, seven to six, I set you.

WILDING'S FOOTMAN Briskly, my boy.

FOOTMAN I set you this.

WILDING'S FOOTMAN How much?   20

FOOTMAN Three halfperth of farthings.°

WILDING'S FOOTMAN Three halfperth of farthings? (*Rises from play*)
I see thou retain'st the spirit of thy ancestors, and as thou wert
born and bred, wilt live and die a footman. Three halfpenny worth
of farthings!   25

FRIENDALL'S FOOTMAN He sets like a small-beer butler° in a
widow-lady's family.

WILDING'S FOOTMAN May'st thou starve under the tyranny of a
housekeeper,° and never know the comfort of board-wages again.

FOOTMAN Well, well, I have my money for all that.°   30

WELLVILE'S FOOTMAN Why, what a pretty° fellow have we here
debauched from us and our society by living in a civil° family! But
this comes of keeping good hours and living orderly. Idleness after
supper in your private houses is the mother of many mischiefs
among the maids.°   35

WILDING'S FOOTMAN Ay, ay, want of employment has thrown him
upon some gentle chambermaid, and now he sets up for good
husbandry,° to father her failings and get a wet-nurse for his lady.°

FOOTMAN Better so than to father your master's bastards, as you do
sometimes; or now and then cheat him of his wench in the   40
convey,° and steal his clap from him.

COURTALL'S FOOTMAN Gad i' mercy,° i' faith, lad.

WILDING'S FOOTMAN That indeed is a sin I often commit, and
sometimes repent of. But, the good with the bad, I have no reason
to complain of my service.   45

FOOTMAN Pray don't trouble your head about mine then.

FRIENDALL'S FOOTMAN Come, come, we have all good places if we
can keep 'em. And, for my part, I am too deep in my master's
affairs to fear the losing of mine. What think you of the family of
the Friendalls, my lads? A public private family, newly set up, and 50
of very fair reception.°

WILDING'S FOOTMAN Ay, Dick; thou hast the time on't indeed.°

FRIENDALL'S FOOTMAN The master of it frank° and free, to make
an invitation to the whole town, and the mistress hospitable and
handsome, to give 'em welcome and content; for my master knows 55
everybody, and contrives that everybody shall know her.

WILDING'S FOOTMAN Ay, marry, sir, there's a family to breed up a
pimp in! You may make a fortune out of such a mistress, before
your master can get her with child.

FRIENDALL'S FOOTMAN My master has been married not a quarter 60
of a year, and half the young men in town know his wife
already—nay, know that he has known enough of her, not to care
for her already.

WILDING'S FOOTMAN And that may be a very good argument for
some of 'em to persuade her to know a little of somebody else, and 65
care as little for him.

COURTALL'S FOOTMAN A very good argument, if she takes it by the
right handle.

FRIENDALL'S FOOTMAN Some of your masters, I warrant you, will
put it into her hand.°   70

WILDING'S FOOTMAN I know my master has a design upon her.

FRIENDALL'S FOOTMAN And upon all the women in town.

COURTALL'S FOOTMAN Mine is in love with her.

LOVEMORE'S FOOTMAN And mine has hopes of her.

WILDING'S FOOTMAN Every man has hopes of a new-married   75
woman. For she marries to like her man; and if upon trial she finds

she can't like her husband, she'll find somebody else that she can like, in a very little time, I warrant her, or change her men till she does.

FRIENDALL'S FOOTMAN Let her like as many as she pleases, and welcome. As they thrive with her, I shall thrive by them. I grind by her mill,° and some of 'em, I hope, will set it a-going. Besides, she has discovered some of my master's intrigues of late. That may help to fill the sails. But I say nothing—I will take fees o' both sides and betray neither.

WILDING'S FOOTMAN If your lady loves play,° as they say she does, she will be so far in your interest,° that he that makes his court to her must have money to recommend him.

FRIENDALL'S FOOTMAN To me he must indeed, if he expects my assistance.

LOVEMORE'S FOOTMAN Come, come, what do you think of my master, Mr Lovemore, for the lady?

WILDING'S FOOTMAN I don't think of him.

FRIENDALL'S FOOTMAN Not so much as she does, I believe you. He's a generous gentleman and deserves very well of her, and me.

WELLVILE'S FOOTMAN My master, Mr Wellvile, is often at your house.

WILDING'S FOOTMAN He follows Mrs Sightly, I can tell you. But if your lady, Mrs Friendall, has a mind to be very well used—not to settle to't, but only by the way of a fashionable revenge, or so, to do herself justice upon her husband—I look upon Mr Wilding, my master, one or other, to be the cleverest cuckold-maker in Covent Garden.

FRIENDALL'S FOOTMAN Not to settle to't indeed, for your master is not over-constant.

WILDING'S FOOTMAN He does not stay in a family, to be challenged into Westminster Hall° by the husband's action of battery, for an assault upon his wife.° He is not so constant.

COURTALL'S FOOTMAN Or if your lady be disposed to the more refined part of an amour, without the brutality or design of enjoyment, only for the pleasure of being talked of, or so forth—

WILDING'S FOOTMAN Your master, Courtall, will fit her to a hair. For he will be as fond of the appearances of an intrigue as she can be. To see him in the chase, you would think he had pleasure in the sport; for he will be as sure always to follow her as never to press her. He will take as much pains to put her undeservedly into a lampoon° upon his account, as he would to avoid a handsome occasion, in private, to qualify her for the scandal.

FRIENDALL'S FOOTMAN In short, Mr. Courtall will do everything, 120
but what he ought to do, with a woman.

COURTALL'S FOOTMAN He has broke off with three gentlewomen, upon my word, within these two months, for coming on too fast upon that business.

FRIENDALL'S FOOTMAN Well, there are pretenders enough.° So I 125
have the profit, let my lady take the pleasure of the choice. I'm for the fairest bidder.

WILDING'S FOOTMAN What, Harry, hast thou nothing to say of thy mistress, Mrs Witwoud?

MRS WITWOUD'S FOOTMAN Nothing extraordinary, but that I'm 130
tired of her.

WILDING'S FOOTMAN She lives, as she used to do,° least at home—has no business of her own, but a great deal of other people's. All the men in town follow her, but 'tis for other women; for she has frightened every one from a design upon her. Then she's a general 135
confidante, and sometimes reports no more than she knows; but that's a favour indeed, from a wit, as they say she is.

MRS WITWOUD'S FOOTMAN If she be a wit, I'll be sworn she does not take me for one; for she sends me very often upon very ridiculous errands. 140

WILDING'S FOOTMAN I think you have a correspondent porter° in every quarter of the town to disperse her scandalous letters, which she is always bantering one fool or other withal?

MRS WITWOUD'S FOOTMAN Four or five always in pay with her.

WILDING'S FOOTMAN But when Horn Fair° comes, that's sure to be 145
a holiday, and every married man that has a wife handsomer than she is, at her proper cost and charges, may expect a fairing,° to put him in mind of his fortune.

MRS WITWOUD'S FOOTMAN I find you know her too well to desire to live with her. 150

WILDING'S FOOTMAN I had rather be master of ceremonies to a visiting lady,° to squire about her how-d'ye's and usher in the formal salutations of all the fops in town upon her day°—nay, though she kept two days a week—than live in a family with her.

WELLVILE'S FOOTMAN Will this damned music-meeting never be 155
done? Would the cats' guts° were in the fiddlers' bellies!

[Enter] Two Pages meeting°

FIRST PAGE My Lady Smirkit's page!

SECOND PAGE Who's there? My Lady Woudmore!

FIRST PAGE At your dear service, madam.

SECOND PAGE O lord! Madam, I am surprised to see your ladyship   160
here.

FRIENDALL'S FOOTMAN What have we here?

WILDING'S FOOTMAN The monkeys aping their ladies; let 'em go on.

SECOND PAGE How can your ladyship descend into these little
diversions of the town, the plays and the music-meetings?   165

FIRST PAGE Little diversions indeed, madam, to us, who have seen
so much better abroad and still retain too much of the delicacy of
the French, to be pleased with the barbarous performances of these
English.°

WILDING'S FOOTMAN That's a touch for° some of 'em.   170

FIRST PAGE Yet there's no staying always at home, your ladyship
knows.

SECOND PAGE Nor being always seen in the Drawing Room,° I vow
and swear.

FIRST PAGE So that, madam, we are almost under a necessity of   175
appearing in these public places.

SECOND PAGE An absolute necessity of showing ourselves sometimes.

FIRST PAGE Ay, but, madam, then the men, they do so ogle one—

WILDING'S FOOTMAN Ah! Very well, Mr Charles.   180

FIRST PAGE Into all the little confusions that a woman is liable to
upon those occasions.

SECOND PAGE I swear my Lord Simperwell has an irresistible way
with him.

FIRST PAGE He ogled me all the music long—I believe everybody   185
took notice of it—so furiously, I could not bear it myself. I vow
and swear, he almost made me blush; and I would rather do
anything to deserve blushing, in another place, than by a country
modesty betray such an unpardonable want of breeding to the
censure of so much good company.   190

WILDING'S FOOTMAN I dare swear for her ladyship, she had rather
do it than blush for't.

FIRST PAGE (to Wilding's Footman) Why, how now, Jack Sauce? (To
the Page) But did I blush, madam?

SECOND PAGE Only for your friends, madam, to see us so neglected.   195

FIRST PAGE Fie, fie, madam, you made your conquest too. I minded°
nobody but my lord; and I vow and swear, I must own it, madam,
he ogles one more like a man of quality° than anybody about town

that I know of, and I think I am pretty well acquainted with all
the soft looks in town.   200

SECOND PAGE One after another we have 'em all. But, Jesu,
madam—

FIRST PAGE Ay, madam?

SECOND PAGE They say the French fleet will be here next summer,
with their Tourvilles,° and their things, and, Jesu, madam, ravish   205
us all.

FIRST PAGE O lord, madam, ravishing us is nothing; but our dear
religion, madam, what will they do to that?

SECOND PAGE Ay, what indeed, madam?

FIRST PAGE I would not lose the gaping galleries of our churches°   210
for the best religion in Christendom.

WILDING'S FOOTMAN You are precious° pages indeed. Betray your
ladies' secrets, before you come into 'em!°

[SERVANT] (within) Make way for my lord there; bear back,
gentlemen.   215

WELLVILE'S FOOTMAN So, so; 'tis done at last. Let's get the coaches
to the door.

> *Exeunt*

[1.2]

> *The curtain drawn up° shows the company at the*
> *music-meeting. After [Musicians perform] an Italian song,°*
> *Lovemore, Wellvile, Wilding, Courtall, Springame, Friendall,*
> *Ruffle, Mrs Friendall, Mrs Sightly, Mrs Witwoud, Fanny*
> *advance to the front of the stage*

FRIENDALL Ladies and gentlemen, how did you like the music?

MRS SIGHTLY O very fine, sure, sir.

MRS WITWOUD [to Springame] What say you to't, young gentleman?°

SPRINGAME (going aside with her) I have something to say to you I   5
like a great deal better, provided you won't laugh at me. (To the
company) But the music's extremely fine.

WELLVILE Especially the vocal part. For I did not understand a word
on't.

FRIENDALL Nor I, faith, Wellvile; but the words were Italian. They   10
sung well, and that's enough for the pleasure of the ear.

COURTALL By which I find your sense is sound.

FRIENDALL And sound sense is a very good thing, Courtall.

    [Friendall] goes to Wilding

WELLVILE *[aside]* That thou wilt° never be the better for.

FRIENDALL Wilding, thou hast been so busy about that young girl   15
there *[indicating Fanny]*, thou know'st nothing of the matter.

WILDING O, sir, you're mistaken; I am a great admirer—

FRIENDALL Of everything in petticoats.

WILDING Of these musical entertainments. I am very musical, and
love any call that brings the women together.   20

COURTALL Though it were a cat-call.°

FRIENDALL Vocal or instrumental! Which do you most approve of?
If you are for the instrumental, there were the sonatas° tonight,
and the chaconnes,° which you know—

WILDING The sonatas and the chaconnes which I know! Not I, sir,   25
I don't know 'em. They may be two Italian fiddlers° of your
acquaintance, for anything I know of 'em.

FRIENDALL Fie, fie, fiddlers! Masters, if you please, Wilding, masters—excellent in their art, and famous for many admirable
compositions.   30

    [Friendall] mingles with the company

COURTALL So, he's fast in his own snare, with his sonatas and
chaconnes. But how goes the world, Wilding?

WILDING The same women every day, and in every public appearance.

COURTALL Here are some faces, I see, of your acquaintance.   35

WILDING Ay, pox take 'em; I see 'em too often to forget 'em. Would
their owners thought as ill of 'em as I do, they would keep 'em at
home. But they are for showing their show still, though nobody
cares for the sight.

    [Wilding and Courtall] mix with the company

MRS WITWOUD *[to Springame]* Methinks 'tis but good manners in   40
Mr Lovemore to be particular to your sister,° when her husband
is so universal to the company.

SPRINGAME Prithee leave her to her husband. She has satisfied her
relations enough in marrying this coxcomb; now let her satisfy
herself, if she pleases, with anybody she likes better.   45

MRS WITWOUD Fie, fie, there's no talking to you; you carry my
meaning further than I designed.

SPRINGAME Faith, I took it up where you left it—very near the
matter.

MRS WITWOUD° No, no, you grow scandalous; and I would not be   50
thought to say a scandalous thing of a friend.

SPRINGAME Since my brother-in-law is to be a cuckold—as it must
be mightily my sister's fault if he be not—I think Lovemore as
proper a fellow to carry on so charitable a work as she could ha'
lit upon. And if he has her consent to the business, she has mine,   55
I assure you.

MRS WITWOUD A very reasonable brother!

SPRINGAME Would you would be as reasonable a friend, and allow
me as many liberties as I do her.

MRS WITWOUD Why, so I will. She has the men, and you shall have   60
the women, the whole sex, to pick and choose—

SPRINGAME One mistress out of.

MRS WITWOUD As many as you please, and as often as you have
occasion.

SPRINGAME Why, faith, that pleases me very well. You hit my   65
constitution,° as if you were familiar with it, or had a mind to be
so.

MRS WITWOUD Not I indeed, sir.

SPRINGAME And I have, as you were saying—

MRS WITWOUD As I was saying!   70

SPRINGAME Very often an occasion for a mistress.

MRS WITWOUD You say so yourself; I know nothing of your
occasions.

SPRINGAME Shall I bring you acquainted with some of 'em? I have
great variety, and have, every day, a new occasion for a new   75
mistress. If you have a mind to be satisfied in this point, let me go
along with you.

MRS WITWOUD Home with me?

SPRINGAME Or home with me will do my business as well.

MRS WITWOUD But it won't do mine, sir.   80

SPRINGAME Then let it be home with you, though my lodging is
very convenient.

MRS WITWOUD Why, this is sudden indeed upon so small an
acquaintance. But 'tis something too soon for you, and a little too
late for me.°   85

SPRINGAME Not to repent, I hope, madam? Better late than
never, you know. Come, come, I have known a worse offer better
received.

MRS WITWOUD And this offer you will make to every woman till it
be received, I dare answer for you.   90

SPRINGAME That's more than you can do for yourself for refusing
it. But the folly fall upon your own head. I have done my part,
and 'tis your fault if you're idle.
   [*Springame*] *goes away.*

MRS SIGHTLY [*joining Mrs Witwoud*] You have been entertained,
cousin.   95

MRS WITWOUD By a very pretty prating fellow, cousin; and I could
be contented to let him show his parts this way as often as he
pleased.

MRS SIGHTLY What! Like a man of honour, he's for making good
what he says?   100

MRS WITWOUD And comes so quick upon that business, he won't
afford a woman a reasonable liking-time, to make a decent excuse
to herself, if she should allow him a favour.

MRS SIGHTLY The young officer has heard enough of your character,° I suppose, not to put it too much into your power of laughing   105
at him.

MRS WITWOUD I'm sorry for't. I would have a man know just
enough of me to make him a lover; and then, in a little time, I
should know enough of him to make him an ass.

MRS SIGHTLY This will come home to you one day.   110

MRS WITWOUD In any shape but a husband, cousin. (*Observing
Lovemore with Mrs Friendall*) But methinks Lovemore and Mrs
Friendall are very seriously engaged—

MRS SIGHTLY I have had an eye upon 'em.

MRS WITWOUD For such a trifle as cuckolding a husband is in this   115
town.

MRS SIGHTLY The men will always design upon our sex; but I dare
answer for her.

MRS WITWOUD And so will I. That if she should fall from the frailty
of the flesh into that folly, she will appear no monster, whatever   120
her husband may be.° What say you to a ramble° after the music?

MRS SIGHTLY I say nothing to't.

MRS WITWOUD A hackney jaunt,° from one end of the town to
t'other?

MRS SIGHTLY 'Tis too late.   125

MRS WITWOUD I know two several° companies gone into the
city—one to Pontack's and t'other to the Rummer°—to supper I
want to disturb strangely.° What say you, coz?° Let's put on our
masks, draw up the glasses,° and send up for the men, to make
their women uneasy. There's one of 'em to be married; it may do   130

good upon her, by showing what she must trust to, if she will have a husband.

MRS SIGHTLY And can you be so mischievous?

MRS WITWOUD Can you resist the temptation?

MRS SIGHTLY I came with Mrs Friendall and must go home with 135
her. Look to your charge [*indicating Fanny*] there.

MRS WITWOUD I have an eye that way.

MRS SIGHTLY We shall see you tomorrow, cousin?

MRS WITWOUD At your toilet,° cousin. You are always my first visit.

[*Mrs Witwoud*] *goes to Wilding and Fanny*

MRS FRIENDALL [*to Lovemore*] Is this your friendship to Mr Friend- 140
all? I must not hear it.

LOVEMORE You see he gives you leave.

MRS FRIENDALL Therefore I can't take it. The confidence° is so
generous, that even that would secure me to him.

LOVEMORE The confidence is as generous on your side; and do you 145
think that will secure him to you?

MRS FRIENDALL I'll ask him, if you please.

LOVEMORE You'll but disturb him.

MRS FRIENDALL (*calling him*) Mr Friendall.

FRIENDALL Ha! What's the matter, madam? 150

MRS FRIENDALL There has happened here a scurvy dispute between
me and one of your friends, sir, as you think fit to call 'em.

FRIENDALL A dispute! About what, prithee? But before I hear a
word on't, Lovemore, thou art certainly in the wrong, in holding
an argument with a woman. 155

LOVEMORE I begin to think so too, sir, for contending with a lady
that will be tried° by nobody but her husband.

FRIENDALL But what's the business? Nothing extraordinary between
you, I hope?

MRS FRIENDALL Believe me, sir, I think it very extraordinary— 160

LOVEMORE Very extraordinary indeed, madam, to be so publicly
exposed for a private opinion.

MRS FRIENDALL And you shall be the judge of the difference.

FRIENDALL No, no, no difference among friends; it must not come
to that. I'll make up all differences between you. 165

LOVEMORE You may do much indeed to set all straight.

FRIENDALL And so I will, i'faith, Lovemore; I'll reconcile all, I
warrant you. But come, what is this mighty matter between you?

MRS FRIENDALL I think it a mighty matter, Mr Friendall, to be so
far suspected in my conduct, that anyone, under the title of your 170

friend, should dare, in your absence, to be so very familiar° with
me—

FRIENDALL How, madam!

LOVEMORE (*aside*) All will out, I see.

FRIENDALL In my absence, so very familiar with you?   175

MRS FRIENDALL As to censure these innocent liberties that the
women allow themselves in the company of their husbands.

LOVEMORE [*aside*] So; she has saved her credit with me, and mine
with her husband.

Mrs Friendall joins Mrs Sightly and Mrs Witwoud

FRIENDALL Why, Lovemore, thou art in the wrong of all this. I   180
desired you to sport off a little gallantry with my wife, to entertain
and divert her from making her observations upon me;° and thou
dost nothing but play the critic upon her.

LOVEMORE I find I was mistaken. But how would you have me
behave myself?   185

FRIENDALL Why, I would have you very frequent in your visits, and
very obliging to my wife, now and then to carry on our other
pleasures the better. For an amusement, or so, you may say a civil°
thing to her, for every woman, you know, loves to have a civil
thing said to her sometimes. But then you must be very cautious   190
in the expression. If she should in the least apprehend that you had
a design upon her, 'twould raise the devil in one part of the family,
and lay him in another, perhaps, where I had a mind to employ
him. Therefore I would have you keep in favour with her.

LOVEMORE I'll do my best, I promise you.   195

FRIENDALL She's inclining, you must know, to speak very well of
you; and that she does of very few of the men, I assure you. She
approves of the intimacy and friendship between us, and of your
coming to the house; and that may stand you in stead° with the
lady you wot of.°   200

LOVEMORE I apprehend you.

[*Lovemore moves towards Mrs Friendall*]

(*To Mrs Friendall*) So, begging the lady's pardon with a design of
doing something to deserve it—

MRS WITWOUD That will never fail with the women, Mr Lovemore.

LOVEMORE I will make an interest° with the masters, to give you a   205
song at parting.

[*Lovemore*] *goes to the music-masters*

MRS SIGHTLY An English song, good Mr Lovemore.

FRIENDALL O, by all means, an English song.

[Friendall] goes [to] the music-masters too

WELLVILE Any song which won't oblige a man to tell you he has seen an opera at Venice to understand. 210

FRIENDALL [*to the Music-Master*] Pray, let him sing the ladies the song I gave him.

MUSIC-MASTER Which song, sir?

FRIENDALL The last.

MUSIC-MASTER 'Tis not set,° sir. 215

FRIENDALL (*turning from him, to the ladies*) Not set, sir!

LOVEMORE [*to the Music-Master*] That's a fault he'll never forgive you.

MUSIC-MASTER Why, really, sir, I would serve any gentleman to my power; but the words are so abominably out of the way of music, 220 I don't know how to humour 'em.° There's no setting 'em, or singing 'em, to please anybody but himself.

MRS SIGHTLY [*to Friendall*] O, but we lose by this!

FRIENDALL Hang 'em, idle rascals. They care not what entertainment we lose, so they have but our money. 225

MRS SIGHTLY Is it your own song, Mr Friendall?

FRIENDALL I must not rob your ladyship of your part in it.

MRS SIGHTLY My part in your song, sir!

FRIENDALL You were the muse that inspired me. I writ it upon your ladyship. 230

MRS SIGHTLY Fie, fie; that pride would ruin me. But I know you say so to every woman.

She turns from him

FRIENDALL [*aside*] Egad, she's i' th' right on't. I have told a dozen so already at the music-meeting, and most of 'em believe me.

MRS SIGHTLY [*to Mrs Friendall*] Does Mr Friendall often write 235 songs, madam?

MRS FRIENDALL He does many things he should not do, madam; but I think he loves me, and that excuses him to me. Though, you may be sure, 'tis with the tenderest concern for my own reputation, that I see my husband daily trifle away his so notoriously in 240 one folly or other of the town.

[Mrs Friendall] goes to Friendall

MRS WITWOUD [*aside*] For her° own reputation, it must be; for the world will believe she turns such a husband to the right use,° whatever she says to the contrary.

MRS FRIENDALL [*to Friendall*] Mr Friendall, pray be satisfied with 245 a good estate, and not imagine, because you have that, you have

272

everything else. The business of writing songs should be over with
a married man. And since I can't be suspected to be the Phillis or
Cloris, 'tis an affront to me to have any other woman thought so.

FRIENDALL Indeed, madam, so far you are right: I never heard of   250
any man that writ a song upon his wife.

    [The musicians perform a song]

SONG

> *Ingrateful love! Thus every hour°*
>   *To punish me by her disdain!*
> *You tyrannise to show your power;*
>   *And she, to triumph in my pain.*   255
>
> *You, who can laugh at human woes*
>   *And victims to her pride decree,*
> *On me, your yielding slave, impose*
>   *Your chains; but leave the rebel free.*
>
> *How fatal are your poisoned darts!*   260
>   *Her conquering eyes the trophies boast,*
> *Whilst you ensnare poor wandering hearts*
>   *That in her charms and scorn are lost.*
>
> *Impious and cruel, you deny*
>   *A death, to ease me of my care,°*   265
> *Which she delays, to make me try°*
>   *The force of beauty and despair.*

FRIENDALL Lovemore, we may thank you for this. But when you
keep your promise to me at dinner tomorrow, and (*speaks to all the
men*) you, and you, and all of you, gentlemen, I'll do you reason°   270
to the good company.

    [Friendall] goes to the door

[*Calling offstage*] Some of my servants there!

COURTALL [*to Mrs Friendall*] Madam, I am very luckily here to offer
you my service.°

MRS FRIENDALL No particular woman must expect it from so   275
general a follower of the sex as Mr Courtall is.

COURTALL A general follower of the sex indeed, madam, in my care
of 'em.

MRS FRIENDALL Besides, 'tis dangerous to be seen with a man of
your character; for if you don't make it an intrigue, the town makes   280
it for you.° And that does most of your business as well.

COURTALL There's no knowing a man by his character in this town; the partiality of friends and the prejudice of enemies, who divide it, always make him better or worse than he deserves.

MRS FRIENDALL If you have no regard to my reputation, pray be tender of your own. 'Tis nowadays as scandalous in a man, who would be thought to know the town (as I know you would), to wait upon a bare face to her coach, as it used to be to lead out a vizard-mask.° But the pit has got the better of the boxes, with most of you, in that point of civility;° and I don't doubt but it turns to better account. 285 290

SPRINGAME [joining them] Indeed, sister, it does turn to better account; and therefore we must provide for ourselves.

  [Springame] takes Courtall with him to Mrs Witwoud.
  Lovemore goes to Mrs Friendall

Why, here's a woman, Courtall. If she had a vizard-mask to encourage me, I could go to the world's end° with her. But, as she is, bare-faced, and an honest woman— 295

MRS WITWOUD You'll do a foolish thing for once: see her to her coach, I dare say for you, to make her otherwise.

SPRINGAME (addressing to her)° Why, if it must be so—

WILDING [to Fanny] You own your aunt is abed; and you see Mrs Witwoud's too busy to mind your going away with me. 300

FANNY I can't tonight; but I'll call upon you tomorrow morning, as I go to six o'clock prayers.

LOVEMORE (to Mrs Friendall) I hope, madam, I may without exception wait upon you.° 305

WELLVILE (to Mrs Sightly) And, madam, I have the title of an old servant° to your ladyship to expect that favour from you.

MRS SIGHTLY Mr Friendall, having a handsome wife in the company, may be jealous;° and you will pardon me, if I am unwilling to give him a suspicion of a man whom I would have everybody think as well of as I do myself. 310

MRS FRIENDALL [to Lovemore] Mr Friendall gives you more opportunities than I can approve of, and I could wish you would not take the advantage of 'em. They'll turn to no account.

FRIENDALL [to Mrs Sightly and Mrs Friendall] Come, ladies, I am your man, I find. 315

  [Friendall] leads Mrs Sightly [out,] Mrs Friendall following

RUFFLE [to Lovemore] What think you of this occasion?°

LOVEMORE You can't have a better. Follow him—and be famous.

*Springame leads Mrs Witwoud [out,] Wilding leads Fanny
out. Ruffle [follows] after the company*

WELLVILE [*to Lovemore*] What have you now in hand?   320

LOVEMORE Why, all my hopes of the wife depending upon the
senseless behaviour of the husband, I have contrived, by this
fellow, before her face too, to expose him a way° that must ruin
him with her forever. Let's follow, and expect the event.°

Exeunt

[1.3]

The street

*Several link-boys and Footmen. [Enter] Springame with Mrs
Witwoud, Wilding with Fanny, and several others*

[FIRST] LINK-BOY Have a light, gentlemen; have a light, sir.

SPRINGAME Light yourselves to the devil.

SECOND LINK-BOY Bless you, master; we can find the way in the
dark. Shall I light your worship there?

SPRINGAME Then call a coach, and thy wit shall be thy reward.   5

*Friendall enters, leading Mrs Sightly with his wife. Ruffle
enters after 'em, Lovemore and Wellvile in the rear*

FRIENDALL'S FOOTMAN° [*calling offstage*] Mr Friendall's coach
there! [*To Friendall*] 'Tis at the door, sir.

FRIENDALL [*to Mrs Sightly*] I must improve° every opportunity with
your ladyship to convince you of the truths I have been telling you
tonight, and [*attempting to give her a letter*] in this billet I give it   10
under my hand° how very much I am your servant.

MRS SIGHTLY Fie, fie, before your wife!

*Mrs Sightly throws it behind her. Ruffle takes it up. Friendall
leads Mrs Sightly off and returns for his wife*

MRS FRIENDALL [*to Ruffle*] Sir, that paper don't belong to you.

RUFFLE Don't be jealous, lady. I know no design the gentlewoman
has as yet upon my person, and I'll belong to you, if this gentleman   15
pleases.

FRIENDALL You're pleased to be merry, sir; but no touching her,° I
beseech you.

MRS FRIENDALL What would the fellow have?

RUFFLE Why, I would have this fellow gone about his business.   20

FRIENDALL My business lies here at present, sir.

RUFFLE You lie there, sir.

> [*Ruffle*] *hits Friendall a box on the ear and draws* [*his sword.*] *The women shriek. Mrs Friendall pretends to hold her husband.*° *The company come about 'em*

MRS FRIENDALL Good Mr Friendall, another time; consider where you are. You are more a man of honour, I know, than to draw your sword among the women. I am sorry this has happened in a place where you can't right yourself without wronging the company. But you'll find a time to do a justice to yourself, and the ladies, who have suffered in the apprehension of such a brutality.° 25

SPRINGAME I'll go along with you.

> *All go off but Mrs Witwoud*

MRS WITWOUD Would the devil had 'em for drawing their swords here. I have lost my little captain in the fray. My charge is departed too, and for this night, I suppose, has left me to make an excuse to the family for her lying abroad° with a country cousin, or so. That rogue Wilding has carried her home with him, and 'tis as well now as a week hence, for when these young wenches once set their hearts upon't, everything gives them an opportunity to ruin themselves. Her aunt Teazall has made her rise to six o'clock prayers to fine purpose, if this be the fruits of her devotion. But since she must fall to somebody, I'm glad Wilding has her, for he'll use her ill enough in a little time to make her wiser for the future. By the dear experience and vexation of this intrigue, being disappointed of many things she expects, she may make a virtue of necessity, repent because she can't keep him to herself, and make an honest man a very good wife yet. 30 35 40

> *Exit* [*Mrs Witwoud.*] *Lovemore, Wellvile, Ruffle return*

RUFFLE I have done my part, and am satisfied with the honour of the achievement. 45

LOVEMORE 'Tis a reputation clear-gained, since there's no danger of accounting for't.°

RUFFLE So, thanking you for this occasion of showing myself,° I am your humble servant. 50

> *Exit* [*Ruffle*]

WELLVILE Who is this hero, pray?

LOVEMORE Why, this is a spark that has had the misfortune of being kicked very lately, and I have helped him to this occasion of repairing his honour upon our very good friend, a greater coward than himself. He has served my ends; now let him serve the town's. 55

WELLVILE But did you observe how the lady behaved herself in the quarrel, to conceal her husband's cowardice?

LOVEMORE What a handsome excuse she made in his favour to the company, when she can never make any for him to herself.   60

WELLVILE This matter, well managed, may turn to account. Though you must not be seen to expose him, you may take the advantage of his exposing himself.

LOVEMORE And let her say what she can upon this subject, I believe no woman can be contented to have her honour, much longer than   65
her fortune, in the possession of a man who has no fund of his own° to answer in security for either.

> Thus, who a married woman's love would win
> Should with the husband's failings first begin:
> Make him but in the fault, and you shall find   70
> A good excuse will make most women kind.

Exeunt

2.1

[*Mrs Teazall's lodgings*]

Mrs Witwoud at a table, with Betty, and a Footman waiting

MRS WITWOUD No news of my cousin Fanny this morning?

BETTY For God's sake, madam, not a word of her lying out tonight.
We shall have the devil to do with the old gentlewoman, if she
knows it.

MRS WITWOUD That's a secret I can keep from her for my own sake,   5
Betty. But how comes this about? I'm quite out of gilt paper.°
Harry, you fetch me two or three quire from Mr Bentley's,° and
call at Mrs Da Robe's,° my mantua-woman's, as you come back,
for letters. And—d'you hear?—give this note to Joe the porter. He
needs no instructions; let him leave it for Mr Wilding.   10

Footman and Betty go out

I find I must meddle in this business; for her visits at this rate will
not only be troublesome to him (as I would have 'em), but in a
little time be public to the whole town. Now, though I am very
well pleased with any matter of scandal, I am so nearly related to
the interest of this girl, I would not have her the occasion of it.°   15
They say the understanding ought to be suited to the condition,
to make anyone happy. Would she were in a condition suitable to
her understanding! She has wit enough for a wife, and nothing else
that I know of.

Mrs Teazall enters to her

MRS TEAZALL O, madam! You're welcome home.   20

MRS WITWOUD Rather good-morrow, cousin.

MRS TEAZALL Rather good-morrow indeed; that's the properer salutation. For you're never to be seen in your lodging at any other time
of the day; and then too, as soon as you're out o' bed in a morning,
you summon a congregation of your fellows together to hear you   25
prate by the hour, flatter everybody in the company, speak ill of
everyone that's absent, and scatter about the scandal of that day.

MRS WITWOUD Why, madam, you won't quarrel at that, I hope. 'Tis
one of the most fashionable, innocent diversions of the town. It
makes a great deal of mirth, speaking ill of people, and never does   30
anybody any harm.

MRS TEAZALL Not with any that know you, I believe. How came you
home last night? The night before, you arrived like a carted° bawd,

justly punished for the sins of the people. You confessed you were
forced to bilk your coach, to get rid of the coxcombs that dogged   35
you from the playhouse; and, being pursued by the coachman and
footmen (for I don't doubt but you gave the gentlemen encouragement enough to come home with you), you looked as if you
belonged to a cellar in some of the alleys you were hunted through,
and had been caterwauling in all the kennels in town.   40

MRS WITWOUD That was an unfortunate night indeed.

MRS TEAZALL Well, deliver every good woman's child, I say, from
such daggle-tailed courses as these are. What will be the end of
'em, I beseech you? You will make yourself as odious in a little
time as you endeavour to make everybody else. This is not the way   45
to get a husband; the men know too much of you already to desire
any more of you.

MRS WITWOUD I don't set up for a husband.°

MRS TEAZALL Marry come up here! You may have an occasion for
an husband, when you can't get one. Husbands are not always to   50
be had at a month's warning to finish another's work. What, 'tis
beneath the character of a she-wit, I suppose, to be constant? Or
is a husband out of fashion with you forsooth? Another woman's
husband° can go down with you, to my knowledge, and as ugly a
rogue too, with as hanging a countenance,° as I could wish any   55
villain I had a mind to be rid of—your diversion, as you call him.

MRS WITWOUD O spare my shame. I own he is my curse, doomed
for my plague—and pleasure.

MRS TEAZALL Spare your shame! I'll say that for you: you have not
been sparing of any endeavour that could bring a shame any way   60
into the family wherever you lived yet, if there was ever a fool soft
enough to throw it upon.° All your relations know you, and are
afraid to have you in a house with 'em. And I suppose you are very
well pleased to be from under their roof, to have your fellows come
after you to my house, as they do, and as I am fool enough to allow   65
of.

MRS WITWOUD For no harm, cousin, I hope.

MRS TEAZALL Perhaps you think it no harm; and, indeed, it can't
easily do you any harm. But, I'm sure, I have one of my nieces
already undone, by your bringing her acquainted with some of 'em.   70
I was forced to marry her, you know, below her rank (for the usual
reason° of this end of the town) into the city, where 'twas less
scandalous, the wives there having a charter° for what they do.
And now Fanny, a very girl,° when I have provided a husband,

and all, for her—for she must have a husband—she takes after her   75
sister, as a little thing will make a precedent for what we are
inclined to. She takes after her sister, I say, and is unfortunately
engaged in a passion for Mr Wilding. And how to prevent it—

MRS WITWOUD Indeed, I must acknowledge I was, in a great
measure, the unfortunate cause of my cousin Biddy's mis-   80
carriage.° But, for my cousin Fanny, rely upon me; nothing shall
come on't. I am now going to Mr Wilding on that account, and
have sent a note to secure him at his lodgings till I come.

   Betty enters

MRS TEAZALL Well, where's this girl? Why does not she come, when
I send for her?   85

BETTY Madam, she went to six o'clock prayers, and is not come back
yet.

MRS TEAZALL God's bodikins! Has she got the trick on't of abusing
the church into the place of assignation already? Wilding has
carried her home with him. That's certain. [*To Mrs Witwoud*] Get   90
you gone after her. Maybe you may prevent his wicked design on
her. Go, go, and redeem her, though you leave yourself in her
room.°

MRS WITWOUD I'm obliged to you, truly, madam.

MRS TEAZALL I dare venture you; you'll not be in love with him.   95
You'll give him as good as he brings; and, let the worst come to
the worst, you have lived too long in the town to be uneasy for any
man or be concerned beyond the pleasure and convenience of the
intrigue. Therefore, I may venture you. A little time goes a great
way in this business. Deliver her, and I won't find fault with   100
you—these three days you shall do what you please.

   Exeunt

2.2

Friendall's house

[*Enter*] *Mrs Friendall following Friendall*

MRS FRIENDALL Nay, Mr Friendall, I know what you will object to
me; but you must hear me out. The concern and care of your
reputation is as dear to me as it can be tender to you, since I must
appear to the world only in that rank of honour which you are
pleased to maintain.   5

FRIENDALL Why, madam, you have as handsome an equipage as any
man's wife in town that has a father alive.°

MRS FRIENDALL This must not put me off. I see you make little of
the matter, to hide it from my fears; and there indeed you're kind.
But 'tis in vain to think of concealing from me what you intend.   10
From what you ought to do I know what you will do, after so base
a wrong.

FRIENDALL A drunken extravagance; the fellow will be sorry for't
when he's sober—

MRS FRIENDALL If you would stay till then.   15

FRIENDALL And beg my pardon.

MRS FRIENDALL That he shall do, if that would satisfy you.

FRIENDALL Satisfy me!

MRS FRIENDALL And let it satisfy you. It ought to satisfy you from
such a one. For I believe he would not have quarrelled anywhere   20
else, nor there neither, but upon the prospect of being prevented,
or parted, or secured° over night, in order to beg pardon in the
morning.

FRIENDALL Ay, madam, but consider—

MRS FRIENDALL Pray consider me, Mr Friendall. I must suffer   25
every way, if you proceed to a revenge—in your danger, which
must be mine; in my honour, which ought to be more yours than
to expose it upon every little occasion. Come, come. In other
things you have a good opinion of my conduct; pray let me govern
here. You may be assured, I'll do nothing to lessen you; the   30
satisfaction shall be as public as the affront. Leave it to me for
once; I won't° be denied. He is not worth your danger.

FRIENDALL Well, you shall govern me.

MRS FRIENDALL What, you are a married man and have a good
estate settled upon you, and should not be accountable to every   35
idle rakehell that has a mind to establish a renown from being
troublesome to public places.

FRIENDALL What then would you propose?

MRS FRIENDALL A small request—not to stir abroad, nor be at home
to anybody, till you hear from me.   40

FRIENDALL I promise you I won't.

   Exit [*Friendall*]

MRS FRIENDALL I dare take your word. His tameness° last night,
and backwardness this morning, in resenting that blow satisfy me
that he is not in a fever for fighting. I don't know that he is a
coward; but, having these reasons to suspect him, I thought this   45

was my best way to hinder him from discovering himself.° For if he had betrayed that baseness to me, I should despise him; and can I love the man I must despise?°

    [*Enter*] *Springame to her*

Brother, I sent for you—

SPRINGAME To make up° this quarrel, I know; and I come to lend a   50
helping hand to the work. I design to be a second in the business.°

MRS FRIENDALL You must be my second then, for I have taken the
quarrel upon me.

SPRINGAME With all my heart, egad. We, who live all the summer
for the public, should live in the winter for ourselves.°   55

MRS FRIENDALL And the women, good captain.

SPRINGAME That's living for ourselves, for 'tis not living without
'em. And a duel now might but interrupt a month of other
business perhaps,° that would be more agreeable to my constitution, I assure you. Then we are to have no fighting, it seems?   60

MRS FRIENDALL For reasons I'll tell you hereafter.

SPRINGAME Nay, there was no great danger of it. I have found out
the gentleman's lodgings and character. We shall strike up a peace
before a bottle's to an end.

MRS FRIENDALL [*handing the challenge to Springame*] This challenge   65
must be delivered as from him;° I trust the management to you.
Only take this in advice: that Mr Friendall wants your assistance
within.° You must stand by him, and oblige the gentleman to make
him satisfaction, without bringing his person in danger.°

SPRINGAME I understand you, and he shall satisfy him, or me.   70

MRS FRIENDALL See him satisfied, and I'll satisfy you with something shall be better to a younger brother° than the false mus-
ters° of a winter's quarter.

SPRINGAME I warrant you.°

    Exit [*Springame*]

MRS FRIENDALL Whatever I think of him, I must not let him fall into   75
the contempt of the town. Every little fellow, I know, will be
censoriously inquisitive and maliciously witty upon another man's
cowardice, out of the pleasure of finding as great a rascal as himself.
How despicable a condition must that matrimony be, when the
husband, whom we look upon as a sanctuary for a woman's honour,   80
must be obliged to the discretion and management of a wife for the
security of his own! Have a care of thinking that way; for in a
married state, as in the public, we tie ourselves up, indeed, but to
be protected in our persons, fortunes and honours by those very

laws° that restrain us in other things; for few will obey, but for the 85
benefit they receive from the government.°

    Servant enters

SERVANT Madam, Mr Lovemore.

    [*Servant*] *goes out*

MRS FRIENDALL° Lovemore here! I know he comes to tempt me to
rebel; but I'm prepared for him.

    Lovemore enters

Good-morrow, Mr Lovemore. 90

LOVEMORE I could not expect to see your ladyship so early. I come
to Mr Friendall.

MRS FRIENDALL May I thank you for the visit?

LOVEMORE I came as a friend, you may be sure, madam. Where your
honour's concerned, I can't be an enemy. 95

MRS FRIENDALL Not reasonably, indeed, to any man that would
injure it, since you are a professed enemy.

LOVEMORE An enemy!

MRS FRIENDALL Unless you will allow nobody to ruin it but
yourself. 100

LOVEMORE Indeed, I would allow nobody to defend it but myself, if
I had the keeping of it. But a happier man has that title, and I can
only hope to be a second in your service.

MRS FRIENDALL I thank you for the service you design me. But that
happier man, as you call him, who has the title, will maintain it, it 105
seems; for he, and my brother Springame, I'm afraid, are gone
about it already.

LOVEMORE Gone, madam!

MRS FRIENDALL An hour ago, before I had notice to prevent 'em.
For Mr Friendall, you may be sure, was impatient for an occasion 110
of righting himself.

LOVEMORE I might have thought so, indeed, madam. Would I had
come sooner.

MRS FRIENDALL You may yet be serviceable to me, sir, though you
are too late for Mr Friendall. 115

LOVEMORE How, madam, I beseech you?

MRS FRIENDALL By endeavouring to prevent 'em. You are acquainted
with the ways of reconciling matters of this honourable nature. I
am going to make an interest° with a kinsman, a colonel of the
guards, myself, to secure 'em.° Let your good nature in this be a 120
proof of your friendship; and command me to my power.

    Exit [*Mrs Friendall*]

LOVEMORE Prevent 'em! Yes, yes; that I must do for my own sake. For if he should behave himself better than I imagined he would, it may secure him in his wife's esteem, and only ruin me with her, who laid the design.   125

    Exit

2.3

Wilding's lodgings

[Enter] Wilding and his Footman

WILDING Have you disposed of her?

FOOTMAN Safe into a chair, sir. She's jogging homeward, lighter by a maidenhead, I presume, than she came, sir.

WILDING The loss is not so light, but she may feel it.

FOOTMAN Heavy enough, perhaps, nine months hence, sir. But have   5
you sent ever a lie° along with her?

WILDING How, sirrah?

FOOTMAN Pardon me, sir. Not that I believe your honour was sparing of your conscience, in saying anything, and swearing to't, that she had a mind to believe.   10

WILDING That you may swear, indeed.

FOOTMAN But she's gone away so very well satisfied with what you have said and done to her, she's above inventing a lie for herself. The first angry word they give her at home, I suppose, you may hear of her. A hackney-coach removes her, and her commodes,   15
upon very little warning; and I expect° when she will send in half a dozen band-boxes, to take possession of your lodgings. But, pray, sir, if I may be so bold—

WILDING Yes, yes; at this time you may be so bold. The service of your wit secures you the privilege of your jest.   20

FOOTMAN Then, pray, sir, why did you take so much pains to persuade this young creature to come away from her aunt, when I know you never design to take care of her yourself?

WILDING Why, faith, I can't make you a very good answer. But the best reason I know of is—besides the reputation of undoing her—it   25
looks kind, at the time, to talk of providing for the woman that does one the favour. 'Twas a very plausible argument to cozen her into a consent, level to° my design of lying with her, and carried to the very mark of love.

FOOTMAN Indeed, it costs nothing to promise,° when nothing can oblige you to pay. And if she depends upon it, at her peril, 'tis she will be disappointed, not you. Though, ten to one, poor little rogue, from the fondness of her own inclinations she guesses at yours, and fancies, from the courtesy she has done you, you will be so civil a gentleman to marry her.

WILDING Not unlikely. There's none of these young girls—let a man's character be never so loose among 'em—but, from one vanity or other, will be encouraged to design and venture upon him. And though fifty of their acquaintance have fallen in the experiment, each of them will still imagine she has something particular in her person, forsooth, to reclaim and engage him to herself. So most of 'em miscarry, upon the project of getting husbands.

FOOTMAN Gad forgive me for swearing; but, as I hope to be saved, and that's a bold word for a footman, I beg your pardon—there's a lady below, in a vizard, to speak with you.

WILDING Get you gone, you rascal. Beg her pardon, and leave to wait upon her.

    Exit [Footman]

She would have been admitted in less time to a privy councillor's levée, though he had laid aside the business of the nation to manage hers. This must be the letter-lady.° She comes a little unseasonable,° if she knew all. If she has experience enough to allow for some natural miscarriages which may happen in the beginning of an amour, I may pacify her that way. 'Tis but swearing heartily, damning the modesty of my constitution, laying its faults upon an over-respect to her, and promising better things for the future. That used to be a current excuse;° but 'tis the women's fault, if it pass too often upon 'em. If she prove an old acquaintance, the coldness of the entertainment will secure me from the persecution of her visits hereafter. But if it be a face I never saw, I may use her well enough yet to encourage her to another appointment. So every way does my business, whatever becomes of the lady's.

    Mrs Witwoud enters, masked

O madam, I beg your pardon.

MRS WITWOUD No excuses, good sir. Men of employment are above good breeding; and I see you have a great deal upon your hands.

WILDING I am a man of business,° indeed, madam; and, as you were pleased to signify in your letter, my practice lies among the women. What can I do for you?

MRS WITWOUD Can't you tell what, sir? You are not the man I took
you for. But you are like our fortune-tellers, who come into our   70
secrets more by our own folly, in betraying ourselves, than by any
skill or knowledge of their own.

WILDING Indeed I should ha' proceeded, as most of those fellows
do—set out impudently at first, taken several things for granted (as
that you were no maid, and so forth), ventured briskly at every-   75
thing—and something might have happened to please you.

MRS WITWOUD Did the lady, just gone away from you, find it so?

WILDING She had what she came for. You would take it ill to lose
your labour yourself, madam.

MRS WITWOUD She ventured at everything, as briskly as you could,   80
I suppose, sir?

WILDING 'Tis a towardly girl indeed, and comes on finely. I have no
reason to complain of losing my labour upon her. She's ready for
running away from her relations already. Are not you a little that
way inclined? Come, come; if you have any troubles upon your   85
spirits, child—

MRS WITWOUD You can remove 'em into the flesh, I warrant you.

WILDING If you have ever a husband that lies heavy upon your
conscience, I have a cordial will drive the distemper from your
heart.   90

MRS WITWOUD Why, that's kind indeed, to make some room for the
lover. But that is not my distemper. I could resolve it myself, if I
had a husband, whether I would make him a cuckold or no. But I
lie under a difficulty of disposing of a maidenhead.

WILDING There I must resolve you;° that case I often handle.   95

MRS WITWOUD But hear it, I beseech you, before you decide it.

WILDING That would do well in Westminster Hall,° I grant you; but
in proceedings of this nature we are always on the plaintiff's side.
Let the sober party° say what they can to the reason of the thing.
You are certainly in the right, in pleasing yourself.   100

MRS WITWOUD 'Twill come to that, I believe. For you must
know, sir, that, being under the discretion and tyranny of an old
aunt—

WILDING You will naturally run away from her.

MRS WITWOUD And being considerable enough° to be followed for   105
my fortune—

WILDING You will certainly be betrayed and sold by her—

MRS WITWOUD To some booby of her own breed,° who, paying too
dear for the purchase, will undo himself to undo me.

WILDING Come, come; you are now under my care. 'Tis my fault,   110
if you miscarry.

MRS WITWOUD And mine too, if I do.

WILDING Let me be your trustee.°

MRS WITWOUD Indeed the woman should cheat the man as much as
she can before marriage, because, after it, he has a title of cheating   115
her as long as he lives.

WILDING If you can't make over your money, make over your—

MRS WITWOUD Common conveyances° both in our sex, sir.

WILDING A maidenhead's a jewel of no value in marriage.

MRS WITWOUD 'Tis never set down indeed in the particular° of a   120
woman's estate.

WILDING And therefore least missed by a husband, of anything she
brings along with her.

MRS WITWOUD If indeed, by the articles of marriage, a man should
covenant for a maidenhead, the woman, in a legal honesty, ought   125
to satisfy the bargain; but the men never mention that, for fear of
inflaming the jointure.°

WILDING And the women never put 'em upon't.°

MRS WITWOUD Out of a conscience in their dealings, to be sure,
for fear they should not always be able to be as good as their   130
words.

WILDING I see, madam, we differ only in our sexes. And now, if you
please, we will beget a right understanding between them too.

MRS WITWOUD How, sir!

WILDING I'll show you how.   135
    [*Wilding makes advances to her, which she resists*]
Have a care what you do, madam; 'tis a very difficult matter, let
me tell you, to refuse a man handsomely. Look you, madam, I
would have you make a decent resistance; a little of it enhances
the favour and keeps up the value of your person, but too
much on't is an undervaluing of mine. Nay, nay, when it once   140
comes to fighting, you often ruin what you would raise.°
Struggling too long is as much to your disadvantage as not
struggling at all; and you know 'tis the same thing to a woman—a
man's being indifferent, as his being incapable to oblige her. Come,
come, enough of this.   145

MRS WITWOUD So I say too, sir. The jest will go no further, I see.
    [*Mrs Witwoud*] *unmasks; he declines into a respect to her*°

WILDING Mrs Witwoud! I did not expect to see you here, indeed,
madam.

MRS WITWOUD I came upon business, Mr Wilding; but the temptation of a vizard-mask, and the pleasure of prating upon such an   150
occasion, has carried me a little beyond it.

WILDING I am obliged to you for a great deal of wit, whatever else
you design me by this visit.

MRS WITWOUD Which now you hardly thank me for, since 'tis
impossible for an old acquaintance to answer your expectations of   155
a new face.

WILDING To show how I value your visit, and the regard I have for
you, I will give some necessary orders in the family to prevent your
being seen in my lodgings, and wait upon you again.

Exit [Wilding]

MRS WITWOUD By this extraordinary care of my reputation, I find   160
he has no design upon it himself. Not that I have any design upon
Mr Wilding; but I am sorry to find that every man has not a design
upon me. For since want is the rate of things, I know no real value
of reputation, but in regard of common women,° who have none;
no extraordinary worth of a maidenhead, but as 'tis a temptation   165
to the man to take it away; and the best commendation of virtue
is, that every man has a design to put it to the trial. It vexes me,
though, to think he should grow so tame upon the sight of
me—not that I believe I had anything in my face that altered him.
Something did; that's certain. By which I find 'tis not enough for   170
a woman to be handsome; there must be a probability of making
that handsome woman kind,° to make a man in love with her, for
no man is in love without some encouragement to hope upon.
Now, from one of my character, who have impertinently prated
away so much of my time—in setting up for a wit, to the ruin of   175
other people's pleasure and loss of my own—what encouragement
or probability can there be, but that, as I have lived a fool, I ought
to die repenting, unpitied, and a maid? If I had died a maid, 'tis
but what I deserved for laughing so many honest gentlemen off
their charitable design of making me otherwise.   180

Wilding enters to her

WILDING Now, madam, you command me.

MRS WITWOUD It shall be to do yourself a favour then, Mr
Wilding—to rid you of an encumbrance, which lies as heavy upon
your pleasures as a wife upon her husband.

WILDING O, defend me from a wife.   185

MRS WITWOUD And from a silly mistress, sir, the greater burden of
the two. A wife you may lay aside, but a foolish, fond mistress will

hang about you like your conscience—to put you in mind of your sins before you are willing to repent of 'em. You know whom I mean, Mr Wilding. You may trust me with the secret, because I know it already.

WILDING That's one very good reason, truly, madam.

MRS WITWOUD My cousin Fanny indeed is very well in her person—

WILDING I'm glad on't.°

MRS WITWOUD Very well to be liked, I mean.

WILDING I mean so too, madam. (*Aside*) Though I have known a clap mistaken for a maidenhead before now.

MRS WITWOUD But she's a girl, and I can guess how very unfit a girl must be to give you any desire beyond undoing her. For I know your temper so well—now you have satisfied the curiosity or vanity of your love, you would not bear the punishment of her company another day to have the pleasure of it another night, whatever you have said to persuade her to the contrary.

WILDING Fie, madam, think better of me.

MRS WITWOUD Better nor worse than I do of all the young men in town. For I believe you would now resign her to anybody else with as much satisfaction as you got her for yourself. I know most of those matters end in the benefit of the public;° and a little of your ill usage, which you will take care to supply her withal, may make her one of the common goods of the town. But that's a ruin I would prevent if I could. Therefore, to save you the labour of getting rid of her—for that's the only design you have now upon her, I'm sure—I came to spare your good nature the trouble, by making you a very fair offer.

WILDING Let's see how reasonable you can be, in another body's bargain.

MRS WITWOUD Very reasonable you shall find me, if you will but give over your farther attempts upon her—which now you may easily be persuaded to, I suppose—and contribute, by your assistance, to my design of marrying her. I will engage my self and interest,° which you know is very considerable in my own sex, to serve you in any other woman of my acquaintance.

WILDING Faith, madam, you bid like a chapman.

MRS WITWOUD Any woman, of any family or condition—the best friend I have I'll befriend you in, and thank you into the bargain.

WILDING Stay. Let me consider—which?

MRS WITWOUD But take this advice along with you. Raise the scene
of your affairs above the conquest of a girl. Some of you sparks   230
think, if you can but compass a maidenhead, though but your
tailor's daughter's, you have settled a reputation forever. Why, sir,
there are maidenheads among the women of quality, though not so
many perhaps. But there are favours of all kinds to be had among
'em, as easily brought about, and at the same price of pains that   235
you can purchase a chambermaid's.

WILDING I'm glad you tell me so.

MRS WITWOUD Why, there's Mrs Newlove, and her cousin Truegame,° Mrs Artist, Mrs Dancer, Lady Smirkit, Lady Woudmore,
and twenty more of your acquaintance and mine, all very fine   240
women to the eye—

WILDING And of reputation to the world.

MRS WITWOUD Why, those very women of reputation to the
world have every one of 'em, to my certain knowledge, an
intrigue upon their hands at this very time; for I'm intimate with   245
all of 'em.

WILDING I see you are.

MRS WITWOUD But, as fine as they seem to the eye, Mr Wilding,
what with the false complexions of their skins, their hair and
eyebrows, with other defects about 'em (which I must not discover   250
of my friends, you know), with their stinking breath in the
morning, and other unsavoury smells all the day after, they are
most of them intolerable to any man that has the use of his
nose.°

WILDING That I could not believe indeed, but that you tell me so.   255

MRS WITWOUD Then there's Mrs Faceall,° a very fair woman
indeed, and a great fortune. As much in shape as you see her, I
have been a godmother to two of her children, and she passes for
a very good maid still.

WILDING She passed upon me, I assure you; for I was very near   260
marrying her myself once.

MRS WITWOUD Choose where you please; but I would not advise
you to any I have named yet.

WILDING Is there any hopes of Mrs Friendall?

MRS WITWOUD Little or none yet awhile, I believe. Mr Lovemore   265
has at present engaged° her. But there's my cousin Sightly! Lord,
that I should forget her so long! That I should be so backward in
serving a friend! She is the fittest woman in the world for you, the
most convenient for your purpose in all the town, easy in her

humour and fortune, and able to make her lover so every way. She shall be the woman.   270

WILDING Would you would make her so.

MRS WITWOUD I can and will make her so. We shall walk in the Mall° this morning. If you think fit to be there, it may introduce the acquaintance.   275

WILDING I'll but° dress and be with you.

MRS WITWOUD I don't doubt but in a little time to give you an opportunity, and the lady an inclination of having it improved. But that must be your business. I'm a-going about mine—to make her a visit. Remember our bargain, sir.   280

WILDING I warrant you.

     Exit [Mrs Witwoud]

       Let whoremasters rejoice; the times must mend,
       If every woman has but such a friend.

     Exit

3.1

Ruffle's lodgings

[*Enter*] *Ruffle and Servant*

RUFFLE A gentleman to speak with me! I am gone to Banstead
Downs,° to the horsematch.

SERVANT There's no match there, sir, this fortnight.

RUFFLE Not this fortnight! I had forgot myself. But you may say I
went out by five in the morning, and you don't know when I come   5
back. Go, tell him so.

SERVANT I have told him already you were within, sir.

RUFFLE Pox on him, what manner of man is he? Does he look like a
man of business?°

SERVANT Not much like a man of business.   10

RUFFLE No, I warrant you. Some coxcombly companion or other,
that visits in a morning, and makes other people idle, not to be idle
himself. But can't you tell what he would have with me?

SERVANT I'll ask him, if you please.

RUFFLE He may be a messenger,° for aught I know.   15

SERVANT I'll bring an account of him.

> *Exit* [*Servant*]

RUFFLE Would he were a messenger. I could be contented to pay the
fees,° to be secured in the hands of the government for a fortnight.
Well, this guilt is certainly very terrible. The blow I gave Friendall
was a very ill thing done of me. It lies heavier upon my conscience   20
this morning than it did upon his face last night.

> *Servant re-enters*

SERVANT His name is Captain Springame. You know his business,
he says.

RUFFLE Yes, yes, I guess at it. I thought what it would come to.
Show him up to me.   25

> *Exit Servant*

I must do as well as I can. (*Strips into his gown and cap*)° There
comes no good of being too forward upon these occasions. 'Twill
require some time to dress again. 'Tis gaining time° at least.

> *Springame enters*

SPRINGAME Good-morrow, sir. [*Giving him the challenge*] I have a
small bill upon you here.   30

RUFFLE A challenge, I suppose.

SPRINGAME Payable at sight,° as you will find it.

RUFFLE You take me unprovided, you see, sir, to answer you at sight.

SPRINGAME I'll stay till you dress, sir, if that be all, to have you
along with me.   35

RUFFLE Ay, ay, sir, I'll go along with you. Never doubt it, sir; you
shan't stay long for me. I may dress time enough for somebody,
if that be your business. I'll do the gentleman reason,° I warrant
him.

SPRINGAME We ask no more, sir.   40

RUFFLE You are his friend, I suppose?

SPRINGAME At your friend's service. I serve upon these occasions
sometimes, by way of second, or so, when I want employment of
my own.

RUFFLE Is fighting your employment?   45

SPRINGAME 'Tis a soldier's employment.

RUFFLE Why, really, sir, I beg your pardon; I'm sorry I must
disappoint you. I never make use of a second, especially in such a
quarrel as this is, where I am so much in the wrong already, that
I am almost unwilling to engage in it any farther myself. Where is 50
your friend, pray?

SPRINGAME Below, in a coach, sir.

RUFFLE O dear, sir, don't let him wait upon me;° bring him up, I
beseech you. And—d'ye hear, sir?—I'm loth to justify an ill thing.
If he is resolved to be satisfied, why, with all my heart, sir, I'll give 55
him the satisfaction of a gentleman; I'll beg his pardon. Pray tell
him so.
          Exit Springame
If fighting be his employment, would he were at it anywhere else,
and I fairly rid of him. I could discover° now that Lovemore set
me on to affront him; that would throw the quarrel upon Love- 60
more. But then Lovemore knows me, and I must expect to be
scurvily used by him if I do. Hang baseness; 'tis but begging
pardon at last.
          Springame enters with Friendall
SPRINGAME [*to Friendall*] A very civil gentleman, brother. He is not
the man you took him for.   65

RUFFLE No, indeed, sir, the captain's in the right. I never justify an
ill thing.

FRIENDALL 'Tis very well you don't, sir.

RUFFLE I am more a man of honour,° I assure you, sir.

FRIENDALL I shall be glad to find you so.   70

RUFFLE Sir, you shall find me so; I scorn to do an ill thing as much as any man. I was last night in the wrong, as every man is sometimes; and I'm sorry for't. What would you have more, sir?

FRIENDALL That is not enough, sir; I must have more.

RUFFLE Why, I beg your pardon, sir. 75

FRIENDALL What's begging my pardon, sir, for such a public affront?

SPRINGAME (aside) So, now he grows upon him.°

FRIENDALL That won't do my business, begging my pardon. My reputation's at stake, and that must be satisfied, before you and I 80 part, sir.

RUFFLE Lord, sir, you are the strangest man in the world. You won't oblige me to justify an ill thing, would you?

FRIENDALL Damme, sir, what do you mean? Not to give me satisfaction? 85

RUFFLE I mean, sir, to give you any satisfaction, in reason. But I can't fight against my conscience if I were to be hanged, sir, not I.

SPRINGAME No, brother, that's a little too hard upon the gentleman. You see his conscience won't suffer him to fight with you.

FRIENDALL Damn him and his conscience! He made no conscience 90 of affronting me.

SPRINGAME But his conscience has flown in his face since,° it seems.

FRIENDALL And now he finds it only in his fears.

SPRINGAME Come, come, you may be satisfied without fighting.

FRIENDALL If you think so, brother— 95

Lovemore enters, [unseen by Ruffle]

LOVEMORE [aside] Pox on't, they're here before me.

[Lovemore] joins with Friendall. [They talk apart]

RUFFLE [to Springame] Captain, I'll beg your friend's pardon in any public place. At the music-meeting, if he pleases—

SPRINGAME That's staying too long for't.

RUFFLE Or in full Mall° before the beaux or the officers of the guard; 100 or at Will's coffee-house° before the wits; or in the playhouse, in the pit before the vizard-masks and orange-wenches, or behind the scenes° before the women-actors, or anywhere else, but upon the stage—and you know, one would not willingly be a jest to the upper galleries.° 105

FRIENDALL You hear what he says, Mr Lovemore.

LOVEMORE I'll do you justice, sir.°

RUFFLE (*seeing Lovemore, he takes heart again*) If none of these offers will serve his turn, sir, if your friend will be satisfied with nothing

but extremities, let him look to himself, let what will be the   110
consequence.° I must do as well as I can with him.

LOVEMORE (*aside*) So, he has seen me, I find.

SPRINGAME (*aside*) What the devil, he won't fight at last, sure!

RUFFLE [*to Lovemore*] Sir, your most humble servant. You guess these
gentlemen's business, I suppose. I have offered 'em any satisfaction,   115
in reason. But, taking me, as you see, sir, at a disadvantage, two to
one, nothing would content 'em, without exposing myself as a rascal
to all the town, sir. Now, sir, you are more a gentleman, I know; and
they shall be damned, before I give 'em any other satisfaction, now I
have a man of honour to stand by me.   120

LOVEMORE Gentlemen, I came to reconcile you, if I can. What say
you?

SPRINGAME He offered just now to beg my brother's° pardon in the
playhouse.

RUFFLE Make your best on't; I did so.   125

FRIENDALL Then let it be tonight in the side-box before the ladies°—

RUFFLE With all my heart, sir.

FRIENDALL For they are the part of the town that a man of pleasure
should secure a reputation withal.° Your servant, sir. Lovemore,
your humble servant.   130

    Friendall and Springame go out

LOVEMORE And hast thou begged his pardon?

RUFFLE And glad to come off so. I was never so put to't to bring
myself off a quarrel before. It had been impossible, if the captain
had not done a good office° between us. But I bore up as soon as
I saw you.   135

LOVEMORE But then 'twas too late. You had sneakingly begged his
pardon before. If you had sent to me at first, I would have brought
you off cleverly. Suppose he had carried you behind Southampton
House,° which he never intended. 'Twas but falling down, or
dropping your sword, when you came there, to have saved all. But   140
now you have ruined your own reputation, and my design upon
him forever.

RUFFLE What could I do? He not only sent me a challenge, but came
himself to carry me along with him.

LOVEMORE How? Send you a challenge, and come with it himself!   145
That's something odd. Pray, let's see the challenge.

RUFFLE [*giving Lovemore the challenge*] There 'tis; make your best on't.
The paper will make admirable crackers for a Lord Mayor's Show;°
every word in't is as hot as gunpowder. I'm glad I'm rid on't.

Exit [Ruffle. Lovemore reads the letter]

LOVEMORE If this be Friendall's style, 'tis mightily mended of late.   150
I have a note of his about me, upon Child,° for money won at play.
I'll compare 'em. [*Takes out the note*] 'Tis not his hand neither.
Nay, then there's more in't. This may be a stratagem of his wife's.
I've seen her hand and think this very near it. It must be so. But
then Friendall's coming for satisfaction is an argument he might   155
send this challenge. But coming at the same time with it himself
is an argument against him that he knew nothing of the matter.
For though he delivers his love-letters, he would hardly deliver his
challenges himself. And, for his coming here, Springame might
put him upon't, from a reasonable probability that this fellow was   160
a rascal. I don't know what to fix upon. This challenge will be of
use to me with the lady. I'll take it for granted that she writ it and
proceed upon it accordingly.

   Exit

[3.2]

St James's Park°

*[Enter] Friendall, Springame, with Mrs Friendall and Mrs
Teazall*

SPRINGAME [*to Friendall*] Brother, if you have no farther service
for me, I must think of employing myself. My walk lies another
way.
   Exit [Springame]

MRS FRIENDALL I'm glad you're rid of this business so handsomely,
Mr Friendall, and that Mr Lovemore was by at his begging your   5
pardon.

FRIENDALL When I undertake things of this kind, I always go
through with 'em.

MRS FRIENDALL This is very well over, and I hope you will take care
to keep out of 'em for the future.   10

FRIENDALL Every man has the misfortune of 'em sometimes,
madam.

MRS FRIENDALL But 'tis a prudent man's part to keep out of the
occasion of 'em. And, in order to't, Mr Friendall, I could wish you
would not make your house, as you daily do, one of the public   15
places of the town.

MRS TEAZALL She's in the right on't indeed, Mr Friendall. You are
very happy in the discretion of a good lady, if you know when
you're well. There are very few women would quarrel with your
good nature in this point, sir. But she has too great a regard to her   20
own and your reputation, you see, not to apprehend the malice of
ill tongues upon the liberties you allow in your family. The graver
part of your friends take notice of it already, and, let me tell you,
sir, are extremely concerned.

FRIENDALL That they are past the pleasures of good company   25
themselves. Why, really, madam, I believe it. But they may say
what they will; I shall do what I please. I live to myself, and not
to the whimsical humour of the graver part of my friends; and so
you may tell 'em, good madam, (going) from your humble servant.

MRS FRIENDALL You won't leave us, Mr Friendall?   30

FRIENDALL I'll go home with you, like a good husband, madam; but
no man of fashion, you know, walks with his wife. Besides, there's
a noble lord I must walk with.

    Exit [Friendall]

MRS FRIENDALL Anything to be rid of my company.

MRS TEAZALL Why, how have the men, at this rate, the impudence   35
to think the women should not cuckold 'em! If I had such a
husband, as old as I am, o' my conscience, I believe I should use
him as he deserved. But that's some comfort. Use him as you
please; nobody will think you wrong him. And, let me tell you, 'tis
a great thing to have the town on one's side.   40

MRS FRIENDALL I'll keep 'em so, if I can.

MRS TEAZALL Nay, faith and troth, you have given him fair warning.
If he won't take it, he must answer himself for all the miscarriages
you can be guilty of in your conduct hereafter.

MRS FRIENDALL There's something more in that,° Mrs Teazall.   45

    Exeunt [Mrs Friendall and Mrs Teazall. Enter] Lovemore,
    Wellvile, following 'em

WELLVILE There's your Mrs Friendall before us. I honour her
character as much as I despise her husband's.

LOVEMORE Though he has 'scaped the public discovery, if she°
knows him to be a coward, it does my business still as well.

WELLVILE If I did not think him one, I would put him to a trial he   50
should not so easily get clear of, for putting a note into Mrs
Sightly's hand at the music-meeting.

LOVEMORE How!

WELLVILE But I owe him a good turn for it.

LOVEMORE It comes into my head, and you shall pay him the good   55
   turn.° What if you put Mrs Sightly upon telling his wife of it?

WELLVILE Ha!

LOVEMORE You ought to do it.

WELLVILE I think so too myself; and you may be satisfied I'll
   do't—more out of a regard to the woman° I value so much, than   60
   any design of promoting your cuckolding the fool.

LOVEMORE Good grave sir, the plot is never the worse, I hope, for
   carrying your friend's interest along with the lady's.

WELLVILE Make your best use on't, Lovemore; I'm contented we°
   should thrive together.   65

   Exeunt [Lovemore and Wellvile. Enter] Mrs Sightly and Mrs
   Witwoud after 'em

MRS WITWOUD You are mightily injured, indeed, madam, to be
   persuaded to come abroad, so much to your disadvantage, such a
   delicate° morning as this is, so much against your inclinations. But
   you'll know your interest better in a little time, and me for your
   friend, I suppose, when you find the benefit of it.   70

MRS SIGHTLY Nay, cousin, the injury may be forgiven, for the
   pleasure of the walk at this time of the year.

MRS WITWOUD Why, the very walk is to be liked, though there were
   nobody in it to like us. But there's a great deal of good company
   in the Mall; and, I warrant you, we'll have our share of the   75
   commendation of the place,° in spite of fresher faces. You are sure
   of your part of it already.

MRS SIGHTLY How so, good Mrs Witwoud?

MRS WITWOUD Why, good Mrs Sightly, there's Mr Wellvile before
   you.   80

MRS SIGHTLY My Platonic lover,° as you call him.

MRS WITWOUD And as you find him.

MRS SIGHTLY I think him very much my friend.

MRS WITWOUD Very much your friend! I grant you indeed, every
   woman that is not wholly insensible°—and one would not be   85
   thought insensible, you know—every woman ought to have a
   Platonic passion for one man or other. But a Platonic lover in a
   man is—

MRS SIGHTLY What, pray?

MRS WITWOUD Why, he is a very unmannerly° fellow. He is not   90
   what he should be; that's certain. As for the matter of respect,
   which we keep such a clutter° about and seem to value so much
   in the men, all that I know of it is, that if any man pretended to

follow and like me, I should never believe what he said, if he did
not do something to convince me. I should think he affronted me   95
extremely, if upon the first handsome occasion he did not offer me
everything in his power.

MRS SIGHTLY How, cousin!°

MRS WITWOUD I hate a blockhead that will never give a woman a
reputable occasion of refusing him. 'Tis one of the best compli-   100
ments a lover can make his mistress's pride, and I never knew any
man that did his business without it.

MRS SIGHTLY Why, Witwoud, thou art mad, sure.

MRS WITWOUD Not° for your Mr Wellvile. If I were in your place,
I should have something the better opinion of him, if he would   105
have a little worse opinion of me. But, between you and me, I
should not like him for a lover.

MRS SIGHTLY He does not pretend° to be one.

MRS WITWOUD Who's here? Wilding and Courtall behind us? That
Wilding, cousin, is a very pretty gentleman.   110

MRS SIGHTLY And Courtall too—very well.

MRS WITWOUD I must bring you acquainted with Wilding.

MRS SIGHTLY No more acquaintance, good Witwoud.

MRS WITWOUD For his discretion and conduct, his good behaviour,
and all that, Wellvile is his acquaintance and will answer for. But 115
his agreeable, easy wit and good humour you may take upon my
word. You'll thank me, when you know him.
        *Exeunt [Mrs Sightly and Mrs Witwoud.] Wilding and
        Courtall enter*

WILDING She's a woman of her word. You see she has brought Mrs
Sightly along with her.

COURTALL I never doubted it. She'll carry her to supper in a night 120
or two. She's never the worse bawd, I hope, for being a gentlewoman.

WILDING A good family indeed gives a countenance to° the profession; and a reputation is necessary to carry on the credit of a
trade.   125

COURTALL Here's Wellvile just behind us.

WILDING Prithee stay with him. I'll tell you how I thrive.
        Exit [Wilding.] Wellvile enters

WELLVILE Good-morrow, Mr Courtall.

COURTALL O sir, yours.

WELLVILE Was not that Wilding left you?   130

COURTALL He's in his employment, sir, very busy.

WELLVILE In pursuit of the women, I know. It hardly answers the
expense, I doubt.

COURTALL You have no reason to say so. There's a lady before us,
of your acquaintance, Mrs Sightly by name, of another opinion. I   135
suppose she thinks such an assurance° as his, in coming to the
point, is more to the nature of the thing than all your ceremony
and respect.

WELLVILE Mrs Sightly!

COURTALL She, sir; the very same. I could tell you a secret, Wellvile;   140
but you are one of those fellows that hate another man should lie
with a woman, though you never attempt her yourself. I confess I
am something of your mind. I think the enjoyment the dull part
of an intrigue, and therefore I give it over, when I see the lady in
earnest.   145

WELLVILE But the secret, Courtall?

COURTALL Why, faith, Wellvile, if you have temper to manage it,°
the secret may be of use to you. Wilding, you know, never
debauches a woman only for himself. Where he visits, in a little
time every man may be received in his turn. You must know, 'twas   150
Witwoud put him upon Mrs Sightly. She knew what she did, I
suppose, and has promised him a good office in her way. Make
your advantage of what I tell you; but not a syllable to anyone.

        Springame enters

SPRINGAME O Courtall! Here are a couple of vizard-masks have set
upon me in the next walk, and I wanted thee to take one of 'em   155
off my hands.

COURTALL I'll stand by you, my noble captain.

        Exeunt [Springame and Courtall]

WELLVILE (*alone*) I'll think no more on't; 'tis impossible.° What's
impossible? Nothing's impossible to a woman. We judge but on
the outside of that sex, and know not what they can nor what   160
they do, more than they please to show us. I have known Mrs
Sightly these seven years. Known her! I mean I have seen her,
observed her, followed her. Maybe there's no knowing a woman.
But in all that time I never found a freedom that allowed me any
encouragement beyond a friend. Maybe I have been wanting to   165
myself.° But then she would not throw herself away upon a
common lover; that's not probable. If she had been affectedly
reserved, I would suspect the devil in her heart had stamped the
sign of virtue in her looks, that she might cheat the world and sin
more close. But she is open in her carriage, easy, clear of° those   170

arts that have made lust a trade. Perhaps that openness may be
design. 'Tis easy to raise doubts. And still she may be—I won't
think she can—till I know more. But Witwoud is, I know her,
everything that's mischievous—abandoned and undone. Undone
herself, she would undo the sex. She is to bawd for Wilding. I   175
know her bad enough for any trade. But bawds have some good
nature, and procure pleasure for pay. Witwoud has baser ends—a
general ruin upon all her friends.

> *Several [lords] pass over the stage. [Enter] Friendall, [who is]*
> *slighted by 'em, one after another*

FIRST LORD [*to Friendall*] I have a little business at present. But I
shall see you at the play.   180

> *Exit [First Lord]*

FRIENDALL In the king's box,° my lord. (*To another*) My dear lord,
I'm your humble servant.

SECOND LORD Another time, good Mr Friendall. You see I'm
engaged.

> *Exit [Second Lord]*

FRIENDALL A pox o' their engagements. A man can't make one   185
among 'em.° [*To another*] O my most noble lord.

THIRD LORD I know you will upbraid me, Mr Friendall. But I'll
recover your opinion and come and dine with you. Let's have Jack
Dryden and Will Wycherley,° as you call 'em. Some of these days
we'll be very witty together. But now I am your servant.   190

> *Exit [Third Lord]*

FRIENDALL [*aside*] This is a very unfortunate morning with me. I
have not walked one turn with a lord, since I came in. I see I must
take up with the men of wit today.—O Mr Wellvile!

WELLVILE Don't let me keep you from better company.

FRIENDALL Faith, sir, I prefer a man of wit to a man of quality at   195
any time.

WELLVILE [*aside*] If she thinks Witwoud her friend after this, 'tis a
sign she's pleased with it, and there's an end on't.

FRIENDALL Why, Wellvile, thou art cogitabund, as a man may say;
thy head is running upon thy poetry.   200

WELLVILE I beg your pardon, sir; I did not mind you indeed.

> *Wilding enters to 'em*

Your servant, Mr Wilding.

FRIENDALL Wilding, yours. But, Wellvile, prithee, what is't to be?
A song? A tribute to the whole sex? Or a particular sacrifice? Or
is't a libel upon the court,° ha? We'll keep your counsel. Or a   205

lampoon upon the town? What, I am a great honourer and humble servant of the muses myself.

WELLVILE A very favourite of 'em, I hear, sir.

FRIENDALL I sometimes scribble indeed for my diversion.

WILDING And the diversion of the ladies, Mr Friendall.   210

WELLVILE And the diversion of all the town, Mr Friendall.

FRIENDALL Why, faith, gentlemen, poetry is a very pretty amusement; and, in the way of intrigue, or so, among the better rank of people, I have known a paper of verses go farther with a lady in the purchase of a favour than a present of fifty pounds would have done.   215

WILDING O, sir, 'tis the only way of purchasing a woman that is not to be bought.

FRIENDALL But, Wellvile, prithee communicate,° man.

WELLVILE Why, if you will have it, I have a design upon a play.

FRIENDALL Gad so, let me write a scene in it. I have a thousand   220
times had it in my head, but never could bring it about to write a play yet.

WILDING No, no; you had it not in your head, sir.°

FRIENDALL I vow to Gad, but I have then, twenty times, I'm confident. But one thing or other always kicked it out again. But   225
I promise you, I'll write a scene for you.

WILDING Before you know the subject?

FRIENDALL Prithee, what is't? But, be what it will, here's my hand upon't; I'll write it for you.

WELLVILE You must know then, sir, I am scandalised extremely to   230
see the women upon the stage make cuckolds at that insatiable rate they do in all our modern comedies, without any other reason from the poets, but because a man is married he must be a cuckold. Now, sir, I think the women are most unconscionably injured by this general scandal upon their sex. Therefore, to do 'em what service I   235
can in their vindication, I design to write a play and call it—

FRIENDALL Ay, what, I beseech you? I love to know the name of a new play.

WELLVILE *The Wives' Excuse; or, Cuckolds Make Themselves.*

FRIENDALL A very pretty name, faith and troth; and very like to be   240
popular among the women.

WILDING And true among the men.

FRIENDALL But what characters have you?

WELLVILE What characters? Why, I design to show a fine young woman married to an impertinent, nonsensical, silly, intriguing,   245
cowardly, good-for-nothing coxcomb.

WILDING (*aside*) This blockhead does not know his own picture.

FRIENDALL Well, and how? She must make him a cuckold, I suppose.

WELLVILE 'Twas that I was thinking on when you came to me.   250

FRIENDALL O, yes, you must make him a cuckold.

WILDING By all means a cuckold.

FRIENDALL For such a character, gentlemen, will vindicate a wife in anything she can do to him. He must be a cuckold.

WELLVILE I am satisfied he ought to be a cuckold; and indeed, if the   255
lady would take my advice, she should make him a cuckold.

FRIENDALL She'll hear reason, I warrant her.

WELLVILE I have not yet determined how to dispose of her. But, in regard to the ladies, I believe I shall make her honest at last.

FRIENDALL I think the ladies ought to take it very ill of you, if you   260
do. But if she proves honest to the last, that's certain, 'tis more than the fellow deserves. (*To Wilding*) A very pretty character this, faith and troth.

WILDING And very well known in this town.

FRIENDALL Gad, I believe I can help you to a great many hints that   265
may be very serviceable to you.

WELLVILE I design to make use of you. We who write plays must sometimes be beholden to our friends. But more of this at leisure.

FRIENDALL Will you walk, gentlemen? The ladies are before us.   270

WELLVILE I have a little business with Wilding. We'll follow you.
      Exit Friendall

WILDING Business with me, Wellvile?

WELLVILE About a fair lady. I'll tell you as we walk.
      Exeunt [Wellvile and Wilding.] Enter Lovemore with Mrs
      Friendall, Mrs Sightly, Mrs Witwoud, and Mrs Teazall

MRS TEAZALL Nay, indeed, Mr Lovemore, as matters are managed between the men and women of the town, 'tis no less a blessing   275
for a lady to have a husband that will but so much as offer to fight for her and her honour, than 'tis for a husband to have a lady that has any honour to defend. There's such a depravity in matrimony, o' both sides, nowadays.

MRS SIGHTLY Why, good madam, is it such a business for a man to   280
offer to fight for his wife?

MRS WITWOUD All that I know is, the man that would not fight for me should do nothing else for me.

MRS TEAZALL You'll have your wit, let who's will blush for't.°

LOVEMORE (*to Mrs Teazall*) As you say, madam, a man of honour   285
is a great blessing in a husband—such as Mr Friendall has shown
himself to be. And here's a lady will value the blessing as it
deserves.

MRS FRIENDALL (*aside*) I must indeed despise him in my thoughts.

MRS WITWOUD (*walking off with Mrs Sightly*) Fulsome and foolish!   290
Let's hear no more on't. They don't think this can blind us.

LOVEMORE [*to Mrs Friendall*] If you were not inclined to it before,
madam, this last behaviour of his would engage you to value such
a blessing as you ought.

MRS FRIENDALL My duty would engage me. [*Aside*] What does he   295
mean by this?

MRS WITWOUD Cousin Teazall, your opinion, pray.
    [*Mrs Teazall joins Mrs Witwoud and Mrs Sightly*]

LOVEMORE [*to Mrs Friendall*] I have something to tell you, madam,
if you would but allow me; this is no place.

MRS FRIENDALL You'll find a time, I warrant you.—Ladies, the   300
Mall begins to thin.
    [*Mrs Friendall*] goes to [*the ladies. Enter*] Wellvile and
    Wilding°

WILDING Well, sir, since you declare yourself in love with the lady,
and I am not, I promise you, and you may trust me, I'll never
follow her more.

WELLVILE I do trust, and thank you for the promise.—Ladies, your   305
servant.
    [*Wellvile*] addresses to Mrs Sightly, Wilding to Mrs Witwoud

MRS WITWOUD [*to Wilding*] O, he's come at last! There's nothing to
be done here. You've outstayed your time. But we'll call at the
chocolate house° in St Alban's Street, as we go home. You may
meet us there by accident, you know.   310

WILDING [*aside*] If I were to be hanged now, I must meet 'em there,
though I have given my word to the contrary.

MRS TEAZALL [*aside, to Mrs Witwoud*] Is that the filthy fellow?

MRS WITWOUD That's Wilding, madam.

MRS TEAZALL I see there's no knowing a whoremaster by his face.   315
He looks like a modest, civil gentleman.

WELVILLE (*to Mrs Sightly*) Your friend, Mrs Witwoud, madam, may
be of that good-natured opinion that Lovemore is familiar with the
husband, only to be more familiar with the wife. But you must be
cautious of what you say, for fear we turn the scandal upon you.   320

MRS SIGHTLY Upon me, Mr Wellvile?°

WELLVILE Pardon me, madam, I have the freedom of a friend. But Mr Friendall declares he is in love with you; and, after that, the good-natured town, whatever they believe, will go near to say that your familiarity with his wife may be in order to the husband.   325

MRS SIGHTLY Contemptible! Sure nobody would think so.

WELLVILE 'Tis an ill-natured age to handsome women, madam.

MRS SIGHTLY Must I suffer, because he's a fool?

WELLVILE You may suffer, because he's a fool.

MRS SIGHTLY This is not only to be accountable for our own conduct, but to answer for all the indiscretion of the men's.   330

WELLVILE You must, madam, for those men's you allow to be so near you.

MRS SIGHTLY It would be but an ungrateful° piece of news to Mrs Friendall, if I should be serious enough to tell her of it.   335

WELLVILE 'Twould be more ungrateful to her, if anybody else did, and would go near to make you serious, if another should tell her for you.

MRS SIGHTLY But who can tell? It may be the cause of a breach between 'em.   340

WELLVILE Nay, madam, if it be considerable enough to make a breach in marriage, you may be sure 'twill make a breach in friendship. And how much that will be to the advantage of your reputation upon such an occasion—

MRS SIGHTLY I am convinced you are my friend, Mr Wellvile, and   345
thank you for this care of me.

　　　[*Wellvile and Mrs Sightly*] *mingle with Lovemore, Mrs Friendall, and the rest*°

MRS WITWOUD [*to Wilding*] This is the aunt would ha' been upon your bones,° I assure you, if I had not delivered you.

WILDING How shall I do to appease her?

MRS WITWOUD There's but one way now to please her. You must   350
know she has been in her time, like other women, in at most of the pleasures of this town. But, being too passionate a lover of the sport, she has been a bubble at all games. And, having now nothing to lose but her money, she declares for lanterloo° and is contented to be only cheated at cards.   355

　　　[*Enter*] *Friendall with Springame and Courtall*

FRIENDALL Why, what do you think, ladies? These gentlemen here, in spite of the temptation of so much good company, refuse to dine with me.

SPRINGAME (*to Mrs Witwoud*) O madam! Are you there?

COURTALL (*to Mrs Friendall*) Your brother has seduced me, madam.   360
SPRINGAME We'll visit you at night, ladies, in masquerade,° when
    the privilege of a vizard will allow us a conversation out of your
    forms,° and more to our humour a great deal, ladies.

   Exeunt Springame and Courtall

FRIENDALL Lovemore, Wellvile, Wilding—you'll follow us?
LOVEMORE We won't fail you, sir.   365

   Friendall goes out with the ladies

MRS WITWOUD [*going; to Wilding*] St Alban's Street.
WILDING Will° tell you more of this.

   [*Exit Mrs Witwoud*]

WELLVILE Wilding, you'll take another turn with us?
WILDING Faith, no, I'm tired. We shall meet at Friendall's all.

   Exit [*Wilding*]

WELLVILE At Friendall's be it then,   370
   Where the kind husband welcomes every guest.
LOVEMORE He but invites; his wife must make the feast.

   Exeunt

4.1

Friendall's house

All the company [i.e. Friendall, Lovemore, Wilding, Wellvile,
Mrs Friendall, Mrs Sightly, Mrs Teazall, Mrs Witwoud]
enters after dinner. [The women converse among themselves,
as do the men]

LOVEMORE Mr Friendall, you have the best wines and the greatest
choice of any man in town.

FRIENDALL There's an elegance in eating and drinking, gentlemen,
as well as in writing.

WELLVILE (*aside*) Or your style would never go down.   5

FRIENDALL How did you like the Lucena I gave you, the Galicia,
the Mountain-Alicant?° You taste the sun in them perfectly,
gentlemen.

WILDING O, plainly, sir!

FRIENDALL Then the Aracina, the Ranchio, and the Peralta, the   10
Carcavelos, the Lacrymae, the Schiveas, the Cephalonia, the
Montalchino, with all the Muscatels°—and to conclude, my single
bottle of Tokay.

LOVEMORE Admirable all, sir.

FRIENDALL A friend of mine that brought the Tokay from Buda   15
assures me, the stones of all those grapes are gold.°

WELLVILE That makes the wine so scarce.

FRIENDALL Nay, not unlikely. But of all the wines of all the climates
under the sun—

WILDING Give me the Greek.°   20

FRIENDALL O, I abominate—

WELLVILE The language, but not the wines; you may relish them
without it.

FRIENDALL Ay, that may be. But of all the wines, pagan or
Christian, in the world, I think the Borachio° the noblest.   25

WELLVILE [*aside*] 'Tis of the roughest kind indeed of beasts. Would
he were in the skin of one of 'em.

WILDING But your Vin de Congress,° Mr Friendall—

FRIENDALL True; but 'tis a Dutch wine and grows in the province
of Zeeland. I have drank it upon the place.   30

WILDING But, Mr Friendall, pray, in all your variety and interest
among your friends in the city, have you not sometimes met with
such a wine as the Vin de Short-Neck?°

307

FRIENDALL Vin de Short-Neck? Yes, I have drank of it at Thompson's,° and was the first that took notice of it. But 'tis a prohibited French wine,° and I have too great an acquaintance with the Members of Parliament not to drink according to law.

WILDING Yours is very good snuff, Mr Friendall.

FRIENDALL Yes, truly, I think 'tis pretty good powder.

WILDING [*offering Friendall his own snuff*] Pray, your opinion of mine; you are a critic.

FRIENDALL [*sampling it*] This is Havana° indeed; but then 'tis washed. Give me your dry powders;° they never lose their scent. Besides, yours is made of the leaves of the tobacco.

WILDING Why, what the devil's yours?

FRIENDALL Mine, sir, is right palilio,° made of the fibres, the spirituous part of the plant. There's not a pinch of it out of° my box in England. 'Twas made, I assure you, to the palate of His Most Catholic Majesty,° and sent me by a great Don of Spain that's in his prince's particular pleasures.

        [*Friendall*] *goes to the women*

WELLVILE And his, it seems, lie in his nose.

FRIENDALL Ladies, what say you to the fresco of the garden? We'll drink our tea upon the mount,° and be the envy of the neighbourhood.

MRS WITWOUD O delicately thought upon!°

FRIENDALL [*to Mrs Friendall*] Madam, which tea shall we have?

MRS FRIENDALL Which the company pleases, Mr Friendall.

FRIENDALL The plain Canton, the Nanking, the Bohea, the Latheroon, the Sunloe, or which?° Ha!

WELLVILE Have you any of the *Non Amo Te*?°

FRIENDALL Faith, no, sir, there came but little of it over this year; but I am promised a whole canister by a friend of a considerable interest in the committee.°

LOVEMORE Then the Bohea, sir, the Bohea will do our business.

FRIENDALL My Bohea, at the best hand too,° cost me ten pound a pound. But I have a tea, with a damned heathenish hard name, that I think I was very much befriended in at an Indian house° in the city. If you please, we'll have some of that.

MRS FRIENDALL 'Tis in my cabinet, Mr Friendall. I must order it° myself for you.

FRIENDALL That, madam, must make the compliment the greater to the company.

        [*Mrs Friendall*] *goes out*

[*To his guests*] *Allons*. You know the way; I wait upon you.
>   *All go out but Lovemore*

LOVEMORE This way she must come. She can't avoid me, thanks to
the honest husband.   75
>   *Mrs Friendall returns*

MRS FRIENDALL Are you one of the gentlemen that love the tea with
a hard name?

LOVEMORE Faith, madam, I must love anything that gives me an
opportunity—

MRS FRIENDALL With any woman that has a mind to improve it.   80

LOVEMORE Of adoring you.

MRS FRIENDALL Me, Mr Lovemore! I was going before, but now
you drive me.

LOVEMORE [*restraining her, and kneeling*]° Stay! This violence,°
If you can call it violence on my knees,   85
Excuses you to all your female forms—°
Nay, to yourself, severer than your forms—
If you should stay and hear me.

MRS FRIENDALL Well, what's the matter?

LOVEMORE Everything is matter of your praise,   90
The subject of fresh wonder—
Your beauty made to tire the painter's art,
Your wit to strike the poet's envy dumb.

MRS FRIENDALL Are you turned poet too?

LOVEMORE Indeed you can inspire me—   95

MRS FRIENDALL With the spirit of scandal I may; a small matter
conjures up a lampoon against the women. But to the purpose, sir.
You pretend business with me, and have insinuated a great deal of
pains all this day to get an occasion of speaking to me in private;
which now, by Mr Friendall's assistance, you think you have   100
ingeniously secured. Why, sir, after all, I know no business
between us that is to be carried on by my being alone with you.

LOVEMORE I'm sorry for that indeed, madam.

MRS FRIENDALL Suppose, Mr Lovemore, a man should hit you a
box on the ear.   105

LOVEMORE Only suppose it, good madam.

MRS FRIENDALL Why, sir, any man that's brute enough may do it.
Though that brute should beg your pardon never so publicly for
the wrong, you would never heartily forgive him for pitching upon
you.   110

LOVEMORE Not heartily, I believe, indeed.

MRS FRIENDALL Why, very well. You keep me here against my will,
　　Against all rules of decency—to me,
　　My sex and character, the worst of wrongs.
　　Yet you will think it hard to be condemned   115
　　Or hated for your light opinion of me
　　That first encouraged you to this design.
LOVEMORE Hated for loving you!
MRS FRIENDALL   Ay, there's the business.
　　Who would not stay to see her worshipper
　　Upon his knees, thus praised and thus adored?   120
　　'Her beauty made to tire the painter's art,
　　Her wit to strike the poet's envy dumb',
　　And all delivered in such a dying tone no lady can outlive it. Mr
　　Lovemore, you might have known me better than to imagine your
　　sly flattery could° softly sing me into a consent to anything my   125
　　virtue had abhorred. But how have I behaved myself? What have
　　I done to deserve this? What encouragement have I given you?
LOVEMORE A lover makes his hopes.
MRS FRIENDALL Perhaps 'tis from the general encouragement of
　　being a married woman, supported on your side by that honour-   130
　　able opinion of our sex, that, because some women abuse their
　　husbands, every woman may. I grant you indeed, the custom of
　　England has been very prevailing° in that point; and I must own
　　to you, an ill husband is a great provocation to a wife, when she
　　has a mind to believe as ill of him as she can.   135
LOVEMORE How if the wife believe too well of him?
MRS FRIENDALL Why, then the folly's hers. For my part, I have
　　known Mr Friendall too long not to know justly what he deserves.
　　I won't justify his faults; but because he does not take that care of
　　me he should, must not I have that regard to myself I ought? What   140
　　I do is for my own sake. Nay, what is past,
　　Which, by your hints, I know you do suspect,
　　I own I did it—
　　Not for the commendation of your wit,
　　Nor as a debt to him, but to myself,   145
　　Foreseeing a long life of infamy
　　Which in his follies I was married to,
　　And therefore saved myself by saving him.
LOVEMORE Your conduct everywhere is excellent;
　　But there it was a masterpiece indeed,   150
　　And worthy admiration.

MRS FRIENDALL And would you have me lose that character,
 So 'worthy admiration', which even you,
 An enemy, must praise, when you would ruin?
 No, what I've done to raise this character   155
 May be an argument I will do more
 To heighten it, to the last act of life.
LOVEMORE And all for the reward of being thought
 Too good a wife to such a husband.
MRS FRIENDALL   How!
 You know him then?   160
LOVEMORE You and I know him.
MRS FRIENDALL   Fit to bear a wrong?
 Is that the reason of your wronging him?
 I want but that.° O, let me but believe
 You injure him, because you know you may,
 And attempt me, because you think it safe;   165
 And I will scorn you low, as you do him.
 You say you know him. Now, sir, I know you,
 You, and your practices, against us both.
 You have encouraged all that has been done,
 Exposing him only to ruin me.   170
 'Tis necessary to believe as ill of you as I can;
 And for the future, till you clear yourself—
LOVEMORE I can clear myself.
MRS FRIENDALL I'll think you capable of everything,
 Of any baseness to advance your ends.   175
 (*Going*) So leave you to your triumph.
LOVEMORE Madam, stay. I must be justified.
 [*Produces the letter*]
 This challenge here has taught me all I know,
 Made me suspect who writ it, and presume
 All I have said to you.
MRS FRIENDALL°   Where had you it?   180
LOVEMORE Ruffle gave it me. I hope you may forgive my knowing
 it, since, by resigning it into your hands [*gives Mrs. Friendall the
 letter*], I give you up the only evidence that can rise up against him.
 Such a piece of news, madam, would have been welcome enough
 to the ill nature of the town; and I might have had my ends° in   185
 such a report, had I encouraged the exposing him.
 But when I saw how near you were concerned,
 I had no other pleasure but the thought

Of serving you.
If I have served you, I am overpaid.   190
If not, I must serve on. For I but live
To serve you.

MRS FRIENDALL My employment calls upon me. Are not you for
tea?

    *Two Footmen with a service of tea enter and go out with Mrs
    Friendall*

LOVEMORE I find I am restored; but I was reduced to the necessity   195
of a lie to come into favour again. But that's a necessity that every
man of honour must submit to sometimes, that has anything to
manage with the women. For a lover that never speaks more than
the truth is never believed to be a lover; and he that won't lie to
his mistress will hardly lie with her. So let his honesty reward him;   200
the lady won't, I dare say for her. There must be a cheat upon the
sense sometimes, to make a perfect pleasure to the soul. For if the
women did but always know what really we are, we should not so
often know so much of them as we do. But 'tis their own faults.
They know we can't live without 'em, and therefore ask more of   205
us than we have honestly to give for the purchase. So, very often,
they put us upon dissimulation, flattery and false love, to come up
to their price. Mrs Friendall went away a little abruptly. I'm glad
she did; for that methinks confesses an obligation which she has
not yet in her power to return.   210

    Wellvile enters to him

WELLVILE Lovemore, your plot begins to thrive. I left Mrs Sightly
telling Mrs Friendall everything between her and Mr Friendall. I
thought fit to acquaint you with it, that you might be prepared. You
know best what use to turn it to. My business is with Mrs Sightly.

LOVEMORE I thank you for the news. They're coming this way; I   215
would not have 'em see us. I must hover here.

    *Exeunt Lovemore and Wellvile. Enter Mrs Friendall and Mrs
    Sightly. [Mrs Friendall carries a letter]*

MRS FRIENDALL I could not have believed it.

MRS SIGHTLY I am sorry you have reason to believe it upon my
account. Indeed, I was unwilling to believe it. I suffered it as long
as I could; but, finding no end of this persecution—   220

MRS FRIENDALL You have used me like a friend, and I thank you.
His note since dinner desires you would meet him at seven at
Rosamond's Pond.° You can't be so hard-hearted to disappoint
him?

MRS SIGHTLY If you have a mind to have a plainer proof of his   225
treachery—

MRS FRIENDALL The proof is plain enough: you say it. Besides, he
has given it under his hand° here. [*Indicating the letter*] And I
believe the gentleman, though you won't.

MRS SIGHTLY Or if you would, let him know you have discovered   230
him, and upbraid him with his baseness before me.

MRS FRIENDALL That would but harden him, or make him vain, by
showing a concern for him.

MRS SIGHTLY If you have any curiosity to be satisfied, I'll go with
you to the place appointed.   235

MRS FRIENDALL I would not have him know either of us.

MRS SIGHTLY Then we must have a man to secure us.°

MRS FRIENDALL We may trust your friend Mr Wellvile.

MRS SIGHTLY Mr Friendall, you must know, thinks him in love with
me—so, being a rival may make him avoid us. But Mr Lovemore   240
will do as well.

MRS FRIENDALL I would not have him know it.

MRS SIGHTLY He knows it already. I made no secret of it, and Mr
Wellvile told it him.

MRS FRIENDALL Then he, or anyone—   245
    Lovemore enters to 'em

MRS SIGHTLY O, here he comes!—Mr Lovemore, we must employ
you this afternoon.

LOVEMORE To serve myself, in waiting upon you.
    The rest of the company [i.e. Friendall, Wilding, Wellvile,
    Mrs Teazall and Mrs Witwoud, accompanied by one or more
    Servants] enter to 'em

MRS TEAZALL Well, here's such a clutter° to get you to cards. You
have drank your tea. What will you do next, I trow?   250

MRS WITWOUD Why, take a nap, or smoke a pipe, anybody that has
a mind to be private.

MRS TEAZALL Would I had one civilly in a corner.°

FRIENDALL (*to a servant*) Get the cards in the drawing-room.
    [*Exit Servant*]

MRS WITWOUD Not till we have the song, Mr Friendall, you   255
promised us.

FRIENDALL Why, faith, I was forced to set it myself. I don't know
how you'll like it with my voice; but, faith and troth, I believe the
masters of the music-meeting may set their own words, for any
trouble I shall give 'em for the future about mine.   260

WILDING Nay, then you ruin 'em.
MRS WITWOUD The song, the song, sir!
FRIENDALL [*sings*]

SONG

> Say, cruel Amoret, how long°
> In billet-doux and humble song
>   Shall poor Alexis woo?   265
> If neither writing, sighing, dying
> Reduce you to a soft complying,
>   O, when will you come to?°
>
> Full thirteen moons are now passed o'er,
> Since first those stars I did adore   270
>   That set my heart on fire.
> The conscious playhouse, parks and court°
> Have seen my sufferings made your sport;
>   Yet am I ne'er the nigher.
>
> A faithful lover should deserve   275
> A better fate than thus to starve
>   In sight of such a feast.
> But O, if you'll not think it fit
> Your hungry slave should taste one bit,
>   Give some kind looks at least.   280

WILDING Admirable well—
MRS WITWOUD Set and sung, sir.
LOVEMORE A gentleman does these things always best.
WELLVILE When he has a genius.°
FRIENDALL Ay, sir, he must have a genius. There's no being a   285
     master of anything without a genius.
MRS FRIENDALL Mrs Teazall, Pam° wants you in the next room.
          Scene draws, shows tables and cards°
MRS TEAZALL I'll make the more of him, when I get him into my
     hands.
WELLVILE (*to Mrs Sightly*) I have something to tell you, worth more   290
     than the cards can win for you.
MRS FRIENDALL Who's for comet?°
LOVEMORE I am your man, madam.
MRS FRIENDALL You play too deep for me.°
MRS WITWOUD [*to Mrs Sightly*] Cousin, you'll make one of us?   295

MRS SIGHTLY I go your halves,° if you please. I don't care for playing myself.

They go in to play. The scene shuts upon 'em.° Wellvile and Mrs Sightly stay

MRS SIGHTLY Now, Mr Wellvile, you have something extraordinary to say to me.

WELLVILE I have indeed, madam. But I should prepare you for the story. There are some friends in it that you will be concerned to have an ill opinion of.

MRS SIGHTLY I have reason to think you my friend.

WELLVILE Then pray give me leave to ask how long you have known Mr Wilding.

MRS SIGHTLY I never spoke to him till this morning, at the chocolate house, as we came from the Park.

WELLVILE I think he's Mrs Witwoud's particular acquaintance.

MRS SIGHTLY That, I suppose, gave him his title of speaking to us.

WELLVILE And she has a mind to bring him acquainted with you. I'm sorry I must warn you of him. I was in hopes it would have died of itself. But his talking to you at the chocolate house, after he had promised never to follow you more, makes me apprehend that he is still carrying on his design upon you.

MRS SIGHTLY A design upon me!

WELLVILE He has a design upon you. And you have heard enough of his character to suspect the honour of any design he has upon any woman. But, such as it is, your cousin Witwoud, and very good friend, for ends of her own which I can inform you in, has undertaken to bring it about. I see you are surprised.

MRS SIGHTLY I pray, sir, go on.

WELLVILE I never pretended to be a friend of Mrs Witwoud's, but now I hate her; and what I tell you is not to ruin her with you, but of nearer consequence—to save you from being undone by her. This is not a secret; I'll tell her of it myself, and my thoughts of her into the bargain. But, madam, you know best how far she has solicited his cause to you, how far my story is probable, and whether you don't think she persuaded you to walk this morning in the Mall in order to meet° Mr Wilding. That was the business of her visit to you, as he tells me, whatever she pretended to the contrary.

MRS SIGHTLY You astonish me.

WELLVILE I am astonished myself indeed, madam—not to find her as I always thought her, fit for any mischief; but to think she can

pretend° to be a bawd and provide no better for a friend, to   335
sacrifice you to a man who would tell all the town of it, as well as
Courtall, and has confessed to me that he never was in love with
you, nor had a thought that way, till she put it into his head and
promised to assist him in't.

MRS SIGHTLY Unheard-of villainy!   340

WELLVILE Faith, madam, if I might advise you, it should be to a
man of honour at least, that can be so tender of a reputation not
to lessen a lady's favour so far to make it the common mirth of the
town. If you have any favours to dispose of, dispose of 'em
yourself. Let not another run away with the benefit of your good   345
turns. I have been an old admirer, madam, and, I hope, stand as
fair, and have as good a title to put in my claim, as any man of her
providing.

MRS SIGHTLY So, sir, then it seems you think I must be provided
for, and therefore these advances must please me. I have some   350
reason to believe what you say of my cousin Witwoud; but I
have no reason to think you very much my friend. She has
betrayed me, and you are pleased to think I deserve it. I thank you
for your caution; but it shall secure me for the future against her
and you. For, as much as I thought you my friend (nay, though   355
I languished for you), the encouragement you are pleased to
make from other people's base opinion of me shall teach me to
despise you.

> *The scene opens. The company [i.e. Mrs Teazall, Mrs*
> *Witwoud, Mrs Friendall, Friendall, Wilding and Lovemore]*
> *rises from play and comes forward*

MRS TEAZALL Nay, nay, I have done with you. If this be your fair
play, there's no danger of your foul.° Why, you make no con-   360
science of cheating anybody out of your own gang.°

MRS WITWOUD Conscience at cards, cousin! You are a better-bred
lady than to expect it.

FRIENDALL Conscience, madam, is for serious affairs. Nobody minds
it° at play.   365

MRS TEAZALL Nay, I'm even right enough served. I deserved it;
that's the truth on't. I must be playing with company so much
younger than myself. But I shall be wiser for the future and play
the fool in my own form,° where I may cheat in my turn.

MRS FRIENDALL If you speak of your losings, madam, I believe my   370
fortune has been harder than yours. In ten sets running with Mr
Wilding, I never turned one, nor had comet in my hand.°

MRS WITWOUD [*aside, to Wilding*] Nay, if you win her money, you
may win everything of her, if you know how to manage your game.

WILDING And, faith, I'll play it as well as I can.   375

       [*Mrs Witwoud*] *goes to Mrs Sightly*

MRS WITWOUD [*to Mrs Sightly*] Cousin, I have won an estate for
you.

MRS SIGHTLY You have undone me.

       Exit [*Mrs Sightly,*] *Mrs Witwoud following*

WILDING [*aside*] I'll watch my time and follow 'em.

FRIENDALL Lovemore, prithee keep the company together. I have an   380
appointment upon my hands and must leave you. We must serve
one another sometimes, you know.

       [*Friendall*] *goes off. Servant enters*

SERVANT Madam, the Jew, newly turned Protestant,° that my master
was godfather to, has brought the essences and sweet-waters he
ordered him to raffle for.°   385

MRS FRIENDALL (*going*) Shall we try whether we like any of 'em?

       [*Exit Mrs Friendall with Mrs Teazall*]

WELLVILE We shall find him a Jew still in his dealings, I suppose.

LOVEMORE You would not have him lose by his conversion, I hope.

WILDING Like other wise men, he's for saving soul and body
together, I warrant him.

       They go in   390

[4.2]

[Friendall's] garden

[Enter] Mrs Witwoud, following Mrs Sightly

MRS SIGHTLY Never think of denying or excusing it to me. I am
satisfied there's more in't than you ought to defend. There are so
many circumstances to convince me of your treachery to me, I
must believe it.

MRS WITWOUD [*kneeling*] I see, cousin, you will believe anything   5
against me. But as I hope to be saved, upon the faith of a Christian,
and may I never rise off my knees into your good opinion again,
if I don't abhor the villainy you lay to my charge. Something I
must confess to you, but I beg you to forgive me. 'Twas unadvised°
indeed, but innocent, and without a design upon you. Courtall's a   10
coxcomb; and nothing but Wilding's vanity or Wellvile's revenge

could be accessary to the ruin of me with you, the only relation I
love and value in the world.

MRS SIGHTLY O, I had forgot the pains you took to secure me,
tomorrow night at cards, at your lodgings with Mr Wilding.   15
Cousin, let me tell you, a bawd is the worst part of an intrigue,
and the least to be said for't in excuse of the infamy. But you had
something more than a lover to provide for me, or you would not
have exposed me to a man that would expose me to all the town.
Is it because I have been your best and last friend—for you will   20
hardly find such another in your family—that thus you reward me
for the folly? Or is it because I am a witness of your shame, that
you would be a contriver of mine? I know—and I look upon it as
a judgement upon the former follies of your life—that you are
notoriously abandoned to the beastly love of a fellow that nobody   25
else can look upon; and, maybe, you are mischievously pleased to
make me as despicable as yourself. There must be the devil in the
bottom on't,° and I'll fly from him in you.

MRS WITWOUD O, don't leave me in this passion. I am utterly
ruined if you go. Upon my knees I beg it of you.   30

MRS SIGHTLY Cousin, I forgive you. What's past shall be a secret
for both our sakes. But I'm resolved never more to come into your
power. So, farewell, and find a better friend than I have been.
    [*Mrs Sightly*] *goes out*

MRS WITWOUD She's lost, and my design upon her, which is yet a
greater misfortune to me.   35
    [*Mrs Witwoud rises. Wellvile and*] *Wilding* [*enter*] *to her*
    [*To Wilding*] O, sir, I am obliged to you—and you are obliged to
yourself for your success with Mrs Sightly. So like a boy, to
discover the secret before 'twas in your power to expose! Away,
I'll have no more to say to you.
    [*Mrs Witwoud*] *goes out*

WILDING So, sir, you have made fine work on't with the women.°   40
    thought I had satisfied you in the Mall this morning.

WELLVILE Sir, I must be better satisfied than I was in the morning.
I find there's no relying upon your word, since, after your promise
never to follow her more, you could excuse yourself to me° in the
Mall, to meet her at the chocolate house.   45

WILDING Nay, then we have both our grievances, and [*drawing his
sword*] this must answer 'em.
    [*Wellvile and Wilding are*] *going to fight; Courtall enters to*
    part 'em

COURTALL Fie, fie, friends, and fighting! That must not be, gentlemen. Mrs Witwoud has told me the matter; and unless you had a fourth man to entertain me, you had even as good put up° 50 again. We are all in a fault, and all deserve to be swinged for't; that's certain. Wilding was a fool for telling me of his design, and I was a fool for talking on't to Wellvile; and Wellvile no wiser than either for making such a bustle about it. Therefore, pray, gentlemen, let's agree in this opinion: that, by our own prating and 55 prying into other people's affairs, we often discover and ruin one another's designs.

        For women are by nature well-inclined;
        Our follies frighten 'em from being kind.

Exeunt

5.1

Mrs Witwoud's lodgings

[Enter] Wilding following Mrs Witwoud

MRS WITWOUD Nay, I don't wonder you thrive no better with the women, when you can part with such an advantage over Mrs Friendall. You say you have won a sum of her, which she would not be known to lose. Why, another man would take the privilege of a winning gamester, upon such an occasion, to press her to a 5 promise, at least, of coming out of your debt.

WILDING I shall improve, I find, upon the advantage of your hints. But Mrs Sightly, madam—

MRS WITWOUD Ay, Mrs Sightly indeed. Was that a woman to throw away upon the vanity of being talked of for her? In the time you 10 were bragging to other people of being in her favour, you might have been everywhere you desired.

WILDING Nay, not unlikely.

MRS WITWOUD I have made all the excuse I could for you—some, too, that in my conscience I thought very unreasonable myself, and 15 could pass upon nobody but a woman that was easily disposed to forgive you.

WILDING If she would but hear what I have to say for myself.

MRS WITWOUD Nay, she's pretty well prepared. But you must not think of speaking to her bare-faced—that she can't consent to for 20 her own sake. You have made the matter so public, she has eyes upon her, to be sure, now. But it happens very luckily—Friendall has a masquerade tonight at his house. There, if you please, I can give you an opportunity of clearing yourself to her.

WILDING I ask no more of you. 25

MRS WITWOUD Never think of defending yourself; for what's past, you were certainly i' th' wrong, and she thinks you so. You know well enough what to say to a woman that has a mind to believe you.

WILDING How shall I know her at the masquerade?

MRS WITWOUD Go, you, and prepare for't; and depend upon me for 30 your intelligence.°

Wilding goes out

I find I am declining in my reputation, and will bring every woman of my acquaintance into my own condition, of being suspected, at least. I have promised more than I can do with my cousin Sightly.

I have lost my credit with her too lately to betray her in the way   35
of friendship. Let me see. Betty!
    Betty enters
You know where the man lives that made my cousin Sightly's scarf.
Go to him from me; desire him to borrow it, that a lady may see
it, who likes it and desires to have one made of the same pattern.
    Exit Betty
I despair of bringing her to the masquerade. I must personate her   40
myself and meet Wilding in her room.° But what may be the issue
of that? Let what will be the issue. The farther he presses his
design upon me, the farther I carry my design upon her; and for
once, in order to my revenge, rather than not expose her, I'll
venture to grant him the favour,° that he may tell on't, and she   45
have the benefit of the scandal.
    Goes out

5.2

St James's Park

    [*Enter*] *Lovemore, with Mrs Friendall and Mrs Sightly*

LOVEMORE Yonder comes Mr Friendall, madam.

MRS FRIENDALL Would I were at home again. I came upon a foolish
    discovery of his actions, to be surprised in a very unaccountable
    one of my own.

MRS SIGHTLY That is, walking incognito on this side the Park with   5
    a man of your character, Mr Lovemore.

MRS FRIENDALL I hope he won't know us.
    [*Mrs Friendall and Mrs Sightly*] *put on their masks*

MRS SIGHTLY He's too busy in his own affairs.

LOVEMORE He comes upon us. I must speak to him.
    Friendall enters

FRIENDALL [*to Lovemore*] You are provided for, I see. The ladies, I   10
    suppose, wish I could say as much for them too. Very genteel
    women both, faith and troth. I warrant 'em women of condition,
    if not women of quality,° by their assignation at Rosamond's Pond.

LOVEMORE You fancy that from the quality of your own intrigue.

FRIENDALL Why, there's something in that too. And the truth on't   15
    is, my assignation is with a woman of quality.

LOVEMORE Mrs Sightly, I fancy, Friendall.

FRIENDALL Fie, fie, why should you think so? But let her be
who she will, if she disappoint me, I'll own it tomorrow to
everybody.   20

LOVEMORE That she disappointed you?

FRIENDALL No; that 'twas Mrs Sightly I had an intrigue with.

MRS SIGHTLY [aside, to Mrs Friendall] A small matter makes an
intrigue of his side, I find.

FRIENDALL (viewing his wife) Sure I have seen somebody very like   25
this lady?

MRS FRIENDALL [to Lovemore, aside] I would not be known for the
world.

LOVEMORE [to Mrs Friendall] I'll bring you off, I warrant you.

FRIENDALL She has the air and mien very much of a lady of my   30
acquaintance.

LOVEMORE Not unlikely, faith. It may be she herself, for aught I
know to the contrary. But if you have a mind to be satisfied—

MRS FRIENDALL [to Lovemore, aside] Lord, what do you do?

LOVEMORE I have no occasion for her at present. This ([indicating] 35
Mrs Sightly) is my woman. She's [indicating Mrs Friendall] but an
ill-natured encumbrance at this time; and you'll do me a favour to
dispose of her.

FRIENDALL Nay, if you are so free to dispose of her, I'm satisfied
she is not the woman I took her for. For, to tell you the truth,   40
Lovemore, I thought 'twas my wife. And, egad, I began to be very
uneasy—not so much for finding her in your company, as that she
should come so peevishly° to disturb me in an affair so very much
above her.

MRS SIGHTLY Why, sir, they say your wife is a very fine woman.   45

FRIENDALL A wife a fine woman, madam? I never knew a husband
that thought so in my life.

MRS FRIENDALL But somebody else may, sir, if you allow her to
make these entertainments for the town that I hear you do.

FRIENDALL Gad so, Lovemore, prithee bring the ladies to my   50
masquerade tonight. There's nobody but people of quality to be
there, for pleasure is my business, you know; and I am very well
pleased to allow my wife the liberties she takes, in favour of my
own.° For, to tell you the truth, the chief end of my marrying
her—next to having the estate settled upon me—was to carry on   55
my intrigues more swimmingly with the ladies.

LOVEMORE That's a convenience in matrimony I did not think of.

FRIENDALL One of the greatest, upon my word, sir. For, being seen
so often abroad, and visiting with my wife, I pass upon the formal
part of the town for a very good husband; and, upon the privilege   60
of that character, I grow intimate with all her acquaintance—and,
by the way, there's hardly a family in town, but I can contrive to
come acquainted with upon her account. There I pick and° choose
in the very face of their reverend relations, and deliver my billets
myself.   65

MRS FRIENDALL You have 'em ready then?

FRIENDALL Two or three always in my pocket. (*Shows 'em*) I write
half a dozen in a morning for the service of that day.

LOVEMORE Hard service, I assure you.

FRIENDALL Not at all. The letters are but copies one of another, and   70
a love-letter should be a love-letter, you know, passionate and
tender, whoever 'tis designed for. Ha! Yonder are two women in
masks! I must not be seen with you. Ladies, you know when you're
well, I suppose, by the choice of your man. Make much of him;
he's my bosom-friend and confidant of my pleasures.   75

MRS FRIENDALL And you of his, I suppose? There's no pleasure
without a confidant.

FRIENDALL Faith, madam, I am of your mind. But Lovemore's a
little too reserved. 'Tis, at present, his fault, from a want of
knowing the town; but he'll mend of it,° I hope, when he comes   80
to have a woman worth talking of. Lovemore, not a word at
home of seeing me here, as you value the fortune of your friend.
Adieu.

    [*Friendall*] *goes out*

MRS FRIENDALL Are you the confidant of the gentleman's pleasures?

LOVEMORE I have not betrayed 'em, madam.   85

MRS FRIENDALL Methinks a friend should have warned me of 'em.

LOVEMORE I would not be thought to do ill offices, especially in
marriage, madam.

MRS FRIENDALL I don't think you would. (*Aside*) Would Mr
Friendall were as tender of wronging me.   90

MRS SIGHTLY You have had a handsome account of their expedition.° And we are both obliged to Mr Friendall.

MRS FRIENDALL I am very well paid for my curiosity of coming
here.° I suppose we shall have a rendezvous of his wenches at the
masquerade. Pray let's be ready to receive 'em.   95

    Exeunt

[5.3]

Friendall's house

[Enter] Men and Women in masquerading habit,° [including] Wellvile, Wilding, Courtall, Springame, Mrs Witwoud, and Betty, [with Musicians]

MRS WITWOUD° [*to Betty*] Wilding has his eye upon us, I see. I have something to say to him in my own person, and then I must change scarves with you. Be sure you are i' th' way.

WELLVILE (*to Betty*) I thought I had known you,° I beg your pardon, madam, for the mistake.   5

BETTY You're very welcome to't, sir. I would have you mistaken; and that you will always be, when you judge upon the outsides of the women.

WELLVILE You are for a stricter examination, I find. There are conveniencies for a full discovery in the next room.° Somebody   10
will show you the way.

[Wellvile] leaves her

WILDING [*aside*] That's Sightly in the scarf, and Witwoud with her, I suppose. I must not be mistaken.

COURTALL [*to Springame*] I like the freedom of a masquerade very well; but it confounds° a man's choice.   15

SPRINGAME Why, faith, I have a mind to be particular,° if I could but hit upon the woman.

MRS WITWOUD [*aside*] And that you shall presently, little captain. I'll put myself in your way.

SPRINGAME (*to Betty*) Behind a cloud, my pretty moon! Shall I be   20
the man in you?

BETTY With the bush at your backside.° You deserve to be whipped for your wit, sir.

SPRINGAME I stand corrected, madam.

[Betty] goes from him

MRS WITWOUD Does she beat thee, little master? Come a' me,° and   25
I'll make much of thee.

SPRINGAME As much as you can of me, I dare say for you.

MRS WITWOUD Come, come; I'll use you better.

SPRINGAME To use me worse. Is not that your design? She has given me my answer at once. You perhaps would linger me through a   30
winter's expectation, and not do my business at last.

MRS WITWOUD What's your business, pray?

SPRINGAME Why, your business, any woman's business that has a mind to employ me in't.

MRS WITWOUD No touching me. I have an unfashionable husband in the company that won't thank you for making him a cuckold.   35

SPRINGAME But you will, I'm sure, if it be but to teach him better manners.

MRS WITWOUD I like your company extremely; but I have a great deal of business, and would willingly be rid of you at this time. But this ring [*giving him a ring*] shall answer for me, till (*going*) I see you again.   40

SPRINGAME Pray redeem it as soon as you can.

MRS WITWOUD Sir, sir, if you have any interest in the family, pray let's have a song or a dance to divert us.   45

SPRINGAME I'll see what I can do for you.

    [*Springame*] *goes away*

MRS WITWOUD You should be Wilding.

WILDING And you should be as good as your word.

MRS WITWOUD The lady is better than you can expect.° That's she in the embroidered scarf. You must not speak to her before the company. Take her aside, by and by, in a corner. She'll thank you for your care of her. Here's more company.   50

    Lovemore enters with Mrs Friendall and Mrs Sightly

I won't be seen with you.—[*Aside, to Betty*] Now, Betty, for the change.

    Mrs Witwoud and Betty go out

WELLVILE Lovemore, I am in disgrace with Mrs Sightly and can't find her, to come into favour again.   55

LOVEMORE That's she, that came in just now with Mrs Friendall. I'll direct you to one by going to the other.

    [*Lovemore and Wellvile*] *go to* [*Mrs Friendall and Mrs Sightly, as the Musicians perform a song*]

        SONG

    Corinna, I excuse thy face,°
      The erring lines which nature drew,   60
    When I reflect that every grace
      Thy mind adorns is just and true.
    But O, thy wit what god has sent?
      Surprising, airy, unconfined.
    Some wonder sure Apollo meant°   65
      And shot himself into thy mind.

After the song, Mrs Witwoud and Betty, having changed
scarves, enter, to be ready for the dance, after which—

LOVEMORE [*to Mrs Friendall*] Some can't get husbands, and others
can't get rid of 'em.

MRS FRIENDALL Every woman carries her cross in this world. A
husband happens to be mine, and I must bear it as well as I can.   70

LOVEMORE I would ease you of it.

MRS FRIENDALL No more upon this subject. You have carried the
argument so far, 'tis allowing what you say, to listen any longer.
But, Mr Lovemore, I will give you what satisfaction I have in my
power; and praise is the reward of virtue, you know. I think you   75
have proceeded like a man of experience in this business and taken
the natural road to undermine most women. I must do you this
justice, that nothing has been wanting on your side.

LOVEMORE I would have nothing wanting on my side, madam.

MRS FRIENDALL And however you came by the knowledge of Mr   80
Friendall's weaknesses, you have improved° 'em as much as they
could bear upon the conduct of his wife. If they have not carried
me as far as you designed, 'tis the fault of my heaviness,° perhaps,
that can't be transported into the woman you'd have me.

LOVEMORE There's a fault somewhere.   85

MRS FRIENDALL Mr Lovemore, some women won't speak so plain;
But I will own to you I cannot think
The worse of you for thinking well of me.
Nay, I don't blame you for designing upon me. Custom has
fashioned it into the way of living among the men; and you may   90
be i' th' right to all the town. But let me be i' th' right too to my
sex and to myself.
Thus far may be excused.
You've proved your passion and my virtue tried.
But all beyond that trial is my crime,   95
And not to be forgiven.
Therefore I entreat you, don't make it impossible to me for the
future to receive you as a friend; for I must own,
I would secure you always for my friend.
Nay more, I will confess my heart to you.   100
If I could make you mine—

LOVEMORE   Forever yours.

MRS FRIENDALL But I am married. Only pity me.°
      [*Mrs Friendall*] *goes from him*

LOVEMORE Pity her! She does not deserve it, that won't better her
condition, when she may. But she's married, she says. Why, that

was the best of my reasons of following her at first; and I like her   105
so well, as she's another man's wife, I should hardly mend the
matter by making her my own. I won't think yet my two months
thrown away upon her. One time or other, some way or other, I
may be the better for her—at least with some other women. But I
begin to believe that every man loses his labour this way sometimes.   110

MRS SIGHTLY (*observing Wilding and Mrs Witwoud*) Who can that
woman be?

WELLVILE Wilding's the man, I know.

MRS SIGHTLY Then it may be my good cousin Witwoud.

WELLVILE Presuming upon the scarf, which is very like yours, I   115
ventured and spake to her. I should have known Mrs Witwoud, I
believe.

MRS SIGHTLY Pray try if you can learn who she is.
    They parle in a low voice

MRS WITWOUD [*to Wilding*] This place is too public for a vindication
of this nature. If you retire into the next room, I may accept of   120
your excuses, upon your promise of good behaviour and better
conduct for the future.

WILDING I'll follow you.
    Mrs Witwoud retires. Wellvile [goes] to Wilding

WELLVILE You will be the man, I see, Wilding. The lady's withdrawn. Don't let her stay for you.°   125

WILDING Faith, Welville, 'tis a fortune thrown upon me; and since
it came without my seeking, methinks you should hardly think it
worth your courting. She'll bring it about one way or other, you
find.

WELLVILE You speak as if I knew the lady.   130

WILDING I would have you know so much: that she is not worth the
honourable care you have of her.

WELLVILE Of whom?

WILDING As if you did not know her.

WELLVILE Why, 'tis not Mrs Sightly.   135

WILDING I have declined it as much as I could in regard to a friend;
but when she follows me—

WELLVILE Mrs Sightly follow you!
    Friendall enters and joins with Lovemore

WILDING No naming names, good Wellvile.

WELLVILE Nay, then I must convince you. I just left Mrs Sightly to   140
come to you. She's now in the company, and I'll carry you to hear
me speak to her.
    [*Wellvile*] *carries Wilding to Mrs Sightly*

LOVEMORE [*to Friendall*] Why, this was a terrible disappointment.

FRIENDALL There are lampoons, sir; I say no more. But I may do myself reason° in one of 'em and disappoint her yet of her disappointment.°   145

Among the women [Friendall] fastens upon Mrs Sightly

WILDING [*to Welville*] Why then, Witwoud has put another woman upon me and abused Mrs Sightly and me. I am satisfied of the cheat, and would be assisting to the revenge of it if I could.

WELLVILE You would not be the instrument to make it public yourself?   150

WILDING No, that I can't consent to.

WELLVILE Then leave it to me. Friendall's a property° fit for our several interests. But Lovemore must employ him.

Wellvile [goes] to Lovemore

FRIENDALL [*to Mrs Sightly*] Faith, madam, I am very fit for your purpose at present. I have met with a little ill usage from a lady by not meeting with her. But you may be the better for it, if you please. You shall have the pleasure, and she shall have the reputation of the intrigue.   155

MRS SIGHTLY I am for all or none.   160

Lovemore comes to [Friendall]

LOVEMORE The rarest accident, Friendall. The reason that you were disappointed in the Park, I can tell you, was, the lady had appointed to meet Wilding here. She is now withdrawn into the next room in expectation of him; which Wellvile, her old lover, suspecting, has taxed him of, and ruined the design. Now, if you would have me,° I'll keep up the jealousy between 'em and give you an opportunity to go in to her.   165

FRIENDALL By all means, Lovemore. This was unexpected, and done like a friend. I owe you a good turn for't. Be sure you keep 'em here.   170

[Friendall] sneaks out after Mrs Witwoud

MRS SIGHTLY (*to Wellvile*) What are you designing upon Mr Friendall?

WELLVILE There's mischief in't; and you may all be the better for't.

[Enter] Mrs Teazall pressing in with a Footman upon the Company

MRS FRIENDALL What's the noise there?

FOOTMAN Madam, here's a rude, unmannerly gentlewoman presses in upon me, and refuses to pull off her mask, as your honour ordered.°   175

MRS TEAZALL You saucy rascal you, I show a better face than thy
mother had, when she laid thee to the parish, you rogue.° Prate to
me, you varlet! And an honester one, though I say it, than any of   180
the company. Here's fine work indeed in a civil family! What, are
you ashamed of your doings, that you won't discover yourselves?

SPRINGAME Mistress, you have the natural privilege of a mask. And,
being disguised in your own face, you may say what you please.

MRS TEAZALL Marry, come up here. Will nothing but a good face   185
down with you?° A woman has a fine time on't with your finical
fancy. (*Looking everywhere for her niece*) But I want leisure° to
laugh at you.

COURTALL Do you know me?

MRS TEAZALL Ay, ay, I guess at you. Learn to speak without a   190
question, you fool,° before you set up for a wit.

COURTALL I know you.

MRS TEAZALL Why, then you may be satisfied I shall think you an
ass.

SPRINGAME Nay, good mother, you had e'en as good pull off your   195
mask. You see you are discovered.

MRS TEAZALL Discovered, you snotty-nosed jackanapes! Would I
could discover your master.° I would send him a note of your
name. You are not yet clean from school and are setting up for the
women forsooth. You have been so used to be turned up for a   200
blockhead,° that you are° for peeping into everybody's back-door
to find as great a fool as yourself. Sirrah, sirrah, a good birch-rod
for your mistress—that would tickle your tail as you deserve.°

SPRINGAME Nay, good your reverence.°

MRS FRIENDALL What's the matter, pray?   205

MRS TEAZALL Why, the wicked ways of living in this town are
matter enough for the vexation of any woman that has a girl to
look after. God's my life! Can't you keep up your masquerades in
the primitive institution of making cuckolds,° as it used to be,
without bringing the young wenches into the mystery of matri-   210
mony before their time? Where's my niece among you? 'Tis a
burning shame to draw away a poor young girl into these deboist,
galloping doings, as you do.

MRS FRIENDALL Good Mrs Teazall, not so censorious. Pray, where's
the harm of a little innocent diversion?   215

MRS TEAZALL Innocent diversion, with a pox to't!—for that° will be
the end on't at last. Very innocent diversion indeed! Why, your
music-meetings, dancing-meetings, masking-meetings, are all but

pretences to bring you together; and when you meet, we know
what you meet for well enough. 'Tis to the same purpose, in good   220
troth. All ends in the innocent diversion.

WELLVILE Nay, faith, the gentlewoman has reason for what she says.

MRS TEAZALL Well, make me thankful for it; there's one civil
gentleman among you. And really there's a great deal of comfort
in opening a poor woman's case° to a discreet, good-natured   225
gentleman. Pray, sir, hear me; and if you don't allow that I have
some cause for what I do, I will be contented never to see coat-card
nor have Pam in my pocket again.°

MRS FRIENDALL But who are you looking for all this while?

MRS TEAZALL An untowardly girl, to be sure; my cousin Fanny,   230
madam. She has undone herself, and my hopes of a husband for
her. Gad forgive me, I have no patience, when I think upon't. Last
night, Witwoud, forsooth, she carries her to the music-meeting.
Then one Wilding, an impudent whoremastering fellow, he carries
her home with him, which I could forgive well enough too, if it   235
ended there. But now, when all things were agreed upon, and Mr
Buttybun° was to give us a supper and sign the writings° in order
to marry her tomorrow, when the baggage was called upon to
perform her part, whip, she had given us the slip, tucked up her
tail and run a-roguing after that fellow again. But I shall light upon   240
her.

LOVEMORE Wilding, what say you to this?

MRS TEAZALL O, sir, are you there? If there be any justice in
England for the women, I'll have you bound to the good behaviour. I'll swear the peace against you myself;° for there's nobody   245
safe, young or old, at this rate, if such whoremasters as you are
allowed to do as you do.

WILDING I am bound already to behave myself like a gentleman. I
do what good I can, in my generation,° but injure nobody.

MRS TEAZALL Sirrah, sirrah, you shall find you have injured my   250
niece, and me, before I have done with you.

WILDING You won't bring it to Westminster,° I hope, to be decided
who has most injured her—I, by being civil to her, or you, by
telling it to all the town.

MRS TEAZALL Why, that's true again.   255

WILDING And let the company judge who appears to be most her
enemy—I, in teaching her a very good trade,° or you, in endeavouring to break her before she's well set up in't.

COURTALL (to Mrs Teazall) Nay, now it goes against you.

WILDING I have put her in a very good way. If she manage it 260
well, she'll make more on't than her mother made of her matrimony.

MRS TEAZALL Nay, 'twas the ruin of her; that I grant you.

WILDING And let the worst come to the worst, if she fails in this
calling, she may begin in another, as they do in the city sometimes. 265
'Tis but setting up for a husband at last.

MRS TEAZALL But that you won't consent to, it seems.

WILDING Faith, madam, I han't seen your niece since morning; and
then Mrs Witwoud obliged me to give over my pretensions to her,
upon the promise of procuring Mrs Sightly for me. 270

MRS SIGHTLY Without my knowledge, sir?

WILDING Indeed, madam, you were not to know of the bargain.

MRS TEAZALL Then you don't know where Fanny is?

WILDING Not I, faith, madam.

WELLVILE We were just complaining of Mrs Witwoud's unkindness 275
to you, as you came in.

MRS TEAZALL Ay, sir, I am beholding to you.

WELLVILE She has been very busy all this night in carrying on an
intrigue between your niece and somebody. They are retired into
the next room. They went out at that door, if you have a mind to 280
be satisfied.

MRS TEAZALL I'm sorry, sir, I han't time to thank you for this
favour. I must make haste, for I'm resolved to be satisfied.

    Scene draws,° shows Friendall and Mrs Witwoud upon a couch
Very fine! Here is a sight indeed!

MRS WITWOUD Confusion! 285

FRIENDALL What a pox! Disturb a gentleman's pleasures! And in his
own house too! Ha! Witwoud here! Nay then, would you had come
sooner. Madam, I beg your pardon for some liberties I have taken
with your ladyship. But, faith, I took you for Mrs Sightly.

MRS WITWOUD [*to Friendall*] I never was mistaken in you. 290

WILDING You see I had too great a respect for you, and therefore
provided you a more deserving—

MRS WITWOUD Fool.

WELLVILE And one that had as good-natured a design upon Mrs
Sightly as you had yourself. 295

MRS TEAZALL Nay, now, gentlewoman, I think 'tis come home to
you, and I am glad on't with all my heart.

MRS SIGHTLY You have paid dear enough for that scarf; you may
keep it for a pattern for your friends, as 'twas borrowed for. I won't

insult over you, and am only pleased that I have 'scaped your   300
snares.

MRS WITWOUD That disappointment is my greatest curse; and
disappointments light upon you all.

  [*Mrs Witwoud*] *goes out*

COURTALL [*to Springame*] This is your mistress, captain.

SPRINGAME And, egad, she shall be mine now in spite of her   305
teeth.° For since I find she can be civil° upon occasion, I shall beat
her into good manners, if she refuses me.

  [*Springame*] *goes after her*

WELLVILE [*to Mrs Sightly*] Everything has fallen so much to your
advantage, that sure the fault I made may be forgiven. What
amends I have in my power, I am ready to make you.   310
My liberty, of what I have to give,°
Is what I value most; and that is yours,
When you consent to let me make you mine.°

MRS SIGHTLY This is too sudden to be serious. When you're in
earnest, you won't need an answer.   315

WILDING [*to Lovemore and Courtall*] They are striking up a peace on
all hands, gentlemen; we shall be left out of the treaty.

LOVEMORE There's yet a lady to declare herself.

MRS FRIENDALL Mr Friendall, I'm sorry you thought it necessary
to your pleasures to make me a witness of my ill usage. You know   320
I can and have passed° many things some women would think
wrongs, as such resent 'em, and return 'em too. But you can tell
how I've behaved myself.

FRIENDALL Like a gentlewoman always, madam, and my wife.

MRS FRIENDALL The unjust world,   325
Let what will be the cause of our complaint°
(As there is cause sufficient still at home),
Condemn us to a slavery for life.°
And if by separation we get free,
Then all our husband's faults are laid on us.   330
This hard condition of a woman's fate
I've often weighed, therefore resolved to bear.
And I have borne—O, what have I not borne?
But patience tires with such oppressing wrongs,
When they come home to triumph over me   335
And tell the town how much I am despised.°

FRIENDALL I see we are both disappointed in this affair of matrimony. It is not the condition you expected; nor has it the

advantages I proposed. Now, madam, since 'tis impossible to make
it happy between us, let us ev'n resolve to make it as easy as we   340
can.

MRS FRIENDALL That must be my business now.

FRIENDALL And mine too, I assure you. Look you, madam, your
own relations shall provide for you at pleasure out of my estate.°
I only article that I may have a freedom of visiting you, in the   345
round of my acquaintance.

MRS FRIENDALL I must be still your wife, and still unhappy.

LOVEMORE [*aside*] What alteration this may make in my fortune with
her, I don't know; but I'm glad I have parted 'em.

FRIENDALL Well, gentlemen, I can't be very much displeased at the   350
recovery of my liberty. I am only sorry Witwoud was the occasion
of it. For an old blown-upon she-wit is hardly an intrigue to justify
the separation on my side, or make a man very vain of his fortune.

LOVEMORE [*to the audience*]

> This you must all expect, who marry fools,   355
> Unless you form 'em early in your schools
> And make 'em what they were designed for, tools.

Epilogue

Spoken by Mrs Barry

My character, not being much in vogue,
Has drawn me in to speak the epilogue—
But, pray conceive me right, not to disparage
That ancient, English perquisite of marriage,
Which, when the priests first made all pleasure sin,   5
Faster than they could cheat us, drew us in
With rites and liberties of cuckolding.
That used to be the custom, and so common,
No girl but wished herself a married woman.
Whether I've done my husband right, or no,   10
Most women may be in the right that do.
Our author does not set up for reforming,
Or giving hints to fools who won't take warning.
He's pleased that other people are pleased too
To help to reap that harvest which they sow;   15
For among all the cuckolds of this town
Who show themselves and are as daily shown,
Our poets may make some of 'em their own.
You find in me what may excuse a wife.
Compare at home the picture with the life,   20
And most of you may find a Friendall there—
And most of you more justly used than here.
Our author has his ends, if he can show
The women ne'er want cause for what they do;
For, ladies, all his aim is pleasing you.   25
Some mettled sparks, whom nothing can withstand,
Your velvet fortune-hunters, may demand°
Why, when the means were in the lady's hand,
The husband civil, and the lover near,°
No more was made of the wife's character?   30
'Damn me', cries one, 'had I been Betterton',°
And struts and cocks, 'I know what I had done;°
She should not ha' got clear of me so soon'.
You only fear such plays may spoil your game.

But flesh and frailty always are the same;   35
And we shall still proceed in our old way,
For all that you can do, or poets say.

The Wives' Excuse: Appendix

> Hang this whining way of wooing;°
>   Loving was designed a sport.
> Sighing, talking, without doing,
>   Makes a silly, idle court.°
> Don't believe that words can move her,   5
>   If she be not well inclined;
> She herself must be the lover,
>   To persuade her to be kind.
> If, at last, she grants the favour
>   And consents to be undone,   10
> Never think your passion gave her°
>   To your wishes, but her own.

EXPLANATORY NOTES

The following abbreviations are used in the notes:

Am	*Amphitryon*
Ghosh	Thomas Otway, *Works*, ed. J. C. Ghosh (Oxford, 1932), 2 vols.
Holland	Peter Holland, *The Ornament of Action: Text and Performance in Restoration Comedy* (Cambridge, 1979).
Jordan and Love	Thomas Southerne, *Works*, ed. Robert Jordan and Harold Love (Oxford, 1988), 2 vols.
Partridge	Eric Partridge, *A Dictionary of Slang and Unconventional English* (5th edn.: London, 1961)
PC	*The Princess of Cleves*
Price	Curtis Alexander Price, *Henry Purcell and the London Stage* (Cambridge, 1984).
SF	*The Soldiers' Fortune*
Simpson	Claude M. Simpson, *The British Broadside Ballad and Its Music* (New Brunswick, NJ, 1966)
Spencer	Christopher Spencer (ed.), *Five Restoration Adaptations of Shakespeare* (Urbana, Ill., 1965)
Stroup and Cooke	Nathaniel Lee, *Works*, ed. Thomas B. Stroup and Arthur L. Cooke (New Brunswick, NJ, 1954), 2 vols.
Summers	John Dryden, *Dramatic Works*, ed. Montague Summers (London, 1932), vi.
Thornton	Thomas Southerne, *The Wives' Excuse or Cuckolds Make Themselves*, ed. Ralph R. Thornton (Wynnewood, Pa., 1973)
Tilley	M. P. Tilley, *A Dictionary of the Proverbs in England in the Sixteenth and Seventeenth Centuries* (Ann Arbor, Mich., 1950)
WE	*The Wives' Excuse*
Wilson	F. P. Wilson (ed.), *The Oxford Dictionary of English Proverbs* (3rd edn.: Oxford, 1970).

Act, scene, and line references for quotations from Shakespeare's plays in the notes are taken from William Shakespeare, *The Complete Works*, ed. Stanley Wells and Gary Taylor (Oxford, 1986).

The Soldiers' Fortune

Epigraph *Quem recitas . . . esse tuus*: 'That book you recite, O Fidentinus, is mine. But your vile recitation begins to make it your own' (Martial, *Epigrams*, i. 38).

Dedication 1 *Mr Bentley*: Richard Bentley, a bookseller, publisher, and stationer in Russell Street, Covent Garden. In addition to *The Soldiers' Fortune*, he was involved in the publication of two other plays by Otway, *The Orphan* and *The Atheist*, a sequel to *The Soldiers' Fortune*. As the following paragraphs suggest, dedicating a play to its publisher was Otway's playful innovation. The more normal practice was to dedicate one's work to someone of status and sufficient wealth to respond to the honour with some 'ready money' (l. 15 below) for the needy author.

25 *think civilly of her*: i.e. think that she is a modest and respectable woman. The remark, however, is double-edged, since 'civil', in addition to its modern meanings, could also in this period mean 'sexually accommodating or inviting'. This latter sense of the word is often in play in all four of the texts in this volume.

25-6 *Faugh . . . seen at it*: Otway is echoing a famous passage in 2.1 of William Wycherley's *The Plain Dealer* (premièred on 11 December 1676), in which the hypocritical, sexually duplicitous Olivia pronounces no woman 'modest' who could see 'the hideous Country Wife without blushing or publishing her detestation of it'. The Country Wife was, of course, written by Wycherley himself.

28-9 *Paddington*: in the 1680s Paddington was still a village separate from London and, with its taverns and eating-places, a convenient place for covert assignations.

30-1 *as easily as . . . a rose*: spiders were believed to turn everything they consumed into poison.

32 *as perfectly . . . by instinct*: cf. Shakespeare's *1 Henry IV*, 2.5. 270-8, where Falstaff falsely claims to have recognized Prince Hal when the latter was disguised as a robber: 'Why, thou knowest I am as valiant as Hercules; but beware instinct. The lion will not touch the true prince—instinct is a great matter. I was a coward on instinct'.

35 *a lady*: 'traditionally taken to be Mrs. Aphra Behn' (Ghosh). No secure proof of the identification has been produced. Behn's prefaces to her own plays, however, do frequently target satirically the pieties of the more censorious of her own sex.

42 *not buried her talent neither*: a mischievous misapplication of the parable of the talents in Matthew 25: 14-30

The Characters of the Play 1 *Beaugard*: the name combines two French words—'beau' (handsome, glorious, lofty, noble) and 'garde' (guardsman, soldier; defence, protection). The French derivation presumably reflects the character's military service abroad.

2 *Courtine*: in French as in English military terminology, 'courtine' can mean 'the plain wall of a fortified place'. *OED* also lists 'courtin' as meaning a 'farm-court or close' within which animals were confined. Its

earliest example of this meaning comes from 1794; but the exchanges between Courtine and Sylvia in 5.1. 103–10 suggest that this sense may have been active earlier.

4 *Sir Jolly Jumble*: three meanings of 'Jumble' appear relevant—two which are still current, 'mix together in confusion or disorder' and 'agitate, shake up', and a seventeenth-century slang meaning which is now archaic, 'have sexual intercourse with'. Similarly, 'jolly', in early modern slang, meant, in addition to its modern senses, 'lecherous, wanton' and (of animals) 'in heat'.

5 *Fourbin*: in seventeenth-century English, 'fourbe' (derived from French) meant as a noun 'cheat, impostor; trick, imposture' and as a verb 'to cheat, impose upon'. Its aptness here refers to Fourbin's account of his origins in 1.1 as well as to his impostures later in the action.

6 *Bloody Bones*: 'a phrase used . . . as the name of a bug-bear to terrify children; also, *fig.* "bug-bear, terror" ' (*OED*).

Prologue No speaker is identified; but the prologue is clearly intended for one of the actresses.

Lord Falkland: Antony Carey, 5th Viscount Falkland (1656–94), who was Treasurer of the Navy 1681–9, and was appointed in 1692 to the Privy Council. His career and Otway's as schoolboys at Winchester College overlapped briefly, and Otway dedicated *Caius Marius* to him in the same year in which *The Soldiers' Fortune* was premièred. Falkland was the offspring of a famous family but, having inherited little patrimony, was a hungry seeker after preferment in the 1670s. In a petitioning letter of 4 November 1675, he lamented how 'tedious attendance, and fruitless applications, and defeated hopes have been the Sting of my necessity' (John Wilmot, Earl of Rochester, *Letters*, ed. Jeremy Treglown (Oxford, 1980), 112). He was thus well-positioned to understand the obsession of Otway's soldiers with their own lack of preferment.

2 *neglect*: 'neglects' (*1681*).

4 *abandoned stage*: the early 1680s were an unhappy period financially for both the acting companies operating in London, though the King's Company was, in fact, in direr straits than the Duke's Company, which performed *The Soldiers' Fortune*. In 1682 the two amalgamated to form the United Company.

13 *nymph of ours to one of you*: i.e. one of our actresses to one of the spectators with whom she was having an affair.

14 *a more powerful saint*: i.e. Elkanah Settle's *The Female Prelate*, a rabidly anti-papist retelling of 'The Life and Death of Pope Joan', premièred by the rival King's Company in May 1680 with great success.

25 *Phillis*: one of the numerous stock names for a mistress used in contemporary pastoral and erotic verse. The plays in this volume deploy

a wide range of these, including Celia, Cloris, and Selina, as also their male equivalents, Amoret, Strephon, Florimel, and so on.

1.1 S.D. [*The Mall*]: walk, bordered by trees, in St James's Park, London, which was a fashionable promenading place in the later seventeenth century.

7 *an honest man*: the modern meaning of 'honest' is operative here; but the phrase also means 'a man of honour'. Its use throughout the play is also designed to evoke the Civil War usage, 'honest party', by which Royalist gentlemen referred to themselves.

10–11 *left our employments abroad*: during Charles II's reign, English professional soldiers served, at various times, in the Portuguese, Dutch, and French armies. As becomes clear later in this scene (see, for instance, ll. 131–4), Beaugard and Courtine have been in the French service. From 1668 individual English soldiers were no longer allowed to enter foreign service independently, but had to be 'joined to organised "regiments, troops, or companies" which had entered into articles with the appropriate prince or his agent in England'. All such bodies of soldiers were 'under a contractual obligation to return to England if and when Charles gave the order' and could not undertake such service without his approval. In effect, the British mercenary business was now 'directed as an instrument of foreign policy' (John Childs, 'The British Brigade in France, 1672–1678', *History*, 69 (1986), 386). The king's permitting British troops to serve in the armies of the greedily expansionist, absolutist, and Roman Catholic France of Louis XIV, in action principally against the beleaguered Protestant Dutch Republic, caused deep concern to many in England. Those worries were compounded by fears that the regiments serving abroad represented a powerful force over which Parliament had no control, the ultimate loyalty of which was to Charles II alone and which might one day be mobilized by him in a bid to impose his own brand of absolutist rule at home. For most MPs, therefore, the army at home and abroad was one of the key political questions of the age, and from *c*.1673 campaigns were mounted to compel Charles II to recall and disband the soldiers in French service. He made occasional minor concessions but only initiated a major recall when in late 1677–8 his own foreign policy had changed and, with Parliament's approval, he was assembling a substantial army for war with France. Indeed, the mass levy of 1678 was only possible with substantial injections of proven officers from the French service. Beaugard and Courtine were evidently among those who returned at this time and took new commissions in the expeditionary force against France. The latter had, however, not long landed in Flanders when peace was signed at Nimeguen. It was then withdrawn to England and soon thereafter—at Parliament's strenuous insistence—disbanded. Men like Beaugard and Courtine, having obeyed the wishes of Charles II and Parliament, were thus suddenly left without military employment. Hence, their sense of betrayal and angry recriminations.

14–16 *loyalty and starving . . . thrive since*: as military defeat in the Civil War engulfed the royalist cause in the mid-1640s, royalist writing began to develop an iconography of honourable poverty to cope with the financial disaster which faced many Cavaliers, whether they chose to remain in England or take refuge in exile. Alexander Brome's 'The Royalist' (1646) is characteristic in its boast that 'We do not suffer here alone, | Though we are begarr'd, so's the King, | 'Tis sin t'have wealth, when he has none, | Tush! poverty's a Royal thing!' The restoration of Charles II to the throne in 1660, however, did not produce a financial settlement which offered satisfactory recompense to all those who had suffered loyally. In 1660 Brome's 'The Cavalier' responded bitterly: 'That phanatical crue | Which made us all rue, | Have got so much wealth, | By their plunder and stealth, | That they creep into profit and power: | And so come what will, | They'll be uppermost still; | And we that are low, | Shall still be kept so | While those domineer and devour'. (For both these poems, see Alexander Brome, *Poems*, ed. Roman R. Dubinski (Toronto, 1982), i. 117 and 111.) Beaugard's disenchanted speech builds on this history of poverty and disappointed hopes.

18 *Alsatia bully*: Alsatia was a nickname for the Whitefriars district in London, a liberty or sanctuary for fugitive debtors, which had also become a favourite resort for many varieties of criminals. 'Bully' carries a range of uncomplimentary meanings in this period, from 'swashbuckler, bravo' to 'protector and exploiter of prostitutes'.

this flopping: 'this a flopping' (*1681*).

20 *iron sword*: this kind of heavy battle sword was the characteristic emblem of the disbanded soldier. In contrast, the fashionable wear for a gentleman was a lighter, shorter sword, often elaborately decorated.

23–4 *the worthy knight . . . of the post*: a 'knight of the post' was a professional perjurer, who lingered in 'the Temple walks' to offer his services to lawyers in cases currently in process. 'Peripatetic' means (1) 'itinerant, homeless' and (2) (mockingly) 'belonging to the school of philosophy founded by Aristotle'.

35 *drudge*: gigolo. Both as noun and verb, the word often carried sexual meanings in this period.

45 *families*: households, companies.

49 *Wapping*: a hamlet of St Mary Whitechapel on the Middlesex bank of the Thames, populated largely by sailors and their families, and notorious as a haunt for prostitutes.

58 *where new levies are to be raised*: i.e. where recruiting is in progress and where, therefore, such as Beaugard and Courtine could expect to

find military employment. Captains, however, could also themselves profit from recruiting. In some levies each recruit was promised an individual bounty ('levy-money'), but the money was initially paid to the relevant captain, who then struck his own bargain with each recruit.

71   *presently*: immediately.

79   *reverend*: worthy of respect on account of age or ability (used ironically here).

92   *Piazza*: an arcade in Covent Garden, another popular place for promenading.

98   *quality*: rank, breeding, social standing (the dominant meaning of the word in all four of these plays).

100 *parts*: abilities, capacities.

101 *presently understanding*: 'presently understand' (*1681*).

105 *The freedom of commerce increasing*: our conversation becoming more relaxed and intimate.

106 *pour passer le temps*: to pass away the time (French).

     and so: and so forth.

110 *where I had an interest*: where I had some influence, i.e. where they would put themselves out for me.

111 *squire*: (1) attendant; (2) pimp.

125 *distinguish*: mark out from the common rank and file.

127 *rascal*: this word, like 'rogue' at l. 131 above, is almost always used at this time with a definite social weighting—i.e. 'rascals' and 'rogues' came from the lowest social orders. The use of either to describe someone of gentry rank could, depending on circumstances, range in tone from playful badinage to outright insult.

131–4 *serving the great monarch . . . Captain Beaugard*: see note to ll. 10–11 above.

138–9 *A black man*: the association of black colouring and ardent sexuality is conventional in the seventeenth century.

149 *upon the toilet*: on the dressing-table.

155 *the philosopher's stone*: the elusive substance which, according to the alchemists, could transform all metals into gold.

157 *Locket's*: a celebrated tavern near Charing Cross.

160–1 *which . . . withal*: with which (a recurrent usage in these texts).

166–9 *'Twas fortune . . . two months' pay*: see note to ll. 10–11 above.

169 *debentures*: a 'debenture' was a certificate given to a disbanded soldier, specifying arrears of pay owed to him. Those issued in the summer of 1678 remained unnegotiable two years later.

176 *wheezing*: 'wheeting' (*1681*).

177 *bags*: i.e. of money.

179 *The laird*: the Scottish 'laird' (i.e. 'God') implies that these miserly citizens were typically Presbyterian Whigs, and therefore, if not actually, then virtually Scots—on all counts, objects of aversion for English Tory gentlemen, who remembered bitterly, for example, the involvement of Scottish armies in the mounting of rebellion against Charles I in the 1640s.

180 *proper*: (1) excellent, admirable; (2) handsome.

184 *redcoat*: the first English soldiers to be uniformly dressed in red coats were those of Parliament's New Model Army, formed in 1645. Despite this association, Charles II's army adopted the same clothing; but where the New Model uniforms were practical and functional, 'that of the Restoration force was Frenchified and a victim of the whims of civilian fashion, especially in the case of the officers' (John Childs, *The Army of Charles II* (London, 1976), 56). The same source (p. 58) offers a detailed account of the dress of a regimental officer around 1680.

191–2 *a particular branch of property lost*: i.e. a property right removed.

195 *the Blue Posts*: a fashionable tavern in the Haymarket, a meeting-place for enthusiastic Tories, 'Church and King' Cavaliers, who loathed Whigs and all they stood for.

199 *preserve correspondence*: continue to act in full accord with their professed friendship.

210 *Ganymede*: in Greek mythology, Zeus's cupbearer and lover, and the type of youthful male beauty.

211 *Rampant!*: (1) brimful of sexual energy; (2) sexually erect (as in some heraldic representations of the rampant lion).

212 *od*: a favourite softened oath of Sir Jolly's, an abbreviated form of 'God'.

225 *delicate*: voluptuous, sensual; pleasing to the palate.

253 *od's fish*: 'fish' here is euphemistic for 'flesh'; hence, the phrase is a softened form of 'God's flesh' (cf. note to 1.1. 212 above).

261 *The Maw*: this, the reading of all the early editions, could be a transcription error for 'the Mall', but may equally plausibly be Sir Jolly's characteristic nickname for the latter.

285 *tantara-rara*: he is imitating the sound of a flourish on trumpets—i.e. Beaugard is always ready for action, military or sexual.

289–90 *in their copper trim*: decked out in gaudy, cheap dress.

300 *virtues . . . crapish*: 'virtues' is presumably the whore's slip for 'virtuous', and 'crapish', unknown to *OED*, may be her malapropism for 'crabbish', since 'scandalous' means 'addicted to, or loving to disseminate, scandal'.

306 *for all you*: for all you care; for all the help or attention you give us.

310 *O law*: an exclamation of astonishment. 'Law' is a euphemistic form of 'lord'.

312 *treat us*: provide us an entertainment of food and drink.

320 *purest*: finest, most perfect.

320–1 *when be dey mun, Papa?*: baby talk: 'when will the men be here, Papa?'

323 *brave*: fine, handsome.

328 *Mally*: this is *1681*'s spelling, which might be modernized as 'Molly', if it were not for the possibility that she is named after the place where she plies her trade.

1.2.3–4 *leading apes in hell*: the proverbial fate of old maids.

17 *set days*: specified, prescribed days, perhaps those on which she has announced she will receive company.

23 *fondness*: besottedness; foolishness, want of sense or judgement.

31–2 *other divertisements . . . my enjoyment*: other pleasures which divert him from having sex with me—the first of a series of suggestions that Sir Davy's true sexual inclinations are not heterosexual. See, for instance, Lady Dunce's later blunt stigmatizing of him as 'Sir Sodom' (2.1.195), his sudden drunken amorousness with Courtine (4.1.415–21), and his rapt celebration of his wife's resemblance to a boy (4.3.21–3).

36–7 *the fits of the mother*: hysteria.

39 *affects*: loves, delights in.

46 *sticks in your stomach*: obsesses you in a way you can't digest or cope with.

51 *engine*: (1) instrument of torture, but also (2) implement, tool.

72–5 *He is one . . . a party*: in the late 1670s the Earl of Shaftesbury and his allies were organizing an opposition—soon to be called the Whig party—to Charles and his government. It was particularly strong and active in London. Sir Davy is evidently a supporter, as his dislike for soldiers (ll. 69–71 above)—in Whig eyes potential enforcers of monarchical absolutism—would confirm.

76 *the Gate-House*: the prison over the gate of the old palace at Westminster.

92–3 *a peruke . . . of combing*: on campaign, officers wore wigs which were parted at the centre and ended in one or two corkscrew curls or 'dildos', tied back into a queue. It was a practical style, designed to facilitate war duties.

93 *man-at-arms*: 'Man a Armes' (*1681*).

97 *protest eternally against*: solemnly affirm my determination never to have dealings with.

104 *at a dead lift*: in a crisis, in an emergency.

114–15 *industry he has procured*: 'industry procured' (*1681*).

134–5 *The pigeon's . . . feet*: a medieval remedy, used well into the eighteenth century, principally for fevers, but also, as a last resort, for other diseases.

138 *interest*: profit, self-advantage.

2.1.16 *as simply as*: as nakedly, as undisguisedly, as.

18 *a little decayed*: fallen on hard times; come down in the world.

31 *against the world*: i.e. in preference to all other possibilities.

33 *to choose*: by preference.

38 *the monster . . . cuckold elect*: 'yonder comes the Monster that must be the Cuckold Elect' (*1681*). 'Monster' in Restoration texts is often used as a synonym for 'cuckold'.

47–8 *an honest man*: a respectable citizen (as distinct from rogues and riff-raff). But Sir Davy's application of 'honest' to himself is, to Tory ears, a horrid misappropriation of a fine old Cavalier term—see note to 1.1.7—by a man of dubious social credentials and anti-monarchical allegiances.

51 *combing and cocking*: combing their wigs and adjusting their hats to the exactly fashionable angle—actions frequently invoked in late seventeenth-century plays as epitomizing the self-display of the metropolitan gallant.

53 *the boxes in the playhouse*: i.e. the part of the theatre where gentlewomen like Lady Dunce were most likely to sit.

71 *dumbfound him*: i.e. strike him from behind with such speed and dexterity that he won't know who has done it.

102 *a vagabond*: a wandering, disreputable beggar; specifically here, a disbanded soldier, without employment or permanent place of residence. Such itinerants were widely feared as threats to order, property, and decency.

106 *by next sessions*: i.e. when the courts next sit.

114 *This is the*: 'this the' (*1681*).

116–17 *this is the king's court*: affrays, duels, and all forms of personal violence were strictly prohibited within the bounds of the Court—they were regarded as occurring in the presence of the king—and were punished with signal severity. St James's Park, which included the Mall, was part of the royal precincts.

120–1 *That's English in my country*: in the seventeenth century 'country' most often means 'region, district', so Beaugard may intend 'that's English in my part of the country'; but he could also be saying, 'What I am asking is plain English, so don't repeat it as if it were something unintelligible in a foreign tongue'.

125 *if you go to that*: i.e. if you provoke me, if you are prepared to push it that far.

130-1 *you may be . . . beside you*: the Jesuits—for English Protestants traditionally the most zealous and dangerous agents of papist subversion—had been pinpointed in the late 1670s as key conspirators in the alleged Popish Plot to assassinate Charles II and replace him with his brother, James Duke of York, a convert to Catholicism. (For an informative history of the Popish Plot, see J. P. Kenyon, *The Popish Plot* (London, 1972). See also Introduction, pp. xiv–xx.) To a gullible Whig sympathizer like Sir Davy it is axiomatic that the Jesuits would have infiltrated 'the last army', i.e. that raised in 1678 against Catholic France. Throughout the 1670s there had been claims that, in defiance of the law, many of those commissioned in the home regiments were practising Catholics, and in 1678 Sir Joseph Williamson was censured by the Commons for illegally commissioning Catholics in the new regiments raised against France. Building on such scares, Whig propaganda constantly linked Catholicism, absolutism, and the threat to liberty and property represented by a standing army whose only allegiance was to the King. It is Sir Davy's own paranoia, however, which makes him suggest that an officer might himself be a Jesuit priest in disguise.

132 *and be hanged!*: and be cursed! to hell with you!

133-4 *Hounslow Heath*: Charles II reviewed the army of 1678 there on 22 May and 29 June of that year.

134 *disguised in dirty petticoats*: i.e. disguised as women. ('Petticoats' does not in this period necessarily mean 'undergarments'.)

cried brandy: hawked brandy for sale.

137 *you worthy villain of worship*: a deliberately disharmonious form of address, since 'worthy' and 'worship' are terms applicable to a gentleman, whereas 'villain', in addition to its familiar modern meaning, still retained its earlier meaning of 'man of low birth'.

142-3 *a free-born subject . . . a rascal again*: Sir Davy is laying claim, as if by right of birth, to the status of a gentleman. He then calls Beaugard—who considers himself to possess that status by right of birth, but whose poverty prevents his living up to it—'a rascal', i.e. one of the rabble or common herd.

153 *putting out . . . under deck*: i.e. like a Turkish warship or pirate vessel displaying Christian colours in order to prey on Christian ships.

167 *for that*: because.

172-3 *satisfied of*: (1) acquainted with, aware of (2) contented with. Sir Davy, of course, doesn't detect the second meaning.

181 *let her alone to*: i.e. she can be trusted to.

191-2 *gives credit to the sex*: puts trust in women.

197 *abused me handsomely*: i.e. betrayed me with someone who was sexually desirable.

221–2 *Or would you . . . did it himself?*: a ferocious joke, which would have reminded a contemporary audience of the fate of Sir Edmund Berry Godfrey, the prominent Protestant magistrate to whom Titus Oates, the primary instigator of the stories about a Popish Plot, (cf. note to l. 130–1 above), disclosed the enormities of the alleged conspiracy. Godfrey's body—hanged, and run through with his own sword—was discovered, shortly thereafter, on 17 Oct. 1678. It was generally believed that vengeful Catholics had murdered him, and the Whigs made much of this; but it was claimed by some of their Tory opponents that Godfrey had hanged himself and that the sword-work was part of a Whig plot to present a suicide as a murder. Fourbin is suggesting that Sir Davy, a Whig, should be treated *à la* Godfrey, only in reverse.

224–5 *stale jakes*: 'jakes' means 'privy', and 'stale' 'stinking of urine'.

234 *makes love to*: pays court to, attempts to woo (the normal meaning in this period).

244 *quarters*: board and lodging for soldiers. Such billeting was often forcibly requisitioned.

263 *my stomach rises*: i.e. I am revolted, repelled.

280 *music-meeting*: public concert. Southerne's *The Wives' Excuse* opens with one.

285–6 *out of his waiting*: no longer in attendance on her, and therefore no longer protected by her presence.

294 *silly*: feeble, debilitated (not only in intellect).

314 S.D. *clumsy*: ungainly, ungentlemanlike.

320 *and be hanged*: see note to 2.1.132 above.

dainty: delightful, pleasing to persons of delicate and fastidious tastes (used ironically).

322–4 *Some honest . . . withal*: patronage in high places and considerable expenditure were required to secure a commission in the relatively small peacetime army of the Restoration. A captaincy in the Foot Guards, for instance, could cost as much as £1,000. In wartime, as in 1678, shortage of officers changed everything, and Beaugard and Courtine, experienced soldiers abroad but with no money or influence to secure them commissions at home in peacetime, could in this brief emergency obtain captaincies.

331 *neck verse*: the first verse of Psalm 60, the ability to read which gave a convicted offender the privilege of being branded on the hand instead of being hanged.

333 *preferred*: promoted, advanced.

334 *a pardoned rebel loyal*: what follows is a Tory characterization/caricature of a typical Whig's progress, from rebellion against Charles I in 1642, through pardon by the Act of Indemnity and Oblivion after Charles II's restoration in 1660, to sedition and party faction in the 1670s.

336 *busiest*: 'busy' here means 'meddlesome, active in matters which do not concern him'.

346 *him to the block*: i.e. Charles I to execution (in 1649).

349 *popular*: i.e. beloved of the lowly.

351 *Rump Parliament*: the remnant of the Long Parliament of 1642, after Colonel Pride had 'purged' it of its more moderate MPs in December 1648. It executed Charles I in 1649, established the Republic, and was dissolved by Cromwell in April 1653. It symbolized, by Otway's time, the temper and excesses of fanatical republicanism.

352 *be uncovered*: remove your hat in reverence (ironic).

354-6 *committee-man ... pardon*: during the Civil War and after its victory Parliament administered areas under its control through local county committees, which fell into the hands of men conspicuous for military and religious zeal rather than for rank and breeding. Such new men, royalists believed, devoted themselves to lining their pockets. One of the functions of these committees was to direct the sequestration—the confiscation—of royalists' estates. These might be recovered on payment of a fine, but were, in many cases, sold off to Parliament's agents and allies.

358 *luxury*: (1) lasciviousness (2) habitual indulgence in the choice and costly.

359 *honest men*: the customary lament of the Cavaliers that their loyalty was forgotten and went unrewarded by the Restoration government, while men prominent against the King before 1660 and their ideological successors after that date prospered under the restored monarchy.

362 *his master*: Charles II. Thus, Whig caballing in the late 1670s is seen as the latest incarnation of the anti-monarchist tendencies which, in 1649, had secured the execution of his father, Charles I.

364 *swinging*: this, *1681*'s spelling, yields a perfectly apt meaning; but Otway may also be playing on 'swingeing', i.e. 'huge'.

365 *keep his cowardice in countenance*: i.e. put a brave face on his cowardice.

367 *come abroad*: 'came abroad' (*1681*).

375-6 *factious clubs these seven years*: such 'clubs'—gatherings for drinking, talking, and planning political activities—met in taverns, coffee-houses, and private residences. There were Tory clubs and Whig clubs; but 'factious' here refers to the Whig variety, of which the most celebrated, and political, was the Green Ribbon Club, which met at the King's Head at the corner of Fleet Street and Chancery Lane.

377 *recorder of some factious town*: the 'recorder' was the principal judicial official, for civil and criminal matters, of some cities and boroughs. For 'factious', see preceding note.

379 *Magna Charta*: the *Great Charter* of English liberty extorted from King John in 1215, widely regarded as a charter of popular liberties.

385 *use to be*: i.e. are accustomed to be, traditionally are.

393 *chairs*: vehicles, wheeled or carried, for one person.

420 *but I am a gentleman*: thus insulted, a gentleman would challenge his abuser to a duel. Though Sir Jolly's line implies that he may push it that far, he is only bluffing; see his aside at l. 434 below.

429–30 *of the spleen*: i.e. of melancholy, of depression.

441 *Though*: i.e. however—a frequent usage in the plays in this volume.

496 *seamstress*: i.e. a woman who patches up his ragged clothes; but also, by implication, a poor woman who is sexually available.

516 *two pennyworth of hemp*: i.e. a length of rope to hang yourself with.

524 *amuse*: delude, cheat, bemuse.

541 *I should speak*: I would like to speak.

542 *keep my countenance*: prevent myself laughing.

550 *bank*: bench.

566 *thirty in the hundred*: this rate of interest is exorbitant and illegal; the statutory maximum was 6 per cent.

574 *on me*: of me.

617 *delicate*: excellent, fine (though needing careful handling).

3.1 S.D. *Covent Garden*: a very fashionable residential area, but also frequently cited in contemporary literature for the libertinism of many of its inhabitants. In Farquhar's *The Twin-Rivals* (1702), 1.1, one character, for example, speaks of it as 'the low suburbs of pleasure'.

2 *a fellow . . . Cain upon him*: i.e. as a soldier he is lineally descended from the first murderer.

24 *owls*: men who fancy themselves nocturnal predators, but are, in fact, easily duped by such as Sylvia.

66 *pretend to vindicate her*: attempt to vindicate her from this scandalous aspersion.

69 *right-worshipful*: honoured sir (a mode of address to someone of greatly superior rank).

349

78–9 *up three pair . . . the Temple now*: up three flights of stairs in the Inner, or the Middle, Temple. These were Inns of Court, where young gentlemen who were in London to pursue their legal, or other, studies lodged in the upper stories of the buildings. These gallants' exploits figure in numerous contemporary tales of sexual adventure and adultery.

83–8 *Swan at Knightsbridge . . . Rosamond's Ponds*: places of assignation of dubious character. Thus, in Congreve's *Love for Love*, 2.9, Mrs Frail seeks to defend her beleaguered reputation by proclaiming that 'If I had gone to Knightsbridge, or to Chelsea, or to Spring Garden, or Barn Elms with a man alone—something might have been said'. The Swan was a tavern; Rosamond's Pond was in St James's Park, on the edge of which was situated a group of tall elms known as Barn Elms.

105 *the purest*: the finest; capital.

109–10 *Bow steeple . . . the dragon*: St. Mary-le-Bow, built by Christopher Wren between the 1670s and 1683. Its steeple was the tallest—221 feet—of all the new City churches, and it was adorned with a weather-vane in the shape of a griffin.

111 *idle*: (1) worthless, trifling (2) foolish.

112 *pretended*: professed, set out to. The tone is 'had the nerve to attempt to'.

114 *the Crown Office*: the office in which all business coming before the Court of King's Bench was initiated and recorded.

115–16 *the statute of Edward 19th*: the correct reference for the statute defining treason is 25 Edw. III, stat. 5, c. 2.

122 *a good riding face*: i.e. the face of one accustomed to, or fit for, energetic exercise (with an obvious sexual equivocation).

124 *in a corner*: playing the military meaning (i.e. 'when his back is against the wall') against the sexual one (i.e. 'in a moment of intimate privacy' or 'when the lady has no chance of escape').

129 *Flanders jades*: i.e. hopelessly out of condition, not 'fit for service'. Horses from Flanders were judged to be of inferior quality.

132 *leap like a buck*: Sir Jolly is playing on the slang meaning of 'leap', i.e. 'mount sexually'; while 'buck' means (1) the male of various animals (including rabbits) and (2) gallant, rake; and 'to buck' means (of rabbits) 'to copulate'.

149 *fop*: fool, buffoon (not exclusively, at this period, someone obsessed with their appearance or clothes).

157 *Sirrah*: a mode of address characteristically used to social inferiors.

162 *silly*: (1) insignificant (2) poor (3) ignorant.

167–8 *not a wet finger*: not in the slightest.

173 *Indeed*: *1681* prints opposite this speech '*(A Letter.)*', presumably a reminder that Lady Dunce needs to bring with her the letter she produces later in the scene.

195 *Sir Sodom*: i.e. he does everything back to front, in the wrong order. But cf. also note to 1.2.31–2.

208–9 *La you there now!*: an expression of derision.

210 *troubled that*: troubled to such an extent that.

213 *simply*: foolish.

260–1 *answer my desires*: do what I ask you, what I wish.

287 *strangely*: extremely.

289 *what he carries about him*: (1) all his money (to be won at cards); (2) all his strength and expertise (in sexual gamesmanship).

305 *Argus*: a mythical creature fabled to have a hundred eyes; hence, an intensely vigilant watcher (used sarcastically here).

327 *bound to the peace*: bound by a magistrate to keep the peace, i.e. to refrain from strife and commotion.

331 *hangdog*: 'hangdog' means 'low, degraded, fit only to be hung like a dog'. It thus reinforces the social disdain and threat in Sir Davy's calling Beaugard 'a rogue', i.e. a poverty-stricken itinerant, vulnerable to the laws which fiercely punished the unemployed and houseless poor.

342 *hand*: handwriting.

355 S.D. BEAUGARD (*reads*): *1681* here, mistakenly, reads '(*Sir* Jolly *reads*)'.

361 *a monster*: see note to 2.1.38 above.

368 *tell you the business won't do*: 'tell the business won't do' (*1681*).

369 *put up your pipes*: give up, admit defeat.

376 *pretty*: cunning, crafty, artful.

396 *communicate*: impart confidentially.

405–6 *in the roasting of an egg*: in the time it takes an egg to cook.

408–10 *the gold medal ... popish relic*: in the late 1670s and early 1680s persecution of Catholics increased, stimulated by the fears aroused by the Popish Plot. A Proclamation of 20 December 1678 instructed magistrates to disarm proven or reputed Catholics. This one was evidently disarmed of his valuables.

419–20 *impertinence*: irrelevance, trivial concerns.

455 *family*: servants, household.

3.2.4 *closet*: small room (often, as here, one set aside for a particular individual's use).

post-night: the mails left London for all parts of the country on Tuesday, Thursday, and Saturday nights.

351

19–20 *let us make stakes a little*: i.e. let us see how much we are prepared to stake, how far we are prepared to venture.

23 *who shall keep them?*: in wagers, the stakes were usually held by a third person, to be given to the winner.

26 *give him over*: abandon, leave hold of, him.

28 *improve*: employ to our advantage, turn to good account.

35 *halloo!*: a hunting-call, inciting hounds to the chase; though here it is Beaugard who is in danger of being hunted.

35 S.D. *gets up*: nothing in the text precisely determines when Beaugard (and Lady Dunce?) knelt, sat down, or lay on the ground—perhaps at Beaugard's 'drunk with this dissolving—O!—' (ll. 32–3).

52 *justified*: have my innocence established or accepted.

67–71 *I shall . . . geese before me*: Sir Davy's disturbance is expressed in a rather generalized parody of the dialect of the heroic drama popular in the 1660s and 1670s. Characteristically, he amalgamates stories chaotically, setting the Asiatic conqueror, Tamburlaine, for instance, incongruously astride the wooden horse with which the Greeks contrived at last to conquer Troy.

4.1.7–8 *the Dolphin*: rooms in inns were often given individual names.

10–11 *the lands of milk and honey*: cf. 'a land flowing with milk and honey' (Joshua 5: 6).

10–15 *When shall we . . . the sun?*: cf. Captain Henry Herbert's reminiscences of service in Lorraine in 1672–4: 'All our knots of officers associated very loveingly together and was a caball of eating and drinking . . . We had continuall musick and dancing, diner and supper, and treates were our sports and pastimes' (*Camden Miscellany XXX* (Camden Society, 4th ser., 39 (1990), 356)).

19 *Champagne*: a province of eastern France, celebrated for its fine wines. English troops saw service there under French command in the mid-1670s. *1681* reads '*Campagne*' here.

25 *portion*: inheritance (from their Cavalier forbears, the 'honest party'—cf. note to 1.1.7).

28–9 *a gentleman . . . one day*: Louis XIV, the French king. The implication is that war against the French may not be far off.

34 *Ask . . . satisfaction*: i.e. challenge him to a duel.

37 *want*: lack.

38 *obedience to public edicts*: see note to above 1.1.10–11.

47 *at stint*: i.e. within tight limits of expenditure.

57 *shop-book*: register of debts.

59 *cock his greasy hat*: instead of taking off his hat—vailing it—as to a gentleman, he sticks it jauntily and jeeringly on the side of his head.

60 *deputy of the ward*: an alderman's officer. The City was divided into wards, each under the jurisdiction of an alderman.

63 *parish jests*: jokes about happenings in his local neighbourhood

78 *damnable*: 'damnably' (*1681*).

86 *a*: have.

89 *Alsatia*: Alsace, on the eastern borders of France, ceded (though on subsequently disputed terms) by the Austrian Habsburgs to France in 1648. Louis XIV took every opportunity to consolidate and extend his authority there. English troops saw service there under French command in the mid-1670s.

93 *arbitrary whoring and your limited fornication*: playing on the contrast between what is permissible under an absolute, arbitrary monarch like Louis XIV and in a limited English monarchy.

104 *a patent*: a grant from the sovereign, under the Great Seal, conferring the—sometimes exclusive—right to an office or privilege.

112–13 *satisfy my experience*: inform me.

114 *sons of Mars, and imps of Venus*: 'son of Mars' was a colloquial term for 'soldier'. Mars was the lover of Venus, and the soldier is conventionally represented as being similarly addicted to the sexual sport of which she is the tutelary deity.

132 *he!*: 'she!' (*1681*).

170 *cocksparrow*: the sparrow is traditionally the most lecherous of birds; hence, 'cocksparrow' here means 'sexual athlete, stud'.

172 *monopoly*: an exclusive privilege, bestowed by the monarch, of trading in, or possessing, some commodity; widely regarded as injurious to commerce and oppressive to the consumer.

173 *correspondence*: playing on 'correspondence' as (1) business relations or dealings; (2) sexual intercourse.

182 s.d. *They go . . . and bottles*: one set of shutters opens to reveal the table set out for the imminent drinking-bout, and Sir Jolly, the soldiers, and the Drawer move from the forestage to the scenic stage. Beaugard then orders the Drawer to 'shut the door'. *1681* includes the Drawer in the following entry, but it seems most logical to us that he would return to the forestage, as the scene closes on the others, and be joined there by the new arrivals.

183 *the land of Canaan*: the 'land flowing with milk and honey' (cf. note to ll. 10–11 above), given by God to Abraham and his descendants (Genesis 17: 8).

204 *cutting of purses*: a cutpurse was one who stole by slitting purses worn at the girdle.

210 *since the Conquest*: since the Norman Conquest of England in 1066. Sir Davy is implicitly boasting of the antiquity of his family.

221 *No trade . . . profess murder*: 'profess murder' here means 'declare myself expert in', as opposed, for example, to making it his trade. He is claiming that he indulges in it as 'a gentleman's divertisement', not as a means of earning a living. Characteristically, however, he contradicts himself in his next speech.

230 *Soft and fair*: i.e. not so fast.

236 *general undertakers . . . a monopoly*: 'undertakers' means 'contractors, those who undertake a task or enterprise'. The effect of their activity is almost as bad as a monopoly (see note to l. 172 above), in that it prevents others undertaking the same line of business.

241 *Algier*: Algiers was a famous pirate stronghold, which harassed Mediterranean shipping, enslaving the sailors and treating them cruelly. But the depredations of corsairs were also felt on the English coast, with hundreds of English people during the century being captured and carried off to the slave markets of Algiers and Constantinople.

242–3 *an apostate Greek . . . renegado Englishman*: the figure of the renegade convert from Christianity to Islam is a potent and threatening one in seventeenth-century England. See N. I. Matar, 'The Renegade in English Seventeenth Century Imagination', *Studies in English Literature*, 33 (1993), 489–505.

245 *embracing the faith*: reconverting to Christianity.

254–5 *siege of Philippsburgh*: Philippsburgh, a French stronghold on the middle Rhine in Baden and vital to the control of Alsace, was besieged and taken by Imperialist troops in 1676. British troops were among those garrisoned there. Fourbin's fanciful tale of taking 'the impenetrable half-moon', however, places them on the side of the besiegers.

310 *Circean charms*: Circe was an enchantress in Greek mythology who transformed all who drank from her cup into swine. 'Charms' here means 'spells'. Bloody Bones's cant in this speech and at ll. 322–58 below has the same derivation as Sir Davy's matching excursion at 3.2.67–71 (see note).

373 *Fee, fa, fum*: the Giant's words from the story of Jack the Giant-Killer provide an apt exit-line for Bloody Bones, who owes his own name to a children's fable (see note to 'The Characters of the Play', l. 6); and its unvoiced sequel—'I smell the blood of an Englishman'—provides one last intensifier of Sir Davy's panic.

381 *The devil's an ass*: proverbial; see Tilley D242, which cites this passage.

382 *those that defy the devil*: cf. the promise by the godparents on behalf of the baby in the Anglican baptismal service to 'renounce the devil and all his works'.

384 *do me right*: i.e. return my toast; drink as much as I do.

386 *of all conscience*: in fairness; by all that is reasonable.

392–3 *idolatry . . . upon the nation*: the Popish Plot, and the prospect of the succession to the throne of James, Duke of York, a Catholic convert, after Charles II's death, had convinced fervent Protestants that Roman Catholicism—'idolatry'—was poised to sweep in and take over the kingdom.

394 *Sir, your humble servant*: Fourbin is declining to answer Sir Davy's question.

395 *a good conscience*: a phrase redolent of the language of the Puritans, for whom 'a good conscience' was necessarily a Protestant one.

398 *set him*: lay the trap for him.

412–13 *tickle my foot*: i.e. provoke me to kick you.

414 *tickle your guts*: i.e. with his sword.

415 *tickle your toby*: whip your buttocks; but with a sexual equivocation on 'tickle' (the slang meanings of 'tickle-tail', for instance, were (1) whore and (2) penis); cf. the drunken amorousness of some of Sir Davy's next speech.

417–18 *circumcised band . . . Reformation cut?*: Sir Davy's neck-band and beard are evidently in the Puritan style, ostentatiously severe and simple.

421 *buttock*: whore (slang).

425 *countenance . . . bribery*: i.e. accept bribes to allow prostitutes to operate untroubled by the court of which he is a justice.

428 *Stokes*: perhaps the chief constable of the Covent Garden area. Thomas Shadwell's *The Scowrers* (London, 1690) relates 'a Skirmish' there between the gang which gives the play its title and 'some drunken Bullies', in which 'Brigadier *Stokes* with a detachment of Quarter-Staves, and rusty Halberts fell in Pell Mell and routed both Parties' (p. 1).

456 *your left ear*: the left ears of rogues and vagrants had formerly been pierced with a red-hot iron as a punishment and a mark of delinquency. Although this practice had fallen into disuse the association of the left ear with roguery was evidently still—jocularly—current.

4.2 s.d. *in the balcony*: in the Restoration playhouse balconies surmounted the doors set in the walls that flanked the proscenium opening. These were used for scenes requiring an upper level.

32 *doing*: copulating.

35 *avast there*: stop there, stop pulling.

40 *Erasmus' paradise*: (1) a fool's paradise, aptly named after the great sixteenth-century humanist author of *In Praise of Folly*; (2) limbo (cf. John Milton's *Paradise Lost*, iii. 495–6: 'a limbo large and broad, since called | The Paradise of Fools').

42–3 *his cry of watchmen*: his posse of watchmen. 'Cry' meant (1) a pack or crowd of people (contemptuous) and (2) a pack of hounds.

45–6 *God prosper . . . safeties all*: for this song and its printed versions, see Cyrus Lawrence Day and Eleanore Murrie, *English Song-Books 1651–1702* (London, 1940), 229.

56 *whelp of Babylon*: Sir Davy's variation on the Whore of Babylon of Revelations 17: 3–6, identified by Protestant exegesis with the Roman Catholic Church, and thence used as a general term of opprobrium.

61 *state-affairs*: i.e. matters too high and important for the likes of you (with the implication that acts of murder were among the responsibilities—and functions—of government).

4.3 S.D. *The scene . . . were dead*: for a reading of this use of the scenic stage as a specific parody of 'tragic style', see Holland, p. 41.

1 *Close, close*: keep quiet and lie still.

8 *if a body desires you a little*: i.e. if I ask you to do it.

25–6 *What, upon my hall-table!*: cf. Lady Macbeth's 'What, in our house' (*Macbeth*, 2.3.87), when publicly told of Duncan's murder. In Davenant's rewriting of the play, the version performed on the Restoration stage, the line became 'Ah me! in our house?' (Spencer, p. 60). In the remainder of the play Sir Davy's dialogue contains frequent echoes of *Macbeth*. The latter was part of the repertory of the company which performed *The Soldiers' Fortune*, having been revived by them earlier in the month (on 2 June 1680) in which Otway's play was premièred. Macbeth and Banquo were roles played by Betterton and Smith, who also played Otway's soldiers.

29 *distracting*: i.e. which threatened me with insanity. The swift repetition of this adjective within a single sentence may be a transcription error.

38 *blind as buzzard*: proverbial; see Tilley B792, which cites this passage. A buzzard is a kind of hawk regarded as effectively untrainable for hunting; hence, a stupid person unable to spot what is going on before him. Sir Davy speaks wiser than he knows.

40–1 *his wounds . . . touch him*: there was a widespread folk belief that a murder-victim's wounds would bleed afresh in the presence of the murderer.

56 *green wound*: fresh wound.

61 *bowels*: believed to be the seat of compassion.

74 *gift of stroking*: gift of healing by means of massage and other methods of gentle friction (with an obvious sexual equivocation).

80 *canary-bird*: (1) a kind of finch; (2) young wag; (3) harlot.

83 *if I set on't*: if I make up my mind to have it.

109 *gin*: if: 'gan' (*1681*).

109–10 *Bonny lass . . . &c.*: for this song and its afterlife, see Simpson, p. 57.

5.1.4–5 *Geneva Bible or a Practice of Piety*: the Geneva Bible, first published in 1560, was an English translation of the Bible produced by English Puritans in exile at the Calvinist fount of Geneva. It became a Puritan *vade mecum* and its possession an emblem of Puritan allegiances. Lewis Bayly's *Practice of Piety* was a popular devotional work, first published early in the seventeenth century, but frequently reprinted throughout it. The alleged equipping of brothel rooms with pious or holy works is frequently played upon in contemporary texts.

17 *limbo*: prison, confinement; but also playing on the theological meaning (cf. his reference to 'Erasmus' paradise', 4.2.40 above and note).

courage: vigour, spirit, sexual drive.

23–4 *ferreting Moorfields withal*: i.e. hunting, scrambling recklessly after, whores. Moorfields had many brothels.

27 *the whip and the bell*: although the phrase 'a whip and a bell' usually had a more general meaning, i.e. 'something that detracts from one's comfort or pleasure' (*OED*), the Maid is clearly using it literally here to threaten Courtine with a beating.

30 *chaplain*: the assumption of intimate dealings between household chaplains and maids is proverbial in the period. The following use of 'exercise' plays on the meaning of 'religious observance'.

33 *rambling*: wandering the town; but with a secondary meaning of 'going out in search of sex' (for the latter, see J. D. Patterson, 'The Restoration Ramble', *Notes and Queries*, 226 (1981), 209–10).

53 *spite of my teeth*: in spite of my adamant resistance.

89 *civil*: see note to Dedication, l. 25, above.

114 *tenement*: building, dwelling-place (not, as in later use, one of poor quality or state of repair); land held of another by any tenure (i.e. not necessarily 'a lease for your life').

127–8 *too much to common*: i.e. already used by many, like common land.

135 *draw articles*: agree the marriage conditions.

137–8 *the ten o'clock office in Covent Garden*: presumably a scrivener's office, at which the necessary documents can be prepared and signed.

150 *whatever is the matter*: whatever the cause of the disturbance may be.

159 *by your wanting a fleece*: the predominant meaning of 'wanting' in the period was 'lacking'; but the options for 'fleece' are more various. It could mean 'booty'; Courtine is penniless (and therefore perforce dependent on the wealthy Sylvia). It could also mean 'wig'; Courtine's may have slipped off during the previous night's exertions. But a third, slang meaning was 'female pubic hair'; Sylvia's innuendo may be that Courtine's failure to find other sexual prey the night before means he is now tagging hopefully after her.

5.2.1–3 *I cannot sleep . . . help myself*: cf. *Macbeth*, 2.2.20–41. Davenant's version introduces numerous detailed changes to these speeches, but none which materially affects Otway's use of the scene here.

5–7 *Ludgate Hill . . . Fleet-ditch*: Sir Davy's nightmare has precipitated him into the infernal heart of a Pope-burning procession. For these outpourings of anti-Catholic hysteria, see S. Williams, 'The Pope-Burning Processions of 1679–81', *Journal of the Warburg and Courtauld Institutes*, 21 (1958), 104–18, and John Miller, *Popery and Politics in England 1660–1688* (Cambridge, 1973), 182–8. These elaborately spectacular demonstrations processed from Moorgate via Ludgate Hill to a culminating conflagration opposite Temple Bar, near where the Fleet river debouched into the Thames.

9 *it has been . . . night*: cf. *Macbeth*, 2.3.60.

11–18 *methoughts I saw . . . like Towser's*: 'Towser' was at this period a name for a large dog kept for hunting or for bear- and bull-baiting. But at the climax of the Whig-inspired Pope-burning processions of the late 1670s an effigy of the Pope was burnt accompanied by one of Towser, i.e. a devil dog, his diabolic familiar. Implicit in these nervous exchanges, therefore, is the fear that they may have seen not Sir Davy's own guard-dog, but something much more terrifying.

49 *critical*: exercising minute attention and careful judgement.

56–8 *Approach thou . . . confront thee*: a parody of Macbeth's speech of defiance to the ghost of Banquo: 'Approach thou like the rugged Russian bear, | The armed rhinoceros, or th'Hyrcan tiger; | Take any shape but that, and my firm nerves | Shall never tremble' (3.4.99–102). (Davenant's text offers only one minor modification—'Hircanian' for 'Hyrcan'—here.) In place of the exotic threats of the original, Sir Davy's demented but parochial imagination substitutes the bear- and bull-baiting offered in London as a spectator-sport on the Bankside and in Eastcheap.

68 *leathern serpent*: a 'serpent' was (1) a wind instrument made of wood covered with leather and (2) a firework which burns with a serpentine motion or flame. Sir Davy's fevered imagination perhaps animates the first into behaving like the second and elides both with the serpent of Genesis.

78 *horrid*: terrible, abominable.

88 *hanged by the neck like a dog*: the comparison is literal; in seventeenth-century England hanging was a punishment inflicted on dogs.

96–7 *Potestati . . . misericordia*: 'To the eternal power by whose benevolence and pity the nations are preserved' (Latin). We assume that Otway is unlikely to have invented Sir Davy's prayer, but have been unable to identify a source for it.

127 *have all my old shoes*: the bequest of clothes, etc., to servants is frequent in seventeenth-century wills.

5.3 s.d. *and discovers . . . [watching]*: 'and discovers Sir Jolly, Beaugard, *and Lady in her Chamber*' (*1681*).

4 *colours*: regimental flags.

18–19 *some cleanlier shift*: some more decent expedient (but playing on 'shift' meaning 'smock' or 'shirt'). Cf. his wife's earlier account of Sir Davy's uncleanliness (1.2.35–41).

23 *should*: would.

37 s.d. *[Sir Jolly Jumble comes forward]*: 'Enters.' (*1681*).

43–4 *Speak to me . . . did it*: a mosaic of recollections of lines from *Macbeth*, 3.4: 'If thou canst nod, speak, too!' (l. 69), 'Which of you have done this?' (l. 48), and 'Thou canst not say I did it' (l. 49). All of these survive unaltered in Davenant's adaptation.

49 *Did you . . . just now?*: cf. *Macbeth*, 3.4.68 and 73.

56–7 *An you go to that*: i.e. if it comes to that; or, if you are making an issue of it.

72–3 *between Charing Cross and Aldgate*: i.e. from one end of the city to the other.

76–7 *like the grass . . . fadeth*: See Isaiah 40: 8.

81 s.d. *through the trap-door*: in the Restoration theatre Banquo's ghost also used the trap-door in the banquet scene (Spencer, p. 77).

90 *a commonwealth's man*: so good a member of the community; but also, so ardent a supporter of, and enthusiast for, the Republican government (1649–60) which ruled England after the execution of Charles I.

91 *ride in a cart*: condemned criminals were drawn to the gallows on a cart.

114–17 *Why, there, there . . . one another*: cf. *Macbeth*, 3.4.111–15.

145 *civillest*: most accommodating, politest.

162 *the minstrels*: presumably a group of street musicians, available for hire for performance in private houses.

210 *Bridewell*: a penitentiary for whores and vagrants in the Blackfriars district of London.

5.4.5–6 *Antony and Cleopatra*: three years earlier the playhouses had premièred two plays based on the story of Antony and Cleopatra—Dryden's *All for Love*, an immediate success, and Sir Charles Sedley's *Antony and Cleopatra*, an equally immediate flop.

20 *Aristotle*: the pseudo-Aristotle Sir Jolly has read is likely to be such enormously popular works as *Aristotles Master-Piece* and *The Problems of Aristotle*, which may derive a few passages from Aristotle on the generation of animals, but which are essentially seventeenth-century

compilations of a quasi-medical nature, physiologically circumstantial, and especially detailed in their treatment of female anatomy and female sexual responsiveness. See Roger Thompson, *Unfit for Modest Ears* (London, 1979), 166–8.

31 *cut a caper*: dance in a frolicsome manner, with high kicks.

32 *Give me some wine*: this may be addressed to Beaugard and Lady Dunce; but Otway may also be imagining one or more servants on stage in this scene.

34 s.d. *Dance*: the music is provided by the musicians whose attendance Sir Jolly ordered at 5.3.162. Presumably the troupe is also imagined to include dancers, or perhaps Lady Dunce and Beaugard dance amorously to the music provided.

39 *into the alcove there*: the staging here echoes that at 4.1.182–6. The food has been revealed on the scenic stage by the opening of a pair of shutters. Beaugard and Lady Dunce now retreat to the scenic stage, and the scene closes in front of them.

71 *Go from the window, . . . my love*: Sir Jolly's variation on a popular old song. Cf. Simpson, pp. 257–9.

134–5 *having no more grace before her eyes*: this is modelled on a characteristic formula in legal indictments, e.g. '. . . stands Indicted as not having the fear of God before his Eyes, being led by the Instigation of the Devil . . .' (*The Tryal of William Stayley*, Goldsmith (1678), 3).

154 *gently*: without harshness; but also, in the manner of a gentleman.

Epilogue 27 *ragged coast*: 'ragged' here means (1) stony, hostile, infertile; and (2) inhabited by starving poets in rags.

29 *They rail . . . penny-post*: to the dismay of the porters, who delivered letters, a London penny-post was established in 1680.

36 *Trincalos and Stephanos*: Shakespeare's *The Tempest* was principally known on the Restoration stage in an operatic version by Sir William Davenant and John Dryden. Among its many other alterations, Stephano the butler and Trinculo the jester (renamed Trincalo) become the master of the ship and the boatswain respectively. Once shipwrecked, they compete furiously, intriguing against one another for the lordship of the island. In l. 40, 'the monster of your barren isle' plays on another *Tempest* character, Caliban.

45 *wrecked*: 'wracked' (*1681*).

The Princess of Cleves

Epigraph *tuque dum procedis . . . tura benignis*: 'And while you walk in front we'll shout together, "Hail! God of Triumph!", offering the incense due to the kindly gods' (Horace, *Odes*, IV. ii. 49–52).

Dedication *Charles, Earl of Dorset and Middlesex*: Charles Sackville (1638–1706), courtier, rake, poet, and patron of poets and playwrights. As a young man-about-town, he was notorious for his escapades and dissipations and was during this period a close friend, and ally in libertinism, of the equally scandalous John Wilmot, Earl of Rochester, who in 'An Allusion to Horace' (l. 60) dubbed him 'The best good man with the worst-natured muse'. Lee received patronage from Sackville in the 1670s. Sackville took little interest in public affairs but supported William of Orange in the 1688 Revolution and was rewarded with the office of Lord Chamberlain (1689–97), whose responsibilities included the licensing of plays for public performance. Hence, this dedication's concluding plea to him to license the performance of Lee's *The Massacre of Paris* 'in its first figure', i.e. with 'two whole scenes' restored to their original place (see next note). The revival was permitted—at Drury Lane on 7 November 1689 in the presence of Queen Mary—and was a great success.

2–10 *This play . . . to pay*: Lee's *The Massacre of Paris*, narrating the events surrounding the St Bartholomew's Day Massacre in 1572 as a parallel to the Popish Plot, was prohibited from performance at the request of the French ambassador. The date of composition of *The Massacre* is uncertain, and competing theories date it to 1678–9 and to 1681. Lee recycled some material from it for *The Duke of Guise* (1682), another play on the same stretch of French history, this time co-authored with John Dryden. This play too ran into censorship trouble—this is what Lee means when he says it 'was notorious for a bolder fault'—and was suppressed after an initial run of perhaps four days. As he narrates here, Lee similarly re-used material from *The Massacre* in *The Princess of Cleves* when it was premièred in late 1681 or early 1682, but excised it from the 1689 printing of the play. His phrasing implies that the borrowings in *The Duke of Guise* ('two whole scenes') were more substantial than in *The Princess of Cleves* ('a resemblance of Marguerite'). Scholars have speculated as to where the cuts in the printed text may have occurred, but no solid information exists. The first encounter between Nemours and Marguerite in the published play is notably brief, and the 1689 printers clearly became confused during the setting of this scene, 2.1, resulting in widely differing states of it in different copies of the first quarto. So, although the scene is eminently playable as it stands, this may well have been one point at which Lee made excisions, producing a manuscript where the markings were insufficiently clear for the printers to be sure exactly what was required of them. Much less plausible to us is another suggestion which has been made—i.e. that dialogue is missing after Marguerite's entrance in 5.3. Nemours has boasted that 'six words in private' will be sufficient to still her fury—a promise he then nonchalantly carries out in a privacy the audience is not permitted to breach. ('After the vacation' means 'at the beginning of the next theatrical season, in the autumn'.)

15–16 *for when they . . . in Nemours*: Madame de Lafayette's novel, Lee's source, was published in Paris in 1678, provoking great acclaim and controversy, and its fame prompted the swift appearance in 1679 of an anonymous English translation, from which Lee worked. The reputation of Lafayette's Nemours as a 'most polished hero' was thus sufficiently established for Lee's shock tactics to work their full effect.

16 *Whetstone's Park*: a lane between Holborn and Lincoln's Inn Fields, and a pick-up place for prostitutes.

17–19 *The fourth . . . his villainy*: in revising John Fletcher's *The Chances* (*c*.1617) for the Restoration stage in the mid-1660s, George Villiers, Duke of Buckingham, supplied an entirely new fourth and fifth act, greatly enhancing and emboldening the roles of the libertine Don John and free-thinking Second Constantia. One plot of Dryden's *Marriage à la Mode* (*c*.1671) narrates the (eventually failed) attempts of a quartet of witty courtiers to commit adultery. The epilogue announces that Dryden 'would not quite the women's frailty bare, | But stripped them to the waist, and left them there'. Thomas Shadwell's *The Libertine* (1675) is a version of the Don Juan story and includes among its hectic events seductions, rapes, and murder. Shadwell's *Epsom Wells* (1672) pairs courtship comedy with multiple adultery. Rochester borrowed two of its characters—the gigolos, Cuff and Kick—for an appearance in his poem, 'Tunbridge Wells' (ll. 143–8). The climax of their story in *Epsom Wells*—two foolish husbands are eye-witnesses to their own cuckolding by the bravos and then seek revenge for their humiliation—provides the source for the undoing of Poltrot and Saint-André in the last two acts of Lee's play.

20 *the gladiator in the park*: i.e. the statue—much commented-upon—of a naked gladiator in Hyde Park.

The Characters of the Play 3 *Bellamore*: this character, like Jacques, Elianor, Celia, and Irene, is Lee's addition to Lafayette's cast-list.

5 *Saint-André*: in the novel a figure of real political weight, a favourite of the king, and an experienced soldier.

6 *Vidame of Chartres*: 'Vidame', from the Latin 'vice dominus', was in early modern France 'one who held lands from a bishop as his representative and defender in temporal matters' (*OED*).

7 *Poltrot*: not a character in the novel, he owes his name to Jean de Poltrot, a committed Huguenot, who assassinated the Duke of Guise in 1563.

13 *Tournon*: this almost certainly fictitious character plays a very different role in the novel—sexually deceitful, but not a bawd for others nor a political game-player.

14 *Marguerite, [Princess of Jainville]*: Lee interpolates her into the action, assigning to her a set of relationships quite foreign to her historical original. See J. M. Armistead, *Nathaniel Lee* (Boston, 1979), 150–1.

18 *La March*: so-called in the 1679 translation; but Mlle de la Marck in the French text. A minor character in the novel, and not involved in the sexual chicanery which is her lot in Lee.

Prologue [by John Dryden] Although unassigned, this prologue is clearly designed to be spoken by one of the actresses. It was first printed, paired with his epilogue for the play, in Dryden's *Miscellany Poems* (1684). Both prologue and epilogue were presumably spoken at the first performance. Lee did not include them in the 1689 first printing of the play, giving preference to his own prologue and epilogue, presumably composed in anticipation of a hoped-for post-1688 revival.

7 *in mode*: i.e. of the kind that is fashionable.

8 *the very bawd*: i.e. Tournon.

11 *stick at mark*: stay loyal to one woman; but playing on 'mark' as 'target in archery' and hence, in sexual slang, 'female genitalia'.

12 *Some Jew has changed the text*: a playful allusion to contemporary theories that self-interested transcription and translation had affected the biblical text. See, for instance, Christopher Hill, *The World Turned Upside Down: Radical Ideas during the English Revolution* (London, 1972), 208–15.

17 *dipped*: mortgaged; indebted.

18 *pox cant 'em*: i.e. may the pox (syphilis) pay them back for their fancy language (their 'cant') and insulting excuses.

19 *perjuria ridet amantum*: from Tibullus, *Elegies*, III. vi. 49–50, 'perjuria ridet amantum | Juppiter' ('Jupiter laughs at lovers' perjuries'). Ovid echoes Tibullus in *Ars Amatoria*, I. 633.

25 *Achitophel's . . . David*: for Achitophel's participation in Absalom's conspiracy and rebellion against David, see 2 Samuel 15. Dryden had recently deployed the biblical story as a parallel to contemporary politics in *Absalom and Achitophel* (1681).

29 *a-padding*: out hunting, like highwaymen ('padders').

31 *the ready money missing*: i.e. they have no sexual energy left to spend on us.

32 *wink*: turn a blind eye.

33 *sink*: avoid mentioning, conceal. But 'to sink a score' meant, in various card-games, 'to avoid calling a small score in order to mislead an opponent'. Thus, 'sink' cues the gambling terms in the next couplet.

34–5 *renouncing . . . trump our hearts*: 'renouncing' means 'failing to follow suit at cards', so the gallants aren't staying loyal to one love. 'To trump' is 'to play a winning card instead of following suit, thus taking one's opponent's card(s)'. So the women will take the men's jewels, while the latter take the women's hearts.

Prologue 1 *the foremost age*: the earliest times; the Golden Age.

15 *make advantage of the allay*: i.e. derive profit from the impurity.

17–18 *Women turn . . . all the night*: i.e. terror of destitution drives women to make a trade of granting their favours. 'The nightmare, according to one tradition, was a "mare" or hag who rode up and down on the chest of the sleeper, causing him to suffocate or have bad dreams' (Stroup and Cooke).

19 *The little mob, the city waistcoateer*: both 'mob' and 'waistcoateer' are contemporary slang for 'prostitute'.

20–1 *Will pinch . . . her dear*: i.e. pretends extreme poverty, by dressing herself in the skimpiest attire, in order to excite the pity and desire of her customer, and thus to extract both fee and alms.

23 *generous*: the adjective's fundamental meaning in this period is 'nobly born'. It therefore also embraces the range of qualities judged to be appropriate to such birth—hence, here, 'magnanimous, free from mean-spiritedness, un-self-interested'.

24–5 *But there's a monarch . . . poets rhyme*: William III, newly ascended to the English throne at the time of the play's printing.

1.1 S.D. *Fiddles playing*: Theatre musicians often appeared on stage in the Restoration theatre, and this is presumably what happens here. At other points, and in other plays, they played from the pit (alongside the spectators) or from the side box nearest the stage. See Curtis A. Price, *Music in the Restoration Theatre* (Ann Arbor, Mich., 1979), 81–7. In the same book, Price (pp. 213–14) gives information about Thomas Farmer's instrumental music for the play.

2–3 *Prithee . . . time and tune*: Nemours wants the musicians to cease their harmonizing—combining and blending individual parts—and to give him some clear rhythm and melody instead.

3 *eunuch*: i.e. castrato or countertenor.

5 *All other blessings are but toys*: a setting of this song by William Turner was printed in *Choice Ayres and Songs* (1683).

5–6 *toys | To his*: trifles in comparison to his.

7 *fancy*: imagination.

11 *when Adonis got the stone*: Adonis was a beautiful youth adored by Venus, who warned him against hunting lest the wild beasts, her inveterate enemies, struck at her by harming him. Disregarding her advice, Adonis was gored in the groin by a boar and killed. Lee conflates this myth with the parallel Ovidian tale of Endymion, who, allowed by Zeus to choose

his own fate, elected to sleep forever and never grow old. In his sleep, he was visited in each passage of the moon by the goddess Phoebe, his lover. In Lee's revision of the Adonis myth, Adonis experiences a nocturnal agony from a persistent erection comparable to that caused by a gall- or kidney-stone, and Venus, kind as always to lovers' pains, alleviates him without disturbing his sleep.

13 *fancy*: imagination; love, and amorous aspiration.

24 *is a great pretender to nature*: i.e. he is an intellectual fellow-traveller of the sceptical wits of the Restoration in rejecting religion's guidance and instead basing his conduct on the 'light of nature, sense' (John Wilmot, Earl of Rochester, 'A Satyr against Reason and Mankind', l. 13).

26 *grin*: grimace, as with pain, anger or distaste.

30 *dauphin*: the eldest son and heir apparent of the King of France.

32 *the President and Council of Sixteen*: during the French Wars of Religion (1562–98), the Council of Sixteen—so-called because its members were drawn from the sixteen districts of the city of Paris—was the instrument of the radical popular wing of the Catholic League which seized control of Paris between 1588 and 1590. Its meetings figure in Dryden and Lee's *The Duke of Guise*. The events of Lafayette's novel are set between 1558 and 1560; but, although he retains the names of characters apt to the earlier period, Lee often seems to be imagining the action as occurring perhaps a decade or two later.

42–3 *lest ravishing . . . sober design*: he is now so aroused that he threatens—how playfully?—to ravish Bellamore unless he goes on his mission immediately.

50 *the method of the queen*: the 'queen' is Catherine de' Medici (1519–89), wife of Henri II of France (1519–59). In Lafayette's novel the more formidable court politician, at least until the king's death, is his mistress, Diane de Poitiers, to whom Lee makes no reference. Catherine de' Medici is a leading player, however, in both *The Massacre of Paris* and *The Duke of Guise*, which presumably explains Lee's spotlighting of her here also.

51 *fond*: (1) amorously addicted (2) foolish.

56 *contracted to her*: engaged to marry her—in the seventeenth century, a formal commitment from which it was very difficult to withdraw.

62 *who loves him as the queen affects ambition*: whose love for him is as intense as is the queen's ambition.

63–7 *Why thus . . . your part*: laid out as verse in *1689*.

63 *Nemours his soul*: the old form of the possessive, 'Nemours' soul'.

70–1 *in the presence*: at court, in the presence of the king and queen.

88 *flux*: (1) continuous stream; but also playing on (2) continuous discharge (as from the sores caused by venereal disease) and (3) 'flux' meaning as verb 'treat medically, purge'.

112 *at Council*: attending the (royal) Council of State; i.e. engaged in the highest affairs of state.

115 *a serenade*: specifically, a musical salute for newly-weds on the morning after their first night together—a custom so thoroughly established that Samuel Pepys, in a diary entry for 16 February 1667, regarded its omission as 'very mean'.

1.2 S.D. [*The palace of Nemours*]: *1689* marks a new scene here. The action, however, may have been performed in front of the same set of shutters as 1.1, or the latter may have opened to reveal Nemours and Tournon in more intimate circumstances.

10 *pleasantest*: most agreeable; merriest, wittiest.

14 *horrid*: abominable, detestable.

16 *there's it*: i.e. this is all there is to it.

19 *such another man*: one of a kind, a man unlike other men.

38 *big*: pregnant.

44 *of the true breed*: i.e. ripe for seduction, and sexually promising.

46–7 *something extravagant . . . and honour*: the phrasing here is extremely elliptical and may have been foreshortened by a transcription error. But, though cryptic, an actor could render it intelligibly, with 'something extravagant, as thy' meaning 'some extreme or wild action, on which would depend your'.

extravagant: outlandish, fantastic.

57–8 *Luxembourg Garden*: the gardens of the Luxembourg Palace, which were open to the public and a popular place of resort both for the fashionable and aristocratic and for the citizenry.

60 *colours flying*: 'flying colours' are military or naval flags displayed in celebration of victory.

63 *consideration*: i.e. weighing the rights and wrongs.

66 *I must quote Ronsard to punish thee*: a reference to the great 'punishment' sonnet by the sixteenth-century French poet, Pierre de Ronsard, beginning 'Quand vous serez bien vieille, au soir a la chandelle' (When you are very old, at evening by candle-light), in which a woman who has rebuffed him with 'fier desdain' ('proud disdain') is invited to contemplate the regrets which will assail her when 'au foyer une vieille accroupie' ('an old woman squatting by the hearth'). Rochester was reputedly an admirer of Ronsard and imitated several of his works.

67–72 *Call all your wives . . . you are great*: Lee has co-opted and emended a passage from Act 1 of Rochester's revision of Fletcher's Jacobean tragedy, *Valentinian* (*c.*1614), spoken by the predatory, libertine emperor to his male pimps: 'Go call your wives to council and prepare | To tempt, dissemble, promise, fawn and swear. | To make faith look like folly use your skill, | Virtue an ill-bred crossness in the will, | Fame the loose breathings of a clamorous crowd; | Ever in lies most confident and loud, | Honour a notion, piety a cheat. | And if you prove successful bawds, be great' (John Wilmot, Earl of Rochester, *Complete Works*, ed. Frank W. Ellis (Harmondsworth, 1994), 110–11). Though not published until late 1684 or early 1685, a version of Rochester's adaptation was in manuscript circulation by the date of Lee's play.

81–2 *They are turning already*: i.e. they (i.e. the wives) are already inclined towards adultery.

93 *Rosidore*: i.e. John Wilmot, Earl of Rochester, who had died on 26 July 1680. On his significance for the play, see Introduction, pp. xxiii–xxxi.

98–9 *Huddled with worms . . . like other men*: see Introduction, pp. xxv–xxvi.

108 *a hesitation in his speech*: no other surviving contemporary account attributes such 'a hesitation' to Rochester.

110 *affectation*: the variousness of the senses, pejorative and complimentary, in which this word was used in the late seventeenth century makes its meaning here difficult to pin down. It could, for example, mean (1) earnest ambition, striving to achieve a difficult goal; (2) studied and apt display; or (3) hollow simulation. Even with (3), the meaning here could either be that they incompetently impersonate the external features of Rochester's verse or that they accurately imitate its shallowest characteristics.

120–1 *leaving the court . . . learn breeding*: the *ne plus ultra* of folly, for the French court was then esteemed the fount and arbiter of taste and style, while the English laboured to imitate it.

131 *second him*: take his part; assist him in duels.

142 *a bill . . . weekly cuckolds*: the weekly 'bills of mortality' were published returns of all deaths occurring in the parishes in and around London. Similar statistics of births and baptisms were also gathered.

145–8 *with the wits? . . . sworn brothers*: Poltrot is being made to display his hapless ignorance. The wits moved in court circles and would have regarded the Lord Mayor and his fellow legislators of the city as totally antipathetic. The 'Common Council' was the Corporation of London's legislature and was, in fact, often at odds with the Lord Mayor and Court of Alderman, who exercised a right of veto over its acts.

152–3 *'O to bed . . . to me, &c.'*: this is the opening line of the refrain from a ballad popular in the 1670s, '[The Lass of] Cumberland, or Love in Abundance'. The ballad begins 'There was a Lass in Cumberland, | a bonny Lass of high degree'. The refrain is: 'O, to bed to me, to bed to me, | the Lass that comes to bed to me; | Blith and bonny may she be, | the Lass that comes to bed to me'. See Simpson, pp. 424–7. Poltrot's authorship claim is therefore blatantly fraudulent.

158 *'Give me . . . country-bred'*: another fragment from a popular ballad. See Simpson, pp. 378–9 and 131.

165 *as wanton . . . boar-pig*: i.e. as sexually arousable or voracious as a young boar. Cf. Shakespeare's *2 Henry IV*, where Doll Tearsheet calls Falstaff 'Thou whoreson little tidy Bartholomew boar-pig' (2.4.232–3). Pig was the prime delicacy sold at Bartholomew Fair, held in London annually on 24 August.

173 *Philomel's*: i.e. the nightingale's.

178 S.D. *without his hat and wig*: an indication of his impetuous excitement at the prospect of the serenade.

184 *put my hand in*: set or started me singing; got me excited

187–8 *their dying from my killing*: he is alluding to the numerous Restoration lyrics which play on the sexual meaning of 'to die'—i.e. 'to reach sexual climax'.

190 *impertinent*: meddling with something (i.e. song-writing) which is beyond you; behaving with insufficient respect to your superior (Nemours).

191–2 *my character . . . wit and sense*: i.e. the poets will choose me as the model for a character-sketch of a man of wit and sense.

197 *as round as a hoop*: i.e. (of his similes) with perfect symmetrical aptness. The phrase is proverbial (Tilley H593).

203–4 *the great Turk . . . St Denis's Gate*: the 'Great Turk' was the Ottoman Sultan in Constantinople. St Denis's gate was the principal northern entrance to Paris. In 1683 a Turkish army reached—and was defeated at—the gates of Vienna.

204 *Orpheus*: in Greek mythology, the supreme musician.

206 *'When Phoebus had fetched, &c.'*: we haven't discovered a ballad with this opening. Simpson (p. 197), however, lists one beginning 'When Phoebus addres'd [*or* had drest] his course to the West', which includes the refrain, 'O do not, do not kill me yet, | For I am not prepared to die'—a couplet which chimes neatly with Poltrot's remark at ll. 187–8 above.

1.3 SONG: this is the promised 'serenade' (1.1.115 and note) and is presumably performed from offstage as the scene-change occurs.

5 *remove*: stir again, become ready for action again.

7 *love, the little scout*: Cupid, with his bow and arrows, is 'the little scout' or spy.

16 *cry*: 'try' (*1689*).

18 *the queen dauphin*: an Englishing of 'la Reine Dauphine', the title held at this time (as wife to the dauphin) by Mary Stuart, future Queen of Scots (1542–87), a significant figure in Lafayette's novel.

19 *own it on occasion*: claim it as your own when occasion calls. In the novel, the letter is the Vidame's, though Nemours is suspected of having written it.

19–20 *I shall put upon your person*: I shall assert to be yours, or done by you.

24–5 *No more . . . own it*: 'No more, But this remember that, you own it' (*1689*).

30 *Good-morrow, my good lord*: *1689* follows this with 'Save you my dear Nemours!'; but it has already provided an exit for Nemours at l. 25 above. No further dialogue is assigned to him in this scene, and it seems uncharacteristic for him to remain silent throughout another display of idiocy from Saint-André and Poltrot. Presumably Lee nodded for a moment, forgetting that he had already removed Nemours.

33 S.D. *three fingers*: Saint-André is signalling how many times he imagines the newly-weds have made love during the night. Poltrot immediately outbids him.

42 *tournament*: a military sport, in which combatants engaged in single combat or in troops, mainly on horseback.

    the great horse: i.e. the kind of exceptionally large and powerful horse which was trained for use in battle or tournament.

53 *out*: (1) in error, adrift from the truth; (2) nonplussed.

56 *colours*: either 'make-up' or 'shades of clothing'.

66 *Chartres*: i.e. the Princess, who before her marriage was Mlle de Chartres.

83 *when the princess led you to the altar*: a mysterious figure, about whom the play provides no further information. No princess leads her to the altar in the novel.

93 *clear*: transparent.

96 *the god*: Cupid.

97 *stygian oaths*: inviolable oaths, such as the gods swear by the river Styx, one of the rivers of Hades.

100 *conscious*: i.e. which makes her feel guilty.

116 *gall*: rancour, asperity of feeling.

121 *riot'st*: 'riotests' (*1689*).

126 *For the great care you wish*: i.e. in exchange for the great responsibility you invite me to undertake.

127 *insensible*: unresponsive, incapable of feeling.

153 *wait you here again*: return to attend upon you here.

168–9 *The sister . . . her for Savoy*: 'Henry' is Henri II, King of France. His 'sister' is Marguérite de France (1523–74), who married Emmanuel-Philibert, Duke of Savoy, in 1559. In Lafayette's novel the Vidame's covert entanglements are numerous and intricate, but do not involve Marguérite de France.

176 *engaged so high*: involved in a relationship with a woman of such high birth.

182 S.D. [*The Princess . . . to Nemours*]: *1689* has 'Enter Iren.' at this point, but provides no earlier exit for her. We have assumed that she remains onstage throughout, but different performance versions are clearly possible.

2.1 [*The Court*]. This editorial scene location is especially speculative; but the scene seems to require a location other than those used elsewhere in the play, and Tournon opens it by speaking about the reverberations of her manœuvres in the Court.

6 *takes the queen*: entertains, amuses, the queen.

15 *design*: 'a scheme formed to the detriment of another' (Samuel Johnson's *Dictionary*); a plan of attack on someone else.

16 S.D. [*followed by*] *the Vidame*: *1689* printed 'The Vidam.' bracketed in the right margin at the end of l. 17, 'apparently to indicate that he stays to one side of the stage' (Stroup and Cooke).

32 *By all extremes*: in the utmost degree.

34 S.D. *Enter Tournon*: Stroup and Cooke emended this, the reading of those copies of *1689* containing this passage (see following note), to '*Tournon comes forward*', arguing that Tournon's earlier 'Be gone, while I attend the business here' indicates that at that point she 'retires back stage to over-hear the conversation of Nemours and Marguerite'. This is an eminently playable possibility, but so also is the sequence of action suggested by *1689*'s direction, which we therefore retain.

31–8 *Hear, hear him, heaven . . . appointed some ladies*: these lines appear in some copies of *1689* and not others. The textual situation is tangled and has been authoritatively mapped by Fredson Bowers, 'A Crux in the Text of Lee's *Princess of Cleve* (1689)', *Harvard Library Bulletin*, 4 (1950), 409–11.

44 *spleen*: i.e. disabling rage.

49 *a lover*: a suitor, a wooer.

53 *prince*: the dauphin.

57 *curb my will*: control my rage (in favour of calm plotting); cf. l. 56.

2.2.9 *Take no notice, and repeat verses*: Poltrot is stealing a trick from Dorimant in Sir George Etherege's *The Man of Mode* (1676). See, for example, 3.3.192–6 in Etherege, *Plays*, ed. Michael Cordner (Cambridge, 1982), 277.

16–17 *What, does ... little ease?*: 'What does the Maggot bite, you must be jogging from this place of little Ease?' (*1689*).

21 *tricing your curls*: i.e. toying with your wig.

24 *amarum*: probably sweet marjoram, whose other names included amarcus and marum (John Gerard, *The Herbal or General History of Plants* (London, 1633), ch. 217). Gerard lists it as 'a remedy against cold diseases of the braine and head, being taken any way to your best liking; put up into the nosthrils it provoketh sneesing, and draweth forth much baggage flegme' (p. 665). Saint-André presumably pauses in mid-sentence to inflict a dose on himself.

31 *there I was with her*: i.e. in that sally I was a match for her, scored off her.

34 *misses*: kept mistresses.

37 *bustle below*: busy herself downstairs—i.e. not in the bedroom—about her household duties.

61 *a breathing*: (1) a chance to snatch a breath; (2) some vigorous exercise.

70 *compass*: (1) besiege; (2) embrace.

71–2 *as one key unlocks all doors at court*: the Lord Chamberlain received a key on appointment, which at any rate symbolized his right and power to enter all the court's chambers.

80 *cuckolds*: 'cuckold' (*1689*).

countenanced: (1) brazen; (2) affecting the appearance and manners of genuine libertines; (3) permitted on sufferance to associate with their betters.

97 *debauchees*: 'debauches' (*1689*).

99 *orange-wench*: a woman who sold oranges and other refreshments in the playhouse; regarded as easily available to men who wanted sex.

110 *Potiphar's wife of mine*: for the attempted seduction of Joseph by Potiphar's wife and its aftermath, see Genesis 39: 7–20.

110–11 *Pharaoh's lean kine*: see the description of Pharaoh's dream in Genesis 41: 17–21.

116 *Tantalus*: in Greek mythology, a Lydian king who was punished by the gods for revealing their secrets. He suffered the agonies of thirst, hunger, and unfulfilled anticipation through being placed within sight of food and water, but not being suffered to reach and consume them.

130–1 *you are ... farther about*: i.e. you are a more subtle plotter and wish to take a more indirect revenge.

135 *ramble about*: see *SF*, 5.1.33 and note.

136 *intriguing*: carrying on sexual intrigues, or secret love-affairs.

142 *her secret*: i.e. that she can keep secrets.

143 *Florence bawd*: Tournon is an agent of Catherine de'Medici, who was a Florentine. But Elianor's remark is probably mainly prompted by the conventional association of the major cities of Italy with sexual corruption.

158 *Cynthia*: the goddess of the moon—Diana or Artemis—who was the protectress of women.

164 *catch him by the forelock*: i.e. seize the present moment (with a play on 'foreskin'). Time is traditionally represented as bald, but with a lock of hair on his forehead, by which—if one acts very quickly—he may be detained.

166 *love like a sparrow*: see *SF*, 4.1.170 and note.

173 *vaults*: (1) makes athletic leaps; (2) mounts sexually.

176 *glasses*: looking-glasses, mirrors.

china-dishes: these had notoriously been rendered sexually emblematic in William Wycherley's *The Country Wife* (1675), 4.3.

177 *closest*: most secret.

180 *powder*: gunpowder.

187 *double-tongued English kiss*: i.e. what in England would be called a French kiss.

194 *distresses*: (1) self-prostration (in love-grief); (2) pressing solicitations.

195 *a quilt imperial*: an emperor's bed.

2.3.2 *my Hephaestion, my Ganymede!*: Hephaestion was a Macedonian general, the intimate friend of Alexander the Great. For Ganymede, see the note to *SF*, 1.1.210.

18–19 *your bawd-barber or bawd-surgeon*: both these coinages play on 'barber-surgeon', the contemporary practitioner whose skills were especially devoted to the treatment of venereal diseases. Among his activities was the use of 'plasters'—poultices—to staunch and heal discharges from sores caused by these diseases. Similarly, Tournon 'plasters' Nemours 'every day with new wenches' (ll. 19–20 below).

21 *termagants*: 'termagant' (*1689*).

27 *Jove and Europa*: Jove assumed the form of a white bull in order to have his way with Europa.

38–9 *Father Patrick*: although the play is set in France, the symbolic Catholic priest appears to be an Irish papist, though the well-known Anglican preacher, Simon Patrick, had been one of Rochester's targets in his 'Satire against Reason and Mankind' (l. 74) and contemporary audiences might well also have thought of him at this point.

55 *pretty entertainment*: agreeable party or meal.

57–8 *full pop*: instantaneously.

70 *points and tags*: i.e. allegedly witty aphorisms and stale quotations.

76 *a pompous state*: a solemn and splendid appearance.

87 *look my troubles*: i.e. by observing the reflection in the water of her care-worn face.

93 *as*: as if.

101 *To which*: in comparison to which.

108 S.D. *[The Prince . . . embraces her]*: *1689* simply has 'Rise.' here.

132 *My mother's death-bed counsel*: the Princess's mother is a formidable presence in Lafayette's novel. She assiduously educates her daughter in the perils of love, 'the little Sincerity and Candor there is in Man', and 'the Happiness and Tranquility that attends a Vertuous Wife' (p. 15). On her deathbed, aware of the Princess's feelings for Nemours, she tells her, 'You must needs be sensible, that you are upon the point of the Precipice', and urges her to 'Reflect upon the Duty you owe your Husband, and forget not also that that's due to me'. She also advises flight from the Court: 'Desire your Husband to take you thence. Fear not to pursue those Paths which at first may seem hard and uneasie to you. How unpleasant soever they may appear to you in the beginning, you will find more sweetness in them in the end, than in the Vanities of the Court' (p. 67).

145 *Speak home and fly not wide*: speak frankly and do not be evasive.

157 *thy creature*: your puppet, at your total command.

157–8 *mould me, | Thy cringing, crawling slave*: 'mould me | Thy cringing crawling Slave' (*1689*).

185–6 *confessing. | His name?*: 'for confessing | His name——' (*1689*).

217 *quarry*: hunted animal.

219–20 *let it come, | The worst can happen*: i.e. let the worst that can happen occur.

224 *out-of-the-way business*: 'out of the way of bus'ness' (*1689*).

226 *the flag's held out*: cf. 1.2.60.

234 *carriage*: conduct, behaviour.

236–8 *she cuckolds . . . in Christendom*: i.e. she is within her rights to cuckold him, and he has as a consequence no grounds on which to institute legal proceedings against her; and the truth of what I say will be confirmed by any bawd in Christendom.

245 *Your servant, sir*: the Vidame is declining the invitation. He had originally thought that Nemours was asking him to be his second in a duel, not to act as his partner in a love-intrigue.

247–8 *an you go to that*: i.e. if that is how you wish to play it.

252–7 *Stand, sir . . . her pleasure*: 'stand', for Marguerite, means 'halt' (as if she were a highwayman commanding his victim); but Nemours uses it to mean 'have an erection'. Similarly, by 'fall to', she intends 'eagerly make love to', whereas, in his reply, he affects to take it as having simply meant 'kneel before'.

262 *how pat she hits me*: how exactly she predicts my moves.

266 *an you go to that*: i.e. if that is the topic you want us to explore.

270 *then I'm sure of thee*: he is smugly confident that, if they once make love, she will be devotedly his.

273 *cork and feathers*: either (1) men are as light and unstable as cork or feathers, or (2) the man is like the cork and the woman like the feathers, and both are fickle and unreliable.

274–6 *Make . . . in Christendom*: i.e. 'cork and feathers' together 'make a shuttlecock', an apt simile for a woman, as the 'battledore' is for a man. Nemours then boasts that he can keep a shuttlecock/woman in energetic play as long as any man in Christendom.

281–7 *primed . . . go off*: a series of sexual double meanings based on terms from musketry. Thus, 'primed and charged' means 'loaded with gunpowder and a bullet', and 'cocked' 'erected the hammer, preparatory to its release by the trigger'. Once the trigger is pressed, the priming, held in the pan, explodes ('the pan flashed'), and the bullet is then discharged ('I go off').

3.1.5–6 *admire in his temper*: wonder at in his temperament or mood.

15 *forked in the book of fate*: predestined to be cuckolded.

18 *to choose*: in preference.

nice and precise: prim and puritanical.

35–6 *an ambassador's merit*: monarchs customarily bestowed gifts—jewels, works of art, etc.—on ambassadors at the end of their embassies.

38 *sex*: nature, kind.

contain: restrain herself, repress her feelings.

46 *running over me*: i.e. devouring me at once.

52–3 *a devil incarnate*: a devil who has assumed human shape.

54 *you make me*: 'I make me' (*1689*).

57 *I shall not hold*: I will not be able to contain my anger.

60 *with the best of my blood*: diabolic compacts were traditionally sealed in blood. But Nemours is punning. Semen was believed to contain blood.

71 *head*: wig.

79 *runners-at-all*: women who undiscriminatingly pursue any available man; possibly, prostitutes.

82 *acting*: freedom of demeanour.

conversation: sexual intercourse.

87–8 *have with you at all adventures*: i.e. I'll pursue you whatever may come of it.

90 *herself so close*: her identity concealed.

92 *MARGUERITE*: *1689* assigns the speech to Tournon.

93 *racks of woman's wits*: i.e. everything that tortures a woman's mind. 'women's' (*1689*).

103 *let him know*: perhaps 'let him have sex with me'. It may, however, also mean 'reveal to him who I am'—i.e. her first plan climaxes here, but she then thinks of a more elaborate plot, which she outlines in the following lines.

107 *extorted gallantry*: i.e. she will manœuvre him, as part of his courtship of her in her disguise, into reviling his previous lover, herself.

114 *task then. When*: 'task, then when' (*1689*).

130 *in masquerade*: in masked disguise.

134 *fury*: i.e. inspired frenzy or extreme passion, as of one inspired by the gods.

138 *house*: 'a sign of the zodiac considered as the seat of the greatest influence of a particular planet' (*OED*)—here, Venus—over a specific individual's life.

138–9 *Thus sung Rosidore in the urn*: see Introduction, pp. xxvi–xxvii.

144–5 *no drop of blood*: see note to l. 60 above.

158 *have 'em in the wind*: are on their scent.

162 *I am that I am*: 'I am, that I am' (*1689*).

164–9 *broadside . . . sister*: a series of sexual double meanings from the vocabulary of naval combat. Thus, 'broadside' means 'the simultaneous discharge of all the cannon on one side of a ship', while the heaviest guns were placed on the 'lower tier' or decks. The most dangerous place for a ship to be holed is 'between wind and water', i.e. in the part of the hull only exposed above water under pressure of the wind; while 'chain-shot' was a charge of two cannon-balls fastened together by a chain.

192 *little Rosamond*: his re-christening of her derives from Rosamond Clifford, the poisoned mistress of Henry II, who was the target of the jealousy of Henry's wife, Eleanor—hence his promise to preserve her 'from my jealous Elianor'.

207 *turn*: turn sour.

214 *Are they . . . sister?*: (1) Have they not paid us back thoroughly, sister? (2) Haven't they treated us justly?

216–19 *Mine 'noints herself . . . teats in the wrong place*: witches were supposed to anoint themselves in order to fly to their sabbat, while leaving a simulacrum in their husband's bed. The extra teats were for their diabolic familiars and the Devil.

225 *a long black thing*: i.e. the priest who conducted the marriage ceremony.

227 *Put the question*: just suppose; but what if.

242 *a horned beast*: i.e. a cuckold.

247 *breeze*: gadfly, which makes horses and cattle restive and inclined to bolt.

260 *endure all jerks . . . shirt up*: endure all blows like a schoolboy stripped for flogging.

274–5 *What a gentle . . . and airy!*: 'What a genteel countenance!' 'How handsome and vivacious!'

287 *cast*: i.e. whom you have discarded.

290 *fancy*: i.e. mode of disguise.

292 *the dumb man, the highlander*: the Scottish highlanders were reputed to possess divinatory, telepathic, and prophetic powers. The reference here, however, sounds specific and immediately contemporary; but we have been unable to identify a likely candidate.

297 *glancing*: 'glanting' (*1689*).

302 *in a corner*: see note to *SF*, 3.1.124.

304 *divorce*: i.e. separation from bed and board, without right to remarry.

305 *the flying label*: i.e. the legal document on which the charges against her are itemized, and which will henceforth therefore 'label' her. 'Flying' presumably means 'fluttering (as it is brandished)' and 'circulating her ill reputation'.

306 *the Whore of Babel*: the Whore of Babylon, as described in Revelation 17: 3–6, was 'arrayed in purple and scarlet colour, and decked with gold and precious stones and pearls, having a golden cup in her hand full of abominations and filthiness of her fornication. And upon her forehead was a name written, MYSTERY, BABYLON THE GREAT, THE MOTHER OF HARLOTS AND ABOMINATIONS OF THE EARTH'.

3.2.13 *the Chevalier de Guise*: in Lafayette's novel Cleves's unsuccessful rival for the Princess's hand, and an astute observer of Nemours's fixation on her.

24–5 *bears the palm . . . of the field*: exceeds in reputation and prestige the generals who command in the field.

35 *not*: 'no' (*1689*).

52 *poise*: counterbalance, match.

63 *mortal*: death-dealing.

78 *nice*: fastidious, scrupulous.

87 *fame*: reputation.

94 S.D. *Enter the Prince of Cleves*: 'Enter Princess C.' (*1689*).

97 *still*: always; enduringly.

113 *yet to seek*: not yet discovered.

113–14 *He will not . . . at names*: he won't admit he is one of the people involved; he names no names.

116 *posted*: literally, announced in a bill stuck on a post; i.e. the common talk of the town.

136 *charm*: i.e. deceive or dupe, as if by magic.

154 *this ought not to be thine*: i.e. you don't deserve this treatment.

160 *It scents too far*: i.e. your treachery is so gross as to be unmistakable.

171 *my pomp of ease*: 'Pomp' here means 'vain show' or 'empty enactment'. She cannot anticipate ever attaining true peace again.

4.1 S.D. *Music, songs, maskers, &c.*: The masquerade is in full swing, as the opening stage picture makes clear. The festivities continue throughout the scene, and other maskers than the named main characters are required onstage at ll. 29 ff. and for the dance at l. 152 and might perhaps circulate at other points also.

S.D. *with music*: i.e. accompanied by musicians.

6–7 *make him a monster*: see note to *SF*, 2.1.38.

29 *my aim*: i.e. my skill as hunter—and as lover.

S.D. *in the habit of a Huguenot*: Huguenots do not appear to have adopted a distinctive style of dress. Lee probably supposed them to be the French equivalent of English Puritans, at least as represented in popular caricature: Tournon's costume is therefore severely plain, decorous, and drab.

31 *Have I the forward*: 'Have I? For the forward' (*1689*). The *1689* reading is puzzling and seems to require emendation. The one we offer proposes that Nemours is asking himself whether the masked woman who made the appointment is among the company on stage.

33 *ejaculation*: playing its sexual against its religious meaning: a short prayer offered hastily to God.

37–9 *Ah, thou unclean person . . . be found?*: pseudo-biblical language. The whole exchange is a parody of Puritan cant.

39–40 *the Philistines*: one of the ancient peoples of south-west Palestine, enemies of the Israelites.

43–4 *Delilah*: a daughter of the Philistines, the paramour and betrayer of Samson (Judges 16).

48 *the lewd orange-women*: see note to *PC*, 2.2.99.

58 *loves her neighbour as herself*: a mischievous misapplication of Jesus's commandment, as in Luke 10:27.

60 MARGUERITE: this speech, and the next two given to Marguerite in this edition, are assigned by *1689* to Celia.

74 *second-sight*: the ability to perceive absent or future things and persons as if they were present to the senses.

75 *so exactly*: 'exactly' (*1689*).

78 *a trunk*: a speaking-tube.

82 *criss-cross-row*: Christ-cross-row—the alphabet, so called from the figure of a cross prefixed to it in children's primers.

88 *impertinences thereunto belonging*: playing on the legal formula of 'appurtenances thereunto belonging'.

95 *In nomine domini bomine*: 'In nomine domini' means 'in the name of the Lord'. It was a customary opening for wills and ending for prayers. 'Bomine' is mere jingling gobbledegook.

99 *cornutoes*: cuckolds. *1689* has 'cornutors' (i.e. cuckold-makers), which seems inappropriate to the context.

102 *Messalinas*: Messalina was the wife of the Roman Emperor Claudius, a furious nymphomaniac and a byword for immorality.

104 *neighing*: 'weighing' (*1689*).

107 *take air*: become public knowledge.

111 *Jezebel*: a wicked and shameless woman; the wife of King Ahab, who suffered the fate Poltrot imagines for his wife (2 Kings 9: 31–7).

122–3 *are all fish downward*: i.e. are totally libidinous. (A 'fishmonger' was, for instance, slang for 'a pimp'.)

123 *Lot's wife is fresh to you*: Lot's daughters slept with their father and might therefore be represented as emblems of wantonness. His wife was apparently a respectable woman, whose sole recorded mistake was to look back towards their lost estate as the family fled from the doomed city of Sodom, for which she was turned into a pillar of salt. Since one meaning of 'salt' is 'lewd, lascivious', perhaps for Poltrot she has become a monumental figure of slakeless salaciousness. ('To you' means 'compared to you'.)

131 *beetle to drive him*: mallet to drive the wedge.

135 *Are you not fitted finely?*: haven't you met your match? Haven't you got exactly what you deserved?

161 *fitted*: punished.

171 *no smelling art*: i.e. she uses no perfumes.

178 *canopies*: 'canopies' here means 'hangings over a bed'—i.e. Nemours expects not just comfort, but the best of furnishings.

207 *Not but I'll*: although I will also.

214 *drudging*: see note to *SF*, 1.1.35.

216 *ramble*: see note to *SF*, 5.1.33.

220 *creation*: power to mould, imaginative art.

238 *crosses*: thwartings, vexations.

243 *obstructions at the waters*: inability to pass urine.

247 *the new-found lock*: presumably a device to gag the victim; or, perhaps, some state-of-the-art chastity belt.

253–4 *such as . . . me to her*: *1689* has 'such as if I fain not, the Princess of Cleve may fix me to her', which is certainly playable. But another, and to us marginally more plausible, reading would treat 'the Princess of Cleve' as the object of 'gain not', and that is how we have punctuated it here.

271–2 *her that gave Actaeon horns*: the huntsman Actaeon surprised the goddess Diana bathing; she changed him into a stag, and he was torn to pieces by his own hounds.

284 *a parting blow*: the apt meaning of 'parting' is 'dying'; so, via the familiar pun on 'dying', 'parting blow' means 'thrust which triggers orgasm'.

297 *Guide him the perfect temper of yourselves*: grant him the perfect combination of temperament which is the prerogative of a god.

302 *kindly*: with perfect naturalness.

341 *conjure*: here accented on the second syllable (as also at 5.3.106).

374 *suit*: petitioning, urging.

381 *Not but*: i.e. although.

382 *as clear from me*: as undefiled by any action of mine.

393 *there's something rises here*: i.e. the Prince is suffering *tremor cordis*, a heart seizure.

394 *I'll wait you home*: I'll assist you to your home.

401 *spleen the gall-less turtle*: i.e. make even the gentlest of creatures—the turtle-dove—venomous with fury.

4.2.3 *agreed upon the writings*: literally, agreed upon the marriage settlement; but here, conspired together to commit adultery.

4 *with a witness*: 'and no mistake'; you can rely on me (playing on signing as a witness to 'the writings').

9 *the main*: the main chance, the chief objective.

10 *presents her*: gives her gifts.

11–13 *when the business . . . his footmen*: discarded by the lord, she survives by selling her favours to his servants.

15 *have it out of her*: get his money's worth from her.

17 *speaker*: orator; but probably, also, the MP with this title who in the House of Commons presides over debates.

19–20 *satis . . . non satis . . . nunquam . . . ignoramus*: respectively, 'sufficient', 'not sufficient', 'by no means sufficient', 'we take no notice of it'—the verdicts a grand jury could pronounce on the evidence for prosecution in the indictments presented to it. The fact that the jury returns a verdict the judge ('his lordship') did not invite cues us to the contemporary allusion. In the final stages of the Exclusion Crisis, Whig grand juries, as at the trial of Shaftesbury in November 1681, frustrated the prosecutions of several major Whig figures by bringing in *ignoramus* verdicts.

30 *I have plover in reserve*: i.e. I have more exquisite fare waiting for me to feast on.

34 *be branched*: i.e. have cuckold's horns bestowed on it.

36–7 *take a jump or practise on the high rope*: i.e. the sleeping Saint-André is stretching and straining as if he were an acrobat or tightrope-walker.

39 *as many bobs . . . 'Poor jack!'*: Democritus, the laughing—or scoffing—philosopher of Abdera (*c.*460–357 BC), mocked and made fun of humankind's invincible follies. 'Bobs' are 'taints, gibes, bitter jests', and a contemporary slang meaning of 'jack' was 'fool'.

40–3 *There's more pride . . . they'll do 'em*: it was a commonplace allegation that the Puritans' humility was merely an affectation of it; as also that the courtiers were the natural predators of—and irresistible to—the wives of the citizenry.

48 *Here's*: here I am.

52 *Confess, and you know what follows*: cf. the proverbial 'Confess and be hanged' (Tilley C587).

86–7 *the plagues of Egypt*: see Exodus 7–12.

88 *tiresome*: fatiguing, troublesome—i.e. her gallant wants to make love again.

94 *'Alloo*: an elided form of 'halloo'—a loud, prolonged cry, to attract attention. *1689* has 'Allo'.

102–3 *your heifer's a-ploughing*: your wife's copulating.

108 S.D. *with Elianor and Celia*: i.e. at the same time as the ladies (but, presumably, not from the same direction).

128 *crocodile*: i.e. hypocrite. Crocodiles were reputed to shed tears over their prey while devouring it.

4.3.9 *throw boldly . . . if I can*: i.e. bravely risk everything on a single throw of the dice and, if I can, win all the money on the table.

15 *the precise*: the morally austere; the Puritan.

19 *cast the dapper cloak*: cast off their finical (dis)guise.

21 *face him*: keep my eye on him.

4.4.1 *Lovely Selina, innocent and free*: *1689* gives no indication as to whether or not the singer and musicians were expected to be onstage. The setting, by John Blow, was published in *Choice Ayres and Songs* (London, 1683), 28–9.

5 *envious*: malicious.

15 *again*: in return.

31 *the remedy of love*: i.e. how to cure (and end) your love.

43–4 *Yet what can . . . shroud?*: i.e. what use are the warnings?

58 S.D. *above*: see note to *SF*, 4.3 initial S.D.

69 S.D. *[Kneels before her]*: it is unclear when Nemours should rise again—perhaps not until the Princess commands his departure at ll. 87–9 below.

97 *let*: stop, prevent.

5.1.4 *Harebrain*: (1) fool; but also (2), since 'hare' was slang for 'whore', sexually addicted.

10 *Trojan race*: i.e. the British, whose ancestors were—according to a popular myth—refugees from Troy.

18 *hot-cockles*: 'a rustic game in which one player lay face downward, or knelt down with his eyes covered, and being struck by the others in turn, guessed who struck him' (*OED*). Poltrot, however, is also thinking of another kind of close bodily contact. The slang meaning of 'cockles' was 'female genitalia'.

19 *of custom*: merely customary, therefore unobjectionable.

21 *'Noli me tangere'*: derived from a Latin motto, 'Noli me tangere quia Caesaris sum' ('Do not touch me, because I am Caesar's'), supposed to have been inscribed on the collars of Caesar's hinds. Poltrot is suffering imperial delusions.

28 CELIA. . . *you fly*: 'Seek, *Celia*, not to shun me, for where'er you fly' (*1689*).

38 *a noseless whore*: venereal disease could corrode, sometimes even efface, the sufferer's nose.

39 *so she*: as long as she.

45 *mere*: unadulterated, perfect.

52 *Flesh of my flesh*: see Genesis 2: 24.

59 *Goody*: short for 'goodwife', a polite form of address to the mistress of a household, here used scornfully.

59 *Bathsheba*: the wife of Uriah the Hittite, seduced by King David, who arranged for her husband's death (2 Samuel 2: 2–27).

63 *like a full-acorned boar . . . and mounted*: a recollection, with the genders reversed, of Posthumus's anguished imagining of his wife's presumed adultery in Shakespeare's *Cymbeline* (2.5.15–17): 'Perchance he spoke not, but | Like a full-acorned boar, a German one, | Cried "O!" and mounted'.

66 *carted bawd*: see note to *WE*, 2.1.33.

69–70 *the confines of our benevolence*: i.e. from my good will; beyond the bounds of my charity. Poltrot is affecting the royal plural.

71 *before the Vidame here?*: but the Vidame is not onstage. Is she threatening to call the Vidame to be a witness? We have no sure answer to this puzzle.

73 *post thee*: i.e. proclaim you as an adulteress. See also note to *PC*, 3.2.116.

79 *cormorant of cormorants*: these sea birds were proverbially regarded as insatiable.

84 *run his fortune*: shared his lot—in particular, here, his property and income.

86 *in mortuis et in limbo patrum*: 'among the dead and in limbo'. The 'limbo patrum' is that part of the borderline of Hell assigned to the righteous who died before Christ's revelation—a melancholy place, but without burning pitchforks.

91 *son of Belial*: i.e. personification of evil. The phrase is biblical in origin, as, for example, in Judges 19: 22.

105 *Mephistopheles*: the devil who, in the story of Doctor Faustus, secured the latter's damnation.

111–12 *if they had seen . . . to pot too*: i.e. Poltrot's 'smock-face'—here, one rendered bloodless through fear—makes him so like a woman that he would have been raped too. ('To go to pot' meant 'to be cut in pieces like meat for the pot' and therefore 'to be destroyed or ruined'.)

119 *use that exercise*: are accustomed to that kind of sexual licence.

122–3 *like the Indian wives . . . not outlive thee*: as in the custom of suttee, i.e. the burning of the living widow with the corpse of her husband, as practised by certain castes among the Hindus.

129 *All flesh is grass*: 1 Peter 1: 24.

139–40 *the man in the almanac*: almanacs offered detailed advice and commentary on matters marital and sexual. Many were particularly exercised by the promiscuity of women and the unfaithfulness of wives. See Bernard Capp, *Astrology and the Popular Press: English Almanacs 1500–1800* (London, 1979), 112–26.

140 *hold the door*: i.e. act as pimp.

5.2.3–4 *always in a milk diet . . . Florentine mother!*: in Lafayette's novel, the dauphin 'had not his health' (p. 55), but it is Lee's addition to allege that this is caused by a syphilitic inheritance from Catherine de'Medici.

16–17 *by the way of consolation*: i.e. to offer condolences to her for her husband's death (though also playing on the idea of 'offering sexual consolation').

30 *lay the dauphin in her dish*: accuse her of sexual dealings with the dauphin.

nose her in the tiptoe of her pride: smell her out at the height of her sexual excitement ('pride' = 'sexual desire, esp. in a female animal' (*OED*, *sb*, 8b).

33 *Petronius*: the Roman sensualist of the time of Nero, who committed suicide by opening his veins and bleeding slowly to death, while discoursing with his friends on light and trifling topics. He was a character in Lee's first play, *Nero*.

38 *The Princess . . . found her fury*: i.e. her discovery that the Princess of Cleves is her real rival has unlocked her fury.

5.3 S.D. *at the state*: this could mean that the body of the Prince of Cleves is lying in state—i.e. ceremoniously exposed to view before interment. But the Princess's later reference to 'this dear remembrancer of Cleves' (l. 88) suggests that 'the state' is, instead, some form of monument to him.

1 *Weep, all ye nymphs, your floods unbind*: in *1689*, this song is printed separately before the play; but it is inserted here in later editions. The setting, by John Blow, was published in *The Theater of Music* (London, 1685), 46–7.

2 *Strephon's*: Strephon was a name Rochester had used in several of his own love poems—both as a spokesman for the ardour of devoted, unrequited love (as in 'A Pastoral Dialogue between Alexis and Strephon') and as an exponent of a debonair erotic inconstancy (as in 'A Dialogue between Strephon and Daphne'). It was also used as a name for Rochester himself in a number of the elegies published after his death. (See, for example, David Farley-Hills (ed.), *Rochester: The Critical Heritage* (London, 1972), 101–4 and 115.) The Princess's mourning for her husband is thus ambiguously interlaced with her grief for the feelings Nemours has aroused in her.

11 *sworn by Styx*: see note to *PC*, 1.3.97.

33 *burden*: (1) refrain; (2) chief theme, leading idea; (3) onerous weight borne.

49 *I find it here*: see note to *PC*, 4.1.393.

50–1 *those violent means . . . my soul*: suicides were, according to Christian doctrine, excluded from salvation.

59 *luckless*: (1) hapless; but also (2) ill-omened.

69   *temper*: self-restraint, self-control.

87   *entertain you*: receive you, converse with you.

94   *the quickenings*: the vivifying onset.

95   *Nor feared him then*: Nor did I then fear Cupid.

104   *discovery*: revelation.

108   *Not but I always vowed*: i.e. which in no ways alters my vow.

117   *as a pest*: either 'as from the plague', or 'as if it were infected with the plague'.

121   *more particularly that of you*: i.e. especially not (think) of you.

128   *without the consequence*: unspecified; but presumably Nemours is to understand something like 'being banished forever from my presence'.

145   *engagement*: coming to an agreement; marrying.

146   *chimera*: a fabulous monster, with a lion's head, a serpent's tail, and a goat's body; hence, a wild and fantastic notion—an idea repeated below in 'the stalking nothing' and 'the bladdered air'.

150   *hurl him to the beam*: i.e. vastly outweigh him.

161   *from*: 'for' (*1689*).

163   *censuring*: judging (not necessarily hostilely).

168   *a sense too nice*: i.e. an appetite too attuned to new sensations.

169   *the man that only could love long*: the only man who could love long.

180   *women*: 'woman' (*1689*).

182   *once*: 'one' (*1689*).

188   *the cross returns of love*: i.e. such perverse, thwarting reciprocation of my love for you.

189   *prejudiced*: hostilely prepossessed by your reading of my character.

198   *brave*: defy.

205   *allowable*: admissible, legitimate.

213   *Which therefore . . . its very being*: i.e. which by this excess turns into its own opposite, vice.

232   *Expect*: wait to see.

248   *on the knee*: Nemours knelt at l. 104 above, and it would appear that Lee may have imagined him as playing all the intervening exchanges from the same position, though other stagings are clearly possible.

256   *state*: estate, fortune.

260-6   *Give me thy hand . . . I love her*: laid out as verse in *1689*, as also are ll. 271-3 below.

262   *all to loose grains*: i.e. to the tiniest fragments.

384

269 *Like the fanatic*: in Restoration usage 'fanatic' meant 'a Nonconformist, an unreasoning supporter of the republican cause defeated in 1660'. Viewing the sixteenth-century French religious wars between Catholic and Huguenot as parallel to recent English experiences was a settled habit by 1681–2.

271 *changeable stuff*: 'stuff' means (1) material to be worked upon and (2) fabric; and 'changeable' (1) mutable and (2) showing different colours under different aspects.

292–3 *though I haul cats at sea, or cry small-coal*: i.e. even though I am put to heavy, menial labour. To cat anchors is to haul them up and hang them on the cathead, the piece of timber which keeps them clear of the ship. To cry small-coal is to hawk—and lug—coal about the streets for sale.

295 *Diogenes*: the Greek cynic philosopher, who lived in a tub and professed an extreme self-abnegation and simplicity of life.

303 *ingenuity*: honesty, sincerity.

306 *death-bed sorrow . . . the man*: see Introduction, pp. xxiv–xxvi.

Epilogue [by John Dryden] 2 *bespattered*: i.e. by the prologue (clearly designed for the same actress).

6 *high-flying*: i.e. ranging widely in search of sexual prey. It is a hawking term.

8 *squandering*: spending his (sexual) resources lavishly.

16 *chamber-practice . . . bar*: 'chamber-practice' is 'advice given by a lawyer in private'. So the line means: 'real-life sexual dealings work by different rules than those of the drama'.

24 *Who gave . . . all his due*: playing ironically on Christ's injunction in Luke 20: 25.

26 *confessor*: accented on the first and third syllables.

28 *telling tales . . . school*: cf. the proverbial 'tell tales out of school' (Tilley, T54).

31 *means*: playing on its theological meanings—(1) processes by which grace works on the soul; (2) public worship—and its secular ones—(1) stratagems, trickery; (2) intermediaries.

Epilogue 1 *What is this wit . . . not name?*: Abraham Cowley (1618–67) composed a famous ode 'Of Wit' (published in 1656), which treats wit as a phenomenon 'which, like the Power Divine, | We only can by negatives define' (ll. 63–4). Therefore, for example, ''Tis not a tale, 'tis not a jest, | Admired with laughter at a feast' (ll. 21–2), and so on. Lee's epilogue follows tactics opposite to Cowley's. It eschews negative formulations, starts by asking 'Is it . . .', and then proceeds to a series of heterogeneous statements each prefaced by ''Tis . . .', the relationship of which to one another appears teasingly haphazard and contradictory.

Cowley's ode also denies that true wit can ever include anything 'At which a virgin hides her face' (l. 46)—a definition which, if accepted, would clearly place a work like *The Princess of Cleves* beyond the pale. At a more radical level, however, a Cowleyan influence is perceptibly at work in this epilogue. In David Trotter's words, Cowley's 'odes represent an abnormal vision, which the reader must adjust or fit himself to as best he can'. They 'define and implement a poetic whose main feature is hardiness: difficulty and lack of connection' (*The Poetry of Abraham Cowley* (London, 1979), 112 and 115). In this, they were influenced by the odes of Pindar, the Greek lyric poet (*c.*522–443 BC)—who was, in Dryden's account, 'known to be a dark writer, to want connection (I mean as to our understanding), to soar out of sight, and leave his reader at a gaze' ('*Of Dramatic Poesy' and Other Critical Essays*, ed. George Watson (London, 1962), i. 271). 'Cowley's interest in "cursive" exposition—the development of thought through associative links' (Trotter, 117) finds a parallel in the riddling, ironic fluency with which definition succeeds definition in this epilogue. Cowley's first stanza asserts of wit that 'A thousand different shapes it bears, | Comely in thousand shapes appears: | Yonder we saw it plain, and here 'tis now, | Like spirits, in a place, we know not how' (ll. 5–8). Lee's epilogue too proclaims wit's diversity and ubiquity, but ostentatiously refuses to restrict it to 'Comely' manifestations.

2 *The rare inducement to*: uncommonly excellent qualities or capacities which earn their possessor a perfect fame.

3 *The art of nature*: an art like nature; or, an art whose products are indistinguishable from nature's; or, neither art nor nature merely, but the quintessence of both.

curious in a frame: highly ingenious and skilful in what it designs or contrives.

4 *a Trimmer*: like Whig and Tory, this term had gained a new political meaning during the Exclusion Crisis, signifying someone who—like George Savile, Marquess of Halifax (1633–95), who wrote *A Character of a Trimmer*—sought to 'trim' or balance between the opposing Whig and Tory parties and by such expedient moderation keep the ship of state on an even keel.

5 *fop*: (1) fool (not necessarily someone addicted to foolish display in clothes); (2) pretender to wit.

in the story: in the historical narrative, to history.

6 *'Tis honour . . . disguise*: an especially enigmatic line. 'In honesty's disguise' could mean (1) disguised as honesty or (2) in a disguise which conceals honesty. In most usages, 'honour' and 'honesty' are near-synonyms, which would perhaps favour (2). Of the two, however, 'honour' might be deemed to bear the more absolute set of meanings,

and the line therefore mean something on the lines of 'It is a man of true honour pretending to be a mere honest fellow'.

7 *Caesar . . . in a prize*: an emperor or king stooping to the level of, or acting as, a hired combatant in a contest for prizes.

8 *Pindar's ramble*: see note to l. 1 above.

nature in misrule: (1) an anarchy akin to nature's or (2) nature turned upside down, as in the old Christmas Feast of Misrule, during which mock dignitaries displaced, and made sport of, the true ones.

9 *A politician . . . a fool*: 'politician'—usually deployed uncomplimentarily at this time—means (1) statesman and (2) crafty plotter. 'Acted' can mean (1) impersonated (see preceding note) or (2) impelled, activated.

11 *The Danaid's filling . . . sieve*: the Danaides were the daughters of Danaus, king of Argus, who, having killed their husbands on their wedding-night, were condemned to draw water everlastingly from a deep well in sieves.

15 *for a clown reviled*: mocked as a fool or buffoon.

16 *A pestle . . . for a child*: the pestle and mortar were the symbol of the apothecary's profession. So, perhaps, 'an adult's implements or tools transferred to a child'.

17 *hardly*: only with difficulty.

18 *artificial*: skilfully feigned.

19 *lays her on*: (1) lies on her; (2) makes vigorous love to her.

20 *gather May*: gather hawthorn blossom; but, also, participate in the rites of May Day (see Robert Herrick's 'Corinna's going a-Maying', with its talk (ll. 52 and 55–6) of 'Many a kiss, both odd and even' and 'the keys betraying | This night, and locks picked').

Amphitryon

Epigraph *Egregiam vero . . . duorum est*: Virgil, *Aeneid*, iv. 93 and 95 (with l. 94 omitted). In his translation of the *Aeneid* Dryden renders these lines: 'High praises, endless honours, you have won, . . . Two gods a silly woman have undone!'

Dedication *Sir William Leveson-Gower, Baronet*: Leveson-Gower (*c.*1647–91), fourth baronet of Sittenham, Yorkshire, was an MP and substantial landowner, whose estates included Trentham Hall in Staffordshire. A strong Anglican, he opposed the succession of the Catholic James II and supported the Revolution of 1688 which deposed him; but he was critical of the performance of William III's ministers, championed the rights of Princess Anne, and, by 1690–1, ranked among the moderate Tories. This combination of Whig and Tory instincts makes him a particularly emblematic figure in the political divisions of his age.

7 *the late Revolution*: the 'Glorious Revolution' of 1688, in which the Catholic James II lost the throne of England and William of Orange, his Protestant son-in-law, acquired it. As a consequence of the Revolution Dryden—a recent convert to Roman Catholicism and a loyal adherent of James II—lost his posts of Poet Laureate and Historiographer Royal and was compelled by financial exigency to return to playwriting.

8–9 *the difference of opinions*: throughout 1689–90 the political world was racked by heated controversy over the justifiability of James's deposition and the rationale and limits of allegiance to him and to his successor. The temperature was also raised by frequent rumours of plots to restore James II. This volatile situation made it imperative for a man in Dryden's situation to cultivate the patronage of men like Leveson-Gower who were known to have been staunch supporters of the Revolution.

19 *acted by a thorough principle*: consistently guided in his conduct by genuine and rooted principles.

21 *a word*: i.e. 'good nature'.

27–8 *begun with . . . Earl of Leicester*: earlier in 1690 Dryden had dedicated his new tragedy, *Don Sebastian*, to Philip Sidney, third Earl of Leicester (1619–98). In the 1640s and 1650s Leicester had played a conspicuous part in Ireland in Parliament's campaigns against Charles I's supporters and had been a member of most of the councils of state during the Commonwealth and Cromwellian Protectorate. Pardoned at the Restoration, he exchanged a political role for that of an energetic and generous patron of poets and men-of-letters. His natural political sympathies remained, however, with the architects of the Revolution.

32 *a lost cause*: i.e. that of James II.

34–5 *as a great wit has told the world*: traditionally identified as Tom Brown, who in *The Late Converts Exposed* (1690) taunted Dryden for the disastrous reverse in his personal fortunes caused by the 1688 Revolution.

35–6 *Sancho Panza*: Don Quixote's squire, who, when left with no alternative but to flog himself, still contrived to avoid most of the blows. See Miguel de Cervantes, *Don Quixote*, trans. Charles Jarvis (Oxford, 1992), 1032.

38–9 *Ovid . . . Pontus*: in AD 9 Ovid, the Roman poet, was exiled by the Emperor Augustus to Tomi, on the shores of the Black Sea. From there he addressed a number of poetical epistles—the *Epistulae ex Ponto*—to friends who were likely to have influence at court.

41–2 *The merry philosopher . . . the melancholic*: Democritus of Abdera (fifth century BC) was known as the laughing philosopher, and Heraclitus (died *c.*475 BC) as the weeping philosopher, because the former derided man's follies and the latter grieved at them.

44–6 *The more reasonable . . . the future*: *Amphitryon* enjoyed immediate and lasting theatrical success.

53 *your country*: i.e. the county of Staffordshire.

56–7 *the names of Plautus and Molière*: see Introduction, pp. xxxii–xxxiii.

59 *unquestioned*: i.e. of undisputed quality.

69 *in representation*: in performance.

71–2 *into their form of play*: into competing in their league.

73 *Mr Purcell*: Henry Purcell (?1658–95), the greatest English composer of the seventeenth century. Dryden's praise of him implicitly retracts his praise of the French composer Louis Grabu in the preface to *Albion and Albanius* (1685): 'When any of our Country-men excel him, I shall be glad, for the sake of old *England*, to be shown my error'. The popularity of Purcell's songs for *Amphitryon* is indicated by the unusual decision to print them at the end of the 1690 quarto. His instrumental music for the play was printed in *Ayres for the Theatre* (1697).

79–80 *the third day*: the profits from a new play's third performance went to the dramatist. On that day his supporters were likely to be present in force.

81–2 *that young Berenice*: Jane Leveson-Gower, the daughter of Sir William, and, later, the wife of Henry, Lord Hyde (the future Earl of Clarendon and Rochester). In 1692 she was one of those who interceded success-fully on Dryden's behalf to secure the lifting of the ban on his penultimate play, *Cleomenes*.

86 *apprehend*: anticipate fearfully.

The Characters of the Play 1 *Jupiter*: king of the Olympian gods; insatiably devoted to sexual adventure, as a result of which he was the father of innumerable children. In *The Hind and the Panther*, part 3, ll. 144–5, Dryden described him as 'Black-browed and bluff' (i.e. with a broad face or forehead) and 'Broad-backed, and brawny built for love's delight'.

2 *Mercury*: the Roman equivalent of the Greek god Hermes, son of Maia and Jupiter, to whom he acted as messenger. He was also patron of travellers, and of rogues, vagabonds, and thieves.

3 *Phoebus*: Apollo, son of Leto and Jupiter; god of the sun, as also of music and poetry. As the sun-god, he coursed daily across the sky in a chariot drawn by flying horses.

4 *Amphitryon*: a Theban prince, son of Alcaeus and Hipponome.

9 *Alcmena*: daughter of Electryon, King of Argus, wife to Amphitryon, and mother to Hercules.

14 *Thebes*: the principal city of Boeotia, in ancient Greece.

Prologue *Mrs Bracegirdle*: it was sometimes Restoration practice, as here, for the prologue and/or epilogue to be spoken by performers not otherwise in the cast. In 1690 Anne Bracegirdle was a rising star and destined, within a few years, to be one of the most popular players in London.

3 *satyr*: Dryden is playing on the erroneous but traditional derivation of 'satire' from 'satyr', a woodland god or demon, partly human in form and partly bestial.

5 *not suffering him to tease ye?*: the prologue which Dryden had written for *The Prophetess* in May 1690 contained some tartly political jibes and was as a result banned after its first performance. Thereafter, his observations on Williamite England were frequently more indirect and coded.

9 *secure your fear*: secure you from the fear of being his target.

12–13 *This is . . . the rich*: i.e. 'poor' and 'rich' in poetic talent; but playing on 'levelling' as associated with the Levellers, the political radicals of the 1640s who aimed to level all inequalities of position, rank, and wealth among Englishmen.

17 *Julian's interloping trade*: Robert Julian was the most prominent of those contemporaries who eked out a living from copying and selling in manuscript poems, including 'lampoons' (l. 19), which were unsuitable—because, for example, of the libellous specificity of their references to particular persons—for appearance in print. 'Interloping' means 'trading without a proper licence' and 'intervening in a transaction to make a profit for oneself'.

18 *on the theatre*: i.e. on stage (as opposed to in verse lampoons).

20–1 *The first . . . they gig*: i.e. one lampoon is certain to generate another in response. 'Jig' here means 'scurrilous, mocking song' (see *OED*, *sb.* 3); but another of its meanings—a mechanical contrivance like a whipping-top—is at work in the next line, with 'gig' meaning 'spin like a whipping-top' and 'whip 'em out' playing on 'whip out' as (1) cause (a top) to spin and (2) draw (a sword or knife). A whirligig of charge and counter-charge, part playful, part lethal in intent, is being evoked. The spinning top, however, begins to lose momentum in l. 23.

29 *draw*: i.e. their swords.

32 *after*: (1) subsequent to; (2) on the model of (as in Genesis 2).

1.1 s.d. [*Thebes*]: no particular setting for this scene is specified in *1690*. The same '*Night-scene of a Palace*' as for 2.1 might have been used. Alternatively, a night sky might have been represented, perhaps on a cloth drop.

s.d. *several machines*: descents from above in machines had been a staple resource of the Restoration stage since the 1660s. The movement could be a simple vertical descent or ascent, or this could be combined with a horizontal movement across the scenic stage or from upstage to downstage within the scenic stage.

6 *consult*: in seventeenth-century usage, this often meant 'a conspiratorial meeting, a cabal'.

8 *Mars and Vulcan*: Mars was the Roman god of war, while Vulcan, a son of Jupiter and Juno, was the god of fire and the working of metals.

11 *Venus*: the Roman goddess of beauty and sensual love, married to Vulcan, whom she cuckolded with Mars.

12 *petticoat affair*: love-affair.

16 *sons of harlots*: both of them were born out of wedlock.

22 *Juno*: the wife, and twin sister, of Jupiter, and queen of heaven; patroness of marriage and motherhood, as well as of riches and power.

spiritual court: in contemporary England the church courts had jurisdiction over matrimonial misdemeanours, including adultery.

23-4 *stood upon his prerogative*: insisted upon his right, as sovereign, to be subject to no restriction or interference.

24 *hit him . . . teeth of*: reproached him to his face with.

26 *in their cups*: drunk.

33 *harnessed . . . Samos*: the peacock was the favourite bird of Juno. This association was particularly strong on the Aegean island of Samos, which was celebrated for her cult and where she was said to have been born.

36 *petitions*: prayers, supplications; also, formal requests, such as are made by subjects to a sovereign.

38 *set up*: stabled.

56 *Much good may do you with*: i.e. you'll gain nothing by.

59-61 *Some mortal . . . Europa*: Cadmus, in Greek mythology, was the founder of Thebes. Semele was his daughter, whom Zeus/Jupiter seduced, disguised as a man. Europa was Cadmus' sister, who was carried off by the same divinity, this time in the shape of a bull.

65 *familiar*: (1) belonging to my family; (2) knowledgeable through intimacy of relationship and contact; (3) taking impertinent liberties.

72-3 *fornicate . . . swan*: for Jupiter as a bull see note to ll.59-61 above. He was an eagle when he mated with Asterie, and a swan when he coupled with Leda. Mercury evidently also knows of a performance by him as a ram.

75 *recreate*: (1) amuse or enjoy yourself; (2) re-create, i.e. reproduce.

79-83 *That when . . . close hypocrites*: though phrased as a general political proposition, this speech must have made the first audiences think immediately of Charles II (died 1685), who had made no attempt to conceal his sexual profligacy and was the father of fourteen children outside wedlock.

87 *hidden from the vulgar view*: concealed from the people's sight.

93–8 *But what is fate? . . . foresight?*: here too, the dialogue teasingly evokes contemporary political controversy. In the debates surrounding the 1688 Revolution the exact nature of the role of divine providence in the dethroning of one king and elevating of another was anxiously pondered and anatomized by polemicists of every political allegiance. See Introduction, pp. xxxiv–xl.

110 *with a vengeance*: in its extremest form; with a curse on it.

113–14 *For you kings . . . prerogative*: the divine-right theory of monarchy, which James II and his supporters maintained, reserved to the king an ultimate right (or 'prerogative') to act outside, and even in opposition to, the laws of the realm if circumstances—of which he was the final judge—made it necessary. Mercury's aphorism, however, is also apt to post-1688 circumstances. In 1690, there was little reason for thinking that William III, whose earlier career had been built on the wreckage of Dutch republicanism, would not keep a careful eye on the maintenance of his 'own prerogative'.

115–16 *If there be . . . of an eternal being*: i.e. if the concept of right and wrong is inapplicable to a god, or has no power to shape a god's actions.

121–3 *I shall beget . . . the world*: Hercules, the son of Jupiter and Alcmena, was a hero of prodigious strength, whose twelve mighty labours included the destruction of a variety of monsters and the amendment of many of this world's ills. On the panegyrical linking of William III and Hercules, see note to 5.1.409 below.

135–8 *a mere country gentleman . . . the government*: a gibe—from a decidedly Court perspective—at those provincial gentry who allegedly devoted themselves to rural and social pursuits, while constantly denouncing the actions of kings and ministers without real political knowledge or any serious policies of their own to propose.

138 *patriots*: cf. 'Gulled with a patriot's name, whose modern sense | Is one that would by law supplant his prince, | The people's brave, the politician's tool. | Never was patriot yet, but was a fool' (Dryden, *Absalom and Achitophel* (1681), ll. 965–8, pillorying the Whigs during the Exclusion Crisis).

143 *grumbletonian*: a contemptuous epithet applied, in the 1690s, to certain members of the so-called 'Country' opposition to the Court, who allegedly obstructed government business with the sole aim of being bought off with offers of office or preferment.

151 *review*: (1) see again; but playing on (2) make a military inspection of.

167 *envious*: malicious.

168 *rage*: act of violence.

172 *lay on*: wager on, lay odds on.

179 *Jove*: i.e. Jupiter. Dryden switches unpredictably between the two names for his leading character.

190 *discover*: unmask.

194 *give down*: let flow.

195 *Let me alone*: leave it to me.

196 *villainous*: lowly, servile, plebeian.

209 *banker's shop*: a 'banker' was someone who dealt in bills of exchange, giving drafts and making remittances.

210 *clippers, and coiners*: clippers pared off the edges of coins and sold the silver and gold thus obtained. Coiners made counterfeit coins.

232 *old Saturn was deposed*: Saturn, or Cronus, the father of Jupiter, was defeated and dethroned as ruler of the world by his son.

233 *Pallas*: Pallas Athene or Minerva, the virgin goddess of wisdom.

235–6 *woe be . . . on his side*: at this point too, the original spectators must have thought immediately of Charles II. See note to 1.1.79–83.

239 *ready money*: playing on the idea of both financial and sexual resources.

255 *holding a candle to*: i.e. assisting.

266 *edified*: spiritually nourished or consoled. Night is responding to the mock-religiosity of some of Mercury's Puritan-derived language—for instance, 'a *reverend, primitive, original* bawd, *from the first hour of thy creation*' (ll. 249–50).

269 *the seven stars*: the Pleiades, generally visible shortly before dawn.

272 *My service to Jupiter*: my compliments to Jupiter; but also playing on the notion that she is at his beck and call.

s.d. *Night goes backward*: if those arriving from heaven descend from above, it is perhaps logical to expect that Night's chariot was flown in from the side wings and moved horizontally across the stage and that she now returns whence she came.

1.2.2 *been indifferent to my choice*: i.e. provoked neither positive nor negative feelings in me.

7 *Sustaining all his cares*: enduring (in imagination) the same anxieties and troubles which burden him.

23 *Everyone in our own vocation*: i.e. everyone has to attend to their own way of earning a living. The phrase is proverbial (Tilley C23), religious in origin, and often, as here, used profanely.

28 *by the same token that*: in confirmation of which; or, and also that.

58 *make my pennyworths*: earn my wages, make a good bargain.

59 s.d. *in the shape of Amphitryon*: i.e. dressed like Amphitryon.

61 *to these*: compared to these.

88–9 *my judge . . . take place*: a judge's authority in his court is indicated by his being addressed as 'my lord'. Phaedra alleges from this title that, even outside the court-room, news about Gripus should take precedence over the concerns of others.

92 *worried*: seized and tugged (as by dogs or wolves).

102 *Betwixt . . . live again*: i.e. between our bouts of love-making (playing on the colloquial meaning of 'die', 'to achieve sexual climax').

103 *success*: outcome

115 *fondness*: (1) tenderness of feeling, but also (2) foolishness. Cf. Alcmena's description of herself in the preceding line as 'the fool of love'.

137 *would fain be coming off*: would like to evade performing your promise. But 'come off' also meant 'ejaculate'.

139 *o' purpose*: with set purpose; with real determination; with effectiveness.

143–4 *Jupiter but laughs | At lovers' perjuries*: see the note to Dryden's prologue to *PC*, l. 19 (p. 363).

151 *the devil a*: not a single.

154–5 *some mere elder brother*: i.e. some dullard. Proverbially the elder brother inherited the family estates, but intelligence was the younger brothers' portion. Phaedra's prayer to Jove is that the child begotten by this night's love-making should be of the kind she names.

160 *As I*: as if I.

169 *the ready*: i.e. ready money.

177 *a very woman*: i.e. the sex in epitome.

180–2 *would . . . their fees?*: officials in seventeenth-century government departments exacted fees for the performance of their functions from those who needed to transact business with them.

183 *worrying one another*: making vehement love together.

189 *of providence be void*: be without divine direction or control.

195 *preferred*: offered to Jove; given preferential treatment.

2.1.16 *waiter*: attendant.

17 *civil*: grave, proper, decent (used ironically).

21–2 *These are . . . the subject*: i.e. if great lords treat their servants in this way, what trust can be placed in their claims—during and after the 1688 Revolution—to be the champions of the people's 'liberty and property' (a key watchword for the 1688 Revolution's advocates and defenders)?

24–5 *the republican spirit*: i.e. the spirit of political radicalism, which harked back approvingly to the levelling agendas of some of the extremer political groups of the 1640s and 1650s. See also note to *Am*, Prologue, ll. 12–13.

34 *beforehand*: in advance of payment, i.e. before offering his 'devotions' to the gods.

39 *the god of eloquence*: Mercury himself, traditionally the patron deity of prose and rhetoric.

43 *lanthorn*: 'lanthorn' is a variant of 'lantern' and *1690*'s preferred spelling throughout this scene, thus enabling Mercury's punning on the cuckold's horns in this line. Presumably the lanterns are also made of horn.

44 *fumbler*: sexually incompetent or impotent.

57 *orator*: the 'orator' is an officer of the University of Cambridge or Oxford whose duties include speaking in the name of the university on state and formal public occasions.

66 *High day*: Sosia's variation on 'Hey-day', an exclamation of surprise.

67 *playing the good-fellow*: revelling.

87 *fee, fa, fum*: see note to *SF*, 4.1.373.

94 *I defy peace and all its works*: a variation on the godparents' promise on the infant's behalf in the Anglican baptismal service to 'renounce the devil and all his works'.

103 *two-legged man*: recalling a definition of man attributed to Plato by Diogenes Laertius, 'implumis bipes' ('a two-legged, unfeathered animal').

134–5 *brought you . . . friend*: i.e. made you a little more humble and polite, friend.

143–4 *remembrance*: a token, keepsake (to recall a specific memory); here, a blow.

145 *flippant*: nimble and disrespectful; with a play on 'flip' meaning 'strike sharply'.

154 *sober sadness*: deadly earnest.

155 *heathen name*: i.e. the Theban equivalent of a Christian name.

170–1 *I was . . . laced Sosia*: playing on the distinction between plain and 'laced' (or fancy) garments, and on 'to lace' meaning 'to lash, beat'.

174 *by my good will*: willingly; if I could have my wish.

187 *beat . . . Pterelas*: 'The islands of the Teleboae . . . are in the Ionian Sea . . . They are mentioned by Homer as the haunts of notorious sea-pirates, and in Greek myth were celebrated on account of the war carried on between them and Electryon, king of Mycenae, the father of Alcmena' (Summers).

191 *tittle*: *1694*; 'little' (*1690*).

199 *now do you*: now it is your turn to.

205–6 *Davus . . . Harpage*: Davus is Sosia's father in Plautus; Harpage, Dryden's addition, is derived from the Greek for 'rapine' and 'a pronged instrument, a rake' and is pronounced with three syllables.

220 *credits*: reputations.

223 *passages*: occurrences.

230 *some false brother*: some treacherous fellow-servant.

253–4 *made an end of me*: vanquished me; consigned this Sosia to non-being.

260 *the patch upon my nose*: Sosia is concealing a syphilitic disaster. See note to *PC*, 5.1.38.

264 *apparel*: appearance.

265 *gives me*: i.e. gives me to believe, makes me think.

279 *expect*: Sosia is playing on 'expect' meaning 'wait for'.

279–80 *what sour fruit that crab-tree bears*: the crab tree is a wild, bitter apple, and cudgels—crab-sticks—were often made of its wood.

287 *his excellency*: i.e. ambassador Sosia.

288 *his credentials*: (1) an ambassador's credentials or letters of credence; (2) Sosia's ability to gain credence for his improbable tale.

290 *lank*: loose from emptiness; drooping, post-coitally languid.

291 *his Almightyship*: *1690* follows this with the start of a new scene, 2.2; but, since the action is continuous and Mercury remains onstage, Act 2 has been printed as a single, undivided unit in this edition.

292 *aloof*: some distance away.

296 *Detracting crowds*: i.e. crowds of detractors.

316 *draw our curtains close*: i.e. the bed-curtains.

319 *lay*: lain.

320 *widowed*: i.e. which has been so long parted from your wife.

324 *strangely*: exceedingly.

351 *so nicely*: with such fine discrimination.

367 *niceties*: delicate and minute discriminations.

374–7 *A lover . . . by conquest*: another passage which teasingly invokes the controversies surrounding the 1688 Revolution. Arguing that William III's title to the English throne was *de facto*, not *de jure*, and ultimately rested on conquest, was not viewed with favour by the new regime. The issues are explored in J. P. Kenyon, *Revolution Principles: The Politics of Party 1689–1720* (Cambridge, 1977). See also Introduction, pp. xxxvii–xxxviii.

393–4 *love has . . . god of me*: a 'lime-twig' was a twig smeared with birdlime to catch birds, while a current meaning of 'lame', and the primary one here, was 'paralysed, unable to move'. 'Lame god', however, also recalls

Vulcan, the god of fire, who, 'lame' in the modern sense, was also besotted by a woman, his wife Venus, who cuckolded him with Mars. In revenge, Mars trapped the lovers in a net and humiliated them before the gods.

398–9 *all interest*: i.e. entirely devoted to self-interest.

413–14 *He sells ... the poor*: Mercury's gibe would have recalled for the original audience the aftermath of the defeat of the Monmouth rebellion in 1685, when there was a brisk trade in selling pardons to delinquents, from which the notorious Judge Jeffreys and James II were both alleged to have profited. In 1690 Williamite troops were in action in Ireland against troops loyal to James. William's recent victories there may have suggested to Dryden that Irish Jacobites might soon be the victims of a similar judicial inquisition. ('As he uses to do' means 'as he is accustomed to do'.)

428–9 *Jupiter in a golden shower*: Jupiter transformed himself into a shower of gold in order to make love to Danae, daughter of the King of Argos.

443–4 *conjure up that sprite*: i.e. call up (as if by magic) that evil spirit.

450 *steal custom*: i.e. steal off without paying custom duties. The payment Mercury/Sosia owes is, of course, sexual.

454 S.D. *knaps her fingers*: snaps her fingers. *OED*, however, also gives 'knap' as 'a cheating-trick with dice'. Is Phaedra perhaps signalling, via a nimble gesture with her fingers, that he is a low-grade conman?

476 *equally*: playing on 'equally' meaning 'equitably, justly'.

481 *take place of*: take precedence before.

491 *honest*: virtuous, chaste.

503 *dunghill-cock*: 'dunghill' here means 'of inferior breed' and 'cowardly', i.e. not prepared to engaged in (sexual) action. As Mercury's following reference to 'Dame Partlet' makes clear, Dryden is thinking of Chanticleer and his wife in Chaucer's *The Nun's Priest's Tale*. In Dryden's own later translation of the tale, 'Ardent in love, outrageous in his play | He feathered her a hundred times a day' (ll. 69–70). Unnerved by a prophetic dream, however, he is accused by her of being 'a cock of dunghill-kind' (l. 139).

514 *You and I ... in a civil way*: i.e. we have had our sexual pleasures together.

518 *Marry come up*: an exclamation of scornful and defiant protest.

536–8 *a woman of the town ... more easily*: i.e. (as in the conventional image of the merchant's wife in seventeenth-century comedy) cajoling her husband with gentle words in order to deceive him more easily.

542 *bastings*: playing on 'baste' as (1) drop fat or butter over, as in roasting, and (2) beat with a stick.

545 S.D. *caduceus*: the wand carried by Mercury as messenger of the gods. It was surmounted by two wings and entwined by two serpents. With it he could impose sleep on whomever he chose.

546 *What, . . . anointed wife?*: analogies between the authority of king over subject and of husband over wife were conventional in seventeenth-century debates on national and domestic hierarchy. Bromia implicitly inverts the accustomed order of the household—bestowing supremacy on the wife—and assigns to the latter an adjective—'anointed'—only appropriate to a monarch.

548 *stupid*: destitute of energy, sunk in inertia.

552 S.D. *alone*: Presumably a set of shutters close before this speech, to mask the somnolent Bromia and leave Mercury alone on the forestage.

556 *type*: reproduction, image.

558 *second*: i.e. reinforcer, supporter (in her matrimonial wars); follower.

3.1.3–5 *the monster . . . stone-cutter's*: Summers explains the first of these as a reference to a story 'that a great devil had appeared to Louis XIV, and although the King was at first frightened he soon learned to join league with Satan'. The second he refers to a contemporary story about the widow of one Mr Pudsey of Warwickshire, a 'well flesh'd and limb'd stone-cutter' who attracted her, and a rumoured bargain with the devil.

11–12 *honest face*: playing on 'honest' meaning 'not duplicitous', i.e. 'not made for lying' (with his wife, who therefore lies with other men).

41–2 *use complaisance to you*: i.e. behave in complete compliance with your wishes or mood.

45–6 *Nothing but . . . cudgel*: parodying the oath a witness takes before giving testimony in a trial.

61 *impertinences*: irrelevancies

72 *As plain as any packstaff*: a 'packstaff' is a staff on which a weary pedlar rests his pack. The phrase—now 'as plain as a pikestaff'—means 'perfectly plain or clear'.

114 *loose and free*: genteelly limber and fluent in his movements.

120 *defended*: forbade entry through.

143 S.D. (*Saluting her*): i.e. embracing and kissing her. This is a crucial moment; as her following speeches make clear, Alcmena immediately perceives the difference between this embrace and those she enjoyed during the preceding night. See Introduction, p. xxxvii.

168 *with usury*: with interest—i.e. giving more in return than he received.

175 *my preventing image*: 'preventing' here means (1) preceding, coming before (Amphitryon himself); (2) anticipating (the joys Amphitryon might himself have enjoyed).

185 *too much of the creature*: this phrase usually means 'too much intoxicating liquor'; but 'the creature' here is clearly Alcmena herself.

201 *recollect your scattered thoughts*: put your thoughts in order, control yourself.

215 *art magic*: the magic that is produced by knowledge in the forbidden arts.

227 *unsociated*: un-Sosiated me, made me no longer myself; but also playing on 'sociate' meaning 'join together in a society'—i.e. Sosia has been made an outcast as well as a non-person.

230 *More words . . . bargain, sir*: i.e not so fast! Cf. the proverbial 'Two words to a bargain' (Tilley W827).

251 *they may carry double upon all four*: i.e. there will then be four doubles—two each of Amphitryon, Sosia, the diamonds, and the goblet.

266–7 *examination . . . magistrate*: i.e a magistrate's investigation into the fact and circumstances of an unmarried woman's pregnancy—a prime spectator-sport for those who, like Phaedra, are greedily inquisitive about others' private affairs.

301 *fame*: reputation.

323 *wait on you*: accompany you.

324 *Expect me here*: await me here.

337 *been predominant*: prevailed sexually. But Sosia speaks wiser than he knows. Planets—here, Mercury—were believed to be 'predominant' over the disposition and destiny of those born during that planet's ascendancy.

338 *a side wind*: an indirect means or method.

339 *how squares go*: how matters stand.

343–4 *a brown study*: a reverie, of a gloomy character.

354 *all things . . . accommodated*: i.e. their quarrel may be settled.

358 *remember*: remind.

360 *still*: constantly, always.

405 *his own*: the truth about himself.

415 *too civilly*: see note to *SF*, Dedication, 25.

431–2 *circumstances*: circumstantial evidence.

435 *love-figure*: figure of speech, piece of lovers' code.

436 *peace-maker*: i.e. the penis.

441 *exalted*: drunk.

450 *Bacchus*: the Roman god of wine.

overtaken: intoxicated.

466–7 *as it makes . . . against you*: as it works for or against your advantage or interests.

467 *to mend the matter*: to make things even worse, to add to the insult.

491-2 *there are . . . dog-days too*: the 'dog-days' covered the period when the Dogstar rises and sets with the sun (*c*.3 July–11 August). Sexual relations during hot weather were commonly deemed imprudent.

493-4 *blear-eyed, like a May kitten*: offspring born in May were proverbially flawed and required tender rearing. See, for instance, Tilley M770.

495-6 *Let the physicians . . . says of 'em*: the popular reputation of physicians in the seventeenth century was low, with the typical charges against them ranging from utter charlatanism to their allegedly being ready to take a life for a small fee. For the latter, see *SF*, 4.1.302–3.

505 *a-trooping*: off soldiering.

511 *the stern goddess . . . cares*: Venus, the god of love.

513 *held it out*: resisted staunchly.

517 *And die . . . can die*: see note to 1.2.517 above.

521 *proved*: put to the proof, experienced fully.

524 *solicit*: do the business on your behalf; but the word could already mean 'importune a woman immorally', a meaning apter here than Phaedra can know.

528 *I won't*: 'I wou'not' (*1690*).

534-5 *What . . . sound*: i.e. with sweet sounds only, unaccompanied with any more tangible reward! 'Cats' guts' are the strings of the violin, and 'rosin' (or resin) is applied to the bow in order to increase the necessary friction.

548-9 *the bloody flux*: dysentery.

551 *in the room on't*: in place of it.

564 S.D. *appear above*: see note to *SF*, 4.3 initial S.D.

569 *Celia, that I once was blessed*: 'despite being in the treble clef it was sung by the baritone Bowman, who also acted Phoebus *ex machina*' in Act 1 (Price, p. 148). Here he reappeared as an unnamed Theban musician, or perhaps a spirit, like those Mercury summons to dance and sing in Act 4. 'This song . . . was published in the 1690 play-book, complete with a six-bar ritornel for two violins and a bass. Whether the symphony is supposed to serve as the dance mentioned in the stage direction is uncertain, though it seems too brief for the purpose' (Price, p. 149).

4.1.2-3 *I would fly . . . thy sight*: the earth is here imagined as ending in a ridge or precipice, from which one might leap into space.

42 *recruits of force*: supplies of strength

70 *hatched upon your tongue*: i.e. mere language, not from the heart.

86 *fondness*: see note to 1.2.115 above.

89 *mould*: pattern, material.

108 *'Many things . . . the lips'*: cf. the proverbial 'Many things fall between the cup and the lip' (Tilley T191).

114 *before the cause is opened*: the language is legal, 'cause' meaning 'litigation, legal process or case'—i.e., like a lawyer, Phaedra won't contemplate obliging Mercury until more substantial payment is hers.

126 *As some enchantment*: as if some enchantment.

138-9 *my planet . . . to malice*: playing on the idea of a planet's predominance. See note to 3.1.337 above.

157 *Midsummer moon?*: i.e. sheer lunacy? Madness was supposed to be brought on by the moon and aggravated by the heat of summer.

158 *gone a-madding*: running mad.

169 *rogue*: cf. note to *SF*, 1.1.127

177-8 *I should bring . . . fool's noddle*: i.e. I would punish you as you deserve if I were not unwilling to harm the good wine bottled in your foolish skull.

200 *citizen*: merchant, shopkeeper.

201 *catch a stomach*: work up an appetite.

210-11 *a crash at the bottle*: a short, intense drinking bout.

216 *Here's a fine business towards!*: Sosia is protesting about what he takes to be the suddenness of Amphitryon's mood change and the unfairness of this angry response to his industriousness. 'Towards' means 'imminent, impending'.

231 *like a dumb dog*: see note to *SF*, 5.2.88.

235 *a process*: (1) the whole of the proceedings (including sentencing) in an action at law; (2) a sequence of events.

250 *plead*: i.e. answer the charges against me.

251 *I warrant thee*: i.e. I guarantee your safety.

252 *under my lord's favour*: with due deference to my lord; craving his permission to speak.

271 *an*: as if.

271-3 *for a brace . . . of plenty*: see 3.1.553-60.

289-90 *something . . . the forehead*: i.e. the cuckold's horns.

312-13 *free-born stomach*: 'free-born' means 'born into freedoms, i.e. rights'— here, that of being fed. The slogan, 'free-born Englishman', was frequently deployed in the debates around the 1688 Revolution and was particularly resonant to Whigs and—see note to 2.1.24-5 above—'republicans'.

313 *subversion of fundamentals*: playing on 'fundamentals' as (1) the lower parts of the body (specifically, the anus) and (2) the fundamental laws and liberties of the kingdom, for the subversion of which James II had been deprived by Parliament of his throne.

323 *stay*: delay, postpone.

359 *compassionate*: take pity on.

371 *hold good intelligence together*: come to a good mutual understanding.

381 *owning*: confessing to be the father of.

389 *make one of 'em*: i.e. be allowed to be one of the two Sosias Phaedra thinks she has seen (instead of being digested totally into Mercury).

390 *incorporate me*: absorb me, incarnate me.

394 *obstinate to stick to me*: i.e. refused to renounce claiming to be me.

395 *my resemblance*: resembling me; or claiming to be me.

428–9 *shift 'em*: playing on 'shift' meaning 'change one's clothes' (cf. his '*suits of persons*').

432 *for thy turn*: i.e. fitted to you sexually, able to satisfy you physically. A slang meaning of 'turn' was 'lovemaking, copulation'.

434–5 *there's a bargain for you*: a colloquial meaning of 'to sell bargains' was 'to return an unexpected, often lewd or obscene, reply to another's question'.

441 *shoeing-horns*: as a shoeing-horn levers the foot into the shoe, so Phaedra's letter—with its untrustworthy show of love to him—is designed to lever Gripus into loving her.

443 *a mere*: unadulterated, the essence of.

454 *a handle to thy iniquity*: i.e. knowledge about her which he can use to blackmail her into compliance.

459–60 *born under the same planet*: Mercury being the god of thieves.

468 *a cast of my office*: a trick of my trade; or a demonstration of my powers.

s.d. *He stamps upon the ground*: an ascent via a trap was often cued on the Restoration stage by a stamp of the foot from one of the onstage players.

s.d. *MERCURY'S SONG TO PHAEDRA*: Purcell's setting of Mercury's song, among other small variants, alters the opening words to 'For Iris I sigh'. Price (p. 149) writes that 'According to a stage direction, Mercury himself is supposed to sing . . ., but the music sources name Mrs Butler [who had also played Night in 1.1] as performer . . . From Purcell's point of view, Bowman would have made a better Mercury than the non-singing Leigh. A surrogate singer here suggests that the songs were introduced at the last moment, leaving Dryden no time to make the alterations necessary to exploit the actor's special abilities'. However, *pace* Price, the heading to the song can be read to mean the song Mercury presents to Phaedra, not one he himself sings.

475 *things of course*: customary things.

476 *the taking for better for worse*: i.e. taking marriage vows to one another.

479 *legend*: history, record; but playing on 'legend' meaning 'story of the life of a saint'.

480 *so equally joined*: joined on such terms of equality; joined in so just an agreement.

S.D. *a fantastic dance*: an early manuscript of the complete *Amphitryon* score in the Fitzwilliam Museum, Cambridge (MS 683), contains a 'Dance for Tinkers', which was the accompaniment for the performers of this 'fantastic' or grotesque dance. 'That it is given only in two parts, treble and bass, might suggest performance by a small stage band' (Price, pp. 150–1).

493 S.D. *A PASTORAL DIALOGUE BETWIXT THYRSIS AND IRIS*: the '*New singers*' 'were none other than the recirculated Bowman and Mrs Butler. Because the latter had just performed the preceding song, she must have dashed off stage and down stairs to catch the ascending trap' (Price, p. 150). Purcell set Dryden's verses 'almost entirely in the declamatory style, except for the formal and rather austere concluding rondeau'. In most such 'amorous dialogues, the singers join their voices near the end to symbolize agreement or mutual gratification. But here, even though Iris says she will yield, Purcell avoids the usual anodyne of warbling thirds and sixths, never quite letting the voices come together' (Price, p. 150).

497 *the shepherd's hour*: i.e. his moment of opportunity.

524 *at the height*: at the highest pitch.

532 *the music*: i.e. the company of musicians and dancers.

533 *a better heaven in store for you*: i.e. a better heaven—Phaedra herself—than that in which Mercury—as god and as planet—normally operates.

539 *interest*: self-interest, personal advantage.

542–3 *Our iron age . . . be sold*: the iron age was the last and worst age of the world, succeeding the ages of gold, silver, and brass. It is also, paradoxically, an age of gold, because in it everything is for sale.

5.1.2 *my proper chattel*: i.e. legally mine ('proper' here meaning 'own'; cf. the legal term, 'chattel personal').

13–14 *point'st to privilege*: i.e. protects the rights of the citizen in his judgements.

14 *veers to prerogative*: i.e. shows bias in favour of monarchical power.

32 *pass my word*: pledge my word.

36 *which*: whichever.

39–40 *lay you by the heels*: i.e. send you to prison.

40–1 *an unlawful, bloody challenge*: duelling was illegal in late seventeenth-century England.

53 *in the forms of honour*: according to the etiquette of duelling.

60 *squeeze the subject*: oppress, and financially victimize, the King's subjects.

64 *methodically*: in the prescribed and proper order.

65 *suffer a non-suit*: the relevant sense of 'non- suit' here is the stopping of a suit or legal process by the voluntary withdrawal of the plaintiff. Thus Gripus attempts to withdraw from the confrontation with Mercury, but is reminded by the latter what as a judge he should have remembered, i.e. that such a 'non-suit' leaves the question of 'costs and charges' still unsettled. Mercury, that is, still wants the cup restored.

83 *livery and seisin*: delivery and possession. 'Livery of seisin' is the proper legal phrase, meaning 'the delivery of property into the corporal possession of a person'.

85 *an Act of Oblivion*: i.e. a promise to forget the past. The term, in its original usage, meant an act granting a general pardon for political offences—in particular, the Acts of 1660 and 1690, by which those who had taken arms against Charles II and William III respectively were exempted from punishment for their deeds.

87 *under my girdle*: under my control.

87–8 *I'll cap verses . . . of the chapter*: i.e. I'll never be lost for an answer in our quarrels. ('Cap verses' means 'to reply to a verse quoted by another with one beginning, for example, with the initial or final letter of the first'; 'to the end of the chapter' means 'right to the end, throughout'.)

94 *All of a piece*: all consistent.

120 *the Gorgon's head*: the Gorgons were terrifying females with serpents on their heads instead of hair. Medusa was the chief of them; and whoever looked on her face was immediately turned to stone.

126 *comedian*: actor.

159 *equal*: equitable, just.

170 *under correction*: i.e. in one's power; but also, receiving a taste of the punishment he usually hands out.

195–6 *It should be . . . their tongue*: the language is Greek, as is confirmed by Jupiter's next speech.

202 *In sadness*: in earnest.

203 *hiccius doccius*: a formula—akin to 'Hey, presto!' or 'Hocus-Pocus'—employed by conjurors in performing their tricks.

207–8 *fifty Attic talents . . . farthing!*: a humorous conjunction of Greek and English money. The Attic talent was equivalent to *c*.26 kilograms of gold or silver.

240 *rose*: 'rise' (*1690*).

247 *This is a case too nice for vulgar sight*: i.e. a servant like Phaedra lacks the delicacy of discrimination to determine a case like this.

249 *its proper choice*: the correct choice; but also, its own choice, the choice her heart has already made (in accepting Amphitryon to be her husband).

254 *false and foolish fire*: i.e. *ignis fatuus*, will-o'-the-wisp.

267 *vain*: empty, futile.

305 *for an unmerciful deity as you are*: i.e. being the unmerciful god that you are.

322 *my wife of the left hand*: a left-handed, or morganatic, marriage is one between persons of unequal rank—here, a god and a mortal. Mercury, however, seems to be adapting it—cf. 'lawful concubine'—to mean also a union unsanctified by the church.

324–5 *You shall . . . a god*: you must excuse me from believing you, even though you are a god.

330 *under black and white*: in writing; therefore, secure.

339 *Mount Parnassus*: a mountain near Delphi in Greece, sacred to Apollo and the Muses.

340 *fobbed off with a poetical estate*: since poets are proverbially impoverished.

355–6 *no more but Mas and Miss*: i.e. Master and Miss. She wants only one child of each sex.

358–60 *The second . . . martyr for it*: the pagan god is allowed by Dryden to glance satirically at Christ and Christ's sacrifice.

362 *separate maintenance*: this normally signified the financial provision made by a husband for his separated wife after the breakdown of a marriage. But Phaedra is building the assumption of separate residences for husband and wife—as perhaps befits a union between a god and a mortal—into the original contract between them.

363 *Act of Settlement*: Phaedra is playfully assigning her deal with Mercury a dignity comparable to that of an Act of Parliament for settling the affairs of the nation—such as the 1689 Act of Settlement 'declaring the rights and liberties of the subject and settling the succession of the crown' after the 1688 Revolution. (Extra clauses added to a financial bill in Parliament were said to be 'tacked'.)

364–5 *I can see . . . best of you*: i.e. it takes no especial wit to work this out. The phrase is proverbial (Tilley M965).

371 *privilege of peerage*: a peer could avoid indictment in the ordinary courts of law by claiming the right to be tried by his peers—thus often, in practice, a jury of his friends and associates—under the presidency of a Lord High Steward.

375 S.D. *on the theatre*: on the stage.

384 *secure thy jealous fear*: banish your suspicions of your wife.

386 *No fame . . . lost*: i.e. having Jupiter as your rival, and the lover of your wife, is no blemish to your reputation. ('Concurrence' means 'rivalry, pursuit of the same object'.)

388 *And, by . . . into a price*: and, by sharing it with you, elevates it into something of great value.

390 *translate*: transform.

396 *in his own despite*: in defiance of Jupiter; notwithstanding the opposition of Jupiter.

404 *a world that wants a Hercules*: Williamite iconography frequently represented the king as Hercules. (See, for instance, Stephen B. Baxter, 'William III as Hercules: The Political Implications of Court Culture', in Lois G. Schwoerer (ed.), *The Revolution of 1688–1689: Changing Perspectives* (Cambridge, 1992), 95–106.) The traditional iconographical associations of Hercules included interpreting him as 'an emblem of Christian fortitude' and as 'a figure of the warrior whose success brings peace and empire' (Baxter, p. 97). In the immediately post-1688 context aligning William with Hercules also implied that his victory over James was just one of his many labours of virtue. In Dryden's line, 'wants' means 'lacks' as well as 'needs'. *Amphitryon* is clearly not the work of a playwright who takes William's Herculean pretensions seriously.

Epilogue 11–12 *In all his reign . . . did begin*: here too the original audience must have thought of Charles II. Cf. the notes to 1.1.79–83 and 235–6 above.

20 *bestowed a star*: (of Jupiter) made his illegitimate children the tutelary deities of the heavens; (of Charles II) bestowed titles of rank (duke, earl, etc.) on his illegitimate children.

26–32 *Severity of life . . . mend our breed*: Dryden playfully proposes that, as the pagan deities were displaced by the Christian God, so Restoration licence has been displaced by Williamite austerity. His concluding lines, however, are recognizably the work of a man who, in *Absalom and Achitophel* (1681), had celebrated Charles (as King David) because he, 'after Heaven's own heart, | His vigorous warmth did, variously, impart | To wives and slaves; and, wide as his command, | Scattered his maker's image through the land' (ll. 7–10).

The Wives' Excuse

Epigraph *Nihil . . . expectatio*: 'nothing is so adverse to those who wish to please as expectation', adapted from Cicero, *Academica*, ii. 10.

Dedication *Thomas Wharton, Esq.*: 'Honest Tom' Wharton (1648–1715), who later became Earl and Marquis of Wharton. He held the office of Comptroller of the Household, a middle-ranking Court appointment, from 1689 to 1702. He was a zealous Whig and ardent supporter of the

1688 Revolution, who was also renowned as a rake, a dissimulator, a swordsman, and the author of 'Lillibullero'. This dedication only appears in three surviving copies of *1692*; see Harold Love, 'The Printing of *The Wives' Excuse*', *The Library*, 5th ser., 25 (1970), 344–9.

2 *man of fortune*: wealthy man.

12 *interest*: influence due to personal and political connections.

12–13 *where most voices are to carry it*: where majority opinion (among spectators in the playhouse) is to decide the matter.

13 *some people*: i.e. people who read the play in manuscript before its première.

23–4 *in the trust and confidence of a friend*: i.e. placing faith in a friend's trustworthiness.

26 *music-meeting*: a public entertainment, featuring vocal and instrumental music, in a music- or concert-room—a recent, highly fashionable innovation.

32 *upon leading her out*: as she was escorted to her coach.

39 *Sir Anthony Love*: this comedy, subtitled *The Rambling Lady* and premièred in 1690, had been Southerne's greatest theatrical success to date.

43 *Cleomenes*: Dryden was at work on this play, based on a story from Plutarch, during the summer of 1691. For its troubled history, see James Anderson Winn, *John Dryden and His World* (New Haven, Conn., 1987), 451–3. Dryden had known Southerne since the early 1680s, when he had written the prologue and epilogue for Southerne's first play, *The Loyal Brother* (1682), and the prologue for his second, *The Disappointment* (1684).

45 *preferred me to it*: i.e. advanced me—in preference to others—to this office of trust.

48–9 *evidence of my cause*: witness in my support.

50 *be as little impertinent as I can*: stray as little from the matter in hand as I can; do everything I can to avoid impudence.

56–8 *to mend my condition . . . a crowd*: to improve my circumstances in life in a manner more apt to my temperament, and therefore in a sphere of action remote from the pressures of public business.

59–60 *I don't know . . . that fair sex*: 'Wharton was in fact a professed libertine' (Jordan and Love), a fact of which Southerne can hardly have been ignorant.

62–3 *pretenders*: aspirants to female favour; amorous charlatans.

67 *an offering of my inclination*: a gift inspired by my respect and affection for you.

To Mr Southerne 2 *while these malignant planets reign*: i.e. while playhouse taste is hostile to intelligent writing (and instead—cf. ll. 7–8—favours farce, the audience's taste for which Dryden often decried).

5 *buffoonery*: here accented on the first syllable, and voiced as three syllables ('buffoonry').

9 *The Spanish nymph*: plays with Spanish-derived plots and Spanish settings had formed a prosperous sub-genre on the post-1660 stage. Dryden's reference here seems to be to a particular recent play; but no apt candidate has been identified, and it is even uncertain whether 'The Spanish nymph' is the play's title or one of its characters.

11 *a monster Muscovite*: 'a reference to the popularity of bear baiting which made serious inroads in attendance at the theatre. *Muscovite* would be a generic term for bear' (Thornton).

15 *So Terence . . . writ*: the Roman comic dramatist, Publius Terentius Afer (*c*.190–159 BC), whose plays were greatly admired in the seventeenth century for the elegance of their language. Interest in Terence's plays had been recently intensified by the 1689 publication of Laurence Echard's translation of them, which decked them out in the language of the post-1660 comedy.

17 *scene*: i.e. play.

18 *Nokes*: James Nokes, who had played major roles in the other three plays in this volume, had recently retired from the stage, his last recorded appearance being in Mountfort's *Greenwich Park* in the spring of 1691.

20 *laboured*: carefully worked, highly elaborated.

22–5 *With such good manners . . . rebuke*: a marginal note in *1692* identifies 'the wife' in l. 22 as 'The Wife in the Play, Mrs. *Friendall*'. These couplets presumably reflect the particular nuancing of Mrs Barry's performance of the last duologue between Mrs Friendall and Lovemore.

28–9 *The standard . . . Wycherley*: Dryden is invoking the great achievements of English comedy in the 1670s, regarded by many contemporaries as having climaxed with the premières of Sir George Etherege's *The Man of Mode* (1676) and William Wycherley's *The Country Wife* (1675) and *The Plain Dealer* (1676). Etherege had died in France earlier in the year in which *The Wives' Excuse* was published.

The Characters of the Play 1 *Lovemore*: Betterton had given this name to an earlier rake role he had written for himself in *The Amorous Widow* (*c*.1670), a comedy still in the repertoire in the early 1690s.

2 *Wellvile*: possibly playing on French *ville* (town)—i.e. Wellvile is a gentleman totally adapted to town mores.

5 *Springame*: 'game' was contemporary slang for 'women who are sexually available', while, in field-sports, 'to spring' meant 'to cause (a bird, especially a partridge) to rise from cover'. Though Springame, however,

can begin the chase, at the play's end his pursuit still remains incomplete.

7 *Ruffle*: As a noun, 'ruffle' meant (1) contention, dispute, (2) commotion, disturbance of peace or tranquillity, (3) defeat, (4) ostentatious or swaggering display, all of which are apt to this character.

10 *Mrs Sightly*: 'Sightly' means 'beautiful'; but an older sense, 'conspicuous to others' view', may also be active here. In the seventeenth century, 'Mrs' was a title accorded to adult gentlewomen, whether married or not.

11 *Mrs Witwoud*: i.e. she wishes to be taken for (accepted as) one of the wits.

12 *Mrs Teazall*: she 'teases all', i.e. irritates or grates upon all the other characters. A 'teasel' is a plant with prickly leaves, and the head of the fuller's teasel is used for teasing cloth.

Prologue 3 *chere entière*: with a gala banquet, with a full-dress feast. The second word is pronounced to rhyme with 'cheer' and 'here'.

5 *she-neighbours*: the 'vizard-masks' of l. 7, i.e. prostitutes.

11 *by foul weather*: by quarrels or disputes.

14 S.D. *To the Maskers*: i.e. to the 'vizard-masks'.

15 *theirs*: i.e. the faults or weaknesses of the 'whoremasters'.

24 *three deep*: the side-boxes contained three rows of seats.

1.1 S.D. *The outward room to the music-meeting*. The stage directions here suggest that this is a discovery scene, i.e. 'the main curtain should rise after the prologue on a scene in which the action is already underway' and in which 'as the rising of the curtain discloses the scene, the stage business of the footmen, gambling, is concluding because the third footman has won all the ready money' (Thornton, p. 27). In addition, the direction at the beginning of 1.2, '*The curtain drawn up*', makes it likely that, although 'Drop curtains' were 'not customary in the late seventeenth-century theatre', 'the company took the trouble to have a specially-painted drop prepared for 1.1, depicting an entrance-chamber in the concert hall, which could itself be raised at the end of the scene to reveal the music-meeting in full swing' (Judith Milhous and Robert D. Hume, *Producible Interpretation: Eight English Plays 1675–1707* (Carbondale and Edwardsville, Ill., 1985), 257). Jordan and Love speculate that the imagined location for this scene is the music-room at York Buildings in Villiers Street, though there was also a rival concert-room in Charles Street, Covent Garden.

S.D. *hazard*: a dicing game, which according to Charles Cotton (*The Compleat Gamester* (1674), 168) was aptly named, since 'it speedily makes a man or undoes him; in the twinkling of an eye a Man or a Mouse'. Cotton also reports that it 'is play'd but with two Dice, but there may play at it as many as can stand round the largest round Table'. The repeated references in the stage directions here to '*rising from play*' may thus indicate that Southerne expects a table onstage in this scene.

1 *WELLVILE'S FOOTMAN*: in *1692* the footmen are simply listed by number. Their dialogue, however, makes clear to whom all but one of them belong. Thus, '*1. Foot.*' is Wellvile's servant, '*2. Foot.*' Friendall's, '*3. Foot.*' Wilding's, '*4. Foot.*' Courtall's, '*5. Foot.*' Lovemore's, and '*7. Foot.*' Mrs. Witwoud's. This leaves *1692*'s '*6. Foot.*' unassigned to an employer. He may belong to Ruffle, but nothing in his lines makes this clear. In this edition, the speech-prefixes for the others have been adjusted to identify their masters; '*6. Foot.*' appears simply as 'FOOTMAN'.

2 *a free cost*: alluding to the custom (perhaps only recently established) of allowing servants free entry to the upper gallery to watch a performance's final act.

4 *a merry main*: the rules of hazard are intricate. But the basic pattern is that the 'caster' calls a number between five and nine and then tries to throw this number (the 'main') on two dice and so win the stakes. If instead he throws a number from four to ten, this becomes his 'chance', and he can win by repeating it on his second throw. If, however, on his second throw, he throws the 'main', he loses and must pay out the amount staked against him.

9–10 *in the apprehension of wanting a supper*: in the expectation of having to go without supper.

10 *board-wages*: payment to a servant in lieu of food.

11 *to the devil with his bones*: dice were called the devil's bones.

15 *Set out my hand*: wager against me.

21 *Three halfperth of farthings*: six farthings, a farthing being worth a quarter of a penny.

26 *small-beer butler*: 'small-beer' was weak, poor, or inferior beer, and the term was used by transference to describe things or people of low rank or quality. Hence, the whole phrase here means 'low-grade servant', 'one whose place none of us need envy'.

28–9 *under the tyranny of a housekeeper*: dependent on a superior servant's whims for the food you receive.

30 *for all that*: in spite of all you can say.

31 *pretty*: fine (ironic).

32 *civil*: well-ordered, grave, sober.

33–5 *Idleness . . . the maids*: cf. the proverbial 'Idleness is the mother of all evil' (Tilley I13).

37–8 *for good husbandry*: (1) to be a good husband; (2) stringent economy.

38 *a wet-nurse for his lady*: the chambermaid would be able to breast-feed her mistress's child as well as her own.

40–1 *in the convey*: in the course of conveying her to him.

42 *Gad i'mercy*: an abbreviation of 'God have mercy'. The apt tone here is presumably genuine or (more plausibly) feigned shock at the explicitness of the other footman's satire.

50–1 *A public . . . fair reception*: i.e. a household, newly formed on the recent marriage of the Friendalls, and so hospitable that it throws open its doors, almost undiscriminatingly, to a wide circle of guests.

52 *thou hast the time on't indeed*: i.e. you have the perfect, most enviable employment.

53 *frank*: liberal, generous, lavish.

70 *hand*: the 1721 edition of Southerne's *Works* bowdlerizes this to 'Head'.

81–2 *I grind by her mill*: i.e. the more lovers she takes, the more tips and bribes I'll receive (playing on the slang meaning of 'mill', 'female genitalia'). But the line is also a variation on a proverb apt to the careless openness of the Friendall household: 'He is my friend that grinds at my mill' (Tilley F705).

86 *play*: gambling; but also playing on a second meaning of the noun, 'amorous sport'.

87 *she will . . . in your interest*: she will be so profitable to you; her interests will so coincide with yours.

108 *Westminster Hall*: the principal law-courts were situated in and around Westminster Hall.

108–9 *the husband's . . . his wife*: a cuckolded husband could sue his wife's seducer for damages. It is Southerne's playful conceit, however, which dubs this an 'action of *battery*'.

118 *lampoon*: 'The Restoration lampoon was a medium-length satirical poem which dealt with its victims one by one in separate stanzas or in groups of a dozen or so couplets. The treatment was customarily scandalous and obscene' (Jordan and Love).

125 *pretenders enough*: plenty of aspirants or wooers.

132 *as she used to do*: as she has been accustomed to do.

141 *a correspondent porter*: i.e. a carrier and deliverer for Mrs Witwoud's plentiful correspondence.

145 *Horn Fair*: this was a fair for the sale of horn goods held at Charlton in Kent, often invoked, as here, for a joking reference to cuckoldry.

147 *a fairing*: i.e. Mrs Witwoud's letters will seek to convince the husbands that their wives have bestowed cuckolds' horns on them—her equivalent of a gift ('a fairing') from Horn Fair.

151–2 *a visiting lady*: one addicted to making and receiving social visits.

153 *her day*: the day on which she has announced she will be at home to receive visitors.

156 *cats' guts*: violin strings, commonly supposed to be made of cats' intestines.

   S.D. *Two Pages meeting*: 'a rare late example of writing for child actors' (Jordan and Love), though they also mention the possibility that young actresses might have played the roles.

167–9 *too much . . . these English*: in post-1660 England French tastes, styles and models had been intensely fashionable, though such fads had also from the start been the target of playhouse satire.

170 *touch for*: witty strike at.

173 *the Drawing Room*: i.e. the great withdrawing-room at the palace of Westminster, in which the King and Queen received company.

196 *minded*: observed, took notice of.

198 *man of quality*: gentleman.

205 *Tourvilles*: Anne Hilarion, Comte de Tourville, was the French admiral who defeated the combined Dutch and English fleets at the Battle of Beachy Head, 30 June/1 July 1690, and subsequently bombarded Teignmouth. Fears of a French invasion were current throughout 1691.

210 *the gaping galleries of our churches*: i.e. the galleries in church from which the ogling gallants gaped at the women in the pews below.

212 *precious*: fine, worthy (used ironically).

213 *before you come into 'em*: before you are old enough (1) to be admitted to their full confidence and (2) to become their lovers.

1.2 S.D. *The curtain drawn up*: see note to 1.1. 'The membership of the society already described are fixed upstage during the performance of an Italian song; it is a tableau that allows the audience to apply the descriptions already heard to the individuals now seen. The man talking to a young girl must be Wilding; the fool must be Friendall and the woman embarrassed by his actions must be his wife, and so on' (Holland, p. 166).

   S.D. *an Italian song*: the taste for French music was on the wane in the 1690s, while Italian music was growing rapidly in popularity.

3–4 *gentleman*: *1774*; 'Gentlemen' (*1692*).

14 *wilt*: 'wot' (*1692*).

21 *cat-call*: a 'cat-call' was a squeaking instrument used in theatres to express disapproval; but the reference is also, of course, to the mating-call of tom-cats. In addition, 'cat' was contemporary slang for 'whore'.

23 *sonatas*: instrumental compositions in the Italian style.

24 *chaconnes*: variations on a ground bass in the French style.

26 *fiddlers*: Wilding's choice of word is deliberately provocative, 'fiddlers' often at this time being used to describe itinerant tavern musicians. Hence, Friendall's indignation. He, on the other hand, seems to believe that 'sonatas' and 'chaconnes' are the names of famous composers.

41 *be particular to your sister*: fix his attention on your sister, single out your sister.

50 MRS WITWOUD: this speech is assigned to her in *1713*, but to Springame in *1692*.

65–6 *hit my constitution*: gauge my temperament exactly.

84–5 *But 'tis something . . . for me*: Mrs Witwoud affects to consider Springame too young, and herself too old, for this sort of thing.

104–5 *your character*: i.e. the report of you in circulation in town.

120–1 *no monster, whatever her husband may be*: see note to *SF*, 2.1.38.

121 *a ramble*: note to *SF*, 5.1.33.

123 *a hackney jaunt*: an excursion in a hired carriage.

126 *several*: separate.

127 *Pontack's . . . the Rummer*: the former was a noted and expensive public-house in Abchurch Lane, while the Rummer is probably a public-house of that name in Fleet Street.

127–8 *to supper . . . strangely*: *1692* has 'to Supper: I want to disturb, strangely', thus perhaps treating 'I want to disturb, strangely' as an independent main clause. It can, however, also be read as a subordinate clause, dependent on the preceding main one, which is how this edition's punctuation interprets it. 'Strangely' here means 'extremely', 'exceedingly'.

128 *coz*: i.e. 'cousin', often used in the seventeenth century as a sign of intimacy and friendship, and not just of blood-relationship.

129 *the glasses*: the side-windows of the hackney-coach.

139 *At your toilet*: fashionable ladies received visitors during the final stages of dressing.

143 *The confidence*: the trust he places in me.

157 *tried*: put to the test; judged.

171 *familiar*: intimate; but also, behaving as if he were a member of her family (with the accompanying right to censure her).

182 *making her observations upon me*: observing what I am up to.

188 *civil*: i.e. mildly flirtatious.

199 *stand you in stead*: turn to your advantage.

199–200 *the lady you wot of*: Lovemore appears to have told Friendall he is pursuing another lady. Her identity remains unspecified.

205 *make an interest*: use my influence, 'make' perhaps suggesting that money will change hands.

215 *set*: i.e. set to music.

221 *humour 'em*: i.e. fit music to their peculiarities and inequalities.

242 *her*: *1713*; 'his' (*1692*).

243 *to the right use*: i.e. by cuckolding him.

252 *Ingrateful love! Thus every hour*: *1692* identifies this as '*By Major-General Sackvile*'. Edward Sackville was a devoted follower of James II and, after the 1688 Revolution, a Jacobite plotter, on whom the government kept a close watch. His words were set, as were all the songs in the play, by Henry Purcell, who 'used only the first two of Sackville's four stanzas. Apparently heeding Mrs Sightly's request for an English song, he set the lyric in the "serious" style', producing 'an exceedingly severe song for such humorous circumstances' (Price, p. 174).

265 *A death*: playing on the colloquial meaning of 'death' = 'orgasm'.

266 *try*: experience, suffer.

270 *do you reason*: i.e. show you my appreciation (by the entertainment I offer).

274 *my service*: i.e. to escort you to your carriage.

280–1 *makes it for you*: spreads word that you have, in fact, enjoyed the woman.

286–9 *'Tis nowadays . . . vizard-mask*: 'Where it was formerly a scandal for a man to escort a vizarded prostitute from the theatre, it is now a reflection on his standing as a man of the world to be escorting an honest woman' (Jordan and Love).

289–90 *the pit . . . civility*: the pit being where the vizard-masks might be expected to circulate, while ladies of honour tended to seek the relative safety of a box.

295 *the world's end*: (1) to the ends of the earth; (2) to a notorious house of assignation, the World's End at Chelsea.

299 S.D. *addressing to her*: i.e. he falls into place beside her to 'see her to her coach'.

304–5 *without exception wait upon you*: attend you to your coach without any moral objections being raised to it.

307 *servant*: devotee, suitor.

308–9 *Mr Friendall . . . jealous*: 'i.e. may imagine that Wellvile is attempting to ingratiate himself through Sightly with Mrs. Friendall' (Jordan and Love).

317 *occasion*: opportunity.

323 *a way*: i.e. in a way.

324 *expect the event*: see what happens.

1.3.6 *FRIENDALL'S FOOTMAN*: assigned by *1692* to '*5 Foot*.'; but Friendall's servant seems the obvious candidate for it.

8 *improve*: make the best use of.

10–11 *give it under my hand*: have written.

17 *no touching her*: no raillery at her expense.

22 S.D. *pretends to hold her husband*: i.e. behaves as if she is restraining Friendall, who, however, has no appetite for a fight.

28 *in the apprehension of such a brutality*: in the fear aroused by Ruffle's action and by anticipation of the fighting that might then immediately ensue.

33 *lying abroad*: spending the night away from home.

47–8 *of accounting for't*: of having to fight a duel as a result of it.

49 *showing myself*: making a public display of my bravery and manhood.

66–7 *no fund of his own*: (1) no honour of his own; (2) no adequate wealth.

2.1.6 *gilt paper*: writing-paper with gilt, or gold-coloured, edges.

7 *Mr Bentley's*: cf. note to *SF*, Dedication, 1.

8 *Mrs Da Robe's*: 'Mrs. *Da Robe* would be from the Italian *roba* meaning *cloak* or *clothing*; however, *bona roba* was a frequent generic term for whore' (Thornton).

13–15 *Now, though . . . of it*: i.e. because she is my close relation, I wouldn't be able to regard her downfall with the scandalous relish I bestow on the comparable fates of others.

33 *carted*: 'carted' means 'paraded through the streets in a cart by way of humiliating punishment'. Such malefactors often suffered bruising, if not direr, treatment at the hands of the crowd.

48 *I don't set up for a husband*: I am not in the market for a husband.

53–4 *Another woman's husband*: a second ghost character, also alluded to at 4.2.25–6, but never seen.

55 *as hanging a countenance*: i.e. as of one who plainly deserves hanging.

62 *to throw it upon*: to use to take the blame for her follies.

71–2 *for the usual reason*: i.e. pregnancy.

73 *having a charter*: the charter of the City of London specified the rights and powers of its corporation and citizens. By analogy, the citizens' wives are here represented as assuming they possess a matching privilege of indulging in extra-marital forays.

74 *a very girl*: i.e. a mere girl.

80–1 *miscarriage*: ill-conduct; mishap.

92–3 *in her room*: in place of her.

2.2.6–7 *any man's wife . . . a father alive*: any wife of a man whose father is still alive, and who therefore has not yet inherited the family estates.

22 *secured*: arrested, locked up (and, hence, secured from having to fight). Duelling was illegal. In addition, the friends and relatives of potential duellists sometimes arranged for the authorities to arrest and confine them in order to prevent them meeting.

32 *won't*: 'wonnot' (*1692*).

42 *tameness*: *1713*; 'lameness' (*1692*).

46 *from discovering himself*: i.e. from publicly revealing his cowardice.

48 *must despise*: 'most despise' (*1692*).

50 *make up*: bring to a conclusion (not 'heal, pacify'; cf. next note).

51 *in the business*: i.e. in Friendall's duel with Ruffle.

54–5 *We . . . for ourselves*: Springame is an army officer, and the summer was the campaigning season. During the winter, officers were often absent from their regiments and at their recreations in town.

58–9 *a duel . . . business perhaps*: either (1) in recuperating from wounds received, or (2), since duels were illegal, in the imprisonment which might result, or in fleeing abroad to evade imprisonment.

66 *as from him*: as if sent by Friendall.

67–8 *wants your assistance within*: needs your help in the next room.

69 *in danger*: *1692* follows this with 'And he shall satisfie him, or me', in mistaken anticipation of Springame's following speech.

72 *a younger brother*: younger brothers were traditionally needy, lacking the status, income and expectations of the eldest brother of a family.

72–3 *false musters*: it was not unknown for dead or otherwise non-existent soldiers to be listed in the muster-rolls as actually serving, their pay being pocketed by the officers.

74 *I warrant you*: I promise you; you can rely on me.

85 *laws*: *1713*; 'Laces' (*1692*).

82–6 *in a married state . . . the government*: the traditional analogies between the authorities of king and husband were still a powerful element in contemporary thought. Mrs Friendall's aphorism reflects the current controversy about the grounds on which the 1688 Revolution might be justified. As J. P. Kenyon demonstrates in *Revolution Principles: The Politics of Party 1689–1720* (Cambridge, 1977), arguments based on the idea of a contract between king and people commanded less assent than arguments in favour of *de facto* abdication deduced from James II's flight from the country. The ideas with which Mrs Friendall experiments are, therefore, of a distinctly radical cast.

88 *MRS FRIENDALL*: this speech, as also her next one, was mistakenly ascribed in *1692* to her husband.

119 *make an interest*: use my influence.

120 *to secure 'em*: see note to l. 22 above.

2.3.6 *ever a lie*: i.e. any lie.

16 *expect*: anticipate.

28 *level to*: in line with, consistent with.

30 *Indeed, it costs nothing to promise*: mistakenly attributed in *1692* to Wilding. *1713* corrects the slip.

50 *the letter-lady*: see 2.1.82–3.

50–1 *unseasonable*: at an inconvenient time (because Wilding is in no condition, after the exertions of his night with Fanny, to make love to her).

56 *a current excuse*: an acceptable excuse.

66 *man of business*: a professional man (like a lawyer or scrivener); but also playing, as the remainder of his speech makes clear, on the slang meaning of 'business', i.e. 'sexual dealings'.

95 *resolve you*: assure you, put your mind at rest; but also, free you from your difficulty.

97 *Westminster Hall*: see note to 1.1.108 above.

99 *the sober party*: the morally orthodox or censorious.

105 *considerable enough*: sufficiently wealthy.

108 *some booby of her own breed*: one of her idiot sons, or some fool from her family; a half-wit like herself.

113 *Let me be your trustee*: the suggestion is that she should convey the administration of her property to Wilding, in order to deprive her future husband of control of it. The property they have in mind, however, is at least as much her virginity as her monetary wealth.

118 *conveyances*: (1) legal transferences of property; (2) sleights-of-hand, trickery.

120 *the particular*: the written statement of the particular items or details (of an estate).

126–7 *the men . . . the jointure*: i.e. if the husband were to make it a formal condition of marriage that his wife must be a virgin, she and her relatives might insist in return that her jointure—the property settled on her in the event of her husband's death—should be increased.

128 *put 'em upon 't*: encourage them to raise the matter.

141 *what you would raise*: desire; the penis.

146 s.d. *he declines . . . to her*: i.e. his behaviour towards her immediately becomes more decorous.

164 *common women*: prostitutes.

172 *kind*: compliant, accommodating.

195 *I'm glad on't*: Wilding is affecting to believe that Mrs Witwoud was assuring him that Fanny was not infected with venereal disease.

209 *in the benefit of the public*: i.e. in the creation of prostitutes.

222 *interest*: influence.

238–9 *Truegame*: as an adjective applied to women, 'game' meant 'prone to venery, engaged in harlotry' (Partridge).

253–4 *has the use of his nose*: see note to *PC*, 5.1.38.

256 *Faceall*: brazen, impudent; mere face.

266 *engaged*: i.e. as in a duel.

273–4 *the Mall*: see note to *SF*, 1.1, opening stage direction.

276 *but*: *1713*; 'but but' (*1692*).

3.1.1–2 *Banstead Downs*: to the east of Epsom, and a venue for horse-racing.

  9 *man of business*: here probably a euphemism for 'creditor, debt-collector'.

 15 *messenger*: a royal official, whose duties included the arrest of intending duellists.

17–18 *the fees*: i.e. the resulting legal charges, and payments exacted by gaol officers for accommodation.

 26 S.D. *his gown and cap*: i.e. his night attire.

 28 *gaining time*: *1713*; 'Gaming-time' (*1692*).

 32 *Payable at sight*: a 'bill' was a promissory note. Just as such a bill had to be paid as soon as presented, so the challenge Springame has brought requires of Ruffle that he should be immediately willing to duel with Friendall.

 38 *do the gentleman reason*: i.e. satisfy his desire for a duel.

 53 *wait upon me*: be kept waiting for me.

 59 *discover*: reveal.

 69 *a man of honour*: conventionally, one who was always ready to defend his honour by duelling, when challenged to do so; but Ruffle reverses the phrase's meaning and discovers honour in refusing to fight when he knows he is in the wrong.

 78 *he grows upon him*: i.e. he is becoming bolder, more bullying, in his behaviour towards him.

 92 *flown in his face since*: rebelled against him; taken the colour from his face.

100 *in full Mall*: i.e. at the most fashionable time of day for promenading in the Mall, when it will therefore be at its busiest.

101 *at Will's coffee-house*: in Bow Street, Covent Garden; celebrated, as Ruffle implies, as the gathering place of wits, including Dryden, Wycherley, and Southerne himself.

102–3 *behind the scenes*: gentry in the audience took to themselves the right of free access to the back-stage area and the players' dressing-rooms.

104–5 *the upper galleries*: the top tier of the playhouse, with seating for the lower classes, including footmen admitted for the last act as a 'free cost' (1.1.2).

107 *I'll do you justice, sir*: I'll be a witness for you that he made these offers, sir.

110–11 *let what will be the consequence*: whatever may be the consequence.

123 *brother's*: i.e. brother-in-law's.

126 *the side-box before the ladies*: see note to SF, 2.1.53.

128–9 *that . . . withal*: with whom.

134 *done a good office*: been of service, acted as a conciliating intermediary.

138–9 *behind Southampton House*: the fields behind Southampton House— which stood in Great Russell Street, then on the northern edge of London—were a well-known duelling-ground.

148 *a Lord Mayor's Show*: the annual procession and festivities, including the explosion of fireworks ('crackers'), on the day, 9 November, on which the new Lord Mayor of London took up office.

151 *a note . . . upon Child*: i.e. an instruction in his handwriting to his banker—Sir Francis Child (1642–1713)—to pay a specified sum of money to Lovemore.

3.2 S.D. *St James's Park*: this presumably reflects the image Southerne expected to be represented on the shutters (probably ones already in use) which the actors would employ. The scene's action, however, is confined to one part of the Park, the Mall.

45 *There's something more in that*: that is a thought of some weight; that would bear further thinking about.

48 *she*: *1713*; 'he' (*1692*).

55–6 *It comes . . . the good turn*: i.e. an idea has occurred to me, which will enable you to inflict on him the retaliation you desire.

60 *woman*: *1713*; 'Women' (*1692*).

64 *we*: *1713*; 'you' (*1692*).

68 *delicate*: delightful, pleasant.

75–6 *the commendation of the place*: i.e. the compliments customarily bestowed on the fashionable women promenading in the Park.

81 *Platonic lover*: i.e. one whose love is free from, or transcends, sexual desire. Mrs Witwoud's tone will, of course, have been sarcastic.

85 *wholly insensible*: totally unresponsive to male attentions.

90 *unmannerly*: ill-bred; but with a play on 'unmanly'.

92 *clutter*: clatter.

98 *cousin!*: see note to 1.2.128 above.

104 *Not*: *1713*; 'And' (*1692*).

108 *pretend*: lay claim; declare himself.

123 *gives a countenance to*: gives a respectable appearance to.

136 *assurance*: i.e. self-assurance.

147 *if you have temper to manage it*: if you have sufficient self-control to cope with it and put it to apt use.

158 *I'll think no more on't; 'tis impossible*: *1692* lays this speech out as prose; but Jordan and Love relineate most of it as verse. We are sceptical about this and have therefore stayed loyal to *1692*.

165–6 *wanting to myself*: failing to do justice to myself.

170 *clear of*: unpolluted by.

181 *the king's box*: at performances not attended by the king or other members of the royal family, the king's box was let out.

185–6 *make one among 'em*: gain access to their company.

188–9 *Jack Dryden and Will Wycherley*: Dryden and Wycherley were both close friends of Southerne's and most probably present at the play's première.

205 *a libel upon the court*: a political satire against the government.

218 *communicate*: share the secret.

220–3 *I have a thousand times . . . in your head, sir*: Friendall means that he has had the intention to write a play a thousand times, but never got round to doing it. Using the same phrase, Wellvile then implies that Friendall has, in fact, never possessed the intelligence or wit to carry out such an intention.

284 *let who's will blush for't*: 'Who's will' is a contraction of 'who as will', i.e. 'whoever will'. The meaning therefore is 'no matter who blushes for it'.

301 S.D. *[Enter] Wellvile and Wilding*: '*Wellvile and Wilding coming forward*' (*1692*).

309 *chocolate house*: a shop serving chocolate as a drink.

321 *Mr Wellvile*: *1713*; 'Mrs. *Wellvile*' (*1692*).

334 *ungrateful*: unwelcome.

346 S.D. *and the rest*: of those named as being on stage, only Mrs Teazall remains unaccounted for. Southerne's memory may be betraying him, or perhaps he imagined other mute promenaders in this scene.

347–8 *upon your bones*: i.e. made a meal of you, devoured you to the very bones; or beat you until your bones ached.

354 *lanterloo*: a cardgame, later known as Three-Card Loo and Pam-Loo

361 *in masquerade*: see note to *PC*, 3.1.130.

362–3 *out of your forms*: not fettered by normal decorum.

367 *Will*: *1713*; 'We'll' (*1692*).

4.1.6–7 *How did you . . . Alicant?*: the wines whose names Friendall recites in this and the following speech are mainly Spanish.

12 *Muscatels*: the early texts read '*Muschatellos*'.

15–16 *A friend of mine . . . gold*: Tokay, a dessert wine from Hungary, was particularly rare and expensive. Buda, on the right bank of the Danube, was at this time far more important than Pest, on the left bank. They were not incorporated into one municipality until 1872.

20 *the Greek*: Greek wines were expensive and fashionable in the seventeenth century.

25 *Borachio*: not a wine at all; but a word, imported from Spanish, meaning (1) a large leather bottle or bag (hence Wellvile's next speech) and (2) a drunkard.

28 *Vin de Congress*: this is a mocking invention of Wilding's, i.e. 'wine of copulation'; but, eager not to appear ignorant, Friendall is cued by its chiming with the recent Congress of the Hague (held in January 1691) into thinking it must be a Dutch wine.

33 *Vin de Short-Neck*: 'Possibly a pun on the then popular Portuguese wine, Charneco' (Jordan and Love).

34–5 *Thompson's*: clearly a vintner's; but no certain identification has been made.

35–6 *a prohibited French wine*: England and France were currently at war; and by an Act of Parliament of August 1689 all trade with France was forbidden for three years.

42 *Havana*: snuff made from Cuban tobacco, which was *not* washed.

43 *dry powders*: dry snuff, made by grinding the tobacco after it has fermented.

46 *palilio*: a variety of snuff, very delicate in its aroma.

47 *out of*: except in.

48–9 *His Most Catholic Majesty*: the King of Spain.

53 *mount*: small artificial mound in the garden.

55 *delicately thought upon!*: i.e. what a delightful idea!

58–9 *The plain Canton . . . or which?*: Friendall now offers a catalogue of China teas. Tea-drinking came into fashion in England in the 1660s.

60 *Non Amo Te*: 'I do not love you', the opening words of Martial, *Epigrams*, i. 32. Wellvile is playing Wilding's game and bamboozling Friendall with a fake tea of his own invention. 'Tea' could be (and was perhaps usually) pronounced at this time to rhyme with 'way', and therefore 'te' in Latin.

63 *the committee*: the Board of Governors of the East India Company, which imported much of England's tea. The war with France had restricted the trade.

65 *at the best hand too*: either (1) from the best supplier or (2) at the most competitive or advantageous price.

67 *an Indian house*: a shop for the sale of East Indian goods.

69 *order it*: see to it.

84 S.D. *kneeling*: Lovemore clearly kneels at around this point. When he gets up again, however, is not specified by the dialogue and will vary from production to production.

Stay! This violence: the lines laid out as verse in this and subsequent speeches in this scene in this edition are printed as prose in *1692*.

86 *female forms*: i.e. the decorums you women impose on yourselves and men.

125 *could*: *1713*; 'and' (*1692*).

132–3 *the custom . . . prevailing*: i.e. such behaviour has become normal practice in England.

163 *I want but that*: (1) that would be the last straw (2) I only need that provocation to spurn you forever.

180 MRS FRIENDALL: this speech is misascribed to Friendall in *1692*.

185 *had my ends*: achieved my objective.

223 *Rosamond's Pond*: see note to *SF*, 3.1.83–8.

228 *under his hand*: in his own handwriting.

237 *to secure us*: to protect us; to ensure our reputations.

249 *clutter*: turmoil.

253 *Would I had one civilly in a corner*: the 'one' is a card, presumably preferably a winning one. As elsewhere, however, Mrs Teazall speaks bawdy without realizing it (cf. note to *SF*, Dedication, 25).

263 '*Say, cruel Amoret, how long*': Mountfort, who played Friendall, was a gifted countertenor. Only the first of the song's three stanzas 'can be sung to Purcell's music, unless part of the humour was an attempt to make the second and third verses fit the tune' (Price, p. 174). It 'is a theatrical representation of an incompetent song, not the work of the fool himself. Purcell both exposed Friendall's venial sins of pomposity and dillettantism *and* produced a piece of roguish charm' (Price, p. 175). The

song's words are ascribed to an unnamed *'Man of Quality'* in the early texts.

268 *come to*: acquiesce, surrender.

272 *conscious*: i.e. alertly observant.

284 *a genius*: an apt bent or turn of mind.

287 *Pam*: the knave of clubs in lanterloo, in which it is the highest trumps.

S.D. *Scene draws . . . cards*: for this kind of staging, see note to *SF*, 4.1.182.

292 *comet*: another card-game.

294 *You play too deep for me*: i.e. 'the stakes are too high', in every sense.

296 *I go your halves*: i.e. 'I'll go halves with you', in respect of winnings and losses.

297 S.D. *The scene shuts upon 'em*: 'A pair of shutters are brought together, concealing the gamesters who have withdrawn into the scenic area' (Jordan and Love).

329 *to meet*: *1713*; 'to' (*1692*).

335 *pretend*: set out to be.

360 *there's no danger of your foul*: either (1) your crooked play can't be any worse than your fair play or (2) then I am not going to risk being the victim of your foul play.

361 *anybody out of your own gang*: anyone who isn't one of your own gang.

364-5 *minds it*: pays any attention to it.

369 *in my own form*: 'With players her own age; an analogy from the schoolroom' (Jordan and Love).

371-2 *In ten sets . . . in my hand*: 'Comet is played with two packs composed of red suits and black suits respectively with the exception of one card—the nine of diamonds in the black pack and the nine of clubs in the red pack—which is "comet" and can be used in place of any other card to continue a sequence. When played as a winner's last card, it doubles the stake' (Jordan and Love). 'Never turned one' presumably means 'never gained the initiative in, or won, a single set'.

383 *the Jew, newly turned Protestant*: a conversion by which he has qualified himself to engage in the many commercial activities forbidden by law in late seventeenth-century England to Jews.

385 *raffle for*: Raffles took the form of a shopkeeper offering a prize of goods from his stock, with contestants paying specified amounts for a number of throws of the dice, and the goods going to the ones who scored highest. Friendall has arranged for one to be staged at his house for his guests' delectation.

4.2.9 *unadvised*: imprudent, rash.

28 *on't*: of it.

40 *women*: *1713*; 'Woman' (*1692*).

44 *excuse yourself to me*: i.e. make your excuses and leave me.

50 *put up*: sheathe your swords.

5.1.31 *your intelligence*: the information you need.

41 *in her room*: in place of her.

45 *grant him the favour*: i.e. allow him to have sex with me.

5.2.12–13 *women of condition, if not women of quality*: i.e. women of some status, perhaps even gentlewomen. The (ironic?) insinuation is that only the gentry use Rosamond's Pond as a surreptitious assignation point.

43 *peevishly*: spitefully.

53–4 *in favour of my own*: in order to further or advance my own pleasures.

63 *and*: *1713*; 'and, and' (*1692*).

80 *mend of it*: i.e. shed his reserve.

91–2 *their expedition*: i.e. the expeditions indulged in by such gentlemen as Friendall (and Lovemore).

93–4 *my curiosity of coming here*: my curiosity in coming here; but also, my (indiscreet) whim of coming here.

5.3 S.D. *in masquerading habit*: all the principal figures, with the exception of Mrs Teazall, remain masked for the greater part of this scene.

1 MRS WITWOUD: this speech is misascribed to Wellvile in *1692*.

4 *I thought I had known you*: he has mistaken her for Mrs Sightly, since she is wearing the latter's scarf.

9–10 *There are . . . the next room*: i.e. they won't be disturbed there and can therefore be as intimate as they like.

15 *confounds*: confuses, muddles.

16 *to be particular*: i.e. target one woman in particular (Mrs Witwoud).

22 *With the bush at your backside*: the man in the moon is traditionally represented with a dog and a thorn bush. Betty's wit deftly converts the latter into a bundle of birch twigs.

25 *Come a' me*: come to me; but also playing on 'come at' meaning 'have sex with' (*OED*, *vb*, 38b).

49 *is better than you can expect*: i.e. is behaving more generously than you deserve.

59 *Corinna, I excuse thy face*: Purcell set this as 'a Scotch air whose limber melody ambles up and down the entire soprano range with deceptive ease' (Price, p. 175). *1692* identifies the song's words as being written '*by Tho. Cheek Esq*'. 'Cheek was a minor versifier of the Dryden circle who participated in group translations of letters by Voiture and Bentivoglio' (Jordan and Love).

65 *Apollo*: see note to *Am*, 'The Characters of the Play', l. 3.

81 *improved*: exploited, taken advantage of.

83 *heaviness*: dullness, want of alacrity.

86–102 *Mr Lovemore . . . Only pity me*: the lines laid out as verse in this edition here are treated as prose in the early texts.

125 *stay for you*: have to wait for you.

144–5 *do myself reason*: justify myself by placing my own conduct in a good light; revenge myself by exposing her conduct and character.

145–6 *disappoint her yet of her disappointment*: make the pleasure she took in disappointing me turn sour.

153 *a property*: a means to an end; a tool or instrument.

165–6 *if you would have me*: if you want me to do so.

176–7 *refuses to pull . . . ordered*: it was the custom at masked parties and balls for new arrivals to unmask briefly so that undesired intruders could be identified. But the footman here is being sarcastic: Mrs Teazall is not wearing a mask.

179 *laid thee to the parish, you rogue*: implying that he was a bastard, abandoned by his destitute and unmarried mother, and brought up at public expense.

185–6 *Will nothing . . . with you?*: is nothing but a pretty face palatable (or acceptable) to you?

187 *want leisure*: don't have the time.

190–1 *Learn to speak without a question, you fool*: 'A legal test for imbecility' (Jordan and Love).

198 *master*: schoolteacher.

200–1 *turned up for a blockhead*: bent over the schoolmaster's flogging-block to be whipped as a dunce.

201 *that you are*: *1713*; 'as you are' (*1692*).

203 *tickle . . . deserve*: she is playing on two slang meanings of 'tickle-tail'—(1) whore, hence her reference to 'mistress'; (2) schoolmaster's rod.

204 *Nay, good your reverence*: please spare me (ironic); or, a reverend lady like you shouldn't speak so grossly (mock horror).

208–9 *in the primitive institution of making cuckolds*: according to their original purpose or design of making cuckolds. In other words, married women, not unmarried girls like Fanny, used to be the gallants' partners during masquerades. Mrs Teazall's phrasing hijacks the language of Protestant ecclesiology.

216 *that*: i.e. the 'pox', venereal disease.

225 *opening a poor woman's case*: an unintentional *double entendre*, since the slang meaning of 'case' was the female genitalia.

228 *in my pocket again*: perhaps simply 'in my hand of cards'; but it may also imply that Mrs Teazall is herself capable of sharp practice as a gamester.

236–7 *Mr Buttybun*: Jordan and Love explain his name via a definition from Francis Grose's *A Classical Dictionary of the Vulgar Tongue* (1785): 'One lying with a woman that has just lain with another man, is said to have a buttered bun'.

237 *the writings*: the legal documents detailing the financial aspects of the marriage settlement.

245 *I'll swear . . . myself*: to swear the peace against someone is to swear that one anticipates danger from them, so that they may be bound over to keep the peace. That, ridiculously, Mrs Teazall does imagine herself, and not just Fanny, to be at sexual risk from the rakes is made clear by the remainder of her sentence.

249 *what good . . . in my generation*: this is the kind of witty misappropriation of religious language to profane use which was targeted by moral reformers during the Collier controversy later in the decade and then led to successful prosecutions of individual actors for speaking comparable lines. This phrase derives, as Jordan and Love point out, from the 'Prayer for a Sick Child' added to the Visitation of the Sick in the Book of Common Prayer in 1662.

252 *to Westminster*: see note to 1.1.108 above.

257 *a very good trade*: the 'very good trade' into which Wilding claims to have initiated her is, of course, that of a whore. The trade metaphor is insolently sustained in his next two speeches. In l. 258, for instance, 'ruin her' means 'disable her from following her trade', a tradesman who 'broke' being one who went bankrupt.

283 S.D. *Scene draws*: Mrs Teazall starts upstage as if to open the offending door, at which cue 'The two shutters are drawn back in full view of the audience revealing a further closed pair with the couch in front' (Jordan and Love).

305–6 *in spite of her teeth*: notwithstanding the fierceness of her opposition.

306 *can be civil*: is prepared to have sex with a man.

311 *of what*: out of what.

311–13 *My liberty . . . make you mine*: laid out as prose in all editions before Jordan and Love.

321 *passed*: overlooked.

326 *be the*: *1713*; 'be' (*1692*).

328 *a slavery*: *1713*; 'slavery' (*1692*).

325–36 *The unjust world . . . despised*: laid out as prose in all editions before Jordan and Love.

343–4 *your own relations . . . my estate*: i.e. her family can stipulate the financial terms of the separation.

Epilogue 27 *velvet*: smooth, fluent, persuasive, seductive. But there may also be an allusion to the velvet patches which were worn to cover face wounds and the depredations of venereal disease.

29 *civil*: i.e. offering no obstacles to his own cuckolding.

31 *Betterton*: 'The phrase is not "had I been Lovemore" but "had I been Betterton". It is not just the character in the play who has failed; Southerne has disrupted the whole pattern of comic form and expectation that was established through the conventional pattern. For the audience, Betterton somehow stood for successful rakishness' (Holland, p. 142).

32 *cocks*: see note to *SF*, 2.1.51.

Appendix 1 *'Hang this whining way of wooing'*: printed in *1692* in 5.3, immediately after 'Corinna, I excuse thy face', but headed '*A SONG*, In the First Scene of the Fourth Act'. This led Jordan and Love to reposition it immediately after 'Say, cruel Amoret' (ll. 265–82) in the latter scene, treating it as an answer to that song, on the assumption that Mountfort, as Friendall, 'sang both songs and that they were heard by the audience-within-the-play as a single bipartite composition' (i. 473). This contradicts early evidence that the song was performed by Charlotte Butler (Thornton, p. 31). Price (p. 176) believes that the song isn't apt to 4.1 and suggests that it 'was probably heard between acts or incidentally during the masquerade'. Thornton, however, argues that it *is* apt to 4.1, but at a different point in the scene from the one favoured by Jordan and Love. Detecting a possible 'pause in the action at this point' (p. 30), he favours placing it between the exit of Lovemore and Wellvile and the entrance of Mrs Friendall and Mrs Sightly at l. 216. It seems to us impossible to reach certainty on the issue, which is why we have printed the song in an appendix. *1692* names no author for the lyrics.

4 *court*: way of wooing.

11 *your*: '*her*' (*1692*).

GLOSSARY

abroad out of doors

acquittance clearing of a debt or other obligation

adad an expletive of asseveration or emphasis

adamantine impregnable, immovable

address courtship

admire wonder at

admiration wonder

adulterate (adj.) of base origin; corrupted by base intermixture; inciting sexual transgression

advised, be consider, act only after reflection

affect (vb.) love

a-fowling hunting birds

again in return

agonize suffer anguish

air demeanour, attitude, manner; melody, tune

airy lively, sprightly, merry, vivacious

allay (n.) alloy, a mixture of metals

allay (vb.) alleviate, abate

allons (French) let us go, come on

allowable permissible, excusable

ambling pacing, walking affectedly

amour love-affair

an if

anotherguess of another sort

antedate expedite, bring forward

apish affected, silly; ape-like

apostate renegade

appoint engage to meet

apprehend understand; imagine, conceive

arbitrement determination, judgement; free choice

arrant out-and-out, unmitigated, rascally, notorious

arras hanging screen of tapestry for a wall

article (n.) condition (in an agreement or contract)

article (vb.) arrange by agreement; specify a condition

artificial ingenious, skilfully feigned

artist schemer, contriver

asafoetida a gum-resin, used as a medicine and in cookery, with a powerful garlic-like odour

assignation appointment to meet, especially a love-tryst

aught anything

awful deserving of, or inspiring, awe

avow affirm

babby baby (in baby-language)

Bacchus Roman god of wine

back (vb.) mount sexually

baffling quibbling, trifling

baggage saucy woman (playful)

balk thwart, frustrate

band (Puritan's) collar, neck-band

band-box light box for holding caps and articles of millinery

banditti brigands

bane poison; source or cause of evil

baneful poisonous

banter (vb.) make fun of, ridicule; impose upon

bastinado beat with a stick

batteries cannon

battledore bat for striking a shuttlecock

beadle parish-officer with the power of punishing petty offenders

beau man of fashion and (often affected) refinement

beck sign with the finger or head

bed-rid (vb.) confine to bed (by a beating)

Beelzebub the Devil

beetle heavy wooden mallet used for driving wedges

beforehand in advance

belie speak falsely of

bellman town-crier; night-watchman

bespeak order, arrange

betimes in due time; before it is too late

betwixt between

bilk cheat; avoid paying what is due

billet note, letter

billet-doux love-letter

billing kissing

bird's-nie a term of endearment

bladdered inflated; swollen into, or like, a bladder

blast (n.) malignant threat

blaze (vb.) proclaim, spread abroad

blowing panting

blow upon take the bloom off; defame

blub swollen, protruding

bob taunt, bitter jest

bobbin finger

bona roba (Latin) woman of extreme sexual promise; whore

booby awkward, ill-mannered fellow; bumpkin

brace (n.) pair

bravado boastful swaggerer, bravo

brave (vb.) defy

brawny possessed of great strength; muscular

brisk full of life and spirit; sharp-witted; smartly dressed

broad (of speech) explicit, frank, unrestrained

bubble dupe, gullible person

bubby breast

buff very strong kind of leather made of ox-hide

bulker itinerant who sleeps on a 'bulk' (a stall in front of a shop); prostitute

bulling cheating; sexually voracious

bully (as term of address) good friend; swashbuckler, bravo; protector and exploiter of prostitutes

Burgundy a French wine, generally red, made in Burgundy

butt mark or mound for archery practice; object of ridicule

buzz busy rumour

by-corner out-of-the-way place

cabinet private room, apartment

cadet younger son; member of the younger branch of a family

cant odd or distinctive talk of any kind; slang

cantharides Spanish fly, an aphrodisiac

capital supremely serious and important; punishable by death

carl strong and sturdy man

carnosity fleshly desire; morbid fleshy growth

carriage conduct, behaviour

case-putter lawyer

cast (adj.) cast-off, discarded

cast (n.) contrivance, device; knack; facial hue, external appearance

cast off dismiss

catch round to be sung by three or more voices

catching captivating; infectious

caterwauling shrieking or crying like a cat on heat; behaving lasciviously

caudle warm, restorative drink

cause case; legal action

censure (vb.) judge

chairman man whose occupation is to carry passengers in a sedan chair

chapman one who buys and sells; itinerant dealer or pedlar

chaqu'un chez lui (French) everyone to his own home

chargeable burdensome, expensive

charm (vb.) subdue or overcome, as if by magic spell; put a spell upon

cheesemonger one who sells cheese

chequer-work pattern of alternating squares of different colours

chevalier member of a French order of knighthood

chit infant, weakling

chits-face baby-face

choose, to by preference

chopping plump, strapping

churning violently agitated, foaming

circumstance fact, detail; piece of evidence

civil decent, refined, polite, modest, respectable; sexually accommodating

clack chatterer; chattering tongue

clam upon (vb.) adhere to, stick upon

clap (n.) gonorrhea; venereal disease

clear free from guilt or blame; unblemished; transparent

close (adj.) hidden, private, secret

close (vb.) cease; be quiet

closet small, private room

clumsy ungainly, and evidently low-born

coat-card court-card (king, queen, knave)

cogitabund deep in thought

colling hugging, embracing

colours military or regimental flags

comet card-game

comfortable imparting comfort; cheerful

commiserate feel pity for

commiseration compassion

commode thing deemed indispensable; tall wired head-dress; chest of drawers

commonwealth state, community

companion associate; fellow (as a term of contempt or disdain)

compassionate (vb.) pity

complaisance eagerness to please; obliging civility; compliance, deference

complot plot together

composition agreement, compromise; mutual concession; settlement

compound compromise, come to terms; agree, for a consideration, not to prosecute; settle (a debt) by agreement for partial payment

condign well-merited, fitting

confidant(e) one confided in or entrusted with secrets, especially in love-affairs

confound confuse, perplex, amaze

conjure implore; adjure, appeal to solemnly; effect by magic

conjuring magic; trickery

conjuror magician

consult cabal, secret meeting

contain hold back, keep in check

contemn despise

contingence chance happening or combination

conventicle nonconformist religious meeting-place

conveyancing legal transference of property; theft, sleight of hand

convoy escort for protection

cordial (adj.) stimulating or invigorating to the heart

cordial (n.) anything which revives or comforts the heart

cordially from the heart

cordial-water beverage which stimulates or invigorates the heart

cornuto cuckold

counsellor lawyer

countenance (vb.) sanction, favour, permit

course (vb.) chase

coxcomb fool, simpleton; affected person

cozen (n.) trick, deceit

cozen (vb.) cheat, beguile

credit reputation; value set upon something or somebody

crimine an exclamation of astonishment

crossness disposition to oppose or be contradictory

cross-questions game of questions and answers in which a ludicrous effect is produced by connecting questions and answers which have nothing to do with one another

cully dupe

cutting penetrating

daggle trail about through the mire

daggle-tailed having the skirts splashed by being trailed over wet and muddy ground; slatternly

daintily delicately

dainty fine, handsome; choice, excellent; pleasant, delightful; rare, pleasing to the palate; fastidious

dally play with (another) mockingly; flirt

damp gloom, dejection; moisture

dapper spruce, finical

dark-lanthorn lantern whose light can be covered

darkling dark; secret, concealed; in the dark

dash (vb.) splash, sprinkle

dashed dispirited, abashed

daubing false pretence; crudely artful pretence

daw jackdaw; simpleton, fool

delicate pleasing to the senses; nicely discriminating

depose lower, put down

descant upon discourse at length about; comment upon

design plot, ruse; plan

didapper pretty, active little bird; sexually nimble woman

dint indentation

discovery revelation, unmasking, successful detection; something detected, unmasked or revealed

dispatch (vb.) make haste

disseize oust, expel

distemper disorder, illness of mind or body

distinguish single out; accord honour to

distracted crazed, mad

distracting maddening

distraction confusion, craziness

diversion entertainment

divert entertain

divertisement amusement, recreation

divulge make publicly known; proclaim (a person, etc.) publicly

doddlepate blockhead, crackbrain

dog (vb.) track or watch constantly, pursue

dog-trick low trick

dog-trot steady or habitual course of action

doings energetic activity; copulation

domine master

don Spanish lord or gentleman

doodle noodle, simpleton

dotterel simpleton, dotard

double (vb.) turn sharply back on one's course in running; act deceitfully

doxy prostitute; mistress; sweetheart

dozing dull, stupefied

draggle-tailed having a skirt that trails on the ground in mud and wet; slatternly

drawer one who draws beer or fetches liquor in a tavern

droll comic or farcical composition; piece of waggery

drone male of the honey-bee; idler, man without employment

drub beat, thrash

drubbing (n.) cudgelling, beating

drudge (vb.) perform mean or servile tasks; toil away sexually

dry nurse woman charged with looking after a child

dudgeon resentment, offended indignation

dun importune for payment of a debt

durance imprisonment

durst ventured, dared

earnest pledge, token of a bargain made

effigy likeness or figure of a person

egad a softened oath, 'By God!' or 'A God!'

eke in addition, also

emmet ant

engine agent, instrument, tool; person devoid of volition or feelings

engross monopolize

engrosser monopolist

entertain admit as a visitor

envious malicious; full of, actuated by, envy

equal even; equitable, just

equipage carriage and attendants; personal ornaments, furnishings, outfit

errant arrant

erring irregular; wavering; straying

essence perfume

even (n.) evening

exception objection

expect (vb.) wait for, anticipate

eyelet-hole small hole

fain willingly, gladly

faith (adv.) in faith, truly

fall to set to work; begin to eat; apply oneself eagerly to

fame reputation

familiar intimate; behaving as if a member of a family or household

family household, including the servants

fancy (n.) imagination; mind; amorous inclination or liking; inventive contrivance

faugh an expression of disgust

feague beat, whip; do for

feat (adj.) neat, nimble, spruce

fellmonger one who prepares skins for the tanner

fernbrake thicket of fern

ferret (vb.) rummage, search about; hunt

fie an exclamation of protest, disgust or outrage

figary vagary, caprice

figure (n.) importance, distinction

fillip strike smartly

fine, in in short; to conclude the matter

finical affectedly fastidious

finished consummate; fastidious

fire-fork fork-shaped instrument for stirring up a fire and putting on fuel

firk whip, beat

fits of the mother hysteria

fitted treated as one deserves, given one's deserts

flashy trifling; trashy

fleece cheat, deceive

flesh (vb.) plunge (a weapon) into flesh

fling (n.) freedom from constraint; witty attack or riposte

fling (vb.) overthrow, get the better of

fluttering aimless, lightweight, trivial; ostentatious

foolmonger one who trades on the credulity of fools

fond foolish; amorously addicted

fop fool; foolishly affected person

for all although, despite the fact that

foremost earliest

formal respectable; precisely decorous

formality precise observance of forms and ceremonies; propriety

forsooth truly (usually ironical or derisive)

forswear swear falsely; forsake sworn allegiance

forward ready; too ready

foul-feeding of debased and gross appetites

frank liberal, unrestrained

fresco cool, fresh air

frippery tawdry trifle

frisk (n.) caper, jig; freak, whim

frisk (vb.) dance, frolic

froward hard to please, refractory, ill-humoured

frowze rumple

frowzy unkempt, disgusting, fusty

fub plump, well-filled creature

full-gorged satiated, glutted

fulsome nauseating, repulsive, coarse, gross

fustian pompous or unnatural style of writing or speaking

gad (n.) an affected form of 'God'

gad (vb.) rove idly or in search of pleasure

gallant man of fashion and pleasure; fine gentleman

gallantry polite or courteous attention or devotion to ladies

galloping hectic, impetuous; dancing rapidly

gathered creased by frowns

gazette news-sheet, giving an account of current events

gemini a mild oath, expressing excitement

generous of good birth; having the qualities apt to such birth; gallant, magnanimous; munificent

gentle well-born, genteel; courteous, polite; mild in disposition and behaviour

gentleman-usher gentleman-in-waiting

gig (vb.) produce, give rise to

gloatingly amorously; with intense satisfaction; disdainfully

God's bodikins an exclamation of amazement and dismay, 'God's body!'

gog, upon the too excited or stirred-up to stay in one place

goll hand

go to an interjection, 'come now!'

gorging choking

gourmand glutton

gramercy great thanks!

green sickness anaemic disease affecting girls about the age of puberty

grinding extortionate

grogram coarse cloth of silk and mohair

gross, in in a general way, without going into particulars

grotto cave or nook in which to retire from the world

gull easily duped person

gunpowder-spots beauty spots produced by means of gunpowder

gypsy cunning rogue; saucy rogue

habit dress, clothes; outward appearance

hackney coach for hire

half-moon semi-circular fortification

half-perth halfpennyworth

hand handwriting

handy delivered with the hand

handsome apt, proper, convenient; favourable

hangings tapestry or other wall-hangings; bed-curtains

hank hold

hard by close by, near

hard case situation involving pain or hardship

hart deer

heart-cherry heart-shaped variety of the cherry

heavy grave, despondent, wanting in vivacity

hector bully, blusterer

hectoring blustering, bullying

hector-at-large completely unrestrained bravo, bravo with whom no-one will dare meddle

hidebound (of cattle) with the skin clinging close to the back and ribs as a result of bad feeding; stingy, niggardly, mean; restricted in outlook

high-flown soaring high; socially elevated or ambitious

hilding contemptible, worthless person, good-for-nothing

hist hush; shh . . .; listen

hogshead large cask

hoity-toity flighty, giddy

honest chaste, sexually virtuous; honourable, of good birth; royalist; true to one's word

hopeful of great promise

hop-o'-my-thumb dwarf, pygmy; small bird

horn-mad mad with rage at having been cuckolded

horrid exciting horror; abominable

hospital almshouse

hout an exclamation of disapproval and contempt

how d'you greeting, salutation

huff (vb.) bluster; treat with arrogance and contempt

hummer woman of extreme sexual energy

humph (vb.) make a sound signifying disdain or distaste

hunch (vb.) shove, thrust

huzza (n.) shout of encouragement, applause or raillery

huzza (vb.) acclaim mockingly, throw contempt at

idle insignificant, useless; frivolous, empty-headed; unoccupied

impart make known

impertinence irrelevance; impudence

impertinent irrelevant; impudent; meddling with what does not concern one; trivial, absurd

imprecation oath; entreaty; prayer

imprimis in the first place

improvable capable of being made more accommodating

improve make good use of, turn to account

inconsiderate rash

indite compose, write

ingrate ungrateful

insensible unaware; incapable of emotion; unresponsive

insinuating artful, cunning, flattering

insult on exult contemptuously over

interessed self-interested

interest profit, self-advantage, self-interest; influence

interlope intrude, trespass; trade without authorisation

intrigue secret love-affair

item a term used to introduce each new article or provision in a formal list

jackadandy little pert fellow

jackanapes ape, monkey; impudent fellow

Jack Pudding buffoon, clown, merry-andrew

Jack Sauce impudent, saucy fellow

Jack Straw nonentity, worthless fellow

jade worthless worn-out horse (or person); hussy, minx

jealous ardently devoted; vigilant in guarding; suspicious of another's infidelity

jilt (n.) strumpet

jilt (vb.) deceive, delude

jingling senseless, repetitive sound

jog (vb.) move away at a heavy or laboured pace

jogging moving on or off

juggler magician

justice-broker trafficker in justice, seller of justice

kennel gutter

kickshaw worthless, trumpery thing

kilderkin small (18 gallon) barrel

kindly genially, benignly; fittingly; naturally

kindness love, affection

kine cattle

kitchen-stuff kitchen refuse, especially fat from pots

knock-down irresistible, overwhelming

knot decorative bow

lambkin little lamb; young, inexperienced girl

lampoon virulent or scurrilous satirical poem (often upon named individuals)

languishing (of music) communicating tender emotion; drooping, pining away

lanterloo card-game, an old form of loo

Lawd 'Lord!'

lay in get in (a supply)

leaguer military camp

leally truly, faithfully

lease (n.) set of three

let (n.) hindrance

let (vb.) hinder, prevent

levée morning reception of visitors (especially by a person of distinction)

lewd low, common; ill-bred, ill-mannered; unprincipled; good-for-nothing; lascivious

liege loyal

light into (or **upon**) happen upon or into; select

limb (vb.) dismember

link-boy/ -man attendant for hire who escorted others with a torch in dark streets

lodge (vb.) go to one's lair or home

lolling drooping and dulled (through drink); sauntering

lubberly lazy; awkward, clumsy

lug pull

lusty hearty, massive, substantial

luxurious devoted to ease and pleasure

luxury lasciviousness, lust; habitual use of the choice or costly; refined and intense enjoyment

madcap wild, rash, free-spirited person

maggot fad, whimsical fancy

maidenhead virginity

main (n.) match, game, bout; object aimed at, end, purpose; a number (in the game of hazard) called by the player before throwing the dice

mannerly well-behaved

mantua woman's loose outer gown

mantua-maker dressmaker

marry come up an exclamation, expressing scorn and disdain

maw Stomach; throat; appetite

mere pure

meridian culmination, highest point

methinks it seems to me

mettled spirited, 'game'

mien bearing, appearance

milch-cow cow 'in milk'; woman producing many children

milksop coward

mind (vb.) notice, pay attention to

minikin little darling

mischievous dangerous, likely to inflict harm

miscreant villain, wretch

miss kept mistress

mode fashion

moiety half

month's mind strong desire or inclination

monument effigy, funeral image

mooncalf one born misshapen; congenital idiot

mortify subdue by severities and penance; humiliate; deaden, deprive of life

motion gait

mould (n.) plastic form, make, matter

mouse (vb.) pull about good-naturedly, but roughly

mumble chew, as with toothless gums

mum 'not a word', silence

mun a meaningless expletive, used in addressing both males and females

mystery skill, art

napkin small towel

nauseate render abhorrent

necromantic magical

new-blown freshly blooming, just blossomed

nice calling for very fine discrimination; fastidious

nicely slightly, by a narrow margin

niceness fastidiousness, delicacy

nicety delicate discrimination

nick (vb.) nickname; hit with precision; catch unawares

nick, in the at just the right moment, at the precise instant

niggard (adj.) ungenerous, stingy

niggard (n.) miser

nimble quick-witted, alert

nominate mention, name

nonage infancy

object person or thing seen

occasion need; opportunity; provocation

office duty, service

one or other altogether

orange-flower white flower of the orange tree, from which a fragrant oil is distilled

orison prayer

ort scrap, leaving

outhector face (somebody) out, intimidate

outhuff get the better of (somebody) by treating them with arrogance and contempt

out upon't an exclamation of protest

overmatch more than a match

overtaken intoxicated

own (vb.) acknowledge

pap breast

parle talk, confer

particular special, unique, distinctive

part quality, attribute, talent

passage incident, happening

pattern copy, likeness; exemplary instance

paugh an exclamation expressing impatience or disdain

pension allowance of money, stipend

perquisite benefit incidental to a particular employment

peruke false head of hair

pet, in a in a sulk, in a fit of indignation

physic medicine

physician doctor

pickle sorry plight, predicament

piece, of a coherent, whole, homogeneous

pink pierce, especially with a sword or rapier

pinking blinking or winking in a sleepy or sly manner

pin-money money allotted by a husband to his wife for private expenses

pish an exclamation expressing contempt, impatience or disgust

pitch on (or **upon**) select, fix upon

plaguy (adv.) confoundedly, troublesomely

play gambling; sexual dalliance

pleasant giving pleasure, agreeable; amusing, witty; ridiculous

pledge drink in response to another's health or toast

plunge (n.) strait, distressful difficulty

point (n.) tagged lace used for fastening clothes

point (vb.) appoint; indicate

pointed piercing, penetrating

politic sagacious, crafty (often, affectedly so)

pomp show, appearance

ponderous weighty, important

portion dowry; inheritance

post (vb.) travel with speed; fix (a notice, etc.) to a post or board, make public, announce

posted made public, proclaimed

post-haste, in with all possible speed

pot-valiant brave due to drink

pound (vb.) put in a pound (an enclosure in which straying animals are confined)

pox venereal disease

praemunire fix, predicament

pragmatical meddlesome; self-important, conceited

prate talk foolishly; chatter

prating (adj.) idly chattering

prating (n.) rattling; foolish, idle chatter

precise prim, formal; puritanical

preferment advancement in condition, status or position

prefer advance, promote

pregnant swelling

premise something already said or noted

presently immediately

pretend attempt; profess

pretended alleged

pretty cunning, clever; ingenious, artful

prithee I beg you, I ask you

probatum est (Latin) it has been proved

process course of legal proceedings

proper distinctive, particular; personal, own; genuine; handsome; apt

property tool, implement, instrument

proportionable well-proportioned

protest declare, affirm

prove experience; test, try

provender food

pug a term of endearment; whore; imp, demon; monkey

pugh an exclamation expressing contemptuous disdain

pule whimper

pulvillio perfumed powder

pump elicit information by artful means; exert or push oneself (to achieve a result)

pumpled pimpled

punk prostitute

puny junior, inferior in rank

pure fine, excellent; absolute, clear

purlieu land on the edge of a forest; suburb of a town; place where one is free to come and go

puzzle (vb.) perplex, bewilder; complicate, mix up

quaint elegant, refined, ingeniously elaborated

quality high or gentry rank or position in society; birth and breeding

quandary (vb.) perplex

quarter place where soldiers are billeted

quelque chose (French) something

quest give tongue, yelp, like a hunting-dog; search (for game)

quit repay

quondam former

quotha says he (or she)

ragout highly seasoned stew of meat and vegetables

rakehell debauchee; thorough scoundrel

rally (vb.) banter, jest at

rank offensive, indecent; lustful, licentious; rancid

rascal low, unprincipled fellow; person of the lowest class; rogue

rattle (n.) sharp reproof

ready (n.) ready money

recreant (adj.) renegade, false

recruit (n.) reinforcement, renewal

recruit (vb.) refresh, reinvigorate

redcoat soldier

remembrancer memento

renegado renegade, especially a Christian who becomes a Mohammedan

repartee (vb.) retort with ready wit

reserve something stored, or set aside, for future use; additional player kept in reserve; refuge

reverence respect

revolution change, transformation

right-worshipful of superior rank; deserving especial respect

ringo eryngo, the candied root of the Sea Holly, formerly used as a sweetmeat, and regarded as an aphrodisiac

riot (vb.) revel; indulge to the full (in a pleasure)

roaring riotous

rogue (n.) vagrant; dishonest person; servant (mostly derogatory or ironic)

rogue (vb.) live like a rogue or vagrant; play the rogue or rascal

roisterous roistering, given to noisy revelling; swaggering

Roman (of a nose) high-bridged and, therefore, emblematic of sexual potency; (of a face) imposing, distinguished

rondeau a poetic form using only two rhymes throughout, and with the opening words repeated as a refrain

rouse become vigorously active

rub up revive, reactivate

ruddy suffused with health and vigour

ruffling swaggering, blustering

rugged threatening in appearance; wild, untamed

sack a white wine, especially from Spain or the Canary Islands

sadness, in seriously; after mature consideration

sake-sake, for for the sake of some person understood but not specified

salt in heat, lecherous

sanguine abounding in blood, and, therefore, ardently amorous in disposition; sanguinary, bloody

satyrion reputedly aphrodisiac herb

sauce-box impudent person

saucily impudently

save you God keep you: a greeting or a farewell

savour taste, smell

savourly with relish

'sbud a softened oath, 'God's blood'

scandalous addicted to (spreading) scandal

'scape escape

scot and lot parochial tax levied for the defraying of municipal expenses

scour beat, treat severely

scowering brawling, roistering

scrip small bag

scurvily wretchedly, shabbily

scurvy sorry, worthless, contemptible; discourteous

'sdeath an exclamation of impatience, a softened version of 'God's death!'

set (vb.) bet, bid

several different, distinct

severally in different directions

shambles meat-market; slaughter-house

sharp (of taste) sour, unpleasantly stinging

sharp-set hungry

sherru beshrew it, a plague on it

shift (n.) expedient

shift (vb.) change one's clothes; bestir oneself

shift, make a contrive, succeed

shog (n.) spasm, shaking condition

shog (vb.) shake to and fro

shrewdly seriously; extremely, intensely

signature seal, especially one made with a signet-ring

silly deserving of pity; helpless, defenceless; unsophisticated, simple; foolish, contemptible

sincerely truly, in good faith

sirrah sir (mostly used as a superior or disdainful mode of address to an inferior)

slap-dash in a precipitate, improvisatory manner

'slife a softened oath, 'God's life!'

sloe fruit of the blackthorn

sly-cap sly or cunning person

smack taste, flavour

smacking kissing noisily

smart (adj.) keen, vigorous; pert, forward; quick, active

smart (n.) pain, grief

smooth-faced beardless, clean-shaven; ingratiating, plausible in manner

snap seize, catch suddenly

sneaking self-prostrating; contemptible, mean

sneaksby mean-spirited person

snuff up inhale

sol-la a meaningless scrap of tune
something (adv.) somewhat
sooth truth; in truth
soothe cajole; appease; humour
sophister person reasoning with specious arguments
sordid low, unworthy
sot fool, blockhead
souse suddenly; headlong
sow-cat she-cat
span very short expanse or length
spark young man affecting smartness or display in dress and manners
speak for order
spice slight touch or trace (of some defect or disorder)
spirit vital power or energy; the normal operation of the vital functions which sustain life
spirituous containing the volatile elements
spit skewer; sword (sarcastic)
spleen anger, indignation; melancholy
splendid shining brightly
splenetic peevish
sprite spirit
squab reserved, quiet, demure
squalling screaming loudly or discordantly
squire servant, follower; pimp
stale lover ridiculed to amuse a rival
start (n.) impulse, sudden spasm of intense emotion
start (vb.) spring up suddenly; move away precipitately, recoil; react with abrupt astonishment
state estate, possessions
stay (vb.) halt, restrain
stew (vb.) stay excessively long in bed
stews (n.) brothels
stick (vb.) thrust (dagger, spear, etc.) into
stickle in take an active part in support of
still always, constantly
stint (n.) allotted portion or measure
stint (vb.) restrict, limit
stint, at on a scanty allowance; with limited means

stomach appetite
stout resolute, dauntless
straggling vagrant
strangely extremely, in an exceptional manner
stuff cloth; nonsense, rubbish
stummed adulterated
stupid lethargic; sunk in inertia
success outcome, result
succubus demon in female form supposed to have sexual intercourse with sleeping men
suit (n.) petition, appeal
summa totalis (Latin) sum total
swain rustic wooer or lover
swash swashbuckler; noisy, swaggering braggart
sweet-water liquid perfume
swim (n.) smooth, sliding movement
swimming wavering, giddy
swinge (n.) power, authority
swinge (vb.) chastise, thrash
swingeing huge, immense; tremendous; powerful, potent
swordman skilled fencer; soldier
synod assembly
table-book memorandum-book
taking captivating, alluring
tallow-chandler maker or seller of tallow candles
tartar Mongol or Turkish warrior; savage, barbarian
tax (vb.) accuse, censure; prescribe or impose (something on someone); challenge
tear (vb.) rant, bluster
temper (vb.) modify by blending or mixture; moderate
tender (vb.) have a care or regard for
termagant turbulent woman; virago, shrew, vixen
terra incognita, in (Latin) in an unknown country
tester sixpence
throughly thoroughly
tilting ready and eager for an encounter
tinsel of superficial splendour, but no intrinsic value; deceitful
tittle smallest part

toper hard drinker
topping pre-eminent, egregious
touchstone test, criterion
touse dishevel (hair, dress), rumple (bed-clothes); indulge in rough love-play
towardly promising, propitious; obliging, tractable
towards in preparation, imminent
toy trifle, matter of no importance; odd conceit, whim
tract course, continuity
traffic trade, business
train (n.) retinue
translate transform
transport (n.) rapture
treat (vb.) provide entertainment; negotiate
trencher plate, platter
trice instant
tricing plucking, tugging
trip dance
troth truth; in truth
trow/I trow 'I wonder', 'that's what I want to know'
truckle behave servilely
trull prostitute
trumpery worthless or showy item
truss tie up; hang
try test, probe
tuffle little tuft
ubiquitary omnipresent
ud's-bud a softened oath, 'God's blood!'
unaccountable insignificant, of no worth
unadvised indiscreet, ill-judged, rash
uncase take off; remove (a disguise)
unconscionable unscrupulous; unreasonable, unjust
unfleshed uninitiated
untap ejaculate
untoward, untowardly perverse, uncooperative, intractable; adverse, ill-starred; ungraceful, indecorous; slow-witted
unvaluable invaluable
upbraid rebuke

urchin vagrant
vagabond vagrant
vagary freakish prank; caprice, whim
vapours nervous disorders
varlet knave
vent (n.) emission, discharge
vent (vb.) utter, release
venture, at a by chance; at risk, at a disadvantage
verily truly
virginals spinet (an old keyboard instrument)
vitals interior organs essential for life
vizard mask
vizard-mask mask covering the face; woman wearing such a mask; prostitute
vulgar pertaining to the common people
wag droll, mischievous person
wagtail whore
wamble be queasy
want lack
warrant promise, assure, guarantee
well-qualitied endowed with good qualities; of good birth
well-knit strongly and compactly built
wheedle piece of insinuating flattery or cajolery
wheedling enticing or persuading by flattering, soothing words
whip (adv.) suddenly, in an instant
whirl violent or confused disturbance; vibration
whitely pale of complexion
whoremaster lecher; pander
wight creature, man (archaic)
without outside
wittol acquiescent cuckold
word, at a concisely, in brief
worm-eaten decrepit, antiquated, outworn
worry harass, assail; bite and shake
worshipful entitled to respect on account of rank
wot know
yoked to coupled to, matched with
yoke-fellow spouse